COMPUTERISED TEST GENERATION FOR CROSS-NATIONAL MILITARY RECRUITMENT

A Handbook

Computerised Test Generation for Cross-National Military Recruitment

A Handbook

by

Sidney H. Irvine

Press

Amsterdam • Berlin • Tokyo • Washington, DC

ISBN 978-1-61499-362-9 (print)
ISBN 978-1-61499-363-6 (online)
Library of Congress Control Number: 2014931477
doi: 10.3233/978-1-61499-363-6-i

Publisher
IOS Press BV
Nieuwe Hemweg 6B
1013 BG Amsterdam
Netherlands
fax: +31 20 687 0019
e-mail: order@iospress.nl

Distributor in the USA and Canada
IOS Press, Inc.
4502 Rachael Manor Drive
Fairfax, VA 22032
USA
fax: +1 703 323 3668
e-mail: iosbooks@iospress.com

LEGAL NOTICE
The publisher is not responsible for the use which might be made of the following information.

PRINTED IN THE NETHERLANDS

FOR MARGARET

CONTENTS

FOREWORD

The advent of the 1980s was a portentous moment in educational and psychological assessment. Rapid advances had been made in a number of foundational fields: The cognitive revolution remade our understanding of how people learn, act, and solve problems. Microcomputers made digital technology and interactive capability available anytime, anywhere. Statistics offered more powerful ways of modeling complicated problems, again in real time. The two-fold challenge now was to figure out how this potential could come together in a principled way to advance assessment, and to put it to work to do astonishing things that had never been done before.

The British Army Recruitment Battery (BARB) is just such a thing.

In this book Sidney Irvine tells the story of BARB, his BARB. It traverses a widespread network, interleaved with connections to thousands of people contributing on BARB itself or working on seemingly unrelated projects years before, from mathematical equations to warrior vernacular, from a postwar army camp in the Mideast to the Britannia Royal Naval College to ivy-covered research labs in Princeton. The result after many years and many adventures is BARB: A computer-administered recruitment test battery which creates, on the fly, brand new parallel tests for every examinee, grounded in psychological science, created and scored with high reliability, and demonstrated valid for the purpose for which they were designed.

At several points in the discursion, Sid refers to our work, some of the many elements that contributed to BARB intellectually and at certain points directly, and which was furthered by what we learned from Sid and BARB. We unashamedly admit the collegial association, and offer some observations from our perspectives.

Bob's connection is the assessment framework he developed with Linda Steinberg and Russell Almond, called Evidence-Centered Design, or ECD. ECD aims to draw out, then make explicit in language and representations, the underlying connections in assessment arguments. Just what is it that one wants to make inferences about, as informed by whatever capabilities that are at issue and whatever purposes are in mind? What kinds of things do we need to see people say or do or make, in what kinds of situations, to get evidence to back our claims? What forms of task design, evaluation, scoring, and analysis embody the argument in the "pieces of machinery" that constitute an operational assessment? The resulting framework builds on foundational principles of assessment to help understand and design familiar kinds of assessments, but more importantly, to create new ones made possible by the foundational advances mentioned above—in particular, BARB. Confluences between ECD and BARB occurred in a joint study of mixed strategies for mental rotation tasks, a conference presentation and chapter on ECD in the Irvine and Kyllonen volume on item generation, and on-going informal conversations during Sid's visits to Educational Testing Service in Princeton.

A particularly intriguing – and for BARB, crucial – line of research was a theory of task generation. Pioneering work such as Jack Carroll's on the cognitive processes that underlie test performance helped bring out some of the connections, and that of Susan Embretson that pointed the way to how to integrate cognition, task design, and psychometric analysis. Task generation was a natural extension of this line of work. Isaac was funded by the Office of Naval Research in the 1980's to pursue what many (including the funding agency!) considered an idea with limited potential, namely item generation coupled to the theories of cognition that were emerging as part of the "cognitive revolution." Isaac initially focused his work on spatial ability for which there was a growing cognitive foundation. It would be many years before item generation would become a widely accepted approach. Sid, however, unbeknown to us and probably most American researchers, was deeply engaged in the development of BARB at the same time and quickly recognized the 'grammatical' implications of the research taking place in the States for automatic item construction. It was no accident that Sid found out about this work as it was happening (before there was a Google), even though it would remain inaccessible in obscure technical reports for years before it appeared in journals. Sid had a long-standing connection with ETS, especially to Sam Messick, visiting ETS frequently, making it his business to find out about the on-going research.

In a Zen koan, Master Hyakujo brings out a drinking water jar, puts it down and says "You cannot call it a water jar. Then, what will you call it?" Isan kicks the jar over and walks away. In a psychometric koan, Dr. John Anderson asks "What would tests be like if there were no fixed item files, no IRT (item-response theory) - and no money?" Dr. Sidney Irvine swallows: then he recruits ideas, psychologists, software engineers, armed services funders, a network of researchers and personnel experts; works for 15 years of fits and starts, through successes and "surprises"; creates, tests, and validates BARB; produces its successors in the United States and Europe, and finally writes a book about the experience. Not so pithy, but a damned good answer, in the same spirit!

Isaac I. Bejar & Robert J. Mislevy
Educational Testing Service August 27, 2013

PREFACE AND ACKNOWLEDGEMENTS

This book has two goals. The first is to provide an evidence centred account of how to generate computer-delivered tests for recruitment *where each applicant is presented with a test that is a parallel form of its prototype.* Moreover, it begins in an era when recruits had little or no experience of computers, so that an important focus is on the discovery and use of the first principles that proved so essential while the *British Army Recruit Battery* was developed by a small team at the Human Assessment Laboratory in the University of Plymouth from 1986 onwards. The research involved was totally funded by United Kingdom Ministry of Defence Contracts 2021-12 and 2021-15 for a decade.

The British Army Recruit Battery, to become known as BARB, was the first mass testing system to be created where each new applicant was presented with unique parallel forms of the tests used to screen for qualities considered necessary for success. BARB went operational in 1992, and is in action today throughout the United Kingdom. There has been no comprehensive account of its development until now: and according to experts, BARB's individual and unpublished official reports contain a major British contribution to psychometrics. With reference to these by kind permission of the Information Department of the Ministry of Defence, unique features in this book outline the necessary cognitive theory for producing multilingual forms of the tests and include the frameworks for test creation. Moreover, the narrative produces details of important independent validation studies with both paper-and-pencil analogues and computer-delivered versions, encompassing the unique characteristics of military criteria.

The second goal is to demonstrate cross-cultural development across a number of North Atlantic Treaty Organisation services. Entirely new test forms, using automatic item-generation were validated at the United States Air Force Research Laboratory at Brooks Air Force Base, San Antonio, Texas from 1997 to 1999 due to the award of a United States National Research Council Associateship. Such were the resources available that the cognitive tests became an integral part of the creation of computer-delivered vocational interest, personality and health-related quality of life instruments validated and standardised on thousands of military personnel. During the past decade, English language versions were translated and used experimentally by the German Bundeswehr; and operationally in selecting military personnel in Belgium from 2006 onwards. There are descriptions of the translation processes and the results of the extensive use of the tests in multiple forms. Moreover, special studies of potential item bias using multiple parallel form tests are included, contrasting the two main Belgian language groups, Flemish and French, with immigrant minorities.

All of these accounts pursue the aims of the book. Throughout, there is a continuous military context, so that results are recorded and stories told about the very large numbers of participants in various national military forces. But that was not the main purpose. The issues encountered – computer delivery for people who had never seen a computer before, predicting item difficulty to avoid using item-response theory, validation, diversity and fairness to minorities – all of these are fundamental today. Any reader with a working knowledge of correlation should be able to understand, and perhaps even enjoy their pursuit and temporary closure. The solutions offered whenever they were met along the way *provide a handbook and guide to modern recruit test construction using the tests illustrated in the book as examples of what can be done using microcomputers in a straightforward and uncomplicated fashion.* Experts may unreasonably find that there is much to be learned from the careful application of well-established cognitive theory, perhaps as an antidote to the pain of understanding the increasingly complex mathematics used in the design of adaptive tests and inventories.

The book has four parts. The first is technically the most robust, dealing in Chapters 1 to 6 with the painstaking work involved in the production of cognitive tests for the British Army Recruit Battery. Part 2, involving Chapters 7 to 9, contains validation studies using the British Army Recruit Battery and its sister tests, used in the Royal Navy and in a special study with the United States Air Force in 1994. The second generation of tests was developed in The United States from 1997 to 1999; and in Germany and Belgium from 2000 to 2006; and included an examination of their fairness to Belgian minorities in 2011, using differential item functions – all collected in Chapters 10 to 13. The last part of the book is a departure from cognition, beginning with a review of attempts to use motivational and social measures in the search for attributes that reduce attrition – a perennial and costly adjunct to recruitment. Chapter 14 is a historical account of work undertaken, followed by evaluation of screening procedures and, in the last chapter, evidence that health-related quality of life questions are the best indicator of what appears to be a constant percentage of losses during phase one of training.

No book as extensive as this one could have been written without the help and collaboration of others, lasting for a quarter of a century or more. Featured are a number of forewords by colleagues and observers who witnessed or have been involved in the pertinent fields of enquiry. Each section has a personal point of view that does much to inform and enliven the discussion. The acknowledgements are many but the sentiments expressed are few, namely, my unqualified thanks, respect and admiration for their many various and valued contributions, verbal, written and motivational.

The work began at the University of Plymouth and constant references to the work of members of the Human Assessment Laboratory are attestation to their concerted and unique contributions. I list them alphabetically: Janet Collis, Peter Dann, Ian Dennis, Jonathan Evans, Paddy Tapsfield (seconded from the Ministry of Defence), and David Wright. Throughout the research the Head of the Department of Psychology, Steve Newstead, was unstinting in his support administratively and collegially, helping to organise the landmark NATO Advanced Study Institute in Athens in 1984 that proved so exhilarating and important in the run-up to the creation of BARB. Nevertheless, BARB and all the related applications that were to follow BARB could not have become operational without complete financial support under contracts 2021/12 and 2021/15, from the Ministry of Defence and the cooperation and active participation of their own psychologists from the Army Personnel Research Establishment and the Senior Psychologist (Naval). Without major involvement by Dr. John Anderson, Dennis Blyth who died 'on active servisce', Paul Cawkill, Chris Elshaw, Pam Gould, Andrea Hampson, Paul Jacobs, and Niall Leavy, and administrative guidance from Elaine Porteous and from Ken Corkindale and Vic Schmitt (both now deceased), none of the research in the United Kingdom could have occurred. Not least, I am honoured to acknowledge permission from the Information Management Department of the Ministry of Defence, to quote and use tables and figures from a large number of internal reports produced for Crown Copyright United Kingdom Ministry of Defence contracts 2021-12 and 2021-15, from 1986 to 1996. These are clearly indicated and referenced throughout. No longer a young partner in the enterprise, but a senior official in the Department, Paul Cawkill volunteered to guide the necessary transit of the draft manuscript, requiring technical approval by Professor Bob Madahar, Chief Technologist, and thereafter by the Legal Department. With his patience and good humour the task ceased to be a major concern for me: and, truly, my gratitude is heartfelt! Wider reference has been made to documents shared with the German Bundeswehr and the Belgian Defence Force, while more detailed accounts of non-cognitive test development may be found in relevant technical manuals edited by me. At all times, copyright acknowledgements are inserted.

In the United States, for almost a decade, the major influence throughout information exchange was the work of the Air Force Research Laboratory at Brooks Air Force base, San Antonio, Texas: particularly that of Raymond Christal, Pat Kyllonen, Bill Alley, Valerie Shute, Bill Tirre, and Malcolm Ree among many others; and not forgetting the evening style of Richard Roberts, a 1997-99 visiting Australian associate now at ETS with Dr. Kyllonen. My main debt, in the day to day operational work involved in the construction and validation of the Lackland Tests during my tenure as Resident Associate Scientist from September 1997 until April 1999, fully supported by the United States National Research Council, was to Richard Walker, Computer Programming Manager, and Janice Hereford the Data Processing Manager. Working with them on a daily basis from specifications to encoding the software for test development was one of the most informative and influential experiences in my professional life. Latterly I moved my desk to their office, with all the other programmers, so critical was their contribution and so important was constant contact and review of events at Lackland. The Lackland Tests were adapted to serve the international commercial world under the direction of Laing Mewhort, their current owner, and Arlene McGurk from their Mindmill headquarters in Northern Ireland. No longer their consultant, I am most grateful for permission to refer to aspects of the *Mindmill Test Manuals*, originally authored, and registered where appropriate with the British Psychological Society.

While at Brooks Air Force Base, I was pleased and honoured to act as an informal advisor (at the request of Dr. Kyllonen) to Thomas Kutschke, on attachment from the Psychological Service of the German Bundeswehr. After his return to Germany, a request to conduct a trial of the Lackland Tests for the Bundeswehr was received. He, with Sybille Schambach, Wolfgang Weber and Johannes Wulf, were the force behind the use of the first translated versions of the generation software in 2002, which continued to be constructed by Richard Walker, acting as an independent consultant, until 2008 when the commercial versions of the tests were first acquired by Mindmill.

This continuity was most important when, like BARB in the United Kingdom, the tests went operational under contract in recruit offices nationally to select all Belgian Defence Force Personnel in 2006 and to the present day. Special thanks are due to François Lescrève, Yves Devriendt, Didier Ghilain, Christophe Coussement, Annemie Defranc, Veerle Tibax and Jacques Mylle, for extended efforts in making the tests operationally valid for different language groups and minorities in Belgium.

When the manuscript was drafted, colleagues and friends were approached to write short forewords to various sections of the book with which they were particularly familiar. Acknowledged world authorities Bob Mislevy and Isaac Bejar of Educational Testing Service agreed to write the main foreword from the perspective of automatic item generation. Dr. John Anderson, whose question to me started it all, was the man to comment on BARB and its basic propositions. Not only that, he has followed the manuscript since its early drafts and made several editorial comments along the way. Paul Cawkill was able to give an active service view of the extensive validations in the Royal Navy. Dr. Pat Kyllonen knows more about the scope of the Lackland Test versions constructed at The Air Force Laboratory than anyone else; while François Lescrève, Johannes Wulf and Thomas Kutschke were first hand witnesses of the research in Belgium and Germany respectively. Lastly, Dr. Mike Matthews, Professor of Engineering Psychology at West Point, and the author of a popular book on Military Psychology agreed to offer a viewpoint on the attrition chapters that complete the book. Their various contributions shed light and bring wisdom to bear on an unavoidably lengthy discourse that has taken some three years to put together.

For bringing the book to publication IOS Press executives Maarten Fröhlich, Anne Marie de Rover, Paul Gijsbers and Carry Koolbergen have more than earned my respect and appreciation for their advice and support. Professor Brenda Wiederhold introduced me to them and I hope her faith in the project will be justified. Professor Jamie Hacker Hughes not only volunteered to write the cover notes, he has obtained permission, in his role as Director of the Institute for Veterans and Families at Ruskin University to house and preserve the archive of original sources for the book. I am twice indebted to him for his generosity and enthusiastic support. In providing camera ready copy, I have had to structure the chapters and proof-read. For any oversights despite my best efforts – the laws of chance dictate that there may be some – I apologise in advance.

Finally, however, there are three persons without whose continual encouragement the contents could not have appeared. Dr. John Irvine made changes in the manuscript happen when he asked some months ago if the book were to be simply a history or was meant to deal with psychometric issues. A major revision followed. Dr. Craig Irvine too, always asked pertinent questions about the chapters he read: and he suggested a few weeks ago the use of point inserts to highlight important sections. Finally, my chief debt has always been for the past half century and is now, to my wife Margaret.

This book is dedicated to her, of course. It could not be otherwise.

Sidney Irvine
September 26, 2013

Part 1:

Five Lessons for a Generation of Tests

CHAPTER 1

MACDONALD'S ASKARIS: FIVE LESSONS FOR BARB

At the outset, the major issues that confronted the production of a new test series for recruits who had never seen their like before are discussed in the context of a little known work of great significance. It was a project in the hands of a small team in the Middle East towards the end of the Second World War. In it, the quest for new tests presages almost precisely what happened in Plymouth some forty years later when a group at the university were asked to create BARB, *The British Army Recruit Battery*. The group in the Middle East had to learn lessons before tests could be adapted to the cultural setting; and these lessons showed that success or failure depended on answers to five questions. What was the recruit culture? What instructions would they need to understand the tests? What kinds of tests were necessary? What qualities did the tests measure? Would they predict success in career roles? In effect, the lessons and the questions posed by them constructed the syllabus for studying how to adapt psychometric tests to cultural contexts where they had never existed.

MACDONALD'S FIVE LESSONS FOR BARB

Understand the recruit culture

Provide clear and simple instructions

Choose the right tests

Discover what qualities the tests measure

Show that the results predict success

THE ARCHAEOLOGY OF EVIDENCE-CENTRED PROTOCOLS: AN UNHERALDED MILITARY CAMPAIGN

Parallels to the problems facing the team devising BARB in 1986 were found in the archives. The five most important lessons in the pursuit of test construction excellence were learned in work completed in the Middle East in the period 1944-45. Indeed most, if not all of the *operational* problems encountered in devising tests for computer delivery had been solved in an almost unknown report (Macdonald, 1945) on those encountered *when tests for screening and allocating conscripts in the world war of 1939-45 were adapted for use with a large cohort of soldiers who had never before experienced them.* What were the difficulties of using tests from one culture in another? How were they resolved? Did they forecast the issues and provide lessons in transposing tests from paper-and-pencil to computer-delivery? Did they still exist as a basic evidential structure for test design and operation in military cultures?

TESTING MACDONALD'S ASKARIS, 1944-45

A large body of cross-cultural work in Africa and elsewhere (cf. Irvine & Berry, 1988) in the decades following 1960 had shed some light on the inadequacy of psychometric debate when there was no proof of the equivalence of test scores among the groups being compared. Long before this, a small military unit (which included ten test administrators, one female typist and a carpenter), under the command of Lt. Col. A. Macdonald, attempted to adapt conventional tests that had been used for selecting British Army personnel during the period 1941-44. The team goal was to create a culturally equivalent selection battery for use with perhaps the most extraordinarily diverse sample of adult male volunteer recruits ever assembled in the history of military psychometrics. A total of 1855 men from no fewer than 64 different tribal groups in Kenya, Tanzania and Uganda were quartered in a base camp somewhere in the Middle East. In the space of a year, he and his co-workers effectively set standards for ensuring that tests introduced to a new cultural context and used for recruitment measure what they are intended to measure. Attempts to adapt recruitment tests to the computer context can be compared with Macdonald's achievements - which is why they are summarised at the outset. In microcosm, this chapter reveals what lessons would have to be learned in constructing BARB; and focuses clearly on the nature of the work. There were five different problems: and these were identical to those confronting the BARB team in 1986.

THE FIVE TEST ADAPTATION LESSONS

Perhaps nothing written about the history of psychometrics reveals as much about test adaptation and new test construction for recruits who had never experienced them before as a unique 65-year-old study of soldiers (known as Askaris[1]) from the tribes of East Africa. The little known work of Lt. Col. A. Macdonald, which is as relevant today as it was in 1945, produced five elementary lessons.

1. The overwhelming cultural component was illiteracy among the Askaris: but Macdonald's material consisted of paper-and-pencil and performance tests used on literate and numerate UK conscripts and volunteers since 1940.
2. Whatever the original English language test form was, instructions had to be verbal, after translation into Swahili, an East African *lingua franca*.
3. The research team had to choose tests, adapt them if necessary and administer them successfully.
4. Every test was scored by hand, in hot, dry conditions; results recorded on paper and calculations computed using slide rules.
5. What the tests measured had to be proved using the technology available.

In short, the Askari test culture introduced elements that would *radically* determine how the tests could be used and scored, having causal effects. One might have hoped that Macdonald's campaign would be part of tests and testing legend by now and that this account would offer no new insights for the construction of BARB. Psychometric history is neither simple nor straightforward. Its inclusions and exclusions are not necessarily a reflection of their scientific worth, in every aspect from simple puzzles to complex personality domains.

---

1   Askari is an Arabic, Urdu, Turkish, Somali, Persian, Amharic and Swahili word meaning "soldier".

LESSON 1: RECOGNISING DIVERSE CULTURAL CONTEXTS: THE RECRUITS

In July 1944, an officer in the Middle East was tasked with assessing the value of 'scientific methods of selection' (Macdonald, 1945 p. 64)[2] for allocating African recruits to military roles. He recognised three problems: devising the tests, administering them, and showing how their application could improve selection procedures. The recruits to be used in the project (his *reagents* in Spearman's memorable 1904 term) were male Askaris, from Kenya (646), Uganda (598) and Tanganyika (611), a grand total of 1855 men in the Pioneer Corps[3.] At the time, there were 209,127 East African personnel enrolled in the British Army. Today, there are approximately 80,000 service personnel in the British Army, and none of them are Askaris[4].

The East African Soldiers

Macdonald is careful to point out that the policy in the composition of African Units was to have a proportionate mix of personnel from all tribal groupings. He is equally careful to emphasise that his sample is large, although purposive, with as reasonable a claim to be representative of the cultural mix as the exigencies of the service might have allowed. At the outset, he stresses the lack of a single language, and the need for Swahili, an East African *lingua franca*, as the only means of communication (Macdonald, 1945, pp.5-6). As the report unfolds, further details of the nature of the sample emerge, sometimes by implication. For example, one of the tests was discontinued because of the lack of a criterion by which to judge its effectiveness, another proved too difficult because of the need to understand English. Simply put, the men available were not, at the virtual end of the war

THE AFRICAN ASKARI CULTURE

'The Japanese have not yet recovered from the terrific hammering they suffered at the hands of the Askaris of the 11th East African Division. During the time these fine troops fought with the 14th Army, they have shown a capacity to understand the most intricate of mechanical contrivances, an ability to perform the most exacting of military duties and, although shelled, mortared and sometimes ambushed, have shown consistently a very high standard of skill, courage and devotion to duty. It is rather difficult to believe that these great masses of raw human material, uncivilised and credulous, could have been turned into such very efficient soldiers. Africans have been trained as Infantrymen, Gunners Sappers, Signallers, Military Police, Mechanists, Drivers and Nursing Orderlies - to mention but a few of their Army jobs. They have fought In Italian East Africa, Madagascar and Burma. Although certainly the finished product of endless patience during training, they have more than repaid the effort that was spent on them.' (Loc. cit. p.71).

---

2   All references are to the original page numbers of the report.

3   The Pioneer Corps was essentially a labour force assisting the Engineer Corps in construction projects.

4   There is a Ghurkha Regiment.

employed in the type of work that required the acquisition of specialised skills. This was no reflection on the ability of the recruits: but it was an implicit commentary on the decisions that had to be made about where and how to employ them at the time. In the insert are words attributed by Macdonald to a senior staff officer. African Askaris when trained could do anything asked of them. With this firmly in mind, detailed observations of the behaviour of the troops available for testing were undertaken. These reinforced the view that the recruits available were neither trained for, nor were not expected to carry out, the roles of other Askaris employed during the active conflict in the Far East as infantry, signals operators, anti-aircraft gunners, police, mechanics and nursing orderlies. The war was virtually over and all that remained was to demobilise the troops. It was Macdonald's job to occupy them actively with a goal in mind, adapting test for recruit selection.

Ethnic Diversity
The recruits were 1855 male Askaris, from diverse tribes in Kenya (646), Uganda (598) and Tanganyika (611). Today, it is doubtful if any test user would be able to use such a sample for selection without attempting to show that the tests were fair to all the different language and national groups. No such problem faced Macdonald in 1945, but the very complex mix of his participants would raise questions asked about 'fairness' in the context of ethnic differences. That may not have seemed important when there was so much else for Macdonald to do, but he would not have escaped criticism if any modern sample of recruits had come from such a wide spectrum of social and linguistic differences. Jacobs (1997) conducted a study on fairness after BARB went operational using a total 20,000 recruit cohort, with favourable outcomes. The same social concerns arise in Chapter 10 when the results of administering tests in Belgium and Northern Ireland are analysed in areas of sectarian and linguistic differences.

Figure 1.1: Diagram of Macdonald's Agility Set-up

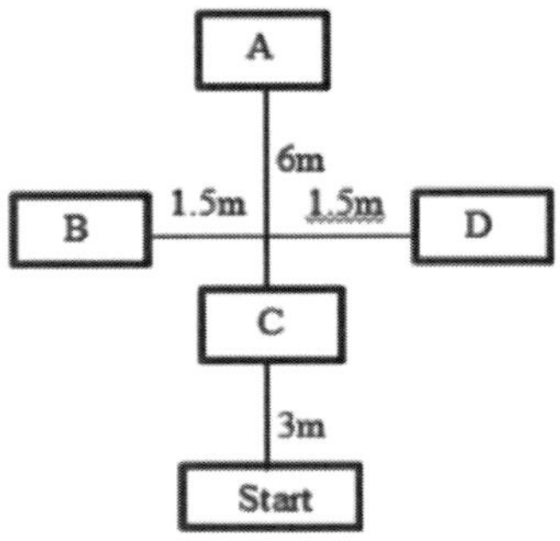

LESSON 2: INSTRUCTIONS AS THE KEY TO PERFORMANCE
The instructions and diagram (Figure 1.1) of a test called *Physical Agility*, a prominent ability dimension marker in the system (see Table 1.3) are examples of Macdonald's unique achievements in a multi-language environment. The task was one combining agility, coordination and task achievement. Performance *was measured by the speed*

at which a given pattern had to be run[5], during which 16 rings were placed in sequence over 4 standards in fixed positions labelled A, B. C and D. Because of the size of the rings and diameter of the poles, manual dexterity demanded proper placement. The instructions to testers fully explained the nature of the task in Table 1.1. As in all cross-cultural testing, prior supervised practice is essential – just as it was with computer-delivered testing. The extract in Table 1.1 from the procedure does much to show the priorities and goals of the 'patter' not only for this, but also for every single one of the tests.

Table 1.1: Instructions for the Physical Agility Task

THE PHYSICAL AGILITY TASK

Eight rings were on a standard at point A, eight at point B. These had to be transferred in sequence from A to C and from B to D, the sequence being Start-A-C-B-D-A-C-B-D until all rings were transferred from A to C and from B to D.

The diagram shows the distances to be covered and the relative position of rings on standards A and B at the start. A practice run in one's own time was given before a speeded trial.

Principle	Practical Demonstration
Pretest Example	(i) The tester gives a complete demonstration to the squad i.e. he sits down at the starting base with his back to the sticks, gives himself the orders: 'Ready' (PAUSE): 'Set! (PAUSE): Go!" and transfers all the rings in correct sequence - at speed.
Prior Practice	(ii) Each man comes out and has a trial run in his own time until the tester sees that he understands the procedure. He is then returned to the starting base and given his timed run.
Monitoring	(iii) The tester watches carefully throughout to see that any of the standards that are knocked down are put up for the man, to shout 'Not on!' if a ring sticks, and to warn the subject which standard to go to if he gets muddled.
Motivation	(iv) The men are encouraged to cheer on each performer.*
Feedback	(v) The score is announced clearly at the end of each run and the competitive, spirit kept alive.
Score Model	(vi) A man's score is the time taken for one complete run from the word 'Go! to the click of the last ring on D.

The instructions to recruits as to how to carry out a prescribed sequence are important not just for what they are, but for what they implied for the future and in present-day computers. Demonstration, prior practice, monitoring, motivation and feedback are the precepts illustrated and to be followed, even, or especially, on

---
5   Run Time over 1500 metres is a measure used to assess British Army Recruits today (Cf. Johansen, 2011).

screens. This task alone illustrates an abiding concern for test users. Scoring tests has ever been an issue. Accuracy? Latency? Both? The physical agility example describes in miniature the efforts required by Macdonald's team to ensure that the recruits knew what to do for each one of the different tests; and what scoring system to adopt with the results once they became available.

LESSON 3: THE CHOICE OF TESTS
Table 1.2 shows the tests used during the assessment of nearly 1900 men during 1945. For convenience, descriptive statistics, edited and rounded to whole numbers, are included. Examination shows that of the sixteen tests used, *all but three were performance tests, familiar in Britain and elsewhere, requiring actual manipulation of test components.* The exceptions were an adaptation of *Raven's Progressive Matrices (1938); an elementary test of English Comprehension; and an elementary Arithmetic Test of simple calculations.*

Table 1.2: Tests Used by Macdonald 1944-45

Source		Label	Mean	SD
MESP Test	6	African Matrix Test (1944 Revision)	22	6
MESP Test	7	Pegboard Manual Dexterity	201	23
MESP Test	8	Reversible Blocks Manual Dexterity	225	36
MESP Test	9	Screwboard Manual Dexterity Test -	112	34
MESP Test	11	English Comprehension	19	18
MESP Test	16	Physical Agility	60	5
MESP Test	19	Mechanical Assembly (Form A)	79	26
MESP Test	20	Mechanical Comprehension	18	4
MESP Test	24	Cube Construction	28	12
MESP Test	26	Fourth Corner Test (1944 Revision)	18	6
MESP Test	27	Block Design	40	23
MESP Test	30	Picture Completion	11	3
MESP Test	53	Arithmetic Attainments	19	12
MESP Test	54	Mechanical Assembly (Form B)	24	7
MESP Test	55	Formboard (Circular Insets) .	45	10
MESP Test	56	Formboard (Square Insets)	39	7
MESP Test	58	Ishihara Colour Vision Test.[6]	-------	-------

A glance at Vernon and Parry's (1949) all but forgotten account of personnel selection in 1939-45 during the Second World War confirms that Macdonald was using tests originating in the 1930s in various occupational selection enterprises: and already had exposure in selecting British soldier, sailor and airman conscripts. They were familiar enough to Macdonald and his contemporaries. Experts recommended their use in the services: and there was nothing better at the time. They were there, for good or ill, to trial with his Askaris. But how, that was the question.

---

6   Given to 373 men of whom 97.9% had perfect colour vision, discontinued because of staff shortages (loc.cit, p. 23).

Modifications Were Needed

Macdonald arrived at the final set of tests only after a lot of preliminary research. The report contains details of a restandardisation of the *Penrose-Raven Matrices* test (see Chapter 4), including complete item analysis and changing the order of 26 of the 46 items in the original version (pp. 24-28). The empirical effort involved, with detailed spoken translations of instructions required is hardly credible by today's standards.[7]

Other performance tests were invented, including pictorial and figural completion tests. These required the study of cards, of which perhaps the best example of is the *Fourth Corner Test* (loc. cit. Appendix B: *Middle East Selection Project* Note 26 gives complete instructions). The test itself consisted of 50 cards on each of which were designs with a part missing. Each card contained a pocket with six shapes in it, one of which supplied the missing element. A full item analysis is tabulated detailing the changes in item order for the version finally used (pp. 30-34). Almost as an aside, the report mentions that the preliminary work on test construction involved 1000 soldiers from Lesotho (loc, cit. p. 30) previously tested for their suitability as members of Anti-Aircraft units. New tests appeared, but the effort was considerable without a theory to determine the difficulty of the items. BARB's tests had to solve this perennial problem.

LESSON 4: ALLOCATING SCORING MODELS

In its description, mention was made of the scoring model adopted for the *Physical Agility Test*. Not right or wrong, as for the great majority of the tests used in the safari into Askari performance, but the *time to completion* when all of the rings are correctly placed on the four standards (Run Time). More than one model of scoring was in use - and the correct choice was to be a much more complex question for all computer-delivered tests some sixty years on (Thissen & Wainer, 2001). Automatic scoring and recording of test responses in computers were to make three models available, accuracy, latency and learning during the test. The opportunities were expanded beyond conventions with no model for immediate resolution.

IMPLICATIONS OF FIRST FOUR LESSONS FOR BARB

Only the complete instructions in Appendix B of the report tell the full story about how to administer and score the various tests. Each test has standardised spoken instructions (called *'patter'*) in both English and Swahili. *Above all, they show and demonstrate in detail how to complete each of the various tasks.* The test administrators must ensure supervision and checking; whilst the verbal *'patters'* typically contain several elements of repetition. *Every presentation emphasises the need to focus attention. The goal for every test is to teach the recruits the test content; and how to complete it after practice.*

With BARB there would be no human intervention. The computer screen, with no voiceover, would have to do it all. However, where test presentation was concerned, innovators had begun almost anywhere, with Binet giving individual performance tests, or Piaget asking a child apparently innocuous questions about

---

7   Macdonald did not produce reliabilities. Because these tended to be speeded tests with short time limits and more than one trial, individual internal consistency estimates were not considered adequate. However, the highest intercorrelation of any two performance tests was .58. If the correlation of .58 between parallel forms of the same test is used as an estimate of test-retest reliability, then this must be regarded as moderate. The highest estimates of reliability that could be calculated from the data available were the communalities of a factor analysis. These ranged from .73 to .37.

amounts of plasticene present in different shapes, or levels of water in long and short glasses. Alternatively, one could examine the beginnings of large-scale paper-and-pencil group testing of United States Army recruits using the Alpha and Beta tests during the 1914-1918 war. *Whatever form of delivery is used, test administration assumes that all participants have equal status when the test proper begins.* Stimuli as test items are assumed to mean the same for every participant, whenever and wherever they are used. If by some chance they do not, then individual or group results cannot logically be compared. This much was known from cross-cultural work on a large scale in the period from 1960 to 1980 (see the extensive bibliography for sources in Irvine, 1986; Irvine and Berry,1988, 2010; Lonner & Berry, 1986). There is one final lesson, where debates continue to flourish. Macdonald learned to cope with the perennial difficulties of validating the tests in military cultures. Even today, they are no less troublesome.

LESSON 5: PROVING WHAT THE TESTS MEASURED
Having constructed, altered, standardised and administered the test battery to some 1900 men, Macdonald and his team then showed, in 1945, an extraordinary and by today's criteria, exemplary pursuit of the required psychometric qualities of their tests. After thorough analyses of how the items behaved, they had altered the order of some; invented others. When imported tests failed to live up to expectation; they shortened the time taken in repetitive tasks; and stopped using those that did not seem to work. That accomplished, the question of what precisely the remaining tests measured in East African recruits who had not been exposed to them before, remained uppermost in their minds. Validity studies had to be carried through in spite of the almost overwhelming challenges of paper-and-pencil collection and hand calculation of data on a very large scale, if their work were to be completed to professional standards. They had no calculation aids except slide rules.

Two Validity Types
Given the end-of-war circumstances of the project, where no long-term follow-up was possible, there were only two different kinds of validity available to Macdonald for judging the military effectiveness of his tests: *criterion validity* with concurrent proficiency ratings and *construct validity* based on what patterns were made by the tests when they were correlated with each other.

THE CRITERION

'factors, outside the control of the [test administration] unit, tended to decrease the value of the correlations obtained'

(Macdonald loc. cit. p.71).

Predicting Proficiency Ratings
The key question was the value of the tests in predicting how well the soldiers performed their current duties while waiting for demobilisation at the end of hostilities[8]. Much prejudice existed about the abilities of 'Africans' who tended to be lumped together, although Macdonald argued strongly in favour of

---
8   There was, as his quotation (loc. cit. p.71) shows, little doubt about the diversity and value of their abilities on active service against the Japanese forces.

diversity. Could the study provide direct evidence that was not hearsay?

Ratings[9] were sought to calculate the degree of success of individuals within companies whose roles were restricted by the end of the war in Europe to garrison duty. The ratings were from Unit Rating Boards consisting of a British Officer, a British NCO and an African NCO, whose assessment was the first one sought. Experienced psychometricians have long realised that perhaps nothing is as certain to be unreliable as a proficiency rating provided in the field, by busy staff members at seemingly low cost to the researchers, but perceived as an externally imposed burden by the raters themselves. Macdonald collected these ratings, nevertheless, on a five-point scale of efficiency, knowing full well their fallibility; tactfully expressed in the insert. After the ratings were collected from different units, comparisons with them and test performance were made, although no correlations within each unit are reported. Inspection of the data indicates that no reliable pattern of correlations existed, in spite of all the effort. The Unit Rating Boards found the task too difficult, because they did not have sufficient information about the men to make sound judgements. Instead, companies were compared on the basis of performance in each of the tests and placed in order of merit. Clearly different levels of performance were visible among the companies, although no information about their roles is provided by Macdonald. Additionally, correlations were calculated using various individual tests as the criterion. Multiple correlations ranged from .28 to .31, uncorrected for reliability or homogeneity. Funnily enough, comparisons with results in infantry regiments with various army tests and BARB, seem to suggest little improvement over time (see Chapter 7).

Although the quest for criterion validity met with anticipated difficulties and barriers, providing no clear cut affirmation of the value of the tests for allocation to different roles, there was as yet one other key question that could be answered. Even if it were not practicable to predict effectiveness in garrison camps where there was no defined military role, what did the tests mean after all the effort expended? Did the tests behave in such a way as to suggest that the same framework of abilities existed for the Askaris as was evident in work on English speaking recruits? For the answer, the intercorrelations of the tests themselves had to be analysed by the best methods available at the time.

Table 1.3: Macdonald's Basic Test Groups

Group A	Group B
African Matrix Test (1944 Revision)	Pegboard Manual Dexterity Test
Cube Construction Test	Reversible Blocks Manual Dexterity Test
Fourth Corner Test (1944 Revision)	Screwboard Manual Dexterity Test
Block Design Test	Physical Agility Test*
Arithmetic Attainments Test (Elementary)	Mechanical Assembly Test (Form A)
Formboard Test (Circular Insets)	Mechanical Assembly Test(Form B)
Formboard Test (Square Insets)	

Construct Validity

A large section (ten pages) of the report (loc. cit. pp. 47-57) describes what domains or factors might underlie the correlations among the various tests; but even then, the

---

9   Limitations of ratings as a criterion measure are discussed in Chapter 15.

complete details provided fail to convey the enormous effort involved in producing the conclusions reached. Days, if not weeks, of effort must have been involved in the calculations, probably by slide rule, to reach their conclusions. Today, the same result arrives after a few seconds of calculation, given the basic data, as in Table 1.3.

To seek closure, Macdonald's team members conducted a group factor analysis of the kind pioneered by Burt and Pearson. Sketched by Vernon (1961, pp. 4-7); and available circulated by him during his work for the armed services in 1941-45 (Vernon and Parry, 1949), his notes were handed down to generations of students supervised by him at The University of London Institute of Education thereafter[10]. The result was the reduction of the data contained in the correlations to two basic factors or test groups that were helpful in interpreting the correlation patterns made by the various tests. Macdonald extended his analysis to bring together the *African Matrix, Arithmetic and Fourth Corner* tests as a subgroup, suggesting that the *English Comprehension Test* be associated with them. He contrasted them with the remaining performance tests of perceptual and shape matching contained in the first factor, thereby splitting it into two related factors. He then identified a second major frame work, consisting mainly of dexterity and coordination tasks all identified in Group B. He proposed a final solution of three factors.

Factor Analysis Cultures: A Word to the Wise.
The cultural context of factor analysis is always a relative one and diversity is assured. If a reanalysis of Macdonald's correlation matrix were conducted today, what would the outcome be? What construct validity structure would emerge, Macdonald's or Vernon's (1961, p. 106) or another structure entirely? What lessons would be learned? To find out, Macdonald's original correlation matrix (loc. cit. p. 49) was duly copied into SPSS and a number of objective factor analyses carried out. However, three factors emerged with the following interpretation adduced. The first was a spatial factor; the second factor described the ability to reason given figural analogies and mental arithmetic within the constraints of working memory; and the third was one of speed of dexterity and physical coordination, identified by the pegboard, reversible blocks, and physical ability tests. The intercorrelation of the factors was in fact considerable (ranging from .57 to .74), suggesting an *overall generalised capability to learn new skills to 'a crude level of stability' (cf. Ferguson, 1954, 1956) under instruction.* The test situations together were one opportunity to acquire procedural knowledge for men confined in barracks with little to do while awaiting discharge and repatriation to their homelands.

WHAT FACTORS?

Factor Analysis Cultures:

A word to the wise – they are relative, not absolute

BARB: THE FIVE LESSONS

Armies everywhere are large, diverse organisations. Although today, the uniformed members British Army could fill a football stadium with 80,000 seats, in 1986 the aim of any new ability test battery was to select 11,000 recruits from the 45,000 applicants who applied every year. They had, after undergoing basic

---

10   The author has a copy, given to him by a colleague, the late Cyril Rogers, a student of Vernon.

training, to be able to perform to the standards required in more than 200 different employment groups. In that year, at the request of the *Army Personnel Research Establishment* (APRE), a revaluation of the *British Army Entrance Tests* (AET86) took place at the Human Assessment Laboratory of the University of Plymouth. Design and content of the tests used by the Army at the time of the review were based on a forty-year-old test battery, first produced during the second world war, known by Macdonald, described in Vernon and Parry (1949), but updated and re-normed from time to time. The hour-long group test session, administered by trained recruiting staff, contained five hand-scored tests in paper-and-pencil called *Instructions, Problems, Dominoes, Verbal Reasoning and Numbers*. School syllabuses had changed greatly since their introduction, and education targets in literacy and numeracy were no exception. Moreover, the individual test contents were well known and subject to much exposure over the years. A new generation of tests had become necessary. Above all, individual testing in a secure computer-delivered network had to replace group paper-and-pencil administration, regardless of what that might entail. Five years of research on adapting tests to military and computer cultures were to follow.

PUTTING TESTS INTO COMPUTERS: AN OFFICIAL VIEW

A year after what came to be known as the *British Army Recruit Battery* (BARB) system went operational throughout the United Kingdom, Chris Lewis-Cooper (1993) produced a statement of the official thinking behind the need for change. First, paper-and-pencil group testing followed by hand scoring had encountered difficulties in the long-term. The recruiters trusted and believed in AET 86, 'their' test battery but the results they provided did not inspire unqualified confidence. Scoring was one concern, because about 12% of the test results on inspection were incorrect because of scoring errors. However, scoring errors were not by themselves a major administrative issue if training were to prove effective. The group-testing context for administering of the tests was perhaps more sensitive: and not without its social implications. The *Army Entrance Test 86* was completed in paper-and-pencil form by batches of recruits. Memories of school tests were known to hold negative connotations for applicants seeking a new start. In that respect alone, the prospect of an individual, computer-delivered session was a modern image likely to attract optimistic attention.

A second and serious problem, inherent in the use of single forms of tests, was test security. This was much more critical because technical revisions were almost inevitable if compromise of existing versions were both recurrent and widespread. Moreover, the routine maintenance of security was a weighty administrative burden. Because only one form of each test operated, the test manuals, test papers, with their answers, all had to be security classified. According to Lewis-Cooper, there were about 25,000 classified documents relating to the tests, costly to administer and almost impossible to keep track of. It was hardly surprising that amendments or alternate forms of the tests were in that context alone, very expensive and time consuming options.

AET 86
WHY CHANGE?

Errors

Security

Knowledge Base

Attrition

Costs of amending *Army Entrance Test 86* were large but more important were the effect in the tests of the level of acquired knowledge required to perform adequately. What was AET86 threshold needed to gain entrance correct, when the knowledge itself was not necessary for carrying out everyday tasks in basic training, the barrier to further coursework? Much of the test content required *declarative knowledge* (facts learned from others) of a kind not taught to every applicant in every school. Given this view, there were two implications. First, training costs would not reduce, nor results improve, by testing all applicants for knowledge available to only a few. This risked bypassing valuable assets in the general population by selecting from an artificially reduced pool. Second, the Army has always counted on their being a large number of highly capable school leavers being motivated to succeed in practical tasks. Development potential was primary; all else was secondary, because good second phase training would fill the need given an acceptable minimum standard. The search for recruits since 1945 had not broadened to examine new testing possibilities. Although alternative test forms had been explored,[11] no new tests were introduced.

The Last Straw
Perhaps the worst point about the Army Entrance Test was that it did not seem to be working. Of the 16,000 recruits selected annually at that time, about 25%, or 2,750 recruits were being discharged for one reason or another annually. From analysis of discharge reports, at least 2% of the entry (320) did not have the ability to keep pace with the training. Each lost recruit was costing an estimated £3,000, meaning that the test was failing to find the disadvantaged 2%, and costing a million pounds every year.

The aim was a new generation of tests based on sound theory and practices that had never before been attempted. If successful, these new measures of aptitude for military service could contribute to, and even alter, the methods of psychometric testing in the United Kingdom and elsewhere. Moreover, such was the scope and vision of the project that it promised to make continuous development of the Army manpower programme's essential tool - its selection procedure - a cost-effective recurrent rather than a capital cost forced on the system whenever, as in the past, the entrance tests were judged to have outlived their usefulness. This proved to be the starting point in the formulation of what came to be known as EDC or *evidence-centred design* (Mislevy, 2011, Mislevy et al, 1999, 2002). Within a few months, the whole focus of the work had initiated a radical approach to test construction. A new generation of tests for recruitment, BARB, was on its way.

BARB: THE AET86 REPLACEMENT

Because the tests had to screen thousands of applicants annually, the practical issue was how to develop an expert system of testing that answered as many relevant questions about the potential of a candidate as possible, within the time available, interviews and background checks notwithstanding. Suppose recruits appear on the doorstep,

---

11   Dr. Malcolm Killcross informed me in 2012 that he researched computer-delivered adaptive tests for APRE, but these were never implemented. However, an account can be found in his unpublished PhD theses (Killcross, 1976). The team at Plymouth were not made aware of this development, and his work was not consulted, valuable though it would undoubtedly have proved at the time.

BARB

*Not one test for all,
but new tests for
one and all.*

having expressed an interest in a technical, logistic, or an armed combat role, and the cost-benefit time limit for assessing the potential of unreferred applicants is decreed from on high as one hour. How could, in the early days of computer-delivery, interactive computer-based testing do more than traditional right/wrong scoring model approaches, seemingly acceptable, and thoroughly integrated with the existing mind-set? *The British Army Recruit Battery*, destined to replace AET86, went into operational service in the South West and South East regions of England in February 1992; and thereafter in all Army Career Information Offices throughout the United Kingdom. *At that time, BARB was to be unique in the world of testing because it could, if required, and did in fact, deliver a 'new' version of its six tests to every applicant in the knowledge that every new test had the same selection and psychometric characteristics as the previous one.* Not one test for all, but new tests for one and all. The replacement for AET86 was so unlike its predecessor that it could not, and was not, received in silence by recruiters. For staff accustomed to the prestige and power invested in the administration, scoring and interpreting paper-and-pencil tests, was BARB more of a threat than an aide?

Two technical issues confronted the Human Assessment Laboratory team before the archetypical BARB tests they created could be appreciated fully. One was the collection of evidence for the psychometric framework considered necessary for constructing recruitment tests. There were lots to consider; although when the literature background to construction is re-examined in the light of day, not much seems to have changed in the past quarter of a century (Campbell & Knapp, 2001, Irvine & Kyllonen, 2002, 2010, Mislevy, 2011, Thissen & Wainer, 2001). The other was the pursuit, through laboratory experiment and simulation, of a basic understanding of what the very idea of computer administration for each individual implied for selecting quality recruits; and what it can still do today. Above all, a computer-delivered system was new world for constructors, users and recruits. Macdonald's lessons were general ones. BARB was a special case. What were the particular lessons to be learned in 1986? And how would a military lesson plan be structured?

MILITARY CULTURE DELIVERY PROSPECTS

In 1986, one had to assume that the system would be an expert one. With job-specific information at its disposal on the one hand, it had to present tests, tasks and inventories, whose theoretical substructures are understood, to applicants. To reach its target, the system had to take account of and selectively use, all of the information, including the responses of the recruit, from the moment the procedure began. Machine systems could be programmed for such a task, because they had existed for some time in other scientific studies where details had to be recorded and managed. Such technological scoring and storage capabilities were of lesser importance than the psychological suppositions determining the rules that the system applied in assessing the personal qualities needed to reach a stable classification point for the candidate.

THE FACTS OF THE MATTER

Putting tests into a computer might to a newcomer in 1986 have seemed to be a simple matter of translating the paper-and-pencil forms into a computer screen, preceded by instructions and asking the applicant to indicate an answer by pressing a key on a regular or specially adapted QWERTY keyboard: or a special console. From the outset this line, simply translating the AET86 tests and their items into computer-delivery forms, was a non-starter for two reasons. First, putting the existing test items on to a screen was not going to work. At that time, crude 'translation models' were, if not operating, then undergoing extensive trials in the United States. They were not successful, according to reliable sources and observation of early attempts to put existing test items on screen. Moreover, this would only prolong the use of all the individual AET tests already under pressure from over-exposure. Second, people in all occupations in Britain were largely unaccustomed to computer use. In 1986, no computerised delivery facility existed for recruit testing: and one had to be created if trials were to be conducted. When the proposal to introduce a new computer-delivered battery of tests for screening potential recruits for the British army was first discussed, a lack of computer awareness and contact among the recruits was the cultural context to be recognised. Very few homes or schools in the United Kingdom had computers. Nowadays such a state of affairs would immediately seem naïve because of everyday exposure to the internet, mobile phones, touchscreens, interactive games and all the technology available to children from the time they can read and write – or even before they are fully literate. *If computers were the test vehicle, the tests had to be adapted to two cultures, the computer itself; and the prediction of training results for army recruits who had no prior experience of using computers and keyboards.* These were two quite different problems, one machine based and the other people-centred. And there was one more. The military training experience was by all accounts a special culture with laws unto itself with firm consequences for criterion validity, as Chapter 7 fully asserts. Perhaps three, not two, cultural adaptations, each requiring a different knowledge base, had to be made before BARB could be introduced with any prospect of success.

THE LESSONS FOR BARB

Macdonald's was the first attempt at standardisation using adapted tests in the history of cross-cultural testing: and it was in a military setting. The result was not an accident. It was to provide only the first example of a recurring pattern evident in all countries where recruits for all manner of occupations were confronted by computer-delivered tests requiring procedural knowledge and manipulation of information in working memory. Elaborate Swahili instructions and supervised practice, involving *the successful acquisition of procedural knowledge* were essential to the execution of the tests, which was the whole aim of Macdonald's research. He had uncovered one of the fundamentals of recruit adaptation, learning novel procedures within the command structure of military cultures. BARB had to follow his example. In short, solutions would allow theory behind the BARB tests to become operational in 1992 and to continue (Irvine, 2013b) to create a new generation of tests for the next 21 years.

The rest of this book takes Macdonald's five lessons, cultural adaptation, test choice, instructions, scoring and meaning, as the model for a new evidence-centred approach to the construction and use of tests for recruitment. Using international studies in Europe and the United States to provide a broad testing landscape, a handbook and guide to success for practitioners and students alike is the consummation greatly desired. The range of studies in the various countries is vast. A short insert at the start of each chapter highlights its contents. Other periodic insertions direct attention, not without a sense of humour, to salient issues. Most compelling, perhaps, are those personal perspectives of people[12] who took part or observed. They have contributed forewords to individual sectors or chapters. While all else may fail, their vision is clear and enlightened.

---

12   John Anderson, Isaac Bejar, Paul Cawkill, Thomas Kutschke, Pat Kyllonen, François Lescrève, Mike Matthews, Bob Mislevy and Johannes Wulf.

CHAPTER 2

LESSONS 1 AND 2: CULTURE CONTEXTS AND TEST INSTRUCTIONS

LESSON 1: RECRUIT AND COMPUTER CULTURES

This chapter provides an outline of those elements of computer-delivered test principles needed for understanding the operational issues that were faced in 1985, but are the self-same issues today in the comprehension and use of computer-delivered tests. Different sorts of cultural components had to be understood for the BARB adaptations to take place. The emphasis, following on from the historical analogy provided by Macdonald's work, is necessarily applied; but the background to the thinking that went into the construction of BARB in 1986 is not widely known. The adaptation of tests to the cultural setting was as important a concept for BARB as it was for Macdonald in 1945, for Irvine (1965), and Irvine & Berry (1988) in their review. It survives even now, with unresolved theory and practice issues (Fatimilehin & Hunt, 2013).

LESSONS 1 AND 2 CULTURE CONTEXTS AND INSTRUCTIONS

Find the attributes for success in initial training

Review computer-delivered testing in military units – USA Belgium Germany

Limitations of computer delivery in item presentation

Comprehend how different presentation modes become elements for radical changes

BARB's psychometric framework:

The Anderson Question

THE RECRUIT CULTURE: FUNDAMENTALS OF PROCEDURAL KNOWLEDGE

Low levels of school attainments reached by many recruits past and present are a fact of army life: but the BARB test results had to prove relevant to initial training demands. What were these demands and what tests were most likely to predict success or failure by a potential recruit? If cross-cultural experience were to prevail, tests constructed without knowing what the cultural demands were would be useless. Insiders' experience was essential. Today, a scan of the internet reveals many sites with advice to new recruits. Potential applicants take it seriously because it comes from experiences that seldom, if ever, have changed during the whole of the last half century. Many visits made to British training depots and discussions with long-serving armed forces members revolved around BARB and its needs. Consensus, regardless of national identity is not difficult to find, in pamphlets or on the internet. United States services veteran Rod Powers[1] gives advice on do's and don'ts in basic training: and Figure 2.1 summarises them. Their content can be classified into what has to be learned, facts (*declarative knowledge*) or know how (*procedural knowledge*). Two thirds of them are about procedures. Facts to accumulate amount to a quarter; and only one tenth are about physical skills. The recruit's fundamental need is to *learn what to do and even more significant, what not to do* to avoid undue attention and sanctions from instructors.

Figure 2.1: Proportions of Knowledge Types

FUNDAMENTALS OF RECRUIT CULTURE

To be successful in basic training, recruits carry out spoken orders without question or hesitation; learn new procedures and acquire specialised military skills (such as aiming and time and distance estimation) that demand perceptual speed and orientation skills. They have to read signs; and attend to notices containing their names. With people they have never met before they build and maintain their self-esteem by learning these skills. Success depends on the approval of instructors on whose behaviour recruits exert no counter-control.

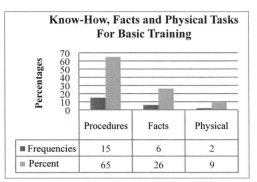

For discipline to exist, 'know-how' or procedural knowledge has to be learned rather than the accumulation of facts. Success under rules that apply for 24 hours of each day in a total, command environment depends on know-how: simply stated, but for many hard to acquire (Kiernan, 2011). There is no visible means of escape, except withdrawal. Even today, with all the technological changes that are evident in simulation environments, visits to training battalions and newspaper reports confirm the prescribed behaviour of instructors and recruits. From all the evidence observed and reported, the insert contains a summary mission statement. It lists the outcomes the new BARB tests had to predict if they were to be both reliable and valid. BARB had to work within, and predict the success of recruits in achieving, these non-negotiable realities. For a comprehensive discussion of the unique military motivation culture of success and failure in initial training, see Chapter 14.

MILITARY CULTURES USING COMPUTER-BASED TESTING IN 1986.

By 1992, the date by which BARB went operational nation-wide, much work on computer-based testing has already occurred, in the United States and in Europe:

---

[1]   Edited from an article on *How to Survive Boot Camp* by Rod Powers in website About.com/US Military

and it largely dates from the availability of the technology at affordable prices. The literature begins to grow from Carroll's (1980) pioneering work onwards, although computer-delivered experiments had appeared in the experimental cognitive science literature for many years. Christal (1984) sets the military marker in his compendium of tests for which software was available, and which were being tried out by the US Air Force basic research project in the cognitive correlates of learning, usually known as *Project LAMP*. Early progress reports of this approach were in circulation, and became formally available in a comprehensive account by Fairbank, Tirre & Anderson, (1986). *Project A* for the US Army was proceeding in parallel, as the comprehensive volume by Campbell & Knapp (2001) was eventually to show, although there were official reports released under closed circulation during the 1980s. Moreover, Hornke (Hornke & Habon, 1986: Hornke, 2002) and Goeters (Goeters& Rathje, 1992; Goeters & Lorenz, 2002) were independently leading attempts at item generation in Germany. A narrower definition of recruit test construction soon followed (Dann & Irvine, 1987). Edited international collections of papers on advances in computer-delivered assessment (Dann, Irvine & Collis, 1991, Irvine & Kyllonen, 2002, 2010) mark progress during the decade.

Four Military Sources
In the search for a solution, and in particular what tests to use and how best to construct them, four relevant military models of computer-based measurement, defined initially in official publications, provided direct operational measures of computer-based testing in applied contexts. They formed a compulsory stage in the review process for item-generative theory. In order of discussion they are the *US Army Project A* (Peterson, 1987; Campbell & Knapp, 2001); The *USAF Human Resources Laboratory's Project LAMP* (Kyllonen, 2010), whose experimental tests are best sourced in Fairbank, Tirre & Anderson, (1986); the development of computer-delivered tests in the German armed services; and trends in the Belgian Defence force.

Because much development of experimental tests capable of use in item generative systems occurred in *Project A* and LAMP, work in these two major projects was scrutinised in the period leading up to the production of unlimited parallel forms in the *British Army Recruit Battery*. These sources are not exclusive: and because detailed studies of the use of item generative tests occurred in Germany and Belgium (see Chapter 12), brief summaries of computer-delivered test systems in these countries are included, with a final highlight on pilot selection in Germany and the UK. Understanding of their various contributions is an essential part of the first lesson, existing: how to adapt computer cultures to ensure that recruits with limitations in educational achievements understood the questions and how to answer them.

UNITED STATES ARMY PROJECT A: THE WASHINGTON CROSSING

Project A (Peterson, 1987; Campbell & Knapp, 2001) was begun in 1980: and at its best it could be said to represent a decisive manoeuvre to lead the revolution in military assessment. It was an extensive, and costly (requiring approximately 400 person-years), investigation by the US Army Research Institute. Diverse measures designed to be useful in predicting recruit selection and retention were trialled empirically; an extraordinarily broad enterprise in applied psychology with cognitive, motivational and attitude domains constructed on a large scale. The various studies were concerned with the choice of tests to use in military contexts; and how to define their interrelations and limits. Above all, work required new versions of computer-based cognitive tests to evaluate their particular contribution. The reports are treasure troves of assumptions, methods and results.

PROJECT A: COGNITIVE TEST SCOPE
The *Project A* cognitive tests fall into three types. The keystone element is the *Armed Services Vocational Aptitude Battery* (ASVAB) series that is a well-known battery of ten aptitude measures heavily reliant on acquired knowledge. Readers will find examples of the ten basic ASVAB test types in Table 2 of Chapter 9. Next is a recognisable battery of six paper-and-pencil psychometric 'factor marker tests' derived from the ETS Factor Kit (Ekstrom, French & Harmon, 1976) which in their turn owe a great deal to Thurstone (1938). Last is a set of computer-based tasks that are in the 'perceptual and psycho-motor domain', although there is much evidence to suggest that they test more than that. These computer-delivered tests are detailed (Peterson, 1987, Peterson, 2001) but they are summarised in the insert. Together the last two types in the series define a missile tracking and aiming group of tests. The tests can further be defined by various diagrams that characterise the demands made on the participants Campbell & Knapp, 2001 pp. 87-88). Ostensive definitions emerge from the demands of a special console *(The Pedestal)* needed to record responses, using various latency measures, to record times to completion, and accuracy measures. Not least, construct definition arises from a conventional factor analysis of the correlation matrix of all the tests used in the study (ASVAB, paper and pencil, computer-delivered experimentally dependent derivatives).

SIX *PROJECT A* TEST PARADIGMS

Simple and Choice Reaction Time (Latency To Solution);

Speed and Accuracy (Object Recognition and Comparison)

Short Term Memory (Sternberg Probe)

Working Memory (Frame-at-a-Time Arithmetic)

Movement Judgement (Cannon Shoot)

Target Tracking (Target Shoot)

PROJECT A RESULTS
Much information and insight emerge from a full description in the volume by Campbell & Knapp, (2001, Chapter 5). Here, though, comments are confined to the essentials of *Project A* whose test adaptations had the greatest relevance for BARB immediately after its production in report form by Peterson (1987). There are general observations grouped under headings of construct validity, reliability and delivery interface, the properties that related to all computer-based tests in use at the time.

Construct Validity

The most outstanding features of the computer-based tasks are the centrality of the computer-based measures of perceptual speed and of working memory. These form bridges between traditional *Armed Services Vocational Aptitude Battery* (ASVAB) entrance tests and the experimental series of paper and pencil tests based on the Thurstone-inspired ETS Kit (Ekstrom, French and Harmon, 1976). Three or four mathematical factors will reproduce the matrix. That is, performance depends, respectively, on learned declarative knowledge and skills, on attentional or working memory capacity; and on speed of encoding information and verifying this against information stored in fast-access memory.

Aiming and Tracking Tasks

The aiming and tracking tasks of the computer-delivered battery correlated substantially with static spatial tests and with working memory tasks, which the theory demands, correlated moderately with processing tasks involving arithmetical and mechanical information, and correlated only slightly with ASVAB Total, which can be taken as a verbal-educational marker. This important study suggests that time-estimation may be related to the constructs of speed and working memory inasmuch as the classes of tasks that define these constructs depend on reconstructive processes. *The cumulative evidence for aiming and tracking to be part of a general sub-system is more substantial when Project A results are added and considered as a whole. Time-estimation tasks were validated for British Army recruits (Cf. Chapter 9).* However, tasks that required complex apparatus were difficult to justify, as the work in *Project A* was to show. The following sections on reliability and the delivery interface provide the rationale for careful consideration of the task type and its response requirements.

Delivery Interface

The delivery interface used in the *Project A* experiments is shown in a diagram in Campbell & Knapp (loc. cit. p. 94), termed *'the response pedestal'*. This unique interface with its imposing title was a complex piece of equipment, designed for two-handed tracking coordination as well as recording answers to tests on a concept keyboard. There are all together fourteen different response keys to be recognised, learned and mastered if fluency is required as a prelude to reaction time reliability: ten buttons, two 'gear levers' and two slides. Different manipulation procedures are required for each family of computer-delivered tests. Because the time to master and automate the procedures of the console must have been considerable, and transfer from one task to the next was not apparently built into the test sequence, one can only speculate about the contribution of what one might define as the 'pedestal sources of variance' that attend all the latency measures. As the test-retest reliabilities for simple reaction-time tasks were relatively small (Campbell & Knapp (loc. cit. p. 109), a hypothesis for this must be the amount of error variance in latencies attributable to learning and relearning the console. This result, and visible *Project A* pedestal complexity were the main factors in the decision to use touch screens in the BARB, because at no point were two-handed

THE PROJECT A PEDESTAL:

Its Buttons - and Bowing Out?

coordination or multiple response keys necessary for initial recruit screening. In fact, the results quoted in Campbell & Knapf, were available in Petersen's (1987) restricted report on *Project A. These convinced the BARB team that touchscreens were the only option in Britain in 1986.* Today, touch screens are every child's birth right. In 1986, they were even in their rudimentary form, fundamental to the adaptation of British Army recruits to computer culture. Only a decade later, a restricted movement mouse interface had become a realistic alternative with enlarged screens in work completed at Lackland Air Force Base during 1997-99 (Chapters 10 and 11).

Score Model Reliability

Experimenter induced artefacts of slopes, difference scores, ratios and the like that are notoriously unreliable (when the average intercorrelation of two measures approaches their reliability, the reliability of their difference scores or scores derived from differences approaches zero). However, the internal consistency of computer-based measures within test sessions is generally good; but test-retest correlations, (see Campbell & Knapp, 2001, p. 107) were much lower and gave some cause for concern if individual change measures of timed tasks were contemplated. However, these lower reliabilities could reveal that procedural learning had occurred between sessions, disrupting the ranks of individuals. Irvine (1979, 1981) reports considerable procedural switch among students carrying out repeated trials at a simple coding task over a six-minute time span.

PROJECT A REVISITED

The edited *Project A* account, derived from original restricted reports, occupies more than 600 pages in Campbell & Knapp, (2001). It details and evaluates the construction and try out of many types of tests, notable for the care with which these are specified and used. It is also salutary in two respects. The attempts to translate conventional cognitive tests to computers did not always meet with the success and use that perhaps they merited. Moreover, the types of analyses used on the data to reveal the domains and constructs of the tests (invariably principal components and varimax rotations of data matrices) represent a systematic interpretational focus. Finally, there remained unknown effects of the 'pedestal variance' on latency data. Despite these idiosyncrasies, it made pioneering contributions to the coherence of theory that emerged from the use of computer-based tests on a large scale. Specifically, the underlying and apparently essential, cognitive test domains of *perceptual speed and working memory* were confirmed in this, the most comprehensive application of then current instrumentation. *One must not forget that only Campbell & Knapp have provided full and comprehensive results from recruitment tests involving interests, motivation and personality, together with validity studies. Emphasis on cognitive tasks alone does not do their landmark work justice for its comprehensiveness and reach beyond the framework of item response theory.*

USAF PROJECT LAMP: FORT SUMTER FIRED ON?

The US Air Force *Project LAMP* based in Brooks AFB, San Antonio, Texas, might possibly be perceived, if not as a challenge and rebellion by another service arm against army efforts in Washington, then as a potential southern state rival. Kyllonen, (2010) records the only comprehensive summary account of the enterprise in existence, with nearly 150 reports and published sources that had been circulating for years; *but not a single reference to Project LAMP exists in Campbell & Knapp (2001)*. Unlike *Project A*, it did not set out to apply cognitive, affective and conational domains to a grand selection and allocation design. Its aims were much more limited, and specific: to trace the relationships of cognitive abilities and skills to speed, amount and permanence of learning. From the outset, the tests and tasks were computer-based and at the same time, the project was both theory and model oriented. The work focussed on describing those measures that would predict efficiency in simulated service functions.

Project LAMP; Five Distinguishing Marks.
While the first focus is a programmatic effort at model building, the second is the availability of large numbers of participants. The third, important for efficiency, is a stable computer-delivery environment, first established in 1981, and a long-serving technical backup team providing programming and analysis skills. The fourth is a capability to decentralise aspects of the work by contracts let to Universities, Colleges and Research Corporations.

A final and quite crucial observation emphasises the kinds of measures used in *Project LAMP* (and indeed most modern psychometric studies). Many of them seem quite simple to do. That is, they presuppose a low level of formal education. Carroll (1981) had labelled them *Elementary Cognitive Tasks* (ECTs). To confuse their ease of comprehension with simplicity of cognitive function would be a fundamental mistake (just as erroneous as calling all figurally or symbolically presented tasks *non-verbal* without first filming the obvious subvocalisation of participants). All of these features enabled *Project LAMP* to conduct systematic experimental validation of measures and models very quickly. Perhaps the only note of caution is the knowledge that the interface for early work was a modified QWERTY keyboard: and later work used a mouse-controlled cursor.

USAF PROJECT LAMP

Project LAMP owes much of its inspiration to Christal (1981, 1985, 1988) Christal & Kyllonen, (1986), Kyllonen & Christal, (1986, 1988, 1989, 1990) .

Synthesis is provided by Kyllonen's foreword, and in several of his publications: Kyllonen (1985, 1986, 1987, 2010) Kyllonen Tirre & Christal, (1988, 1991) and Kyllonen & Woltz, 1988).

Several test type innovations are apparent in Woltz (1987) and in Tirre and his associates (1987a, 1987b)

LAMP's Four Sources Model: Reconstructing g?
Research for the project was conceptualised and eventually rooted in the *Four Source Framework* (Kyllonen & Christal, 1988). This is reproduced as Table 2.1 which summarises the argument used by Kyllonen showing how he and his colleagues have arrived at measuring

aspects of *Declarative Knowledge, Procedural Knowledge, Processing Speed and Working Memory.* The constructs are defined in this way because they are considered to enter into learning in different but complementary fashion. Kyllonen (1996 pp. 55-7) describes how he *tried to verify the four source model by administering twenty-five tests to 350 volunteers. Total test time was 6 hours, each test taking about 15 minutes to complete.* Some if not all of these tests and tasks could be further categorised by using Carroll's eight item families or domains, although they were not derived from them. Kyllonen's four source framework was to prove an enduring one for LAMP.

Table 2.1: Kyllonen's Framework for Four Source Test Construction

	Verbal (V)	Quantitative (Q)	Spatial (S)
Processing Speed (PS)	PSV	PSQ	PSS
Working Memory (WM)	WMV	WMQ	WMS
Declarative Knowledge (DK)	DKV	DKQ	DKS
Procedural Knowledge (PK)	PKV	PKQ	PKS

Precisely what defines the predominance of any one set of skills or abilities or degree of knowledge is the nature of the learning that is occurring and the particular stage in the learning sequence that the subject has attained. The research had three phases: first, distinguishing Processing Speed from Working Memory by differential validation of these constructs; second, distinguishing Ryle's 'knowing that' from 'knowing how' by separating tasks of procedural learning from tests of acquired knowledge: and third, they attempting to derive a taxonomy of learning skills (Kyllonen & Shute, 1988) with which to infuse computerised learning tutors. The measures of learning in the tutors would represent the four constructs used for the classification of predictors. How did the results of the *Four Source Framework* relate to the task of generating tests in computers?

The 'g' of Processing Speed?
Kyllonen describes a number of experiments designed to assess whether information-processing speed can be generalised across diverse content. His conclusion stems from the technical problems of isolating speed of encoding, speed of search, speed of comparison and speed of retrieval from estimates of latency from derived measures. He concludes that speed of processing is generalisable across content within processing stages, but not across them. That is fast encoders are fast at all encoding tasks, but fast encoders are not necessarily fast searchers or fast comparers.

Operationally, the most compelling finding of the series was the high correlation (.5) between speed of semantic search for meanings of words *(Happy is a positive word, sad a negative word: to which category does laugh belong?).* Latency to indicate positive or negative is the dependent variable) and declarative knowledge measured by vocabulary test scores that are found in IQ composites. In paired-associate and list learning when the study time was extremely short, the same type of semantic search task predicted recall in the region .3 to .5. Reaction times in quest of semantic certainty proved promising for predicting learning outcomes. This series also revealed that speed of semantic search is a meaningful construct. Clearly, the residual problem was how to measure this without resorting to item-banks that require renewal. The fact that speed or latency is the important variable relaxes the restraints that accuracy would place upon item-generation.

THE WORKING MEMORY CONSTRUCT.

The major success of the work on *Project LAMP* (even if it did nothing more it would be judged a major scientific contribution by this work alone) was the standardisation of a series of processing tasks that underscore the role of working memory in problem solving and remembering rules of procedure in the early stages of learning. *These working memory tasks pioneered the use of the computer screen to control the amount and above all the sequence of subject information.* This enabled estimation of the efficiency with which a learner can retain, retrieve, rehearse and maintain information while transforming it mentally by use of personal (and of course invisible) strategies. Because of the combination of cognitive and psychometric disciplines in the BARB team (Evans, Evans and Dennis, Newstead Dann & Collis, Irvine and Newstead) the work of Baddeley and Hitch in working memory tasks was well known and applied early in the search for item generative tests of power and precision. An example of early work is available.

THE WORKING MEMORY CONSTRUCT

The major success of the work on Project LAMP (even if it did nothing more it would be judged a major scientific contribution by this work alone) was the standardisation of a series of processing tasks that underscore the role of working memory in problem solving and remembering rules of procedure in the early stages of learning.

Working Memory in Action.
A construct validity study of the LAMP battery showed that a Working Memory Factor emerged which subsumed reasoning. A speeded-quantitative factor was defined by the ASVAB number operations, but it attracted variance from the ABCD task involving mental manipulation of the letters of the alphabet (Hockey & Maclean, 1986 pp. 419-20) The task requires the transformation of letters in memory by stepping forward a fixed number of places in the alphabet e.g. $S + 2 > U$. This can be done for more than one letter $SI + 3 > VL$, and in addition by stepping backward $PD - 1 < QC$. A verbal factor loaded by the ABCD task and the Baddeley AB sentence verification task that Irvine Dann & Evans (1987) feature as a task that could be computer-generated.

Working Memory and Procedural Learning.
Kyllonen & Woltz (1988) report a series of experiments using procedural learning tasks with moderate and high attentional demands. They included several measures of processing speed and efficiency as predictors. The studies are important for the way in which the learning tasks were constructed. The example in Figure 2.2 below shows just how demanding the application of if-then logic can be when the instructions are

first learned before they are applied; or even when given concurrently with every item until learned. The memory demands are formidable: and for any with limited attention spans, almost impossible.

Figure 2.2: Project LAMP Instructions for Learning Task

DECLARATIVE RULE SET FOR PROCEDURAL LEARNING TASK

If new number note if digit-word (seven) or digit-symbol (7)

If digit-word, check if odd or even.
If digit-word odd, check if at bottom
If at bottom, press L, else D.

If digit-word even, check if at top
If at top, press L else D.

If digit-symbol check if big or small.
If big, check if at bottom
If at bottom press L else D

If small, check if at top
If at top press L, else D

It forms a concept-learning task whose declarative rules are specified. As such, it is an early example of an attempt to use a D-Model, by learning rules in the classifying of information. The computer-based programme displays digits (e.g.7) or words that have the same name as a digit symbol (Seven) at the top or bottom of the screen. When that happens, the stimulus can be processed. Note that *odd and even* are categorical priors. Moreover, it is a classic example of controlling the nature and the difficulty of the task by using the screen as a necessary *radical*. Paper and pencil analogues could be constructed, although complex and uncertain in their outcomes. Without using a computer screen to display each item consecutively, with or without the rules, it could not be done.

A second series of tasks concerned the simulation of a real visual transformation task, learning the concepts involved in three different figural representations of electronic logic gates for determining current flow, mastery of which is essential in servicing complex circuits. The electronic *Logic Gates Task* has procedural rules of the same complexity as the concept learning task just described. Two important studies of the relation of cognitive tasks to success in learning to identify and differentiate these tasks (Christal, 1990, Irvine & Christal, 1994) were carried out; and the later study is reported in full in Chapter 9, the Plymouth Laboratory pursuit of reliable military criteria.

LAMP SHEDS LIGHT ON RESPONSES

Note, finally, that at the early stages in project LAMP *a standard typewriter QWERTY keyboard was the interface.* The response keys for L and D responses in Figure 2.2 were in the middle row of the keyboard, but they still had to be found among others. Perhaps less daunting than the pedestal used in *Project A*; but no less a factor for applicants with no experience of the standard keyboard. The lessons from the United States campaigns were learned. Touchscreens became the BARB interface.

LAMP: WORKING MEMORY THE KEYNOTE

For both types of tasks, learning verbal and visual concept transformations, concordant results emerged. First, there were different stages of procedural learning. These stages formed a continuum defined by the increases and decreases of correlations with different classes of cognitive tests from first to last trial. Next, what predicted success in one stage did not necessarily predict success in subsequent stages. The results are reported by Kyllonen & Woltz (loc.cit.) in terms of derived variables that need more explanation than can be given here, and perhaps some psychometric caution. Nevertheless, measures derived from working memory tasks were the constant elements in the equation. Error rates in the learning trials correlated most highly with working-memory performance in the early trials. Time to complete the trials correlated most highly with the same measures in the later stages. Rate of execution (component efficiency) as measured by latency also had important contributions to make in the later trials. *In short, working memory measures predict error rates (Accuracy) in early learning trials and time to complete (Latency) in later trials.*

Confirmation from a number of studies of the centrality of working memory tasks leads to these conclusions about their relationship with intelligence and learning. They share large proportions of variance with what have hitherto been regarded as widely different tests - such as reasoning, verbal, spatial and perceptual measures of intelligence; they reveal parsimonious prediction of learning rates in early trials and speed of execution in later trials. Consequently, the involvement of working memory in the efficient performance of tests of second and third order is a plausible hypothesis that allows theoretical determination of what it is that the *Alphabet Forward and Backward* paradigm measures. Because these early forays and expeditions into computer-delivered tests contained examples and recommendations, they offered insights, prescriptions and, not least, revelations about what to follow: and perhaps more salutary, what best to avoid if misadventures were not to be repeated.

EUROPEAN RECRUITMENT USING COMPUTERISED TESTS : THE 1980s

The commentaries in Chapter 12 by Johannes Wulf and François Lescrève give important perspectives

Independently, Belgian and German military psychologists had begun to experiment by adapting tests to computer delivery

EUROPE: EARLY COMPUTER-BASED MILITARY TESTING

In Germany, military psychologists had begun to experiment by adapting tests to computer delivery (Wildgrube 1983; Storm 1999). Academia was not far behind. Studies on the adaptation of individual figural test types were forecast by Hornke (2002) and Hornke & Habon (1986) investigating the factors making figural tests like *Raven's Matrices* difficult. Pilot selection proved an early focus for first generation computer-delivered tests at the Hamburg Aeronautical Selection Centre (Goeters. 1979; Goeters and Rathje 1992; Goeters and Lorenz (2002, pp. 339-60); and in Britain, Bartram's 1985-8 studies on *Micropat*, are discussed and referenced in the closing section of the chapter.

THE LESCRÈVE BELGIAN DEFENCE SYSTEM
The present-day GCTB (Computer Delivered Test Battery) system currently employed for the Belgian Defence Force (BDF) gradually developed over time under Col. Francois Lescréve from basic paper-and-pencil tests used in recruit selection. Test batteries in the BDF contained cognitive, personality and motivational group tests. Group observational tasks also appear in the officer selection system (Devriendt, 1999b, Van Beirendonck, 1998). Initially, these were paper and pencil test batteries. In common with other NATO forces, the Belgian system relied upon medical and psychological standards, as indicated by Mathieu, Dubois & Viaene (1987). The Belgian Defence Force started variants of automated selection from 1970 onwards, and development during the 1980s and 1990s under the leadership of Lescrève advanced through various technological stages (Lescrève, 1993, 1995a, 1995b, 1996, 1997a, 1997b, 1998, 2000). Lescrève's colleague Schreurs (2001) describes the progress made. Their efforts reveal a comprehensive allocation system that is computer controlled and validity driven, an advanced and unique framework for military selection discussed in Chapter 12.

During the seventies automated processes were introduced at the Recruitment and Selection Centre in Brussels. Punched cards scored and stored paper-and-pencil test results. In the eighties, the first computer-assisted system became operational. In the second half of the nineties, a new version was developed. From 2001 onwards, paper-and-pencil testing ceased and a completely integrated computer-delivered selection procedure existed in local recruitment offices throughout Belgium in Flemish and French. This meant the removal of redundant tests and the provision of a single recruit test battery for the screening of all applicants, regardless of their role preferences. Like the tests in Britain the United States and Germany, they were adaptations of commonly used tests of verbal, numerical, spatial and mechanical aptitude and information.

Figure 2.3: Outline of Three-day Selection Sequence in BDF

Day1	Day2
Information (Part 1)	Medical Examinations[2]
Intellectual Potential Test[3]	*Lunch*
Lunch	Physical Fitness Tests
Motivation Test	**Day3**
Information (Part 2)	Interviews
Biodata Form[4]	
Additional Tests (as required)	

As the contents in Figure 2.3 show, the central selection process at the reception centre in Brussels, largely devised over several years by Lescréve, was comprehensive and had points of inclusion and exclusion for different reasons. On Day 3, fully qualified psychologists of officer rank carried out personal interviews, an unusual event for the assessment of enlisted men and women. The *California Personality Inventory* was translated and used as a preliminary profiling device; and the results made available before the interview took place. It is still used today.

Selection took place in stages but initial screening occurred nationally in *Maisons de Defence* (MdD) - recruitment offices in all major centres in Belgium. Further medical, psychological and group testing were centralised in Brussels only if the Belgian MdD initially approved the applicant. The central system in Brussels is currently part of a military hospital complex and by the turn of the century had fully equipped test centres capable of testing 60 applicants at any one time. Recently, first phase testing in the MdD recruitment information centres ended and all potential recruits have to journey to Brussels for complete appraisal, involving cognitive, personality and medical screening. This contextual background contributes to the complete understanding of the Belgian GCTB selection studies detailed in Chapter 12 where the computer-delivered tests are validated. In Chapter 13, a special study of Differential Item Functioning (DIF) examines the same tests for their fairness to females and males: and in particular, minority immigrant groups that are compared with majority native-born Belgians in both official languages, French and Nederlands (Flemish).

CONSCRIPTS IN THE GERMAN BUNDESWEHR CONTEXT

A complete English-language historical account of test development in the Bundeswehr was not immediately apparent. After several enquiries, materials by a officials of the ministry of defence were found and constituted the available background (Fritscher & Koch, 1975; Steege, 1976; Buchtala, 1977; Birke & Wildgrube 1978). According to Wildgrube, (1983), the first empirical phase started with the *Aptitude Classification*

---

2   Candidates who pass the medical selection are admitted to the physical fitness tests. The others are sent home after the lunch break.

3   Candidates who pass the Intellectual potential test may continue. The others are sent home after the lunch break.

4   Experimental tests or tests for specific entries.

Battery (EVT), the standard test battery for entrance into the Federal Armed Forces and similar to the ASVAB.

Table 2.2: Bundeswehr Computerised Batteries, 1983 and 2000

Test Name	Test Name	
1983 Battery*	**2000 Computer-Delivered Battery**	
Word Analogy Test(WAT)	FDT	Figural Reasoning
Figure Reasoning Test (FDT)	WBT	Verbal Reasoning
Arithmetic Reasoning Test (RT)	RT	Number Skills
Spelling (Orthographical Test; RST)	RTHST	Orthographic (Spelling) Test
Mechanical Ability Test (MT)	MT	Mechanical Ability
Electrotechnical Comprehension Test (EKT)	EKT	Electrical Principles
*paper-and- pencil provided for notes	RP	Reaction Time
	FT	Radio Operator Test
	SIG	Signal Detection
	DOP	Auditory Discrimination
	IQN	General Classification Index

From Wildgrube's account of paper-and-pencil test content, it seems as if the speeded paper-and-pencil tests described in 1983 had been successfully transferred to computer-delivered form. Initially six subtests (the subtests without graphic items) were on the computer in two parallel forms. Four more subtests were not on the computer (e.g. radio test, test for reaction rate) measured special aspects and were speeded tests.

All six tests on the computer had time limits and all items unanswered were presented again. Testing time varied between 45 and 75 minutes, because some applicants required more time for the practice items. On a single day, approximately eight persons were tested at each test station. Gradually, the Bundeswehr system was expanded and improved, until by the year 2000, when experimental tasks were first tried out nationwide, (Irvine et al. 2000, Irvine 2003), ten different tests were administered by computer, using a console interface, and automatic calculation of overall classification scores were included. There is a full description of the tests in Chapter 12, following a foreword by Johannes Wulf and Thomas Kutschke.

PILOT SELECTION: THE HAMBURG
IDENTITY AND A UK PARALLEL,
BARTRAM'S MICROPAT

PILOT SELECTION

The Hamburg Identity :

Goeters and Rathje

Bartram's Micropat

Although the Bundeswehr system might seem to be a careful transmission of paper-and-pencil tests into computers, followed by expansion into a broader frame of reference, the outstanding pioneering work of Goeters and Rathje (1992) in the *DLR Aerospace Centre* in Hamburg was to prove one of the first operational demonstrations of item generated tests for specialist aircrew selection. Rathje was able to produce multiple forms of pilot aptitude tests: and these went operational as a selection battery for potential trainees. The work of the Hamburg Aerospace Centre is unique in the field of pilot selection because of its reliance on item generative tests. It was a landmark contribution to military test construction from German scientists, owing much to the thinking apparent in the doctoral dissertation of Goeters (1979), which conducted a special study of repeated trials involving the *Wegfiguren Test*. A multiple parallel form version of this test was trialled by the BARB team successfully predicting item difficulty (see Chapters 4 and 7).

The pilot selection work in the previous decade had to await its fullest description in Goeters and Lorenz (2002, pp. 339-60). They describe how a comprehensive pilot selection battery was conceived first around a number of paper-and-pencil multiple parallel form tests (called PARAT tests), which were added to with traditional fixed-version tests, and finally translated into a computer-delivered system. Because the parallel forms had no fixed item bank, Goeters and colleagues were able to distribute pre-test information describing the nature of the tasks, setting a prime example for all those who could employ the multiple parallel form principle in test construction. Goeters and Lorenz illustrate and describe item types (loc. cit. pp. 346-49). Their data shows very close mean and variance results from three different forms of the six PARAT tests. The structure of the tests when allied to more traditional entrance tests (p.355) revealed four factors named *quantitative reasoning, spatial orientation, perceptual speed and mechanical comprehension*. Prior to 1990, the Plymouth and Hamburg groups knew nothing of the work of the other laboratory. Thereafter, information was exchanged: and a cooperative study of the English language BARB tests conducted with native German speakers in 1996 with the PARAT comprehensive battery. Results failed to throw more light on PARAT structure or validity. Their only substantial correlation was with an estimate of English language proficiency provided by using the BARB subtests.

HELICOPTER PILOTS AND COMPUTER-BASED TASKS: MICROPAT
Although not originating in Germany, another similar military computer-based testing model for pilots was in operation, invented by Bartram (1987). Because this work was carried out independently and was contemporary with BARB, it proved important in deciding what kinds of tests could be used and how they might be scored: and to discover if there were elements in common with the other aviator test projects. Initially constructed for British helicopter pilot selection, generalisation to fixed-wing pilots proved possible (Bartram, 2002). At the risk of oversimplifying and doing the system a summary injustice, one may describe it as a variety of computer-delivered procedural learning tasks in which one has to use gross and fine motor coordination in single and dual task families resembling those found in simple flight simulators. The scores used to predict degree of training success and relationships with established selection tests for pilots and observers emerged from trials at a number of operations grouped under functional names, such as *Adtrack, Landing, Schedule, Dualtask*. These names represent discrete series requiring mental coordination of diverse and complex ergonomic demands.

Although no explicitly stated construction theory underpins MICROPAT, the mental model of procedural effectiveness was operationally defined in a prediction study of 105 Army helicopter pilots, using 35 measures from which a final 10 yielded a multiple R of .50 (corrected for shrinkage) with reported degree of success in Advanced

Rotary Wing training. One may note in parenthesis the limited size of the sample used by Bartram to reduce the 35 possible predictors to 10. This caution aside, the Bartram data is a testimony to an attempt to marry the kinds of control over variables witnessed in small experimental contexts to simulator situations using humans. Like all the early attempts at computer-based assessment described it represents a special psychometric context. It was a very important pointer to the complexities of scoring models once computers become available. Two aspects were noteworthy: the effects of more than one trial (learning models) and the use of experimentally dependent test scores to make composites.

Effects of More than One Trial
A feature of the data presented by Bartram is the amount of change in structure as measured by the intercorrelations of measures from first to second trials in a series. Not only do mean levels change, *but the intercorrelations change also.* When this happens, a hypothesis requiring investigation is the suspicion that what is going on in the participant's head in the first series is not what is happening in the second. The interpretation of individual or average gain, if the scores do not mean the same thing, from early to late trials then becomes problematic. The low reliabilities of many of the measures reported by Bartram are more evidence of the same dynamism in the model.

Experimentally Dependent Structures
Second, there are a number of statistical problems inherent in repeated measures that generate a number of derivative scores from a small subset. Bartram reports the generation of at least 35 measures. For example, in a single mental arithmetic subtraction task, not only are speed *(Ttsa)* and accuracy *(Ncsa)* initially recorded overall, they are finally defined in a composite score *(Mtsa = 100*Ttsa/Ncsa)* based on the results of the last 25 trials. This is only one example of multiple score derivation from one subtask. The numerous scores derive from a restricted number of tasks by creating qualitative differences using scoring algorithms. Because these are experimentally dependent on a few basic measures, their reliabilities were low, reflected in their random correlations with other reliably measured variables. Finally, experimental dependence in the measures cannot produce random error variance, which correlational models demand. Limited sample sizes increase the risks of reification of chance associations; and the use of factor analyses given all of these circumstances is almost certainly artefactual (Roberts, 1959). Using derived scores needs great sophistication in design and equally great caution in execution. Bartram's work prompts a full discussion of scoring models in Chapter 5.

The value of MICROPAT is nonetheless exceptional; not only in what it defined when it did in early days, but also in how it succeeded in spite of external psychometric constraints, which are functions of operational needs and small numbers of pilots available in the trials. The Plymouth team owed much to Bartram for demonstrations and full access to his reports.

THE 1990 TEST FRONTIERS AND BARB

Much initial research had occurred, all of it inspired by the new computer culture opening for test development, but not all of it focussed on the need to develop multiple forms for use in high-stakes selection and screening. Even now, the results of *Project A* have not produced diverse forms of the measures developed with such skill and persistence. The adventures of LAMP have never realised their enormous potential for test development. Much of test use is still constrained by traditional test types administered using complex interfaces. Touchscreens exist in current versions of BARB, but they are not widespread in computer-delivered test delivery, in spite of their everyday use in supermarkets and job centres, not to mention i-pads and mobile phones. The focus provided by Carroll, Sternberg, Eysenck, Kyllonen and Snow was critical to test development. The search for what made items difficult had begun in the construction of BARB, leading to its nation-wide operation by 1991, after much basic research. Computerisation brought many challenges, not the least of which was the modern analogue to Macdonald's Lesson 2: how to use the computer to instruct, score, tabulate and report on every test.

A CULTURAL GENERATION DETERMINANT: THE ANDERSON QUESTION

Whatever aspects of test construction the military cultural contexts were to influence, there was to be one unalterable demand made on what went into the novel BARB system in the first place. The then virtually unknown use of item-generation to produce infinite numbers of tests in real time was to provide the fundamental building block for the BARB computer-delivered system. Given computer-delivered tests, with the need for effective test security and fairness to all applicants, this was seen as the ideal solution but it was a worrisome step in the dark. Dr. John Anderson of the Army Personnel Research Establishment outlined the blueprint for the nature and construction of BARB tests with an indelibly memorable, seemingly facetious, but fundamental question. *'What would tests be like if there were no fixed item files, no IRT (item-response theory) - and no money?'* It was, for all that, taken seriously: and is hereafter referred to as *The Anderson Question*. What evidence could be produced for a reply? After a careful preliminary review of the computer-based test and cognitive paradigm literature (Irvine, Dann & Evans, 1986), and the organisation of a major NATO advanced study institute (Irvine & Newstead, 1987, Newstead Irvine and Dann, 1986) the essence of the question was found to be practicable as early as 1987. The review showed that items in specific cognitive domains could be generated, not in an *ad hoc* empirical manner by individuals, but in computers from substantive theory

THE ANDERSON QUESTION

What would tests be like if there were no fixed item files, no IRT (item-response theory) - and no money?

The Anderson Question: Fundamentals
Where does one begin to answer the question raised by John Anderson - perhaps the most influential military psychometric question for large-scale test use of the past twenty-five years? *What could recruitment tests be like if there was no fixed item bank, avoiding computer-adaptive format, without using expensive and labour-intensive methods of equating parallel forms (such as item response*

theory) and ensuring parity? Answers to *The Anderson Question* were not found immediately. Given that the computer would be the medium of test delivery, there were two implicit issues inherent in the problem. What theory was robust enough for constructing the tests: and how were the tests to be delivered and scored? One had to begin somewhere: and the starting point called for guiding principles.

THE PRIMACY OF RADICALS AND INCIDENTALS
At the time, a great deal of interest was being shown by tests constructors on the nature of cognitive tasks that could become test items with a substantial pedigree. The puzzle was how to construct them in a way that would make computer algorithms for their production a consistent reality. The items had to be produced and scored automatically. Not only this, but algorithms had to determine and record the difficulty levels of the items, otherwise parallel forms could not be constructed. One very important concept was provided by Behar's (1986a, 1996b, 1996c) reports on computer-derived techniques for estimating the difficulty of items where a figure was hidden inside an overall pattern, known as *hidden figures tests*. He perceived the tasks of generating items as creating a *language* for which a grammar was the logical foundation. No other single quote had quite as much influence on how BARB was first conceived The evidence centred design (ECD) approach can be simplified when its stages are seen to correspond to simple sentence grammar, providing definitions of content and its constructs (subject), encoding them in a process (verb), and then simulating the product to predefine its validity (object). From Bejar's key conceptualisation, it was a relatively easy matter to define two quite different elements of item syntax. Given *The Anderson Question*, two constructs proved to be central to every aspect of test construction. They are simple to understand and difficult to put into practice. They are *radicals and incidentals* (Irvine 2002).

> ## THE BEJAR KEY TO GENERATION
>
> *'A generative approach to psychometric modelling incorporates response modelling, item development and validation.....The response modelling and item development become a single process once we have written the grammar for the item type in question'* (Bejar, 1986).

Radicals and Incidentals
One was the knowledge and use, in the structure of an item, of elements that would *always* change its difficulty. These constant change elements were *radicals*. Whereas radicals would be present in the grammar, or logic, of items of equivalent difficulty, additionally there had to be knowledge of what aspects of an item would make no difference to its difficulty, but would serve to make the item, on the surface, *seem different* from its previous examples. These were *incidentals*, necessary surface additions, irrelevant in the prediction of what proportion of respondents would provide the correct answer, but they ensured the serial independence of successive, phenotype items once a genotype item with a known level of difficulty had been generated.

As the design for BARB progressed with a number of studies of *radicals and incidentals*, what to include in BARB and what to leave out gradually surfaced. A word of caution, perhaps, is necessary - and not only to the wise. Radicals are not all the same. There are those that come with cognitive experiments: and others that come, perhaps unannounced and unforeseen, with the use of the computer itself. There are others that come with knowledge of what program structure or grammar to change in an item that will make it more or less difficult. For almost a century, paper-and-pencil was the established technology for test delivery to groups. Various methods of representing items, multiple choice responses, hand and machine-scoring, were well tried and accepted. Computer-production on screen, however, was a new but essential cultural context for the transcription of items. Early experimentation brought awareness that this was fraught with uncharted sources of difficulty. For example, Christal (1987), compared paper-and-pencil and computer-delivered tasks in the USAF Laboratory at Brooks Air Force Base and found that the tests, once transferred from one medium to another, sometimes like any normal child behaved beautifully, and at others in an unpredictable fashion giving rise to much parental concern and even sleepless nights.

ITEM RADICALS AND INCIDENTALS

Radicals are those theoretically consonant structural elements of items, which, as quasi-independent variables, will cause statistically significant changes in item-difficulties measured by error rate and/or time to completion. Incidentals are those surface semantic characteristics of items which preserve serial independence but, when allowed to vary randomly within item strata, will exert no significant influence on item-difficulty.' (Irvine, 2002, p. 12).

LESSON 2: INSTRUCTIONS AND RESPONSES IN COMPUTER CULTURES

Discussion thus far has taken a firm line. Operational definitions of tests are not completely derived from first cognitive principles, however much one would like that to happen. Whereas in the past, paper and pencil delivery of group tests restricted the range of operational variables, including constant concern for security that demanded precise examination dates nationally, computer-based testing can be said to have increased variables to such an extent that they needed specification. The history of testing shows that, as tests become used, and usage provides operational definitions of constructs, so evidence appears to confirm the status of certain measures and to relegate others to a hold or discard pile. These decisions do not come by themselves. Test forms arrive, deliberately or by unconscious habituation, from what is available and has credibility at the time. Without doubt, tests in computers have defined, by hardware, by software and by knowledge-based systems new operational dimensions, all created for score production according to preconceived paradigms. For BARB, the unknowns were how to use the computer to produce instructions and items that were completely understood; and how to create tests from knowledge of what made its items difficult. It was as simple, and as problematic, as that. In fact, retrospectively how to present the questions to recruits who had never experienced computer before might have been labelled *The Irvine Question.* Experience of administering novel tests in Africa with children and adults made him the prime source.

INSTRUCTIONS ON SCREEN AS ITEM RADICALS

Display

Information

Response

HARDWARE RADICALS AFFECT ITEM DIFFICULTY
Theory is carried forward operationally in every use of tests. But for recruits whose reading threshold was estimated at that of 11 year-olds who had never encountered a computer, the most important context for the use of BARB was the use of the microcomputer itself. Its importance lay not in the computer's operating system, but in how the ergonomics of test delivery would influence the instructions essential to understanding and answering items, and hence, test construction.

The computer can be a variable, or more exactly can be made to define a number of influences on difficulty, or *radicals*, that will shape the nature of the process to be measured. These variables are *display mode, information mode, and response mode.* The importance of these modes is that they should always be recognised as *radicals, controllable and with predictable effects on item difficulty.* They should never be *incidentals*, because they would randomly effect outcomes and produce unreliable items.

Display Mode
Display Mode in computers is predominantly visual. It can be a completely static representation of an item (as if it were transferred without change from paper to screen): a ticker-tape, where a sentence is delivered at a fixed rate as the words appear to travel across a screen: or a wholly dynamic item where parts actually move or rotate (as in an arcade game environment where movement is a precondition).

Figure 2.4: Display Radicals

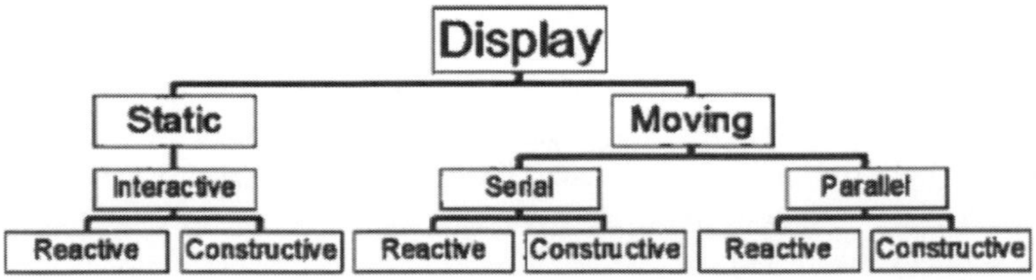

The amount of movement in computer-based test items is a display variable not available in group testing, although apparatus tests (using puzzles, cards, beads, jig-saw pieces) administered to individuals also introduce degree of movement and manipulation of the apparatus as a source of variation, for example in the so-called *non-verbal* Performance Scales of the WISC and WAIS that are misnomers. These particular scales require verbalisation based on responses to movable, and moving, apparatus.

Information Modes
Information Modes can vary in the *quality, amount, order, pace and medium* of presentation. For example, much of information delivery in traditional testing is quasi-linear processed serially, fixed by what may be printed on a page of given size. It is most controlled in the medium of verbal items and least controlled in figural item medium where subjects are free to extract what they will in whatever order they so prescribe.

Figure 2.5: Information Radicals

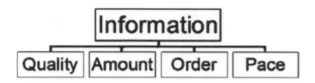

In using the computer to determine amount, order, pace and medium of information delivery, test constructors may control the range, and by implication the difficulty effects of all of them. By knowing that range for each variable, the test constructor can choose to limit or extend it. Note that in Figure 2.5 the information categories in particular, may vary within each one. Quality refers to the amount of degradation on the screen. Order, pace and amount of information are not necessarily correlated attributes, although in practice they are likely to be. Finally, another category (Modality) to distinguish prose from representations from geometrical figures in visual displays needs to be specified. Auditory delivery is not a forgotten condition: simply mentioned, and not elaborated here because it was not used in BARB and its successors.

Response Input
Response Input is perhaps one of the least obvious but most important variables in computer-based testing. How one makes the response is no longer a form of multiple-choice on the printed test or on a separate answer sheet, but can vary from standard computer keyboards to modified keyboards, to custom-made consoles (including joysticks), to analogues of paper and pencil involving pressure-sensitive touch screens. These are qualitative differences that do not represent a single continuous variable. Hence, for any specific type of test, form of response must follow function. In the figure, the response modes are ordered left to right in the degree of manual dexterity needed to make a response (apart from voice, a separate issue). A touch screen involves no more than a finger press, whereas a console can be a major learning task in itself. Modern computer games differ in the elaboration of their input consoles, but even very young children learn to use them with remarkable speed after hours of practice. However, the time needed to learn the interface was never a matter of concern for recruits in the 1980's.

Figure 2.6: Response Radicals

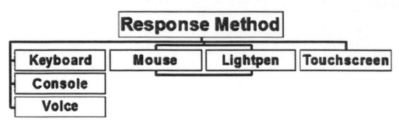

Of course, recording an accurate answer in a test without a time limit is a relatively trivial task whatever the mechanics of it. The true-score variance in subjects is not related to the speed with which they record the answer, or if it is, time to complete all the test items is of no consequence. In any timed test, speeded or not, where the number of completed items is the basis of success, the variance introduced by the form of response is critical in paper and pencil as well as computer-based tests. In either form, hunting around for the correct location for the answer will invalidate the test or reduce its reliability. In general, in comparison to the relatively few ways in which responses are made in paper-and pencil tests, nearly all computer-based tests may be largely circumscribed by the idiosyncrasies of the response mode. *In 1986, when the construction of BARB was authorised, recruits to the British Army had seldom if ever seen a computer, let alone used a QWERTY keyboard or mouse. It did not then take much imagination to realise that a touch screen interface could be the only practical way forward.*

THE SCREEN'S PRIMARY FUNCTION: MAKING THE BARB ITEM SIMPLE
Even if paper-and-pencil analogues were successfully trialled, routine transposition of item types on paper to a computer screen was never an option. From the outset, it was seen to involve a special requirement as the example below will show.

This is a complete representation of a semantic item requiring the identification of 'the odd-one-out'. *Presented on a single screen, touch screen pressure on the box containing 'scent' is all that is necessary to record an answer.* Within a restricted cursor framework previously defined, experienced computer users can respond quickly and accurately using a 'mouse' to direct the cursor. From the outset, each item of this type is a form of 'dramatic unity' with its own 'actors' and 'distractors' immediately present, so that time, space and subject matter are preserved on a single screen. Crucially, no change of location (second screen) or materials, or recording more than one time period from start to finish are necessary. *Not all BARB items were so elegantly constructible, but the goal of single screens, preserving unities of time, space and subject matter, was always borne in mind and pursued whenever possible.* Given principles, practices and ideals to pursue in knowing how to present the tests, the next step was to construct test items that could fulfil their aspirations as valid measures of recruit success.

INSTRUCTIONS AS RADICALS:

SPEARMAN 1904

'The chief part of this time was devoted to instructing and practising them, and to finding out what was the lowest age fit for such a collective experiment. Despite all precautions to secure reliable results, I was unable to quite convince myself that such uncultured children could be treated adequately without elaborate individual attention.' (Spearman, 1904).

ARTEFACTUAL INTELLIGENCE

Five lessons were apparent in the Macdonald report; the second concerned with instructions, the key to performance based on understanding what the item is about and how to respond with a potentially correct answer. The more recent history of cross-cultural testing is full of campaigns where stimulus identity has proven no substitute for functional equivalence (Irvine, 1983; Lonner & Berry, 1986; Irvine and Berry, 1988, 2010). But, ironically perhaps, evidence for the difficulty of testing in untried contexts had been available since the beginning of the 20th century. Recognisably one of the most influential publications, and certainly one of the most famous, on the nature of abilities tested by 'simple' procedures was, and perhaps still is, Spearman's (1904) paper on the nature of intelligence.

His contribution was to propose, from the test results, a theory of intelligence dependent on a single factor g. For more than a century, much debate has attended his conclusions about how responses to simple stimuli and apparently more complex abilities are related to each other. Such discussions about the nature of intelligence have been endemic since 1904 and Irvine, (1983, p. 47) shows that a new theory comes along every decade; but very little, if any, attention has ever been paid to Spearman's detailed description of how he collected the data. Without a doubt, discussion has overlooked the painstaking attempts made by Spearman to ensure that the sample of English rural village children who attempted his cognitive tasks and tests (his *'reagents'* as he quaintly described them), understood what was required to respond meaningfully. When he tried to administer some of the tests collectively to a whole group of local children in the home culture of the village school, there was a self-confessed conclusion, shown in the insert. Almost a century later, unlike many mainstream testing adventurers into the abilities of minorities, cross-cultural psychologists, without the benefit of hindsight, had the same declared aim as Spearman. Items taken directly from a conventional test were useless until by careful presentation and elaborate individual attention they tested what they were supposed to.

COMPUTER RADICALS AND TEST MEANING: A SIMPLE EXAMPLE

Unless the effects of test formats were known in both psychometric and cognitive process frameworks, the prediction of item-difficulty, the backbone of multiple parallel form construction, would be difficult if not impossible. In attempting a hesitant step forward, one of us wrote a sketch for a paper that states *the nature of the experimenter context problem for test construction* exactly. It begins 'Why is there always a general factor?' Some progress came when the computer itself began to be used to present items in different ways. Imagine a simple item presented wholly on a single screen.

Figure 2.7: Consider a Test Item on a Single Screen

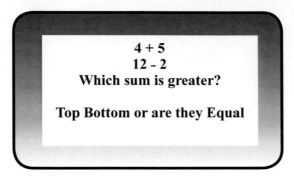

        Unlimited time is given and this simply transfers a paper-and-pencil item to a computer screen. Nothing changes except the participant now sees the item at eye level and not on a desk surface. If single computer screens provide a collection of items with similar structure, measured performance will be highly dependent on the speed and accuracy of relatively simple arithmetic manipulation; and would thus be highly correlated with other measures of 'mechanical' arithmetic. Such sets of arithmetic items, if put into three parallel forms of tests like Guilford's examples of his multifactorial framework, are likely to define a separate, lower order 'number fluency' factor. The so-called arithmetic tests would require speed of encoding symbols and the read out of a set of automatic tables mentally accessed within the individual for the answer. In addition to psychometric or factor definition, latency models of such automated processes in simple arithmetic had been in place for some years (Groen & Parkman, 1972, Parkman, 1972). Models such as these measure intra-individual parameters that successfully differentiate efficient from inefficient performers. On the other hand, if the target item is embedded in a test constructor's context that includes a whole range of arithmetical problems, involving verbal descriptors, these are likely to be presented, at least conventionally, in order of difficulty. As such, they are virtually certain to require different algorithms for their solution from one item to the next.

SCREEN RADICALS CREATING 'G'
But even if the item were to remain 'unchanged' but *presented in the computer in a wholly different fashion, using the screen as a device,* the result could be a *radical* change in what is being measured. A good example exists in computer contexts (a critical change) the 'frame-at-a-time' presentation of mental arithmetic items where the order of presentation of essential information including is randomised. The exposure time for each screen (the *pace* radical) would itself alter the difficulty of the item. Even if unlimited time were given for each screen, *a random frame at a time strategy* would change the character of the problem entirely. Performance on simple arithmetic test items presented a frame at a time is likely to (and indeed it does, Christal, 1991) correlate with performance on a much wider range of other measures. What is being measured has altered because of the *radical* screen context prescribed by the experimenter. Not so much an exercise in simple arithmetic, more a calculated, and predictable, demand on working memory capacity, close ally to *g* (Kyllonen, 1996).

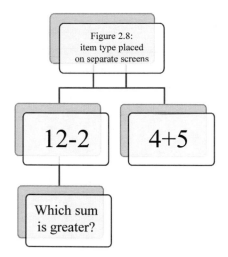

Figure 2.8:
item type placed
on separate screens

12-2   4+5

Which sum
is greater?

Figure 2.8 is a diagram that helps to show what the effect would be if the same simple arithmetic problem is in sequence, one screen at a time. The diagram shows the sums in order, but they could occur randomly in any screen, except the last. Using the frame at a time format for presenting simple arithmetic calculations in memory transforms a whole series of paper-and-pencil items into a general factor, not of fluency, but of working memory, closely allied to g. Of course, the more calculations required before the question is asked, the greater the number of answers that need to be stored and retrieved from memory. This kind of information-processing demand, for which arithmetic operations is only a vehicle, could be correlated with other measures, excluding parallel forms which would introduce experimental dependence and extra factors. Whenever the same processing demands are hidden in seemingly different incidental contexts - verbal reasoning, spatial rotations, search for one of a number of complex shapes in a field, the resultant covariance matrix would and should yield a general factor, very likely to be working memory induced by the form of computer presentation. The specific item content would be incidental. That is why there could always be a general factor. Such illustrations are the logical extension of the proposition that general intelligence could be measured partly because of a serendipitous experimental artefact - the attempts of examiners to produce items from a lack of knowledge of the processes behind the right answer. If one takes this as a plausible context for the presence of g, one can set out to test it. With a target for test construction of specific constructs measured in non-overlapping ways, it ought to be possible to measure performance in current tests of intelligence economically from screen-controlled measures of process. Only if these measures proved, after all the experimental controls had been exerted on the potential for artefactual overlap, that the process measures were irrevocably correlated, could g survive as a construct. This argument is not very far away from the rationale provided by Kyllonen in an influential series (Kyllonen, & Christal, 1990; Kyllonen, 1996). To take the argument further, the fundamental question is not only 'What does this test measure?' but also 'What evidence provides the radicals that make this item difficult?' Furthermore, if it is possible to identify the causes of difficulty at or beyond the point of individual performance, thereby experimentally controlling for unplanned computer influences on response production, then this information is the answer to the question 'What does the item measure?' Note that such an approach is not inconsistent with g as a construct. It makes identification of where such a construct may be found more specific. Spearman might well have smiled at such a conclusion, because he insisted that tests revealed to the user not so much about the nature of intelligence as where it might be found (Spearman, 1927, pp.75-76). Who would credit Spearman as the godfather of the evidence centred design movement?

SIMPLY PUTTING THE ITEM ON THE SCREEN

An oversimplification would be to conclude that the problem of how to present an item on a screen would be solved once the understanding of the issues had been brought to bear on test production. However, the summary principles that were derived from this overview were stated in mock-heroic form as *Dann-Irvine-Murphy's Laws* (DIMS) of computer testing. And here they are. The first law recognises that information displayed on a screen is not the same as the same information on a printed page. In fact, large amounts of text on a screen are often ignored.

This law was in part derived from previous cross-cultural experience of test presentation in Zimbabwe, where instructions were always given verbally, with items constructed on flannel-boards, or velcro-sticking illustrations, one step at a time, with much repetition (Irvine, 1964). *The consequence for BARB was the creation of a novel series of test instructions. Applicants were shown how to do a test one sentence at a time, with step-by-step illustrations on screen.* Tickertape presentations were used, with redundant text moved from centre focus points to upper levels when the next step was explained. The whole enterprise was to use the screen as a means of emphasising a single explanatory phrase or sentence in the structured instructional sequence, with the least in the way of distraction[5].

THE FIRST DANN–IRVINE MURPHY LAW

'The greater the area of screen covered by instructions to the candidate, the less effective they will be.'

THE SECOND DANN–IRVINE MURPHY LAW

"The more keys and buttons on the response interface, the less the test-retest reliability of item latencies.'

SIMPLY ANSWERING THE QUESTION

The second controlling factor in computer delivered testing is the *response*. The report by Peterson, (1987) on the experimental tasks in *Project A*, the US military project detailed by Campbell & Knapp (2001) described how a number of tests were computer-delivered using an interface described as a *pedestal*. Impressive as this lofty nomenclature seemed, because a wide array of cognitive and psychomotor tasks was presented needing co-ordination, the results of using the 'pedestal' or modified typewriter keyboards in tasks where simple, timed responses were required were varied to say the least: and in many instances, might well be judged unsatisfactory where quick responses and high reliabilities were required. Similarly, even modified use of the QWERTY keyboard in *Project LAMP* gave rise to the same doubts. Insights, generously provided by the authors of early reports led to the formulation of this fundamental second law for the BARB test construction team - more keys, less reliability.

---

5   Dr. Peter Dann's exemplary work in encoding the instructions in this fashion was an innovation that is still the standard to emulate today.

THE THREE LAWS OF COMPUTERISED TESTING

Less is more on screen: and more is less

Less is more in the response mechanism:　and more is less

The more one uses item-generation and the less one uses IRT,　the less the likelihood of compromise in any test

THE COMPUTERISED ADAPTIVE TESTING CULTURE AND BARB

Computerised adaptive testing is an endemic characteristic of computer-delivered systems depending on IRT, whether erroneously used for selection or not. If computerised adaptive testing (CAT) is used for selection, only the easy items are needed for rejects, the others are redundant (Lord, 1979). On the other hand, in computerised adaptive testing involving thousands of applicants annually, where high scores are the target, only the difficult items need be stolen: the easy items are irrelevant to the final standing (Wainer 2002). In this key source, Wainer argues that the cost of producing the most difficult items in any system depending on them as the common core to provide parallel form equivalence far outweighs their value. Moreover, because the difficult items appear more frequently than others, being less plentiful they are the most likely to be compromised. He concludes that to maintain test security the increase in production of difficult items had to be exponential[6].

The Anderson Question always was wary of the hazards of item response theory, an integral part of CAT; and foresaw the potential difficulties of using IRT as a means of equating norms, although the effects of the ETS scenario were never anticipated. Because of cooperation with ETS, from 1986 onwards, knowledge of the consequences of undermining computer delivered tests that did not depend on infinite numbers of items of equivalent difficulty was shared. By 1994, relief at the decision taken not to use computerised adaptive testing and/or item response theory for BARB was understandable with reports of the major success of compromising one of the most widely used tests employing both IRT and CAT adaptations in the United States, *The Graduate Record Examination* conducted for the College Board by ETS. The arguments for rejection of item-response theory and computerised adaptive testing score models that were in vogue at the time of BARB's development await the reader in Chapter 5. Perhaps they might still seem to be applicable in 2013, although denial could well be a defence mechanism for continuation.

CONCLUSIONS FROM COMPUTER DELIVERY OF ITEMS

In the determination of the form and function of BARB tests, three main principles were always invoked, derived from awareness of the effects that constant screen presentations could have on item difficulty, and repeated exposures of core items required by IRT. In the development period 1986-91, they became the three *laws* of computer-based testing. Perhaps they have survived to the present day. Application

---

6　This led to Wainer's Law, seen in context in Chapter 5.

of these principles in a consistent way was designed to minimise the effects of introducing unknown hardware *radicals* that would change the nature of the test and hence alter what was being tested in the applicant. Effects on item difficulty from failure to read the screen adequately, or hunting around on a response input for the correct button to press were deemed neither desirable nor excusable. Nor was IRT deemed necessary if the difficulty of the items in a test could be predicted well enough to ensure the delivery of an infinite number of parallel forms. Even if the *Anderson Question* were not answered by the three principles, their application made the answer more likely. It will not have escaped notice that they are all based on one simple tenet: *more is less and less is more.*

CHAPTER 3

LESSON 3: WHAT TESTS TO CHOOSE: EVIDENCE-CENTRED SOURCES

Two Psychological Cultures: Correlational and Experimental
The search for evidence found a useful general model in Cronbach's much-quoted address to the American Psychological Association. Thereafter, correlational cultures are scrutinised. These contrast British and American schools of thought. Then quasi-experimental sources involving latencies and evoked potentials are evaluated before moving on to identify cognitive elements that combine to form *radicals* that change item difficulties or remain as appearance-changing *incidentals*. Because tests are the vehicle, traditional ability theories involving the analysis of correlations were first in line. The others follow in sequence, each adding a piece to the jigsaw.

Cronbach's Paradigm
In his presidential address of 1957 to the American Psychological Association, Cronbach (1957) discussed at length what he termed *The Two Disciplines of Scientific Psychology*. One discipline uses main effects to study performance on any one task; and the other uses correlations of many variables in the quest for construct definition. It is possible to paraphrase and apply Cronbach's views about predicting behaviour to test items. The ideal theory is what Cronbach terms 'a redundant network' theory where a network permits prediction of item difficulty from past experience of and/or present characteristics of organisms. For test construction, this model translates to (Stimuli→Radicals and Incidentals→Universal Item Difficulty). To make this happen, as Cronbach rightly argued, there has to be a confluence of evidence from the two disciplines. In 1986, the evidence was reviewed in the quest for the important antecedents to predicting item difficulty, the identification of *radicals and incidentals*. Part of the review was a request to Kline (1988) to examine the British cultural influence on ability measurement. His response, in Irvine & Berry, (1988 pp. 187-207) provides details of the development in Britain (and elsewhere) of the two frameworks from Spearman (correlational) and Galton (experimental) in the period prior to BARB.

LESSON 3:

SPOILT FOR CHOICE?

Cronbach's dream: unifying evidence sources

Psychometric cultural values: British and American

The latency IQ; attention and fundamentalism

Components and hierarchies: Sternberg and Carroll

THE CORRELATIONAL CULTURES OF PSYCHOMETRICS

Ability constructs find their widespread definition in individually-administered tests and in group test analogues alike. Table 3.1 shows just how many revisions have taken place between 1904 and 2004, with no firm or final agreement. A new theoretical slant occurred every decade or so. The understanding of their precepts and origins is a prerequisite to modern decision-making involving tests. Such has been the dominance of group testing that ability constructs are largely operational in those individual tests, and analogue paper and pencil tests, operationalised in group administration. Results from millions of participants are the major empirical legacy of psychometrics. Not until Irvine (1979) reviewed cross-cultural factor analytic studies was it possible to submit that legacy to a single mode of analysis to clarify the structures revealed by testing. Until then, different schools of thought debated structures of intellect and methods of test construction. A constraining sense of what tests are of most worth has not always produced good science; but it cannot be ignored, since it represents an important theoretical input. This is a form of *Utility Theory*. Briefly, this defines scientific advance in terms of what society deems useful at any period of adaptation to ecological press. It provides the key to understanding (Miles, 1957) that is important for theory construction and development.

Table 3.1: Ability Theories Since 1904

Date	Authors	Theory
1904-27	Spearman	One general factor and a number of specifics
1920-40	Thurstone	A limited number of primary abilities
1920-50	Thomson	Group factors, associationist
1920-60	Burt-Vernon	Hierarchical, essentially g, verbal and spatial
1940-70	Guilford	Multiple and distinct
1950-82	Eysenck	Biophysical Factors
1960-80	Cattell	Two broad factors qualitatively distinct
1976-90	Carroll	Hierarchical Group Factors (Distributive Memory)
1977-90	Sternberg	Componential information processing
1980-1990	Snow-Kyllonen-Christal	Interactionist reconstruction of g from working memory
2000-	Various g ' brain maps'	Deconstruction using brain scans

What, in 1986-1996 could a cross-cultural perspective, exemplified by Macdonald's work in 1945, contribute to a new generation of tests for military selection? A cross-cultural perspective begins by realising that the persons who use tests and those who undergo them take part in a social exchange that imbues tests with more than cognitive content (Irvine, 1979, 1985, 1986b). Because these social exchanges are culturally transmitted, tests results cannot be assumed to have objective scientific life. For example, a major barrier to progress in theories of abilities (and hence in consistent test construction) has been the fundamentally different, socially mediated interpretations of the same results by American and British scientists (see Carroll, 1993, pp. 35-52).

Even if the mathematical formulations behind the theory were identical, these have been interpreted each within a frame that is imposed by a definite sense of value. And the British and American value frames are very different. General factors began with Spearman and independent ability clusters with Thurstone. The transatlantic gap has never disappeared, even with interventions from Donders, Binet and Piaget.

Correlation Subcultures: British Hierarchical Models
Ever since Spearman showed that it was possible to account for a great deal of the covariance between measures of ability by mathematically transforming a square correlation matrix into a single row or numbers, called a factor, the quest for a structure of ability by using tests has pursued hierarchies of general and specific aptitudes. This notion, synthesised by Vernon (1961), but owing much to work by Burt (1917), and Thomson (1939) recognised that not all problem-solving skills had the same degree of generality. Some skills extended to a wide array of problems, while others were specific to a restricted range. Ferguson (1954, 1956) saw the issue in terms of the degree of transfer that was possible between one family of tests and any other.

Social Consequences in Britain
This 'general intelligence with some specifics' approach to abilities revealed by the correlations of tests was part and parcel of the tripartite division of British secondary schools following the decision to ensure free secondary education for all in 1944. Grammar schools, highly prized by parents and pupils, required students whose profiles showed them capable of those activities where a great deal was left to the student to solve alone. This ethos required pupils to use abstractions and algorithms; and called for fluency in the production of arguments in prose. Requiring less general, and more specific groupings of skills were vocational-technical schools and secondary-modern schools. There, more direct prescriptions for work were given; and the work was more specific in its demands. In spite of protests to the contrary, this formal 'apartheid' has been replaced by an informal one in large comprehensives where students are put into streams or sets by initial screening by measures that carry the assumptions of hierarchy with them in their construction. Not surprisingly, General Certificate of Education results from examinations conducted at the end of secondary school have been good indicators of how well students could use verbal, mathematical and scientific algorithms to solve problems.

The consequences of valuing generalisable abilities are very are evident in the quite illogical attributions attached those who do well in tests of intelligence. They are regarded as being good at everything, while those whom the test system rejects are far too often perceived quite wrongly as good at and good for, nothing. One can hardly show surprise when all but 16 percent of the population object to tests that are about to consign them to inferior status, for whatever reason. The social legacy of using

SOCIAL PSYCHOMETRICS:

Spearman's g and Educational Apartheid at 11+

Grammar Schools

Technical Schools

Secondary Modern Schools

general ability tests in British schools is the tendency to reject all tests by those whom they seek to serve. IQ tests have no status for the school-leaver seeking training or a job with a future, the adult made redundant by new economic or technological theories, and above all, minority ethnic groups who are stereotyped as under achievers in mental tests of all kinds.

THE WAYWARD FREEDOM FACTORS - STALKING OR STACKING?

Guilford's Artefactor Triads

Cattell Rejected

Jensen Vilified

American Cultural Models: Aptitude Independence

Thurstone (1938) was fully aware that little difference existed between his own work and that of Spearman. Only some of his successors understood that Thurstone's insistence on not one, but a number of distinct primary abilities stemmed from his realisation that the technology of finding the common elements in correlations among tests produced mathematical answers that were neither final nor psychological. He preferred parsimonious, fixed and psychological solutions: and those sprang from 'simple structures'. These seemed to be most apt when they produced a limited number of abilities, whose relation to each other was a question that was then secondary to their accurate description.

This question of their relation to British general-factor theory had been resolved in Thurstone's mind by 1947. The ideal of distinct and unrelated abilities was pursued in the United States until it mushroomed under Guilford (1956) in his elaborate schema of a large number of separate, cell-like abilities none of which was necessarily related to any other. Operational proof depended on triumvirates of tests that were scarcely experimentally independent of each other. As the number of abilities multiplied, so parsimonious description disappeared, and under review by Carroll, (1972) science faltered. The persistent notion of multiple separateness and distinction in human abilities had been contradicted empirically by Cattell (1963) and criticised by many others, yet it was supported by a North American educational value system rooted in the proposition that all men - and women - were created equal. Just as all men (and women) were of equal value under God, so were abilities and skills. This is most evident in the construction of a diverse curriculum in which any educational activity is as valuable as any other. Credits are of equal value in the award of the high school diploma. Diplomas are not, officially, of higher or lower order. They attest to what applicants can do well by personal inclination and a unique combination of abilities that exist as a right under the American constitution.

No Going Back unless g is Decomposed

Multiple factor theory was useful to those who organised schools in the way that they did. In fact, when Jensen (1969, 1982, 1985, 1988) tried to reassert the primacy of what became known as *psychometric g*, his scientific arguments were submerged in a social minority context that refused to entertain them because it could not. They challenged too severely the social mobility ethos that found comfort in the notion of a large number of discrete abilities all of equal rank. There was no use for general ability theories in a decade of civil rights litigations, riots, and examination of social conscience over the Vietnam War. Revivals of fundamental, basic ability theories were, simply, un-American activity. Sternberg, however, was able to restore interest by his own work and collections of contributions by others, of which the most important, perhaps, was the Snow, Kyllonen & Marshalek (1984) model based on a topography of ability and learning correlations, elaborated by Kyllonen (1985, 1986) in his work for the USAF laboratory. Carroll's (1993) definitive work on factor analytic studies of tests signifies the end of debate about the number of abilities: and the beginning of a new focus on the nature and functions of elementary cognitive tasks, examined towards the end of the chapter. He owed his early inspiration[1] to a visit to Thomson (1939), in Edinburgh shortly after the Second World War; and thereafter showed a preference for hierarchical group factor interpretations that Thomson would undoubtedly have applauded.

THE LIQ?

Speed and Fundamentalism

Pay Attention

React - it's Time

Evoke your Potential

APPROACHING THE LIQ[2]: NEW WAVES BUT OLD PROBLEMS

Faced with the need for creative task construction, psychometricians who wish to measure 'elementary cognitive' functions can choose from a number of them. The problem is exactly the same as that faced by those wishing to measure individual differences by using printed tests of abilities. Which, if any, to choose? If factor analysis by itself is not sufficient, and it seldom is, what might constitute proof of their validity? Techniques for validating constructs, even in robust effects, are well known. The requirements of Campbell & Fiske (1959) have been quoted for more than fifty years. Not only must they be correlated with similar tasks, but also with dissimilar tasks so that they are defined both by what they measure and what they do not measure. Studies that have attempted to meet those demands are absent from the citation indices, except Carroll's (1980) laboratory report and his summation (Carroll, 1993). Apart from this, to use the cognitive tasks found in the experimental culture for psychometric purposes was not a new departure, as those first administered to village children by Spearman (1904) clearly show. They were nevertheless analysed, in ways that are indistinguishable from the countless other paper and pencil tests that have claimed to measure some aspect of ability on limited evidence; and hence, provided no theoretical advantage.

The conclusion from the period immediately prior to 1986 was that new methods of measuring abilities had flourished with speed, but with disorder. Theoretical advance can only be fostered when the ingenuity that created the measures is turned to systematic efforts to validate them as constructs. Carroll, Eysenck,

---

1 He was very proud of a small black and white photograph he had taken of Thomson, displayed on the wall of his office in North Carolina in 1976, seen during a visit with him.

2 The Latency IQ (Irvine, 1986a).

Hunt and Sternberg all made important contributions. It could be said that the use of cognitive tasks as if they were merely sophisticated test scores is too easy and obvious a target. Not much will be gained by the claim to have delivered a *Latency IQ, or LIQ*. To characterise new attempts to produce a reference system for tests as part of such an enterprise would be misleading, since paradigm shifts had changed the face of psychometrics beyond recognition. In particular, the work of Sternberg and Eysenck might be produced as signs of the times. The restraining hand might belong to Carroll. Moreover, measuring intelligence by methods not involving tests would contribute to the multi-method framework demanded by Campbell and Fiske.

THE CULTURES OF MENTAL SPEED AND FUNDAMENTALISM
The third strand in conventional ability theory, fundamentalism, was apparent in Eysenck's (1981) edited collection *A Model for Intelligence*: and this is often ignored in the run-up to thinking about abilities and their means of measurement. Early in his career, Eysenck's awareness of the need to distinguish speed from accuracy and persistence was clear from involvement with Furneaux (1952, 1960) in the development of the Eysenck-Furneaux paradigm and re-emphasised in his *Model for Intelligence* (Eysenck, loc. cit. pp.6-10). Its revival owes much to computer-inspired revival of interest in latencies, but the evidence is coherently marshalled in a demanding mathematical treatise by White (1982) and is given some empirical impetus by Berger (1982) whose work is also a useful history of the notion of speed of mental functioning.

While the distinctions among speed to complete a test, accuracy in answering and persistence in the face of difficulty are intuitively certain, few have undertaken to relate the three constructs to a consistent theory. Eysenck attempted this as part of his biological approach to behaviour; and this included the measurement of ability and personality functions. The arguments he employs to link speed measures with genetically inherited capability to process information may not be wholly convincing either in their assumptions, logic or inferences. Nevertheless, the evidence of interest in speed functions early in the history of mental measurement is striking: equally one realises that speed could not be measured with any accuracy using paper and pencil tests. Ironically, without using group paper and pencil tests, the large numbers of participants that would be needed to stabilise correlations would take many years to collect. Psychology has seldom shown any sign of willingness to delay either publication or gratification. In the past, measures of speed were confined to specialised laboratories using small numbers of participants, as Welford's (1980) comprehensive book on the story of reaction-times makes plain. Today, however, microcomputers have brought measures of speed to hundreds of participants. The relationship between speed and accuracy can be fully explored; and this relationship need not necessarily be seen in an Eysenckian fundamentalist context. In fact, it very seldom is.

COMPUTER MODELS OF ATTENTION: DIVIDE AND CONQUER?
One of the most popular areas of investigation had been a focus on ability from the point of view of attentional tasks, particularly those purporting to assess divided attention and high workload (Hunt, 1987, Stankov & Horn, 1980, Stankov 1983). Similarly, Jensen's excursion into individual differences (Jensen, 1982, 1988, pp. 106-145) using reaction times had taken on the mantle of divided attention with a set of tasks that are quick to administer. But the tasks employed by Jensen and others,

(Vernon, 1983; Vernon and Jensen, 1985) bear no symbolic or theoretical consonance with those of Stankov. Neither Stankov nor Vernon and Jensen's tasks are in any way comparable with those preferred by Lansman, Poltrock and Hunt (1983) in their pursuit of ability to focus and divide attention. In the space of a few publishing years more tests of attention were exhibited than had probably been developed in the previous half century.

The canon of parsimony had been somewhat neglected in pursuit of innovation. The important unifier of such neophiliac plenitude is scoring - not using accuracy but latency to complete these tasks that are emerging as micro-based. This emphasis on speed made White's (1982) mathematical model linking speed, accuracy and persistence the only wholly consistent theoretical statement. But no exhaustive validation of White's theory of thirty years ago has since occurred in the field of divided attention, which is ideal for such a purpose. Instead, laboratories have gone their own way. Examination of the participant interfaces with the microcomputers they used reveals no consistency. These important determinants are as idiosyncratic as the tests themselves. Notable exceptions were the programme of work carried out in the USAF Project LAMP, the comprehensive overview and bibliography of which has emerged only recently in an account by Kyllonen (2010)[3].

Operating with Reaction Times

Tasks that still require effort, but perhaps less of it, were pursued by Jensen in an attempt to get closer to general intelligence. These have been simple and choice-reaction time tasks. But these, too, were the participant of extraordinary claims. Some systematic scrutiny may be returning to the movement if the critical notice served on Jensen's reaction time series by Longstreth (1984) is taken as more than a minority view. Irvine (1983e), in a comment on work by Jensen on choice reaction time tasks as measures of intelligence in Eysenck's (1982) collection, made the point that the literature on the instability of reaction-time tasks is too voluminous to ignore, and that these tasks are neither pure nor simple. In detail, Welford's (1980) book on reaction times demonstrates that whole careers have been built in experimental psychology by changing the instructions and response modes for what appears to be the simplest of all cognitive tasks and then arguing about the outcomes as if the products (latencies) from the participants were the result of identical sequences of operations within them. Carroll's work examining elementary cognitive tasks (ECTs) using a computer program as a yardstick of process sequence, made such claims difficult to maintain. In the narrower route of ability measurement, calling a measure a reaction time, and then giving it to minority groups (Jensen, 1982) seemed all that had to be done to ensure both publication and controversy. The lesson from Jensen's exercise in assessing population differences in ability, using reaction times, came under close scrutiny as new frameworks for occupational assessment were sought. Neither psychometrics nor ethnic minorities are well served by gratuitous group comparisons. On the other hand, one of the very best studies[4] in the speed/intellect area with majority and minority groups is that by Verster (1983, 1987). It has the virtue of impeccable construct validation and was conducted in South Africa on white and black participants of both sexes.

---

3   Currently head of a research group at ETS Princeton.

4   Unfortunately largely unread, only six recorded attributions on web search in 2013.

NOT CONSCIOUSLY ATTENDING: NEUROLOGY AND ABILITIES

All of the work reviewed so far has assumed conscious effort by the participant. Suppose a measure of ability could emerge without any conscious effort at problem solving or reacting to stimuli were to appear. What then? Would it advance the theory of abilities? Would the measure be valid in predicting everyday recruit competence? Would social values sanction it? Would it be cost beneficial? All of these questions attend any radical departure from cognitive measurement. Such a line of research with its roots in the Galton tradition has been extensively reported by Eysenck (1982) and his colleagues A. E. Hendrickson (1982) and D. E. Hendrickson, (1982). This work has two quite distinct phases, the production of empirical relationships among measures, and the development of theory that explains them.

The empiricism is easy enough to describe but costly and hard to replicate. First, *Averaged Evoked Potentials* (AEPs) of neutral auditory stimuli (clicks in headphones) were clinically determined for each participant by the experimenter. By attaching electrodes to the scalp, the lengths of the wave following the onset of the stimulus were found by an averaging algorithm. In addition the variance of the waves over all trials was determined for each participant. When the results of these measures were correlated with IQ total, the length measures and variance measures each correlated .7 with the IQ total. When length and variance measures were combined in a posthoc composite, their correlation with IQ reached .82. The trouble with that work is *reported inability to produce an objectively scored wave.* When the computer produced scores based upon an algorithm for determining AEP wave length, they showed zero relationship with IQ. Only clinical intervention by Elaine Hendrickson produced a waveform that correlated. This would not result in any general use of the AEP, or any other measure where entry to a restricted range of occupations demanded objectivity (Irvine, 1983e).

SPEED NO ANSWER WHEN THE GOING GETS TOUGH?

SUMMARY

Three quite novel approaches to ability measurement, from those requiring much effort, to those requiring no effort at all were examined. Their attraction lies in the way that abilities can be accessed using novel measures that are not obviously tests. Novelty is one advantage, but the lack of consistent attempts to model performance on these tasks makes them difficult to recommend. The most important contribution of this work, whether on high attentional, demand or low attentional demand tasks *is recognition that processing speed is a centroid in the assumptions of the scientists involved.* Accuracy scores are not avoided, but there is a growing awareness that the utility of speed scores decreases as items take longer to solve. There is a cross-over point from the validity of speed scores of items with very short latency (Hi validity) to those requiring longer latencies (Lo validity) and revealing errors. As errors increase, so the validity of accuracy scores takes over the predictive role. This conclusion is evident in many studies, is most clearly and progressively determined by Verster (1987), but has no unified theory for its explanation. Irvine (1986a, pp. 21-24) coined the expression the LIQ, or latency intelligence quotient to define the intention of the movement, concluding that 'new waves' of apparently simple cognitive tasks intended to provide an IQ derived from latencies had not solved construct validity issues that accompanied theory revisions ever since Spearman, in 1904.

STERNBERG'S HOLISTIC THEORY: RADICAL CULTURAL RELATIVISM

The introduction and production of computerized tasks have been made possible by current cognitive conceptions of information processing. In fact, textbooks on human abilities are characterised by headings derived from that approach. Modern holistic approaches complete the framework for a radical approach to mental measurement. In our view, integrated, or holistic theory has had a number of advantages. First, it has led to a better delineation of the issues in model building. Specifically, it has distinguished processes from products: and both of these from the contexts in which they operate. Above all, holistic theories provide keys to understanding (Miles, 1957) the nature and limits of measurement. The fullest account of what is generally known as *triarchic theory* appears in Sternberg (1985a). Of some operational relevance is Sternberg's insistence on the *context of measurement*, an aspect that is singularly absent from fundamentalist conceptions of ability. How unique was Sternberg's approach, and what are its points of contact with, and advantages over its rivals?

TRIARCHIC THEORY

A major reformulation of the concept of general ability termed triarchic theory, derived from Sternberg's (1977) earlier work on '*components*'. At that time, Sternberg introduced component-theory, avoiding the whole factor-analytic approach because he judged that it had not the power, scientifically, to advance our knowledge of intellect. Sternberg's paradigm eschewed psychometric tests, and instead defined the information content of reasoning in terms of stages of processing. The important elements in his threefold definition of intelligence (or generalisable sets of skills) are specified as adaptation to novel stimuli; rate of automatization

THE TRIAD

Stimuli Adaptation

Fluency Rate

Contextual Demands

(or making fluent what is learned); and adaptation to the context of measurement. Additionally, Sternberg argues that the mechanisms of functioning in a purposive, problem-solving manner be specified. These are based in the componential frame that specifies executive processes, performance components and knowledge-acquisition components. Latency was used as a measure of the process; and we can characterise his effort as part of the L-Model (latency) movement. When Sternberg describes components, dynamic images clothe the metaphors for theories that are currently being considered useful. Take this definition of a component by Sternberg (1984b) as an example. *'The component may translate a sensory input into a conceptual representation, transform one conceptual representation into another, or translate a conceptual representation into a motor output.'* Translations, transformations and representations are not static entities or simple elements of discourse. On the contrary, they are extremely complex constructs with great category width.

Measuring Components

Sternberg's components are nevertheless latency based, and in that they share with Eysenck's, Hunt's and Jensen's and Stankov's work, a common concern for speed of execution. Sternberg himself defines *duration, difficulty and probability of execution* as the markers for components. This can be compared with the much earlier transatlantic excursion by Furneaux, Eysenck and White (White 1982) into *speed, accuracy, and persistence* in relation to problem parameters such as difficulty and discriminating power. There is precious little between Eysenck and Sternberg operationally in the long run - except in Sternberg's attention to context, implying relativity rather than absolutism. When two scientists as different in assumptions as Eysenck and Sternberg agree on these basic approaches to measurement, they point to the elements of performance that may be modelled in tasks where accuracy, speed and more than one trial are needed.

KEEP TRI-ING?

Perhaps

One has to specify the links between short term memory components and the mobilisation of long term memory information in tasks that simulate training. How does learning affect performance? Sternberg needs '*metacomponents*' to account for this. Metacomponents are ghosts in the machine without tasks to define them. Not much about executive processes is known except that their existence as constructs is central to information-processing paradigms (Detterman, 1984). Equally, Irvine (1984) speculated that the Sternberg theories may be incapable of full operational definition. However, Sternberg (2008) has since produced a lengthy chapter illuminating a series of experimental attempts at external interventions to improve intelligence test scores. The effect sizes and consequent success of the interventions were limited; and at the end Sternberg has recourse to Spearman's two factor theory as the most influential of all constructs for use in training and selection. Sternberg's demonstration of attempts to measure components is his major contribution. The heuristic impetus provided by distinguishing the stages in processing test items has been considerable.

SUMMARY

Sternberg's (1985b) *Triarchic Theory* has existed for more than 25 years but with only limited statement in operational terms, and subsequent exploration (Sternberg, 2008). The conclusion from the decade of work prior to the construction of BARB was that new methods of measuring abilities had flourished with speed, but with disorder. Practical progress could only be made when the ingenuity that created the measures is turned to systematic efforts to validate them as constructs. Carroll, Eysenck, Hunt and Sternberg all made important contributions. Those who integrate them operationally and at the same time avoid the recurrent problems of individual differences research in multicultural contexts could produce coherent measures of abilities, skills and their correlates in motivation and interests. Performance models of the type advocated by Carroll seemed to hold out the best possibility of measurements that are context-responsive yet are process-determined. How these contributed to the construction of BARB is now reviewed.

THE PROCESS OF THE PRODUCT – SEQUENCES AS *RADICALS*

CARROLL'S UNIVERSALISM: TEST PARADIGMS AND ITEM DIFFICULTY

Carroll will probably be best remembered for his attempt to revise and restructure ability theory in his last great work *Human Cognitive Abilities* (Carroll. 1993). But his output during the previous twenty years was equally powerful and influential. A watershed occurred with the publication of Resnick's book, in 1976, called *The Nature of Intelligence*. This collection is especially important for an attempt by Carroll (1976) to produce a new structure of intellect not by applying more tests, nor by constructing new ones, *but by examining known tests*. The conventional methods of factor analysis were put aside, in order to apply theory associated with cognitive tasks to psychometric tests. *They were scrutinised by specifying a model of memory, as well as other cognitive characteristics, by Carroll himself, using a computer program which he devised*. Thereafter, with the help of this semi-expert system, each test was examined to determine its cognitive task demands. The study emerges as the very first use by a psychologist of a computer to aid in the evidence-based restructuring of psychometric test items by means of a cognitive model of memory. The result was, indeed, a 'new structure of intellect' (Carroll's own sub-title); but there was not a single participant interrogated, except Carroll himself. In his next work, Carroll (1980) he took a related, but updated approach.

He began to examine, by much the same means, the task demands imposed by the burgeoning use of microcomputers to employ cognitive tasks as measures, not of accuracy, but of speed of response. In this extensive monograph, he provides an improved system for the analysis and construction of paradigms and of the tasks that define them. Carroll's examples of how reaction time measures can be seen to differ significantly in their demands on the participant (by adopting a computer based system of interrogation of the task) are crucial for the evaluation of claims made for the generalisability of reaction-time measures. The object is to relate experimenter events to the corresponding mental events of the participant. Reaction time tasks, by this scheme, show infinite variety. But models of performance can emerge from such analyses. These performance models are essential to the production of useful cognitive tasks and tests.

Computer-Based Cognitive Tasks
In one of the most compelling analyses of tasks that could be used to assess intelligence, Carroll (1980b) set down a definition of eight basic cognitive task paradigms to categorise the majority of tests under scrutiny. He did not claim them to be exhaustive but they provided a useful and much needed framework in which to fit new measures. Carroll's framework, seen in Table3.2, specifies the cognitive paradigms for each family of task, allows referencing of these tasks with traditional psychometric constructs, and enables domain studies to be formulated as part of the ongoing process of construct validation. Any new model of mental measurement was then required to relate effectively to progress in structuring intellect from cognitive-process paradigms, as distinct from a traditional test base. Attempts to create

BARB had thereafter to reference measures to paradigms and processes, rather than to reproduce standardised test scores from items contained in conventional paper-and-pencil tests. Dann & Irvine (1986) devised a handbook of cognitive tests, after detailed analysis and consideration of the Carroll paradigms and correlated various examples of computer-delivered tests with them. The handbook was a major influence on the final choice of tests and their design in BARB.

Table 3.2: Carroll's (1980) Eight Cognitive Task Paradigms With Examples

Paradigms	Examples
1. Perceptual apprehension	Word recognition threshold
2. Reaction time and movement	Choice reaction time
3. Evaluation/decision	Dichotic listening task
4. Stimulus matching/comparison	Posner tasks
5. Naming/reading/association	Word naming
6. Episodic memory read-out	Digit span
7. Analogical reasoning	Verbal, figural analogies
8. Algorithmic manipulation	Mental arithmetic in base (other than) 10

What Makes Items Difficult, I Guess?[5]

As part of demonstrating the utility of the 'person characteristic function', Carroll conducted investigations of the characteristics of what makes items difficult. Several examples are to be found in an overview of this material in Carroll (1987). Carroll's concordant experimental work (Carroll, 1983a, 1986a, 1986b, 1987) was devoted to using item-response theory. Unlike Lord (1980b) who assumed that items vary in their powers of discrimination and of difficulty, he demonstrated that when the tasks do not vary much in their discrimination power, and are homogeneous in what it is that they measure, functions can be developed. Examples of successful prediction of what makes visualisation items difficult in a number of apparently different tests were not casually chosen. Carroll's subsequent factor analysis of spatial test intercorrelations produced a single general factor. The implications for the construction of an optimum referent task for the factor are plain. The tasks require a number of mental rotations in which verification of a same or different target is complicated by obverse or mirror images. Should these human requirements be met by computer algorithms that combine to stabilise difficulties over trials, then multiple parallel forms can be constructed from theoretically consistent estimates of item-difficulty that can then be verified on small participant pools. Carroll's uniqueness lay in the active pursuit of theory to estimate item and ability parameters that circumvent much of the awkwardness and complexity of IRT methods. Approaches to predicting item difficulty for BARB are reported in Chapter 4.

THE END OF THE BEGINNING: A SUMMARY

Structural theories, each within its own psychological culture, have made significant progress since Spearman. Tests produced a massive empirical database. Examination

---

5   Carroll's answer when I asked him in 1977 in the Thurstone Laboratory what the issues in measurement would be in the next decade.

of it, after nearly a century, expanded empirical horizons and narrowed the search for structure. Emphasis on paper-and-pencil examination results produced a growing reluctance, by any who perceived themselves as disadvantaged, to undertake tests of any kind: and many recruits seemed to have a dislike of classrooms and paperwork. A model, or models, for cognitive performance that would maximise the utility, and hence acceptance of systems of appraisal was required for social and political acceptance. These trends underpinned the major changes in test development that characterised BARB. They arose from a base in human information-processing anchored in psychometric constructs. However, the tests had to be presented and scored, using the potential of computer technology. What was the best way forward?

THE 'SHOOT OUT' IN ATHENS

(1984 et seq.)

Computerisation: Paying Close Attention
To summarise: the extent of the work that had to be reviewed before BARB could be constructed is found in the following collections; Freidman, Das and O'Connor, (1981); Sternberg (1984b, 1985a, 1985b); Eysenck, (1981). Even with the evidence of these sources, the examples and content of lectures given at the ASI for NATO held in Greece, in December, 1984[6] (Irvine & Newstead, 1987; Newstead, Irvine and Dann, 1986) were among the most influential. Carroll, Eysenck, Hunt, Sternberg and Vernon were all present to summarise their current thinking, while Irvine provided a critique of several cognitive item types that were due to find their way into computer-delivered systems (Newstead, Irvine and Dann, 1986, pp. 1-26). From all the available sources, a study of the simplest tasks was undertaken, hoping to answer *The Anderson Question*. From those requiring high concentration to others that seemed to demand no apparent task effort, analyses of conscious attention was the keynote. Then the use of holistic theories as operational models was considered. In particular, Sternberg's attempts to put into action a theory based on three aspects of human adaptation were placed in the perspectives of veterans at the NATO institute. Moreover, applications from published military sources, concentrating on those for whom operations and results are explicit were included. Finally, computer-derived taxonomies of data description, particularly those developed by Carroll, set limits to the claims from any single measurement paradigm.

---

6   Referred to by participants as 'The Shoot Out in Athens' because of the presence of theorists such as Eysenck and Sternberg with very different approaches and cognition models. However, Carroll, Vernon, Hunt, Berry, Irvine and others were able to prevent gunfire. In the end, a contextual view of intelligence theory seemed to satisfy most of the large number of participants.

CHAPTER 4

LEARNING LESSON 3: TESTING TESTS IN THE LABORATORY

This, perhaps the longest chapter in the book, is central to the understanding of what the team in the laboratory at Plymouth understood before moving forward. There were four tasks: how to simulate item construction and solution using the computer alone, with no participant other than the programmer: decoding item structures to separate radicals from incidentals: applying incomplete block designs to test production. By the end of the chapter, the complex elements of design are set out clearly. Finally, a comprehensive list of achievements using radicals and incidentals with which to predict item difficulty is the outcome of various successful laboratory experiments in the decade following 1986.

TESTS: A TESTING TIME

- *Item-generation forerunners*

- *Jonathan Evans's simulations*

- *Isaac Bejar's 'grammar' at ETS*

- *Tasks with strategies*

- *Working memory in item difficulty*

- *Test format using incomplete block designs to maximise information*

TEST CHOICE:
GATHERING EVIDENCE

Currently, the various approaches to producing multiple parallel form tests have been largely codified within two construction frameworks. One is known as *evidence centred design*, (ECD) and the other *the linear logistic test model* (LLTM). Both of these are referenced with examples of prominent publications at the end of the chapter. Essentially, the first (ECD) specifies the kinds of evidence test constructors should seek and apply to the item structure. The precise definition of constructs in both tests and criteria, the item structures and alternates, the methods of verification – all leading ultimately to computer simulation that will replace the massive empirical data production needed for item-response parameters. The second, the linear logistic test model, has also been used as a partial solution to the ever-present problem of using large numbers of participants to produce the data necessary for a single item. Today's formulations have followed what is now recognised as a turning point in the discipline, the collection of studies by early pioneers in Irvine & Kyllonen (2002), reviewed with foresight and precision by Gierl & Leighton (2004). The attempts to construct BARB have been, *de facto*, evidence centred, being concerned with intelligence theory, alternative measurement models, the nature of the outcomes to be predicted, the knowledge

required and for tests construction by using computers, and scoring. It had to follow
these routes, given *The Anderson Question*. Precisely what kinds of evidence might
be centred in the final design of BARB is now provided by the examples that follow.
The road to ECD began with BARB and its contemporaries; and in particular with the
contributions by Collis, Dann, Dennis, Evans and Wright at Plymouth.

In retrospect, some may argue that the road to predicting item difficulty began
early in the last century, in Cyril Burt's laboratory when he and his colleague Penrose,
helped J. C. Raven to produce his master's thesis in which the *Progressive Matrices
Test* was first uncovered. In a handwritten letter to the writer[1], in April 1967, Burt
explained the principles behind what he termed the *Penrose-Raven Test* as follows,
using the diagram below, drawn on the letter.

> *What was ...important was that it could be systematically constructed on a scale of
> increasing complexity, like a mathematical 'matrix' of rank one, two, three etc. Multiply
> a determining row of size by a determining column of shape (3 lines, 4 lines, 5 lines
> for example, and you got a 'matrix of rank one' (Take in Diagram) ...Superimpose
> a matrix determined by colours and you had a compound matrix of rank 2. Insert
> dots in the middle and you added a further complication. When Raven registered for
> M.A. by research in 1935 or thereabouts, it seemed a promising topic (Burt, personal
> communication, 5 April, 1967)*

In the extract in Figure 4.1, Burt goes on to describe Penrose's role. The letter is really
about what a Matrices score could portend, but his comments describe one of the very
earliest attempts to predict the difficulty of items from their constituent components.

Figure 4.1: Burt's (1967) Diagram on Matrices Item Difficulty

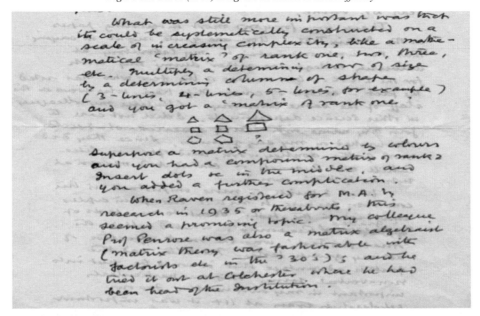

---

1   In response to an early draft of Irvine, S. H. (1969b). Figural tests of reasoning in Africa: studies in the use of Raven's
Progressive Matrices across cultures. *International Journal of Psychology, 4,* 217-228.

A more detailed formulation of the rationale is contained in the foundation article by Penrose and Raven (1936, pp. 97-103). They were the first to show how to construct items of increasing difficulty using analogues based on matrix algebra, in which Penrose was an acknowledged authority. Penrose and Raven illustrate eight ordinal and additive elements of different complexity from which it is possible to predict item difficulty (Loc. cit. pp.100-102). The items become progressively more difficult as the rank of the matrix increases by adding successive overlays of radicals needed to create them. Hence the appropriateness of the name *Progressive* Matrices. Perhaps more attention might have been paid to test construction by applying their rationale for the construction of *Raven's Matrices* than mistakenly claiming its scores as a measure of 'pure g'- a viewpoint so unacceptable to Burt that he wrote in 1967 that he would have 'expunged' it from Raven's thesis if it had been present - which of course it was not. What the test might or might not measure is still a matter of debate, although modern item-generation techniques (Hornke, 2002; Kunda, McGreggor, & Goel 2009) reveal more about the verbalisations required to disentangle visual complexity with progressive difficulty.

Moreover, Burt's insights were not the only evidence for difficulty paradigms, like those expressed by Penrose and Raven that could be used to produce item cycles of increasing difficulty. A notable and relatively unknown example of parallel form success is to be found in the *Spiral Nines Test* (CSIR, 1960) developed by Oscar Roberts for the National Institute of Personnel Research[2] in the 1960s. Roberts was able to produce parallel forms of paper-and-pencil tests based upon ten cycles each of six different test types. The standardisation was such that a person completing only the first cycle of six would have a stanine score of 1. Completion of two cycles yields a stanine of 2, and so on until a top score of 9 would be gained by completing 9 cycles correctly. Item response models were not in use, but Roberts was able to demonstrate their outcome, hence *Spiral Nines*. Fascinating as these early examples were, they afforded little more than curiosity at the time, and a hope to emulate them if possible in a different culture and another age. But they, and others like them, should be recognised as tests with strong evidential credentials, worthy of recognition as early examples of success in predicting the difficulty of items from their elements.

VIRTUAL DIFFICULTY WITH COMPUTER-BASED ITEM GENERATION

Early paper-and-pencil trials were run in parallel with laboratory research at Plymouth: and the code for computer generation and record-keeping was begun. The operational BARB battery of computer-based tests of basic cognitive abilities used procedures to construct test items from algorithms based on prior knowledge of factors which affect item difficulty. Peter Dann (Dann, 1993) provides a full description in the complete BARB foundation code document. A lot of thought was necessary before the basic abilities cluster (ABC) tests were to appear. Some examples of early computer-based efforts described in this chapter show their influences on the final set of BARB tests. The outcome was to prove unique in the development of military tests. *A new parallel form of equivalent items was constructed in real time and administered to each applicant.* Nothing like this had been used nation-wide. Since its operational use in 1992, over half

---

2   The South African NIPR psychometric research under its director, Simon Biesheuvel was a notable cross-cultural contribution, often in the face of opposition.

a million individual tests have been produced for Army applicants. The tests arrived only after work in the laboratory, and elsewhere, demonstrated that code could solve an item and reproduce it with an index of its difficulty. The critical breakthrough was by Evans in Plymouth and Bejar at ETS Princeton, both working independently.

EVANS'S EVIDENCE CENTRED SIMULATION DESIGN IN 1986: SPATIAL MAPPING AND RANDOM WALKS

There was one critical issue. What would make the tests difficult, and what would not affect difficulty? And there was the hitherto hidden agenda in the computer itself. What could writing the code to generate the items in the computer reveal about the difficulty of the items themselves? At the survey stage only, some clues about how to answer the first question emerged. As they are listed, the problems fall into order of importance, and the sections that follow address the first two of these as the critical issues, devising a performance model and programs to generate and predict the difficulty of the items. There is no such thing as absolute machine difficulty, although there appear to be some universals that determine difficulty within broad limits for humans. What goes into the machine is, therefore, a model of performance that generates valid indices of difficulty, as Jonathan Evans was to demonstrate so vividly in the earliest days of experiment within the Plymouth laboratory. Initially conceived as a student project, a method used to initiate research at low participation cost, he developed a spatial mapping task (Figure 4.2) for use in the Plymouth laboratory (Irvine, Dann and Evans, 1986, pp. 82-86). The task was to find the way from one room to another, given a starting point, in the least number of moves. The room plan is complex, as the illustration shows.

Figure 4.2: Evans' Simulation 24-Room Plan Layout for Learning

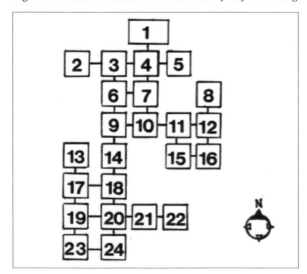

Evans's choice of a somewhat unusual task had three main purposes. First, it opened up the possibility of a whole new family of learning tasks that PPTs (Paper and Pencil

Tests) could not have foreseen. Next, the task can only be presented interactively by the computer, allowing a computer test of the participant's learning rate - or ability level if one wishes to build in that option. *Third, it was probably the first demonstration of how to predict item difficulty for humans when it might be impossible, for all practical purposes, to involve human participants to get base line averages.* Simulation was the option, now part of the vocabulary and syntax for item-generation (Mislevy, 2011). In fact, in this task, item-difficulty could not be accurately predicted employing one-trial attempts with human participants - unless one had unlimited resources.

THE COMPUTER AS EVANS'S SOLE PARTICIPANT

Evans's computer program has no memory of what it did in the last trial, so it never learns from previous trials. It does, though, have an excellent memory for what it has just done in the only trial it is allowed. So it simulates an applicant with one attempt allowed. Finally, it is somewhat single-minded and obstinate. Once committed to a track it doggedly goes down that track until it comes to a dead end, retracing steps until it can take an unexplored track that was previously ignored in its random walk. When it arrives adjacent to a target, it will automatically go to the target, ignoring any side-tracks that may still be open. One feels certain that some job description in one of our armed services must exist that his program fits perfectly, although some students may not be unjustly described by its persona, except, of course for their limited working memories, which can be built into the program.

Figure 4.2 provides what the participant never sees, a plan of the 'rooms' in the house. The participant is given only verbal instructions, for example to walk in a certain direction north, south, east and west, and is given a verbal label for the room, to arrive at the hall from a bathroom or bedroom or broom closet. Each room had a label. Room 1 was the hall, Room 4 the sitting room. Room 11 the kitchen, and so on. The details of the programme construction must be taken for granted, but some description of the program as if it had certain human characteristics may not be amiss. With the map before us, a parsimonious sequence is easy to plot. Starting from 1, about 32 moves would be as good as one might hope for, representing a perfect learning of the task - explore every room at least once. This is well below the random walk average of more or less 43 moves for the same starting point. Taking the limen for the item as 43, one can now express the difference between this and 32 as a positive 'ability' function. This capacity in the test constructor generates a threshold or 'limen' value that a learning model depends on.

Predicting Difficulty

The task, and not perchance, resembles a computer game. How difficult is it? Difficulty will obviously increase with the number of rooms in the house. Hence, the number of rooms to be traversed becomes our best estimate of any single item difficulty. For the explore sequence, that is visiting every one of the 24 rooms in the house once, varying the start point, 100 computer trials for each starting point (shown by the numbers 1,2,3,4,5,6,7 and 8 on the layout) were run. Depending on the starting point, the means ranged from, in round figures, 38 to 46 moves. The average of the means from all of these points was 42.49, with a standard deviation of 2.35. The mean of the 8 values has 95 percent confidence limits of plus or minus 1.66. It becomes a reasonable inference from this that starting point is not quite a random influence on the number of moves, and that number of rooms may be a first estimate, but not an explanation of item difficulty.

Simulation and Difficulty

The walk version of the puzzle attempts to predict item difficulty more accurately, or at least to get a rationale for any theoretical value. We asked the computer to walk from two positions 4 and 24. The targets were as follows. Taking station four as the starting point, walk to 10, 12, 17, and 22 in turn; and, from the other starting point, 24, walk to 18, 13, 7, and 16 in turn. These walks were meant to represent rooms that were 2, 4, 6 and 8 linear stops distant, ignoring the side tracks and other exits from rooms along the way. Figure 4.3 shows the averages for walking randomly through these stops, with 30 trials per walk.

Figure 4.3: Average Random Moves by Linear Distance from Target

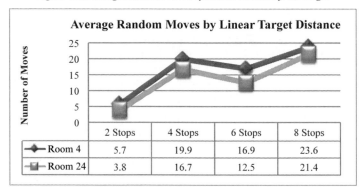

	2 Stops	4 Stops	6 Stops	8 Stops
Room 4	5.7	19.9	16.9	23.6
Room 24	3.8	16.7	12.5	21.4

The average for 30 trials as shown in Figure 4.3, not evenly split, was 3.8. When this problem was run 500 times in the computer, the average number of steps was 3.944. Armed with this information, as the key to predicting item-difficulty, one may account for the apparently high number of steps in the 4 stop condition. The penalties for taking an inappropriate turn are functions of the random depth search along blind alleys; and they are severe if one has no long-term memory from trial to trial. While the joint probabilities of these moves could be calculated, as showed on the simplest example, to yield a theoretical mean, their complexity is daunting.

The Markov Chain estimates account for the design (exit locations) features of the puzzle and the number of rooms in the house, and allow 'limen' difficulties for each type of task. Difficulty values from human naive participants used once as single links in the Markov Chain would be impossible without unlimited resources of time and money. From these machine estimates, improvement over chance by humans can be attributed to learning. And learning can be simulated in the machine. The total time in running all of these complex Markov chain simulations (explore as well as walks) in the computer of the day (a small departmental Bleasdale Computer, which networked BBC Micros), was no more than 45 minutes. Programming took Jonathan Evans somewhat longer; and the realisation by psychometric authorities that simulation was an essential part of parallel forms design, about two decades more.

Conclusions

Item generation in pattern matching paradigms had already been accomplished by 1986; machine indices of difficulty based could be calculated; and the matrix patterns derived in the process of problem solution could be used to regenerate clones, or in

Bejar's definitive term *isomorphs*. Machine problem-solving strategies articulated by Evans is even today not fully established as psychologically valid; but success in regenerating items that relate well to established indices of item-difficulty means that a certain kind of truth is economically determined. Simulation, as a construct, has enormous category width, and forms of statistical simulation to reduce the massive amount of pilot testing to estimate variation among items thought to be isomorphs was foreseen by Fischer (1973) whose linear logistic test model (LLTM) has been widely pursued and extrapolated into various IRT paradigms, constrained (Embretson, 1999), Bayesian (Sinharay & Johnson, 2003) and hierarchical (Glas & van der Linden, 2003). These and other similar statistical attempts are reviewed by Griel & Lai (2012a) and their own derivation of the LLTM model demonstrated in the production of parallel forms of mathematics items.

VERBAL REASONING ITEM RADICALS:
DEFINITIVE CODE BY EVANS – AND SOME CONCEPTS FROM RIPS

Jonathan Evans (1982, Ch. 4, pp. 49-70) had already provided all that is necessary for multiple parallel forms of transitive inference tasks to be created. Apart from this, the concurrent research most easily applied to item-generative methods was the work by Rips (1984) on reasoning items of the formal logic 'If p then q' type. These were once a staple diet in the compulsory first year logic courses taught at certain centres of excellence north of the River Tweed, but are now relegated to the function of instruments of torture to a select band of psychology students. The virtue of formal logic as a test-bed is that the items are relatively closed as a set, and that the types of inference rules and the number of steps that have to be taken to solve them easily identify all the set members.

EVANS's

ITEM GENERATION WITH POPLOG:

structuring and generating a collection of items from a hypothetical model of performance

finding solutions to these items and keeping track of them

reporting these solutions in a form specified by the test constructor

performing as many trials as were necessary to produce estimates of the various difficulty parameters required to maximise information from scores

Given a known universe of discourse, Rips set out to build a system. The particular model considered here is ANDS (A Natural Deduction System) implemented as a computer program. In essence, ANDS consists of two components: the inference rules themselves, which exist as separate subroutines in the program; and a working memory that stores the steps in the proof (Rips, 1984, p.123). The ANDS model, like any other concerned with deductive reasoning, has its share of criticism as a complete cognitive model. That issue, although germane, becomes secondary to the effectiveness with which it predicts the proportions of incorrect responses per item type. Rips provides some convincing data (loc. cit. pp.136-137). To summarise these results, the correlation between predicted and actual mean error rates was .78. A replication study yielded a correlation between observed values in the first and second studies of .86. This work by Rips was to provide confirmation of the general approach to predicting item difficulty already published by Evans (1982).

THE EVANS EVIDENCE-CENTRED REASONING PARADIGMS
The second study is one of the earliest examples of simulation as an extension of parallel forms theory, now systematised as part evidence centred design (ECD developed at ETS (1999) outlined in Mislevy, Steinberger & Almond (2002) and described for practitioners in Mislevy's (2011) account. The concepts learned from study of the work of others were important, but the aim was to construct tests in such a fashion that would distinguish between elements that would always change item difficulty (radicals); and those that would change an item's outward appearance but make no difference to its difficulty (incidentals). Thanks solely to the voluntary efforts of Jonathan Evans two applications of a powerful programming language (POPLOG & LISP, 2013) were able to simulate functions that are necessary for the following purposes:

Evans Generates and Solves Grammatical Transformation Tasks
The first item-generation breakthrough for the laboratory was a simple version of a grammatical transformation task considered to be a three-minute test of reasoning (Baddeley, 1968, 1981; Baddeley & Hitch, 1974), and generally recognised as a sentence verification task involving grammatical transformations, with increasing loads on working memory. The item type may be described as deceptively simple. A statement is made about the order of two successive letters. This is followed by a representation of the sentence. Finally, a question asks if the letter sequence is a true or false depiction of the content of the sentence. The example is perhaps simpler then the description!

- **Example: A follows B: = AB. True or False?**

In summary, it is as a *sentence verification task* with a symbolic representation of the sentence content requiring transformation to arrive at a truth value. A useful account of the various nuances of grammatical transformation tasks is available in Greene (1970) and further illuminated in Carroll (1980, pp. 166 et seq.) who categorises the Baddeley task as Stimulus Matching/Comparison under his paradigm framework (Loc. cit. p. 74). Evans's solution to item-generation and subsequent production of answers and estimates of difficulty wholly within the computer were not affected by the ease or difficulty of writing code. They were very much influenced by the availability of a model for task solution that had some basis in intuition (that is, it had user acceptability) and a lot of basis in experimentation with human participants. Evans makes quite clear in the code, that *the programme as written is in response to the experimental findings about how humans solve the problem. It is not written as a programme for the machine to solve the problem as only it could.* The full explanation of the program, with 20 examples, is given in the original report (Irvine, Dann & Evans, 1986, pp. 87-93). Here perhaps one might emphasise the shortness of the program required to generate the items, to solve the problems and keep track of the steps undertaken.

To make these and countless others like them possible, Evans encoded a procedure to construct the item by choosing the sentence frame, and randomising the letters to be used, and randomising the letter order. Another procedure checked for the presence of passives and negatives, prior to transforming the statement into an active affirmative and incrementing the difficulty list with each transformation. Examples of the output using only one verb (follows) and two letters (D and F) are seen in their original form in Table 4.1. The output of the generation program traces the solution, showing the transformed versions of the sentences and printing out a difficulty list. This list contains a base time (B) plus the code N for a negative transformation and P for a passive transformation. It also has a separate parameter for the T type of verb (VP - precedes, VF follows) which may also affect the latency. The task modelled here is a simple version, illustrating the techniques involved which could be extended to much more complex variants, and to other reasoning tasks. According to the model, the response times would be given by the sum of the parameters in this list. The relative difficulty of the items can be inferred from the number of steps involved. To estimate actual item difficulty it would of course be necessary to obtain the parameter values by experiment or from publications. Empirical work would verify the assumed increase in latency with each step.

Table 4.1: Automatic Item Generation Pioneered

Evans' (1986) Automatic Item-Generation

PROBLEM 1

Statement: D follows F   Letter pair: F D

** [D follows F]

Solution **<false>

Difficulty ** [B VF]

PROBLEM 2

Statement: D is followed by F   Letter pair: D F

**[D is followed by F]

**[F follows D]

Solution **<true>

Difficulty** [B P VF]

PROBLEM 3

Statement: F is not followed by D   Letter pair: F D

** [F is not followed by D]

** [D is followed by F]

** [F follows D]

Solution ** <false>

Difficulty ** [B N P VF]

The relative difficulty of the items can be inferred from the number of steps involved. To estimate actual item difficulty it would of course be necessary to obtain the parameter values by experiment or from publications. Empirical work would verify the assumed increase in latency with each step. The further development of this basic task by the addition of another level, demanding solution of two sequences in problems of this kind, comes in Figure 4.4.

Figure 4.4: Extended Baddeley Task Type in 6 Screens

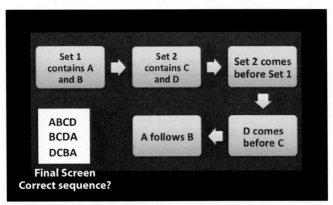

The answer to the problem, although straightforward as long as one has all the information before one's very eyes, becomes much more difficult to generate accurately in working memory *if each statement is delivered serially, a screen at a time, and then disappears before the next arrives.* The screen *radical* can add a dimension to the Evans structure: and it often does. Many mistakes occur if each one of the statements is given in turn by a computer, only to disappear off screen when the participant indicates readiness for the next. In fact, it might prove almost impossible for many, because of rehearsal and maintenance demands in working memory. In that particular condition, involving six successive screens, distinguished and power-wielding visitors to the lab were protected from the rigours of this task, especially if their seniority in rank was also accompanied by seniority in years.

Nevertheless, given Evans' POPLOG approach, to rank items like these in order of difficulty, depends on the number of transformations (involving negatives, use of the passive voice and information pace) required to arrive at the correct answer. Here was an explicit direct transfer from cognitive theory to right and wrong models of test construction, a fulfilment of the prescriptions made by Cronbach as early as 1957, but never realised until the *Anderson Question* appeared. Even if right-wrong scoring were adopted, the use of the computer meant that, if latency to key press was recorded, 'working out time' enacted by each time spent on successive screens, or item demands could be extracted as a bonus. Assuming that simple and complex versions are testing the limits of working memory, then there are two different ways of estimating ability: speed to execute low-level demand, if no errors worth recording were found; and speed and/or accuracy in executing high-stress demand. The value of this type of item is the addition of the levels of complexity until the probability of a

BEJAR'S GRAMMAR

'A generative psychometrics, then, involves a 'grammar' capable of assigning a description of every item in the universe of items and is capable of generating all the items in the universe.' Bejar & Yocum, 1991

BEJAR'S PRESCRIPTIONS

§ *Devise a performance model for item solution*

§ *Program the computer to solve and generate items*

§ *Relate computer difficulty to human difficulty*

correct response is a chance phenomenon for the individual. In short, it becomes possible to validate the test using only internal criteria and to use the computer to simulate solutions by participants of different 'ability'.

BEJAR'S GRAMMAR:
SPATIAL ITEM PRODUCTION

A test item is no more, and no less, than a composite of a number of unique elements, each of which may or may not affect the difficulty of that item. In the construction of most paper-and-pencil tests, experience and guesswork were applied before the difficulty of the item was provided after trial and error. To depart from these conventions, still in use under the guise of item-response theory, a new approach was essential. In any item formulation, either by hand or by computer, one had first to construct a 'grammar' for the item, as Bejar (1986a,1986b,1986c) made abundantly clear with his prescient work on predicting the difficulty of figural test items using a computer-based program. Although the domain area is spatial, the item types are different. They are rotational tasks requiring visualisation (Shepard & Metzler, 1971) and *Embedded Figures* (Ekstrom, French & Harmon, 1976, p. 21). In the laboratory at Plymouth, work proceeded on spatial mapping, reasoning, verbal structures and strategies – all designed to find out what item elements would predict their difficulty. Important though these experiments were in evaluating item types to use, Bejar's formulation of his generative models (Bejar & Yocum, 1991) describes the essence of the automatic generation problem. The requirement was a 'grammar' capable of describing every item in a generic type, but also capable of generating the items themselves. The required 'grammar' is analogous to the structure of a simple sentence. There is a subject (item content), a verb (the algorithms that produce the item) and an object, (the prediction of item difficulty). *It was perhaps the most important statement of the decade, because of what it implied - the structure of the evidence leading to simulation was essential for item-generation to succeed.* It provides a number of prescriptions for different types of evidence implicit in the materials supplied by Evans.

Bejar's work at ETS provided important confirmation of the early laboratory work at Plymouth. He pioneered two important studies of spatial tasks, one involving rotation, and the other embedded figures: and in doing so traced a path that deserved to be followed but was ignored for a decade or more in the United States.

Three-Dimensional Rotation
This can be constructed and rotated on computers with high resolution graphics; and can be manufactured in them from current graphics methods, although Bejar does not attempt this. Instead, he pre-constructed the items and presented them at fixed angles of disparity. The outcome was a confirmation of the Shepard & Metzler (1971) 'physical analogue' approach. They discovered that the time to verify two figures as identical increased with the size of the angle of disparity between the two figures, as if a mental parallel to an actual physical rotation were occurring.

Figure 4.5 Examples of the Shepard and Metzler (1971) Tasks

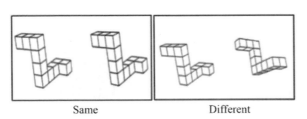

| Same | Different |

Here are two examples of the rotational tasks. Participants have to compare two shapes and decide whether they are the same or, if they prove to be mirror-images, different. *Incidentally, when rotational tasks were used in BARB, special attention had to be given to instructions and trials that actually rotated images on screen to demonstrate that the figures would or would not match. This was a crucial feature of the system.* The illustration is useful in understanding why such tactics were necessary with the recruit population. Moreover, any verification of the match or mismatch in a computer had to programme the rotation itself to determine the outcome. The analogues from Bejar's studies were many. Bejar concluded that the relationship between angular disparity and item difficulty in the 'match' condition is linear, determining a criterion for item generation. Response-time 'envelopes' were determined so that an item could be transposed to right-wrong scoring treatment from latency after a fixed interval. In this case 5 seconds was a convenient cutting point. Because the non-match items did not fit the linear increase model for positive matches, Bejar was left with two different mental models for which no common problem-solving 'grammar' exists.

Hidden or Embedded Figures Difficulty.
Bejar had complete success with his second item-type, embedded or 'hidden' figures. In fact, this proved to be historically definitive. The task in hidden figure items is to determine whether a specified target figure is embedded in a background matrix of intersecting lines. Bejar not only produced a means of detecting the target in a matrix, but effectively generated clones from matrices of given complexity values, an astonishing achievement whose impact might have been far greater had it been widely applied.

In this study the approach has been to postulate a theory, in the form of a computer program, of how participants solve these items. The program solves the items correctly but in doing so records the difficulties it encounters. The difficulties exhibited by the program are highly correlated to psychometric difficulty, thus suggesting the validity of the model. The next step is to 'turn the program around' and have it generate items of known difficulty. (Bejar, 1986a, p. 8.)

The illustration[3] in Figure 4.6 shows the general idea of automatically finding a potential difficulty value for an embedded figure matrix of 42 intercepts. The target figure itself, embedded in the complex pattern, has seven sides. By use of the Hough (1962) transform (see Ballard, 1981), the target is scrutinised in the computer for a match at every line intersection, or node. If one line overlaps, a value of 2 is recorded; and so on until a perfect match is made, giving a score of 14 when all 7 sides of the target figure fit an identical shape in the large matrix. Although Bejar gives no details about how to calculate machine indices of difficulty, some observations are possible from the matrices provided.

Figure 4.6: Bejar's 1986 use of the Hough Transform with Embedded Figures

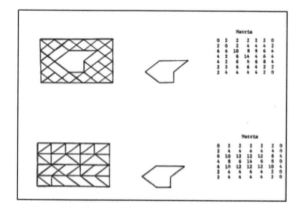

Summing the numbers in the matrix of the easy item gives a much lower value than the sum total in the matrix alongside the difficult item. *An average value of the line match score can be derived, low values indicating easy items.* This gives a machine-generated item difficulty index b', which can later be correlated with b, observed psychometric difficulty. The values at each of the 42 points are also used in an item generation or cloning process, because the machine must produce these by line subtraction, iterating and back-tracking until a desired fit is obtained. Bejar (1968a) provides evidence for the success of this process (loc cit. pp. 9-10 and Annex A) *by successfully cloning two hidden figure items with contrasting levels of difficulty.*

Like Evans's work on reasoning items, this was one of the earliest examples of automatic item generation without using any participants to determine a difficulty value for any single item. Using the same series of items, Ippel (1986) confirmed the psychological robustness of the attempt to fit machine solutions to cognitive performance in his doctoral thesis on the determinants of performance. He confirmed in a meticulous series of experimental studies what Bejar's computer-derived embedded figure model assumes. In brief, difficulty increases with the number of lines on the matrix; and some targets are easier to find than others using various individual

---

3   Shown by kind permission of Isaac Bejar.

strategies. Both Bejar and Ippel showed how evidence led to simulation, while Evans was independently having success with automatic generation of reasoning and spatial learning tasks in Plymouth.

The Key: Item Grammars

The subsequent BARB 'grammars' were to contain logical statements for the construction of items from those 'radical' elements that change their difficulty, and those 'incidentals' that make the item seem different from others but have no effect on the difficulty of the item. Chapter 6, where the BARB concepts were extended, contains additional examples of the application of these basic concepts. Much was required before the grammars were found and the language of item generation changed from oral tradition with an orthography of its own. A necessary step was to determine how learning a relatively simple strategy, explicitly or implicitly (and not knowingly) during the test might affect or even alter its structure. Fortunately, some previous work on a classical item type used in intelligence tests was relevant to the enquiry.

LEARNING DURING THE TEST: DSST AND ROTATION TASK EXPERIMENTS

Three main influences on participants' performance were obvious when long-service and 'simple' *Digit-Symbol Substitution Tasks* (DSST or, popularly, CODES) were given as repeated measures in paper-and-pencil format, implying learning over trials. If others like it were to emerge, what would affect their difficulties? Important in the quest for radicals that would predict item difficulty, the main effects on DSST performance were predictable from cognitive theory. *Two elements were initially involved, the amount of information contained in the symbols: and the size of the set of symbols to be encoded.* Table 4.1 shows how set size and symbol information can be varied, using sets of five, seven and nine typewriter symbols *compared with a rotated F font using four F ninety degree rotations and four mirror images.* The rotated F requires much more effort to recover the relevant information than the symbol set because the F shape is constant and the rotations are complex. Given these external conditions, were there factors *within* individuals that would affect difficulties while they took the test, such as conscious use of strategies or the effects of learning that they were not aware of?

Table 4.1: Illustration of Different DSST Task: Set Sizes and Symbol Information

Sets of Digits and Substitutions								
Symbol	%	@	!	$	&	*	£	#	?
Digit	1	2	3	4	5	6	7	8	9

Rotated F ⇕ ⇕ ⇕

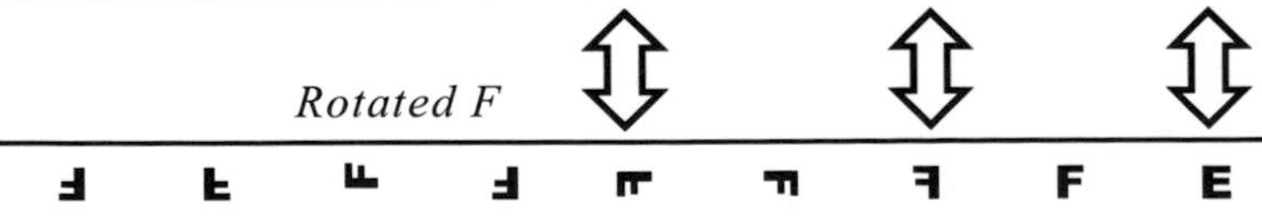

Symbol	⅃	Ŀ	⊔	⅃	�障	ᒣ	⅂	F	E
Digit	1	2	3	4	5	6	7	8	9

Number of Items in the Set

To compare external effects, the number of items in the set to be coded was varied using Miller's (1956) principle of the magic number 7, plus or minus 2. This defined the three different set sizes (5, 7, 9), between groups to represent different demands on working memory. Performance was a linear function of set size, for both sets of symbols, not only in the Plymouth University laboratory (Birch, 1981), but in real-life group-testing paper-and-pencil trials conducted in Africa (Irvine, Schoeman & Prinsloo, 1988), Canada (Gorham, 1978, Jennings, 1979) and Samoa (Stanko, 1979). The increase in performance due to coding progressively larger sets was linear when transformed to bits by the function $Log2\ N$ where N is the number of items in the set. This effect was an extrapolation of the Sternberg (1966) probe in the memory set task.

Loss of Information

Invariably, when the amount of information contained in the symbol decreased, making discrimination difficult, performance declined (Royer, 1971). To illustrate, it is possible to make up to 8 symbols, as Royer did, all of which are functions of F in various rotations of 90 degrees clockwise (see illustration); and another four of the same rotations for its mirror image, and to make up a ninth by using a very similar E or modified F. In this and in similar low discrimination conditions, compared with the normal maximally discriminable symbols, performance sharply decreased. Therefore, the effects of learning on performance on DSST tasks are minimised when it is very difficult to discriminate between pairs of symbols. If the symbols are easily perceived and recognised, the rate of learning is uncontrolled during encoding: and this raises the question of what meaning to attach to scores at different stages of completing a test of several trials at the same type of task. There is no guarantee that the abilities needed at the beginning of the first trial are those that will be used at the end of the last trial by every participant.

Pre-Learning the Codes

Little was known about the use of learned strategies to affect how the task was solved, or what abilities were involved. Some prior knowledge did exist from work in Canada with M.Ed. students. In particularly apt DSST series (Jennings 1979)[4], using the conventional symbols and digits, participants were asked to pre-learn, and commit to memory, the digits with their respective symbols. When the task was given, using the set size variations, there was no key to the paired symbols at the top of the test page, as there would have been under normal conditions. Retrieval from long-term memory (LTM) storage was necessary to complete the test. Results from this were compared with a control group, with the normal test format of search for the symbol at the top of each page, requiring cognition and working-memory storage with the prompt present.

In the retrieval from LTM condition where the codes had been pre-learned, information processing constants were achieved from average scores. Performance was then a function of the number of bits of information processed (set size) *and the number of times* that a set was run through 'the processor'. For example, a set of five digits and symbols, repeated in a total of 25 items, had been run past participants 5 times. If a set of 7 were involved, 35 items would have to be processed to run the set through 5 times; and a set of 9 would be run through five times after 45 consecutive

---

4   A M.Ed. student supervised by the author at Brock University, St. Catherines, Ontario, Canada

items. In the retrieval condition, evidence of constant processing values existed for the idealised individual. *From such results, a performance model of task difficulty can be determined, based on indices of discriminability, set size, and repetitions in the central processor. From this, test items could be created with certain knowledge of their degree of difficulty.* This was a big step forward. Was a similar model available from the traditional test format, with no pre-learning?

The model derived from recall data did not hold for the normal testing condition, with the key at the top of the page always visible. This prescribed a different approach to the code recognition and encoding paradigm to reflect the findings of Allison (1960) and Bunderson (1967), who demonstrate that 'abilities' used to perform various cognitive tasks change as the task is learned. Nevertheless, there is no universal law of individual strategy use. Jennings discovered that the coordination of skills to solve DSST in its traditional paper-and-pencil form varies greatly for individuals. *There is no guarantee that the abilities needed at the beginning of the first trial are those that will be used by every participant at the end of the last trial. In fact, most participants in the recognition- search condition successfully recalled from memory the correct symbols for the 9-item digit set after three trial blocks of two minutes.* This does not mean, however, that they used recall from memory in later trials to produce the substitutions.

TASKS USING STRATEGIES

• *Information load varied*

• *Pre-learning the pairs*

• *Strategic rotations*

• *Strategies change what is measured*

FINDING THOSE 'COACHED' IN A SPATIAL TASK

The use of strategies was an issue that was part of the experimental context of learning models implicit in repeated trials at the DSST. In fact, the earlier paper-and-pencil Canadian work of Jennings deliberately set out to determine strategic effects of pre-learning symbol pairs. A more controlled computer-delivered experiment with Naval Cadets was possible using a triangle rotation task. This moved the strategy-difficulty problem into another era. A cooperative study with Educational Testing Service (Mislevy, Wingersky, Irvine and Dann, 1991), made it possible to predict the mean response time per item to a rotation task involving the rotation of two right triangles, originally with 30 and 60 degree angles as complements to the 90 degree right angle. In this experiment, the score model was latency (L Model) where difficulty was judged to increase as time spent on a solution became greater. *Item difficulties changed when the triangles varied in their line lengths, angle of rotation, and when identical or mirror image triangles were being compared.* When the triangle's line lengths were altered this became a *radical*, so that the complementary angles changed, and the mirror image triangles became more difficult to distinguish from their 'normal' identity.

Figure 4.7: Effect of Adjacent Side Length in Right Triangle Comparison

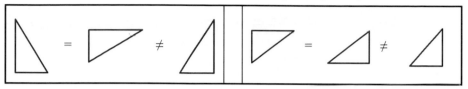

Specifically, the study was able to compare results from participants given a simple observational strategy[5] for solving the problems, that did not involve rotation, and those who had not been informed. Use of the strategy did not make the problems any easier when the side lengths on either side of the right angle became almost equal, producing an 'equilateral' shape. The results of strategy use when the use of the strategy was increasingly time consuming was the focus of attention.

Latency was almost perfectly predicted knowing line lengths, angle of rotation and identity vs. mirror image (R=.92). The simple examples in Fig. 7.2 provide an exercise in rotation with identical and mirror image forms where side lengths are varied. Attempts to solve the puzzle should leave the impression that the longer the side next to the right angle the easier it is. This early, almost prophetic, result underlined the need to ensure that item-generative formats took account of coaching that could introduce strategies that provide the correct answer *but involve procedures that had little or nothing to do with what qualities the item was designed to measure.* Although this item type was not used in BARB simply because it was prone to strategy compromise, the experimental series was important for determining the extent of *external (construction)* radicals and *internal (strategic)* radicals on item difficulties. The *Rotated F* test became a feature of BARB because the accumulated information from the experiments confirmed the effects of rotation on difficulty, and using a strategy seemed more complex than the visual rotation itself. Moreover, a single participant having repeated trials over a 10 day period with the BARB system perceived that eventually he 'knew' the answer to the rotated F questions without actually seeming to do the rotation. In short, no conscious attempt at rotation was apparent. The irony, perhaps, of this work lies in its cooperation with ETS, where the effects of coaching and compromise were to be dramatically demonstrated on the Graduate Record computerised (adaptive) versions a few years later (Wainer, 2002).

CONCLUSIONS

These modest results began to reveal what might be attempted, and what difficulties might be encountered, in a programme of basic research to determine the relationship between performance on a task that has survived in IQ batteries from the beginning of the century and some asymptotic level of competence in the individual. The CODES example was discussed in to illustrate the nature of an unsolved D-Model problem in which main effects would have to be modelled. This is a consequence of the general strategy, advocated from the beginning, of employing tasks whose main effect parameters, and psychometric history are understood before embarking with them into new cultural contexts, such as computer-delivered systems for naive participants,

---

5   Starting at the right angle, move the eyes in a clockwise direction. Note if the long or short side is encountered. Now move to the next triangle. Repeat the process. If sides of the same length are observed, the triangles are identical. If sides of different lengths are encountered, the triangles are different. This strategy was passed on by a cadet in the Royal Navy Engineering Academy when I asked him how he solved the item.

or perhaps as Spearman might have termed them in such circumstances 'reagents'! Note that these were laboratory experiments. Operational contexts with computer equipped testing facilities were to come, but they had to be worth the effort and expense. Without proof of the effectiveness of new tests, they would not be used. The extremely rare operational, accurate and reliable field criteria for definition and use of a learning task were training results collected on anti-tank missile gunners (Chapter 7). These, and the logic gates learning material collected at Lackland AFB (Chapter 8) proved to be a critical part of the evaluation of learning parameters and their prediction, using conventional and computer-delivered test performance. The outcomes of theoretical issues explored in closed experiments did not, however. stand in the way of closure. There was a narrowing of focus, nevertheless. There was a growing consensus that the measurement of working memory was a key to regulating item difficulty.

ALPHABET RECONSTRUCTION: WORKING MEMORY AT WORK

Letters and steps as radicals

Students and soldiers compared

Wolz confirms linear models

TOWARDS WORKING MEMORY FOR BARB
The centrality of working memory as a construct for the BARB tests to define and use was emerging. Again, the need was to find a simple task whose literacy demands were minor, fully concordant with prescriptions that eleven year olds should have no difficulty with its specifics. *The Alphabet Recoding, or AFB (Alphabet Forward and Backward in the BARB series)* was a key test in an investigation of the influence on deductive reasoning of reconstructing information in memory. It came to the notice of the team during the 'shoot out in Athens' or. More formally, the important NATO Advanced Study Institute (ASI) held there in 1984. Originally revealed in Hockey, Maclean and Hamilton (1981) and included (Hockey & Maclean, 1987 pp. 419-420) in the Advanced Study Institute Proceedings (Irvine & Newstead, 1987; Newstead, Irvine & Dann, 1986). The task was, in real-estate terms, deceptively simple. Letters of the alphabet were presented in a quasi-arithmetical format, such as G + 2 or, more difficult with two letters widely dispersed, VF-2, or made even more difficult with three letter each requiring three steps backward, HXP -3. The correct sequence in working memory is found after moving forward or backward in the alphabet. It proved to have a very high loading on a reasoning factor, *but most critically, the AFB working memory task involves no obvious reasoning element whatsoever*. This implied that individual differences variations in reasoning performance are, procedural knowledge apart, functions of working memory and/or attentional capacity (cf. Kyllonen, 1996).

Work in the Plymouth University laboratory by a senior student (Chittenden, 1986) with the forward version of the task first marked its promise as a predictor of intelligence test scores among Army personnel (Figure 4.8), and as involving a higher order working memory factor. He administered this to two groups, one of soldiers and one of students. Highly significant group mean differences in latency *for Alphabet Forward* items at different difficulty levels existed between the two groups, soldiers and university students. Despite obvious differences in achievement levels, item difficulty could be predicted very accurately for both groups, rank correlation of difficulty with increased load being well-nigh perfect. The task showed positive and moderate correlation with verbal intelligence scale scores.

Figure 4.8: Chittenden's Alphabet Task Latencies: Students vs. Soldiers

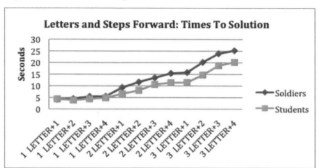

Figure 4.9: The Alphabet Task Radicals

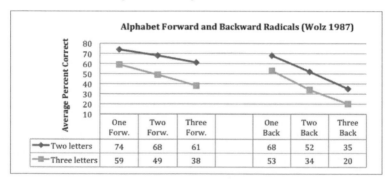

	One Forw.	Two Forw.	Three Forw.		One Back	Two Back	Three Back
Two letters	74	68	61		68	52	35
Three letters	59	49	38		53	34	20

The Wolz results in Figure 4.9 show that the slopes of correct answers against numberof steps forward in the forward series of two compared with three letters are linear and parallel, and so are those for the backward series. The backward and forward slopes are not, however exactly parallel with each other. The series shows that there are processes relating to the number of letters presented that affect difficulty, and there are processes relating to the lag - or steps forward or backward. The lack of parallelism between the forward and backward slopes could mean that backward counting in the task requires different reconstruction in working memory than forward counting. This series confirmed Chittenden's (1986) original work at Plymouth, begun earlier, with latencies on the forward version of the tasks where both student and soldier latencies showed linear increases with item complexity.

VERBAL RADICALS IN WORKING MEMORY: SIMPLE AND ELABORATE 'CODES'

Bejar and Evans demonstrated how it was feasible to use the computer to determine a kind of 'virtual difficulty' using figural and spatial orientation items, where declarative knowledge was not a primary condition for their solution. Similarly, the potential for using a verbal radical 'grammar' to some types of declarative knowledge items is considerable. Prior to forming BARB, the case for applying it in algebra items was available Mayer, Larkin & Kadane (1984, pp. 255ff.). This potentially important area was another for the specific purpose of item generation for recruit selection. It provided a key to understanding, when the contribution of Mayer and his colleagues was examined. They seemed to have enough evidence to help design grammatical forms for the construction of algebra items. The work could be used in two ways: to analyse existing items in order to predict their difficulty, or to be part of the evidence required to create an expert system for item generation, both of which were seen as essential stages.

VERBAL ENCODING RADICALS

Code 1. The elaborate code is: In MOD, John's overseas travel budget is £90,000 more than that of Ken. Only five years ago John's overseas travel budget was £11,000 less than three times Ken's overseas travel budget. What is Ken's overseas travel budget?

Code 2. The formal (cloning and generative) form of this question is: Find a number such that 9 more than the number is the same as 11 less than three times the number.

Code 3. In stripped down algebraic equation form the question is: $x + 9 = 3x - 11$. Find x.

The core of the system is an attempt to produce a cognitive analysis of problem solving in algebraic problems in 'parallel' verbal and equation formats. The difference in working out solutions to elaborate verbal and skeletal 'equational' representation of the same problem, one might note, rests on the different storage needed to comprehend the 'codes' for the same calculation. For example, consider the insert example with three codes; *elaborate, formal, and basic equation forms*. Their working memory demands are different.

Generating items of the types Code 2 and 3and to perform the algorithms for their solution requires fewer steps than those required for Code 1, analogous to the different demands on working memory. Three different questions, simple in themselves demand an increasing number of equations to provide the answers, beginning with one equation and then needing the formation of others as the questions demand more inferences. The problem and the three questions of increasing difficulty are on page 82 for study at leisure and convenience!

Specifying the Difficulty Index

Just as Bejar was able to use the Hough Transform to place the embedded figures items on a scale of difficulty, the question of interest is how to use the expert system's procedural knowledge, or rules, can determine how difficult each item is, and hence, to put the item generation rules in touch with reality. For example, Mayer, Larkin & Kadane (1984) describe a series of categories that are employed to demonstrate the 'state' of any attempt at solution. This is a function of the number of calculations to be performed, and the number of 'moves' either on paper or in working memory. The coherence of the scheme is verifiable from very high multiple regression coefficients with time to solution, where the independent variables were number of calculations and number of moves (loc.cit. p.260). The examples show how their system can be applied.

These three examples begin to reveal a system for categorising difficulty in terms of retrievals (memory operations) and transformations; and, of course, difficulty in algorithms can be given further refinement by indexing from frequencies of common computational errors. Although other strategies may solve such puzzles, the grammar that seems to be most useful in determining degrees of difficulty based on cognitive process identification and frequency is contained in the Mayer concepts MOVE, STACK and COMPUTE (p.267). These concepts help to distinguish types of operations that can be entered into an equation to provide answers to what makes items difficult. When that question begins to be answered, item-generation is possible. A similar example is provided with a full explanation of the implications of linear representations for item difficulty in Evans (1982, p. 64) The Mayer approach is concerned with constructing a cognitive frame of reference of mathematical knowledge types. By applying this to the analysis of mathematical questions, one may produce an expert system that will performance-model solutions. Generating items from the components identified by Mayer could be a straightforward enough task. However, this is only one useful approach for understanding the relative complexity of mathematical items. Dennis (1995) was to develop his own design for generating mathematics items and others when asked to expand the BARB framework for the Royal Navy - essential reading in Chapter 6.

The Air Force receives 10 times as much money for test development as the Army. The Navy receives 20 times as much as the Marines. The Air Force receives 40 times as much as the Marines.

Questions: Level 1.

Does the Air Force get more than the Army?

$$AF > RMY?$$

Equation 1. AF = 10RMY

Answer Q.1. Is (Air Force more-than Army) Yes.

Involves 1 retrieval, 0 substitutions:

Assigned to difficulty level 1.0

Questions: Level 2.

Does the Army get more than the Marines?

$$RMY > M?$$

Equation 2.   NV = 20M
Equation 3.   AF = 40M

From Equations 1, 3,
RMY = 4M (Equation 4)

Answer Q.2. Is (Army more-than Marines) Yes.

Involves 2 retrievals and 1 substitution:

Difficulty Level 2.1

Questions: Level 3.

Does the Navy get more than the Army?

$$NV > RMY?$$

From Equations 1, 4 (requiring retrieval of 2, 3)
N = 5R (Equation 5)

Answer Q.3. Is (Navy more-than Army) Yes.

Involves 3 retrievals and 2substitutions:

Difficulty Level 3.2

COUNTERBALANCING DIFFICULTIES: A TEST GENERATION FRAMEWORK

Before embarking on Macdonald's third lesson plan how to score the tests, and dealt with in the next chapter, there is one more problem following successful item difficulty prediction that had to be researched in the laboratory. Given predictable item difficulties, and code in the computer to use the radicals and incidentals, the test items still had to be organised in such a way that any scoring system could deal with the patterns made by the answers to them. Flexibility was needed so that economies of scale could be linked to maximum information about the capabilities of the recruits. The next section offers an example of how it was conceived, using typical mathematics questions in response to a request from army training staff (Irvine, 1994)[6]. The paths to conclusions converged in code elaboration, calculation requirements, the number of moves, and not least, *a design for ensuring that there were enough examples in any test to ensure adequate repetition of these; and as a special treat for item analysts, that every item type was compared against every other at least once.*

PREREQUISITES
There were a number of issues to resolve. The first priority was *to obtain a clear set of baseline prescriptions in mathematics from those who train candidates for technical roles.* Eventually, a generous response from the staff in Army technical training establishments to a request from The Human Assessment Laboratory for a sample of past examination papers, made available to not only specimen sets of items given to recruits on arrival, but work sheets, curriculum outlines and a series of test papers for instructional modules. With a first-hand evidence of what trainers were looking for, a clear and informed understanding of the nature of the test construction parameters became possible. Moreover, worked examples in the modules themselves provided exact specifications of the know-how required by the trainees to attain mathematics performance levels. The materials available from the training organisations were the platform. The next step in the process was the application of computer-based prerequisites. Although we did not realise it at the time, the ECD paradigms were already in operation.

EXAMPLES FROM ARMY APTITUDE TEST
How a block of items may be constructed is based on the first three items printed in an initial test of mathematics in the Army Apprentices College, Harrogate. The items have to be solved without the use of a calculator. Here is the first item in the pretest.

- **Item 1.** ....18 - (- 4) + (- 3) - (5)

This item is a 'package item' that involves the mastery of a number of stages in calculation using the basic operators of addition and subtraction (illustrated in Item 1). The Mayer approach can be applied to determine the number of phases. Mastery is also required in multiplication (repeated additions of constants) and division (repeated subtraction of constants) and involving positive and negative numbers, as will be evident from a glance at Items 2 and 3, which complete an item series, but because they do not cover every possible combination or permutation, they are best seen as an incomplete block;

- **Item 2.** .... 20 - 3 × 6 = ?
- **Item 3.** .... 17 ÷ 4 - 2 = ?

Applicants answering all three items correctly would, it is assumed, signal to the instructor that they had mastered the various sub-sets of knowledge and skills that are implicit in these three 'packages'. Failure in any one of them would not, of course, show where the breakdown in skill and knowledge application had occurred, or what

---

6   Material in this report used with permission from MOD. All examples are Crown Copyright.

had caused it. Proposed item types for positive and negative concepts are in Table 4.2. Any of a number of human errors involving lack of factual knowledge, inattention, working-memory lapse as well as incorrect application of learned rules, could have been responsible. If these items define a number of goals to be achieved, however, there will emerge, when they are applied to a population of entrants, two categories: those who can do them *'the proficiency group'* and those who cannot *'the learning group'* These groups can be used to provide stopping rules for testing and for devising models of scoring. Analysis of these three item types shows that they are dependent on an understanding of three items of *declarative knowledge* prior to performing any mental operations necessary for solving the problem.

Table 4.2: Sample Items on Concepts of Plus and Minus

In the following[7], a number or situation

is	
either **positive**	**+ 6**
or **negative**	**- 12**
or **zero**	**A nil-nil draw.**
Indicate what each of the examples is	
4 degrees below zero	**plus, minus, zero**
A handicap of 4 kg	**plus, minus, zero**
Goals for 34; Goals against 21	**plus, minus, zero**
A flat battery	**plus, minus, zero**

DEFINING THE UNIVERSE OF SKILLS

To begin with, one might assume that applicants who cannot identify positive and negative numbers will not be able to do any of the rest of the sequence. This produces only three concepts, positive and negative and zero. However, there are encoding contexts in which these operate, in numbers, in temperatures, in bank balances, in goals for and against, in electric current, and so on. It might be wise first to find out the extent of generalisation of the concept of positive and negative. Other examples of generalisation might include *9 degrees Centigrade*; and, with a certain cultural bias, *Game abandoned after rain.* Political bias might be deduced from *National Insurance deduction from pay*, and would certainly be excised by the editorial committee: who might also ask for references involving female and male attributes to be counterbalanced and any reference to sectarian origin to be omitted. If positive and negative numbers were not understood by the applicant, it might be desirable to discontinue appraisal at this point, although experience suggests that people can add and subtract without knowing much about positive and negative operators. So further assume that the

---

7   In this item the probability of getting an item right by chance is .33 for each example. The various probabilities of getting all, none or some right by chance can be calculated, leading to confidence scoring, as in Chapter 5 or in forms of proficiency scoring involving stopping rules based on Wald's confidence limits for samples of proficient, learning and pre numerate groups (Kalisch, 1980). Moreover, probit analysis could be used to estimate thresholds, given BARB scores as an ability 'dose rate', if one will pardon the expression.

POSITIVES AND NEGATIVES.

$+ x + y = z$ *(Type 1)*

$- x - y = z$ *(Type 2)*

$+ x - y = z$ *(Type 3) or with zero (Type 4)*

$- x + y = z$ *(Type 5) or with zero (Type 6)*

applicant can add and subtract basic number bonds. Moving on to test know-how in use of operators (here plus and minus only) and using only two numbers, the total domain is only six types. If a dimension based on results being either plus, minus or zero, this yields 8 types of items that are required to test the concept because Types 3 and 5 could expand to have items with three rather than two choices. However, use of this format to determine competence in number bonds requiring carrying will increase the size of the set. When at least one number is such that mental addition will require manipulation in working memory, the set is increased by a separate Cartesian factor of 2, even if the operation requires carrying or not. This gives a set of 16. Suppose, now, a third term is provided, w. This, too would carry a plus or minus sign, and the three term domain would have a set size of 32. These variations would define a total domain set of 8 two-term, 16 two-term with or without carrying, and 32 three term with or without carrying, or 56 items. Such a large number is best managed within subsets.

Before leaving this domain, one should note that the very first item in a proficiency test used by the army was a 4 term item with carrying:

- **Item 1. ....$18 - (-4) + (-3) - (5) = ?$**

Because the test administered to new arrivals fixes a threshold for proficiency, the question now becomes what set of item types, containing the prerequisites for the threshold, will predict proficiency or learner status. One can immediately observe that this 4 term item type alone is capable of producing 64 variants, whose parallel forms, created by using equivalent number bonds, run into many thousands. Transfer of what has been demonstrated to specifications for most if not all foundation mathematical domains is feasible for instructors and thereafter is only a practical exercise for computer analysts. Items 2 and 3 presented at the outset are, for example, already pre-assembled in a subtest of ARCOM *(Army Regular Commissions Board Battery)* Eight items, each requiring sixty seconds or more for a domain may be far more than one can afford to give in a short test - and the requirement is a scientifically constructed incomplete block that in the shortest possible time establishes the status of the candidate as *proficient* or *learning.*

The goal is to produce many items that take a short time to do but which predict with accuracy the status of the applicant. The second aim is to provide a flexible format for diagnosis and remediation, if this is part of training. Table 4.3 attempts to itemise seven different examples of seven different aspects of the kinds of knowledge required in the army tests. The reason for this will become apparent when an incomplete block design for item presentation is detailed in the next section.

INCOMPLETE BLOCK DESIGNS: EXAMPLES

Like most models of general application, the incomplete block design principle seems simple in hindsight. The test items can be constructed around generic item types in which one or more given answers to a number of linked questions is presented as a target to verify. The candidate is thereby required to work through each question in turn to decide if the answer to that item in the set matches comes within the range of possible answers offered. The links in the questions have to be designed and presented in sequences that estimate and map knowledge structures. To be economical of time and to be able to cover as much of any specified domain of mathematics as possible, a progressive knowledge requirement may have to be built into each item set for which a target answer is offered. Item sets can never exhaust all the elements of basic laws of arithmetic operations, algebra, Euclidean and co-ordinate geometry in a single test, but they can systematically sample the domains in as few items as possible, and from these samples predict knowledge structures in parallel and supplementary areas.

BLOCKS IN TEST DEVELOPMENT

For the purpose of identifying in a computer-driven test format the knowledge and skill thresholds in mathematics of Army entrants, a subset of items can be constructed around any given theme or domain, and inferences can be made from the pattern of results about the entire knowledge structure of the entrant when the items increase the extent of knowledge in its complementary forms of knowing that and knowing how. These progressive samples of domain knowledge and skills are called *blocks*. If the domain contains a lot of elements, the *block size* will necessarily be large. Even then, a good estimate of knowledge can be made from an *incomplete block*. If one considers traditional examination papers to be examiner-selected incomplete blocks of items, because they can never exhaustively test the domain - which is why students 'spot' questions successfully - there is nothing very novel in the notion of item sets as blocks (cf. Kendall, 1948; Kendall & Gibbons, 1990).

SEVEN CATEGORIES IN THE MATHEMATICS DOMAIN

An incomplete block design was chosen so that the seven mathematical varieties shown in Table 4.3 could if necessary be distributed in 7 blocks of 3 items each, so that each item appears a total of 3 times (replications) and every item can be compared against every other once, and in this case order effects are counterbalanced. In non-counterbalanced designs, the order of the blocks can be randomised, or dependent on the answer to any one item within the block. Although the item varieties are repeated as identical items, the actual delivery of them would produce items of identical difficulty for each type, but they would seem different. They would apparently seem *incidental*, but their underlying structure would be determined by *radicals* so that they were of identical difficulty. The same design can be used in the production of other types of mathematics items. Examples given in Table 4.3 illustrate seven different mathematical problems.

Table 4.3: Examples of Seven Mathematical Items for Incomplete Blocks

	Seven Mathematical Types for use In Incomplete Block Design
Mathematics 1	**Addition and Subtraction of Positive and Negative Number Sequences** 1a. 9 + 7: 1b. 12 – 7: 1c. 7 – 16: 1d. - 8 + 9 – 2: 1e. 15 - 7 – 8: 1f. 23 - 21 - 8 + 2: 1g. - 7 + 11 - 9 - 3 + 15
Mathematics 2	**Multiplication and Division with and without (Brackets)** 2a. 8 x (+6): 2b. - 5 x (- 8): 2c. 7 x (- 6): 2d. - 4 (3 - 8): 2e. (3 + 5) x 2: 2f. (16 ÷ 4) – 2:2: g. 12 ÷ 3 + (6 - 2)
Mathematics 3	**Fractions** 3a. 1/2 + 2/5: 3b. 7/16 – 1/4: 3c. 3/4 x 5/9 :3d. 3/5 ÷ 9/10: 3e. 2 1/2 x 1/5: 3f. 3 2/3 ÷ 11: 3g. 1 1/2 ÷ 2 1/2
Mathematics 4	**Conversions Fractions and Decimals** 4a. 1/10: 4b. 3/5: 4c. 2 1/4: 4d. 0.20 : 4e. 0.05: 4f. 0.125: 4g. 5.750
Mathematics 5	**Indices and Powers** 5a. $3^3 \times 3^4$: 5b. $2^4 \div 2^3$: 5c. $(3^2)^3$: 5d. $3^2 + 3^2$: 5e. $5^2 \times 5$: 5f. $2^3 - 2^4$ 5g. $2^3 \div 2^{-4}$
Mathematics 6	**Simple Algebra (Transpositions / Equations)** 6a. $x = 5 \times 4$: 6b. 20 = 5y: 6c. 20 = y/5: 6d. 4 = 20/5a: 6e. 2c - 10 = 22: 6f. 35 - 2z = 15: 6g. 16 - 2b = b + 7
Mathematics 7	**Simple Algebra (Factorisation)** 7a. 3a + 6 : 7b. -2y + 4: 7c. b^2 + 3b: 7d. 2ab - $6a^2$: 7e. $y^2 - c^2$: 7f. $a^2 + 2ab + b^2$ 7g. a^2 - 7a + 10

THE ELEGANCE OF YOUDEN SQUARES

An example of how to use incomplete blocks scientifically to reduce survey time and costs, to enable performance modelling, and to diagnose proficiency levels is now appropriate. In Table 4.4 are seven different item types, based on the properties of numbers, emerging from the last section, Applying the principle of incomplete blocks to item distribution in groups, one can designate each item type *A to G* , as a *variety*. Here there are seven varieties, but there could be more, or they could be spread more widely over the whole area, as the last section shows.

The lower half of the table shows the formal arrangement of the items. Nevertheless, if item blocks are constructed systematically in patterns from Cartesian sets of knowledge factors or elements, *schemes can be devised for item generation that will attempt to cover domains from as few items as possible, consistent with a reliable estimate of the knowledge of the individual.* No CAT system will be necessary and no IRT is required. Fortunately, incomplete blocks of items present few problems to computers in selection and presentation of items from larger complete blocks, and the statistics of estimation from blocks have been available in biological science for nearly a century. The applications of incomplete blocks are appropriate when item types are initially being tried out within domains, or, if the number of item types is not too large, in any block size that seems efficient. In test development, the design can be used to try out parallel items generated by the computer or by writing teams from specifications. Suppose there is an initial item pool enough for 3 parallel forms, in this case 21 different items, three of each variety. A different parallel item could occupy the position given for any one variety, thus testing 21 items in all.

Table 4.4: Incomplete Blocks with 7 Varieties: Numeracy Domain

Variety A	Variety B	Variety C	Variety D	Variety E	Variety F	Variety G
2 + 3	7 - 3	5 - 0	- 3 + 5	8 - (- 1)	2 + (3 − 5)	3 - (- 3 - 2)
Block1	**Block2**	**Block3**	**Block 4**	**Block5**	**Block6**	**Block7**
2 + 3	7 - 3	5 - 0	- 3 + 5	8 - (- 1)	2 + (3 − 5)	3 - (- 3 - 2)
7 - 3	5 - 0	- 3 + 5	8 - (- 1)	2 + (3 − 5)	3 - (- 3 - 2)	2 + 4
-3 + 5	8 - (- 1)	2 + (3 − 5)	3 - (- 3 - 2)	2 + 5	7 - 3	5 - 0

For example item variety A1 is 2 + 3. If there were 3 parallel items of this type, A2 could be 2 + 5, and A3 could be 2 + 4. If A1 is used on the first occasion that an Item Type A is required (Block/Sample 1), A2 could be substituted in Block/Sample 5 and A3 in Block/Sample 7. Similarly 3 parallel forms for all 7 different Item Types could be developed and put into the correct block. As a first approximation, items appearing in training modules have been taken as panel judgements. From items actually given to entrants to teach them the foundation skills, samples have been assembled to produce 7 illustrative blocks of 7 items used in module proficiency tests. Blocks of 7 are shown here only because of convenience. They could be, and were, blocks of various sizes first demonstrated by Youden (1940) and having many design applications.

BLOCKS FOR TESTING INDIVIDUALS

Incomplete blocks are also appropriate to deliver in succession to individuals to estimate their proficiency without using too many items. Every item type is compared against every other once. With as few item types as 7, one could include them all, but test time would be soon used up if every domain needed 7 items. From a block of 3, an estimate of individual proficiency can be calculated. If the first block is not enough, because the participant has made an error in one or more item varieties, a parallel form of any one of this or any of a number of item varieties could be given in the next block to test the hypothesis that this area is mastered or is still in the process of being learned.

Taking an example from the first block containing items using Types A B D, suppose an error is made in Type D (-3 + 5). If diagnosis is the aim, the next block delivered by the computer using the BARB system could then contain a parallel form of the item   (e.g. - 2 + 4, or - 4 + 6). In this series it is Block 3, which also contains 5 - 0 and 2 + (3 - 5), item types involving zeros and the use of positive and negative operators. *In short, a probe may be followed by an extension of the skill structures.* If the first error were a slip or a chance mistake, the second series would correct it. If it were a knowledge structure deficit, the next sequence of items would confirm it.

BLOCK SCORING ALTERNATIVES

Scoring for individuals in these circumstances provides many opportunities not available in conventional test formats. Above all, in selected groups for technical training, the instructors want to know the chances of an entrant having *proficient or learning status.* Conditional probability scores produce a risk factor. Candidates would have everything from a 100 percent chance of being proficient to a 100 percent chance of being a learner. Of course, they may have no chance of being either because their thresholds are so low that it would be counterproductive to admit them given the prerequisites of the training programme. If the prerequisites were to change, then the profile for learners and proficient entrants would also change, but these changes would have to be transferred to the computer for implementation as Lescrève (1997b) warned some years ago. With probability parameters in place, stopping rules for testing for admittance are easy to install.

In the area of initial test construction, using parallel items one would compare item parameters within item types but between blocks to test the hypothesis that the items were parallel within varieties. With fairly large national samples, incomplete blocks of items are very economical frameworks for developing large numbers of new items. A carousel system developed specially for BARB was programmed to test large numbers of items in a very short time. Parallelism is not complicated if item difficulty variations in graduated item-banks are counterbalanced in blocks of relatively small size through the application of algorithms (Armstrong, Jones & Wang, 1994). These variations are then *incidental* to forms with identical group means. However, if one wishes to vary difficulty in a predictable and construct-congruent way where there are no item-banks, then the elements of items that change their difficulty have a root-causal or *radical* function. These elements produce parallel forms that are both reliable and valid.

PLYMOUTH PREDICTIONS OF ITEM DIFFICULTY

The broad canvas of work in the laboratory testifies to the range of options that faced the team in the quest for answers to *The Anderson Question.* The outcome was not just a sketch of experimental results, but the construction and portrayal of prototypes, following decisions about how best to score the new generation of computer-delivered tests. The outcome had to be assessed against the one criterion that would be both reliable and valid. Given the actual difficulty values of items in trials of the various tests, how well were they predicted? From the outset, work in Plymouth distinguished between *incidental* elements of items and *radical* elements, defined and illustrated in Chapter 2. From 1986 to the turn of the century, predicting classical item-difficulty (p-values) from radicals in items succeeded in a variety of tasks in Plymouth and elsewhere. For example, in Carroll & Johnson (1991), *Block Counting*, and two of Thurstone's (1938) orientation tests (*Flags, Hands*), *Shepard's and Metzler's (1971) Rotation Task*, the *Seashore Pitch Test* and a Vocabulary test were all used. The p values for items were predicted from observed item radicals with a multiple R ranging from .72 at least and .99 at best. Table 4.5 summarises a variety of successful predictions in the decade following the beginning of the project, and directly related to the final composition of BARB.

Table 4.5: Multiple Correlations of Radicals with Item Difficulties

Author	Test Type	Multiple R
Carroll & Johnson (1991)	*Block Counting, and two of Thurstone's (1938) orientation tests (Flags, Hands), Shepard's and Metzler's (1971) Rotation Task, the Seashore Pitch Test and a Vocabulary test*	**From .72 to .99**
Woltz (1987))	*Working Memory*	**n/a**
Chittenden (1986)	*Alphabet Reconstruction*	**.99**
Irvine et al. (1990)	*Rotated F*	**.84**
Mislevy et al. (1991);	*Triangle Rotation*	**.92**
Dennis (1993)	*Directions and Distances*	**.88**
Wright and Dennis (1992)	*Cube Folding*	**.92**
Dennis, Collis & Dann (1995). Dennis (2002).	*Verbal Comprehension, Vocabulary, two tests one with concrete[a] the other using abstract[b] words*	**.85 .94[a] .84[b]**
Dennis (1995)	*Numeracy*	**.97**
Tapsfield (1996)	*Path Tracing Wegfiguren Test*	**.97**
Embretson (1996)	*Mathematics*	**.79**

As far as the work in large scale applications was concerned, results were very promising in the domains of working memory (Woltz, 1987; and Chittenden 1986) as outlined; spatial orientation (Irvine et al. 1990; Mislevy et al. 1991; Wright and Dennis, 1992; and further advances in literacy, numeracy and reasoning made by Dennis (Dennis 1993, 1995; Dennis, Collis & Dann, 1995). Another study in the Human Assessment Laboratory (Tapsfield, 1996) involved the figural path-tracing *Wegfiguren*[8] test (Kirsch, 1971, Goeters, 1979) where item difficulty was predicted almost exactly

PREDICTING ITEM-DIFFICULTIES FOR BARB TESTS

Even in specific technical contexts, Dennis (1993) was able to forecast with good accuracy p-values for a directions and distances task for navigator selection that was

---

8   A computerised version was developed by Nigel Barlow and David Wright, University of Plymouth.

WHAT MAKES ITEMS DIFFICULT?

Plymouth predictions of item difficulty from radicals and incidentals

composed of verbal instructions. The correlation of this verbal instructions test with other spatial orientation tasks was substantial. Wright and Dennis (1992) had equally promising results in constructing a visualization test based on cube-folding, with a single factor at six levels predicting these bands of difficulty with R = .92. Perhaps the most salient work in the whole field of predicting item difficulties lies in his report (Dennis et al.) where the p-values of verbal comprehension tasks were successfully predicted (R=.85) using sentence type, degree of grammatical transformation and word length in a linear model..

A vocabulary test of semantic categorization, closely allied to verbal analogies, was successfully modeled using semantic theory and word frequency, with a final R of .94. A version of this involving only abstract words was modeled to produce a prediction of p-values with R=.81. This work shows the strong influence of cognitive performance models in the approach taken by Dennis. With the same emphasis he has also modeled numeracy items (Dennis, 1995) with similar success in predicting difficulties with R estimated at .97. That this is no isolated phenomenon is clear from the work of Embretson (1996) who reports a multiple R of .79 in predicting Rasch model difficulties of mathematics items from a more eclectic empirical perspective.

The strength of these various approaches can be gauged from the average proportion of variance explained by the studies for which R is provided. This is .796 equal to R of .89. Moreover, the approach taken, of identifying radicals and incidentals involved in cognitive modeling, transfers elegantly across domains. Given such results, the construction of aptitude and achievement tests from item-generation theory principles would had two consequences. First, parallelism would be achieved; and second, item-response-theory would then have parameters that are more or less independent of contexts or domains. That is, certain cognitive parameters of items would generalize. In some contexts, particularly in mass screening where the capacity to process new information was the primary construct, item-response-theory could be dispensed with entirely; or reinvented to incorporate time to complete the item as another major area of concentration (see Dennis & Evans, 1996; Evans & Wright, 1993; Mislevy et al. 1991; Wright, 1990, 1992, 1993, 1997).

EVIDENCE CENTRES: SOME BASIC CORE TESTS

During the decade from 1976-1986, the technology of testing changed with the theory, and demonstrated two main developments. The first principles of computer use in testing mental abilities were stated in Brooks, Dann and Irvine (1984) and standards were formalised (Bartram, Beaumont, Cornford, Dann & Wilson, 1986). The second popular direction stemmed from attempts to fit item-response parameters necessary for adaptive tailored testing: but this was not an avenue to follow when producing multiple parallel forms from test items whose difficulties could be predicted accurately from cognitive theory. Following the initial experimental work just described, an internal report called *A Handbook of Computer-based Cognitive Tests* (Dann & Irvine, 1987), provided the second necessary and preliminary tactical frame.

From Long Lists to Paper-and-Pencil Analogues

Groups of tests that additionally satisfied a fundamental set of the eight[9] cognitive paradigms established by Carroll (1980) provided a long list. These began to define an experimental battery for construct validation of new tests. All of the task types thought to be relevant were represented in it. Even from this knowledge base, the difficulties of making decisions because there was no previous experience in delivering them to participants with no previous computer exposure were considerable. Table 4.6 shows the preliminary long list classification frame as tests were sought for BARB.

Table 4.6: Dann's Taxonomy of Generic Task Types

Task /Test Type	Factor	Generative	Score[10]
Alphabet Plus or Minus	Gf	Yes	A
Arithmetic Operations	Gf	Yes	A
Transitive Inference	Gf	Yes	A
Baddeley and Hitch Task	Gf	Yes	A/L
Letter Checking	Ps	Yes	A/L
Target Identification	Ps	Yes	A/L
Reaction Time	Motor S	Yes	L
Divided Attention	Gf	Yes	A/L
Time Estimate (Wall Task)	T	Yes	A
Intercept Estimation	T	Yes	A
Shooting	T	Yes	A/L
Dot Separation	Gs	Yes	A/L
Word Categorisation	V	Yes	A/L

Specific applied requirements coexisted with the choice of tests and evidence for these was also sought. A few of these preliminary tasks might determine the general training capability of recruits in core military skills as parsimoniously as possible; allowing extra time to determine technical aspects of recruit performance. The long list collated after extensive research by Peter Dann recognised the centrality of working memory tests as parsimonious estimates of a general training capability, not altogether different from aptitudes necessary to learn all the basic skills. However, self-imposed constraints on the aptitudes to be assessed and recorded by computers were ease of understanding, simplicity of response and the use of simple numeracy and literacy domains. The second requirement in the long list was a start to defining 'core military skills' for recruits, beginning with aiming and tracking. Whether or not they would ever use one in action, basic raining demanded that they had to be able

---

9   Perceptual Apprehension, Reaction Time and Movement, Evaluation/Decision, Stimulus-Matching/Comparison, Naming/Reading/ Association, Episodic Memory Readout, Analogical Reasoning, Algorithmic Manipulation.

10   These scores were provisional: A is accuracy, L Latency.

to use a rifle. These skills were somewhat distinct from other ability domains but, for good reason, had to be tested and the results examined, as in Chapter 9. Perhaps the preliminary phase was complete, but it could not be moved on using computer trials, except by simulation The list of possible tests drawn up for future trial could only be evaluated at a new specially constructed test centre established at Army Personnel Selection Centre (APSC) at Sutton Coldfield by courtesy of the Officer Commanding, and his staff. While this was being built and assembled, convenient analogue versions of a core set of BARB tests were administered in groups using multiple paper-and-pencil forms. Printed analogues were not simply an option, but a basic requirement for early research and development in a computerless landscape. Beginning with paper-and-pencil analogues of some of the tests in the long list had effects on future development because they were known to be effective before the computer-delivered test centre was ready. *This meant that some of the tests listed would have to join a queue, although there was no guarantee that successful paper-and-pencil analogues would test the same qualities as automatic item-generation versions in computers.*

AUTOMATIC ITEM GENERATION TODAY

These attempts to provide rule-based examples of what may be done to generate items, to solve them, to find test formats and provide indices of their difficulty are as helpful as any other publicly available. The rules for item construction were already proven in two languages (see POPLOG & LISP, 2013). They are also implicit in the *Hough Transform*. Given these, and adequate performance models in the cognitive literature, the common practice of employing large numbers of human participants for test construction came under serious review. Since then, and especially since the publication of Irvine and Kyllonen (2002), with more than 250 references in recent literature, automatic item generation has moved from these beginnings to becoming a major focus of test constructors efforts to ensure that tests are both different in appearance but identical in function.

The international extent of the work in evidence today is perhaps an indicator of automatic item-generation's arrival as a scientific discipline that may yet change test construction demands - from empiricism on a massive scale, to theory as the prime requirement. Major contributors to the field in the USA included Bejar and Mislevy, who have continued their early involvement. In Britain, an advance in the production of high-level reasoning items was recorded by Newstead et al. (2002). Work in Belgium by relative newcomers, such as Lievens & Sackett (2007) provides a very comprehensive summary of item-generation progress since its origins and gives powerful evidence of domain extension to include situational judgment scenarios. Arendasy and colleagues in Vienna (Arendasy, 2005, Arendasy et al. 2007) list an impressive series of aptitude tests with a high degree of success in predicting item difficulties. In Canada Gierl (2007, 2009), Gierl & Lai (2012), and Gierl, Lai & Turner (2012) have shown in two very recent extensions that mastery of the field depends not just on radicals and incidentals, but on the use of construction architecture such as Mislevy's (2011) ECD and statistical alternates such as LLTM (Fischer, 1973, 1996). Moreover, Gierl has recently produced his own test construction software IGOR (cf. Gierl & Lai, 2011, pp. 11-12) with good prospects for the future of the field.

CHAPTER 5

LESSON 4: SCORING WITH AUTOMATIC ITEM GENERATION

In 1985, when the BARB system was at the planning stage, answers to *The Anderson Question* were going to determine what the tests were and what they would measure. The previous chapter is proof of near closure. There yet remained the problem of how to score the tests, even if one knew how to construct them using evidence-centred design, thereby predicting item difficulty from cognitive attributes. In effect, if *The Anderson Question* were feasible without IRT, the calibration of items necessary for the equating of parallel forms of the same type of test would not be necessary. Even after ways forward for test design had been charted, conclusions about use of the scores from the system perhaps presented a greater challenge than any that had been met already. The limitations of paper-and-pencil and pencil scoring using templates no longer existed. Within the computer, it was possible to record every stage of item completion, and to include relevant information in the record of progress through the tests. What was the most effective way to score a parallel form test, maximising its reliability and validity when complex military criteria are involved? Would it be possible to score the tests in ways not previously available in paper-and-pencil modes?

BARB SCORING MODEL OPTIONS

· *the IRT and CAT options*

· *scoring models: R, L and D*

· *conventional scoring models*

· *binomial confidence scores*

· *latency filters in item generation*

· *Plymouth scoring experiments*

· *cusums and time envelopes*

This chapter begins with the place of item response theory in multiple parallel form tests where common equating items were redundant. Then the issue of computerised adaptive testing needed resolution. Much research on test scoring has assumed that questions must progress in difficulty until failures occur. Alternatives to IRT include right and wrong (R), latency (L) and learning or dynamic (D) scoring options. Power scores involving combinations of accuracy and time to complete are outlined, including cumulative sums or *cusums* trialled in the laboratory. Moreover, time envelopes involving simulation studies were studied using multiple parallel forms. After establishing the principles for the BARB test system, the scoring formula for future tests was built into the test output content.

SCORING PARALLEL TEST FORMS: THE IRT OPTION

By 1988, research had produced prototype tests from algorithm-generated items whose difficulty parameters were within a relatively narrow range. When this occurs, methods of assessing the limits of individual differences in human performance need not depend upon increasing the difficulty of the items to points where individuals equal in ability are predicted to fail. Computerised adaptive testing (CAT) using item-response theory was a direct outcome of this practice, and a full account of past and present test scoring methods is available in Thissen and Wainer (2001). However, neither computerised adaptive testing nor item response theory was destined to be part of the final answer to *The Anderson Question*. Given evidence-centred designs, a simple reference frame would be adequate for tests where parallel forms of tests provided very small mean score differences among forms. An infinite number of parallel forms, each with its own set of items, changed the scoring framework. Nevertheless, there was a case for considering IRT in combination with computerised adaptive testing. It was, after all, the test makers' bandwagon of the era.

The eventual decision, to abandon IRT followed a systematic resolution of the issues using psychometric performance models, with some emphasis on stimulus sampling theory. With these frames of reference for construction, the next step was to apply principles for item generation, using as examples tasks already classified psychometrically, and some types of tasks scheduled for inclusion in the battery of cognitive tasks under construction. Why was IRT not applied in 1985 as solution to compiling parallel forms of tests, regardless of the scoring procedures adopted?

IRT ASSUMPTIONS

Using stored information about item behaviour, takes each response as an estimate of ability until a desired precision level is achieved.

Predicts performance from abilities supposed to underlie response to item just completed.

Estimates ability scores from samples of performance with error limits.

ITEM-RESPONSE THEORY: A RADICAL SOLUTION CONSIDERED

The vogue for IRT had emerged during the seventies and much of computer-based testing in use from 1985 until 1994 had been operationally constrained by the degree of involvement of the system in the extant item-response theories and their applications. The characteristics of an item-response model are summarised in the insert.

The book by Thissen and Wainer (2001) on test scoring gives a complete overview and reference guide for IRT. The origins of practices with a form of item-response theory can be traced to Binet, if one so chooses, and not without good reason. The basic idea is evident in Binet or Wechsler IQ-type tests individually administered to children. An example from normal practice will make this clear. Using age as a guide to ability, the administrator enters the test at some recommended point, presents items until the child fails a sequence of them, revealing that the probability of passing the next item is, if not zero, then as near chance as makes no difference to true-score variance. A score based on the number of items answered correctly uses a conventional metric. The resulting index of an underlying trait or ability is a 'mental age'. The next child may be older or younger: and consequently begin with quite a different series of items to establish mental age, but usually with some as a common core. However, stimulus identity is not a prerequisite for comparisons, or for assignment of an ability level or threshold. Nevertheless, the results for each person - indices of ability or IQs - are assumed to be directly comparable.

In computer language, we have a series of 'If...then' subroutines. 'If x years old, go to item y.' 'If...then' routines also characterise the scaling procedures, which will first depend upon assigning item responses to computer memory locations, followed by some arithmetical summations, and so on. In short, transferring existing test items to automation is neither original nor exciting, since the computers we have today can fulfil all of these 'interview' functions, and the necessary clerical transformations for scoring, without any loss of reliability or validity (Brooks, Dann and Irvine, 1984).

THE ADAPTIVE TESTING CASE FOR IRT

Even so, in 1985 many different IRT models existed, depending on how many aspects of item behaviour were required to define the nature of the item. Fundamentally, a choice would have to be made among the three basic types of item architecture that were commonly pursued and debated: the Rasch model (Rasch, 1960, Rasch, 1961; Rasch, 1966a: Rasch, 1966b), the normal ogive model (Lord and Novick, 1968), the two parameters logistic model (Birnbaum.1957), and the three parameters logistic model (Birnbaum, 1968). The history of IRT development since Birnbaum introduced the notion to ETS in the 1950s was compelling. Even for tests with no need for the boundaries of IRT there was a model to emulate.

In essence, expert opinion was required to inform a decision. One source available in 1986, the basic textbook on IRT (Hambleton and Swaminathan 1985), was essentially making the case for IRT in all its forms, in spite of an admission on the very last page (loc. cit. p. 310) that classical scoring of tests was often appropriate. Evaluative stances on IRT by its most eminent practitioners were also available. In 1979, Weiss had initiated a Computerized Adaptive Testing Conference in Minnesota (Weiss, 1980). One of its features, *Symposium and Discussion: State of the Art of Adaptive Testing and Latent Trait Test Theory* (loc. cit. pp. 436-452) had immediate relevance to decision-making. The contributors were Gerhard Fischer University of Vienna, Frederic Lord Educational Testing Service, James Lumsden University of Western Australia, David Weiss University of Minnesota, and John Carroll University of North Carolina at Chapel Hill. The most telling consequence, from the point of view of BARB, was the verdict of these experts on the use of item response theory for computerised adaptive tests *in recruit selection contexts.*

Computerised Adaptive Testing: A Viable Option For BARB?
Fred Lord, whose influence on the field has been paramount (See Wainer and Messick, 1983) had devised at ETS the basic techniques for parsimonious estimates of ability, based on responses to as few items as possible, as early as 1959. The original work was designed to make existing tests better; but it was transferrable to emphases on equating parallel forms. Without being able to predict item difficulty from the item

content without expensive empirical trials, a number of common items was needed to equate new test forms, using IRT. The programme of work by Lord and Wingersky (Lord and Wingersky, 1983; Wingersky and Lord, 1983) was a fulcrum in creating adaptive forms of the ETS flagship, the *Graduate Record Examination*, (or GRE) in computerised adaptive testing form. These two reports deal with applied mathematical solutions to equating scores from two dissimilar tests, including the very interesting question of *how many common items need be administered to different samples to ensure that the items that are not common are comparable*. The answer - from two to five common items - formed a tribute to the theoretical power of IRT. Lord (1983), in quite a short note, addresses the problem of how to estimate ability when some items are omitted. Although the answer applies to right-wrong questions, the solution can translate to latencies. This would mean estimating mean latency, using a probability algorithm to ignore outriders.

Computerised adaptive testing (CAT) was an administrative possibility for BARB because it offered greatly reduced testing time covering a number of abilities. The Kaplan blow (Jacobson, 1995) to daily computerised adaptive testing was well into the future and was to post-date the operational use of BARB, and *Wainer's Law* (Wainer, 2002) appeared only in the next century. As early as 1980, however, there was a consensus[1] that computerised adaptive testing was not ideal for selection purposes, summed up by Lord.

'An important point is sometimes ignored in the consideration of adaptive testing: Adaptive testing is most useful when it is necessary to measure well at both extremes of the ability range. It is not at all useful if all that is needed is to divide a group of people into those who will be accepted and those who will be rejected' (Lord, 1980, p.439).

Moreover, Lord when reviewing the IRT model that involves estimates of item difficulty, discrimination and guessing (three parameters) makes a comment that supplements *Wainer's Law*, which advocates stealing only the difficult items in a computerised adaptive testing system. *Lord's Corollary* in its complete form states:

'Under the 3-parameter model, if it is desired to estimate the ability of low-level people, the difficult items should not be scored but thrown away, since they just add noise to the score. To go to an extreme, the 3-parameter ability estimate for a low-ability person may be based on the person's responses to just two or three items out of the entire test' (loc. cit. p.440).

This technically sound and administratively convenient conclusion, with its impenetrable logic, raised the prospect of politically defending *an objection by rejected applicants that they were allowed to take only three items in each of the BARB tests while the successful applicants were given many more 'chances'*. Admirable as the qualifications of powerful ministry of defence committee members might be, explanations of the mathematical foundations of computerised adaptive testing would hardly serve to lessen their anxieties about sanctioning any computerised adaptive system depending on item response theory. If BARB showed IRT to be unnecessary, all recruits would have equal opportunities.

---

1   Only Weiss disagreed with Lord, Fischer, Lumsden and Carroll.

CAT Item Responses and Item Difficulty

With a CAT system for BARB unlikely, one would have perhaps been able to stop consideration of item response theory as an option worth pursuing. But it was not quite as simple as that. Some years earlier, Weiss(1973) had examined in a lengthy report scoring methods where knowing the difficulty of the test items was a prerequisite to understanding the nature of the test and scoring it outside the boundaries of classical test theory. Both Weiss (1980, pp. 444-446) and Carroll (1980a, pp. 449-450) had independently used this approach where knowledge of item difficulty could be used to calibrate tests and define the place of individuals within them. More was to follow: Trabin and Weiss (1983), and in the NATO meeting in Athens Carroll (1987), provided examples with real and simulated data of how the difficulty of an item could be related to the probability of passing it by individuals with different levels of ability. They called this a person characteristic *curve* (PCC, Weiss) or *function* (PCF, Carroll). Regardless of primogeniture, the alliance of predicting the difficulty of items without large-scale empirical and costly empirical determination required by IRT methods made the Weiss-Carroll approach worthy of consideration as a scoring alternative to classical test theory. The procedure had merits, particularly if the difficulty of each item could be determined without exhaustive trials with large subject pools, all of whom were behaving impeccably without guessing characterised by random key-pressing, but its feasibility required complex scoring methods whose transparency was by no means guaranteed for operational use in mass screening.

ETS AND THE KAPLAN 'SILVER BULLET'

There is, however, one essential review, and with it a devastating critique, of the use of item-response theory use in computer-delivered tests when, as in BARB, the same test or forms with common items were used nationwide on a daily basis to intended applicants. Perhaps only the inimitable Howard Wainer could have done both while representing the very organisation that had most to lose from his analysis (Wainer, 2002). This was written almost a decade after BARB had eschewed IRT and had, instead, gone operational *with a system that had employed a new parallel form of each of the BARB tests to every new recruit.* What did Wainer reveal a decade later that seemed to justify in retrospect, the final approach taken on how to generate and score the BARB tests?

In 1994, when one of the most influential of selection tests designed by Educational Testing Service (ETS) for selection to university graduate studies throughout the United States, the GRE or *Graduate Record Examination* had been adapted for computer presentation and administered, not annually, as in the past using paper-and-pencil, but continuously on demand in various centres, a major conflict arose. This was between Kaplan Education Centres and ETS (Jacobson, 1995). Essentially, the Kaplan organisation devised a system that if used, would compromise the computer-delivered GRE almost completely. It was, like all successful attacks, a very simple one. Kaplan employees took the GRE examination over a few weeks, with instructions to memorise key items and pass them on to those who followed. This strategy effectively made the GRE in its nation-wide computer-delivered form at that time, redundant, with enormous costs to ETS. This sent a signal to those who had believed IRT could shorten the time to assess capabilities; expand the universe of testing from annual orchestrated competitions to assessment at convenience; and ensure as many individual repetitions as were deemed necessary to make the grade.

The Kaplan virus contaminated the ETS transcontinental graduate examination express, even if a cure were possible. Today, with internet applications of tests, it takes only a print screen key to freeze items, copy them and then use them for compromise in so-called coaching psychology enterprises.

Wainer's Law: How to Beat the CAT

'Steal the difficult items in a CAT system;
the easy items do not matter.'

Lord's Corollary to Wainer's Law

'If it is desired to estimate the ability of low-level people,
the difficult items should not be scored but thrown away
since they add noise to the score.'

Wainer pinpointed the fundamental flaws of using the same sets of key items as milestones of ability in the daily use of tests, with elegant and illuminative examples and data sets (loc. cit. pp. 288-296). First, *as a necessary consequence of the IRT model,* a very small proportion of items in the Graduate Record Examination had continuous usage. The most difficult of these were the targets for compromise, because the easy ones did not matter. *And, he stressed, the most difficult items were the most costly to create, standardise and stabilise.* However, as Lord insisted, computerised adaptive tests were virtually useless where selection was the goal. Only the easy ones mattered under any selection system where a lower bound score means rejection after a handful of items. Second, the abilities of a professional writer of test questions set the limit to the level of difficulty of an item, not any relevant theoretical algorithm. The third 'controlling' factor in computer-delivered testing is the frequency of test use when distributed to a number of 'clients'. If a test or test series is available once per year, as in annual school examinations, or, in some cases, infrequent competitions for jobs or university places, the chances of test compromise through security failures are more remote. With clients tested on a daily basis, no single form of a test will survive for long. CAT in a client based system was shown by Wainer to expose the same key items on every test occasion. Detailed analysis disclosed that 80 % of interactions with the applicants were confined to 40% of items. Wainer's arguments, a decade after it went into service, vindicated the design of the tests used in BARB, and other series: and his caveats require answers by IRT model users even today. For web-based recruitment purposes, to establish the IRT paradigm for equating forms of computer-delivered tests, the necessary repetitive use of key items was a bridge, not just too far, but leading to disaster in the daily application of tests on a nation-wide basis.

Even if the arguments advanced by Lord and Wainer, had been available and considered at the time, IRT was discarded as an option for BARB and its successors because of the success with which item difficulties could be predicted from their cognitive and psychometric models. After rejecting IRT, what were the available scoring options for BARB's multiple parallel forms? The remainder of the chapter reviews them.

SCORING MODELS: WHAT SCORES AND WHEN?

How variance among individuals is assessed affects how consistently a test measures any quality. In classical test theory, the basic 'rule' - means writing an item that consistently satisfies two independent criteria: (1) that it measures what it is supposed to measure; and (2) that a known proportion of the group for which it is intended should know the right answer. Ideally, the same people should continue to get the items in the test right, so that the items discriminate consistently between high and low scorers. If this holds, a collection of items will maximise true-score variance and minimise error variance, ensuring high reliability. Scoring thereafter is a formula where the correct answers determine standings.

SCORING TESTS

Right and Wrong

Latency to Answer

Dynamic or Learning

Confidence Scores

Cusums

In a move away from the question of technique, one uncovers questions of psychological substance. Scoring the items in one way or another will make a difference to their meaning, as well as their utility. From the earliest days of test construction and laboratory experimentation three basis types of score models have existed (Irvine, 2002) and they give different answers to the same question: how should the test be scored? The first, upon which all traditional test construction procedures were developed, is an accuracy, or *right-wrong* approach, which is the R-Model. The second a laboratory product, is a speed of execution, or *latency* model - the L-Model. There is another determinant of test performance, which has particular force in latency determination, learning – giving rise to *dynamic* or D-Models, such as may be circumscribed by the use of cumulative summations *cusums* (Page, 1954, Barnard, 1959, Wright, 1993, 2002, Wright and Dennis, 1999). Each of these provides knowledge necessary for an evidence centred solution to predicting item difficulty. The paradigm constraints of each approach provide a key to understanding how to pursue the goal of predicting of item difficulty.

THE R-MODEL PSYCHOMETRIC TRADITION
The R-Model is the one still in widespread use today, and has produced structural theories that attribute performance to a number of abilities - or, according to some, latent traits – that samples of items from the various ability domains will measure empirically. Given criterion performance, predictions depend on individual regression equations using the information available in the right answer score, after adjustment for possible guessing effects. Item response theory (IRT discussed earlier) developed almost entirely from the dichotomous R-Model approach: and, as the success of the

use of IRT in improving R-Model tests demonstrates, it is a powerful staple paradigm when the model has gone through successive stages of refinement. The R-Model has its analogies among production cars, namely the Model T, the Mini-Minor and the Volkswagen Beetle. R-Models and production cars, though, are many and varied. Irvine (1983) points out that one ability theory every decade (see Chapter 3, Table 1) have come about since Spearman. Fortunately, an empirically-based revaluation of their theoretical utility can be witnessed in Carroll's comprehensive reanalyses of data matrices and, most importantly then, and now, of the types of cognitive tasks for which difficulty parameters were deemed possible (Carroll, 1980, pp. 242-64, 1983a, 1983b, 1986a, 1986b, 1986c). These sources, more than any others, parsimoniously account for most of the variance among factor-analytic theories that have prescribed what right-wrong items to include in tests, or performance samples, and still rank as the definitive statement on the limits of R-Models as we understand them today. The value of R-Models to computer-based testing is summarised in point form for reference as the basis for evidence centred design.

R-MODEL FUNCTIONS.

1. Specification of the involvement of ability functions in task performance

2. Differentiation of tasks into domains of varying generality and specificity

3. Variety of scoring models that enable the precise estimation of ability

4. Means of developing computer-based performance models

L-MODELS IN EXPERIMENTAL LABORATORIES
Latency or speed models have also had a long history. Furneaux (1952) is identified as a pioneer of a psychometric approach to the investigation of speed-accuracy relationships. White (1982), who has produced a working version of the relationship, with the addition of persistence, puts his work with Eysenck into IRT context in a modern update. Mathematical solutions apart, the current cognitive frameworks for L-Models originate in experimental performance research. The flowering of the movement in the decade prior to the construction of BARB is witnessed in Hunt, Frost and Lunneborg (1973), Hunt and Lansman (1982), Carroll (1976), and even earlier in Baddeley (1968). Approaches relevant to BARB item construction included word-recognition models (Adams, 1979), inductive reasoning (Pellegrino and Glaser (1982), and spatial aptitude (Pellegrino and Kail, 1982). Its origins are in reaction-time paradigms, essentially; and the dependent variable has been latency or time to complete the answer in a single task, or a number of them in part or in whole.

Eight Test Types with Latency Paradigms
Even with a multitude of experimental studies involving reaction times or their derivatives, there were, according to Carroll (1980) *eight basic paradigms of cognitive tasks* where research into the time taken to inspect, decide and react to an apparently simple event has been both extensive and historically important. In his fundamental

review and analysis, Carroll (1980, p. ii) lists them (see Chapter 3 Table 2), realising, of course, that they have full expression in tests where accuracy measures were commonly used: He devotes the next 250 pages to a detailed analysis of each of the eight paradigms of what he defined as *elementary cognitive tasks* (ECTs). Later developments by a number of authors ensured a profusion of varieties, pure and hybrid, with little evidence of their systematic investigation or construct validation (Irvine, 1986a, 1987a). Nevertheless, Samejima (1983a, 1983b) made available a general item-response solution to L-Model items that need to estimate the ability of the participant from item performance based on latency to complete. Bejar (1986a, 1986b) used this approach in fitting LOGIST parameters to computer-generated items of a figural type, requiring 'visualisation ability'. Finally, Dann and Irvine (1987) produced a handbook of cognitive tests for appraisal in which the field was essentially summarised and described for the development of multiple parallel form tests based on knowledge of their experimental and psychometric qualities – the core of item-generation.

Heuristics for the Use Of Performance L-Models Begin to Emerge
A collection, edited by Sternberg (1984a) gives some useful examples of these. The surprising finding, perhaps, is the number of claims for high correlation between the speed with which some apparently simple tasks (where difficulty levels are almost 100 percent, i.e. error free) are executed and IQ. Not only does Baddeley's (1968) three-minute reasoning task make such a claim, but Brand and Deary's (1982) work on inspection time thresholds, extensions of verification tasks involving upper and lower case letters (Irvine and Reuning, 1983, Irvine Schoeman and Prinsloo, 1988), and several encoding and transformation tasks using arithmetic operations (Christal, 1985a, 1985b), emerged as likely candidates for L (or Latency) IQ measures. It was an exciting but contradictory period, and the work done in studying it did not bring decisions about how to score the BARB tests any easier.

L-MODEL SUMMARY AND CONCLUSIONS
1. The parameters of scoring in L-Models can vary. They include total and average latencies; measures of individual dispersion; intercepts and slopes when progressions along the same continuum exist for individuals; ratio and difference scores. Psychometrically naive use of traditional latency score ratio and difference permutations when they are used to produce correlations, represent various degrees of experimental dependence. Resolution of L-score parameters is essential before they can be incorporated prudently into multiple regression equations.
2. There is the phenomenon of the '.3 barrier' which puts RT correlations with IQ at around that level, in spite of protestations to

L-MODEL ATTRIBUTES

1. The parameters of scoring in L-Models can vary

2. There is the phenomenon of the '.3 barrier'

3. There are crude limits to stability

4. The speed-accuracy dilemma has to be resolved

the contrary. See Fairbank, Tirre and Anderson (1991) for confirmation of the population figure based on a very large sample of US servicemen.

3. There are crude limits to the stability of chronometric L-Models using Elementary Cognitive Tasks (ECTs). Briefly, if the tasks take too long to complete, the relationship between latency and its determinants seems to get 'noisy'. At that time, latency ceases to predict the ability level as effectively as the accuracy, or R -Model.

4. This observation portends the last contribution of L-Models. The speed-accuracy dilemma has to be resolved, although much progress was made by evidence-centred simulations of speed-error trade-offs by Dennis and Evans (1996).

Conclusions

L-Models and the eight task paradigms that define them make available, from their particular performance (i.e. main effects) models, clues to item difficulty given initially by the latencies that are taken to complete the tasks under various manipulations. These clues are amplified by the study of the relative importance of main effects or manipulations that increase latency until the probability of correct response for the individual reaches a chance level. The confirmation of robust main effects allows a transfer of information from L to R Models, since they can be translated as facets of difficulty. Their systematic manipulation facilitates programming, and brings a logical, as well as psychological rationale for item generation and estimation of ability parameters.

D-Models: The Dynamics of Learning

The use of dynamic or learning models to provide evidence for test item-construction is seldom observed and the literature is sparse. No control for learning during the test seems capable of being exercised. Psychometrics has shown little interest in rates of learning during the test, for reasons that are partly a function of assumptions about abilities, and partly the reliance on paper and pencil conventions in group testing. Practical barriers have included the labour involved in recording and calculating score functions that are not just the sums of items judged to be correct. *The main theoretical hindrances to D-Models have been the assumption that abilities are fixed entities; and that any test, administered once, can provide a stable estimate of whatever ability is measured by it.* Nevertheless, there have been opportunities for progress. Learning does take place during repeated trials at tasks that are identical. Improvements are made with progress through the system. The 'learning curve' is an expression used by many who have no real understanding of what is meant by it, or its complexities. One might, with reason, hope that contrasting behaviour at the beginning with behaviour at the end of the task to be learned, would be a helpful way to characterise individual differences among recruits faced with a large number of new learning demands during initial or secondary training. Nevertheless, to use information from what might be learned during a test performance has never been easy, and it has never been satisfactorily resolved using difference scores, using gains or losses from beginning to end, including repetitions, as the foundation stones for building a model of individual differences. The reasons for the failure of difference scores to contribute are not far to seek, because of one incontrovertible fact.

Simply put, most difference scores are very likely to be of low reliability. Why should this be? The statistical rule that casts doubt on any proposed use of difference scores is simple to apply. *When the positive intercorrelation of any two tests approaches their individual reliabilities, the reliability of a difference score calculated by subtracting one from the other approaches zero!* One can imagine a number of trials at a task with the number correct or the time to complete the task being recorded. Differences could be calculated, only to find that the unreliable difference scores were not valid predictors of any subsequent performance, whereas the original scores had some validity. Puzzlement might well ensue, if one were not to be aware of the universality of the statistical artefact created by using difference scores. An elegant but nonetheless concurrent summary of the argument with a proof was given by Guilford (1954, pp. 392-3): and at the same time the date of the reference may remind the reader of how long this has been known, but with so little effect among educational league-table followers at large.

'Crude Levels of Stability'
First, the broad outlines necessary for accommodating the notion of learning during the test are found in Ferguson's (1954, 1956) definition of an ability as *'a skill learned to a crude level of stability'*. This is not only consistent with modern information-processing approaches to cognition, it leaves open the possibility of incorporating measures of learning rate, specific to a family of tasks, within the framework of assessment. With the reliability of difference scores always an issue, psychometric explorations in 'learning during the test' are understandably uncommon. In the course of fifty years, reports by Allison (1960) and Bunderson (1967) seemed very promising, but they were largely ignored by test users because they were labour intensive. Only one application of the extensive mathematical model-building of Estes (1978, 1981), has found its way into psychometrics Estes (1974) clearly understood the potential of Royer's (1971) experiment with the *Digit-Symbol Substitution Task* (DSST), more popularly known as *Coding or Codes,* in the WISC. The relevance of this to BARB was shown in Chapter 4.

    Until Cronbach and Snow (1977) reanalysed Allison's work for the relation of ability tests to learning parameters, they rested in obscurity. Work from Snow's laboratory (Snow, Kyllonen and Marshalek, 1984) was primarily concerned with mapping learning and ability parameters, but enabled learning approaches to assessment to go forward. Perhaps the closest one might get to observing this model in paper-and-pencil form is in Thurstone's tests, *each of which was based on a single item type, requiring the participant to do a number of them in succession.* This approach, continued in BARB and ARCOM (see Chapter 6), implies that people will with experience of the test cope with the item type, and in so doing learn strategies for dealing with it effectively until they reach asymptote. In doing this, given a constant level of difficulty for the test items, participants can work at a constant pace that depends on their efficiency when the test is timed, but not speeded. There is a difference between a carefully timed and a speeded test that is all too often ignored in the literature.

EXTENDING BOUNDARIES OF D-MODELS
Undoubtedly, a formidable obstacle has been the assumption that abilities are fixed entities, and that the test, administered once, can provide a stable estimate of whatever ability is measured by it. Work from Snow's laboratory was concerned with mapping learning and ability parameters, a route followed extensively in Project LAMP by

Kyllonen and Christal (Kyllonen, 2010). Nowhere at that time, was more successfully attempted and achieved, but with less influence on military testing, than the output from a project entitled *Complex Learning Assessment*, founded by Christal and developed extensively by Kyllonen and Shute (Shute and Kyllonen, 1990, Kyllonen, 1996). Because of close cooperation with LAMP during the periods prior to and during the creation of BARB, the general directions and summary findings of learning experiments and their potential for D model use had been freely shared. What did the experiments using computer-driven software designed to teach people how to carry out simple and difficult procedures show that was so important?

PROJECT LAMP: THE COMPLEX LEARNING ASSESSMENT (CLASS)
The CLASS and later Cooperative Laboratory (Co/Lab), measurement units were initially projects for collecting data on complex learning tasks. They were to prove central to the life of LAMP, so that the tests created could demonstrate power to predict learning. Without any hope of receiving learning criterion measures in the relatively short computer-delivered testing time allocated during recruit training at Lackland, learning had to be measured in the laboratory using tasks with face validity for service use. Among these were electronic logic gates (Christal, 1991, Irvine and Christal, 1994) circuit learning, where recruit efforts served as criteria against which LAMP, ASVAB and later, ARCOM tests could be validated. Over a period of time CLASS and Co/Lab evolved into ends in themselves, concentrating on artificial-intelligence-based instructional systems.

The Classic LAMP/CLASS Laboratory Study
The first, and never to be repeated classic LAMP/CLASS laboratory study, administered a complex series of cognitive and learning tasks to participants of from 260 and 350 students and other volunteers. Over 7 days they were administered the CAM 1 battery (12 hours), the ASVAB, the BRIDGE tutor containing at least 25 problems to be solved through trials, hints and error corrections. USAF personnel could not be used, because the study took 40 hours to complete and training needs simply could not accommodate this time demand. Many learning indexes were generated, including the number of hints requested, number of errors, and the respective negative slopes over problems 1-25. The various requirements included pre-tests (a) knowledge of domain-specific concepts; (b) learning concepts and definitions; and (c) three post-tests: code-recognition test, code rearrangement test and code writing test. As if that were not sufficient, mood and personality inventories were completed. The inordinately complex data set demanded and received several analyses whose complexities are revealed in the two key reports of what was to prove the most far-reaching computer delivered learning laboratory enterprise of the century (Shute and Kyllonen, 1990; Kyllonen, 1995). Evaluation of the key construct of working memory, with delineation of its role in learning were the aims. Given the importance of this cognitive concept in the removal of the logical primitive function associated with the notion of g, this material deserves the fullest appraisal and exposure. What did the experiment show?
    First, scores used to estimate working memory capacity correlated with the ASVAB general factor close to unity (Kyllonen, 1993). Next, three orthogonal learning factors were estimated from pre-tests, learning indicators, and post-tests: (1) general learning; (2) tutor-specific learning; and (3) transfer learning. Kyllonen's summary is proof of success. In a latent variable regression analysis, there was only

one primary determinant of general learning, working memory capacity (r = .91). With the orthogonal, tutor-specific and transfer-specific learning factors, working memory capacity was still an important determinant (r =.51, .39, respectively), but prior knowledge of programming and math concepts were also significantly related (r = .42, .48, respectively). Because of the amount of learning that was provided by the tutor, the finding about the importance of working memory was quite remarkable (Kyllonen, 2007, p. 16). Fundamental though this was, it could do no more than signpost routes for item definition and generation given LAMP's priorities. Perhaps the best example of potential impact is found in Lohman, Pellegrino, Alderton and Regian (1987) where practice effects on various cognitive tasks are illustrated, and in the extensive review of cognitive task structures in Fairbank, Tirre and Anderson (1991, pp. 51-101). In short, the extraordinary and unique work of project LAMP did not necessarily tell us what item generation might mean, but where it might be found. This is what the team at Plymouth discovered when they experimented with the well-known *Digit-Symbol Substitution Task* found in IQ batteries. What *prevented* learning was the clue to item construction.

D-MODELS SUMMARY

Repetition, or practice, decreases latencies

Retrieval models in learning are different from recognition models.

Baseline performance is difficult to establish.

Asymptotes imply a departure from linearity

Scoring is complicated, particularly if unreliable difference scores or slopes based on only a few trials are used

D-Models Summary

D-Models, because of their dynamism, are difficult to refine, use and explain. There are some simple, and perhaps obvious, points of substance in the insert. They provide a good indication of the psychometric dilemmas facing the constructors of tests with limited times and a wide range of specific skills as the content vehicles. To determine learning rates when the demands are many and varied is no simple operational task.

USING CONVENTIONAL SCORING MODELS: THE LAST ANALYSIS

To conclude the review on scoring, key sources were researched: and these are listed in the references. Concerned with relevant theory and applications, they provide an essential ostensive definition of the forces then at work. They include Carroll (1976, 1980b, 1983a, 1983b, 1986a, 1986b, and 1987); Dann (1993); Hambleton and Swaminathan (1985); Hunt (1980, 1981); Hunt, Lunneborg and Lewis (1975); Irvine and Newstead (1987); Kail and Pellegrino (1985); Lord (1980a); Neimark and Estes (1967); Newstead, Irvine and Dann (1986); Sternberg, 1984, 1985a, 1985b; Thissen and Wainer (2001) and Wainer and Messick (1983).

Most of these were contemporary with the initial development of BARB, except that on stimulus sampling, which deserved some revaluation for use in artificial intelligence environments. The advantages and disadvantages of four different paradigms for future work in item-generative methods were examined. These included R-Models, L-Models D-Models, and IRT models that are robust and for which a detailed technology existed. Several examples of how tests had been scored in the past were examined to review their potential for BARB and parallel form tests in general. These were perceived as somewhat 'opportunistic', because they grew up in the framework of paper-and-pencil group tests, mainly hand scored.

VARIETIES OF FORMULAE

Right-Wrong for guessing

Latency scores and derivatives

Binomial Confidence Scores

Cusum Distributions

CONVENTIONAL OR OPPORTUNISTIC SCORES

Several conventional methods of scoring tests for speed and accuracy were uncovered in the literature review for BARB. While each one had merits, under scrutiny they may be described as mainly opportunistic. By opportunistic is meant that the scores derive from the constraints of paper-and-pencil test administration cultures; and the unintegrated goals of experiments using latencies. In group test administration using pencil and paper delivery, *right, wrong and omitted* items form the only observable categories[2]. In all scoring formulas for accuracy, assumptions exist about what these three item categories mean, since the participant is seldom asked or interviewed. If speed is subsequently calculated from a fixed time limit, the average speed to complete an item has to be estimated from all the information about right, wrong and omitted items. Speed scores similarly become functions of the assumptions made about the contribution to estimates of true-score variance to omits and wrongs. The scoring methods may be *ad hoc* to the test context, and because they form no *a priori* definition of the context itself they are constrained by the *opportunities* for scoring that are presented – hence opportunistic.

A rational alternative requires the application of a simple principle.

Collections of items can be used as for assessing speed and accuracy only when inferences justify the assumption that performance is based on the use of skills that are relevant to the solution of the items.

In other words, the participants are trying to solve the problems before them: and are responding in a non-random manner. If that inference cannot be made with confidence from any sequence of items, then it is pointless to give a value to the outcome expressed as either accuracy or a speed score, or some amalgam of both. Other procedures for basing accuracy and speed scores on confidence limits established for individuals are offered as an alternative to opportunistic methods.

---

2   Only 'abandoned' of the alternatives, never seems to be mentioned: but 'keypressers' in computer-delivered tests presented and interesting category. See Chapter 7.

These methods do not preclude subsequent reference to estimates of capability from population norms.

FORMULAS FOR SCORING ACCURACY

The conventional accuracy score that takes no account of speed is a *ratio* of rights to total items completed. In items that are homogeneous and easy, slow participants who have a high success ratio are indistinguishable from those who are fast with the same success ratio. Such ratio scores seem to be counter-intuitive to the empirical evidence that shows those participants most likely to succeed in work activities to be both fast and accurate. Ratio scores are customary in fixed test treatments when all have attempted or are required to attempt the same number of items. Traditional essay-type examination marks expressed as percentages of a maximum are everyday examples of accuracy scores based on a ratio. Psychometric tests tend not to use percentage accuracy scores. They usually correct for guessing. Such scores are the main concern in this section.

Scores Adjusted for Guessing

There are two basic formula scoring equations in traditional methods of psychometric test construction. All formulas are based on the assumption that for any item the participant knows the correct answer *R* and chooses it, the participant chooses the wrong answer *W*, omits the item *O*, or guesses randomly from one of the *k* alternatives. To describe them briefly helps to establish the notation to be used hereafter.

The first formula is based on the assumption that the participant would improve a score to the extent that all omitted items could have been guessed.

$$Xadj = R + O/k \qquad\qquad Formula\ 5.1$$

Where *Xadj* is the corrected score derived from the observed number correct *(R)* and the number of omitted items *(O)* and *k* is the number of alternatives in a multiple choice format..

An alternative *Xadj^* formula is the *rights minus wrongs* correction where *W* is the number of errors. Here, the effect is to decrease the observed score by estimating the number of correct items that may have occurred as a result of guessing.

$$Xadj^\wedge = R - \{W/(k-1)\} \qquad\qquad Formula\ 5.2$$

Although equations 5.1 and 5.2 will produce values that are numerically different for each participant, equation 5.2 is a linear transformation of 5.1 and if the two corrections are used on the same test scores, the results will yield a correlation of unity.

Rights With and/or Without Wrongs? Additional Considerations for Guesses

Formula scoring has additional techniques that may be empirically derived, the best explanatory examples of which are still to be found in Guilford (1964 pp. 489-493) and in Dubois (1965 pp.404-406). These include weightings for right and wrong scores, criterion or factorially determined for prediction in specific situations. Guilford provides some pertinent examples of what might be attempted by differentially weighting right and wrong scores. Dubois is typically much more analytical in his evaluation of such procedures. He correctly points out that when rights and wrongs are strongly correlated, and negatively so (as in easy and timed tests), subtracting wrongs from rights simply includes more of the variance already captured by rights. In other cases, wrongs have little variance compared with the variance of rights, making the use of scoring formulas of little or no value. Only when wrongs have considerable variance, and have low relationship with rights and show definite negative correlation with the criterion, would empirical determination of their weights in a regression equation be worthwhile. For the most part, conditions favouring empirical determination of scoring formulas by regression against a criterion are favourable when a substantial proportion of items are omitted; and when intercorrelations of the three variables - rights, wrongs and criterion - show that the multiple correlation of rights and wrongs with the criterion is greater than it is with rights.

Again, illustrative reviews of empirical studies of formula scoring include that by Diamond and Evans (1973). They found that reliabilities, and hence estimates of true-score variance were not any the better for use of formulas involving rights, wrongs or omits. Corrected scores tended to produce slightly higher validities, but not appreciably so, and for no obvious reason. Moreover, Lord (1975) suggested that instructions to examinees were not precise enough to verify the application of a random guessing model. Nevertheless, empirical studies involving precise instructions to candidates showed that when participants attempt and give an answer to all items, they achieve more than when instructed to guess (Bliss, 1980). Finally, Lord (1983) in a response, outlines a maximum-likelihood case for using the normal correction for guessing formula when all items are equivalent. In short, using formula corrections to estimate accuracy scores depends on a number of assumptions. The rationale is less likely to be one derived from a theory of performance than from preferences for one set of assumptions over another.

SPEED OF RESPONSE SCORES IN PSYCHOMETRICS

Latencies, or speed of response to a standard stimulus over trials, have a history going back to Galton and Wundt. They permit study of each trial where times are not categories, but can be perceived as part of a distribution, for groups between participants for one or more trials and for individuals over all trials (Restle and Davis, 1962). The distribution of trial latencies for any single participant can provide measures of central tendency and variance for individuals. Much has been made of this flexibility, particularly by Jensen (1982, 1988) who regards scores based on individual variance over trials to be as critical as individual means, without seeming to recognise that a scatterplot of intra-individual mean reaction times and variances must tend to form an experimentally dependent triangle. Family size and order of birth is a perfect analogue. When plotted they form a triangle with a theoretical correlation value of .5 (Irvine, 1964, pp. 198-199)[3]. This value can also be compared with Hendrickson's (1982) empirical correlations between string lengths and their variances in latency-derived averaged evoked potential measures of .55 -.59 in different small samples.

---

3   This was pointed out to me by the late Oscar Roberts, of the South African Institute of Personnel Research. Much of what I learned about the adaptation of tests in other cultures was due to him and the published work of Biesheuvel and Reuning.

In short, latency means and variances for individuals calculated over trials are experimentally dependent because participants operating at the limit of very quick performance *must* have small variations, while the propensity for large variation increases only as the mean latency increases. Eysenck (1988) argues that this very variation is the underlying cause of large latencies, but that seems too simplistic when the scores are experimentally dependent. The sampling problem with any large variation is that the mean value has a large standard deviation, giving large confidence limits for estimation from a small number of events. A comprehensive attempt to score items of moderate difficulty using latencies is the report by Tatsuoka and Tatsuoka (1978). A cogent case is made for applying Weibull (1951) distributions to such items in criterion-referenced tests. Their techniques are applicable to work-rate tests (cf. Reuning (1983) for an excellent review with examples) where items were completed with a high degree of accuracy.

SOME TYPICAL SPEED OF CORRECT RESPONSE FORMULAE

A prior issue is the method of calculating the mean average response, and this is worth some examination. The first method is to calculate the arithmetic mean for R items and to ignore latencies for W and O items (R = Rights, W = Wrongs, O = Omits). This is defined as the *latency of rights* or **X*lr*** model. In this formula, no allowance is made for very fast and/or very slow response times.

X*lr* = average of latencies for R items   **Formula 5.3**

A second is to calculate the arithmetic mean but to develop a stopping rule to omit random outriders, particularly at the outset, which is likely to be the slow end of the distribution, using individual or group variance estimates to define outrider limits. This is defined as the *truncated or trimmed latency of rights **L*rt*** model.

X*lrt* = Average of truncated latencies for R items   **Formula 5.4**

Opportunistic Accuracy/Speed Scoring Methods

Methods that do not ignore but penalise participants for incorrect responses are customary and violate the assumption that wrong answer latency is not interpretable. These methods utilise the total time spent on the test in a ratio score involving total time to complete all items expressed as a function of those items that are judged correct. Two recent variations are described, and their relationship determined. One observed in operational use by Bartram (1986) is the following expression:

100 (Total Time/Number Correct in final 25 items)   Formula 5.5

This is an average value composed of the sum of the time to complete the correct items (R) plus the sum of the W (wrong) item times divided by the number of correct trials *in the last series of 25 items*. It has the effect of increasing the average time by that required to produce a number of wrong or omitted answers. If one substitutes total of test items for total time, the formula can be recognised as an inverse percentage.

Another in use at the time (Alderton, 1989) was the formula

Proportion Correct/ Geometric mean latency (R + W)......Formula 5.6

Geometric means are *de facto* derived from the arithmetical mean by logarithmic transformations of raw scores. Transformations of latencies into log latencies do not alter the information content, although the density functions of the distributions of latencies would change with logarithmic functions, for the most part treated as lognormal. Armed with this information, one can deduce that Formula 5.5 and Formula 5.6 are perfectly correlated, even if their values are different. Number correct is the limiting factor.

Restating the Problem

These are typical of many attempts to estimate ability from latency data. What they all have in common is tacit agreement that estimates of ability should be based on correct response totals. The problem seems to be how best to estimate the latency for a correct response, and having estimated it, provide a theory for estimating ability from it. The two opportunistic latencies formulae (5.3 and 5.4) obviously penalise those who are both slow and inaccurate, implying a power or efficiency function based upon latency *and* accuracy. Individual differences in the speed-accuracy trade-off do not help clarify them. Nevertheless, they are typical of many in the experimental literature. Just as the assumptions of the tester are the determinants of corrections for guessing, so they may quite idiosyncratically (or opportunistically if the scoring formula chosen leads the highest correlation with a criterion) inform the choice of equation.

BINOMIAL CONFIDENCE SCORES AS ESSENTIAL LATENCY FILTERS

The point of departure for is the need to have confidence in the sample of items scored *before* using latencies, and the need to resolve, or control, the speed-accuracy trade off.

Bevans (1963) in an unpublished manuscript made available to the team, demonstrated the use of the binomial theorem (as did Kalisch, 1986), to produce a system that Bevans called *confidence scoring* to take into account the number of items attempted in a generous time limit and the accuracy with which they were completed. He illustrates his system (Bevans,1966) using *Raven's Advanced Matrices*, a power test of increasing item difficulty, administered with eight choices per item under a fixed time limit. His term, *cred score*, applied to confidence scoring, seemed particularly appropriate applied to very short latencies if they were to be regarded as expressions of superior performance, and not as expressions of frustration by respondents at the demands of the tests.

KEYPRESSERS AND LATENCIES

Binomial Confidence Scores

Cusum Distributions

In short, non-randomness is a prerequisite to the use of latency models. Essentially, the *cred score* is an expression of the experimenter's confidence that the participant is not using a guessing strategy to produce a succession of right and/or wrong answers.

Alternatively, the participant is assumed to be using cognitive functions consistently to obtain, or to fail to obtain, right and/or wrong answers. If the items are constructed from a theoretical position, then inferences may be made about what these cognitive functions are.

Grounds for Removal of 'Keypresser' Latencies?
A similar, and convenient probabilistic approach, based on the binomial theorem was demonstrated by Wright and Dennis (1992) in their development of spatial orientation tests for the Royal Air Force. The formula is designed to produce a z score based on the number of items correct and the number wrong.

General Formula
The formula can be generalised to multiple choice tests with any number of alternatives. In its general form as a normal approximation to the binomial it could be written as follows:

Let X be the number of correct items, n be the number of items attempted. Let a be the number of alternatives. A z score showing the probability of a random response series will result,

$$z = (X - n/a) / \sqrt{(n\{a-1\}/a^2)} \qquad \textbf{Formula 5.7}$$

This formula will produce a normal distribution of scores so that *any z score greater than 1,.67 can be used with confidence, but any value less than 1.67 is likely to be the product of random guessing.*

An example based on a score of 5 made from 16 items attempted on a test *whose items have four choices* produces a z score formula of

$$z = (X-n/4) / \sqrt{(3n/16)} \qquad \textbf{Formula 5.8}$$

In this formula X is the score made; n/4 is the total of number of items (n) attempted divided by the number of alternative answers (a), in this case, four. The chances of a score being random are fewer than one in twenty whenever a value of z is greater than 1.67. Any value for an individual of less than 1.67 would indicate a score of little or no confidence. This would mean that any latency score based on the items attempted would be unstable and should be rejected. A typical pattern is that of a 'keypresser' where a large number of items are attempted with a very short average latency but with a z score showing no credibility.

A Worked Example
A recruit completes 16 items (n) and gets 5 of them (X) correct. The test items have four alternatives. How confident could we be in taking his times to complete the items to be a reliable indication of his speed?

$$Z = (5 - 4 / \sqrt{(12/16)}$$

$$Z = 1/.87 = 1.15$$

In this example, there is no confidence in this score because the Z value is less than 1.67, and any latencies derived from the item responses would be discounted.

This approach was used extensively in the account of military test development in Chapters 10 to 13 after 1996; and especially whenever studies of the time taken to complete items were involved in estimating abilities. *Latencies, whenever they were employed, were confined to those scores where credibility beyond the limits of chance had first been established.* This strategy eliminated 'keypressers' who were responding randomly as quickly as possible. See Chapter 11 for compelling evidence of the effect of 'keypressers' on test reliability. A large number of participants completed multiple parallel form computer-delivered tests at Lackland Air Force Base and it was possible to isolate 'keypressers' and examine their motivation.

PLYMOUTH SCORING EXPERIMENTS

There has been general agreement that following multiple task completion, latencies are justifiable for those items that are correct. If the item is wrong, one cannot assume that the participant's time taken involves parallel processes to those in the correct answer. Latencies have thus been conventionally measured for correct, but not for wrong answers. Even after the decision had been made to observe the conventions, three team members[4] worked together to explore viable alternatives to opportunistic scoring with combinations of accuracy and latency.

Specifically, inherently unreliable difference scores among repeated trials would not help in defining a dynamic or learning model for test applications. Instead, they examined various options, where time and correct responses interacted. Wright (1993, pp. 391-395) and Wright and Dennis (1999) applied CUSUMs (cumulative sums) to test score sequences. The CUSUM charts enable the tracking of small shifts in process, incorporating a series of data values. Wright showed how individual score plots against elapsed time to answer can be used to demonstrate different learning and/ or performance rates when scores adjusted for guessing are plotted at intervals along the cumulative time taken to complete the test. Given confidence scores, CUSUM slopes can predict outcomes at a fixed time limit, thereby reducing testing time.

Figure 5.1: Two CUSUMs for Test Performance (After Wright, 1993)

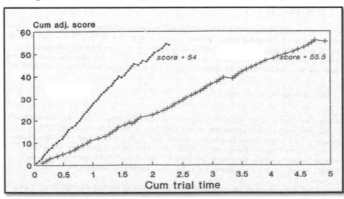

---

4   Ian Dennis, Jonathan Evans and David Wright.

Figure 5.1 introduced by Wright (1993) tracks the progress and shows the difference between two participants, both with virtually the same score on a semantic identity/difference vocabulary test adjusted for guessing, but plotted against the time recorded for solving the items in sequence. The two participants have almost identical adjusted scores, the final heights of the CUSUMs being 54 and 55.5 respectively. However, the one on the left of the chart works at a much faster rate than the one on the right, reaching the score adjusted for guessing in about half the time. Had the test been stopped after 2 minutes rather than when all 60 items were completed, one score would have been approximately 25: and the other 50 - about twice that of the other. This timed test score, which reflects speed as well as accuracy, is proportional to the slope of the CUSUM graph. It may be obtained by dividing the final height (i.e. the adjusted score with correct as +1 and error is calculated as $-1/(k-1)$ where k is the number of choices) by the total latency in minutes, or the log mean latency in centiseconds or milliseconds.

TWO QUESTIONS

1. How credible is the score derived from responses within a given time envelope?

2. How can a stopping rule be developed by combining item generic types and time envelopes?

Wright showed that use of the resulting 'power scores' increases the correlations of the test with the general training quotient of the 1986 Army Entrance Tests. Wright and Dennis (1992) expanded this model to include a range of spatial tasks. They showed not only that the CUSUMs could differentiate work rates in rotated symbols, cube folding and related tests (and by implication learning rates) but that they could as in medical research, isolate those whose scores could be excluded because the CUSUMs showed no increase in slope when the score was plotted against elapsed time. De Olivera and associates (2008) give proof of the practical use of the CUSUM principle with medical trainee progress in trials involving accurate alignment of anaesthetic needle to ultrasound beams. Many trials were necessary before reaching the necessary level of skill and, more to the point, some trainees learned a lot more quickly than others did. Many appeared to have great difficulty in reaching the criterion for success, regardless of the number of trials undertaken (maximum 25). De Olivera then extrapolated the results to suggest that only completion of more than 100 trials would ensure confidence based upon accuracy and, by implication, safeguard the wellbeing of patients. If used in this fashion, CUSUMs become a logical development of the item-generation paradigm in forecasting a stopping rule. Wright's ingenuity was not confined to this paradigm. He saw further advantages to using latencies in concurrence with verified accuracy scores. One of these was the potential of time'envelopes' where the time to complete an item was curtailed..

TIME ENVELOPES AS RADICALS IN ADAPTIVE TESTING
Wright (2002) and Wright and Dennis (1999) in two seminal papers, show how it is possible to put different generic item types into time capsules and thereby to alter their difficulty level. The delivery of items in blocks with different time envelopes for items permits a sampling framework to be developed. Moreover, given confidence

in the accuracy of responses to an array of items of any size within a given time, it ought to be possible to estimate with some precision the ability of an individual if the distribution of average latencies is already known. As before, there are two questions to answer.

This published work grew from a series of five reports by Wright and his colleagues, Dennis and Evans (1990,1991); and Evans and Wright (1992,1993,1994) and a publication by Dennis and Evans (1996). Evans and Wright (1994) found part answers in an unpublished detailed report. Computer simulation studies were based upon the logistic models of a fixed-time transitive inference task, with a substantial working memory loading, derived from BARB by Evans and Wright (1993). Using simulation techniques and Bayesian estimation procedures, they showed that time envelopes could be put around test items using the screen as a control. Logistic models once fitted to the items, which remain unaltered as generated, can alter difficulties by the use of time constraints, permitting an ingenious adaptation of item-response theory. The technique of Bayesian estimation and its application in an adaptive testing algorithm is explained (loc. cit. pp. 6-7).

Additionally, a variant of this test with higher item discrimination was postulated and simulations were conducted thereafter with two assumptions: (1) all items are presented with a fixed time limit; and (2) this limit can be varied in adaptive versions of the test. With both adaptive and non-adaptive procedures, more reliable measures can be obtained by using Bayesian estimation than by R-Models involving percentage correct. The improvements are greatest are when the items have substantial discrimination indices and when it is permissible to shift the time limits to adjust item difficulty to the ability level of the participant. Whenever working memory capacity is low, then high time settings may be required for transitive inference and other item types dependent on working memory capacity; and these would nullify any adaptive advantages. Finally the possibility of developing a procedure using fixed, but optimal time allowance is raised and outlined. In retrospect, Evans and Wright offered BARB the bridge between R and L Models and opened up an option of using IRT within all item generative tests with controlled screen delivery. It was a unique opportunity, but like much basic science, not introduced operationally either in BARB or in any of the subsequent tests. Extended use could only have followed if those responsible for the tests had themselves enough technical knowledge to be confident in the outcome following explanations to high-ranking officials who, having never pretended to be psychometricians, nevertheless had the final word and the power of veto, if necessary. Commercially, it would have had even more barriers to cross, even or perhaps especially, in today's HR personnel climates where elementary statistics is a rare requirement for role enactment.

AN OPEN QUESTION: WHAT SCORING MODELS TO USE ON ITEM GENERATIVE TESTS?

The research conducted in the laboratory led to several observations and conclusions. Initially, because trials of the tests were in paper-and-pencil, accuracy models were compulsory. And at that time these were required whenever there were no extensive computer systems for automated test administration. Similar paper-and-pencil forms were also introduced in the United States prior to complete computerisation. The results confirmed the use of scores corrected for guessing and their companion, the confidence score based on the binomial theorem brought to notice by Wright and Dennis. Latency scoring was still a possibility. The first extended opportunity, prior to 1990 occurred in the United States when a modified version of BARB was used to measure individual differences in the ability to learn electronic logic gates (see Chapter 8). After 1996, the wholesale use of computer-delivery meant that studies in the USA, Germany and Belgium produced both accuracy and latency data. If possible, the average log latency per item completed was recorded, following the work of Dennis and Evans (1996) on the speed accuracy trade off. Latencies were used where the non-random nature of the test score was first established.

USING THE BINOMIAL THEOREM TO PROVIDE A STOPPING RULE
Here two possible versions of the system are outlined. The first stops testing when the average speed for item solution fails to increase. The second establishes population parameters for item latencies for a given item type and then sets out to estimate the status of any individual on the whole test from a sample of items delivered in different time envelopes. This accepts Wright and Dennis's (1999) proposition that the speed-accuracy trade-off can be exploited to extend the range of item difficulty for generic item types.

When Does the Participant Reach Asymptote in Time to Solution?
To answer this question by applying the binomial theorem seems to represent an empirical solution with some theoretical justification. Having satisfied oneself that the candidates' responses scored for accuracy have a very remote possibility of being produced randomly, an average latency for those items correctly answered in the first set (i) of n samples of serially ordered groups of items of convenient size is determined. Thereafter, the group of items i(n) is categorised according to whether each item correctly completed is faster or slower than the average latency of the i(n-1) group. The binomial theorem once more provides a confidence score, with the advantage that each successive group of items can be compared with a previous group (or rolling if this is preferable) average. The stopping rule would operate whenever p<.05 that this new group could have random distribution of latencies around the mean of the previous set. Confidence scoring using the binomial theorem may be used to scale individuals first on their accuracy for a completed series. One may then decide if their speed is increasing, or whether it has reached constant velocity within crude limits of stability. In conjunction with cusums charts, a learning model can be developed.

Group Membership as a Sampling Problem
An interesting parallel development of probability theory is apparent in an unnoticed paper by Linhart (1959) whose work on the binomial theorem attempts to estimate the consistency of psychological tests with dichotomous scoring. In a run of k items assumed to test for the presence or absence of an attribute A in a sample of n participants it is not known whether a participant has an attribute A or A-(not A). The decision about whether the participant possesses A (and belongs to that group) is a function of the probability Pi of obtaining the result A from A types and the same probability Pi of obtaining the result A- from A- types. Methods are given for providing confidence limits for Pi when n = 1 and k has any value; and for any

n where k = 2, 3; and for obtaining approximate confidence limits for large n where k has any value. The extension of this logic to various levels of ability associated with the completion of generated item classes (either correctly or correctly within a predetermined time limit) is not difficult to imagine. Consider M ability or time levels each associated with completion of homogeneous items of different difficulty. One can then estimate the probability of a person belonging to any one of these categories using the Linhart model or its later maximum likelihood or Bayesian variations using a logistic model. The logistic model is fully reviewed in Thissen and Wainer (loc. cit. pp. 74-109). Linhart's work was perhaps the first to apply the potential in item-response patterns to solve a psychometric classification problem (Hector and Hudson, 1958). This predates Birnbaum (1967, 1969) and Birnbaum's (1968, loc. cit. pp.395-479) core contribution to Lord and Novick (1968).

Group Membership and Differential Item Difficulty
Finally, and significantly, the work of Holland and Thayer (1986) on Mantel-Haenszel (MH) procedures for testing the probability of non-chance differences in item-difficulty between groups determines groups that are maximally differentiated by accuracy on any single item; and contrasts those groups for whom item-difficulty is invariant. In the context of item-generation procedures, their tests of item functioning are IRT independent, although they coexist with IRT models. The use of MH tests first on accuracy to test for ability-group invariance and then for latency to maximise group variation has certain attractiveness. And it returns us to the problem addressed in the first instance - how to solve operationally problems associated with examining item responses first for accuracy and then for speed. A particular difficulty in the investigation of differential item functions (DIF) awaited anyone who had produced multiple parallel forms of items that were analogues of each other but were not identical, and scattered over a hitherto unimaginable number of test forms. In Belgium a solution was found: and a complete account exists in Chapter 13.

Part 2:

BARB: The British Army Recruit Battery

Dr. John Anderson on BARB

Head of Personnel Psychology Division/
Assistant Director Army Personnel Research Establishment

In 1985, I was the head of a small unit within the Army Personnel Research Establishment. The unit's role was to provide technical support to the Army Staff in the area of manpower supply: recruitment, selection, training and retention. At that time, the Army's, soldier selection process faced a number of problems, both technical and administrative, which Professor Irvine delineates in Chapter 1. In addition, the existing tests pre-dated many changes to the role of the soldier. The bolt-action rifle had long since become a museum piece. In addition to its sophisticated rapid-fire replacements there were missile launchers, radios, electronic countermeasures and the complexities and diplomacy of peace-keeping duties to be mastered. The long-overdue successor to the AET would have to be a robust measure of ability to learn, as far as possible independent of the educational background of the recruit.

Other factors also had to be considered. Traditional psychometric tests have a shelf life. Their utility is a function of the test-taker's unfamiliarity with the material: validity generally declines with repeated exposure. In practice, this means that tests must be replaced by alternative versions at regular intervals. This process is, if done properly, expensive in both time and manpower. This is partly due to a lack of rigour: in a previous revision of AET the production of test items resembled a craft skill, not a science. In consequence, large quantities of the test items generated by the cottage industry of item writers were rejected after extended trialling. The statistical sieve of item analysis was necessary because no means of predicting the difficulty of an item, other than the writer's best guess, existed.

The cost and complexity of the task meant that replacement versions were produced only rarely, to the general detriment of test validity.

At the time, the use of computers was expanding rapidly. Computer-based testing (CBT) was being actively researched, especially in the USA, but the focus was on using computer terminals to deliver the test material. Could the process be taken further: could one capitalise on the rigour of computer programming to create computer-generated tests: Computer-generated, GT, not CBT? Could one imagine a computer declaiming in Churchillian fashion "Give me the rules, and I will finish the job"? There were certainly established tests whose constituent items could be completely described by rules. The uncertainty was whether the range of abilities which could be measured by rule-dependent tests was sufficient for the Army's needs.

These thoughts led to the placing of a very modest 1-year research contract with what was then Plymouth Polytechnic, for a postgraduate to be supervised by Professor Irvine. Initial results were encouraging: the contract expanded in time and scope, the Polytechnic became a University, and Professor Irvine and his colleagues came up with radical (if he will forgive the pun) answers to what he termed "The Anderson Question". Those answers, and more importantly, the thought processes which gave rise to them and the constraints on their practical validation in the field, are set out in detail in the first nine chapters. They offer an unique viewpoint over the fields of aptitude testing and cognitive theory, a viewpoint which led to major practical applications.

CHAPTER 6

BARB: FROM PAPER AND PENCIL ANALOGUES TO PROTOTYPES

This chapter contains examples in various item formats of the trial analogues of the six final computer-delivered tests in BARB[1]. And a table shows where each test was used. Each item type is described in turn. Additions to the BARB item repertoire were constructed for the Royal Navy and the Royal Air Force. They too are illustrated together with the accuracy of their item difficulty predictions. Paper-and-pencil analogues are followed by descriptions of the computer-delivered versions together with the core foundation references required to determine item radicals and incidentals. Finally, the results of the first trial of BARB, conducted on a platoon of twenty-eight volunteers show that initial optimism was based on an experimental cross-over design involving the simplest of parallel forms in paper-and-pencil and hand-scored format, going inexorably back to the future while waiting for computers and touchscreens.

OPERATIONAL FRAMEWORKS: PAPER-AND-PENCIL ANALOGUES

The first operational framework for BARB was necessarily paper-and-pencil because the microcomputer base at the Army Personnel Recruit Centre had to wait until a building was created to house the initial 30

---

1   All BARB examples in this chapter are reproduced by permission of the Ministry of Defence Of Great Britain and are Crown Copyright.

microcomputers and server. The illustrations given below for future reference are closer to the computer-delivered versions than their printed analogues. Where appropriate, easier and harder item types are shown with answers and brief instructions. The abbreviated labels are commonly used in tables describing test results. The insert and the index of abbreviations show these for *Letter Checking Arithmetic Encoding and Comparison, Alphabet Forward and Backward, Rotated Shape, Transitive Inference Reasoning Tasks, Vocabulary (Semantic Identity).*

Nevertheless, the operational version of the BARB computer-based testing system eventually contained seven tests. Six of these were introduced for the basic validation studies. An enhanced vocabulary test was devised at a later date following its development for the Royal Navy[2] NPS tests and incorporation with ARCOM[3]. The time estimation task had to await the construction of the computer-delivered test centre at Army Personnel Recruit Centre. Commentary on any one test shows its theoretical origins, and explanatory notes on how it was originally conceived and formulated. The initial computer-delivered BARB series concludes this chapter. Now in Table 6.1 an overview of what tests were used in the various military contexts recounts what versions of the tests were to appear in rapid succession from the Plymouth laboratory in response to requests from officials for selection tests.

BARB

The Magic Number Seven Plus or Minus

Table 6.1: Overview of Parallel Form Tests for Army and Navy Personnel

TESTS 1990-1996	DOMAIN	BARB	NPS	ARCOM
Letter Checking (LC)	Perceptual	X	X	X
Rotated Symbol(RF)	Orientation	X	X	X
Number Distance(ND)	Work. Mem. (N)	X	X	X
Alphabet Task 1(Simple)AFB	Work. Mem. (L)	X	X	
Alphabet Task 2 (Complex)	Work. Mem. (L)	X	X	X
Vocabulary (Odd One)SI/SD	Verbal Educ.	X	X	X
Reasoning (TI 2 or 3 Term)	Verbal (WM)	X	X	X
Sentence Construction	Verbal (WM)		X	
Directions & Distances	Orientation		X	X
Brackets (Parentheses in USA)	Work. Mem. (N)			X
Math Foundations	Proficiency (N)		X	
Vocabulary	Proficiency (V)		X	

---

2   The NPS or Naval Personnel Series was identified by using the reverse initials of the department known as Senior Psychologist Naval, or SPN.

3   ARCOM is the acronym for the Army Regular Commissions Board that selects officer cadets.

The tests most likely to provide a GTI or *General Training Index* were first identified and then made ready for extended trials. They included two serial search tasks in working memory, *Letter Checking and Rotated Shape.* Reconstruction tasks in working memory were grammatical transformations; manipulation of letter sequences of the alphabet in their normally learned order; and simple arithmetic based on distances between pairs of numbers. Perhaps seeming on the surface as simple as ABC, they were referred to as *The ABC Tests,* particularly in their paper-and-pencil mode.

LETTER CHECKING TEST

HOW MANY PAIRS OF LETTERS ARE THE SAME?

Figure 6.1: Letter Checking

C	B	G	D		m	e	a	f
v	t	e	d		C	J	S	H

    0 **1** 2 3 4   **0** 1 2 3 4

The Letter Checking Test was used in detailed psychometric experiments by Irvine & Reuning, (1981) as an extension of the Sternberg (1966) probe in a memory set paradigm with English language participants: and cross-cultural verifications (Irvine, Schoeman & Prinsloo, 1988) were completed in Canada, South Africa and Samoa to confirm the models involved. The results produced indices of difficulty that defined and extended the definition of *radicals*, one set classified as an *extra-hominem radical* Upper vs. Lower Case a-a (match) vs. a-A (extra encoding) because of stimulus qualities. The other was an *intra-hominem radical* depending on an internal auditory loop. This radical involved letter pairs in the English alphabet with auditory similarity *b, c, d, e, g, p, t, v and (z only in USA).* They take longer to process than letter pairs with dissimilar sounds. The letter stimuli times to complete are longer in the different case condition, but the auditory loop effect is constant, regardless of case. Among the most difficult, is, by extension, a *rotated* letter case pair sounding the same, e.g. d p, or D d, because of the steps required to negation. The first example shown contains these auditory loop confusions and, when one attempts this and the second example, perhaps provides intuitive certainty.

NUMBER AND LETTER DISTANCE TESTS

The paper-and-pencil *Number Distance Task* was based on the models provided by Moyer and Landauer, (1967); Parkman, (1972); Groen and Parkman, (1972), showing how the difficulty of decisions based on number retrieval could be estimated from the relative distance of numbers from each other. It is catalogued in the section dealing with the final choice of computer-delivered for the *British Army Recruit Battery.*

FIND HIGHEST AND LOWEST NUMBERS. WHICH OF THESE TWO
NUMBERS IS FURTHER FROM THE REMAINING NUMBER?

Figure 6.2: Number Distance

Easy			Harder		
3	**5**	**9**	**14**	**25**	**5**
a	*b*	*c*	*a*	*b*	*c*

LETTER DISTANCE TEST [4]

IN ALPHABETIC ORDER, WHICH LETTER IS FURTHER FROM THE
MIDDLE ONE?

Figure 6.3: Letter Distance

Easy			Harder		
A	**C**	**F**	**M**	**Q**	**T**
		X		X	

ALPHABET FORWARD-BACKWARD TEST

IN THE ALPHABET, WHICH LETTERS GO FORWARD/BACKWARD
FROM THOSE GIVEN?

Figure 6.4: Alphabet Forward and Backward

Easier			Harder		
	AB	+ 2		QVC	- 2
CD	DE	BC	PSA	OSB	OTA
X					X

---

4   This test was a later addition to the original paper-and-pencil tests. It proved to be an acceptable alternative and in
format resembled the *Number Distance Task* making the instructions easier. Legend, perhaps apocryphal, has it that
an ageing official found the complex *Alphabet Forward and Backward* test, used in earlier studies, too demanding, so
that it had to be impossible for recruits..

Complex Alphabet Task

IN WHICH ROW ARE THE CORRECT LETTERS TO BE FOUND?
THEY NEED NOT BE IN ORDER.

Figure 6.5: Complex Alphabet Task

	A	B	C	+	1
1	A	B	C	F	E	
2	D	A	F	B	C	
3	A	C	E	F	D	

Details of the scale of the prior research on the AFB (*Alphabet Forward and Backward*) task were given in Chapter 4. Versions of the task, of which a multitude of types could be produced, were trialled in cooperation with the United States Air Force Laboratory LAMP program, and Woltz (1987) was able to determine *p* values for the alphabet reconstruction task that had been adopted for BARB. The original alphabet task (e.g. AB +2 =?), initial versions of which were pioneered by Hockey, MacLean and Hamilton (1981), and reported in a second experiment (Hockey and Hamilton, 1986, p. 419) showed that individual differences in the time required to store the information in items of increasing difficulty, accounted for most of the individual differences in solution times. As might be predicted from the original work by Hockey and his colleagues, the *p* values in the BARB experimental versions varied predictably with the number of letters in the stimulus and in the number of steps required to reconstruct the alphabet from memory. The difficulty of the items could be reconstructed, knowing the number of letters to be encoded, and the number of steps forward and/or backward in the alphabet.

These working memory *radicals* were assured, while the *incidentals* were the letters of the alphabet themselves, ensuring random sampling from strata of first, middle and latter thirds. Counterbalancing was applied to the examples from each stratum, knowing, from elementary learning theory, that early and late orders of the alphabet were more quickly accessed than the letters in the middle if alphabet fluency were uncertain. Modified later versions (Figure 6.5) prevented the use of strategies in solving items with limited choice options: and others were produced to accommodate some officials who reportedly found the original too demanding. Raymond Christal once remarked that it was important to have special examples of all types of test items for visiting dignitaries to hand: and these - the 'generals'- versions had to be the easiest possible.

Symbol Rotation (F) Test)

HOW MANY PAIRS MATCH ONLY WHEN THEY ARE TURNED
AROUND

Figure 6.6: Symbol Rotation (F)

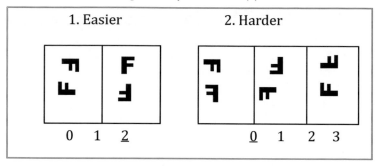

Normally, the two-symbol comparison item was used in trials, following good prediction of p values. Difficulty indices from the more difficult three-symbol *Rotated F Task* used in alternate versions of BARB predicted *p* values with R at .84, (from an officer cadre with restricted range) knowing stimulus characteristics. A number of radicals included the number of same pairs, the minimum number of rotations to find the number of same pairs, the number of parallel stems, among others. The salient quality was the number of rotated pairs of letters that were the same. *Additionally, the more rotations made in the item to verify the number of pairs that matched, the more difficult was the item.* This confirmed previous trends in the experimental 'two-dimensional' series (Shepard and Metzler 1971), and used by Bejar (1986a, 1986b, 1986c, Bejar and Yocom (1991).

REASONING TESTS (TRANSITIVE INFERENCE)
Two versions were used, the easiest requiring inference from two sentences and the more difficult involving three sentences. They are generally referred to in the literature as the two and three term transitive inference series.

REASONING SAMPLE ITEMS

READ THE STORY. ANSWER THE QUESTION

Figure 6.7: Transitive Inference

1. Easy	2. Harder
Fred is shorter than Joe.	Trish is lighter than Sue.
Who is taller?	Fran is heavier than Sue.
	Who is heaviest?
(A) <u>Joe</u> (B) Fred	(A) <u>Fran</u> (B) Sue (C) Trish

Radicals in *Transitive Inference Test* items include the amount of information in a single frame; the use of a time envelope; the number of terms in series (2 or 3); the sequence of Information, (Anchoring Contrast A>B, B>C or B<A B>C); the length of the words used in the sentences; the addition of negatives; and the use of marked or unmarked (e.g. big-little) adjective types. Incidentals in transitive inference are assumed to be names when counterbalanced for sex or ethnic identities, and qualities where the word frequencies are high and of equivalent category widths. Major work on reasoning by Evans (1981; and Evans &Wright (1992, 1993) permitted evaluation and adoption of this task in its variants of two or three terms in the item sequence.

However, one might reflect that its use as a measure of ability to learn was a traditional part of measurement theory and practice (Burt, 1923 p. 95) in the United Kingdom; and in Burt's collection, the two versions identical to those chosen for BARB were expected to be presented to children aged seven and older! In fact, Burt's series of graded reasoning tests (loc. cit. pp. 95-98) could well be perceived as forgotten models for the more complex tasks recommended for item generative tests by Dennis (2002), and Newstead et al. (2002), and whose difficulty could be predicted from grammatical and word frequency components.

ADDITIONAL TEST CREATION: SP(N) SERIES AND ARCOM

Different United Kingdom service arms had different priorities. Tests with a more advanced educational knowledge base were thought necessary for missions needing situational awareness and the selection of technicians and officers. Sponsors of the research requested operational versions of tests involving these and other item types already in use for BARB. Tests judged fit for trial were added to those. In fact, tests to replace one that had many years of use for selecting navigators had a six-week deadline. Parallel forms emerged inside the limit.

THE CUBE-FOLDING TEST
In response to a request from the Royal Air Force, Dennis and Wright (1992) devised a unique cube-folding test capable of large-scale multiple parallel form production. The salient and unique aspects of the test items that made the test such an outstanding example of elements necessary for multiple form production included a basic set of eleven planar shapes requiring to be folded into a cube, only two of which were not capable of providing mirror-image alternatives.

Figure 6.8: The Cube-Folding Test

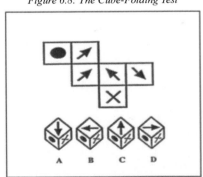

Moreover, only three distinct symbols defined cube sides and, most ingenious of all, *the response alternatives were always the same, regardless of the problem to be solved.* Dennis also made this advance, never seen before in the item type, totally in tune with computer-delivered tests. *Because the four alternative answers shown in Figure 6.8 were used for every item, the item type fulfilled all the requirements of a computer-delivered ideal, the unities of action, time and outcome all on one screen within a single time span.* From two parallel forms of the test, each of 24 items, using more than 200 officer candidates, item difficulties were predicted (R=.93) with R^2 greater than 86 per cent. Parallel form reliabilities, unadjusted for restriction of range, were serviceable at .73 and proved to be capable of improvement. Correlations with the *Rotated F Test* (RF) and Dennis's *Directions and Distances Test* (DIRDIS), which is described immediately below, were positive if moderate: due, as were all correlations with preselected groups, to range constraint. *From the item parameters specified by Dennis and Wright, 49,152 possible items could be generated automatically from the code specifications.*

DIRECTIONS AND DISTANCES (DIRDIS).

Wright and Dennis, (1992) already had promising results in constructing the multiple parallel form visualization test based on cube-folding. Still in the visualization domain, Dennis (1993) was able to forecast with good accuracy *p* values for a *Directions and Distances Test* for navigator selection. This test required the understanding of complex

---

Figure 6.9 DIRDIS ITEM

In a certain town, the cinema is 600 metres North of the supermarket; the supermarket is 800 metres South of the swimming pool.

What direction is the cinema from the swimming pool?

[A] North [B] South [C] East [D] West

---

verbal directions, retention and storage of information and the ability to transform it into a vector; and that progress is slow because the information needed constant rehearsal! The correlation of this verbal instructions test with other spatial orientation tasks was substantial. Once more, the four distractors were constants, and radicals depended on the number of directional shifts

A 'DIRDIS' ITEM
Any attempt to solve the puzzle without any visual aids or paper and pencil assistance to sketch a map, readily confirms that individual items were composed of verbal instructions requiring visual transformation in working memory. The *Directions and Distances* items were, as a trial attempt at the example will show, not particularly easy.

SEMANTIC IDENTITY, GRAMMATICAL TRANSFORMATIONS AND MATHEMATICAL OPERATIONS

Perhaps the most salient work in the whole field of predicting difficulties for items based upon declarative knowledge is evident in the published material on semantic identity, grammatical transformations, and calculations demanding prior mathematical knowledge, completed by Dennis (Dennis, Collis & Dann, 1995). In his initial MOD report Dennis (1995) elaborates how the *p* values of verbal comprehension tasks were successfully predicted (R=.85) using sentence type, degree of grammatical transformation and word length in a linear model. A vocabulary test of semantic categorization, closely allied to verbal analogies, was successfully modelled using semantic theory and word frequency, with a final R of .94. A version of this involving only abstract words was modelled to produce a prediction of *p* values with R=.81. This work shows the strong influence of cognitive theory in the in the production of performance models.

SEMANTIC IDENTITY
This branch of the work shows the strong influence of applied cognitive theory . Two examples (Table 6.2) show the format involving high frequency objects and lower frequency abstractions. The 'odd one out' paradigm was used exclusively (Dennis, Handley, Bradon, Evans, & Newstead 2002). The source provides a complete framework and rationale for the construction of these items.

Odd One Out Item Types
A concrete word vocabulary test of semantic categorization, closely allied to verbal analogies, was successfully modelled using semantic theory and word frequency, with a final R of .94. Dennis was able to predict the relative difficulty of items depending on the perceived semantic distance of an odd word when compared with others. For example, *Tram, Train and Tulip* present very little difficulty because the distance of the category 'plant' from 'transport' is very pronounced. Substitute *Bicycle* for *Tulip* and the problem becomes harder because all of the words are forms of transport, although only one is pedal driven. The example of this approach involving only abstract words, as exemplified, was modelled to produce a more difficult variety whose item *p* values were predicted from theory determined radicals with a multiple correlation of .81.

Table 6.2: Concrete and Abstract Vocabulary Examples

A	B	C	D	E
spade	axe	hammer	trowel	teaspoon

A	B	C	D	E
reflection	happiness	enjoyment	pleasure	joy

VERBAL COMPREHENSION BY GRAMMATICAL TRANSFORMATION: EXAMPLES
The transformation paradigm had been used previously by Irvine (1964, pp. 497-498) as a means of assessing verbal comprehension in secondary school students

in Zimbabwe, where English was a second language. The sophisticated model by Dennis et al. (2002) was completely independent of Irvine's original. Dennis initiated multiple parallel form production that showed how its use could become a powerful and permanent means of equating the difficulty of items. The following examples serve as simply to illustrate a unique approach that has perhaps never realised its full potential in educational measurement. First, there is a concrete example. Then, a framework for its item-generation follows.

Table 6.3: Grammatical Transformation Paradigm[5]

Find the sentence that has a different meaning from the others
  a **The young girl found the older man's glove**
  b **It was the older girl who found the young man's glove**
  c **The older man's glove was found by the young girl**
  d **It was the glove of the older man that the young girl found**
  e **The glove found by the young girl was that of the older man**

Type 1A	Type 1B
It was the AX who Qed the BY's Z. (1)	It was the BY who Qed the AX's Z. (6)
It was the Z of the BY which the AX Qed. (2)	It was the Z of the AX which the BY Qed. (7)
The Z Qed by the AX was that of the BY. (3)	The Z Qed by the BY was that of the AX. (8)
The BY's Z was Qed by the AX. (4)	The AX's Z was Qed by the BY. (9)
The AX Qed the BY's Z. (5)	The BY Qed the AX's Z. (10)

The Construction of the Series
Several sentence types of increasing complexity were used and trialled, but Types 1A and 1B show how simple items like the example shown could be constructed. Where codes are used in Table 6.3, A and B are *adjectives*, X, Y and Z are *nouns* and Q is a *verb*. The items can be produced in multiple forms by *a permutation of any four sentences from the five in Type A_with any one from Type B, or any four from B with one from A*. A total of 12 Item Types were developed of increasing logical complexity. When these are factorially combined (with/without modifiers) and (short/ longer words), 48 item types emerge. In his initial report Dennis showed in detail how the *p* values of verbal comprehension tasks were successfully predicted (R=.85) using *sentence type, degree of grammatical transformation and word length* in a linear model (Dennis et al. 1995).

MATHEMATICAL OPERATIONS
With the same implacable focus, he also provided items requiring a basic knowledge of mathematical principles (Dennis, 1995). Typical items involved an extensive range of operations including decimals and fractions in normal format, and problems in more elaborate verbal structures. Whereas the BARB items required only simple number facts and were of nominal difficulty, these more sophisticated numeracy tasks, derived from knowledge of their radicals, provided complete success in predicting

---

5   This system was devised by Ian Dennis, is Crown Copyright (1995) and can be used only with permission.

an extended range of difficulties with R estimated at .97. That this is no isolated phenomenon is clear from the work of Embretson (1996) who reports a multiple R of .79 in predicting Rasch model difficulties of mathematics items from a more eclectic empirical perspective. Irvine (1995, pp. 9-10) also made a minor contribution in providing a framework for the delivery of foundations mathematics items using incomplete block designs where every item type was compared against every other at least once. Dennis, Handley, Bradon, Evans and Newstead (2002, pp. 53-72) provide a more comprehensive and theory-based account of this work in the item generation collection (Irvine and Kyllonen 2002).

ARCOM ON TRIAL

However, the work by Dennis and colleagues in providing the necessary item frameworks saw its furthest extension in a new collation, called *The ARCOM*, whose acronym is a simple abbreviation of the process undergone by United Kingdom army officer applicants determined by the <u>A</u>rmy <u>R</u>egular <u>Com</u>missions Board. Perhaps by chance ARCOM proved to be one of the most revealing of the new series. Its origin is part of legend, unable to be verified, but supposed to derive from the wrath of a very senior officer. One of his close relatives was rejected for entry to the officer cadet college on the basis of results from a paper-and-pencil test that had been in operation for decades. How was it that officer candidates came to be rejected by out-of-date methods? Were not other ranks selected by modern computerised tests? Updating and, above all, computerisation as in BARB already applied to enlisted men, were mandatory requirements for those competing for entrance to officer cadet academies.

Within six weeks of an unheralded request from officials in MOD, two paper-and-pencil analogue forms of the ARCOM test were assembled and produced for consultation and try out. Staff in the laboratory assembled the tests from items already trialled in experiments. Soon thereafter, these analogue paper-and-pencil forms were trialled by the self-same officials independently by administering to purposive samples of officer applicants. The applicants were additionally provided with a pre-test booklet where the tests were described; and whose practice examples were to be completed prior to undertaking the tests themselves. Results were subsequently reported by MOD officials for 240 participants on Form A and 228 on Form B.

Figure 6.10: ARCOM Paper-and-Pencil Test Form Means

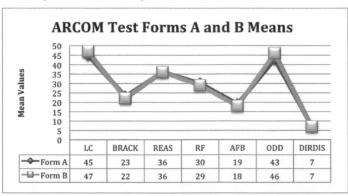

	LC	BRACK	REAS	RF	AFB	ODD	DIRDIS
Form A	45	23	36	30	19	43	7
Form B	47	22	36	29	18	46	7

Figure 6.10 shows the rounded mean values for each of Forms A and B[6]. They are commendably close, the largest mean difference effect size, in the *Odd One Out* vocabulary test, being no greater than 0.3 SD units. This was not deemed large, when the standard error of measurement (SEM) of any one vocabulary test score (based on an estimated test reliability of .84) is ± 3.4 points. Reliability estimates, in effect, were generally good, and often very high.

Table 6.4: Intercorrelations of ARCOM Form A and B Tests

	LCT	BRACK	REAS	RF	AFB	ODD	DIRDIS
LCT	*	.37	.45	.33	.47	.42	.32
BRACK	*.36*	*	.48	.28	.55	.38	.34
REAS	*.34*	*.43*	*	.40	.52	.37	.48
RF	*.25*	*.22*	*.27*	*		.13	.45
AFB	*.36*	*.56*	*.56*	*.24*	*	.44	.50
ODD	*.43*	*.39*	*.40*	*.11*	*.43*	*	.24
DIRDIS	*.29*	*.32*	*.46*	*.38*	*.45*	*.32*	*

Form A Above Diagonal N= 240. *Form B Below Diagonal N=288*

Notes: LCT Letter Checking: BRACK Brackets:Arithmetic: REAS Reasoning: RF Rotated F: AFB Alphabet Forward Backward: ODD Odd One Out: DIRDIS Directions and Distances

The intercorrelations of the paper-and-pencil tests were all positive, with similar patterns (Table 6.4) for both test forms. The vocabulary test proved somewhat independent of the others. Consequently, in both samples, a large parallel form working memory factor emerged, with the largest cluster involving AFB, BRACK, REAS and RF: and a second verbal component was identified. The studies of ARCOM proved to be a microcosm of the standardisation and validation procedures so painstakingly signalled by Macdonald's work among his Askaris, so many years before.

WHAT NEXT ?

Undoubtedly, these preliminary results with ARCOM were promising, but not conclusive. The working memory factor was not unexpected, and the two forms were shown to be parallel enough to be encouraging. *However, and perhaps crucially, there was no evidence of the behaviour of the analogues in computers, because there simply were not enough centres in the UK equipped to demonstrate their effectiveness.* However, a second study in total computer context, available through collaboration with The United States Air Force Research Laboratory at Brooks Air Force Base, was to answer important additional questions and establish a climate of confidence for future joint projects. The results, shown with examples of ARCOM items in Chapter 9, were to prove comprehensive, giving evidence of, practice effects, reliability, construct validity, predictive validity, and, uniquely, a demonstration of the application of three basic performance models available through the use of tests in microcomputers.

---

6   See Table 9.3 in Chapter 9 for examples of tests used in ARCOM.

SUMMATION

The strength of these various approaches in the development of parallel forms depending on declarative knowledge can be gauged from the average proportion of variance explained in studies where the studies show the success with which the proportion of passes for each item is predicted (see Irvine, 2002, p for a list). This is .796 equal to R of .89. Moreover, the fundamental approach taken, of cognitive modelling, transfers elegantly across domains. Certain cognitive parameters of items would generalize. When these recur using relatively easy items, particularly in mass screening where the capacity to process new information is the primary construct, item-response-theory could be dispensed with entirely; or reinvented to incorporate time to complete the item as another major area of concentration (see Dennis and Evans 1996; Evans and Wright 1993; Mislevy et al. 1991; Wright, 1990, 1992, 1993, 1997).

THE SIX MULTIPLE PARALLEL FORM PROTOTYPES FOR BARB

Paper and pencil analogues were a necessary precursor to BARB. The previous pages can do no more than show what they were, but they cannot reveal the extent of the effort involved to get to the point where BARB could be implemented. They can give an overview of the issues involved, the main purpose of the book as a whole, where the account of what happened shows what lessons were learned and what the curriculum for test development in the twenty-first century might contain. This section now reveals what the first BARB system contained, in the knowledge that multiple parallel forms were constructed and used at all times. The illustrations are those best available to give an idea of how the items appeared on screen. Detailed references for the item types and their theoretical frameworks introduce each test. In describing the first, and perhaps the easiest of the BARB tests, a basic counterbalanced framework for test design is added.

BARB'S COMPUTERISED ITEM GENERATIVE TESTS

Letter Checking (LC) Task

Symbol Rotation (RF) Task

Transitive Inference (Who?) Task

Alphabet Forward And Backward (AFB) Task

Number/Letter Distance (ND/LD) Tasks

Semantic Identity/Distance (SI/SD)

Projectile (PJ) Test ('Time Estimation')

LETTER CHECKING (LC) TASK

Psychometric factor: General Speed Gs. Knowledge: Alphabet letters upper and lower case.
Cognitive Model: Semantic encoding and comparison (Sternberg 1966; Posner, Boies, Eichelman, and Taylor, 1969; Reuning, 1978, 1983; Hunt, Lunneborg, and Lewis, 1975; Irvine and Reuning, 1981; Irvine, Schoeman, and Prinsloo, 1988).

This is a test to measure how quickly and accurately people can carry out simple checking tasks. Its origin in BARB derived from comprehensive experimental work by Irvine and Reuning (1981) and extended in Irvine, Schoeman and Prinsloo (1988) wherein the Posner cognitive model was verified as a cross-cultural universal across language groups. The Posner model predicted changes in the difficulty of items depending on what case of letters (same or different) and whether same pairs or different pairs of letters were sought. There are four vertical pairs of letters in each problem. Below the letters, on the screen, are five response boxes with the digits 0 to 4 in them, corresponding to the range of possible answers. In this example there are THREE pairs, ignoring upper and lower case representation, that have the *same name* and the correct answer is 3. The participant needs to study each problem, decide how many pairs have letters of *the same name*, in spite of *the case of the letters being different*, and touch the response box containing the correct answer.

Look at this example:

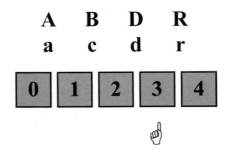

Here are two more examples. The correct answers are shown.

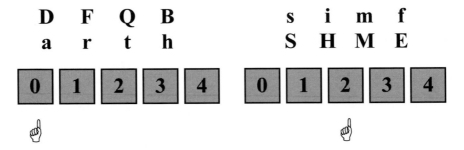

GENERATIVE FRAMEWORKS: LETTER CHECKING EXAMPLE

Previously, the framework for presenting mathematics items in multiple parallel form arrays was detailed. To give one more example of how the tests were *formulated,* an extract from a memorandum circulated among laboratory members for comment on the presentation of *Letter Checking Test* items provides a coherent framework. The focus is on the test just described. It deals with the item type, the number of items to be created in the paper-and-pencil tests that were created for the first trials and the size of a randomised block of items to be generated. *The fundamental principle is the design and production of a block of items that will measure performance in as short a time as is possible without undue emphasis on speed.* Repeated trials at the same type of item ensure that the mental processes involved in the test are sampled adequately to a point of relative stability. These designs were produced with the need to make paper-and-pencil analogues on A4 paper until such time as computers were installed at Army Personnel Selection Centre.

Item Type and Test Size: Although a number of possible letter comparison tasks were possible, (see Irvine and Reuning, 1981) there is only one item type in the test - Different Case-Same Pairs Search (DCSPS) for the number of matches. The item type is shown in the illustration. In a trial with undergraduate students, this type produced a mean of 65.5 in 3 min with a range of 46 to 89. If there are 140-200 items per form for 5 minutes of testing, this requires 60 items per page - 12 rows of 5 for 3 pages gives 180, while 12 rows of 5 gives 120 in 2 pages. With 12 rows of 8, this would produce 192 items in 2 pages. With 5 possible choices per item, 0, 1, 2, 3, 4, meaning that the distractor framework is unchanged for each item.

Block Design: There are good reasons for taking the block of items as 40. The preliminary mean scores suggest that many will manage nearly 3 blocks of 40, while the slowest will manage 2 only. Order will be randomised within each block made up of 40 items as specified, to a limit of 4 of any one solution (all same, etc.) There can be no runs of items, i.e. 1 same, followed by 2 same, followed by 3, followed by 4, though. There are 5 possible item answers (0, 1, 2, 3, 4 the same). Then there have to be 8 of each item answer type randomised per block of 40. These item types must be included. One can use this framework throughout if necessary.

Answer Type: All the same/ different gives only 1 way in which they can be all the same or none the same. That presents no problem. 8 of each are needed xxxx ---- . X denotes position of same-same pair and - a different pair. (16 total).

Answer Type: Three the same yields 4 different solutions, as does One the same (three different) Hence 2 of each solution, xxx-; xx-x; x-xx; -xxx; (three same with x; one same with - shows 16 total).

Answer Type: Two the same gives 6 positions - one of each: xx--; x-x-; x--x; -xx-; -x-x; --x; and two more like this, possibly,(x - - x; and - x – x;) *ensuring serial search to the end of the array,* a total of 8. This means that each solution type will have been tried with the same frequency by each person (on the average); and that order effects are counterbalanced within solution types in a block of 40 items generated in a counterbalanced random design.

This example is typical of the desire to counterbalance incidental difficulty effects produced by the test format and, with randomisation of answer formats within incomplete blocks, to ensure that if there were any effects that were not foreseen they would remain unbiased. Moreover, priming effects, that would occur when the same letters were repeated a number of times (making them perceived more quickly) were considered to be minimised by the random format and the relatively short test duration.

THE REMAINING CORE TESTS

The remaining BARB tests are now described along with the theoretical frames necessary for determining their use in item-generation protocols encoded so as to produce a unique parallel form for each new potential recruit. Block designs are not given for these, although an account of the construction of blocks for the next test, *Symbol Rotation,* is available in Irvine, Dann and Anderson (1990). On the whole, the remaining tests are more difficult than those demanding elementary literacy and numeracy, but the results showed a high degree of accuracy, especially when pre-test information and try-out analogues were available in information booklets. Nowadays, the entrance test information is available on line.

SYMBOL ROTATION (RF) TASK

Psychometric Factor: General Visualization Gv
Knowledge: Recognition of F and its mirror image.
Cognitive Model: Spatial Rotation (Shepard and Metzler, 1971; Just and Carpenter, 1985; Bejar, 1986a, 1986b, 1986c).

This is a test to see how quickly people can turn shapes around in their heads. The problem is to find - given a set of vertically opposite pairs of shapes - how many pairs in the set have two shapes the same. The basic BARB Symbol Rotation test displays two pairs of symbols from a complete set of four F shapes, and their corresponding mirror images. Shapes 1 to 4 are an 'F' shape at rotations of 0°, 90°, 180° and 270°. Shapes 5 to 8 are mirror-images of 'F' shapes at the same rotations. Given a 'font' where the numbers 1 to 8 are rotated F shapes as shown, it is convenient to provide sets of random numbers in a suitable block design and convert to shapes.

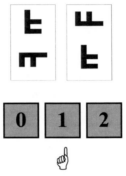

The example shows a typical item in the RF test. Note the pairs to be compared are 'boxed' to ensure that there is no doubt as to which pair is to be compared, and to focus attention on each pair. The two symbols that make up the first pair (in the first dotted-line box) are the SAME symbol at different rotations; in the second pair one symbol is a rotated 'F' and the other is a rotated mirror-image 'F' - so these are DIFFERENT.

The correct response, as shown above, would be '1' because only one pair contains symbols that are the SAME, after mental rotation. The BARB system asked for comparisons of two pairs of symbols; but more difficult versions involving the comparison of three pairs were prepared for use in the ARCOM (Army Regular Commissions Board) tests. These were subsequently used for extensive study in the Royal Navy and with USAF recruits in predicting learning efficiency.

TRANSITIVE INFERENCE (WHO OR TI) TASK

Psychometric Factor: Fluid General Intelligence Gf.
Knowledge: Comprehension of simple sentences; use of comparatives and negatives in assigning meaning.
Cognitive Model: Decisions based on structural determinants of sentences (Clark, 1969, 1970; Clark and Chase, 1972; Evans, 1982).

This is a test of simple reasoning ability. Each problem is about who is taller or shorter or brighter or duller - or something else - than another person.

An item in the simple test could look like this on the first frame on the computer

> # Fred is not as short as Bill.

Participants can study this simple sentence for as long as they need to understand it. When ready with the answer they must touch the screen. The sentence will disappear and a question will then be shown with two possible answers in response boxes. This appears on the second screen.

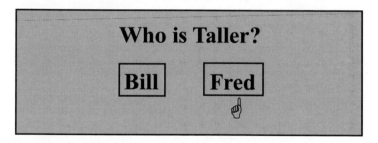

The above example shows that the participant would touch the box with 'Fred' in it for the correct answer. The time to encode the first statement and the time to choose the answer are both recorded. More difficult versions of the Transitive Inference task involved three terms. For example, here are analogues.

(Screen 1)

> # Jack is taller than Bill.
>
> # Bill is taller than Fred.

(Screen 2)

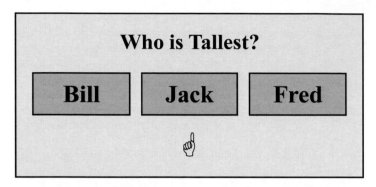

Later versions of the three term series task involved items to deter strategies such as ignoring the repeated term – here Bill – and simply guessing on the remaining two, would result in failure. Nothing is ever as simple as it may seem at first glance.

ALPHABET FORWARD AND BACKWARD (AFB) TASK

Psychometric Factor: General Memory Capacity Gm.
Knowledge: Alphabet letters in sequence from first to last.
Cognitive Model: Reconstructive memory task (Hockey, Maclean, and Hamilton, 1981; Hockey and Maclean, 1986; Woltz, 1987).

This is a test to see how quickly and accurately people carry out simple memory tasks. To solve the problems you need to know the alphabet and the order of the letters in it. The problem is to find what letters come next when you are told to move forwards or backwards in the alphabet. Look at these examples.

A + 1 = B.   **1 step <u>forward</u> (+) from A is letter B.**
B + 3 = E.   **3 steps <u>forward</u> (+) from B is letter E.**
R - 1 = Q.   **1 step <u>backward</u> (-) from R is letter Q.**

Here are examples with two letters.

A D + 1 = B E.

One step forward (+) from A is B <u>and</u> one step forward (+) from D is E

B E - 1 = A D.

One step backward (-) from B is A <u>and</u> one step backward (-) from E is D

The problem is on the screen with three empty response boxes underneath it. As soon as the problem is solved the screen must be touched.

A problem appears on screen:

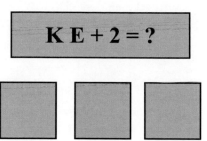

After the screen is touched, three possible answers appear *on the same screen* below the problem, one in each box:

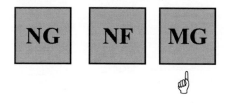

The correct answer (indicated above) has a response deadline of approximately two seconds. If one of the answers is not selected within the deadline, the message 'Too long!' is shown and the program proceeds to the next item.

NUMBER DISTANCE (ND) TASK

> *Psychometric Factor: Working Memory (Numbers) Mw.*
> *Knowledge: Order of numbers to specified range. Number facts for one and two-digit subtraction pairs within the range specified.*
> *Cognitive Model: Decisions based on number retrieval (Moyer and Landauer, 1967; Parkman, 1972; Groen and Parkman, 1972).*

This is a test to see how quickly and accurately people carry out simple number tasks in their heads. Three numbers are displayed each in a square response box. Participants need to find the HIGHEST and the LOWEST of the three numbers and then decide whether the HIGHEST or the LOWEST is further away from the REMAINING number.

Here is an example.

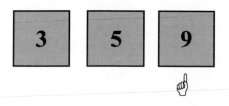

These three numbers are correctly ordered. 3 is the LOWEST and 9 is the HIGHEST. 9 is further from the REMAINING number 5 than is 3 and so the answer to the set '3 5 9' is 9 so the participant should touch the box with 9 in it.

Here's another example:

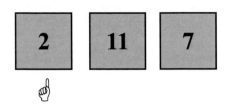

This time the numbers are not arranged in order from lowest to highest; the order has been mixed up. The task is still the same i.e. to find the LOWEST and HIGHEST numbers first and then decide which of these is further from the remaining number. It is marginally more difficult than then when the numbers are ordered lowest to highest reading left to right. The answer is to this example is 2 and the participant should touch the box with 2 in it.

SEMANTIC IDENTITY/DISTANCE (SI/SD)[7]

> *Psychometric Factor: Verbal (Meaning Categorisation) V*
> *Knowledge: Meanings of relatively common words and recognition of similarities and differences*
> *Cognitive Model: Semantic Identity: Collins, A. M. & Quillian, M. R. (1969, 1972); Collins, A. M. & Loftus, E. F. (1975); Glass, A. L., Holyoak, K. J. & Kossan, N. E. (1977); Smith, E. E., Shoben, E. J. & Rips, L. J. (1974); McCloskey, M. & Glucksberg, S. (1979); Rips, L. J. (1984); Rips, L. J., Shoben, E. J. & Smith, F. E. (1973).*

This is a test to see how quickly people can spot the odd word out in a group. Participants are presented with three words in response boxes on the screen. Two of the words will be related in some way; the third is the odd one out.

Look at the following example, already illustrated as an 'ideal' item type:

'Thief' and 'Robber' have the same meaning and so the odd word is 'scent'. For each problem the participant should touch the response box with the correct word. Although this example shows two words of similar meanings, it was possible to construct items where the two words are related as *opposites* (Dann and Tapsfield, 1995).

For example in a triad *Strong, Clock and Weak*, the second word is not related to the pair of opposites about strength, and is the odd one out. Of particular importance in the construction of this test were controls on the frequency of the words and on the degree of semantic distance. See Dennis (2000) for an elegant and informative account of the framework he adopted for constructing similar items in his work for the Royal Navy. Validation of this type of task with the other core BARB tests is described in Chapter 7 where they were used to predict how successfully electronic gate structure is learned. The SI test ran until all 60 items had been attempted, or for a maximum of 6 minutes.

PROJECTILE (PJ) TEST ('TIME ESTIMATION')

Psychometric Factor Memory for Time Intervals Mt
Knowledge: Parabolic Paths of Launched Objects; Gravitational Effects
Cognitive Model; Gibson (1979),(Lee & Reddish (1981); Lee, Young,
Reddish, Lough & Clayton, (1983), Shephard, (1984) Pellegrino &
Hunt, (1988).

This is a test of a participant's ability to estimate the amount of time an unseen moving object (the 'ball') describing a parabolic trajectory will take to travel a known distance. This was known as TP2 and the account of its validation is available in Chapter 9.

For each trial an item is displayed similar to the illustration:

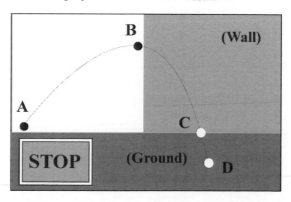

The ball begins at rest at position A and then follows a parabolic trajectory. When the ball reaches the wall at position B it disappears but continues to fall 'behind the wall' as if under the influence of gravity. The participant must judge when the ball would hit the ground (at point C) and show this by pressing the STOP response box. The participant is informed of the position of the ball at the time the response is made (e.g. point D if the time is over-estimated) or a message is displayed if the ball would have left the screen or the participant has exceeded the time allowed for that trial.

In the PJ test the ball moves with three different initial angles at each of four different speeds; each combination of speed and angle is repeated four times giving 48 trials in total.

<table>
<tr><td>

BARB'S WINDOW

Open and Shut Case

</td><td>

THE BARB WINDOW:
ANALOGUES AND EXTENSIONS

Operational use of tests was a primary target. However, there was always good reason to explore the potential of other item types because the design of BARB included a window of 15 minutes to include experimental versions. From the outset, a

</td></tr>
</table>

window of opportunity for test development was an integral part of the design of the computer-delivered system, fully supported by the Army Personnel Research Establishment. With their concurrence, a window was to present new or modified test items for a specified time limit at the end of normal BARB testing at the recruitment centres. Moreover, the window was designed as a 'carousel' that could contain any number of individual tests, limited only by the predilections of their constructors. Only one of these tests, rotated at random, would be given to an individual applicant and the results of that particular test could be referenced against all the other cognitive tests in the existing BARB battery. This meant that a number of tests could be trialled over the same period of time, and that the numbers of applicants attempting any one test were roughly equal. A comprehensive study suggesting an extension of BARB, was provided in a report circulated by Tapsfield (1996) and is reviewed in Chapter 7. The window was not used again for reasons never specified, but reportedly because of 'a need to shorten the time taken to administer BARB'. This decision meant that the inexpensive try-out of replacements could not happen, defeating one of the prime purposes for which the multiple parallel form BARB system was developed.

A LONG TACTICAL CAMPAIGN: THE END OF THE BEGINNING

From this distance, the effort involved to produce the first operational multiple parallel form computer-delivered system to recruits who had never seen a computer before seems to have been great in order to produce just seven tests. However, some comfort might remain when the uniqueness of the product is considered. It had to begin somewhere, and it had to begin with paper-and-pencil analogues, because the military arms were getting ready for computer-delivered operations. One might recall a comment by a commander at Army Personnel Recruit Centre when informal discussions took place about the projected speed of change. He advised patience and restraint; and likened the army to an elephant, slow to move but eventually with relentless advance. What was the first step to be taken by the mammoth, if not startled by the prospects of a mouse when touchscreens were at hand?

Table 6.5: Parallel Forms Analysis (N = 28)

Tests	Form A	Form B	AB/2				
	Means	Means	Mean	SD	rtt	K	Time Mins
Letter Checking	49	48	49	9	.79	80	4
Symbol Rotation	52	56	54	16	.91	110	7
Transitive Reasoning	47	48	48	11	.88	70	5
Alphabet Forward Back	30	32	31	7	.82	60	10
Number Skills	50	48	49	17	.94	80	5
Average	46	46	46	-	.87		
					Totals	400	31

First Trial: A Simple Inexpensive Crossover Design
Two parallel forms each of the normal level ABC tests for providing a general training level index were produced in analogue *paper and pencil form*. A purposive platoon of 28 regular soldiers based at the Army Personnel Research Establishment took part. The senior NCO in charge of the resident platoon was asked by one of the experimenters[8] to provide two evenly-matched teams of 14 volunteers. The actual randomisation of the groups was not essential, since the object was to allow more than one trial at a parallel form of the test, in order to extend the range of responses and to estimate the amount of learning that one repetition on a parallel form might produce. The two groups of 14 participants were administered either Form A or Form B on the first trial and the alternative form on the second trial. Testing took place on a single morning, in two sessions each, including instructions and prior practice, of 1hr. and 10min. with a tea break. Tests were administered by a single male presenter who used overhead transparencies as illustrations and examples. Tests were hand scored using templates.

The summary Table 6.5 shows that the null hypothesis of no differences between forms was upheld for this small group. K is the number of items in a test. Means fell well within the large standard errors produced by small samples; and pronounced score dispersion. Estimated reliabilities were in the range serviceable to good. A second, much larger replication took place using more forms and more participants. This is included in Chapter 7, with the collated evidence for parallelism, reliability and validity in a number of independent studies.

---

8   Dr. John Anderson. He reckoned that the senior NCO knew these men as well as anyone and could be relied to
     provide two evenly matched groups.

CONCLUSIONS

In retrospect as John Anderson's foreword on BARB confirms, this was only the beginning to an enterprise that fundamentally changed recruitment tests for the British armed services and persisted for more than twenty years. Consider how different things were from 1991, when the computer-delivered versions were first available. Every new applicant received a new form of every test in real time. The test window gave a unique opportunity to develop and evaluate new tests parsimoniously. Output was designed to contain not only scores, but the radicals involved in each item, latencies both to comprehend screens and to respond. Not only were the scores used as norms and cut-offs for selection, they, and all the additional information stored in the database had extensive research capabilities because more than one scoring model was always implied in the output. Moreover, security was never an issue, because even the recruiting sergeants did not know the answer to any one test on any one day. To validate the system was Macdonald's fifth lesson. That was in itself a new era not necessarily under the control BARB's creators. Various campaigns, independently designed by MOD officials, or in collaboration with the team at Plymouth, had to follow before proof was available. When one considers that BARB went operational in 1991-92, publication of criterion validity studies involving the computer-delivered system began to be made public at international conferences from 1995. Between nation-wide coverage and the appearance of reports and journals, the negotiations, approvals for access to recruits, data collection and analyses all took their time and their toll of energy. The story of how well the principles involved in parallel form test construction produced measures for successful recruitment and further training begins first in studies with the British Army and then with the Royal Navy, in Chapters 7 and 8 respectively.

CHAPTER 7

LESSON 5: BARB VALIDATIONS USING MILITARY CRITERIA

Essentially, the algorithms responsible for BARB manufacture the tests because the evidence determines a theory-driven production system. It follows that parallel forms of the tests should be produced consistently, with only random variation in descriptive test statistics from form to form. The structural parallelism of the tests, using as few participants as possible, becomes the main issue. In Chapter 6 a trial involving a platoon of twenty-eight recruits was the first step. At the Army Personnel Selection Centre a more comprehensive verification of the paper and pencil tests; and once computers were installed, real-time multiple parallel forms were the goal. The outcomes are the first part of the chapter. The plan depended on data external to the tests themselves, and required substantial testing time with candidates. Their reactions to computers, keyboards and touchscreens were sought and recorded.

BARB'S OUTCOMES

First Step Paper-and-Pencil

The Computer-Delivered Versions: The Interface, Prior Practice, Reliability, Tapsfield's Window

The Criterion Issue

Validation 1993-1997 Basic Training and Phase 2 Results BARB Takes Off: Air Force Studies

Recruitment with BARB: the First Decade

The Second Decade: Johansen's Revisions

Next, the BARB tests had to have stable internal features and confirmed construct validation. The working memory tests correlate well with each other and adequately with tests of declarative knowledge. Apart from construct validity, the tests predict performance in first phase and second phase training. After a review of the criteria used in military studies of validation, the second half of the chapter shows how well BARB versions correlated with the induction phase. The all-important second phase contains different courses for specialist occupations. A complete review of independent studies from 1992 until 1997 evaluates BARB.

PAPER-AND-PENCIL: THE FIRST STEP TO STANDARDISATION

A much more severe test of the hypothesis of test parallelism than a try-out with a platoon of men was hardly a surprise event. More certainty was sought. If the algorithms were correct, one could easily generate two parallel forms, producing many more items per form than required, and creating new forms by simply reversing the pages! Accordingly, Forms A and B from Trial 1 with the platoon were reversed to produce the new Forms C and D, such was the confidence in their parallelism. These were then colour coded by printing on coloured paper of equivalent luminosity. They are referred to as Blue, Green, White and Yellow Forms. During the last week of October, 1988, over 297 recruits were administered what were labelled as the ABC Tests by the same tester. Forms were distributed randomly, so that approximately 80 men took any one form. Session time was 1 hr. 10 min. Experience with applying paper-and-pencil tests in Africa (Irvine, 1986) was applied to devise administration procedures. Overhead projector transparencies were used to demonstrate and construct item types. After each practice item, correct answers were given and hands were raised to show how many had the correct answer. Understanding and motivation were the main goals.

The data included scores on all five tests and previous individual *Army Entrance Test* results, of which the most immediately relevant was a composite score of all the *Army Entrance Test* individual tests called TSG, a score used as a classification index for assignment to training depots. By studying the TSG distributions of participants in the various test colours, bias was detected. The group who had taken the White Form of the tests contained too many highly rated recruits and the Green group too many recruits of below average grades. The means of the tests in these groups were thereafter adjusted for the covariance effects of the TSG ratings.

Table 7.1: Descriptive statistics for ABC Core Tests and AETs (N=279)

							AET1	AET2	AET3	AET4	AET5	N
		LCT	SR	TI	AFB	NUM	Prob.	Instr.	Dom	V. R.	Num.	
Form												
Blue	M	51	56	55	34	52	28	34	32	62	37	79
	SD	9	23	12	14	22	12	10	10	24	15	
Green	M	50	56	51	31	47	29	33	32	60	37	75
	SD	11	18	13	12	22	12	10	12	24	16	
White	M	50	57	54	37	51	32	36	36	63	40	74
	SD	13	22	16	18	21	10	9	11	22	17	
Yellow	M	49	58	53	36	55	32	36	36	69	41	69
	SD	12	19	14	13	20	10	9	10	21	17	
All	M	50	57	53	34	51	30	35	34	63	39	297
Forms	SD	11	21	14	14	21	11	10	11	23	17	
SEM+/-		0.6	1.2	0.8	0.8	1.2	0.6	0.6	0.6	1.3	1.0	
Groups												
HI-LO		2	2	3	6	7	4	3	4	9	4	
Cohen's d		.2	.1	.2	.4	.3	.4	.3	.4	.4	.2	

Note: LCT Letter Checking; SR Symbol Rotation (F);TI Transitive Inference (WHO); AFB Alphabet Forward and Backward; NUM Number Fluency; AET1 Problems; AET2 Instructions; AET3 Dominoes; AET4 Verbal Reasoning; AET5 Arithmetic Numeracy.

Paper-and-Pencil Results from 297 APSC Participants Descriptive Statistics
Thereafter, it was possible to study the results for the purposive sample of 297, knowing
that the random assignment of test forms to different companies did not control for
differences in ability among the companies themselves. *The lesson from this is that
administrative necessity often determines the nature as well as the size of the sample
when group testing is required.* In such a situation the luxury of assigning a recruit
to a computer console at random and thereafter delivering a test form at random does
not exist. Nevertheless, these results provided a preliminary study of form parallelism
subject to sample variation. Results of previously administered *Army Entrance Tests*
provided by the Army Personnel Selection Centre (APSC) permitted concurrent as
well as construct validation of the analogue paper-and-pencil *ABC* core tests. The two
stage results are reported in Tables 7.1 and 7.2:

Standardisation: Checking on Parallelism
A comparison of the parallel forms was not straightforward because of the variation
in the group characteristics revealed by *Army Entrance Test* differences. *Army
Entrance Tests* scores for the groups identified by the colour of the parallel forms
were averaged so that the variation among groups, as identified by colours of tests,
could be estimated. The comparison between the two types of tests is shown in Table
7.2, using the original raw scores and in directly comparable standard deviation units
(Cohen's d) for each test. The table consistently shows that the variation between
parallel forms of the *ABC Tests* is never greater than the test variation for any one of
the *Army Entrance Tests* for the same groups of recruits. In short, the parallel forms
variability is of the same order as that of variation between randomly assigned groups
of participants taking the same AET test.

Table 7.2: Intercorrelations and Factors of ABC and AET tests (N=297)

TEST	LCT	SR	WHO	AFB	NF	AET1	AET2	AET3	AET4	AET5
						Probl.	*Instr.*	*Dom.*	*V. R.*	*Num.*
LCT	1	36	42	39	41	21	31	25	26	33
SR		1	32	28	30	38	20	21	22	20
WHO			1	50	44	32	44	37	44	43
AFB				1	43	26	42	41	32	45
NF					1	32	34	41	26	49
Probl,						1	46	47	62	54
Instr.						48	1	60	54	63
Dom.						46	64	1	44	67
V. R.						64	56	44	1	57
Num.						49	68	65	63	1
						AET	1986	(N=708)		
Factor1	-07	-06	11	16	13	68	72	76	70	82
Factor2	66	52	63	52	56	-02	05	-01	00	04
								N=279	R12	.65

Notes: *AET tests 1-5 described by lower matrix labels. Coefficients in lower diagonal element italicised for
1986 group of 708 recruits. Oblimin Factor loadings (F1 and F2) in bottom rows. LCT Letter Checking;SR
Symbol Rotation (F).TI Transitive Inference (WHO)AFB Alphabet Forward and Backward, NF Number
Fluency; AET1 Problems, AET2 Instructions, AET3 Dominoes, AET4 Verbal Reasoning, AET5 Numeracy.*

Concurrent and Construct Validity

The new information about the tests was contained in their individual correlations with TSG, a weighted composite derived from the five *Army Entrance Tests*, and used by the authorities as an index of occupational level. These correlations represent concurrent validities. They ranged from .50 to .65, values achieved after only a few minutes of testing. This means that they had qualities in common with the *Army Entrance Tests* used at the time, but had some specific qualities in themselves. The table of intercorrelations for all 10 scores that are experimentally independent is Table 7.2. Correlations that were derived from a group of 708 recruits tested in 1986 are also included to judge the typicality of the October 1988 results of the AET tests (Irvine, Dann & Anderson, 1990). The correlations of AET tests appear invariant across the two different samples, while the intercorrelations of the ABC and Army Entrance Tests define two separate but related influences in individual differences in test performance. One is in skills related to school achievements, the other in skills related to efficiency of information-processing on a low threshold of literacy and numeracy. There is also a clear sign of differential validity for the core ABC Tests. They correlate differentially with *Army Entrance Tests* of different types, and moderately with each other, unlike the *Army Entrance Tests* themselves, which have high and fairly uniform correlation with each other.

A Maximum Likelihood (ML) factor analysis[1] of the data matrix, shown in the lowest rows of Table 7.2 produced two factors. In general, the analysis confirms the predictions made about the core tests. One factor identified the *Army Entrance Tests*, with small loadings from the working memory tasks. The other was the working memory information processing efficiency factor that accounted for much of the covariation among the ABC Tasks. The two factors, when subjected to oblique rotational methods, correlated .65. There is a general factor that is not necessarily a determinant, but an outcome of the two complementary domains.

TRIALLING THE COMPUTER-DELIVERED VERSIONS: A NEW ERA

The move to a complete automated system did not occur overnight. First, a building was built at the Army Personnel Selection Centre (APSC) to house 30 computers and server. Once the equipment was ready, it was possible to begin to evaluate some, if not all, of the decisions taken in the construction of the BARB prototype. The very first questions in the move from hybrid trial versions to a completely computer-delivered system were the obvious ones. The choice of tests was no longer an issue. The questions that needed answers were easy to ask, but not so easy to answer. They were unknowns and they are listed in the next insert. The last question was important if test examples were to be provided to applicants before they took the test. Giving practice booklets before taking the test itself was a very real possibility when test security was no longer an issue, because every new applicant was provided with a unique parallel form and nobody knew the answers, not even the recruiting officers. Fairness and equal opportunity on the day were the goals underlying all of these questions. A second technical swathe of them concerned the reliability and validity, of the tests, their stability over time, and, not least, their fairness to minorities. These

---

1   Readers unfamiliar with factor analysis should regard this as a technique widely used to reduce the amount of data in a quest for order and sensible interpretation of the underlying nature of the tests used.

psychometric essentials were not immediately answerable, but were vitally important in ensuring the quality of those who were recruited compared with those who would be left out once the new system was operational.

THE INTERFACE DILEMMA: QWERTY AND TOUCH SCREENS

The work on computer-delivered tests began, knowing that the simplicity of the system was one of the keys to success, both in public relations and in ensuring technical soundness. Work began with samples of recruits who had already been selected by the existing *Army Entrance Tests* (AET). When asked to respond to questionnaires, the recruits apparently found the tests interesting and they appeared to enjoy what was for many their first encounter with what turned out to be a noisy computer environment, with thirty machines in the large room specially built for them. Liking the tests could well be a socially desirable response in an eager recruit, but the physical mode of answering test questions was not. Because the introduction of touchscreens had no precedent, their effect on results was of particular interest; and early research concentrated on contrasting them with modified *QWERTY* inputs, all varieties of mice being at that time so rare that they were not practicable, even if caught. Two early and seminal reports on the use of touch screens and the effects of prior practice were produced (Irvine, Anderson & Dann, 1990: and Irvine & Dann, 1990). Both reports were based on purposive samples of recruits already chosen by the existing *Army Entrance Tests* (AET). The individual test results for the *Army Entrance Tests* were available.

When all the data had been collated, a maximum number of 330 recruits were involved in the analysis of *Touch Screen* (TS) and *QWERTY* (QW) interface effects. The tests used were basic forms of the *British Army Recruit Battery*. Results for each test included scores adjusted for guessing, mean log time per item, and a power score, the adjusted score divided by the mean log time per item. Hand scoring had become redundant. The tests contained the core BARB items that were used throughout the early trials, with the exception of the projectile test, that has its own account in predicting ant-tank gunner training results in Chapter 8.

BARB'S UNKNOWNS

- *Was the system manageable by the staff in the recruiting offices?*

- *Did the applicants enjoy doing the tests in the computer?*

- *Were there any advantages to using touch screens over a modified QWERTY keyboard?*

- *Did the tests behave as one would want them to?*

- *Did prior practice make any difference to test scores on the day?*

QWERTY or Touchscreen?

Fortunately for the pace of progress, the results showed patterns and trends consistent with prior intuition and previous observed practices in the US military attempts at computer-delivery.

Overall, the *QWERTY* (QW) keyboard interface produced *slower average times to complete items, and fewer correct answers* on almost all of the tests. The effects of how the questions were answered by the two inputs compared two groups distinguished by high and low scores on the *Army Entrance Tests*. Below average performers on the *Army Entrance Tests* who used keyboards had consistently worse results compared with recruits of the same ability levels who were assigned to touchscreens. With above average recruits the differences afforded by the qualitatively different *QWERTY* and Touchscreen treatments were neither as strong nor as consistent.

Prior Practice
The enquiry into practice effects in the Army came before the concentrated three pre-test booklet studies in the Navy, reported in Chapter 8. All the materials related to the effect of prior practice on item types, not on identical items whose answers could be remembered. The test results compared paper-and-pencil and computer-delivered prior practice on one of two paper-and-pencil versions of the BARB tests. One version contained the original easier tests and the second an experimental, more advanced, form of the basic BARB tests. The sample size was 149 recruits.

Prior practice always made a difference, producing higher scores in both the easier and more difficult versions. Moreover, when initial *Army Entrance Tests* results were co-varied with the final test results, *those below-average recruits who had practised on the computer-delivered versions showed the greatest practice effects*. This suggested that the reason for below average performance was not so much lack of information, but lack of fluency in basic literacy skills. However, these early purposive studies were no more than indications of the effort needed to standardise and validate the BARB system. The results were not counter-intuitive, but given the nature and size of the samples they were hardly conclusive beyond doubt. But more was to follow once the system was up and running. And, even in paper-and-pencil mode, three independent studies with the Royal Navy reported in the next chapter, were destined to confirm the effects of prior practice.

THE ARMY'S LARGE-SCALE RELIABILITY AND STABILITY STUDIES, 1990-97

The nucleus of a larger team that was to carry on the initial work (Tapsfield 1993, Harris & Tapsfield, 1995, Wright, Irvine and Tapsfield, 1992, Wright and Tapsfield, 1995) completed the foundation work on the computer-delivered BARB tests. Some vital criterion validity studies were carried out independently by MOD officials themselves, who had no vested interest in the success of the BARB system (Holroyd, Atherton and Wright (1995a, 1995b). There were, as before, only two operational questions. How reliable are the tests? How valid were the scores in predicting training success? If a third question arose, its utility lagged behind the others, even if its answer was proof of what the tests measured. What skills and abilities did they measure; and just as important, what did they not measure?

Reliability and Stability over Time
Reliability has more than one meaning, and more than one way of calculating indices of consistency. For the most part, discussion of BARB reliability takes three forms: Scores on timed sectors of the test, given on one occasion, correlated and corrected for length using the Spearman-Brown prophecy formula; Cronbach's alpha, or similar estimates of item homogeneity; test-retest consistency over time when the same

persons are tested twice using two different parallel forms, not the identical test. The re-test can be immediate, or after an undetermined time interval (time-lag), particularly relevant when an applicant takes the tests on a second occasion after the need to improve performance has been advised. Re-test opportunities after initial rejection, the availability of pre-test information either by practice or in pre-test booklets, the consistency of retesting using not identical, but parallel forms, all raise issues of stability of the norms used to accept or reject applicants. From 1993 onwards, one year after nation-wide use of the BARB system in the United Kingdom, results were available to provide the first real insight into the behaviour of multiple-parallel from tests where every new recruit was provided with unique test forms. The history of test use had not prior to this created any precedent.

RELIABILITY STUDIES

Two major investigations[2] into the reliability of the BARB military multiple parallel form tests were conducted (Wright, Irvine and Tapsfield, 1992: Wright and Tapsfield, 1995). The first, using 1877 male and 212 female recruits, established a model for timed tests. The computer output included times to complete test segments without interrupting the applicants, which would have been needed if paper-and-pencil tests were administered in groups. From the results, the tests were divided into timed quarters, and reliabilities determined after intercorrelating the quartets of scores and correcting for the effect of the reduced lengths of the test divisions. The final true score model described was unique in that it enabled the prediction of reliabilities for different times allotted to each test (Wright et al. 1992, pp. 1-5). Reliabilities for each test for times up to 10 minutes per test were estimated (loc. cit. p. 9), and forecasts made about the effects of reducing or increasing individual test times. These permitted the establishment of optimum times that maintained high reliabilities even after taking administrative convenience in recruit office timetables into consideration.

TEST/RETEST RELIABILITY

What Happened in the Interval??

Test/Retest Reliability: What Happened in the Interval?

Test reliability is always important, but it assumes social significance whenever applicants can re-apply for entrance. Army recruiters have never discouraged any one motivated enough to try again. The rules permitted unsuccessful applicants to apply for a retest after a minimum period of 28 days. With BARB in use, the potential recruit was given an entirely new form of each of the six tests in the battery. In his first review, Tapsfield (1993) quoted results from applicants who chose to re-apply during the first year of operational use of BARB. In an extended and definitive study (Harris & Tapsfield, 1995) reliabilities were checked again, with a greatly increased representative sample of applicants. On this occasion, the availability of *pre-test booklets* provided an additional factor in immediate and time-lagged testing. Some applicants did not have, or had not read the booklets by the time they reached the recruiting office, and others did. The Navy's experience (see Chapter 8) with their national sample predated this

---

2   Both led by Dr. David Wright of The mathematics Department, University of Plymouth. The true score model developed was his work entirely. See also Wright, (1993 and Wright, 2002).

result, although with paper-and-pencil tests.

In Table 7.3 the actual reliabilities for the times used in the different conditions identifying the test trials are given. At the same time, the results of the second study, conducted some three years later, with sample sizes with a minimum of 322 per test, are added. The 1995 extension included an assessment the effect of time reduction for the test series, using the Wright forecasting model. The 1993 and 1995 test/retest correlations for the two conditions, time lag and pre-test booklets are shown. The time-lag retest calculated from those subjects who were retested between 28 and 35 days after their initial test. Correlations are substantially lower than in the immediate retest condition, initiating a quest for plausible explanations. Harris and Tapsfield (loc. cit.) offer three possibilities. First, that the tasks set by the various tests are themselves too complex for many army applicants to understand and execute: but this is not supported by the substantial measures of internal consistency and *immediate* test/retest correlations. Another possibility lies in the complexity of the test instructions themselves. Difficult test instructions will affect the least able more than the most able and when they are fully understood, as in a re-test, changes in applicant rank orders will appear.

Table 7.3: Test/Retest Correlations. Immediate and Longer Term Retest[3]

TEST	Same Day			Four Weeks or More		
	1993	1995 Book	1995 No Bk.	1993	1995 Book	1995 No Bk.
Alphabet Forward Back	.80	.79	.80	.57	.51	.54
Letter Checking	.79	.77	.79	.79	.60	.61
Number Distance	.85	.84	.85	.64	.61	.60
Rotated Symbol	.89	.88	.89	.82	.78	.73
Semantic Identity	.75	.84	.75	.86	.83	.78
Transitive Inference	.74	.79	.74	.75	.70	.68
GTI	-	-	-	.88	.81	.77
Sample Size	400+	1972	>322	400+	1248	1007

Third, poorly developed basic skills in elementary addition and subtraction and knowledge of the order of the alphabet can be, and indeed are, improved given time between initial test and retest. Reasoning and semantic abilities, on the other hand, are not likely to change much. Greater improvements for the lowest scorers in test types depending on elementary literacy will radically change the relative standing of applicants. The plausible second and third explanations imply that the *correlations among the number and alphabet tests in the lapsed time retest condition are depressed by educational accident rather than by test design.* Training battalions tend to report, even in 2012, that recruit literacy and numeracy levels are consistently below those necessary for basic needs: reading visual aids, notices and signs; and doing simple calculations.

---

3   Tables 7.3 and 7.4 Reproduced by permission from Harris & Tapsfield, 1995, Crown Copyright. .

Test/Retest Score Patterns in the Time-lag Condition

Figure 7.1 provides evidence, based on averages from raw data in Harris & Tapsfield, (1995, p.17) for marked but uneven changes in test average scores, *the most pronounced improvement being for those recruits who initially have very low scores on the basic skills tests (AFB, LC and ND).* This group of tests also showed the lowest test-retest reliabilities in time-lag conditions, compared with their immediate reliabilities as seen in Table 7.3. Improvements, however, are indications of motivation to succeed, an unmeasured attribute and an intervening variable, one more case study of the vagaries of military criteria, where improvements over baselines reduce validity and reliability. These results are of signal importance in the development of psychometrics because they derive from tests where no memory for correct answers on initial testing can affect the results. Improvements in scores and decrements in reliability *were not memory functions introduced by repeating the same test.* Where major effect size changes like those in Figure 7.1 occur, they demand other plausible explanations. Number and letter tests show big increases, while the semantic and reasoning tests are less prominent. The largest increases are at the bottom of the range, suggesting that even when the literacy levels expected of 11 year-olds determine test construction, the results vary with attainments.

Figure 7.1: Retest Gain Score Contrasts by Initial Reliability Levels

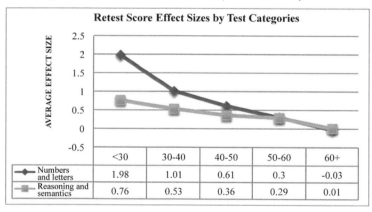

	<30	30-40	40-50	50-60	60+
◆ Numbers and letters	1.98	1.01	0.61	0.3	-0.03
■ Reasoning and semantics	0.76	0.53	0.36	0.29	0.01

The tests showing the greatest increases are the number and letter distance tests. There will be, among those who complete secondary school at the age of 16 having spent 10 years in classrooms, many who do not know with certainty the order of letters in the alphabet: and who cannot mentally carry out simple addition and subtraction. If they are motivated to reapply, it seems likely that in a very short time, they have acquired basic literacy and numeracy skills with dramatic improvement at the bottom of the scale.

Norms and Changes Over Time

Prior to the implementation of the BARB tests, estimates of applicant ability were obtained from extended trials of all tests at what was at the time the central Army Personnel Selection Centre. Data from these trials established provisional, or *anchor norms* for the operational tests. How good were they? Fortunately, the work by Tapsfield (1993a, 1993b) and Harris and Tapsfield (1995) provided substantive answers.

Table 7.4: Estimated And Observed Applicant Norms 1990-95.

	Estimated Norms		Norms 1993		Norms 1995	
TEST	Mean	SD	Mean	SD.	Mean	SD
Alphabet Forward Back	15.2	8.4	10.1	8.3	13.2	9.2
Letter Checking	35.0	10.0	37.3	7.7	41.1	6.8
Number Distance	27.8	11.2	20.8	11.8	25.1	11.5
Rotated Symbol	21.9	8.3	22.4	12.8	27.8	12.9
Semantic Identity	49.5	8.8	48.4	9.6	49.1	9.4
Trans. Inference	33.2	6.9	33.1	8.0	33.0	8.0
Projectile Task	87.3	4.1	89.9	3.9	76.4	8.8

After one year of operational use, the 1993 norms were compared with the anchor norms. In 1995, the exercise was repeated. For most tests, mean adjusted scores (See Table 7.4) for the applicant population fall within one or two points of the estimates. However, for two of the working memory tests involving manipulation of the alphabet (*Alphabet Forward and Backward* or *AFB*) and simple number comparisons (*Number Distance* or *ND*), estimates were optimistic. The *AFB* task yielded an actual mean score of 10.1 in 1993, compared with a trials estimate of 15.2, while the *Number Distance* task yielded a mean score of 20.8 compared with an estimate of 27.8. Table 7.3 has already revealed how dramatic the improvements were in the lowest scoring groups and how these could contribute to an accidental decrease in reliability. This by itself gives no indication as to the real extent of the low scores. Tapsfield (1993b) states that 20% of the applicant population performed at a level no better than chance on at least one of the tests; and that score distributions for every test included cases with scores four and even five standard deviations below the mean.

Not surprisingly, guessing behaviour was found to be most common in the two elementary alphabet order and number distance tests AFB and ND, where, as shown in Table 7.4, the average observed performance in 1993 and 1995 was considerably lower than estimates of average performance. However, even the simple letter-checking processing task that involves nothing more than matching upper and lower case letters of the alphabet, showed levels of accuracy at or below those expected.

Practice Effects
Detailed examination of initial and retest scores found that practice effects were larger than desirable, if the same norms were to be used for those who tried to enrol on more than one occasion. From Harris & Tapsfield's (1995) results summarised in Figure 7.1, the average effect size for an *immediate* re-test was calculated at 0.39 SD units. This increased to 0.60 SD units *after a time lapse* between initial and second test (Harris & Tapsfield, 1995, p.8) of a minimum 28 days. Typically, scores on time-lapsed retest are one half to two-thirds of a standard deviation greater than the initial test. However, the alphabet and the number tasks, produced much bigger improvements in longer term re-testing, *once more supporting the conclusion that improved performance occurs when there is time to review or learn the simple prerequisites for performance on tests requiring the most elementary educational knowledge.* Tapsfield (1993b, p. 17) has summed up the extensive studies of norms and reliabilities admirably. One can do no better than let him conclude.

'Not only is the increment in score larger than is desirable, but it is also persistent. Inspection of score increments for retests occurring up to 100 days after initial test indicates no apparent decrease in increment with time. Any change appears to be limited to an increased variability in retest performance. This has implications for retest policy as it suggests that very lengthy intervals would be required between initial test and retest for practice effects to dissipate. Alternatives to lengthy statutory intervals include the use of retest norms, thereby adjusting scores to counter the effects of practice, or familiarising applicants with the tests prior to the initial test session, in order to minimise practice effects.'

Tapsfield's experience was applied in the second generation of multiple parallel form tests for use in Northern Ireland, the USA and Europe, reported in Chapters 9 to 13. Retest norms were to be standard issues in all future test development. Second time applicants had, in fairness, to be assessed using second time norms.

THE BARB WINDOW: ANALOGUES AND EXTENSIONS

Operational use of tests was a primary target. However, there was always good reason to explore the potential of other item types because the design of BARB included a window of 15 minutes to include experimental versions. From the outset, a window of opportunity for test development was an integral part of the design of the computer-delivered system, fully supported by the Army Personnel Research Establishment. With their concurrence, a window was to present new or modified test items for a specified time limit at the end of normal BARB testing at the recruitment centres. Moreover, the window was designed as a 'carousel' that could contain any number of individual tests, limited only by the predilections of their constructors. Only one of these tests, rotated at random, would be given to an individual applicant and the results of that particular test could be referenced against all the other cognitive tests in the existing BARB battery. This meant that a number of tests could be trialled over the same period of time, and that the numbers of applicants attempting any one test were roughly equal. A comprehensive study was provided in a hitherto unpublished report by Tapsfield (1996).

THE 1996 TAPSFIELD WINDOW: BARB BD EXPERIMENTS - THE 'LOST GENERATION'?
During 1995-96[4], and following independent validity studies, the BARB test 'window' was used for a prolonged period by members of the Plymouth team (Tapsfield, 1996) to examine the potential of five experimental tests that were termed BARB version BD. From the outset, the notion of continuous development of new tests was an integral part of the design of the BARB system. If

TAPSFIELD'S UNDISCOVERED AND UNUSED BARB:

The 'BD' Window

---

4   After Irvine retired in December, 1995, Paddy Tapsfield, A MOD senior psychologist colleague, became Head of Laboratory.

any lesson had been learned in the construction of BARB it was the cost in 1986 and the years that followed, of beginning again, when the old system had been compromised by time and technology.

Tapsfield produced a document for internal circulation at the end of 1996, with a number of innovations. These included the description of a new version of five experimental tests, labelled *BARB-BD*, to distinguish it from the first version known as *BARB-AC*. No published account of his work exists, a major effort at the validation of material at the boundaries of item-generation, alongside his other key contributions to the development of BARB (Tapsfield, 1993a, 1993b, 1993c, 1995, Tapsfield & Wright, 1993, Wright, Irvine & Tapsfield, 1992, Wright & Tapsfield, 1995, Harris & Tapsfield, 1995).

The five tests to be trialled were administered in recruitment offices across the United Kingdom so that data were collected ensuring a different representative random sample of applicants for each of the five tests. This strategy produced results on more than 1800 applicants for each test of which approximately one in five was female, with a total of more than nine thousand potential recruits involved. Individual performance comparisons across several experimental tests were not possible, but each version of the modified tests could be compared with its predecessors. The powerful paradigm and large numbers provided results that show how the horizon of BARB could be economically extended in the exploration of alternative scoring models, a complete review of which is contained in Chapter 5.

TAPSFIELD'S UNDISCOVERED AND UNUSED BARB-BD
Four of the five tests involved in a Tapsfield's *BARB-BD* window-trialled carousel were versions of tasks previously illustrated, either in BARB, or in the Navy Personnel Series (NPS). These were the *The Three-Symbol Rotated F Task, The Three-Term Series Deductive Reasoning Task (Untimed), and the Two Term Series in Timed (TM)* format, the *Wegfiguren or Path Tracing Test,* and an entirely new task type constructed for use in the window. This was called the *CD Task.* Tapsfield's detailed report provided reliabilities, correlations among tests and with the BARB general training index, several factor analyses and complete distribution statistics. Here, only illustrative data is summarised to reveal average differences among different versions of tests purporting to test the same qualities.

Table 7.5: Mean Scores by Type for Female, Male and All Participants

	RF2	RF3	T12	TI2(TM)	TI3	WF
F (N344)	24	19	35	30	6	9
M (N1639)	29	23	33	26	7	14
ALL (N1938)	28	23	33	26	6	13
Mean p Value	.83.	.81	.94	.79	.54	.58

The RF Test proved to be more difficult in its three pair form than in its two pair original, and the difference between female and male performance was of the same effect size, given variances that were almost identical. Reliabilities were good.

The TI Reasoning Test was compared in three versions, the original untimed, two sentence versions, a *timed* two sentence version and an *untimed* three sentence version. The difficulty values decreased markedly from the untimed original of .94 and proved to be much more difficult in the three term series. The time envelope made the two sentence original more difficult, as would be expected, but the general trend of better female performance in verbal comprehension and reconstruction in two-term versions was not upheld in the more difficult three-term test.

The Path Tracing Test

A previous study in the human assessment laboratory had involved the *Wegfiguren*[5] *Test* (Kirsch, 1971). In the paper and pencil versions of this test, reproduced by Goeters (1979, pp. 144 -152) in a repeated trials project, participants followed a drawn path visually on a printed page and count either the number of right or left turns. It was used in pilot selection originally. Estimates of parallelism potential were empirically determined by correlating the order of items in a paper and pencil version produced by Goeters with the radicals identified in the various items. The analogue illustration shows the answer to the first item where R asks for the number of RIGHT turns. The next one, with L in the box, asks for the number of LEFT turns, and so on. If the sequence is attempted, the starting position, the number of turns, and the overall length of the path to be followed - all will be seen to have their influence on difficulty.

Initial interest in the task prompted decomposition of the stimulus for each item used the line length from start to finish, the number of turns, start positions and the number of upside down turns as intuitively certain *radicals* influencing final item order in the test. In 1989, a linear regression model showed that the radical elements in the stimulus predicted p values of individual items with near certainty with a multiple r of .97.

Figure 7.2: The Wegfiguren Test in Paper-and-Pencil Form

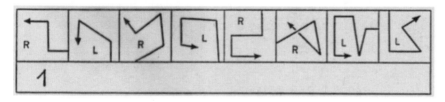

Tapsfield's computer-delivered trials were important because they confirmed the construction in the laboratory of a computer-delivered version, which showed a moving light trace the path to its end on the screen. The *Wegfiguren Test* was a good example of successful creation of a multiple parallel form of a spatial relations task. His work confirmed it as a potential supplement to other predictors of specialised aptitudes. Finally, Tapsfield describes a demanding continuous memory task in which sequences of letters have to be remembered given prior determinant rules for comparison of an existing letter with the one that follows. Results were preliminary, and a follow up not attempted. Having no analogue or research history, comparisons with existing tests were not made.

---

5   An ingenious computerised version was developed by Nigel Barlow and David Wright, University of Plymouth. The paths in practice items were traced by a moving light.

TAPSFIELD'S CONCLUSIONS

Tapsfield's conclusions are important first-hand contributions and these are summarised. He explains that the experimental tests contained in BARB version BD were developed for a number of different reasons. The timed two-term item transitive inference task was seen as a way of reducing test time. For the 3-term transitive inference task and the 3-pair rotated symbol task the aim was to increase difficulty. Results from the 3-pair rotated symbol version offered no greater reliability or validity than was already available from the 2-pair version. The only reason to use it would be an increase the number of alternatives offered with less incentive to guess. The *Wegfiguren* test was included to enhance the spatial domain. It appeared to be adding to the rotated symbol task in the spatial domain and further research for certain groups requiring high-level spatial skills was indicated. None of Tapsfield's 'window' initiatives were operationalised by the sponsors of the research. In fact, the BARB window was discontinued because with it, BARB took more than an hour in the recruitment offices. It shared the same fate as the BARB *Projectile Test*, whose promise is discussed in Chapter 8.

PREDICTIVE VALIDITY RESULTS 1993-1996: THE CRITERION ISSUE

It seems very likely that expertise in evaluating military criteria lags some way behind that involved in test construction. This lack of studies that reveal the nature of military criteria puts new test programmes at considerable risk. Because studies of criteria content and reliability are seldom executed and even less frequently published (but see Jones, 1984), the case study material in this chapter serves as illustrations of problems most likely to be encountered and which will be resolved more quickly than system-wide organisational variation.

EVALUATING MILITARY CRITERIA:

THE REALITIES

The traditional military solution to test validation is to follow the path to valid measurement of robust human constructs that are known to enter into occupational success. All the trends in modern measurement combine to reinforce the view that one must try to find out four things about a recruit that will be of permanent value; and that can be assessed regularly by various means in every military role throughout a soldier's career. These are basic information processing skills - mental alertness or general training index; special aptitudes; physical fitness and eye-hand coordination; and interest/motivational profile. Each will tell us something essential about personnel resources to match against needs. Any systematic review of the content of military selection tests shows that although experiments with non-cognitive tests have occurred in plenty, only one construct - general training capability – has been measured universally in Army recruit selection since 1914. Only recently has there been a complete and systematic review, for the United States Army, of the reliability or validity of non-cognitive composite scores (Campbell & Knapp, 2002, pp. 304-305). Changes in basic measurements would be as important as permanence, because in the long run, the record will not lie.

In using all of these to predict outcomes, one has to be mindful of the view attributed to Cronbach that the simplest way to invalidate a test battery is to use a criterion that is inexpensive, field-based, subjective and unsupervised. If this is a counsel to perfection, it seems hardly surprising; from this distance that Macdonald's criteria of ratings by groups of NCOs and Officers of Askaris in camps awaiting repatriation should prove unrewarding.

EVALUATING MILITARY CRITERIA: THE REALITY
In pursuing criterion, or predictive validity, the aim is to select those candidates whose predictor characteristics maximise the probability of criterion success and minimise the possibility of failure. The mathematics involved is usually the fitting of a linear regression model to the predictor and criterion data. Because so much of selection for enrolment is based on tests of aptitude, the simplest and at the same time most appropriate model for military criterion studies is that criterion behaviour C is a function of ability A in the soldier and the military situation S in which the behaviour is required.

In short, C = f (AS) .... **Formula 7.1**

The discussion that follows tries to find the limits of models of military selection that are patterned after the formula $C = f(AS)$. Any observed measurement of criterion behaviour carries with it individual variation in the ability required to perform the role that constitutes the criterion: and the interaction of that ability with the military requirements. Just as individuals may be expected to vary in their levels of ability, so the situations may be expected to differ in the variables that define them - in particular those variables that are concerned with the logistics of training large groups of people, in moving them from treatment to treatment in an orderly way, and in determining those factors in training that affect performance but which are not captured in ability measures.

MATHEMATICAL AND LOGICAL ASSUMPTIONS
The effectiveness of the test scores in a regression equation is maximised by weighting and adjusting the cut-off points in the predictors and pass-fail rates in performance in training to produce the fewest number of admitted-fails and not-admitted successes. Solutions to these problems are mechanical, complete tables having been available for some considerable time (See Taylor & Russell, 1939). Such models are most likely to capture useable variance in the predictor where ability may be expected to influence the outcome when training occurs immediately after selection in a single training depot. It follows that one of the most debatable contexts for the operation of the model is the long-term or continuous use of the selection tests and their actuarial weightings in large number of different training depots - the norm rather than the exception. That problem is discussed first.

Continuous Use of Cut-Offs
The use of any fixed set of cut-offs for the tests and criteria assumes that the relationship between predictors (entrance tests) and outcomes (proficiency in training or service performance) remains unchanged over time. Almost invariably, such an assumption proves to be theoretically optimistic and practically unsound (Cronbach

& Gleser, 1957). The most common breakdown in the long-term application of the model is failure to make regular and informed adjustments to predictor test cut-offs and profiles. Once people get accustomed to tallying scores and scaling them in a certain fashion, it seems that changes seldom occur. When the system eventually reports training problems or unsatisfactory trainee performance, failures are then laid at the door of the selection tests, often quite wrongly. Research invariably reveals that the logic of the selection model can be discarded by policy changes over the years (cf. Johansen, 2011).

Lack of Fixed Treatments
One of the assumptions of fixed ability (A) cut-off and non-adaptive linear prediction models is a fixed treatment (S) effect. When policy dictates that everyone be treated alike in testing and in training, no adjustment for treatment is needed to stabilise the weights given to different predictors. In soldier recruitment, use of such a fixed treatment model requires that the probability of success is constant from depot to depot and cohort to cohort. If not, then a model for each depot has to be derived.

If the probability of success is not identical from depot to depot arid/or intake to intake, the fixed effects model - using the same cut-offs in the selection tests for everyone - breaks down. The odds-ratios for success would not be constant. Then, either the test or criterion cut-offs should vary, or both, to preserve the policy of equal opportunity from the same test score. If this perfectly logical action were taken, then it might not be politically defensible. Bias could be a correct conclusion, but it would derive from unequal pass rates at the depot, not in test cut-offs. Thus the fixed-model for prediction of success or failure is weakened whenever training depot inconsistency is detected. The knowledge presently available defines four organisational variables that seriously affect the use of fixed-linear models in soldier selection. Any one of them would disqualify the model. All four of them may co-operate in any selection system, regardless of the branch of service.

Four Censors of Criterion Validity
First, the percentage drop-out or attrition from the training depots is not same for every type of training, or year on year. This variability ensures that the weights attached to tests become dysfunctional for failure rates that violate the assumptions of the original weights given to predictors based on percentages of success and failure.

Second, constant changes in staffing are part and parcel of military life although staff permanence is a feature of outstanding training organisations. Staff in training regiments is posted in and out, two years being the norm, and the frequency of such postings is a variable that can be quantified. In fact staff changes are often made deliberately to effect changes in practice - "to give the place a good shake up." This implies that the treatment of recruits (S) may be an unknown and variable function of regular changes in the staff of training regiments. The consequences of staff changes on those variables that define the situational part of the basic $C = f(AS)$ model are unknown, because they have not been studied.

Third, the boundaries shift in the tests without any control for seasonal adjustment, because mechanisms for continuous feedback of results to make compensatory shifts in weights possible at short notice are virtually unknown. Because the results of variability in training depots are always post hoc and because they may not be stable from year to year, the law of supply and demand is an unknown change element whose effects are traceable only in outcomes - differential pass rates. It was not uncommon to hear from recruiting offices that they were 'scraping the bottom of the barrel'. As no modelling of quota effects has ever seemed possible, their contributions to failure rates are neither predictable in nor accountable to the selection procedure.

Fourth, able recruits leave the service in unpredictable fashion before voluntary exit limits (see Irvine, 2013a), even if rated highly in initial training, and are thereby selection successes. This can be correctly judged to be not a failure of selection, but a failure of retention. These failures of retention cannot then be logically included in criteria against which to regress selection instruments used to predict success in previous stages: but they are used for such purposes politically because there is no other useful information available from a screening battery that has no other domains but abilities.

TWO CASE STUDIES:

The Unfit Infantryman

The 'Maladjusted' Naval Cadet

BENIGN CRITERION CENSORS IN TWO SERVICE ARMS

The first case study in how retention rates may be made to vary by altering treatment or (S) functions was provided by the Officer Commanding APSC, Sutton Coldfield during the trial of the BARB system. The colonel's work was focussed on 'D' grade physical fitness recruits. These are recruits whose physical fitness and coordination were at the lowest acceptable level on a four point scale A to D. He decided to ask 'D' rated recruits to spend two weeks at APSC undergoing a graduated and relatively non-stressful orientation to routines and drills calculated to improve coordination, fitness and self-esteem. His two-week physical orientation period for recruits initially judged lacking in physical robustness resulted in all but two out of ten being recommended for next stage training. In a follow up of 500 of these self-same 'D' rated prospects traced over all training depots, the overall retention was in the region of 78%, compared with only a 50% single probability of training success of 'C' recruits going straight to the infantry training depot.

This was a fine achievement. Nevertheless, study of the predictive efficiency of the Physical Fitness Tests used for selection, in ignorance of this work, would show that they failed to predict training success. The relative success of 500 'D' soldiers would confound the initial grades awarded. Because benign intervening treatment was given only to those at the outer rim of the distribution of initial physical ratings, the correlation if all soldiers in all groups were included would certainly be much reduced and would cast doubt on the validity of the physical assessments prior to induction.

One last word. Asked what the secret of his success was, the colonel replied unhesitatingly that it was due to the quality of his officers - the uncharted and unknown qualitative intervening variable. APSC's achievement is an outstanding example of an astute and well-timed empathetic exercise in *retention,* but it serves here as a prime example of the potentially misleading results of embarking on validity studies in *selective efficiency* of tests where the criteria are neither fully understood nor differentiated by construct and/or treatment.

CONTEMPLATING ONE'S NAVAL: OFFICER CADETS

In the next chapter, there is a comprehensive account of work with the Royal Navy. One study of officer cadets at British Royal Naval College, Dartmouth was possible only because of their unique centralised record system and the full cooperation of training staff. The context was not physical fitness, but success in military college examinations. Final marks in a variety of disciplines have served in the past as criteria for selection test validation. Scrutiny of all final examination marks included structural analyses showing that the pass-fail final mark was a heterogeneous mixture because of its specificity. How these examination marks, the criterion for pass/fail at Dartmouth, were moderated, provides the second relevant example. In the discussions with RN training staff, the team was able to create a climate of confidence. Analyses were never to offer or imply criticism of British Royal Naval College examination practices, the understanding being based on the knowledge that examination scores for pass or fail decisions are what they are for reasons of Navy policy. The most important policy aspect of final pass marks was *the customary effect of moderating actual performance to ensure that the threshold for pass had been achieved.* Knowledge of the facts, willingly provided by training staff, was vital to the interpretation of a study of test validities. This usually resulted in low marks being raised to make the pass level, but not the reverse to ensure failure! Without these facts one would draw the wrong conclusions from patterns of correlations between tests measuring abilities and examinations measuring officer candidate behaviour. The comparison with improving the 'D' level soldier is obvious. Too lengthy to describe here, the data analysis model showed that the normal examination practices of moderating and 'adjusting' actual candidate performance produce the following effects: distribution distortion; restriction of range; variance specific to certain types of examination; loss of candidate information by using weighted composites in a final pass mark. Any or all of these may contribute to a low correlation between selection tests and graduation results for officer candidates.

In short, when $C = f(AS)$, knowledge of the construction of C is paramount. Where S includes moderation of actual performance, the correlation between A and C is bound to be reduced. Without that knowledge, the relationship between C and A is not interpretable. If the correlations were used indiscriminately, the errors would actually be much greater than the forecast.

UNCONTROLLED TREATMENT EFFECTS

To conclude from the two quite distinct, but immediately analogous case studies., if criterion domain studies - including some of contextual treatment effects - are not undertaken, then the chances of nullifying the investment made in all new forms of test construction and delivery are very great. Criterion studies must in time lead to maximum likelihood estimates of performance in different training contexts, provided that the system is constructed to make use of the information provided from them. The argument advanced to this point asserts that the regression model we apply to long-term test validation studies in current training contexts is systematically misleading because of four censor mechanisms acting randomly on the S (situational aspects) of military criterion data: The unknown sources of variance

THE FOUR CENSORS

§ *uncontrolled variation in training standards*

§ *staff changes in training depots*

§ *ad-hoc and unmonitored shifts in test cut-offs required to fulfil quotas*

§ *the use of retention measures as criteria*

in criteria used at present constitute the major weakness in any new testing programme. The danger is that perfectly good tests are rejected because the criteria are themselves not subject to validity studies. It follows that the most self-destructive influence on test development is a lack of input into conventionally accepted valid and reliable criterion measures that are psychometric minefields. To summarise: in measurement terms, these four organisational contexts act as arbitrary censors in the selection process. Consequently the tested cohorts of recruits and the criterion elements are not the known constants which the fixed weights model demands. Any belief that there is, or indeed ought to be, or even could be "a satisfactory level of criterion validity" for any test battery used in contextual unknowns is difficult to sustain.

The Limits of Criterion Studies
Several different approaches were able to be tried out in non-operational circumstances. In the chapters that follow, examples of validation using the whole array of predictors, from abilities, to interests, personality and health related quality of life are provided. More importantly, perhaps, different criteria types are shown ranging from combat skills, simulated gunnery success, actual learning of electronic system concepts, and, perhaps looking to the future, job satisfaction and wellbeing.

COMPUTER-DELIVERED TESTS: BARB'S FOLLOW-UP VALIDITY STUDIES

Whatever else may be important for test use, criterion validity is always the key element. Moreover, validity takes many forms, so that there are as many trials to endure as there are forms. In short, the following types of validity are most commonly examined: *content, construct, discriminant, concurrent and predictive.* Each emphasises a different aspect of test use. Although some aspects of validity were pursued in trials during the construction of BARB, predictive validity studies of the BARB system had to follow after its operational introduction in 1992. Although Lewis-Cooper (1993) alerted the test construction team to questions arising from discussions with army trainers and testers that only validity studies could resolve, published evidence emerged when independent research results were published some years later.

EXTERNAL VALIDATION

Jacobs, Holroyd, Atherton and Wright in Phases 1 and 2

PREDICTIVE VALIDITIES
Undoubtedly, the most detailed search, involving

the greatest variety of army jobs and roles, is for evidence of predictive validity. If test scores predict success in training, then cut-offs for entrance to different training courses can be determined so as to provide the highest number of successes and the least number of failures. Correlation coefficients are used as indices of the degree of success or failure of tests because, as many psychology graduates today may fail to explain when asked, the Pearson correlation coefficient is the index of agreement that minimises errors of prediction. Most important were the several independent studies that took place, using BARB scores as predictors of training outcomes. In general, there are two stages in army training, Phase 1, in acquisition of basic army procedures, drills and know-how. Phase 2 is specialist training in a particular branch or force. Because the jobs in the army are equally as diverse as any multilateral industry, the criteria are manifold and of no guaranteed reliability.

Phase 1 Basic Training
Holroyd, Atherton and Wright (1995a, 1995b) examined the validity of BARB as a predictor in Phase 1 using a purposive cohort of 200 soldiers. A correlation of .26 between BARB scores and overall, conglomerate ratings at first sight seems to be scarcely adequate, but as in all conglomerates, detailed study provides an alternate view. Course criteria were marks on eight written tests and the ratings, provided by the training staff, on different field-based training exercises. *A hallmark of the work was the special attention given to collecting reliable information on a weekly basis, (Holroyd, Atherton and Wright, 1995a, p.180) and to correcting for differential rater effects.* When all was said and done, BARB scores predicted written test performance in basic training, with correlations varied from as high as .49 to a low of .05. Individual facets of variable results are shown in correlations with written tests of NBC Defence (r =.49), Military Law (r =.46), Military Education (r =.34) and Health & Hygiene (r =.37)), with an overall median .30 in the selected group. This is generally agreed to be much higher in the general recruit applicant population. BARB scores were equally successful in significantly predicting performance ratings in 10 fields, including Drill (.28), Skill at Arms (.30), Map Reading (.27) and Security (.45).

Jacobs's Phase 2 Specialist Training Performance
It could be remarked that the phase one study was exploratory, and scarcely conclusive, having used data from only 200 recruits. Basic training does not equip an entrant for the job that eventually has to be done. Here is Jacobs' own view (Jacobs, 1996, p.245).

'The Infantry performance ratings that correlate most strongly with GTI scores are maturity, common sense and weapon handling ..... Both common sense and maturity could be expected to have a relationship with general intelligence. The correlation between weapon handling and GTI scores could also be expected as good performance in weapon handling requires recruits to effect procedures, follow instructions and apply knowledge that has been acquired during training. Although significant, most of the other correlations are at best moderate in size. Whilst it could be argued that the mental demands of Infantry training are less than those in other arms, and that as a consequence GTI should have less of a relationship with training success, the fact that many weaker recruits are given remedial training, may serve to mask BARB's ability to predict training success. The observed correlations may therefore underestimate the true relationship between BARB and training performance.'

Phase 2: Jacobs' Specialist Training Enquiry as the Hub.
His definitive BARB validity studies Jacobs (1995, 1996) are comprehensive both in scope and in numbers assessed. He delivered results from 11 different job categories spanning nine different arms and services including trainees in the Royal Artillery, Royal Engineers, Infantry, Royal Logistics Corps, Army Medical Services, and Adjutant General's Corps, having collected data on 3,700 recruits (Jacobs, 1995 loc. cit. p. iii). He lists the GTI mean scores and ranges for different jobs, highs associated with logistics and engineers and lows with infantry (loc. cit. p.7).

Table 7.6: Correlations Between GTI Scores and Training Performance

Army Corps	Written Theory	Effectiveness	Exercise Scores
RA (All courses combined)	.45 (N=295)	.35 (N=368)	
RA Signals Basic Course	.56 (N=129)	.52 (N-121)	
Royal Engineers	.19 to .35(N=510)		
Infantry		.00 to .25 (N=699)	
Royal Logistics (Supply)	.21to .29 (N=202)		.03 to 34(N=157)
Army Med. Combat	.14 to .22(N=265)		
Adj. General. Corps Clerical	.42to .65 (N=65)		.01 to .24 (N=65)

There are five main criteria: these include written theory test scores, effectiveness ratings, field-based practical scores, pencil and paper based exercise scores, and number of first time passes. Table 7.6 is adapted from Jacobs, (1996 pp. 246-47), with correlation ranges and numbers in the groups assessed. It both illustrates and confirms the extent and degree of success of the BARB General Training Index (GTI) used throughout his work as the measure to correlate with training outcomes.

The follow-up correlations using BARB scores showed that they could be used in a number of different training courses for specialists. For example, BARB correlations with Royal Artillery written tests approach .50. and with effectiveness ratings in gunnery modules in excess of .52. Equally good indices were found in predicting success in clerical tasks in the Adjutant General's Corps (.65 and .46 with written tests). More modest outcomes were found among Royal Engineers, with final effectiveness ratings and BARB's general training index (GTI) correlating .35. The conclusion was that good predictions were found in four job types, moderate to good in three, low in three more (loc. cit. p. 23). Overall, Jacobs showed BARB to be a much more satisfactory predictor of Phase 2 training than of Phase 1 training.

Similar detailed follow- ups were conducted by Holroyd, Atherton and Wright (1995a, 1995b). These covered Phase 1 and Phase 2 training depots. Although the numbers in each different study were varied, because one group at a time was the focus, the range of individual performance measures was large, minimal from infantry and larger through signals, logistics and engineers. The mean correlation from 34 measures was .28 with a standard deviation of .08, giving confidence limits of .12 through .44. The best results were in Phase 2 after initial training. Their conclusion sums it up.

'Thus, it was no surprise to find that some of the highest correlations were between BARB and measures of Phase 2 training performance, rather than performance in Phase 1 where factors such as physical fitness, motivation and military compatibility have an important influence. Even though more data have still to be collected both from the arms and corps included in this paper and from further arms and corps, it is clear that BARB can offer a good prediction of elements of training. '(Holroyd et al. 1995b, p.183).

These foundation outcomes were quickly followed by its successor, (Jacobs, Cape and Lawton, 1997) *increasing the numbers assessed to include 5,723 recruits from in 10 arms and services.* This larger follow up study confirmed the patterns in Table 7.6. Overall, BARB proved to be a cost-effective predictor of performance in Phase 2 training, even after lower levels of prediction were found in the Combat Medical Technician and the Combat Infantryman courses. The records also included average GTI score profiles across all the arms and services. *These showed that recruits with higher GTI scores achieved better results in training than did recruits with lower GTI scores.* Where numbers of female recruits allowed analysis, the results were similar to those for males, with no apparent differences in degree of relationship. GTI scores for female recruits in training were as effective predictors as they had been for males.

CONSTRUCT VALIDITY
Principal component analyses of the BARB computer-delivered tests have consistently reported single factor solutions with moderate to high component loadings (Tapsfield, 1993, 1995; Kitson & Elshaw, 1996).   A preliminary analysis with *QWERTY* touchscreens involved the individual tests of the AET battery *(Problems, Instructions, Dominoes Verbal and Arithmetic , known as PIDVA* and the BARB Battery. The tests in each battery were factor analysed separately. Each analysis produced a general factor, allowing a single weighted factor score for each battery to be calculated. Then the two factor scores were correlated. *This general factor was generally interpreted as one of working memory, with specific contributions from the test content, verbal, numerical, spatial awaiting the addition of other tests to identify them.* Further controlled studies were possible during the test development period at APSC. Two are reported, important because they analyse results from the AET and the computer-delivered BARB tests, including the Projectile Task (PJ) and field trial scores from a large number of anti-tank gunners. The results of the analyses were consistent in all respects.

Two factors accounted for the correlation matrix patterns. One was the verbal-educational content of AET (PIDVA) and the other was the working memory factor defined by the BARB tests. The two factors correlated to a major degree, with a value of .70. It is more prudent to point out that their covariance between the two factors identified largely derives from *the common dependence of Army Entrance Tests and the British Army Recruit Battery tasks on working memory and fluency in encoding and comparison processes in semantic, numerical and figural reconstructions.* Such an interpretation effectively removes the barrier to test development and understanding imposed by the use of the logical 'primitive'[6] term intelligence. It also moves towards

---

6   A logical primitive is a term that does not require further breakdown of the term because it is final as well as complete in itself. Other functions can be derived from it, but it is primary.

the fusion of experimental and psychometric approaches to psychological measurement advocated by Cronbach (1957) and still being pursued today. *The Projectile Task* was very much an outsider in the analyses, having a high degree of specificity, which might have been expected from its quite different demands on attention, requiring estimations of time and distance. In the next chapter, the PJ task is put into its proper context and the complete study of its usefulness discussed.

When BARB is combined with other tests in other services, then the opportunity for finding out what BARB tests relate to is enhanced. Lawton (op. cit. p. xx) reports a result of analysing 1,988 Royal Navy Recruit Test (RT) scores using paper-and-pencil analogues of the BARB tests that produced a two factor solution, one of working memory and a second that was an outcome of using two spatial tasks, one of which used the Rotated F item format. However, when a national sample of 1,000 Navy recruits was tested, using the same types of test, a three factor solution identified the now familiar working memory, a second verbal educational factor and a third combining tests of numerical skills. All three factors were intercorrelated, implying a second-order factor of general training suitability.

BARB TAKES OFF: AIR FORCE STUDIES 1996-97

The computer-delivered BARB system was easily incorporated into existing computer networks at home and abroad; and where these were not ready, machine scoring of paper-and-pencil versions made their use attractive in other military contexts, where once again, adaptation and research could take place. In RAF Ground Trades, BARB's paper-and-pencil forerunners consistent with the Royal Navy material (Jones, Dennis and Collis, 1995) were used with the Royal Air Force Ground Trades (Kitson, and Elshaw, 1996). Indices of trainability derived from BARB and its analogues correlated in the range 0.60 to 0.69 with total entrance scores from existing test batteries, rising to .78 if corrected for range restriction. Because these correlations straddle modality of presentation and quite different test construction principles, the BARB tests, with advantages of low literacy demand and multiple parallel forms, were consistent in screening applicants. This ingenious 'cross-cultural' report by Kitson and Elshaw (1996) was particularly relevant. Although conducted at the request of the Royal Air Force, and also involved British Army recruits who were administered the RAF *Ground Trades Test Battery* (GTTB). This RAF battery yields two index scores, the *General Ability Index* and the *Ground Technical Index*. Kitson and Elshaw concluded that the army sample of 422 recruits was comparable to, although not identical with, a RAF population. They were assessed as being slightly less able than RAF recruits, but the results were relevant to those who might be tempted to join the RAF. The BARB *General Training Index* correlated .66 with the RAF *General Ability Index* and .52 with the RAF *Ground Technical Index. The BARB individual test scores produced a multiple correlation of .70 with the General Ability Index*, and .58 with the *Ground Technical Index*. These were very convincing results for those who might advocate the use of BARB as a tri-service screening device. In fact, Kitson and Elshaw concluded that BARB together with more comprehensive tests of numeracy and literacy could match or improve upon the *Ground Trades Test Battery* for selecting RAF ground trades.

THE ROYAL AUSTRALIAN AIR FORCE TRIALS

Perhaps the last mile in the march towards confidence in the generalisability of the BARB prototypes is travelled in this admittedly short account of the extensive study of the BARB system in the Royal Australian Air Force (RAAF). The material in this section is a summary of extensive and detailed official reports produced by Greig and Bongers (1994, 1995) and Bongers and Greig (1995) and as such can never do justice to the completeness and detail of these reports.

The Australian decision to trial BARB recognised a need to introduce computer administered testing because, as in Britain with the Army, administrative changes made their old paper-and-pencil system redundant. Fairness in administration and scoring accuracy were prerequisites of changes and computer administered tests would ensure those. Nevertheless, the RAAF chose to trial BARB for three reasons. First, BARB employed *elementary cognitive tasks* (ECTs) requiring an educational achievement level of an eleven year old. Second, BARB was potentially capable of being a screening test for both enlisted and officer applicants, as Collis et al. (1991) had amply demonstrated. Third, the item-generative algorithms in the BARB program provided parallel forms, which permit test-retests almost immediately if required because there are no item-specific memory effects inherent in single-form tests.

Given the possibility of similar outcomes in Australia, but using RAAF personnel, BARB was trialled at the Australian Defence Force Recruiting Unit in Sydney, where it was administered in computer-delivered form to all applicants scheduled for selection testing for enlistment or commissioning to the Royal Australian Air Force over a three month period. Data was available from all of the tests used in the selection process. Although some entrants had supplementary tests for specialist roles, all applicants had previously taken the core RAAF tests *WA (Word Knowledge), MX (Arithmetic) and C (Clerical Abilities),* used to calculate the ground staff general ability index. All applicants for commissioned rank were administered *Test B42,* a general ability test by the Australian Council for Educational Research, but restricted to the Australian Defence Force.

RAAF TEST RESULTS

Greig (1997, pp. 41-43) reported that the mean *General Training Index* (GTI) the weighted sum of the individual BARB tests, for the Australian enlistment group was significantly higher than that of a sample of 4,394 British soldier applicants (effect size of 0.55): and that of the RAAF commission group was significantly higher than the GTI index for airmen (effect size of 0.80). No differences between the means for males and females on the GTI were large enough to make comparisons meaningful. Male and female means on the individual BARB tests, however, showed differences on some of the tests. The *Rotated F, Projectile Task & Number Distance* tests provided higher means for males; but females had better performance on *Letter Checking.*

These findings were considered by Greig to be consistent with earlier studies, where the sex differences on individual tests counterbalanced each other so that, overall, there was no sex difference on the GTI requiring operational variation in cut-offs for admission. The distribution of the GTI scores suggested that while the BARB tests require only a limited array of mental operations, BARB performance relates to a wide range of abilities. The correlation matrix revealed limited dispersion around the average index of .41 for the matrix. This provided a rough indication of how much the BARB tests had in common when applied to RAAF personnel. Apart from test *PJ*, the correlations were relatively homogeneous, so that the GTI itself was a composite of similar abilities.

Relationship with RAAF Tests: First Study Construct Validity.
Multiple correlation coefficients were obtained for the BARB scores with the General Ability Index as the dependent variable, and for the BARB scores with the *RAAF Commission Test* as the dependent variable. The multiple correlation coefficient obtained for the Australian enlistment group (R=0.75) is similar to that obtained by Kitson and Elshaw in their study using Royal Air Force selection test indexes as the dependent variables in that the multiple regression for the *RAAF Commission Test* also produced a Multiple r in the range of 0.72. The potential value of the BARB as a screening test battery is reflected in these findings, in the near-normal distribution of the GTI, and in the finding that the GTI provides equal opportunities for men and women.

The Second RAAF Study: Criterion Validity
BARB was thereafter administered a cohort of all Australian Defence Force Recruiting Units to all applicants to the RAAF, with what was by then the recognised procedure of a touch screen interface and advance information given in pre-test booklets. The data analysed for 1086 RAAF Airmen applicants, and 1797 RAAF commission applicants produced normative and correlational findings consistent with those of the initial trial. Furthermore, confirmatory factor analysis of the larger sample produced a two factor solution with sound goodness of fit indicators (Bongers and Greig, 1997). When follow up was conducted, the validities in much smaller samples in various occupations showed only a limited degree of correlation with training organisation outcomes, albeit with what is reported as *a variety of local, and unverifiable criteria* (Greig and Bongers 1998). These results were undoubtedly a disappointment to the authors, after so much promising work, but confidence in BARB remained unshaken. Greig concluded that the difficulties of establishing validity stemmed 'from the problem of finding 'a clear criterion' (loc, cit. p,12). The history of test use with military criteria tends to repeat itself.

Finally, a footnote. The psychometric properties of BARB were also evaluated with a Canadian Forces sample with descriptive statistics and normative tables for the two primary language groups in that country (MacLennan, 1995). That study, however, used only three pencil and paper forms of the BARB tests, one of which *(Letter Distance)* was not part of the computer administered battery used in Australia.

RECRUITMENT WITH BARB 1985-1995: THE FIRST DECADE

From its theoretical beginnings to its operational trials in all three UK service arms and overseas, the BARB system had shown that multiple parallel form production was successful, that the tests were reliable, could relate well to existing screening measures, could predict training outcomes and could preserves security and provide fairness at a very small operational cost compared with its predecessors. The results that occurred were, in light of the variation and uncertainty in military criteria, more than adequate for the use of BARB as an initial screen.

Fortunately, the process did not stop there. BARB had produced tests that were designed to predict the rate at which know-how or procedures could be learned. That was the next mission. Moreover, the criteria against which the tests could be judged were of a different order from those gathered in the field without supervision. They were validated against verified records of progress among Royal Marine commandos, British Army gunners and The United States Air Force ground crew. These three criterion studies are reported in Chapters 8 and 9. That was not the end of the United Kingdom's ongoing affair with BARB. Irvine (2013b) outlined its progress over 21 years. BARB did not stand still in the midst of organisational changes.

Johansen's 21ˢᵗ Century Revisions
In the years to follow, and by 2009, Johansen (2011, 2012) had revised the whole recruitment procedure, although BARB was still in use. Literacy and numeracy tests, auditory comprehension and interviews were additions to BARB. Those who satisfied the requirements at a preliminary recruit office stage underwent a further series of appraisals in residence at a selection centre. How Johansen used this framework, and with what outcomes for predicting training success, are shown in Chapter 14.

Fundamentals With The Royal Navy

by Paul Cawkill
Senior Psychologist,
Human Systems Group, Defence Science & Technology Laboratory (Dstl),
United Kingdom Ministry of Defence

An objective introduction to this chapter would state that it is an overview of the fundamental computer-based testing work carried out with the Naval Service (i.e. Royal Navy and Royal Marines) in the early nineties. However, such detachment would belie the personal memories this chapter evokes as I was there to witness the work undertaken nearly a quarter of a century ago. This chapter therefore, not only describes the complex technical aspects underlying the development of the computer-based tests, it also acts as an historical record of the pioneering work and the people involved. It is also written in a relaxed and flowing manner, which for those of who know him is typical of Professor Irvine's inimitable style.

In 1989 I started working with the Office of the Senior Psychologist (Naval) (SP(N)), Ministry of Defence, London. This small group of Occupational Psychologists worked directly to the Naval Service and were responsible for recruitment, selection, training, and retention of Officers and Ratings/Other Ranks. SP(N) had an illustrious history in terms of recruitment and selection dating back to the Second World War, where the forerunners of many of the selection tests used today were first developed. Much of the pioneering work from those heady days was undertaken by one of the British greats of Occupational Psychology – Professor Alec Rodger (1907-1982). A Cambridge psychology graduate, he worked in the War Office and eventually rose to be Senior Principal Psychologist in the Admiralty during the 1940s. He then began his long association with Birkbeck College, University of London, retiring as Professor of Occupational Psychology in 1975. Professor Rodger always believed that psychologists should conduct their work in such a way that was scientifically sound, administratively convenient, and politically defensible. This was to be a central tenant for all the SP(N) psychologists who followed in his wake.

Sadly, unlike Professor Irvine whose thesis was supervised by him, I never got to meet the great man, or be part of the exciting work he was responsible for developing. However, when I joined SP(N) there was another wind of change building momentum in military recruitment and selection – that of computer-based selection testing. The Naval Service became aware of the work being undertaken by the University of Plymouth on behalf of the Army Personnel Research Establishment (APRE) in what eventually became known as the *British Army Recruit Battery* (BARB) (see Chapters 1 to 7). The man spearheading this pioneering work on behalf of the UK Armed Forces, and in turn acting as a champion for a new era of computer-literate Occupational Psychologists specialising in recruitment and selection, was Professor Sidney Irvine. In terms of the Naval Service, the ABC Tests were born, and on this occasion I was there, and playing a part in the innovative work that had such an impact on Naval selection processes.

This chapter provides a comprehensive overview of the development of the Naval ABC Tests, which includes test development best practice, e.g. construct, concurrent, incremental, and predictive validity, and of course reliability studies. It details the thorough approach involving testing across all ranks in both the Royal Navy and the Royal Marines, involving both Standard and Advanced test batteries, prior to the development of a Combined battery. The beneficial impact of using pre-test booklets is also featured prominently, particularly with regard to female applicants. Cognitive ability is not the only issue addressed as interests and personality are also considered. Entrants could be classified into their respective branches using careers direction and personality measures, thereby adding an extra dimension to support the cognitive approach. More than twenty-five technical reports covering four years of work are condensed into 17 pages of text: and one can argue that it hardly does the subject area justice, but hopefully it provides a flavour of what was and what may be, both to the interested reader and also to the scientists carrying on Professor Irvine's work.

CHAPTER 8

ON BOARD WITH THE ROYAL NAVY

The most complete evidence for the application of multiple parallel form tests in paper-and-pencil versions to erstwhile recruits comes from a three-year long paper-and-pencil study originated by the office of the Senior Psychologist (Naval), known as SP(N). Its significance was all-important because it produced cumulative evidence of the underlying benefits of item generative tests. Running in parallel with the work in the Human Assessment Laboratory, the many reports extended it greatly. From 1989-1993, twenty-three different studies were completed on the feasibility of what were known as the *Navy Personnel Series (NPS)* tests[1]. An indication of the scale and thoroughness of the work carried out can be gained just by reading the titles of the published reports by the office of the Senior Psychologist Navy, SP(N) in Figure 8.1. The extensive fieldwork was recorded in great detail by Dr. Janet Collis, Paul Cawkill and their colleagues, after internal review and commentary by SP(N) senior officials. They have been grouped for convenience by the divisions in the Navy structure at the time: and this grouping is used in the summaries. Unusually, perhaps, they were circulated for all to read, in the army or navy offices. Given the range of research completed, no justice can be done in a comparative study emphasising some efforts more than others; but three deserve special attention in context. First, the enormous range of standardisation and validation undertaken before the computerised tests were put into practice. Second, effects on test performance in three different pre-test practice booklet trials issued before the testing session. Parallel form tests could not be compromised by pre-tests, but

BARB'S SISTER SHIPS

THE NAVY PERSONNEL SERIES

Comprehensive reports of test versions throughout the Service

ABC Tests Standard and Advanced validations

Normative results from the First National Sample

Branch Profiles and Predictive Validity

Pre-Test Booklet Use as Practice Effect

Royal Marine Combat Readiness Predicted

First Use of Interest and Personality Measures to Predict Branch Membership

---

1   The initials NPS were not without significance as SP(N) reveals.

their effects were important in resolving the need for second-try norms if recruits had more than one attempt at the tests, which the booklets provided. Last but not least, there were two very special studies: one with Royal Marine Commandos estimating the validity of cognitive tests in learning combat skills, and the other introducing tests of interest and personality to predict job classifications. A single chapter cannot do justice to their impact.

NATION-WIDE USE OF MULTIPLE PARALLEL FORM TESTS
In the beginning, the Royal Navy had, at the time of trial, no centre or network for computer-delivery of tests to large groups. The tests to be trialled had to be paper and pencil parallel forms of the generic test types in the prototype BARB series, with some modifications. For the Navy trials, the tests are referred to by their initial label, the *Navy ABC Tests*. The term was designed to give the impression to recruits and participants that they were easy to do, and because the items often depended upon the English alphabet. Two levels of these tests were compiled initially - Standard and Advanced. Those constructed at a basic literacy level were the *Standard* form. The second group of tests was more difficult and this is known as the *Advanced* series. After initial trials, a single *Combined* version was produced; and this version was used in the predictive validity studies. The final, *Combined* set used most of the *Advanced* tests and the simpler form of the *Alphabet* task known as the *Letter Distance Test*. The various item types have been illustrated in Chapter 6.

ABC STANDARD AND ADVANCED TEST BATTERY RESULTS
Preliminary work was with the easier form of what were then known as the *ABC Tests*, for want of a more imaginative name. These had only two terms in the reasoning test and two rotated symbols to match. The label was meant to convey *the low knowledge threshold required* for their performance. The tests proved hard enough to do well at for those who have problems with processing information accurately and efficiently. They certainly were not 'as easy as *ABC*'. The eventual form of the *ABC Tests* was based on the *Advanced/Combined* forms of the *Navy Personnel Series*. The *ABC* Standard Battery tests were administered to RN non-technician ratings undergoing training at HMS Raleigh (Collis & Irvine, 1991a). Internal consistency, construct, concurrent and differential validity were all demonstrated at levels appropriate for preselected populations. The *ABC Tests* showed good concurrent validity with both selection/assessment tests (RT and T2). The existing Recruiting Test (RT) was the strongest predictor of its analogue -T2 performance - but *ABC* test performance could be employed as a powerful addition to RT. The same battery was applied to WRNS recruits (Collis & Irvine, 1991b) with similar results.

Figure 8.1: List of Studies with Naval Personnel, 1991-95²

Naval Ratings

Cawkill, P. (1993). A study of the performance of RN/WRNS/QARNNS ratings and RM other ranks applicants on the Plymouth Combined *ABC* Test Battery. SP(N) Report TR 304.

Collis, J. M. & Irvine, S. H. (1991). The Plymouth Standard *ABC* Battery for RN non-technician ratings under training; validity and reliability studies. SP(N) Report TR 266.

Collis, J. M. & Irvine, S. H. (1993). The *ABC* Combined Battery for RN/WRNS non-technicians; further validity studies. SP(N) Report TR 313.

Collis, J. M. & Irvine, S. H. (1991). The Plymouth *ABC* Battery for WRNS rating entrants; validity and reliability studies. SP(N) Report TR 267.

Naval Artificer Apprentices

Collis, J. M. & Irvine, S. H. (1991). The Plymouth *ABC* Standard Battery for Artificer Apprentice entrants; validity and reliability studies. SP(N) Report TR 265.

Collis, J. M. & Irvine, S. H. (1993). The *ABC* Combined Battery for Artificer Apprentices; further validity studies. SP(N) Report TR 311.

Naval Officer Candidates

Collis, J. M. & Irvine, S .H. (1991). Predictive Validity and Utility of the *ABC* Battery with Royal Navy officers under training. SP(N) Report TR 261.

Leavy, N. A. & Collis, J. M. (1991). The Combined *ABC* Test Battery: Trial at the Admiralty Interview Board 1990/1991. SP(N) Report TR 282.

Leavy, N. A. (1993). The Advanced *ABC* Test Battery and its relationship with Fleet Board and OOW course performance. SP(N) Report TR319.

Royal Marine Commandos

Cawkill, P. (1992). A validation study of the T2 test battery against RM other rank training performance. SP(N) Report TR299. Ministry of Defence, UK.

Cawklll, P. & Collis, J. M. (1991). The Plymouth Combined *ABC* Test Battery for Royal Marine other rank entrants; validity and reliability studies. SP(N) Report TR269.

Collis, J. M. & Irvine, S. H. (1991). The Plymouth *ABC* Battery for Royal Marine other rank entrants; validity and reliability studies. SP(N) Report TR 263.

Collis, J. M. & Irvine, S. H. (1993). The *ABC* Combined Battery for Royal Marine Other Ranks; further validity studies. SP(N) Report TR 312.

Collis, J. M. & Irvine, S .H. (1993). A study of Royal Marine other ranks training data: coming to terms with the criterion. SP(N) Report TR 316

Leavy, N. A. & Collis, J. M. (1991). The Combined *ABC* Test Battery: Trial at Commando Training Centre, Royal Marines, Lympstone - March 1991. SP(N) Report TR 282

Personality and Interests of Naval Personnel

Beard, C.A. & Collis, J. M. (1991). Personality and Vocational Interests of Naval Officers under training: the prospective utility of objective motivational assessment. SP(N) Report TR260.

Collis, J. M., & Beard, C.A. (1993). The use of personality and vocational measures for allocation of Royal Naval ratings: some preliminary indicators of validity. SP(N) Report TR (315),

Test Development Studies

Cawkill, P. (1991). The potential use of an audio recording for the transmission of instructions and the administration of the *ABC* test sessions to ratings/other ranks. SP(N) Report R 159.

Collis, J. M. & Irvine, S, H. (1993). The effects of pre-knowledge, retest and types of test administration on computer generated cognitive tasks in a group of Royal Navy and Royal Marine entrants. SP(N) Report TR 314.

Dennis, I. (1993).The development of an item-generative test of spatial orientation closely related to test SP80A. SP(N) Report TR307.

Dennis, I. (1995*). The structure and development of numeracy and literacy tests in the Navy Personnel Series.* Report for Senior Psychologist (Naval). Human Assessment Lab., University of Plymouth, Plymouth UK.

Leavy, N. & Collis, J.M. (1991). The use of an audio recording for the transmission of instructions and the administration of the *ABC* test sessions at the Admiralty Interview Board. SP(N) Report R 153.

---

2   All SPN reports in Figure 8.1 are Crown Copyright as of the date listed: and references to them, relevant data summaries and content are made with prior approval of the Information Department of the Ministry of Defence. The same conditions apply to all APRE official reports referred to or quoted elsewhere.

Within that framework, there were key questions to be answered. One needed to know how reliable and how valid the new tests were, knowing that satisfactory selection tests, of a traditional nature, were already in use for naval recruitment, known simply as *The Recruiting Tests* (RT)[3], which defined the operational battery used for selecting Navy Ratings and Royal Marine Other Ranks. This contained four traditional verbal, figural, technical and quantitative tests of ability. *The RT tests assumed levels of numeracy and literacy associated with secondary school education involving minimum credits in general certificate of education examinations.* Before one could realise the future benefits of automatic parallel form production and test renewal passed on by item-generation theory, any new battery had to prove as effective in predicting training performance as the tests already in use.

Table 8.1 contains descriptive statistics for the advanced/combined and basic versions of the series. Time limits for the tests were standard, and they are given in the footnote below. The time limits were determined to enable a reliable measure to be produced in the shortest time interval possible. This is a factor to bear in mind. All are reported in scores adjusted for guessing (ADJ) Scores. That is, each test score has been adjusted for guessing using a standard correction based on the number of choices for each item type, using the formula *Adjusted score = Number right - (Number wrong/k-1) where k is the number of multiple choices for that particular test.* From these results, it is possible to compile profiles of performance for each group reported. This gives rise to occupational profile norms that can be used to designate bands of test performance appropriate to different job categories.

Table 8.1: Summary Statistics for the Advanced/Combined ABC Battery

	N		LC	RF	TI	ND	AFB LD
RN Officers	294	Mean	57	33	38	54	45*
(Univ. Grads.)		SD	9	11	13	16	13
RN Officer	436	Mean	45	29	29	42	39
Applicants		SD	7	10	7	14	11
Royal Marine	49	Mean	47	28	30	39	44
Officers		SD	7	10	10	15	11
RN Apprentice	158	Mean	42	28	30	37	32
Artificers	.	SD	9	10	8	14	11
RN/WRNS	1732	Mean	40	19	22	25	27
Non-Tech. Ratings		SD	9	10	7	12	12
Royal Marine	165	Mean	29	27	28	24	35
Other Ranks		SD	13	13	11	9	12
RN Ratings	264	Mean	39	21	22	27	27
Applicants		SD	8	11	8	14	11

*Note: Some means proportionally adjusted for time differences *Alphabet Forward & Backward Test. All other means in this column refer to the easier Letter Distance Test*

---

3   At that time there was another Navy series called the *T2 Tests* (discontinued post 1995). In many ways they resembled the RT Series, demanding declarative knowledge acquired by study. Any results from tests administered under slightly different time limits have been proportionally adjusted. Time limits and abbreviations were as follows. Letter Checking (LC) 4 min. Symbol Rotation (SR) 5 min. Reasoning (TI) 6 min. Alphabet Forward and Backward (AFB) 10 min. Number Speed and Accuracy (ND)5 min. Letter Distance (LD) 5 min.

The means and variances of the definitive Table 8.1 permit some relevant observations, the most pertinent of which is the high standing of the technical rating results when compared with officers in the Navy and in the Marines. These two groups - officers and technicians - have significantly higher scores than other entrants, particularly in working-memory based tests. These differences reflect policy decisions in the Navy about the levels of test performance necessary to complete initial and second-level training. The tests actually used to select these trainees were not, at the time of the trials, the '*ABC Tests*'. They were the closed RT (*Recruitment Tests*) used by the services. Different educational standards were needed for admission to the different categories. These thresholds are a concurrent validity criterion. Did the test average differences reflect the higher and lower education standards necessary for entrance? Based the different requirements for officers, artificer apprentices and naval ratings, the descriptives' linear average increase patterns in the table are proof of concurrent validity of the parallel form tests.

The obvious comparisons are between the Artificer (Technical) ratings and the other non-commissioned cohorts. The technical trainees show performance in all tests comparable with that of officer cadets. This serves to show the sensitivity of the tests to the higher entrance standards demanded of the technical entrants. The differences among the other groups are not large, apart from the traditional visualisation/spatial orientation gap between males and females. However, there are applicant group differences underlying the male-female divide, and the difference in the symbol rotation task is by no means a simple phenomenon, although its effect size is substantial and contradictory to all the other male-female average differences in the table, where females outscore men non-technical applicants.

Concurrent Validity with Navy RT Battery
In the attempt to predict the original Navy Recruit Test results from the *ABC* scores, the *Reasoning Test* (transitive inference) was the most effective test in regression analyses. When the same tests were given to Royal Marine Commandos similar patterns appeared, with cohort averages showing standard effect sizes of some importance. The pre-selection effect for artificers is evident in their position at the top of the rankings. Second, the Women's Royal Naval Service entrants show good performance on all tests, except the customary gender-associated lag in tasks demanding mental rotation of symbols. Indeed a major study by Beard & Collis (1993) using multiple discriminant functions showed that some Women's Royal Naval Service entrants could be classified as artificers and as Royal Marines from their ability test profiles. Results for Officers include scores from the Admiralty Interview Board tests, situational interviews, and group behaviour appraisals. These are referred to as the *AIB* results. These became interim or concurrent criteria against which to validate new tests for *Officer Candidates*. Additionally, cadet training records from the Britannia Royal Naval College (BRNC) were acquired for those actually accepted into the Navy as *Officers under Training*.

THE FIRST BRITISH NATIONAL SAMPLE
Initially, in test development, samples are purposive. As has already been demonstrated in this chapter, they are available and convenient, but not necessarily representative. To obtain a national sample of recruits from offices nationwide during a fixed period is

a bonus seldom afforded to test developers. Such was the interest and goodwill of the authorities, that results from a British national sample derived from 1,000 applicants for openings in the Royal Navy, *interviewed and tested with paper-and-pencil tests at every recruit office in Great Britain* were made available. As such they provide the basis for national norms in the age range. As an applicant population, however, they represent those actively seeking employment, and motivated to perform well on the tests. These participants also were administered the Navy *Recruit Tests*. These were the tests that decided their entrance to the service. Because they were given at the same time, they provide concurrent criteria against which to judge the effectiveness of the *ABC Tests*, and a reference frame for construct validation. Unlike previous work with recruits already selected, no range restriction on test scores was capable of modifying the results.

Table 8.2 gives the means, standard deviations and estimates of reliability for all applicants. The averages and spread of scores for females and males are also given to enable estimates of the extent of gender fairness. No previous national sample had included identifiers for men and women. The observed male-female differences are consistent with better female performance in scanning letters and alphabet fluency. Symbol rotation tests produced male averages that are greater than those for females, as was found in the early trials of the tests, but the effect size in the national sample is much less than before. In combined totals, nevertheless, these differences tend to compensate for each other. Similar female-male patterns of results were encountered with trials of BARB tests in Australian air force applicants. (cf. Bongers & Greig, 1997; Greig, 1997: Greig & Bongers, 1996).

Table 8.2: *Descriptives and Reliabilities for a Royal Navy National Sample (N=943)*[4]

	Female N=159		Male N=784		ALL N=943			
	Mean	*SD*	**Mean**	*SD.*	**Mean**	**SE**	**SD.**	**rtt**
LC	39.8	*11.2*	35.2	*12.0*	36.0	±0.4	12.0	.92
TI	17.6	*7.1*	17.0	*7.1*	17.1	±0.2	7.1	.84
ND	21.5	*12.5*	22.7	*12.9*	22.5	±0.4	12.8	.92
LD	26.6	*13.5*	21.8	*12.8*	22.6	±0.4	13.1	.94
SR	20.3	*15.4*	26.3	*16.2*	25.3	±0.5	16.2	.94

The results are typical of the results associated with the *ABC Tests*. There is good dispersion of scores; reliabilities are very high in what is an unselected population (unlike previous studies with selected populations). Reliabilities in the national sample are confined to indices of internal consistency. It was not possible to re-test the sample but for comparison at this stage, other reliabilities for specialist groups with smaller numbers were calculated, both internal consistency and split half. These results confirmed the high reliability of the individual tests, even when administered to pre-selected groups where the distributions of scores are likely to be reduced.

---

4   Crown Copyright 1993. LC - Letter Checking; TI - Transitive Inference; ND - Number Distance; LD - Letter Distance; SR - Symbol Rotation

Concurrent Validity in the British National Sample
Because the *Navy Recruiting Tests* (RT) were given at the same time as the *ABC Tests*, concurrent test background data exists to permit estimates of validity. There were substantial correlations between individual *ABC Tests* and Navy Recruit *Tests* total in the national sample. The highest were between the *Reasoning and Number Distance Tests* and *Navy Recruiting Test Total*, both being in excess of .5.

A stepwise regression model showed that the best fit total was achieved by combining four tests, *Reasoning, Symbol Rotation Number Speed and Accuracy and the working memory Letter Distance test*. The final coefficient was .65. With almost 1,000 cases to work with, each additional test added significantly to the improvement. The significance of the change for each step was set at the .001 level, to ensure a robust equation. The result showed that the *ABC Tests* and the *Navy Recruiting Test Total* have much in common. When the relative times taken to complete the two test batteries are considered, there is considerable economy in applying four short screening tests, available in multiple forms, and selective use of educational content tests thereafter.

Factors Analysed in the British National Sample
The next question concerned what the *ABC Tests* measured when they were correlated with the *Navy Recruiting Tests*. A factor analysis was repeated using exactly the same methods as before. An objective reduction method was used; and when applied to the *ABC* and RT correlation matrix two factors were found, consistent with previous findings of information processing in working memory and foreshadowing replications in the USA and Europe. The analysis provided a maximum likelihood solution of two highly inter-related factors (r =.70). One of these was the *ABC Test* capacity to process new information, involving working memory, and the other the *Navy RT Test* verbal educational factor with a pronounced knowledge threshold influence on performance.

NAVY BRANCH PROFILES AND PREDICTIVE VALIDITIES
Much time and effort were spent by Dr. Collis[5] to follow-up the test surveys in various special branches of the Royal Navy. Examination of these reports in Figure 8.1 shows that approximately half of them refer to validation studies. Two representative outcomes, from the many illustrations available in the originals, are shown. The first, Figure 8.2, tabulates mean scores, showing different average score profiles for various branches.

Figure 8.2: Profiles for Selected Branches

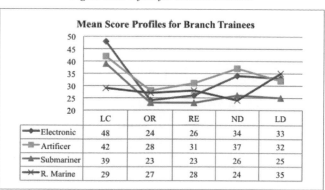

	LC	OR	RE	ND	LD
Electronic	48	24	26	34	33
Artificer	42	28	31	37	32
Submariner	39	23	23	26	25
R. Marine	29	27	28	24	35

---

5   In cooperation with Niall Leavy and Paul Cawkill, now a senior psychologist with MOD.

Many more branches were profiled, but these illustrate the different performance levels associated with special functions. The Artificers and Electronic Warfare trainees have generally similar performance patterns and levels. Royal Marines and non-technician Submariners show more moderate levels of capability. Great care was taken to compare the results of using existing *RT* tests with those from the newly created parallel forms of the *ABC* standard and advanced systems, at this juncture all machine scored paper-and-pencil versions with special answer formats involving mark recognition software. In general, the experimental tests predicted outcomes to a variable degree, but no better than the existing Royal Navy tests. When the two different kinds of tests, the *RT* and the *ABC* series were combined, improvements in prediction were observed.

DETAILED FOLLOW-UP OF PHASE 2 TECHNICAL TRAINING OUTCOMES.
The Royal Marine study, described in detail later in the chapter, was not unique in its significance. The opportunity to conduct a unique phase two training follow-up with *Artificer Apprentices* (ARTAPPS) was grasped with results, that, although quite unexpected in the original plan, nevertheless provided one more valuable lesson on the need to exercise care and caution when recruits come forward for surveys. Even if the original plan was disturbed, sometimes a benefit can emerge. Printing and preparation of the *ABC* tests now enabled scoring using an optical mark reader.

A total of 196 artificer apprentice entrants were tested with the *Combined ABC* battery during the first week of their initial training. *A pre-test instruction booklet had been issued to all candidates at the Careers Information Office.* The *Combined ABC* battery tests were administered approximately 6 weeks after the *ABC* pre-test instruction booklets had been given to the candidates. Of these, 158 entrants had completed the pre-test instruction booklet and 38 had not. Only at the first testing session did it become clear that a number of entrants had not completed instruction booklets: and all subsequent sessions had to include flagging of candidates' test papers to mark the lack of pre-test experience (book/no book). Follow-up results were calculated on those who had completed the booklet. Royal Navy selection scores were collated for each candidate and merged into the *ABC* data file which was subsequently analysed. The psychometric characteristics of the Combined *ABC* battery proved to be highly consistent with that reported previously. Its internal correlation and factor structure is invariant across versions. The types of relationship between *ABC*s and existing selection tests were also consistent with previous reports.

Table 8.3: Predicting Global Criterion Results in Various RN Branches

	ART	A_{EM}	W_{EM}	M_{EM}	MI_{EM}	STW	RM1	RM2	RM3
Global Criterion	.36	.24	.40	.34	.34	.35	.41	.76	.45

Notes: ART(Artificers) The subscript EM means Engineering Mechanic throughout as in A_{EM} (Air Engineering Mechanic) W_{EM} (Weapons) M_{EM} (Marine) MI (Missile) STW (Steward) RM (Royal Marines 1,2,3 where numbers show training phases over 30 weeks).

Table 8.3 summarises the correlations of the *ABC* tests in various combinations with global stage training criteria. In general the correlations now reported are lower-bound estimates of test efficiency because of restriction of range in the selected population; and because of the heterogeneous nature and low coefficients of generalisation of global assessments. Many individual subject correlations are higher than those shown here. Because of the fairly high numbers of subjects followed up, the correlations are operationally of some value. Correlations are moderate to high: and when corrected for variance in populations of applicants, they would increase markedly. All of them are usable, depending on how the cut-off scores for entrance are determined. The high correlations with the Royal Marine cohort deserve special notice, and they are discussed in the context of other studies predicting military 'know how' in Chapter 7.

The Criteria
Complete training data were available. The requirements for success in Part II training for Artificer Apprentices are first, a knowledge of engineering systems allied with ability in maths; and second, a demonstration of naval knowledge and ability to write a formal letter, a technical description and a balanced essay (general and communication studies). The training data showed three of the final exams are highly correlated and represented the requirement for fluency in engineering science and maths. They depend to a large extent on procedural knowledge. The remaining exams bear little relationship with the first set. They either require declarative knowledge specific to naval issues (knowledge of rank badges, different classes of warship and so on) or they test literary skills (essays and letter writing) rather than answers that require mathematical and/or engineering calculations. The psychometric structure of the data bears this out and shows two relatively independent main features of the criterion.

Predictive Validity
The predictive validity of the *ABC* battery showed moderate success in predicting MAT (Maths) by *Letter Distance* and MES (Marine Engineering Science) by *Number Distance*. *Number Distance* also predicted the final exam mark. Two of the five final exams were based on declarative knowledge - a type of performance measure which the *ABCs* do not claim to predict. The predictive validity of the RN selection tests showed RT part scores were not as powerful as RT Total and the set of 'Artificer-specific' assessment tests in their prediction of training success. RT2 (Literacy) had some moderate success in predicting success on the declarative knowledge exams suggesting that essay-type format was indeed required for these exams. The predictive power of *RT Total* in particular was such that *ABC Tests* added little to the regression equations.

Incremental Validity Contexts
Whenever tests already exist, such as the Navy RT tests, new tests have to show that they can reach the same level of efficiency at less cost, or add significantly to the predictive power of the tests already in use. When this happens, incremental validity is demonstrated. There were occasions when the RT tests were best. They predicted formal, academically based training outcomes better than the *ABC Tests*. This is not surprising, because the *ABC Tests* were deliberately constructed from a base of basic

literacy and numeracy. Consequently, they have no educational content prerequisite to the formal coursework, whereas the RT tests do.

On the other hand, whenever previous educational background is irrelevant to the specific military or practical content of the training syllabus - weapons training, fieldcraft, survival skills, officer of the watch, and so on, the *ABC* test was often the best predictor. Finally, there are many studies where a combination of scores from the Navy RT tests and the *ABC Tests* improved prediction dramatically. In short, the *ABC Tests* provided incremental validity over and above the RT tests in practical contexts, and they helped out in other training situations to improve the overall efficiency.

Discussion

Trainability for the group of Artificers studied is operationally defined as success in a set of final written exams. The measure of success is therefore based on a conglomerate of tests relying both on specific declarative knowledge and (more heavily) on mathematical attainments. Both RT and subsequent assessment procedures specifically test and select out for mathematical ability and they also contain elements of mechanical comprehension and literacy. In a sense, the RTs are telling us that a test of essay writing (RT2) successfully predicts ability to write future essays. A test of numeracy (RT3) successfully predicts ability to pass future exams that require numeracy. A working-memory battery with low educational threshold as a rationale for its construction would not predict classroom-based training outcomes as successfully as RT. Despite this, factor analysis of composite data blocks suggests that training totals have a moderately strong relationship with working memory. Factor analysis using composites of all data blocks offers a three factor solution where training total loads .55 with a maths/engineering factor and .49 with a working memory factor. Rate of learning is only marginally less involved in differentiating good trainees than prior technical knowledge. Both are required in an efficient set of predictors.

PRE-TEST BOOKLET INFORMATION: SERENDIPITOUS EFFECT REPLICATIONS

Multiple parallel forms permit the widespread distribution of pre-test information without compromising the test given on the day. Three different studies of their effects were possible in the Royal Navy trials, *all being event-related rather than planned, so that their operational use was mimed.* They involved Artificer Apprentices, Royal Marines and the National sample. Because they proved so similar in their effects, their influence on the use of pre-test information in operational selection was profound. These 'by-products' were just as important as the two other special developments in the Royal Navy research, the Royal Marine Commando validities and the use of interest and personality tests 'blindly' to identify branch members with great and quite unexpected accuracy.

PRE-TEST BOOKLETS

THREE EXAMPLES

Accident

Murphy's Law

National Proof

The Artificers
Data available from a study of Artificer Apprentices was an early example of the effects of pre-test instruction booklets on test scores. Those entrants who worked on the booklet produced *ABC* scores which were very comparable (taking into account a change in test version) with those reported earlier where 'live' administration had been given on the day of the testing session. Because 25% of entrants in this group did not work through the pre-test booklet prior to the administration of the *ABC Tests*, a 'natural', if accidental, and serendipitous treatment effect was produced. If the pre-test booklet was an effective method of ensuring fairness, by ensuring equal awareness of requirements and providing an incentive to adequate preparation, then those who failed to complete it should reveal some disadvantage in the tests themselves. Nevertheless, in this particular group of highly selected entrants, performance without the pre-test booklet may not have proved as disadvantageous as it might be with less able groups. Procedures were adapted to meet the given state of affairs. Each record in the data set was labelled according to whether or not the entrant had completed an instruction book. Means and standard deviations were calculated for each group (book/no book) and an ANOVA was used to examine the differences. To ensure differences were not due to factors other than experience with a pre-test booklet, RN selection data was examined for the two groups, using the navy Recruitment Test Total. No significant differences occurred in RT scores for the book/no book groups. However, significant differences in test performance occurred on two out of five ABC tests. In all cases performance by the book group surpassed the no book group. Effect sizes were big enough to warrant further investigation, suggesting that improvements were related to prior experience with the various test types *because the test items are never identical from booklet to test form*. The information in the booklets has to be perceived as an externally imposed *radical* that changed the difficulty of the test.

Figure 8.3: *Differential Lympstone Test Scores With and Without Pre-test Booklets*

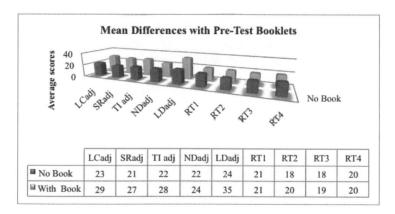

	LCadj	SRadj	TI adj	NDadj	LDadj	RT1	RT2	RT3	RT4
■ No Book	23	21	22	22	24	21	18	18	20
▨ With Book	29	27	28	24	35	21	20	19	20

Murphy's Law in The Lympstone Study: What Happened on the Day
The special study of Royal Marine Commandos is unique in the prediction of success in learning combat skills. The work at the training depot at Lympstone was almost a microcosm of what researchers propose and Murphy's Law disposes. What was discovered on the day testing was to begin proved to be another pre-test booklet

demonstration. The *Combined ABC* tests were to be administered to all new recruits in paper-and-pencil form approximately 6 weeks after the ABC pre-test instruction booklets had been given to the candidates. Testing took place during the first week of training at Lympstone. Test sessions were administered by a trained Personnel Selection Officer, who controlled time limits for the test and dealt with any problems. High hopes for a trouble-free, productive period of work at Lympstone were in place. However, at the very first testing session Murphy's Law was in force.

A pre-test booklet, containing examples and practice items for each test had been issued some weeks earlier at the Careers Information Office to all candidates, who were told to complete it before reporting to Lympstone. Prior to the testing day itself, no checks were enabled to ensure that all candidates had worked through the booklets; and, of course, a number of entrants had not done this. Consequently, each record in the data set had to be categorised (book/no book) to show if the recruit had completed a pre-test booklet. Of the 203 entrants tested with the *Combined ABC* battery during the first week of their initial training, 165 entrants had completed the booklet and 38 had not. Initial descriptive statistical procedures were performed both on whole group data and on separate 'book/no book' subgroups. Means and standard deviations were calculated for each group and analysis of variance was used to examine the differences. Because of significant performance differences between the 'book/no book' groups[6] detailed follow-up analyses were performed on 'book' groups only.

Significant differences between the 'book/no book' in test performance occurred on all but one (*Number Distance*) of five tests. In all tests performance by the book group surpassed the no book group. To ensure differences were not due to factors other than experience with a pre-test booklet, RN selection data was examined for the two groups. The *Recruiting Test*, used for selection of ratings and other ranks comprises four parts; *RT1 (Reasoning), RT2 (Literacy), RT3 (Numeracy) and RT4 (Mechanical Comprehension)*. The RT Total is an unweighted sum of all four part scores and is one factor in determining an applicant's suitability. There are minimum RT Total scores for entry into each branch of the Service and part score minima may be also required for some branches. *No significant differences occurred in RT scores for the 'book/no book' groups*. Because the RT selection tests for Marines showed no advantage for those who had read the pre-test booklet, prior knowledge of what was required to do the ABC battery was held responsible for superior test performance in the ABC battery, there being no sampling bias. From this point onwards, further analyses were performed on 'book' groups only.

Pre-Test Booklets in the National Sample: The Shape of Things to Come
Once more, a check on whether the pre-test booklet had been available prior to completing the ABC Tests showed that in the national sample, some had used the booklet and a minority had not, offering a comparison of its effects on a representative group. This one-time opportunity was the impetus for looking again. Using the database a univariate analysis of variance was performed on each test, with sex as a fixed and book/nobook as a random factor. RT total was available and was used as a covariate, so that the means shown in Figure 8.4 are all adjusted for the effect of the measured general ability level of the applicants.

---

6   A deliberate book/no book study was used in the USA for the Logic Gates trials in the USA and the ARCOM test results standardised accordingly. No such good fortune here, but the results spoke for themselves, in spite of Murphy.

Figure 8.4: Pretest Booklet Effects in the National Sample

Pretest Booklet Effects by Sex of Entrant

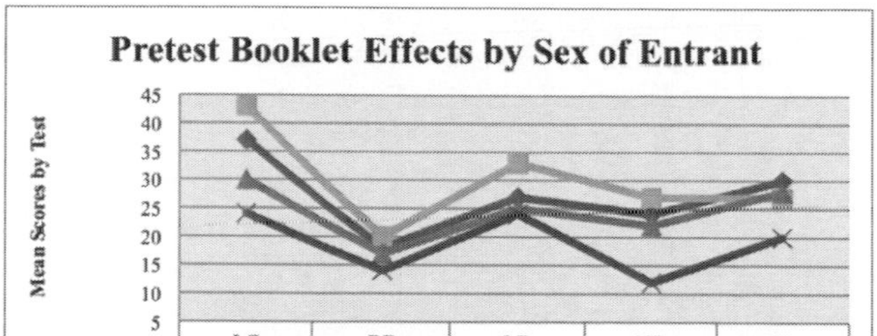

	LC	RE	LD	ND	SR
M Book	37	18	27	24	30
F Book	43	20	33	27	27
M Nobook	30	17	25	22	28
F Nobook	24	14	24	12	20

Notes: Numbers for Entrants: M Book 747, F Book 152; M Nobook 36 F Nobook 7

In every instance, the covariance effect of RT was highly significant. The only other consistent effect was the interaction of the two factors, sex and book/nobook. Inspection of the table shows that female applicants who completed the pre-test booklet outperformed males on all but the symbol rotation test, while males who had not completed the booklet outperformed females. While the proportions not completing the booklets were the same for females and males, with only seven females not having completed the booklet prior to testing, no comparisons were attempted

Nevertheless, the simple conclusion from the interaction effects in this study is a salutary one. Female and male performance differences are most probably due to different composition of the male and female sample applicant samples. Females who apply have quite different pre-existing aptitude profiles from males. *A straightforward, blanket comparison of males and females in the national sample would be inappropriate and systematically misleading.* Similar conclusions attend results of comparisons of men and women in the Belgian armed forces shown in Chapters 12 and 13 and for sectarian groups , also in Chapter 13. The national sample cast a long shadow.

THE UNIQUE ROYAL MARINE COMBAT SKILLS STUDY

One may begin with a truism. There is probably no more demanding training experience than that required for combat readiness under the most extreme conditions. Book reading will not provide tactical know how and precise drill performance. Only if accurate records exist to show to what extent these combat routines have been learned, can predictions be made with any confidence. The Royal Marine depot at Lympstone, in England, is the control centre for producing internationally renowned Special Forces. In completing their pioneering work Dr. Collis and her colleagues were given confidential access to personnel training records, identified only by code numbers. The *Combined ABC* battery was administered to Royal Marine other ranks entrants with the aim of predicting training results. The importance of the study lay in the availability of written and practical training scores collated over a 30-week training period. This includes the most demanding and comprehensive training modules necessary for an elite special operations corps.   In these, procedural knowledge is a paramount requirement, while factual knowledge must also to be demonstrated. Because of the extensive amount of data collected, comparisons with then current Royal Navy Entrance tests (RT) and the Combined and Basic ABC battery of item generative tests as predictors of training results were possible. Moreover, the structures of the test batteries and the training criteria were explored. Finally, the use of a pretest practice booklet, already discussed, threw some light on the role of prior knowledge of test items before taking the tests themselves – and in particular, comparisons with recruits who had not seen the practice booklet prior to initial testing at the recruit training camp.

THE ROYAL MARINES:

COMBAT SKILLS PREDICTED USING RELIABLE CRITERIA

Before the Lympstone work was begun, various forms of the ABC battery had been trialled with different groups of Naval entrants. The basic level battery showed good concurrent validity with both selection and assessment tests (Collis & Irvine, 1991). Other studies indicated that one version (referred to as the Combined ABC battery) is suitable for all levels. This combined version produced large differences between officer and entrant average scores, confirming the use of the battery for an initial basic abilities filter (Leavy & Collis, 1992). Moreover, a substantial trial of the combined version of the ABC battery was undertaken between July and December 1991, involving entrants from all ratings/other ranks cohorts. The aims of the study were to confirm the psychometric characteristics of the Combined ABC battery, to explore the psychometric characteristics of the training criteria, and to determine the extent to which ABC test performance predicts training outcomes.

Table 8.4: Predictive Validities for Royal Marines Training Data (N=165)

Criterion	RT only	ABC only	ABC and RT
Written examinations			
Military Knowledge	0.63	0.39	0.67
First Aid	0.45	0.30	0.48
Map Reading	0.52	0.44	0.63
Fieldcraft	0.47	0.42	0.56
Field exercises			
Exercises	0.45	0.51	0.61
Field Firing	0.35	0.35	0.44
Weapons	0.33	0.45	0.53
Final training outcomes			
Overall Ratings	0.42	0.41	0.57

The capabilities of the Navy RT tests and the ABC battery are shown in Table 8.4. Regressions using each set of tests and both together were conducted and the multiple correlations are reported. *This summary Table 8.4 produces what is generally recognised to be some of the highest validities produced in any study of combat readiness.* Caution dictates that the sample is both purposive and small, compared with large number groups evident throughout the volume. However, the 95 per cent confidence limits of the median correlations in the region of .45 are .56 as upper and .32 as lower bound estimates. The final training rating correlation of .57 has limits of .65 and .44. Why are the results so unique? A plausible answer was provided through an elegant study by Cawkill (1992) where the detailed breakdown of the course structure, assessments and scoring weights for RM trainees was given. A special feature of Cawkill's report tells of great care exercised in assigning marks and scores for these various, and quite different tasks. He provides an invaluable frame of reference, with each component described and weighted in the overall grade. Although his is a restricted report, its significance as far as the Lympstone study is concerned, lay in *making clear the almost total emphasis on procedural learning* in the assessments collected over the 30-week training period. For example, under the label of *'Exercises'*, its category width is seen to include infantry teamwork, speed marches, strategies for coping with terrorist activities, the construction of defences, assault formations and the use of special equipment, laying and detection of mines and other operational tasks. *'Weapons'* covers competence with and maintenance of various weapon types and *'Field Firing'* is a simulated patrol and firing exercise with live rounds. This type of information, perhaps not generally known in 1992, is available today on the internet for intending applicants. *In the complete span of studies reviewed in this volume, no other training depot was able to provide criterion results in such detail.*

The relative success of the correlations of the selection tests, compared with results from other training camps, must in contrast be due to the underlying reliability of the criterion measures. Given criteria of this standard, *The ABCs* were able to predict all essential field-based modules and a final performance rating. In each case the RTs added to those predictions although *The ABCs* proved to be the more powerful combination when each battery was used in isolation. This study illustrates, perhaps better than any other in the series, how the relative independence of the two batteries, the ABC and the RT, maximised predictive validities when the criterion data is *at the same time* expensive to produce, supervised, and field relevant. The ABCs were not designed to predict learning in quasi-classroom environments; such as naval colleges: this was best predicted by the educational content of the current RT battery. Alternatively, training modules demanding procedural knowledge were closely related to ABC performance.

In Chapter 7 the caveats of predicting performance when using military criteria were made clear. The final word on this is a comparison of the British Army validity coefficients reported by Holroyd, Atherton and Wright (1995a, 1995b), Jacobs (1996,) Jacobs, Cape and Lawton, (1997).for infantry training and summarised in Table 7.6. They range from .00 to .29. The Lympstone experience, as described by Cawkill, raises once more the perennial question of how well the screening tests might perform in all military contexts where such meticulous record-keeping was the norm. The need for continuous criterion evaluation is the signal contribution of the Royal Marine study, another fine example of which can be seen in Macpherson (2011).

A LANDMARK: THE POWER OF INTERESTS AND PERSONALITY

Prior to this, little or no material on the use of non-cognitive measures has been reported, apart from a mere mention of Johansen's (2011) account of integrating the judgements of recruiters about recruit behaviour in situational exercises. Much earlier, a student supervised by Dr. Collis undertook a most important study that was to have far-reaching consequences. In it, *The Careers Direction Inventory* (Jackson, 1986) and *The Personality Research Form* (Jackson, 1984) were administered first to Royal Naval officers stationed at Britannia Royal Naval College (BRNC), Dartmouth (Beard, 1990, Beard & Collis, 1991); and later to groups of Artificer Ratings, WRNS Recruits, and Royal Marines (Collis, & Beard 1993). From the first study of Officer Cadets, a core personality profile was apparent. Further subtypes of personality emerged, of which perhaps one of the most difficult to accommodate within a command training environment was an apparent 'aggressive/defensive' type. Valuable as this first trial of the effect of adding interest and personality scores to ability measures was, perhaps the most revealing motivation study of the decade was its immediate successor, (Collis & Beard, 1993); and which was to prove a landmark in the formulation of work in motivation after 1996 (Irvine, Kyllonen & Roberts, 2000; Irvine, 2004, Irvine, 2013).

A NAVAL LANDMARK:

THE UNTAPPED POTENTIAL OF INTERESTS AND PERSONALITY

A definitive breakthrough occurred when the data on different occupational groups of Navy non-commissioned personnel were combined to show what happened when ability, interest and personality tests were used to classify the groups into their known respective branches. Because admission to training was then, and probably still is, largely controlled by ability test results, any notable improvement in accuracy of classification, attributable to interest and personality tests, could be evaluated from the group prediction baselines established by ability tests. Any second stage classification improvement could be revealed when interest scores were added; and the final outcome when personality profiles were included to produce all three different sources of information. Given such a comprehensive data set, comparisons could be made about the potential contributions of non-cognitive measures to the allocation of recruits to special roles within the Navy.

Identifying Artificers, Marines and Logistic Support Staff
Three job categories were available: Royal Navy Artificers *(Technical)*; Royal Marines *(Combat)*; and Women's Royal Naval Service (WRNS) *(Mainly Logistic And Keyboard-Related Functions)*. The *Navy Recruiting Test* of abilities and the Jackson (1984, 1986) tests of interests and personality were administered and scored. The question was, how accurately could an individual be classified as an Artificer, Woman's Royal Naval Service trainee, or Marine Commando, using the measures available? First, all the different test scores were correlated together, and the actual membership of the three different groups was recorded. Then, using discriminant

function analyses, it was possible to observe how well these entrants were identified, first by their initial ability test score patterns; and then to note any improvements in accuracy after adding in cumulative fashion the vocational interest test choices and, finally the personality test scores. Table 8.5 shows the result of this strategy. All entries are the proportions correctly identified,

Table 8.5: Service Branch Classifications Ability Interest and Personality Test Results.

Test Types	Service Category	Classified as Artificers	Classified as Marines	Classified as WRNS
Ability Only				
A	Artificers	.85	.08	.07
A	Marines	.48	.36	.16
A	WRNS	.26	.20	.54
Plus Interests				
A+ I	Artificers	.92	.07	.01
A+ I	Marines	.20	.77	.04
A+ I	WRNS	.13	.08	.79
Plus Interests and Personality				
A+ I+ P	Artificers	.94	.05	.01
A+ I+ P	Marines	.15	.85	.00
A+ I+ P	WRNS	.09	.06	.85

Note: Data first reported in Collis & Beard, 1993, Crown Copyright. Entries are proportions

Dramatic increments in predicting membership of different branches are apparent, particularly in the Royal Marines and WRNS categories. Vocational interests improve the prediction based solely on *Recruiting Test* results. Finally, the addition of personality test scores to these two different sources gives a prediction rate for all three types together. Only two discriminant functions were needed to produce this degree of accuracy, with very favourable odds ratios. Comparable rates of increase over the ability tests are from just over half to 85% for WRNS *and for Marines a remarkable increase to 85% from the initial 36% baseline*, with an overall success rate of close to 90%. The ability tests had very little to do with the Marine profile, whereas interests and motivation profiles separated them from the other branches. The prediction rate for Artificers is not as dramatic as it is for the others, but, as previously observed, apprentices had been preselected for their ability profile, essentially mathematical and spatial ability scores. For Artificers, prior acquired knowledge was the key to their acceptability. Even then, a 10% increase in accuracy for Artificers to 94 % was possible.

Although the reports by Collis and Beard commended, with more than a little justification, the use of motivation tests to improve allocation of Royal Navy applicants, their studies did not result in the accepted use of vocational interest and/or personality tests for entrants to The Royal Navy, or, indeed, anywhere else. However, they were not to be forgotten when the opportunity arose to replicate the procedure using different populations with similar, but not identical tests in the United States (Irvine, Kyllonen & Roberts, 2000). By the end of the century, elements were in place (Chapter 16) so that computer-delivered versions could identify random, guarded and socially desirable patterns of responses, the main reasons behind official reluctance.

CONCLUSIONS: THE SP(N) ACHIEVEMENTS

If the account of work requested and supported throughout by SP(N) had ended at this point, its achievements would still be notable for their thoroughness; and for the light shed on the success of paper-and-pencil versions of the parallel forms in assessing the potential of Naval recruits on land, sea and air. Stable tests predicted branch differences; widespread training success; and an extension to interest and personality domains met with unquestionable promise. Core item types had been identified; strategies for delivery had been outlined and demonstrated using overhead projection and recordings in group presentations in both purposive trials and national samples.

But to end it there would do an injustice to one of the most innovative evidence-centred applications of cognitive principles to automatic item-generation for test construction, carried out on behalf of the Royal Navy by Dr. Ian Dennis and colleagues: and thereafter finding full expression in other contexts, such as ARCOM (*Army Regular Commissions Board Battery*). The Royal Navy request for a broader range of tests was undertaken: They included mathematical, spatial orientation, grammatical transformation and reasoning tasks whose outcomes as components of ARCOM have already been illustrated in Chapter 6. In a comprehensive trial at Lackland Air Force Base in the United States, they came to be established as a major predictor of procedural learning more powerful than the great ASVAB itself. Full details of the trial of the prototype Royal Naval tests using electronic gates as learning tasks follow in the next chapter, Chapter 9.

In many ways, the ABC tests and the versions used in ARCOM were vital sister ships essential to the success of combined operations. The aim of producing computer-based tests of known cognitive functions, from theoretically-driven algorithms, in unlimited quantity and with consistent descriptive statistics had been realised. Without the large-scale trials and follow-up validations undertaken by The Royal Navy, the computerised BARB provided for the army would have had no firm precedent.

193

CHAPTER 9

GUNNERY AND ELECTRONICS: LEARNING TO KNOW HOW

Two More Studies of Learning How To
Fortunately, it was possible during the decade to explore what individual differences are effective in producing learning outcomes among military personnel in radically different training exercises. Three different studies with three different types of procedural learning were the focus of the work with the different forms and test types of BARB. The first, using Royal Marine Commandos and reported in the previous chapter, was concerned with the prediction of training success, not only learning facts from the training manuals, but also in the hard physical environments involving mastery of weapons, fieldcraft, and survival skills. *This early study had to use hand or machine scored paper-and-pencil versions of the tests, to predict training records and instructor ratings of success.* Two more were completed with computer-delivered versions. In retrospect they were adventures in the real world of computer-delivered testing. They tried to predict elements of totally different skills learned at the *second phase* of training. Gunnery in the UK and the learning of electronic logic gates in the USA could hardly be further apart. Moreover, the BARB and ARCOM tests were used alongside existing traditional tests, the AET 86 in Britain, and the all-powerful ASVAB in the United States.

The gunnery trial with British soldiers explored the how well the BARB computer-delivered test of time estimation (PJ) might predict the success rate of anti-tank gunners under training and recruited by AET 86. The contrasting trial examines the effectiveness of computer-delivered tests in predicting how well electronic logic gates were learned by USAF ground operations recruits for whom logic gates were a totally new experience. In that series, the ARCOM tests, whose origin lay in previous requests for a broader framework for the Royal Navy, was contrasted with the ASVAB as a predictor of learning rates. The work on acquiring procedures was to provide two object lessons for today's students.

THE TRIALS OF LEARNING

Two second-phase training trials

Contrasting Tasks: Gunnery and Understanding Electronics

Time estimation as historical psychometrics

Why choose electronic gates?

Construct Definition: What did AET86 and The ASVAB measure?

Was it worth it?

First, technology has shown just how redundant the gunnery experiment has become, with guided missiles and laser targeting in the hands of untrained users wreaking havoc in local wars. It was a historical psychometric exercise because the BARB test created especially for the purpose was the first to be discontinued. For all that, it had inestimable value by showing what the construct of time-estimation was, by demonstrating what it was not - neither like the other BARB tests nor like the AET86. In the USA, apart from confirming earlier work with working memory tests, ARCOM dramatically opened the door on the ASVAB battery by using accuracy and latency scores as a key to its better understanding. Finally, perhaps the most telling issue of all, *like the Marine study, the gunnery and gates trials had the exceptional gift of reliable criterion data.* Perhaps this chapter should be read as an example of what outcomes can be in military psychometrics when there can be no doubt about the relevance and accuracy of the performance that was being forecast by test results. Simulators actually recorded how often the gunners hit the target. In the USA work, the computer itself presented the gates symbols, and scored the attempts by recruits to learn them. One could hardly have done better in a quest for valid and reliable criteria.

PUTTING BARB'S PROJECTILE TEST TO THE TEST

Whereas the majority of the BARB tests were designed to predict the ease with which new skills could be learned and used, the BARB Projectile Test (PJ) was created to predict success in acquiring specialised skills with weapons involved in tracking and aiming. An analogue illustration of the test and some basic references were given in Chapter 6. Before detailing the results of reliability and validity trials with the test, the theoretical frame used at the time for the operational definition of tests of time estimation is provided. The literature covers the main issue: how it is that actions requiring the estimation of trajectories, paths and intercepts may be processed in the brain. The chapter contents are derived from the two main sources in the insert, models of time estimation in different species and pre-trials of estimation tasks with IRT models by Wright (1990).

First, work in modelling how humans

ESTIMATING TIME INTERVALS

First, work in modelling how humans can represent events that need to be referenced in time is reviewed, including basic literature on the preconditions for accurate interception of a moving object, usually a ball, in various games and sports. The BARB test was based on the movement of a ball.

Second, extensive data from three computer-based, dynamic repeated-measures tasks was collected and evaluated to select one of them to predict success in aiming and tracking, using a standard ground to air missile simulator in use at the time. In the summing up, theory and empiricism are reconsidered before offering some prescriptions for future work in the domain.

can represent events that need to be referenced in time is reviewed, including basic literature on the preconditions for accurate interception of a moving object, usually a ball, in various games and sports. The BARB test was based on ball movement.

Second, extensive data from three computer-based, dynamic repeated-measures tasks was collected and evaluated to select one of them to predict success in aiming and tracking, using a standard ground to air missile simulator operating at the time. In the summing up, theory and empiricism are reconsidered before offering some prescriptions for future work in the domain.

THEORETICAL BASES OF AIMING AND TRACKING

If the goal is to predict aiming and tracking performance, what should be measured in what contexts; and what can be measured in restricted testing situations? Because aiming and tracking are co-ordination skills, requiring much practice for fluency, many processes are likely to be involved in their execution. Like pilot aptitude, aiming and tracking may need to be measured using a special simulator. But whenever trainee screening is restricted by administrative convenience in a cost-benefit testing context, theory should help to construct tests that predict operational performance at relatively low cost.

The Anecdotal Consensus on Aiming and Tracking.

There is an intuitive certainty that aiming and tracking have to do with processing spatial information flow from contexts, self-monitoring, and decision-making. For example, marksmen make estimate the effect of micro deviation caused by single system movement (tremor in the gun barrel, for instance in static targets); and in 'catch up' barrel movement (in clay pigeon and skeet), which are dual system patterns. Outfielders, in another context entirely, but closely related to what is required in the BARB test, talk about 'getting a good jump on the ball'. They are able to predict the ball's eventual landing point and get there in time to catch it. Without successful prediction of outcomes, often in 'blind' contexts (serving a tennis ball tossed into the sun) intercepting a moving and downward accelerating object would not be possible. Musicians such as pianists or guitarists will talk about critical passages in high-speed performance where memory errors of even a minor nature have catastrophic knock-on effects on note sequence. Finally, there are people whose living depends on the maintenance of fluent repertoires of psychomotor skills, where there simply is not time to initiate and execute each one independently (Lashley, 1951).

The anecdotal approach is consistent. Complex motor sequences imply long-term memory for patterns of movement, even if they are verbally inaccessible, leading to automatic run-off. *Memory for sequences, and intervals, implies that they can be encoded, even if the codes are not accessible to the performer. In short, everyday speech refers to hand-eye co-ordination; but much of expert eye-hand co-ordination relies on accurate prediction of outcomes based on prior experience.*

A BASIC PSYCHOLOGY FOR AIMING AND TRACKING

Eye-hand co-ordination presupposes two kinds of memory, and sense of timing:
- **generalised memory for kinesthetic outcomes** athletes, and in particular gymnasts and platform divers work well once they 'get the feel of' the exercise.

- ***working memory*** involved in the particular kind of information processing required for decision-making.
- ***a sense of timing*** crucially as far as tracking and aiming may be concerned: and what can plainly be described as a sense of timing in perceptual context.

In summary, some of the skills in tracking and aiming depend on remembering the sequence of established muscular programs. They are temporal and context-related. During learning, working memory is involved whenever predictions have to be made that require conscious and control-regulated action.

PRECEPTS OF TIME ESTIMATION[1]
The capability to extract information that initiates psychomotor sequences on perceptual cue, is probably much more fundamental in all species survival than is generally realised. The work of Lee (Lee & Reddish 1981; Lee, Young, Reddish, Lough & Clayton, (1983) found that gannets and humans are equally capable of plotting intercepts in similar accelerating contexts, gannets altering wing conformation prior to water entry and humans in jumping to anticipate the rate of descent of a volley-ball. This work confirms the adaptive capacity to extract from a moving perceptual flow those invariant characteristics of information that enable prediction of outcomes and the running of psychomotor sequences. The central strand of theory behind the construction of time estimation task to predict aiming and tracking is contextual: and it is universal. The general framework is Gibson (1979) who ecological approach to visual perception is consistent with more general theories of cognition in context developed by cross-cultural psychology. Information flow from what Gibson calls *surface characteristics* of objects and events is filtered and processed by what humans in different cultural contexts bring to the events themselves. Much of this processing of perceptual events in habitual and automatic; and it consists in *extracting fixed properties in the context of information-flow.* It is not easily accessible to the beginner. Least of all is it capable of verbalisation for rehearsal.

INFORMATION NEEDED FOR CORRECT TIMING
A considerable body of literature exists about athletic performance in intercepting the flight of a ball so as to catch it or to hit it with a bat; and most of it is referred to in Golby (1989), whose empirical work on the amount of information needed to make correct contact with a moving ball is referred to later. Under conditions of constant speed in a straight line as when a car or train is approaching, where the cue is distance, only a correct judgement of distance could, *ceteris paribus*, result in crossing the road or track unhurt. Again, if time were the only cue, estimation of time to impact would be an essential for safe crossing. Of course, in non-linear and accelerating or decelerating conditions, such as most ball-games, the equations are much more complex; and it is difficult to imagine a human system with a large number of independent functions each under separate control. *One has to assume a general control system able to operate under very complex, dynamic estimation conditions.*
    The most important finding for construction of the BARB tasks was the

---

1   The literature review here is what was available during the period. It does not pretend to do more than show what was at the team's disposal in constructing the projectile tasks. On reflection, it still seems useful.

growing evidence that *one need not see the target at all times* in order either to hit it (Whiting, 1968; Whiting, Gill & Stephenson, 1970), or (Bahill & McDonald, 1982; Golby, 1989). Whiting's work showed that even with a ball in darkness during the latter part of its flight, it was possible to catch it if visibility for 200 msec. was assured. This raises the question of how much time is needed prior to contact to use information made available during the interval of the ball's flight. Lee (Lee, Young, Reddish, Lough & Clayton, 1983; Lee & Reddish, 1981; Lee, Lishman & Thomson 1982) argue that accurate prediction of time-to-contact (hereafter defined as TP) is crucial. Because the cue is visual, as long as viewing time exceeds the time required for visual-motor processing (c.100-150 msec), performance could be error-free. A test of this position was made when De Lucia and Cochrane (1985) confined sight of the path of a baseball travelling at 60 mph under 'game' conditions to one of three segments, initial, middle and late. Information from any of the three sectors ensured successful performance. Screening of any one sector had very little effect. Golby (1989) attempted a replication of the previous experiment in another fundamental component of English culture - cricket - where the ball travels for 21 yards - and reached more or less the same conclusions. Under all conditions when the middle seven yards of the ball's trajectory were hidden performance gave an approximate 75% overall safe hit rate. Most surprising, perhaps, was a 76% success rate when *only the middle seven yards interval* was allowed for cueing.

Eyes on the Ball, Chaps!
Review of this evidence leads to a general proposition about the role of working memory in such performance. First, consider the nature and significance of the advice 'Keep your eye on the ball'. This may be what coaches tell novices to do, but the ball need not be followed all the way until it hits the bat or racquet. From the reported research on experts, such advice is blatantly a case of information from the environment to be able to put a number of different skills together. 'Early preparation' is a construct much used by coaches, particularly in awkward shots like backhands in racquet games. Expert batters, like expert trackers and aimers require functioning working memories for multimodal forms of information. They may be able to deploy attentional resources differently from novices, but *the judgement of time intervals from limited and incomplete data capture in working memory* seems to be central to successful outcomes, whatever the status of the performer.

The conclusions for the operational definition of tasks that predict eventual mastery of complex aiming and tracking have to focus on those aspects of performance that are central. These have to include the processing of visual (or other contextual) information to enable correct time estimation for contact; and under conditions which depend on enforced storage of information to enable prediction of outcomes from incomplete information. There seems to be more than enough evidence to propose that a general ability to estimate time could underlie success in aiming and tracking. One might call this TE or time estimation.

THREE AIMING AND TRACKING TASKS

In the United States, as part of US Army *Project A*, a comprehensive study of the predictors of gunnery, using simulators and a complex battery of predictors is reported by Smith & Graham (1987). The sample was 95 officers in training. The measures were extensive; and the scores were complex - groupings of accuracy and latencies for different parts of tests. The gunnery criterion was itself predicted by working memory tasks giving a multiple R of .73. Relevant certainly, and recommended for a number of reasons, but this was unavailable to the BARB team at the time[2]. The immediate emphasis was on a task that demonstrable relationships with the skills needed to hit a moving target. Pellegrino & Hunt (1989) had demonstrated the use of 'wall tasks' that show a computer-presented object in movement either in linear or parabolic fashion, with constant velocity or in acceleration mode. Details are given for the three different types of aiming and tracking tasks that were devised for BARB, using the wall paradigm, where a ball is seen prior to reaching a wall, disappears behind it and reaches some point, unseen. The task is to estimate the time at which the point of contact is made. The score is then an error score, either early or late from a zero point of complete accuracy. As for the dependent variables, speed and accuracy in the early and late tracking phases (Dennis & Evans, 1991) are obviously of interest, as are their interactions. Clearly, a number of tasks involving the construct TE can be devised. The construct TE in humans could, from the experimental evidence, be of a general nature, with extensive individual differences in estimating moments and points of contact across contexts.

THREE TRACKING AND AIMING TASK TYPES

Wall Tasks

Projectile Tasks

Collision Tasks

LINEAR WALL AND PARABOLA TASKS (TE1 AND TE2)
Three TE tasks were devised by laboratory members as candidates for trial. They conformed to the requirements set down for all other tests in the BARB series. They were computer-generated in real time from hypotheses about what aspects of the tasks would alter their difficulty. Blocks of items were derived from the Cartesian set of speed, distance and start and finish points of moving displays. Scoring was a function of time error in pressing a key to meet a task requirement, such as prediction the time at which a moving object would land at a fixed point (task TE1, *Linear Wall Task* and TE2, *Parabola Wall Tasks*). The third task type, explored in the laboratory but not used, predicts the time at which two objects moving at right angles to each other would coincide .

The Wall and Parabola forms of the time estimation paradigm are 'wall tasks'. They consist of moving displays in which an object is perceived as moving across a monitor from left to right in linear (TE1 *Wall Task*) fashion along the ground, or in parabolic arc (TE2 *The Parabola or Projectile Task*) through the air, until it disappears behind a wall. Although it is no longer visible, recruits have to assume that it travels along a prescribed path until it arrives on a spot whose distance behind the wall is shown (TE1), or arrives back on the ground after completing its parabolic arc. The last sector of travel is always hidden behind the wall.

The tasks require estimation of time to land on a prescribed spot from data visible in the pre-wall part of the trial, storage of that information and use of it to reconstruct the hidden part of the trajectory so that a keypress can be made to make

---

2   The author discovered it on the internet in 2011.

the object land exactly on the spot. This kind of task assumes that an 'isomorphic' model (Shepard and Metzler, 1971) of the path and speed of the object is possible. The time interval to meet target behind the wall is identical with that required to cover the same distance in the pre-wall segment, but that time interval will begin at a variable time behind the wall in *The Parabola Task*, whenever the zenith of the object does not coincide with the wall itself.

Error Sources
Additionally, some obvious sources of error in these tasks help to focus on their theoretical appropriateness:

Pre-wall data-processing
1. Error in estimating distance
2. Correct distance but incorrect time estimation

Post-wall data-processing
3. Memory for pre-wall interval length decays.
4. Path 'image' poorly reconstructed in working memory
5. Interval not reconstructed in working memory
6. Keypress timing error - control system mishap

These errors are perhaps obvious; and there are undoubtedly more. Success at the task depends on extracting information from the data-driven phase (pre-wall) so as to make accurate predictions with the 'eye-off the ball' (post-wall) in working memory.

RELIABILITY STUDIES
Reliability studies were completed on TE1 and TE2. Both were carried out on large groups of United Kingdom *Army Personnel Selection Centre* (APSC) recruits with a variable N, but which did not go below 100 cases for any single correlation.

TE1: The Wall Task.
This is the linear wall task, known familiarly as 'the rolling ball task'. A ball appears to roll behind a wall and the recruit presses a key when the ball coincides exactly with a stationary target ball visible behind the wall. Wright[3] (1990) produced an elegant mathematical study, using IRT methods, to estimate the information available in items where the error is a continuous variable. In this version, a block of trials consists of 16 items, in which 4 approach speeds are combined with 4 target distances behind the wall. Items are randomised within blocks. Each recruit completed 4 blocks, and the dependent variable was the average timing error over 4 trials at each of the 16 items. A total of 1785 recruits completed the task. Most of the reliable information about recruit performance was obtained from a subset of 4 items at a short distance away from the screen, with speeds varying from 1 (fast) through 4 (slow). The average intercorrelation of these 4 subtests or 'testlets' was .34. The reliability of a test consisting of sets of these items was estimated as .67. This modest value showed that this test would require revision.

     The poorest results, in terms of reliability, were combinations of slow ball speeds and large distances behind the wall. This combination produced answers of

---

3   David Wright and Pam Gould were co-authors on the original report. They made the data possible.

so great inconsistency that the trials on these items provide no useful information. In terms of theory it suggests that slow travel speeds and long intervals put the ball out of sight for so long that it was impossible to maintain the memory of its time interval. Alternatively, and/or additionally, recruits were frustrated by inaccuracies in these conditions and their performance destabilised because of interaction effects. One could only speculate.

TE2 The BARB PJ Time Estimation Task Structure And Reliability
TE2 is a parabola task, eventually called *The Projectile Task* (PJ) or in football parlance, 'hang time', being the time the ball is in the air from start to finish. The ball appears to move from ground position at varying angles and speeds, describes an arc and returns to ground level after disappearing behind a wall, so that the last part of its flight is not visible behind the wall. For this task, *mean relative error of time estimation* for the ball to reach the ground was calculated for each of 8 blocks of trials. The logarithm of this error was used as the dependent variable. TE2: The average intercorrelation of the 8 blocks of trials was, unlike those for the first time estimation task, TE1, reasonably consistent across all blocks, leading to an estimate of .88 for all eight blocks together.

Figure 9.1: The BARB Projectile (PJ) Task

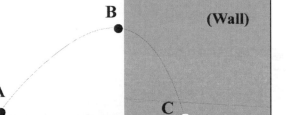

PJ RESULTS

Predictive validity from simulation data

Final Trials Predicted well

Trials intercorrelated showing similarities

Projectile Task Intercorrelations of Trial Blocks

	T1	T2	T3	T4	T5	T6	T7	T8
Trial 1	-	37	33	30	27	24	27	26
Trial 2		-	42	38	33	30	30	28
Trial 3			-	37	30	34	32	33
Trial 4				-	35	33	37	31
Trial 5					-	35	37	36
Trial 6						-	36	36
Trial 7							-	40
Trial 8								-

Furthermore, the table in Figure 8.1 shows that the correlations of the last trial, number eight, decreased almost linearly with each previous trial from .40 to .26. The correlations between adjacent trials were constant. Individuals were learning as the trials proceeded, showing that their 'skills had reached a crude level of stability' in Ferguson's (1959) memorable definition of an ability. D models were not far away in this experiment.

PREDICTIVE VALIDITY OF THE BARB PROJECTILE TASK

The *Projectile Task* was correlated with the criterion data from tests of proficiency using a portable missile launch-simulator at four different intervals during training. The criterion results are numbered CT1 to CT4, representing the order of (CT) criterion tests. The error score on the *Projectile Task* is labelled TE2E. Because it is an error score its correlation with training success would be negative, but here the results are represented as positive correlations to remove minuses.

Table 9.1: Correlations of Performance with PJ Task

	Projectile	CT1	CT2	CT3	CT4
Projectile Score(TE2E)	-	25	29	49	42
Criterion Stage 1		-	52	40	51
Criterion Stage 2			-	66	67
Criterion Stage 3				-	84
Criterion Stage 4					-

Note: Bold values are negative correlations with signs reversed.

The Results Reveal Two Important Patterns.

As was seen in the previous table showing the correlations of *the Projectile Task* with each other, each missile launch performance measure correlates more closely with its immediate neighbour than with any other and these correlations increase at time goes by. This is a typical learning pattern in a complex learning task, showing that rank-orders of trainees are more stable at the end of the training than at the beginning. Similarly, *The Projectile Task* correlations increase for the later trials, because the criterion measure variance is stabilising, that is the training measures are increasing in their internal consistency. If the first two trials were corrected for unreliability, to match the .84 correlation of the last two trials, the correlations would approach the same values as for the later trials. Detailed scrutiny of the results revealed that *The Projectile Task* was good at identifying unsatisfactory trainees; but success rates, assessed by the proportions teaching training performance standard, were high. From these and other considerations, it was recommended that the proficiency standard be raised for trainees admitted after screening by *The Projectile Task*, rather than standards remain constant while admitting fewer trainees.

THE CONSTRUCTS OF THE PROJECTILE TASK: WHAT DID IT MEASURE?

The Projectile Task was involved in construct validation where the domains were defined by the content of the AETs (*Problems, Instructions, Dominoes, Verbal, and Arithmetic*) and the BARB Battery (LC, RF, AL, TI and ND). The subtests TI to

T8 were taken as independent trials for this purpose, partly because of their modest intercorrelations, and after signs in preliminary analysis that the time-estimation tasks were not all together orthogonal to tests in the cognitive batteries administered previously or concurrently to the recruit population. For the purposes of examining more thoroughly the cognitive structure of *The Projectile Task* the firm definition of a time estimation factor (TE) using 8 marker variables was an important first step. Nevertheless, every effort was made not to overinterpret the factors emerging from the analysis in the knowledge that the variables T1 to T8 are not truly independent[4] of each other, and as a consequence, their communalities may be artificially inflated. A maximum likelihood analysis of all 17 variables was carried out.

Table 9.2: Oblimin Rotations with Factor Correlations

Variables	Oblimin Rotated Factors			
	1	**2**	**3**	**C**
AETs (PIDVA)				
Problems		76		57
Instructions	27	50		51
Dominoes	37	36		46
Verbal		79		61
Arith./Math	28	58		66
BARB				
Rotated F	39			18
Transitive Infer.	62			53
Alpha Forward/Back	74			51
Number Distance	66			51
Letter Checking	57			31
PJ Task Trials				
Trial1			49	25
Trial2			59	35
Trial3			60	36
Trial4			60	36
Trial5			57	33
Trial6			57	33
Trial7			59	35
Trial8			57	33
	1	**2**	**3**	
Factor	-			
Intercorrelations		70	45	
			35	
			-	

Note: C is the communality from Maximum LIkelihood extraction

Three factors were predicted from all the previous work on factor extraction with AET and BARB, when two factors best fitted the data when the projectile tasks

---

4   I realised that by putting all the PJ trials into the analysis I was creating an 'artefactor' that my one-time mentor Oscar Roberts (1959) would have expunged. However, the Oblimin rotation shows the correlation with the trials and the other factors. Maybe he would have forgiven me. S. I.

were not included. In the first analysis, the ML procedure extracted three factors from the data independently of our estimate. The Oblimin pattern and structure matrices are shown (Table 8.3) with factor intercorrelations to draw some theory-based conclusions about process involvement in parabola tasks as operationally defined. The numbers are rounded and loadings below .25 and decimal points omitted.

THE THREE CONSTRUCTS

Previous work with the PIDVA and BARB tests confirmed the basic two-factor structure of the domain sampled by these tests. The BARB factor is a *processing efficiency* construct with consistently high loadings on working memory tasks. The second PIDVA factor has been a *verbal-educational* factor associated with traditional AET type tests. The two factors correlate usually in the region of .6, defining a higher-order construct, which has been defined as a general training index. These previous analyses are once again confirmed here, with a two factor-solution for the AET and BARB tests emerging as before, albeit with a slightly higher intercorrelation of .7, indicative of a higher order general factor.

PJ STRUCTURES CONFIRMED

Chaiken Kyllonen & Tirre confirm time estimation factor.

The Time-Estimation Factor

The addition of the *Projectile Task* trials defines *a third, time-estimation factor based upon isomorphic reconstruction of paths in working memory*. The factor correlations show this to be only moderately correlated with the two other factors, and in the same amount. This pattern shows that those skills most entering into successful completion of AET and BARB tests, although required to a small extent, do not account for the range of individual differences measured in the *Projectile Task*. Its moderate but useful correlation with BARB (.45) showed it, at this stage, to be an important addition to screening for aptitudes necessary in a large number of weapon-handling contexts. If a form of working memory was involved, it was 'working 'on a different plane from that required by the other BARB tests. If working-memory capacity and (domain-specific) knowledge are the big two in abilities research, to round out the picture, the big three would add time-estimation to the list. Time-estimation (or temporal processing) ability can be measured with any number of tasks that require an individual to remember or retrieve a time interval, then to report it back through some kind of response.

Some years after the BARB study was reported, Kyllonen's extensive work in the LAMP project for the USAF included a study of time estimation (using 161 graduates) (Chaiken, Kyllonen, & Tirre, 2000). Even with a small sample of highly educated participants, the results confirmed those from the large group of recruits. Two main conclusions emerged: (a) a wide variety of tasks - dynamic spatial, mental counter, time interval estimation--all measured the same ability and (b) that time estimation capability was an important supplement to working-memory capacity in accounting for performance on an wide range of psychomotor ability tasks. As in the BARB study, most of the psychomotor learning factor variance was unique, but was related to processing speed. The correlations of the three factors in the LAMP project were very similar to those shown in Table 8.3, Initial psychomotor performance is constrained by working-memory limits and the ability to keep track of time.

DISCUSSION

Whatever capabilities the tasks possessed, they predicted late and, with correction for assumed unreliability, early trial success in the artillery school. Elements of theory embodied in the tasks as constructed advance the proposition that unless a time interval can be encoded, then it cannot be learned, or held in memory. While this seems to be a sound basis for present frameworks for item-generation of such tests, the mechanisms of encoding are little understood, especially in the kinaesthetic

---

A RETROSPECTIVE INTERLUDE

This work with the projectile task was in many ways a source of satisfaction because a new test had been created, with a 'testlet' scoring procedure invented by David Wright, and a criterion of great certainty provided by Pam Gould. All the necessary parts of the jigsaw had made a complete picture. One more indicator of the importance of their efforts was forthcoming when a review of the results requested that for security reasons, no mention of the average accuracy of the gunners should be made; because that would let any potential enemy how to counteract their efficiency - a consummation indeed.

Just as satisfactory, but on another landscape entirely, was the work on learning to identify electronic gate pathways, that completes this chapter. It gives full rein to the creativity of Ian Dennis, whose applications of cognitive theory to the issues of parallel form construction seem, in retrospect, too little developed and scarcely recognised. His work was mentioned in the previous chapter. It speaks for itself in his contributions to the ARCOM tests that are the central theme of the first cooperative research done in the United States Air Force Laboratory with Raymond Christal and Pat Kyllonen at Brooks AFB.

---

domain. If used as a screening device, improvements in performance and lowering of training time would both be consequences of the size of the validity coefficients. When BARB went operational in 1991, it was an important item; but by 1996, this test had been discontinued. To date, no official explanation for the omission has been forthcoming; and to be fair, none has been requested.

LEARNING LOGIC GATES AT LACKLAND AFB

This research was carried out under a joint services technical co-operation agreement It involved the resources of The Human Assessment Laboratory, University of Plymouth, Plymouth, UK; and The USAF Laboratory, Brooks AFB, San Antonio, Texas, USA. The aim of the work was to confirm, in a quasi-operational context, the findings of an earlier report by Christal (1991), who first demonstrated that experimental, computer-delivered tests of cognitive functions could predict the initial and later stages of electronic logic gate identification with greater effectiveness than the battery of tests known as the *United States Armed Services Vocational Aptitude Battery* (ASVAB)..

WHAT DOES THE ASVAB REALLY MEASURE?
Much has been written about what the ASVAB measures and what the scores predict (Carretta & Ree, 1996; Earles & Ree, 1992; Kass, Mitchell, Grafton & Wing, H. 1983; Maier & Sims 1986; Ree & Earles, 1991, 1992; Ree, Muffins, Mathews, & Massey, 1982). The individual tests, when correlated, have been said to produce a large general factor, perhaps conveniently called *psychometric g*. Some might assert (see Roberts, 1959) that *psychometric g* is not necessarily proved to be a psychological factor, but is no more or less than a statistical artefact derived from the extraction of a first principal component. That caution notwithstanding, the ASVAB general factor is more plausibly interpreted as a general declarative knowledge educational factor, accounting for more than 60% of all the variance (Welsh, Watson & Ree, 1990). On the other hand, several analyses advocate the use of *four group factors, Verbal (WK and PC), Speed (CS and NO), Quantitative (AR and MK) and finally, Technical (AS, MC and EL)*. From these broad groupings, certain vocational composites have been routinely calculated, based on studies of how well the various test combinations would predict training success in the various branches of the US armed services. These composites have been recorded in applicant profiles along with a general aptitude score, the AFQT. An excellent overview of the debate and possibilities is found in Ree & Earles, (1996, pp. 151-165). Two manuals for the ASVAB, in use at the time of collecting data, provided a great deal of cumulative evidence for the success of the battery in allocating recruits to training programmes and predicting outcomes (AACD, 1984; USMEPC 1984). As late as 1997, the ASVAB in conjunction with a high school diploma, was still being presented in international meetings as the main protection against attrition (TTCP, 1997, pp. 60-64).

Here, for readers who have no previous knowledge of the ASVAB framework, a short description of typical items is included. The ten subtests used at that time are listed, with their standard abbreviations in Figure 9.2. The whole battery took more than two hours to administer, and contained over 300 items. Much is written about the ASVAB, but few examples of the individual tests, apart from official handbooks, seem to exist.

Figure 9.2: Summary Outline of ASVAB Test Content

General Science. (GS 25; 11; .83) This test contains 35 standard form vocabulary items requiring scientific knowledge 'Which of the following foods contain the most fat? (a) fish (b) cheese (c) bread (d) tomato.'

Arithmetic Reasoning (AR 30; 36; .87). This test consists of 30 arithmetic word problems, such as the following: 'Fred worked a total of 21 hours for 5 days of the past week. How long is Fred's average workday? (a) 4 hours, (b) 4 Hours 10 minutes (c) 4 hours 15 minutes (d) 4 hours 12 minutes

---

Word Knowledge (WK 35; 11; .88). This test consists of 35 vocabulary items, requiring identification of synonyms   'The sky is overcast today. (a) sunny, (b) rainy, (c) cloudy, or (d) stormy.'

Paragraph Comprehension (PC 15; 13; .72). This test consists of 15 paragraphs, each 1-to-3 sentences long, followed by a multiple-choice question, for example:
'To survive basic training, a recruit has to obey orders without question, never complain, and stay as inconspicuous as possible.'
According to the passage, to survive, a recruit must
(a) make sure he is noticed; (b) complain when necessary; (c) stand to attention when spoken to; (d) keep quiet and do what he is told.

Numerical Operations (NO 50; 3; .70). This is a test of 50 number-fact calculations (e.g., 3 x 7- ? (a) 10, (b) 14, (c) 18, (d) 21). One may complete as many of the items as possible in the short time limit.

Coding Speed (CS 84; 7; .73). This has 84 items designed to measure how quickly one can find a number in a table. Working memory storage is involved. An item shows a word followed by five 4-digit number strings (e.g., (a) 4579, (b) 5793, (c) 6134, (d) 7064. The task is to (a) find the word's number code in a key consisting of 10 word-code pairs placed on top of the page, then (b) select the letter corresponding to that number code. Participants have 10 minutes to complete as many items as possible.

Auto and Shop Information (AS 25; 11; .83). There are 25 questions about automobiles, repair shop practices, and the use of tools. .' Some of the questions include drawings of common tools or parts. An example is: 'A shock absorber is part of the (a) brakes, (b) steering (c) suspension, (d) fuel system

---

Mathematics Knowledge (MK 25; 24; .84). This test contains 25 problems, mainly algebra, but also calculations involving area, percentages, and simple geometry, like the following: 'If $5X = -7$, then $X = :$ (a) 1,25, (b) -5/7, (c) -7/5, (d) 5/7.'

Mechanical Comprehension (MC 25; 19; .78). This test has 25 questions relating to general mechanical and physical principles. The questions are normally accompanied by drawings.
For example, a drawing may show a pulley of more than one wheel with an arrow indicating the direction of one of the ropes. The question might be 'Which of the other wheels is moving in the same direction as wheel X? (a) Wheel Y, (b) Wheel Z, (c) Both Y and Z, (d) None of the wheels.'

Electrical Information (EI 20; 9; .72). There are 20 questions relating to knowledge of electrical, radio, and electronics information. Some of the questions contain drawings, while others do not.
Here is an example: 'Which of the following is the best conductor of electricity? (a) Brick, (b) Wood, (c) Copper (d) Leather.'

The information In brackets shows the abbreviation, the number of items, the time in minutes and the alternate test form reliability.

ARCOM, ASVAB AND ELECTRONIC GATES

BARB tests were extended in 1990-93 in two forms - a paper-and-pencil version for the Navy, called The Navy Personnel Series (Collis & Irvine, 1994) and in a second modification for screening potential Army officers called the *Army Regular Commissions Board Battery* (ARCOM). Both modifications were based on item-generation theory (IGT) so that multiple parallel forms of the tests could be generated from algorithms - a necessary prerequisite of computer-delivered adaptive tests with feedback. Given these types of tests, it was important to have available for each recruit results on tests that required a high-school graduation level of education, and that included measures of various kinds of technical knowledge. The ASVAB series contains just such a selection of measures, with mechanical, electrical and science knowledge tests as well as tests of mathematical knowledge and verbal comprehension. Finally, a criterion measure was required which involved novel learning of a

ASVAB STRUCTURES

Much discussion and debate but little in the way of consensus

technical nature, in which accuracy of a high level could be attained, so that speed of functioning could be assessed against a low error rate. Christal (1991) had used electronic logic gates in his first experiment, and it was appropriate to use this series again. Moreover, a pre-test booklet was available to provide a case study of the effect of prior experience - a paper-and-pencil outline of what the tests measured, with examples and a scoring key. Whereas the work with pre-test booklets among Royal Navy personnel (Chapter 8) was with analogue paper-and-pencil test versions, this was the first opportunity to gauge the effect of pre-test booklets on computer-delivered tests.

PRELIMINARY RESULTS: CHECKING OUT THE ARCOM WITH THE ASVAB

At Lackland Air Force Base 303 recruits were administered a computer-based version of the ARCOM Battery of eight tests, each given within its own fixed time limit. One group was given a pre-test paper-and-pencil booklet and its completion was checked before the ARCOM tests were administered. The second group took the tests without prior exposure. Unlike previous experience with the Royal Navy, the completion of the booklet was manually checked before the trials were begun, so that the effect of previous exposure to, and prior practice, using paper-and-pencil analogue items, on the computer-delivered ARCOM could be assessed.

Eight Logic Gates learning trials, computer-delivered, were completed at the end of the ARCOM Battery. Logic Gates Trials (Gates) were scored for percentage correct and average time per item. Test outcome variables were scores adjusted for guessing and the average latency per item in milliseconds. In addition, the ASVAB scores for each recruit were obtained from records, enabling comparability of the groups assigned to the book-no book condition, a lesson learned from the work with British soldiers. To remove the effects of differential pretest booklets treatment on ARCOM test variables, Z scores were calculated for each person within treatments.

Table 9.3: Pre-test Booklet Results: ARCOM Tests with USAF Recruits

		N	Mean	SD	Effect
ARCOM Letter Checking	Book	152	43.9	7.9	
How many vertical pairs same?	No Book	151	39.0	9.6	0.53
n m r q	Total	303	40.7	9.3	
J M H Q					
ARCOM Number Brackets/Parentheses	Book	152	17.4	9.2	
$12 - (3 \times 2) = ?$ [A] 9 [B] 18 [C] 6	No Book	151	17.5	9.3	0.01
	Total	303	17.5	9.3	
ARCOM TI Reasoning	Book	152	22.6	8.7	
Joe is heavier than Bob.	No Book	151	20.2	7.6	0.29
Bob is lighter than Bill.	Total	303	21.0	8.1	
Who is lightest? [A] Bill [B] Bob [C] Joe					
ARCOM Symbol Rotation	Book	152	21.1	10.5	
How many vertical pairs same?	No Book	151	18.2	11.0	0.26
	Total	303	19.1	10.9	
0 1 2?					
ARCOM AB Forward and Backward	Book	152	11.2	8.0	
AB + 2? = FG CD DE	No Book	151	11.8	6.9	-0.08
RDZ -1? = PDW SFX QCY	Total	303	11.6	7.3	
ARCOM Odd One Out	Book	152	41.8	8.7	
Hot Duck Cold	No Book	151	33.6	7.5	0.93
	Total	303	36.3	8.8	
ARCOM Number Distance	Book	152	20.2	9.4	
Find high and low numbers. Which of these is	No Book	151	16.9	8.8	0.36
further from remaining number? 4 11 7	Total	303	18.0		
ARCOM Directions and Distances	Book	152	3.1	3.6	
In a certain town, the cinema is 500 metres North	No Book	151	2.5	3.2	0.18
of the supermarket; the supermarket is 900 metres	Total	303	2.7	3.4	
South of the swimming pool. What direction is					
the cinema from the swimming pool?					
[A] North [B] South [C] East [D] West					

Learning from Practice: Pre-test Booklets Effects on ARCOM.

Table 9.3 gives the effect sizes in SD units when the pre-test booklet was used before ARCOM was administered in computerised form. It also contains examples of the kinds of items used in each of the ARCOM subtests. Perhaps it is worthwhile recalling that pre-test information about multiple parallel form tests never reveals the items actually present in the test. The outcomes were varied, from minor, unimportant effects to major increases, particularly in simple perceptual speed and vocabulary tasks. However, the effects were noticeable; and made a case for ensuring that the advent of parallel forms made prior paper-and-pencil practice test experiences more likely to produce viable computer-based test scores. Nevertheless, to eliminate the effects, however large or small, all ARCOM test scores were converted to Z-scores *within each treatment*, so that relative performance standings were unaffected by participation in the pre-test trial. Figure 9.3 shows that prior the ASVAB scores made prior to enlistment showed that the two treatment groups were counterbalanced. ARCOM differences were a function of prior exposure to item types.

Figure 9.3: ASVAB Check on Pretest Booklet Effects

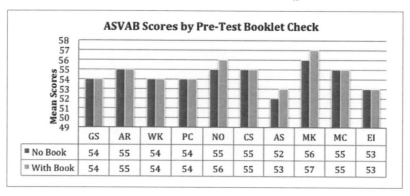

ASVAB Scores by Pre-Test Booklet Check

Mean Scores	GS	AR	WK	PC	NO	CS	AS	MK	MC	EI
■ No Book	54	55	54	54	55	55	52	56	55	53
■ With Book	54	55	54	54	56	55	53	57	55	53

Table 9.4: Factor Structures of ASVAB and ARCOM by Scoring Model Type.

Corect Answers Adjusted	Factors 1	2	ARCOM Latencies and ASVAB R/W	Factors 1	2
ARCOM Parenthesis	.73	.12	*ASVAB General Science(GS)*	.78	-.07
ARCOM TI Reasoning	.69	.18	*ASVAB Mechanical Comprehension(MC*	.74	-.02
ARCOM Alphabet Forward/Backward	.66	.08	*ASVAB Electronic Information (EI)*	.73	.14
ASVAB Coding Speed(CS)	.66	-.17	*ASVAB Word Knowledge(WK)*	.64	-.13
ASVAB Mathematic Knowledge(MK)	.65	.35	*ASVAB Auto and Shop Information(AS)*	.62	.22
ASVAB Arithmetic Reasoning(AR)	.62	.43	*ASVAB Arithmetic Reasoning(AR)*	.59	-.42
ARCOM Letter Checking	.60	.02	*ASVAB Mathematic Knowledge(MK)*	.52	-.44
ARCOM Odd One Out Vocabulary	.59	.34	*ASVAB Paragraph Comprehension(PC)*	.47	-.14
ASVAB Numerical Operations(NO)	.58	-.17			
ARCOM Number Distance	.51	.15			
ARCOM Symbol Rotation (F)	.42	.34			
ARCOM Directions/Distances	.33	.33	ARCOM Parentheses: Lat.	-.15	.67
			ARCOM ABC Back/Forward: Lat.	.20	.62
			ARCOM Odd One Out Lat.	-.24	.61
			ARCOM Reasoning: Lat.	-.30	.61
ASVAB Electronic Information (EI)	-.10	.79	ARCOM Number/Distance: Lat.	.12	.54
ASVAB Mechanical Information (MI)	.08	.79	ARCOM Symbol Rotation: Lat.	-.06	.51
ASVAB General Science(GS)	.13	.79	*ASVAB Coding Speed(CS)*	.06	-.51
ASVAB Auto and Shop Information(AS)	-.22	.69	*ASVAB Numerical Operations(NO)*	.04	-.50
ASVAB Word Knowledge(WK)	.27	.64	ARCOM Letter Check: Lat.	-.19	.40
ASVAB Paragraph Comprehension(PC)	.24	.44	ARCOM Direc/Distance: Lat.	.19	.37

Notes: Extraction Method: Principal Component Analysis. Rotation Method: Varimax with Kaiser Normalization.

TEST SCORE MODELS IDENTIFIED

Two quite different test batteries, ASVAB and ARCOM, and two scoring models for ARCOM, one traditional R or Right/Wrong and the other the average time per item for each different test were uniquely available. It was possible to analyse the intercorrelations of the tests, using the ASVAB scores as a constant R model, and also examining the effect of the latency scoring system in ARCOM. The sample of 351 recruits was used and the results of extracting two factors from the correlation matrices.

Given a working memory battery alongside its test scores, the major focus of the ASVAB is revealed in the *very strong acquired knowledge base of the great majority of its tests*. Finally, when the correlations between the two factors were calculated, the resulting relationship was small, being 0.33. In short, to endow the ASVAB with the status of an IQ, or as has often been the case, status as 'psychometric g' with all the ambiguities of that label, could be somewhat misleading. Moreover, Christal's awareness of large individual differences in working memory processing capability regardless of the amount of knowledge acquired in the past, was fundamental to the realisation that Spearman's *g*, the general factor originally derived from R models, could no longer be seen as a *logical primitive*, or a construct that could not be broken down further

In fact, working memory had been established as a construct capable of measurement in more than one scoring model: and for which theoretical bases had been established (Baddeley, 1968; Baddeley and Hitch, 1974; Kyllonen 19996; Kyllonen & Christal, 1990). *The important outcome was the unchanging nature of the factor structure*. The ASVAB tests showed a predominant acquired knowledge underpinning, while ARCOM had a predominant working memory foundation, regardless of whether Right/Wrong or Latency scoring was used. Most significantly, however, is the consistent identification of *Coding Speed, Numerical Operations, Mathematical Knowledge and Arithmetic Reasoning* with working memory capability, measured either by accuracy or time to complete the items.

WHY LOGIC GATES?

Tests are defined in computers by the kinds of knowledge that are required to be stored and brought to bear on responses to produce scores in real time. For example, output files for individuals are written in such a way as to make them amenable to treatment by algorithms that transform the data from one format to another, usually for scoring purposes. Alternatively, even in the simplest of output conditions, simultaneous scoring for speed and accuracy may be specified - latencies as well as right or wrong responses. In Chapter 5, three different approaches to modelling mental test and work-task performance were described. Definitions have been offered first, for R-Models, that are robust and for which a detailed test technology exists. Next. the possibilities inherent in L-Models, that are traditional experimental cognitive tasks for which large differences between participants have been observed, were revealed. Finally, the challenges of deriving D-Models that take into account learning rates within participants were recognised. Even in traditional analysis of variance designs, variation within participants can be extensive. Each of these models of treating test answers contributes to our knowledge of performance. Each approach is presented as a key to understanding limits in modern test construction: and as a means of determining their utility. Christal's experiments in learning electronic logic gates provided a focus for examining the relationships among all three models. The measures available made a broad frontal attack on the problem possible.

Kyllonen (1996, pp. 63-66) answers the question about why logic gates were such an important part of the study of learning new concepts. Gitomer (1988) first developed logic gates learning tasks to discover how it was that some electronic engineers were better at diagnosing system faults than others. He tried many approaches, but the only test that accurately distinguished good from not so good trouble-shooters was the logic gates task. Christal and Kyllonen both recognised the tasks as involving procedural learning (know-how) as distinct from acquired factual knowledge. It assumed a central role in the extensive research a carried out in the research programme known as *Project LAMP*. What were the three logic gates tasks and how were they used?

Figure 9.4: Three Types of Logic Gates: AND, OR, XOR

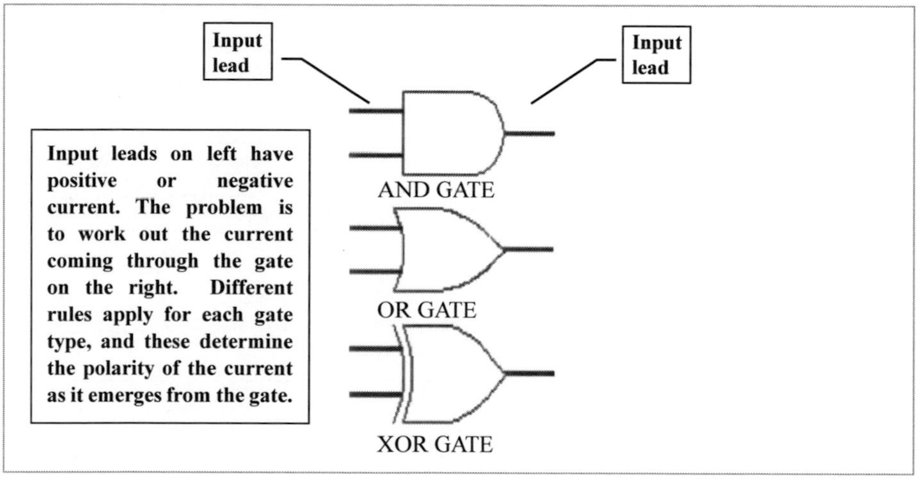

Logic gates are used in diagrams of electrical circuits. Each has a different shape. Only three were used in this study and they first had to be recognised by recruits who knew little or nothing about them. In a short training course on the shapes of AND, OR, and XOR electronic logic gates, participants were asked to recognise each gate by shape and name. Recognition practice was given before the learning trials were begun. by presenting 30 gates shapes on the screen in turn. The task was to label the shape by pressing a key. Each screen was displayed for a limited period, and then the next item automatically appeared. After each incorrect response, a screen displayed all three gates and their associated names for 10 seconds. The keyboard was 'locked-out', except during the period necessary for answers to questions.

Following practice, eight 36-item blocks of mixed AND, OR, and XOR gates, were used to provide indices of how well the gates were learned. Left leads were labelled H or L to indicate high or low input. From the rules for each gate, the output current had to be predicted by pressing a key labelled H or L. After each incorrect response, there was a 10-second feedback frame showing the pictures and rules for all three gate-types, with the missed gate type highlighted. Summaries providing percentage correct and median response time were given at the end of each testing block.

THE EIGHT LOGIC GATES TRIALS

The statistical treatment of the data was exhaustive, and the results concentrate on trends in the Logic Gates trials, factor analyses of the test results in right-wrong and latency scores, and regression analyses to illustrate the predictive power of cognitive factor scores, test composites and individual tests when correlated with the eight Gates trials. Table 9.5 shows the results of the repeated learning trials at the Logic Gates by pre-test treatment group, in order to demonstrate that the different test administration procedures used in the ARCOM Battery had no discernible effect on the Gates trial performance. Mere inspection of Table 9.5 reveals no statistical differences between groups either in percentage correct or in average latency in seconds per item. The trends are identical, showing very high accuracy is attained in a very short time, and a corresponding decrease in latency to respond. The intercorrelations among trials (not shown here) for each presentation condition were of the same order, leading to the decision to combine both groups for factor analysis and for regression purposes, following the production of Z-scores for the ARCOM test results within treatment groups.

LOGIC GATES

What the trials showed and what best predicted individual differences in learning them.

Table 9.5: Electronic Gates Learning Trial Results

	Gates Learning Trial Number							
	T1	**T2**	**T3**	**T4**	**T5**	**T6**	**T7**	**T8**
Percentage Treat1	77	85	88	90	93	94	94	94
Percentage Treat2	78	85	88	90	91	93	94	94
Latency Treat1	22.94	18.98	16.83	14.99	14.13	13.56	13.24	12.58
Latency Treat2	23.63	18.86	16.73	15.38	14.51	13.54	13.05	12.74

Inspection of the percentage correct scores in the Gates trials revealed typical departures form normality, and loss of variance as the trials proceeded. Average latency scores for items within blocks approached normality, but towards the end of the trials some bottoming was apparent. With high accuracy, it was possible to combine and at the same time to normalise the Gates trials score distributions by dividing each accuracy score for each recruit by the recruit's own log average latency per item, giving a power function of learning efficiency.

PREDICTING GATES LEARNING

There only remained the task of predicting how well and how quickly the Gates Learning Tasks could be learned. It was possible to use the percentage of gates learned in each trial, and the average time taken to provide the correct answer as criteria. And every possible test score outcome from ASVAB and ARCOM could be used as predictors. The final puzzle was to determine what combinations of measure would best predict success in learning the gates. For this purpose, all the scores available were used to see what combinations would be consistent in predicting learning efficiency. This meant entering all ten ASVAB scores, seven ARCOM test scores adjusted for guessing and the seven average times per test item scores for ARCOM tests. The method used was a stepwise regression, which means that only the most effective predictors are used until the addition of more predictors would provide no more reliable information about the strength of the prediction and the size of the multiple correlation.

ASVAB or ARCOM?

What the predictions showed and with what success.

Figure 9.5 Multiple Regressions: Relative Strength of Logic Gates Predictors

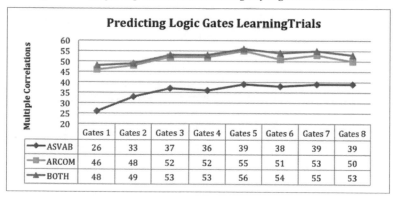

	Gates 1	Gates 2	Gates 3	Gates 4	Gates 5	Gates 6	Gates 7	Gates 8
ASVAB	26	33	37	36	39	38	39	39
ARCOM	46	48	52	52	55	51	53	50
BOTH	48	49	53	53	56	54	55	53

The results were consistent and really very straightforward. A multiple correlation approaching 0.5 was observed for accuracy and speed of learning using the ARCOM tests. The same result was obtained even when the ASVAB tests were put into the equation with the ARCOM tests. The ASVAB tests alone were much less successful, and this result with minor variations held for all 8 Gates learning trials. Figure 9.5 shows the relative and combined strength of the predictors.

The results of predicting Logic Gate learning effectiveness using only the factor scores were uniformly acceptable, with multiple R varying narrowly between .40 and .48, with variance accounted for in the low 20 percent range. The most consistent finding in all the analyses carried out is the *primacy of the working memory factor, followed by both speed of encoding and speed of working memory operations* and the same patterns emerged when individual tests were used. The specialised knowledge factor makes only one appearance, and comes at the very end of an equation. Verbal comprehension contributes a little, but consistently, at the end of four equation series. No fewer than four and no more than six individual tests were generally needed to achieve this result, and almost invariably, the ARCOM working memory scores, accuracy and latency were found to be the predictors whatever trial was being investigated. Most consistent were *Odd One Out, Directions and Distances, Rotated F, TI Reasoning, Alphabet Forward and Backward,*. Perhaps naturally, latency measure best predicted speed of learning, while accuracy contained a mix of score types. *Speed of gates identification and naming was best predicted by the ARCOM efficiency score, created by dividing the standard score for percentage correct by the average time per item block. This effectively produced a rate of learning index.* The Gates learning efficiency score was predicted equally well (within rounding error of a single correlation) by the R Model sum of the ARCOM scores adjusted for guessing, or the ARCOM work rate score which is the R Model score divided by the average time per item in the block.

PROCEDURAL KNOWLEDGE LEARNING AND SCORING MODELS

What scores would prove to be best and in what circumstance? This chapter has concluded three case studies of what outcomes might be achieved, in combat skill, time estimation for aiming and tracking, and logic gates learning. In all three studies, the results were definitive. The accuracy and speed at which novel technical material will be learned depends not on the amount of previously learned technical knowledge, but rather the extent to which the recruit can marshal mental processes of working memory effectiveness, speed of symbol encoding, speed of executing operations in working memory, and verbal fluency. The different scoring models adopted in the various studies produced virtually the same outcomes.

1. The primacy of tests of working memory in predicting field-based criteria among Royal Marine commandos was established as part of an extensive three-year validation study of the Navy Personnel Series (Collis & Irvine, 1994) (see also Chapter 8). Field-based competencies include novel learning experiences such as orientation, map-reading, field-firing and trekking. These criteria are somewhat analogous, in terms of novelty and irrelevance of acquired technical knowledge, to logic gates learning.

2. The development of a time estimation task showed the relative independence of time estimation from the rest of the BARB battery and its potential as a predictor of missile-launching training success when measured against practice involving moving targets. It was a departure from the normal validation study because it outlined a new domain of work, not previously undertaken with British personnel.

3. In predicting logic gates learning the ARCOM tests, whether right-wrong or latency scored confirmed a previous study carried out by Christal (1990), where his LAMP project experimental tests of accuracy and speed of mental processing were more effective than ASVAB tests. They also lend weight to the contention by Kyllonen & Christal (1990) that general intelligence and working memory are closely related. Moreover, the ARCOM tests used here, essentially BARB derivatives, were constructed from a theory of algorithm-determined item-generation, and had no educational prerequisites except secondary school numeracy and literacy.

CONCLUSIONS

In a number of contexts, regardless of country of origin, cognitively-referenced tests have proved effective in predicting the rate at which learning of new concepts will occur. The diversity of the criterion situations shows promise of validity generalisation whenever novelty can be assumed. At Lackland, a power model of speed relative to accuracy was the best fit. Individual differences in the power to complete tasks in two apparently diverse domains are derived from speed of retrieval of categories and the icons that define them. The most powerful single test in ARCOM was the *Odd One Out* word category discrimination task. *This test had an accuracy rate well over 90 percent.* When a confidence score derived from number correct adjusted for guessing, is divided by the average time to complete an item, giving a cognitive rate index, the skills involved map powerfully on to the accuracy and speed with which the shapes of logic gates as determiners of current flow are remembered and discriminated. If one had to seek a definition of the processes in the *Odd One Out* task, the observation of relations and the eduction of correlates might suffice, provided the phrase *in working memory*, were added.

FOOD FOR AFTERTHOUGHT?

The most intriguing aspect of the work is the absence, at present, of a comprehensive theory that will explain why it is that tests which present little or no apparent difficulty to the participants predict rates of learning of new materials better than those constructed on an advanced knowledge base using items of increasing difficulty.

This, of course, is Spearman's definition of intelligence with a caveat derived from the modern revision of *g* from its origins as a logical primitive that could not be subdivided, largely enabled by the work of Snow, Kyllonen, Baddeley, Evans and others. The force of working memory was established in the production of tasks that would enable, if not the ever elusive definition of a concept of *general* intelligence, then the surety of where it might be found with greater cognitive precision.

Part 3:

The Second Generation

The Research at Brooks Air Force Base

by Patrick C. Kyllonen, Ph.D.
Senior Research Director, Academic and Workforce Readiness and Success, Educational Testing Service (formerly Technical Director, Manpower and Personnel Research Division, Air Force Research Laboratory, Brooks Air Force Base, San Antonio, Texas)

As part of his work for the U.K.'s Army Personnel Research Establishment (APRE), beginning in the early 1980s Professor Irvine established relationships with a number of research centers in the U.S. that were engaged in similar efforts. These included Doug Detterman's individual differences lab at Case Western Reserve University, the U.S. Navy's Personnel Research and Development Center then in San Diego, Educational Testing Service in Princeton New Jersey, and what was then called the Air Force Human Resources Laboratory (AFHRL) in San Antonio, Texas (later, the Air Force Research Laboratory). These relationships were mutually beneficial. In the case of the AFHRL the relationship evolved from occasional visits to joint conferences (the Spearman Seminar series), then from regular collaborations, to a yearlong National Research Council fellowship by Professor Irvine in 1997.

As Professor Irvine points out, an opportunity for tremendous progress in our understanding of cognitive ability testing was afforded by a fully equipped computer laboratory established at Lackland Air Force Base and the availability of a large pool (up to 30,000 per year) of Air Force enlistees who were assigned to participate in lab activities during their basic military training. The laboratory was set up by Raymond Christal (assisted by Johnny Weissmuller) in 1982 through support by the Air Force Office of Scientific Research, a basic research funding body.

The lab at the time was unique, predating the Apple computer, and the IBM PC. It was initially equipped with 30 TERAK 8510/a 16-bit CPU microcomputers, with 128K memories, and 8-inch floppy disks. Upgrades to standard PC systems running DOS, then later Windows software were made a few years later, with technology upgrades occurring periodically.

The main purpose of the laboratory and the activity was to explore the idea that aptitude testing might be "reinvented" due not just to technology advances but to advances in cognitive psychology research through the efforts of scientists such as Earl Hunt, Robert Sternberg, Richard Snow, Robert Glaser, James Pellegrino, Patricia Carpenter, Marcel Just, John Anderson, Steve Kosslyn, Lynn Cooper, David Lohman, Walt Schneider, Harold Hawkins and many others. Marshall Farr of the U.S. Office of Naval Research had supported these scientists through a basic research program for a number of years beginning in the late 1970s and continuing through the 1980s. Research management staff from the U.S. Air Force Office of Scientific Research, including John Tangney, believed that the Air Force could take the research findings emerging from Farr's basic research program to build and validate new information-processing tests that might supplement or replace the existing Armed Services Vocational Aptitude Battery, which had not undergone much change since the 1950s. It was in this context in and with these common goals that Professor Irvine collaborated with staff from the Air Force Human Resources Laboratory in a quest for low-cost alternatives. The two partners built a healthy collaboration involving a core series of potential tests, and a number of joint publications, perhaps the most significant of which was an edited volume (Irvine & Kyllonen, 2002), containing contributions from recognized pioneers in a science of item generation for test development that has only now come of age.

CHAPTER 10

FROM PLYMOUTH TO THE USA: ANOTHER GENERATION

From 1996 until 2006, new test development took place in the Great Britain, The United States, Germany and Belgium with the police and military organisations of those nations. Interest in multiple parallel form tests continued from the time that BARB became operational, especially in circumstances where a single-form test or tests had been in existence for some time: and where there were concerns about coaching organisations that had provided help, whether bound by ethical constraints or not, to applicants for competitive entry to service arms and corporations. In particular, a request was made by a regional police force in Great Britain to replace an existing single test by a multiple-form one. This request proved to be the impetus for a new series of tests somewhat like BARB, but for security and other reasons, with items that bore no resemblance to it.

THE SECOND GENERATION

The Brooks Air Force Base Connection

The Paper and Pencil Analogues

Planning the scoring possibilities for computer-delivered versions

The preliminary paper-and-pencil results

The tests were designed for mass screening, wherever procedural knowledge was the requirement for successful training in role execution. Although paper-and-pencil forms were used the police service tests proved to be a starting point for computer-delivered versions. In the present chapter, emphasis is on the test frameworks developed during the decade, and in particular a detailed validation carried out at the USAF Laboratory at Brooks AFB, San Antonio, from 1997-98. Consequently, in Chapter 11, success in languages other than English, requiring translation of the test generation software into major European languages, Dutch, French and German is revealed in national scale studies in Belgium and Germany involving armed services entrants.

THE UNITED STATES STRATEGIC BASE

The extensive studies at the United States Air Force Research Laboratory[1] in Brooks Air Force Base in the USA were able to demonstrate, using large and representative groups of recruits, a rational evidence-centred alternative to adaptive testing using item-generated tests where item-response theory technology is not necessary because

---

1   The author was a US National Research Council Associate from September 1997 to April 1999. Without this support, most gratefully acknowledged, close scrutiny of a new generation of psychometric tests, all computer-delivered, with large numbers of recruits in another military culture could not have occurred.

the various forms of the tests do not have to be rescaled. Previous attempts to construct items to broad difficulty bands in the *British Army Recruit Battery* series had been successful in removing the need for item-response theory. New paper and pencil mode tests, different from those in *British Army Recruit Battery,* had been constructed for use in Northern Ireland. Here was another opportunity to prove the underlying theoretical test construction model using both paper-and-pencil and computer delivered versions of the tests. Brooks Air Force Base had for many years been the development centre for the ASVAB prior to its move to San Diego in the Naval Research Headquarters. Contacts with scientists at Brooks had existed for more than a decade: and in 1997 it was the home of LAMP, the foremost research project in computer delivered testing for the USAF. It enjoyed a unique advantage in test development because it had, at the end of basic training, *access to every Air Force recruit for a period of four hours in a building with computer network for test delivery*. Cohorts of these recruits, who came from all over the USA to nearby Lackland Air Force Base for a six-week induction period, volunteered to undergo trials of the new tests from September 1997 until April 1999. Here was a test construction venture into a new military culture. Given multiple parallel form tests where working memory, the key to learning new procedures, was foremost, what did the ASVAB tests measure, by comparison with the new generation of tests? That was a question that had a history of debate, typified by the work done previously with ARCOM in the Logic Gates learning study: and the work that was to follow provided some debate, if not a conclusion.

PAPER-AND-PENCIL AND COMPUTER-DELIVERED PHASES
In pursuit of these goals, two trials of the prototype tests were carried out at Lackland Air Force Base, San Antonio Texas, beginning in September, 1997. Because there was no prospect of having access to participants using computers at Lackland for the three months prior to January 1, 1998, improved and extended computer delivered software was developed and tested. Generative programs written for the test types available prior to September 1 provided paper-and-pencil versions to be completed by those extra recruits who were randomly redundant in the limited-seating computer complex.

     By the time computer-delivered testing was begun, the generative software was capable of producing four reference files for each form of the six tests used. These files were (1) a paper-and-pencil analogue, (2) a scoring key, (3) a file for insertion into the computer for delivery, and (4) a reference file with details of the construction of the form. *This file also contained a random seed number that could be used to deliver identical item-order versions of the same tests in any language[2] where translation of the test construction elements had first been verified.* These additions provided necessary evidence for parallel form design. Data collection for the paper-and-pencil analogues began almost immediately. The second study involving computer delivery of the tests began early in the following year using a standard mouse interface with restricted travel so that the cursor was never lost.

---

2   This proved critical when generated for different language groups where exact order equivalence was a necessity, particularly in Belgium where Flemish, French and German were all official testing languages.

NATURE OF THE TASKS AND THEIR USE

Given a new start to test production[3], a complete framework was required. Not only did it need to provide scores for individuals, it had to provide research data for theory construction. The need was for two different kinds of computerised delivery forms. The first was operational; the second strategic. The version in use at any one time will determine the progress made towards the goal of psychometric utility. The strategic version is concerned with data at the level of detailed item and test form analysis. First, the most basic of versions is described. It reflects what will happen if no progress were made beyond item-generation in parallel forms. In that limited sense it is a product that can be evaluated at the construct validity level. At the same time the benchmark for strategic data collection is made. Then, the strategic version is outlined, and with this the possible conditions that provide data at the item level to establish a model. Doubtless, readers understand by this stage that paper-and-pencil analogues cannot control the flow of information about individual items as computer-delivery on successive screens can. Individuals are constrained by reading speeds and comprehension given a sheet of paper with questions on it. As was shown earlier, screens can be programmed to control the speed, amount and quality of information. One must expect some differences in any two test series, when delivery modes are different, even if the items are identical. The computer changes the nature of the test item if item-delivery is contextually dependent and under the control of test constructors in the search for predictors of item difficulty.

THE USAF TRIALS WERE A WATERSHED.

The outcome from the two computer-delivered *Lackland Test* results proved to be quite different in its implications for ability testing from anything discovered in other military contexts. Unlike the work prior to this, both accuracy and latency scoring models were capable of being compared and correlated. Potential sources of difference in test performance, including a regulated trial of pre-test booklets, were also explored. All of this occurred against the normal standardisation efforts involving the normative, reliability and validity protocols necessary for successful test administration.

PLANNING THE SYSTEM OPERATIONAL MODEL

The operational model for work in the USAF Laboratory was designed around its well-established computer-delivered test system, permitting parallel form delivery of each of the primary tests working within a self-contained Windows environment. They were generated from specifications and from software developed after December 1995 and prior to September 1997, subsequently refined for languages and local network needs. The items were delivered in fixed order. Each test, however, had fixed time limits designed to permit working at a self-induced pace without stressing the need for speed over accuracy. As far as possible, a single-screen format for item-presentation was adopted: and the system run within Windows as a 'black box' program. Some tests

---

3   With Richard Walker, sometime Chief Test Software Scientist for the USAF Laboratory, Brooks AFB whose work, and the data management service provided by Janice Hereford, were never emulated. None of the work undertaken after 1996 could have succeeded without them and their colleagues.

required more than one screen, the last screen being an answer verification context consistent with the item type. Although touchscreens would still have been the first choice, the suites at Lackland AFB, where the work was to occur, were equipped with a mouse interface. Because of this, and because of the advances made in computer use in the United States in more than a decade since the framework for BARB had been established, the input mechanism was to be a mouse or light pen with restricted cursor travel limits so that the cursor could not be lost on screen. Mouse practice was always given within an interactive game-like format.

POTENTIAL OUTPUT FILES
Output files were required for individuals and for items. The item files are essentially the baseline strategic data involving radicals and incidentals. These were organised on individual items within a single test basis, according to categories specified in the strategic version section. The individual files were organised as tests within individuals. Various output files were needed in order to construct reports for each individual. The report for an individual is what the viewer could access in the operational version.

Data Organisation for Norms Files as Look-Up Tables for Traditional Scores
All individual data was stored after the tests were scored according to a key, or keys developed by the computer at the same time as the test forms were generated. Scores may be adjusted for guessing, transformed, or otherwise modified.

Scores Files
Item responses were scored as right or wrong for each test and the totals adjusted for guessing by a standard formula. They were also scored for the time taken to complete the item. Both of these types of scores were recorded. SCORES files were accumulated for each person and stored in a convenient form along with appropriate ID data. In parallel, each individual score is stored by test. This is the individuals-within-test file. The function of NORMS files was to provide, on their conversion, a look-up table to generate a graphic display and/or a verbal report for each subject. All individual scores were stored in the SCORES file. Eventually, each individual score was referred to the NORMS file for each test when sufficient numbers were tested to create anchor norms. Retest norms were also created.

THE SCORING OPTIONS

Accuracy Scores

Average Latency per Item Correct

Screen Stage latencies

The preliminary paper-and-pencil results

Norms and percentile ranks

Scoring Parameters
Here are the basic structures for the types of scores created for the prototype.

1. *ADJ Scores* The first score is the ADJ or adjusted score – adjusted, that is, for guessing. All scores are likely to be affected by guessing strategies. Each score for each of the tests was adjusted by a correction factor. The general formula is ADJ =

R – [W / (k-1)], where R is the number Right, W is the number Wrong, and k is the number of alternatives in a multiple-choice format. Each test may have a different k-1 value depending on the number of alternative answers. These scores, and others based on use of the binomial theorem were also used as 'confidence scores' to determine whether very fast latencies were the result of random guesses.

2. *Percent Accuracy Score* The percent accuracy score (PAC) is the percentage ADJ score of those completed. After the number correct has been adjusted for guessing by the general formula given above. The general formula is PAC = ADJ / (R + W), where R is number right and W is number wrong.

3. *Latency Scores* In addition to scores based on correct answers, there is a need for scores based on time to complete the items in the test (LAT). These are derived from the distributions and means of the response times for each individual, within each test. In short, just as every test has scores based on correct responses and errors, so every test has scores derived from time to complete its items. The summary score used for the most part (LAT) is represented as the mean of the log latencies in milliseconds to complete each item. That is, the milliseconds for each complete item are recorded, transformed into logarithms, and then summed and averaged. At the same time, the standard deviation (LSD) of the log latencies for each item is computed for each individual. Finally, the standard error of the mean (LSEM) for each person for each test is computed. This is LSD /Ö N, where N is the number of items attempted for that particular test.

- Three latency measures per individual per test were compiled.
- The mean log latency in milliseconds to complete single items in any one test.
- The standard deviation of these individual item logarithms.
- The standard error of the mean of the log latencies in milliseconds per item.

NEW TEST TYPES

Error Detection Test

Alphabet Test

Number Fluency

Odds and Evens

Word Rules

Reasoning Categories

Transitive Inference

Orientation Test

4. *Scores of Standing* When scores such as these were produced for individuals, they are not on a uniform scale. Hence, they cannot easily be compared, and they give no indication of standing relative to the performance of a group of peers. For reporting purposes, these scores have to be related to group performance. The unit of standardisation chosen was the percentile rank. This is derived from a table of frequencies that is converted into cumulative percentages. Percentiles can be calculated and assigned for ADJ scores and for LAT scores.

Implications for System Construction
When the prototype was constructed, its main function was to provide baseline data for the difficulty of generic item types, without time limit, and to determine the distribution of times to correct completion and to incorrect completion. The parallel form specifications for the proposed study required that the tests be referenced to known cognitive dimensions; that mental models

for the tasks be predicated; and that there be no item bank for any test, only a series of algorithms for its construction in real time in the computer. Essentially, the theoretical frames described in Irvine, Dann & Anderson (1990) and Irvine (2002) were relevant to the construction of a brand new set of tests bearing no outward resemblance to any in operation at the time within the armed services in the UK. The test types invented for try-out are first described in their paper-and-pencil analogue forms. *Chapter 11 shows the screen presentation formats of computer-delivered items*.

SHORT DESCRIPTION OF THE NEW TESTS: THE TESTS OF BASIC SKILLS

Initially, five tests were derived directly from these principles and a sixth (the simple *Alphabet Test*) requiring knowledge of the order of letters in the alphabet was added for use in Europe at a later data. Computer screen illustrations of the test types are given at the beginning of Chapter 10, where minitests were created for use in the challenging Belgian diversity studies. The tasks within each test tended to be invariant within each test, and working-memory based. Each, however, had specific variance in a domain that is non-random. The

ERROR DETECTION

descriptions and illustrations are based on paper-and-pencil analogue versions. Unless stated otherwise, test comprehension thresholds assume only elementary literacy and numeracy attainments associated with completion of primary school education.

The *Error Detection Test* (ED) measures the speed with which features of letters and numerals are perceived to be the same or different, and the detection of mismatches. The construct- *Perceptual Speed* - is a recognised building block in the development of literacy skills and clerical accuracy.

> *Knowledge:* Alphabet letters in upper and lower case.

> *Psychometric Factor:* General Encoding Speed Gs.

> *Performance Model:* Semantic encoding and comparison. (Sternberg, 1966; Posner, Boies, Eichelman & Taylor, 1969; Hunt, Lunneborg & Lewis, 1975; Irvine & Reuning, 1981; Irvine, Schoeman & Prinsloo, 1988).

Correct	Copy	Answer
Q1		
TS 92351	TC 72304	[0] [1] [2] [3] **[4]**
Q2		
psfhqou@ibjlmd.net	pskhqou@ibjlmd.net	**[0]** [1] [2] [3] [4]

A perceptual speed task involving comparisons of symbol sets in pairs. This involves serial search to the end of the array and reporting on the number of errors detected when an original is compared with a copy. Errors range from 0 to 4. An incomplete block design is used as a frame for item generation. The instructions require the candidate to compare the correct version on the left with the copy on the right and to detect the number of errors made. The tasks comprise automobile number plates, postal codes, e-mail addresses consistent with modern office environments. Various national forms of these are employed. In the computer delivered version, the correct and copy versions are vertically opposed on the same screen.

The *Alphabet Test* (AB)[4] was not used in the USA, but appears in the Belgian studies. It is included here with all the new tests developed after 1995. A common Belgian names version is shown. Each different language version presents a short list of common surnames in that language. They have to be put in the correct alphabetic order. This is done by clicking on them in turn. Errors are indicated and have to be corrected. Scores are given for fluency and accuracy. This is a feedback test conducted on a single screen. if an error is made then it has to be corrected before progressing to the next name on the list, or the next item. When the third name is correctly ordered, the last name is automatically determined and the item is complete. The pool of common names is never less than one thousand, and every item has a list of four. The items are graded in sections of increasing difficulty, related to the proximity of the initial letter of the name and, where the initial letters are identical, the order of the subsequent letters.

> *Knowledge:* Alphabet letters in upper and lower case. Order of letters in alphabet.

> *Psychometric Factors:* General Encoding Speed and Semantic comparison

> *Performance Model:* Semantic encoding and comparison. (Sternberg, 1966; Posner, Boies, Eichelman & Taylor, 1969; Hunt, Lunneborg & Lewis, 1975; Irvine & Reuning, 1981; Irvine, Schoeman & Prinsloo, 1988; Clark, 1969; Clark & Chase, 1972).

Alphabet Test Example	
Wrong Order:	**Correct Order:**
2:Denooz	1:Beuken
1:Beuken	2:Denooz
3:Pirard	3:Pirard
4:Sittauer	4:Sittauer

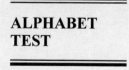

ALPHABET TEST

The *Number Fluency Test* (NF) is designed to elicit number skills unaided by calculators, or close attention to number precision in computing situations: and items require only basic numeracy in addition, subtraction, multiplication and division and the comparison of two products in memory.

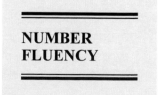

NUMBER FLUENCY

Knowledge: Order of numbers to specified range. Number facts for one and two-digit addition and subtraction pairs within the range specified. Involves simple multiplication and division of whole numbers.

---

4   The abbreviations used in the system are all listed in brackets for reference. Descriptions apply equally to the GCTB Battery installed in Belgium.

Psychometric Factor: General Memory Capacity (with Numerical Specific) Gm.

Performance Model: Decisions based on number retrieval (Moyer & Landauer, 1967; Groen & Parkman, 1972; Parkman, 1972).

Which is greater? Top, Bottom, or are they the Same?

$72 \div 8$	$30 - 2$	$19 + 8$	$7 + 13$	$68 \div 2$
$21 - 9$	$10 + 18$	$17 + 9$	$27 - 6$	17×2
[1] T B **S**	[2] T B **S**	[3] **T** B S	[4] T **B** S	[5] T B **S**

A working memory task based on numeracy using 16 combinations of operators, plus, minus, multiply and divide. Two calculations, one on the top line and one on the bottom line, are to be performed mentally. The answer involves comparison of the two products and reporting which is the greater, Top or Bottom - or if their products are the Same.

THE WORKING MEMORY TESTS

Working memory is concerned with the immediate processing of new information with sufficient reliability to allow a new action to follow. Working memory tasks have proved to be among the most consistent predictors of learning new skills (Collis, Tapsfield, Irvine, Dann, & Wright, 1995; Christal, 1991; Kyllonen, 1996; Kyllonen & Stephens, 1990; Kyllonen & Soule, 1988). These studies found that working memory capacity was the major determinant of learning procedures novel in the experience of the participants, ranging from military fieldcraft exercises to logic gates and programming computers.

Odds and Evens (OE) is a test of comparisons. It is easy to understand. The test requires the correct identification of odd and even number sequences, given a set of rules for the order of three numbers. One must compare the order of rules with the actual order of numbers and decide how many match. The test is designed to represent work tasks that require normal working memory skills unaided by look-up tables or instructional manuals. Rules prescribe the order of odd and even single-digit numbers or symbols.

> ***Knowledge:*** Of the concept of Odd and Even numbers and the identification of written out versions of numbers one through nine.
> ***Psychometric Factor***: Working memory Mw.
> ***Performance Model***: Working memory models from Christal (1988) Clark (1969) Kyllonen & Christal (1988), Kyllonen (1996). Decisions based on number retrieval (Moyer & Landauer, 1967; Groen & Parkman, 1972; Parkman, 1972).

How many numbers match the order of the rules?

Category Rules	Example	Matches				
Odd Odd Even	**Nine Five Ten**	Q1	[0]	[1]	[2]	**[3]**
Even Even Even	**Four Seven One**	Q2	[0]	**[1]**	[2]	[3]

Both words and symbols for numerals were used in the German versions to compare the effects of increased encoding and load in working memory of the word versions in German. The rules are then serially compared with the array of odd and even digits and the number of digits conforming to the rules are reported. In Germany alternate versions of the Odds and Evens tests was devised. The rationale and explanations can be seen in Chapter 12.

ODDS AND EVENS

This particular version was based on symbols for Odd ◆ and Even ○

Regel	Zahlen	Antwort				
						F1
◆ ◆ ○	**Sieben Eins Fünf**	[0]	[1]	**[2]**	[3]	
						F2
◆ ◆ ○	**Neun Sechs Drei**	[0]	[1]	[2]	**[3]**	
						F3

In the computer delivered version, and unlike the paper-and-pencil version, the rules and the examples are presented on separate screens. When candidates are ready to match the memorised rule with the example, the second screen and answer template are presented.

The *Word Rules* (WR) test is a semantic version of the *Odds and Evens* test just described: and the formats are identical. It is used whenever more emphasis on verbal comprehension is required by the job description. The test requires the correct identification of word sequences given a set of rules for their order. Because it has vocabulary common to the *Reasoning Categories* test, these two tests are not given together. Category rules prescribe the *order*

WORD RULES

of examples of the categories. The specific *Word Rules* examples are compared with their categories and the number of matches with the correct order is recorded. It is a semantic analogue of the *Odds and Evens* test.

In the computer delivered version, the rule and the example are presented on separate screens. When candidates are ready to match the memorised rule with the example, the second screen and answer template are presented.

Knowledge: Of the categories of everyday concepts and identification of concrete versions of these.
Psychometric Factor: Semantic Working Memory WM Semantic.
Performance Model: Working memory models from Christal (1988) Clark (1969) Kyllonen & Christal (1988), Kyllonen (1996). Decisions based on semantic retrieval (Clark, 1969; Clark & Chase, 1972).

How many words match the order of the rules?

Category Rule	Example	Matches
Q1 **Insect Insect Country**	**Butterfly Britain Mexico**	[0] [1] <u>[2]</u> [3]
Q2 **Bird Vegetable Bird**	**Cucumber Pea Turnip**	[0] <u>[1]</u> [2] [3]

VERBAL REASONING TESTS

REASONING CATEGORIES

The verbal reasoning tests are powerful, but they are constructed from simple categories and sentences so that the threshold of understanding is not a barrier to performance. These tests concentrate on following instructions, learning rules for processing information and drawing conclusions. Good performance on the *Reasoning Categories* (RC) test depends on memorising a list of categories, such as *building* and *tree*, and putting it in a prescribed order. Then the order has to be matched exactly with specific examples, such as *school* (for building) and *pine* (for tree) to answer the question. It is designed to simulate work tasks that require memory for a number of 'if-then' instructions or procedures.

Knowledge: Categories of objects and identification of concrete instances.
Psychometric Factor: Verbal Reasoning G semantic.
Performance Model: Baddeley, (1968), Baddeley & Hitch (1974), Christal (1988) Clark (1969) Kyllonen & Christal (1988), Kyllonen (1996).

Find the list that matches the rules

Rules 1	Rules 2	Rules 3	Rules 4
bird above insect	things above living	living above things	clothes above tool
tool above clothes	insect above bird	tool above clothes	insect above bird
living above things	tool above clothes	insect above bird	things above living

Write the number of the correct answer below the set that fits the rules for each question							
slacks	eagle	pliers	fly	pliers	fly	slacks	eagle
pliers	fly	slacks	eagle	slacks	eagle	pliers	fly
fly	pliers	fly	slacks	eagle	pliers	eagle	slacks
eagle	slacks	eagle	pliers	fly	slacks	fly	pliers
	1	2	4		3		

Rules are given for the order of four words in a column. The set of rules must be matched with the correct set of words from eight possible solutions. The emphasis is primarily on deductive reasoning, involving reordering of the categories and then identifying the concrete semantic instances of the reordered categories. In the paper and pencil version, answers are recorded by inserting the number of the item that matches one of the eight possible solutions. All referents are visible at all times. In the computer delivered test, each item is presented separately on a separate screen from the answers. Candidates have no reference to the question once they signal that they know the correct order of categories. In the second screen they must identify the correct set of concrete examples matching the revised category order. The load on working memory is greater in the computer-delivered than in the paper-and-pencil version.

This is a short basic literacy level of the test *Deductive Reasoning*, (TI) in the well-known *Transitive Inference* format. The *Transitive Inference* tasks have been used wherever work functions demand simple deductions from a small amount of information.

DEDUCTIVE REASONING
Platoon further than Regiment
Brigade further than Regiment
What is nearest?
A Brigade B:Platoon C:Regiment
Correct answer: Regiment   Answer Position: 3

DEDUCTIVE REASONING

Knowledge: High frequency vocabularies relevant to occupation. Use of comparatives involving directions, dimensions, distances
Psychometric Factor: Verbal Reasoning G semantic.
Performance Model: Evans, 1982: Christal (1988) Clark (1969) Kyllonen & Christal (1988), Evans, Newstead & Byrne, (1993);(Kyllonen (1996).

The literacy threshold is low, but the mental demands are significant in each of two variants, standard (two-term series) and advanced (three term series as illustrated). In the computer version, the item statements are presented on the first screen. When the respondent is ready, the alternative answers are given on the second screen, requiring storage in working memory. Safeguards against guessing strategies were encoded in the item construction rules.

THE VISUALISATION TEST

This requires the translation of verbal directions in to a two-dimensional figural representation. Persons with high aptitude for technical training out-perform those for whom the path to technical excellence has proved longer and more difficult. The test has particular promise for identifying potential navigators and air-traffic controllers. The *Orientation Test* (OR) is based on the relative position of two arrows of different colours that point in one of four directions. The orientation of two arrows is verbally described. This description has to be transformed mentally to a figural representation, and then visually identified in one of eight possible solutions. It is used in technical and executive testing programs. In the computer delivered version, the answers are shown on a separate screen to increase the power of the test. The arrows are normally coloured black and yellow, but an optional red and green version may be substituted by the test user where an elementary pre-screen for red-green blindness may be necessary.

ORIENTATION

> **Knowledge:** Recognition of shape and its orientation.
> **Psychometric Factor:** General Visualisation Gv.
> **Performance Model:** Comparison of sentences against pictures. Spatial orientation of symbols. (Clark & Chase, 1972; Shepard & Metzler, 1971; Just & Carpenter, 1985; Bejar, 1986 a, 1986 b, 1986 c).

Find the pair of arrows that match the description

1			
	↘ ↗	↖ ↙	↖ ↘
Down Left ABOVE Up Left	**X**		
White ABOVE Black	↘ ↙	↙ ↖	↖ ↗

Verbal rules in the form of directions, above, below, up, down, left and right are provided for the identifying pictures of two arrows, one placed above the other. Six possible configurations are provided. The task is to identify which of the six configurations matches the given verbal rules. The visualisation task requires good working memory skills and stresses the all-important reconstruction demand requiring undivided attention.

THE FIRST STUDY: TESTING WITH PAPER-AND PENCIL ANALOGUES

Two forms of the new tests were generated. For convenience they simply referred to here as *Lackland Tests*. Personnel were trained in test administration and the writer was present either as administrator or proctor at Lackland Testing Facility on Tuesdays and Wednesdays whenever possible. The *Lackland Tests* were prepared for use in crossover format, where two forms of a test are used, the order of which is randomly assigned to any individual. Two forms of each test listed in Table 10.1 were tried out. Participants were given Form A or B on the first occasion. On the second, retest administration, the alternate form was given. From such crossover designs, trialled with paper-and-pencil BARB tests ten years before this, parallelism, test-retest parallel form reliability, gain scores from test forms and the relationships between analogues of test types in the two forms, can all be calculated without confounding memory effects inherent in repeating the same (identical) items twice. Because the US Armed Services Vocational Aptitude Battery (ASVAB) scores were made available after ensuring anonymity, concurrent and construct validity studies of the two series, The ASVAB and *Lackland Tests* were carried out. The congruence with the trials undertaken with BARB and the AET86 will, perhaps, be taken as evidence that lessons had indeed been learned. Between September and December 1997, 146 recruits were tested in groups of no more than 40 at a time. In every instance, each test was explained, demonstrated, and prefaced by practice items whose answers were reviewed by the group as a whole and verified by each participant, with the help of proctors. The tests were given in a fixed sequence. The same sequence was observed for the re-test phase. The retest followed a rest interval and the completion of unrelated personality and vocational interest inventories. From observations made and questions asked by the recruits, the tests were well received. Here are the names of the tests, time limits and abbreviations used throughout.

Table 10.1: Abbreviations Used and Time Limits for Lackland Tests

THE LACKLAND TESTS					
ERROR DETECTION TEST (4 MINUTES)					
ED1ADJ	ED2ADJ	ED1PC	ED2PC	ED1LAT2	ED2LAT2
Forms 1 and 2 adjusted for guessing		Forms 1 and 2 percent correct		Mean olog latencies of items attempted	
NUMBER SKILLS FLUENCY (5 MINUTES)					
NF1ADJ	NF2ADJ	NF1PC	NF2PC	NF1LAT2	NF2LAT2
Forms 1 and 2 adjusted for guessing		Forms 1 and 2 percent correct		Mean log latencies of items attempted	
REASONING CATEGORIES TEST (8 MINUTES)					
RC1ADJ	RC2ADJ	RC1PC	RC2PC	RC1LAT2	RC2LAT2
Forms 1 and 2 adjusted for guessing		Forms 1 and 2 percent correct		Mean log latencies of items attempted	
ORIENTATION TEST (6 MINUTES)					
OR1ADJ	OR2ADJ	OR1PC	OR2PC	OR1LAT2	OR2LAT2
Forms 1 and 2 adjusted for guessing		Forms 1 and 2 percent correct		Mean log latencies of items attempted	
ODDS AND EVENS TEST (4 MINUTES)					
OE1ADJ	OE2ADJ	OE1PC	OE2PC	OE1LAT2	OE2LAT2
Forms 1 and 2 adjusted for guessing		Forms 1 and 2 percent correct		Mean log latencies of items attempted	
WORD RULES TEST (4 MINUTES)					
WR1ADJ	WR2ADJ	WR1PC	WR2PC	WR1LAT2	WR2LAT2
Forms 1 and 2 adjusted for guessing		Forms 1 and 2 percent correct		Mean log latencies of items attempted	

PRELIMINARY USA RESULTS: PAPER-AND-PENCIL IN A CROSS-OVER
DESIGN

In general, the aim of producing parallel forms of the tests for USAF recruits was realised when paper-and-pencil versions were trialled. Some inconsistencies were the results of cohort confounds in the experiment, because it was not possible for administrative reasons to randomise the order of tests within cohorts. The test-retest correlations were good to excellent, considering the range restriction in the samples. In the applicant population they would be higher. Practice effects were expected and were reasonable, around half a standard deviation for a second chance using a parallel form.

Even at this stage, the need for second trial norms for applicants in real life had been recognised in BARB outcomes. Overall, the effect size differences between the two USAF test form forms fluctuated but in standard deviation terms it was very low – lower in fact than the differences observed in the British Army Recruit Battery trials with different tests constructed with the same aim (Irvine, Dann & Anderson, 1990).

TEST VALIDITIES

The ASVAB results for the participants were available from records, as indeed they were throughout all aspects of the work. The individual ASVAB test components and the occupational quotients were on record: and they were used as criterion and as construct reference variables. A modest attempt was made to predict one of the quotients, the AFQT, which is the *Air Force Qualifying Test* percentile, by regressing the *Lackland Test* scores using stepwise methods.

For this purpose, the somewhat unusual step of using *the first test attempted*, which was Form A for some and Form B for others, was adopted. Because this increased unreliability in the independent variables, some risk might be apparent. However, unreliability will not change test vectors, simply reduce the overall correlations. Hence a more severe trial of validity was conducted than if only one form had been in use. Three *Lackland Tests* were required to reach a final value of .50 and they entered the equation in the following order, *Reasoning Categories, Number Fluency and Orientation*. At this point, the addition of more tests would not have produced a significant increase, given the relatively small sample involved.

A trial factor analysis of all the tests with the individual ASVAB test components was conducted,

PRELIMINARY PAPER AND PENCIL RESULTS:

SUMMARY

Highly reliable

AFQT predicted using alternate parallel forms

Four Tests are Best Fit for ASVAB composite

Two Factor Solution for all ASVAB subtests together with Lackland Tests

to find out what it was that the new tests might be assessing, because the ASVAB structures were well known, through many studies. A parsimonious two factor solution emerged, a function of Maximum Likelihood Factoring and a Promax Rotation of axes. The familiar emphasis on verbal-educational knowledge within the ASVAB test was revealed in the first factor. This domain was contrasted with a capacity to process new information in the second factor, whose cognitive underpinning was working memory efficiency. There was only a moderate correlation between the two factors, which can be accounted for by range restriction in the ASVAB tests and any unreliability induced by taking the first parallel form of test with a cohort confound. These conservative results are the least that might be expected with paper-and-pencil purposive trials. In fact, Chapter 11 shows what occurs when the confounds are removed and the test administration is controlled by computer.

CHAPTER 11

USA: THE COMPUTER-DELIVERED 'SECOND' PHASE

ANOTHER GENERATION: THE LACKLAND TESTS

Two Phases of Computer Delivered Study

Latency Scoring Models Revisited

Accuracy and Latency Concurrent and Construct Validity Studies

The Final USAF Campaign

Doubtless, readers understand that paper-and-pencil analogues cannot control the flow of information about individual items as computer-delivery on successive screens can. Individuals are constrained by reading speeds and comprehension given a sheet of paper with questions on it. As was shown in Chapter 2, screens can be programmed to control the speed, amount and quality of information. One must expect some differences in any two test series, when delivery modes are different, even if the items are identical. The computer changes the nature of the test item if item-delivery is contextually dependent and under control. The USAF trials were a watershed. The outcome from the two computer-delivered *Lackland Test* results proved to be quite different in its implications for ability testing from anything discovered in other military contexts. Accuracy and latency models were capable of being compared and correlated. Potential sources of difference in test performance were explored. All of this occurred against the normal standardisation efforts involving the normative, reliability and validity protocols necessary for successful test administration. Macdonald's fourth lesson, how to use the test scores, was capable of repetition, using latencies.

Computer-based forms were first administered to cohorts of Lackland inductees during the early part of 1998. These were variants of the types illustrated in the tables of the previous section. For the most part, the items required two screens: the item was presented under no time restraint in screen one and the answer had to be found in screen two. The exception was the number skills test where three screens were used, a separate screen for each of two simple mental arithmetic calculations, and the third for the verification of the answer. Times had changed since 1986, when BARB was conceived, although touch screens would have still been the preferred interface. Most USAF recruits were familiar with computers; and had used a mouse interface: and if they had not, they could opt out. Pre-test mouse practice was given when a number of bug-like creatures on screen had to be removed in turn by chasing them with the cursor and clicking to destroy them. Moreover, the cursor was constrained during a test item so that it could never disappear off screen, nor could move out pre-planned zones for each type of question on the first screen and its answer on the screen that followed. These details might seem at first glance to be trivial, but in practice, they were to be essential for the smooth running of the test sessions and the reported wellbeing of the volunteers.[1]

Figure 11.1: The Error Detection Test

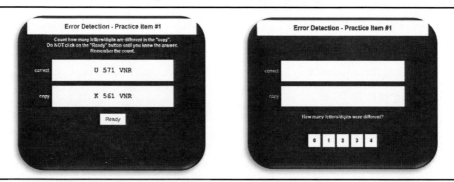

Figure 11.2: Number Fluency With Working Memory

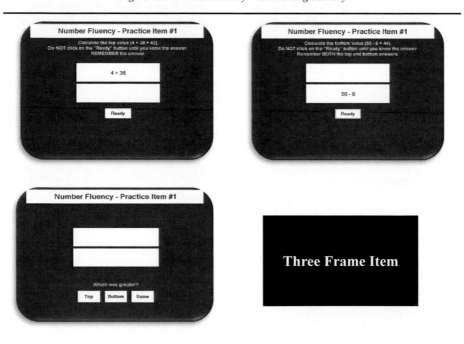

---

1   Richard Walker's vast experience and immaculate programming were responsible for these techniques and their implementation. His work throughout was inspirational, and the data management unparalleled.

Figure 11.3: Odds and Evens Working Memory

Figure 11.4: Deductive Reasoning – Transitive Inference Three Term Series

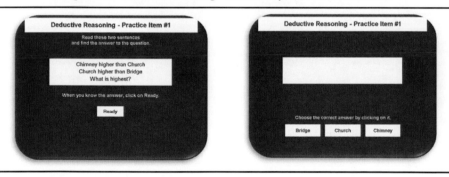

Figure 11.5: Word Rules Semantic Identity

 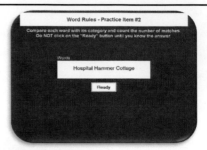

Figure 11.6: The Alphabet Order Test Used in Belgium

Figure 11.7: Orientation – Figural Representation of Verbal Description

Examples of the various computer screens used in item presentation for the tests are provided in Figures 11.1 to 11.7. They reveal the number of screens required for presentation and the deliberate application of the principle that less on the screen leads to maximum understanding of the test requirements. The illustrations are designed to show the overall principles of item presentation with minimum of instructions, clarity of presentation and economy of scale. Scrutiny reveals that the computer-delivered versions are similar in content to the paper-and-pencil analogues, but the use of screen radicals increases the load on working memory.

FIRST PHASE IN THE COMPUTER DELIVERED STUDY.

The first phase employed 367 recruits and involved just two parallel forms of the tests. These forms were administered in series after rest pauses and other non-cognitive form completion. Forms were administered at random at each computer station. Scores were adjusted for guessing, using the standard adjustment formula. The average log latency per item for each test was recorded for each screen exposure. Previously, the question of different models of test scoring, accuracy and latency, was raised (Chapter 5). Here was another, more controlled opportunity to explore the relationships between accuracy and the time taken to produce a response to a question.

LATENCY SCORING MODELS REVISITED

Was the additional information useful? Did it make any difference as to how computer delivered tests could be used? The results included descriptive statistics, reliabilities, construct and concurrent validities, comparison of scores adjusted for guessing with scores derived from latencies, and data on the effect of controlling for accuracy in comparing such scores. The second phase involved 1500 USAF Recruits and employed 11 parallel forms of each of the *Lackland Tests*. The procedures adopted for the first phase were followed throughout

PHASE 1: DESCRIPTIVE STATISTICS AND RELIABILITIES
Table 11.2 contains the descriptive statistics, internal consistency estimates and test-retest correlations for accuracy and latency scores adjusted for guessing. The results reveal good dispersion for the number of items in the test, low increases due to practice between parallel Forms 1 and 2 except where learning is a planned part of the test form (as in the *Reasoning Category Task*) and good to excellent internal consistency and test-retest-parallel-form correlation.

The Percentage Correct (PC) column shows the average item difficulties for each test. They are uniformly high, showing that recruits are accurate in their answers to relatively easy tasks. The variance among the adjusted scores, for all the easiness of the items, indicates large individual differences in work rate. Because the accuracy rate is high, and when the variance in the adjusted scores is relatively low, so the correlations between parallel forms accuracy scores get smaller. This is an example of correlation attenuation due to restriction of range. Percentage accuracy scores, however, have a useful role to play as moderator variables, as ensuing calculations were to prove.

Table 11.1: Descriptive Statistics Internal Consistency and Test/Retest Reliabilities

		PC	ADJ Scores		Log Latency		Rel. adj	Rel. adj	Rel. lat
TEST	N	Mean	Mean	S. D.	Mean	S.d	R_{TT}	$R_{T/RT}$	$R_{T/RT}$
ED1ADJ	367	97.8	29.8	6.7	3.87	.09	.75		
ED2ADJ	367	92.9	29.2	7.6	3.84	.10	.82	.75	.71
NF1ADJ	367	87.6	27.6	11.6	3.92	.12	.87		
NF2ADJ	367	86.8	28.4	11.2	3.88	.15	.86	.84	.67
RC1ADJ	367	72.5	16.4	8.5	4.25	.22	.91		
RC2ADJ	367	77.5	20.6	10.3	4.14	.27	.93	.77	.56
OR1ADJ	367	86.7	17.9	6.5	4.20	.13	.80		
OR2ADJ	367	85.4	20.6	9.0	4.10	.21	.91	.74	.47
OE1ADJ	367	90.0	30.6	10.3	3.83	.11	.89		
OE2ADJ	367	89.5	32.2	11.0	3.78	.12	.91	.73	.51
WR1ADJ	367	89.3	29.3	9.2	3.84	.11	.87		
WR2ADJ	367	89.9	31.2	10.0	3.79	.13	.89	.75	.44

Notes: Rel.adj is reliability for accuracy score adjusted for guessing: Rel.lat is reliability of the latency score: Rtt is internal consistency: Rt/rt is test re-test

Table 11.1 proves just how much lower the test-retest correlations of mean log latencies from parallel forms of tests are than those for work-rate scores adjusted for guessing. Undoubtedly, some of this is due to mouse input, but much of it may be due to the low latency averages of recruits who become '*keypressers*' who have probably given up on certain tests. In fact, the term '*keypressers*' was one regularly used to describe recruits who, for whatever reason, had apparently decided to finish the test as quickly as possible. This means, of course, that a very short average time to complete a test item was not necessarily a sign of high ability. Far from it. While in operational mode negative scores can be corrected, for example by providing a second trial, always assuming motivation to succeed, the appearance of negative adjusted test scores using an accuracy or R model for any single test administration has to qualify results investigating scores using latencies, or L models. The results show just how true this proved to be.

One more result of importance: those *Reasoning* and *Orientation* tests, whose items have long latencies, are the most demanding of working memory and have total completion times for each item in the range 12.59 to 17.78 seconds. The conclusion is straightforward, and worth remembering. *When items take longer than ten seconds to complete, latency scores require special care in interpretation and detailed investigation.*

LATENCY SCORING MODELS REVISITED

Figure 11.8 is a dramatic summary of the intercorrelations of accuracy scores with the mean log latency per item for each of the six tests used in the phase one experiment.

Figure 11.8: Test Scores and Item Speed Correlations by Trial

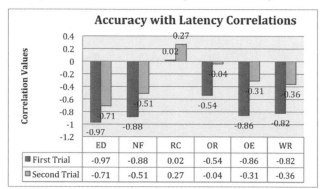

	ED	NF	RC	OR	OE	WR
■ First Trial	-0.97	-0.88	0.02	-0.54	-0.86	-0.82
▢ Second Trial	-0.71	-0.51	0.27	-0.04	-0.31	-0.36

Correlations are shown for the first and second trials. First trial correlations are always higher than those for the second trial. Tests where the items are easy to understand and to complete have substantial negative correlations between total scores adjusted for guessing and the time to complete each item. These are *Error Detection, Number Skills, Odds and Evens,* and Word *Rules.* The difficult tests, by comparison, have a different outcome, the correlations being much lower for *Orientation* and becoming so small for *Reasoning Categories* as to become negligible and drift over to a positive relationship, although only the second trial correlation is significant, the standard error of zero r with a sample of 367 being ∓ 0.05. This result, if it does not make latency models redundant, certainly underlines the risks of assuming that the average speed with which an item is completed is a good guide to underlying ability to perform the task itself. To shed some light on the relationship between adjusted scores (work rates) and latencies which is characterised by low correlations in Chart 1, the 21 recruits identified as having low accuracy scores in *Orientation* were omitted: and this raised the correlation between average time to complete and accuracy scores in the *Orientation* test to -.83, which is on a par with the rest of the results. A second check was undertaken for the other difficult test *Reasoning Categories*. Excluding those (59 recruits in total) who had less than 70 percent accuracy in the *Reasoning Categories* test had the same outcome. The correlation between work rate and latency increased from zero to -.62, better than before but not all together as spectacular a correction as in the *Orientation* Test. Methods of dealing with random response patterns was one of the concerns in phase two, where 1512 recruits were involved. In this, a 'confidence score' was used as a filter for '*keypressers*' in the first test trial to illustrate their effect on latency-work rate relationships. The strategy of first calculating the 'confidence score' before using latencies was an integral part of resolving scoring ambiguities.

ERROR DETECTION LATENCIES AS PREDICTORS OF WORK RATE.
The final set of results for this section is really an introduction to the problems posed by considering alternatives to scoring item-generative tests. Some inkling of what

might happen is given by the short summary of some preliminary results linking latency with scores adjusted for guessing.

Table 11.2: Blocks of Latencies Regressed on Error Detection Test Adjusted Score

Latencies as Predictors of Accuracy				
BLOCK	R	R Square	F	p
First	.810	.652	137.9	.000
Second	.837	.697	169.3	.000
Third	.811	.653	138.8	.000
Fourth	.819	.666	143.7	.000
ITEMS	R	R Square	F	p
4,8,12,18	.835	.694	207.9	.000
11-20	.877	.763	119.1	.000
1-20	.894	.793	117.7	.000

The test with the highest correlation between the total score adjusted for guessing and the mean log latency of items attempted is the *Error Detection* test. The *Error Detection* test in its computer-delivered Mark 1 version is given in two screens (see Figure 11.1) with the correct and copy versions of number plates, zip codes and e-mails vertically opposed in centre screen. The task is to detect the number of errors in the copy and to report that answer on the second screen when ready. Recruits proceed at their own pace. Latencies are recorded for the first screen (solution time) and the second screen (verification time), and total trial time. Each latency in milliseconds is converted to a logarithm. The test format consists of the presentation of small samples of items parcelled into an incomplete block design. This data allows exploration of the use of latencies from incomplete blocks of items as predictors of final score

LATENCY IN THE BEAUTY OF DESIGN

Because the items are presented to the recruits in blocks, with a design for ensuring complete sampling of item types and processes in 56 items, a Youden (1940) square design using 11 blocks of 5 and one extra at random, it is instructive to regress the log latencies for each item in its block of five against the final adjusted accuracy score. In the top half, Table 11.2 summarises the multiple correlation of each of the first four blocks of five items with that total score. In the lower half of the table, results are shown for *item sequences*. The first set, items 4, 8, 12, and 14 were those that entered into the regression first in each of the previous four blocks. These four items by themselves account for 69 percent of the common variance. Similar predictions are possible for sets of ten and twenty items. In the final model of items 1-20, stepwise regression terminated after using only 12 items.

To conclude, all is not lost when latencies and accuracy scores correlate substantially. Given incomplete blocks of items where item types are first stratified randomly, a small number of items will predict a total score derived from longer tests with more than adequate accuracy. As one colleague remarked, adaptive testing does not need IRT when this kind of outcome is possible. Of course, item-generation to ensure fresh sets of items not contained in any item bank was all the while taken for granted in this comment. *Clearly, though, the lower the correlation between accuracy and latency scores, the more difficult it would be to use average item time to shorten the test.* This simple conclusion may seem to be all too obvious. It was not obvious when BARB was first mooted in 1986, testified all too plainly in Chapter 5 on scoring models. A decade later sufficient data had justified the cautions and uncertainties.

THE END OF THE AFFAIR

Accuracy and Latency Concurrent and Construct Validity Studies
The availability of ASVAB data for the Lackland inductees is a permanent bonus to researchers because it provides an opportunity to perform basic validity studies using actual admission criteria as the dependent variables for regressions, and the ten ASVAB tests scores that are used to make composites for admission and job allocation as a construct reference frame for data reduction methods. Chapter 9 contains examples and discussion about the ten ASVAB subtests; and recounts previous debates about what the scores mean when the ASVAB and ARCOM were correlated together. To provide an estimate of the concurrent validity of the experimental tests, the *Air Force Qualifying Test Score* (AFQT) composite score derived from individual ASVAB tests was used as the dependent variable. The six experimental tests were regressed on this score, using the standard stepwise model, and the results for the first and second trials are reported. A multiple correlation of .65 with the AFQT composite was obtained from four tests entering the equation in the following order, *Reasoning Categories*, *Number Skills*, *Orientation* and *Error Detection*, whose total testing time is 23 minutes[2]. This value can be compared with the paper-and-pencil result of .505. Among Air Force applicants, as distinct from the inductees, the .65 correlation is likely to exceed .80, based on the range restriction in the AFQT criterion, and conservatively assuming that range does not increase for the experimental tests. When repeated with results from the second trial, the correlation was .57 using *Number Skills*, *Reasoning Categories*, *Orientation* and *Odds and Evens*

In summary, the concurrent validity studies of the item-generative tests provide proof of their power and parsimony. Percentage accuracy scores show that recruits can get the correct answer, but that the rate at which they complete the items is a variable in which individual differences are marked. Moreover, these individual differences in work rate at tasks where correct answers among those items attempted are the rule rather than the exception, correlate in predictable fashion with much more varied, content-specific tests of the ASVAB, which are generously timed, but calibrated to provide questions where correct answers are expected from only half of the population tested.

CONSTRUCT VALIDITY: ACCURACY AND LATENCY SCORES
Past studies of item-generative tests with similar properties have been conducted with *British Army Entry Tests* and *Royal Navy Recruit Tests* and with *Royal Australian Air Force Tests*. Results have led to the conclusion that they form a strong working memory factor directly involved in the learning of new materials and in the processing of information prerequisite to that kind of learning. On the other hand, more traditional

---

2   See Chapter 12 for a similar outcome in the Bundeswehr trials.

entry tests such as the *Army Entry Tests*, the *Navy Recruit Tests* and the ASVAB, are known to predict performance on tasks where previous educational knowledge and achievements are necessary for their completion. In Chapter 9, the study of the relative efficiency of ASVAB and the ARCOM item-generative tests in predicting the learning of electronic logic gates (Irvine and Christal, 1994) showed that the item-generative tests were the more powerful and consistent predictors of new learning experiences. In a largely confirmatory exercise, the ASVAB test scores and the item-generative test results (adjusted scores and mean log latencies of items attempted) were factor analysed. All 367 cases were used for adjusted scores and 332 were used for the latencies after removing 'keypressers' in either the *Reasoning Category* or the *Orientation* tests. In all analyses a Maximum Likelihood Analysis was carried out followed by a Promax rotation. Parsimony dictated the study of a two factor solution. In both accuracy and latency score analyses, the results are remarkably similar. *The latency factors are all but identical with those for the work rate scores on the item-generative tests,* only the lower reliability of the latter accounts for any minor fluctuations in factor loadings and a slightly lower factor correlation coefficient. The preferred two factor solution in Table 11.3 confirms a demarcation between the ASVAB and item-generative tests.

Table 11.3: Two Factor Solutions for ASVAB and Item-Generative Test Scores

Accuracy And Latency Factors

ITEM-GENERATIVE TESTS

Lackland Test Accuracy Scores			Lackland Test Mean Log Latency		
Number Skills NF1	**.83**	-.10	NF1LAT	**.86**	.03
Odds Evens OE1	**.65**	.11	OE1LAT	**.67**	.00
Error Detection ED1	**.63**	-.10	ED1LAT	**.64**	.09
Orientation OR1	**.49**	.28	OR1LAT	**.56**	-.16
Reasoning Categories RC1	**.42**	**.39**	RC1LAT	**.38**	.05

ASVAB TESTS

Accuracy Test Scores			Accuracy Test Scores		
Numerical Operations(NO)	**.61**	-.23	Numops(NO)	**-.61**	-.17
Math Knowledge(MK)	**.61**	.07	Mathknow(MK)	**-.54**	.11
Coding Speed(CS)	**.54**	-.14	Codespeed(CS)	**-.48**	-.05
Arithmetic Reasoning (AR)	**.53**	.29	Arithreas(AR)	**-.49**	**.31**
Auto&Shop(AS)	-.30	**.79**	Autoshop(AS)	.21	**.72**
Elec.Info.(EI)	-.13	**.78**	Elecinfo(EI)	.09	**.77**
Mech. Comprehension(MC)	.02	**.71**	Mechcomp(MC)	-.03	**.68**
General Science(GS)	.03	**.64**	Genscience(GS)	-.04	**.69**
Word Knowledge(WK)	-.03	**.61**	Wordknow(WK)	.00	**-.62**
Para. Comprehension(PC)	.13	**.48**	**Paracomp(PC)**	-.13	**-.51**

Factor Correlation =.44   **Factor Correlation =.39**

The working memory functions of the item-generative tests separate out from the ASVAB battery those tests that have most reliance upon the cognitive processes in working memory. These include all those where mental calculations have to be performed in arithmetic, mathematics and committing symbol sequences to memory (the so-called *Coding Speed* test). The second ASVAB dominant factor is without any doubt acquired information/declarative knowledge best described as verbal-educational. Much of the traditional ASVAB 'general factor' variance is due to large individual differences in acquired knowledge,. This can be contrasted with the low knowledge threshold of the item-generative tests ensures that recruits who perform poorly do not do so for knowledge deficiencies. The ASVAB can, given the *Lackland Tests* as proven markers of processing information capacity, be finally recognised for what it undoubtedly is, *a test of acquired knowledge with elements of working memory*. This result is identical with that found by Irvine et al. (1990) when the *Army Entry Tests* were factored alongside the BARB battery.

SPEED AND ACCURACY DEFINE THE SAME FACTORS

Diversity and Fairness

In phase one, sex differences, group identities, ASVAB entry scores and other categories were explored, but a much more thorough analysis of the various influences on performance, with standardised effect sizes, was possible in phase two.

CONCLUSIONS FROM PROVING STUDIES: PAPER-AND-PENCIL AND COMPUTER-DELIVERED

The goal of using item-generation algorithms to produce tests of information-processing capabilities was achieved with USAF recruits. The tests functioned with good test-retest reliabilities, high internal consistency and demonstrable validity. They did so with completely computer-delivered forms or traditional paper-and-pencil analogues. This does not only mean that adequate operational definitions of the tests have been achieved. Because their construction is anchored in strong performance models, they have a theory that permits rational explanations for success and failure in the tasks themselves.

THE FINAL USAF CAMPAIGN

Closure in test development is reached when enough has been done to ensure that the tests meet the most exacting standards that can be applied. For computer-delivered tests in 1998 these standards were still being resolved, as far as operational matters such as the interface, practice, scoring and reporting were concerned. In the technical, psychometric domain, the standards of reliability and validity applied regardless of test form. Given the added dimension of item-generation to produce multiple parallel forms not relying upon IRT, computer-delivered forms had to be demonstrably both parallel and reliable. The pilot study with 367 applicants had largely resolved basic issues. What remained to be done?

The large sample available at Lackland proved to be ideal for exploring what aspects of the multiple parallel form tests of six different types of tests were most likely to affect performance. How much did a re-test influence test scores? Was the gain in a second-try score through practice on the first one more influential than receiving a different parallel form from someone else? Did either of those factors count more than the border zone around a single score produced by test unreliability in every type of test, regardless of its construction principles? These were legitimate areas of enquiry concerning test form factors, but there was more to follow. Extraneous elements affect all who take the tests indiscriminately. But there are elements that affect some groups of participants and not others. How great were the differences in performance associated with sex differences, with self-declared group identity, and, perhaps most interesting of all, with the occurrence of one or more negative scores that could only have occurred through a series of chance responses to one or more tests?

Accuracy below a certain threshold in the first group of 367 participants identified those recruits whom we now call *'keypressers'*. This describes what they do, press mouse keys as quickly as possible to get to the next test. This behaviour can have more than one plausible explanation. It may simply be a consequence of not understanding the test instructions; or of finding the demands of the test too much and not persisting. Persistence, however, may be allied to test context. If recruits were generally demotivated, the removal of 'keypressers' in *one* test would result in improvement in *all* tests. However, the improvement in latency and work-rate correlations was found to be *specific to performance on the tests concerned.* If some of the recruits have not persisted in a test, then these results show that there is room for persistence, the motivational parameter added to speed and accuracy by White's (1982) comprehensive scoring model for tests. Fortunately, measures of the health-related quality of life among recruits at Lackland were able to shed some light on poor performance on the more difficult tests. Given 1512 recruits, of whom 999 were men and 513 were women, there was a good chance that some answers would emerge to what made the scores on the tests vary, among them form and motivation differences.

Figure 11.9: Eleven Parallel Forms of Lackland Tests Compared

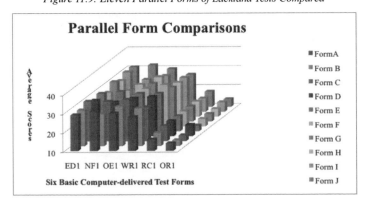

ELEVEN ITEM-GENERATIVE FORMS OF EACH TEST
A large sample of US Air Force inductees collected over a 12-month period was given a number of psychometric measures. Among these were 11 generated forms each of *The Lackland Tests*, including *Error Detection, Number Fluency, Odds and Evens, Word Rules, Reasoning Category* and *Orientation* tests. On the first testing occasion, the

test forms were randomised among recruits. On the second occasion, test forms were randomised once more with the proviso that no one could take the same form twice. Recruits were tested over a period not exceeding 3 hours in total with breaks during any one session. The *Lackland Tests* were the first to be administered. Conditions were standard in a purpose-built computer suite, which was air-conditioned. Testing was at all times supervised by trained civilian staff with extensive experience. Records were searched for the *Armed Services Vocational Aptitude Battery* scores of the recruits and these were added to the files when all personal identity data had been removed. Demographic information included age, sex, social affiliation (ethnic identity), first language spoken and laterality (handedness). Complete test records were available for 1512 recruits, of whom 513 were female and 999 were male.

Table 11.4: Multiple Parallel Form Means: Effects of Unstable Scores on Retest Reliability

	ED1	ED2	NF1	NF2	OE1	OE2	WR1	WR2	RC1	RC2	ORI*	OR2³*
Mean	30.1	32.1	28.8	30.8	30.3	32.3	28.9	31.0	17.4	19.5	13.9	16.6
S_D	6.4	7.1	12.0	13.0	10.2	11.7	10.3	11.8	10.6	11.7	5.8	8.5
N=1512												
Mean	29.8	29.2	27.6	28.4	30.6	32.2	29.3	31.2	16.4	20.6	17.9	20.6
S_D	6.7	7.6	11.6	11.2	10.3	11.0	9.2	10.0	8.5	9.0	6.5	9.0
N=367												
	ED1	ED2	NF1	NF2	OE1	OE2	WR1	WR2	RC1	RC2	ORI	OR2
No Neg. Mean	30.4	32.9	29.7	32.3	31.5	34.2	30.2	33.3	19.4	22.1	14.6	18.1
S_D	6.3	6.5	12.0	12.3	9.4	9.9	9.4	9.8	9.5	9.9	5.5	7.6
N=1311												
	ED1	ED2	NF1	NF2	OE1	OE2	WR1	WR2	RC1	RC2	ORI	OR2
One Neg. Mean	27.9	27.3	23.3	21.1	22.4	19.5	20.3	16.5	4.6	2.3	9.8	6.5
S_D	6.9	8.9	11.0	13.1	11.6	14.5	11.6	13.5	8.2	6.2	6.2	7.6
N=201												

Group Effects on Reliability

		ED	NF	OE	WR	RC	OR
Rtst/rtst	N1512	.69	.81	.67	.68	.77	.66
Rtst/rtst	N367	.73	.84	.73	.75	.77	.74
Rtst/rtst	N1311	.77	.85	.70	.71	.73	.68
Rtst/rtst	N201	.34	.51	.35	.31	-.31	.27

P Values for Effects

	ED1	ED2	NF1	NF2	OE1	OE2	WR1	WR2	RC1	RC2	ORI*	OR2³*
Form	.52	.67	.40	.42	.35	.56	.50	.07	.87	.29	.15	.10
Sex	.01	.11	.08	.05	.13	.32	.02	.69	.37	.55	.39	.24
Group	.02	.01	.75	.40	.15	.51	.01	.08	.34	.04	.02	.10
AFQT	.00	.00	.00	.00	.00	.00	.00	.00	.00	.00	.00	.00

Note: The Orientation time limit was reduced for second phase with lowering of mean scores.

---

3   *Orientation* was given with a reduced time limit and shows a different average compared with the *Orientation* average for the 367 proving trial recruits. Moreover, the *Error Detection* and *Number Fluency* tests were altered to improve their quality control features. Their averages are also different from those for the 367 trial recruits.

How Parallel Was Parallel?

Inspection of the lower half of the comprehensive overview in Table 11.4 is particularly rewarding because it demonstrates the relative effects of test forms on test results compared with group effects normally associated with test performance. The probability of non-parallelism is remote.   Other effects are pronounced. Multivariate analysis of variance was carried out for each test score adjusted for guessing, with test form and social affiliation as random variables, sex as a fixed effect and *Air Force Qualifying Test Score (AFQT)* as a covariate.   The recruits, as volunteers and not random samples of the population, give no assurance that other influences are distributed randomly.   Differential cohort attributes will invariably affect performance, as results in Belgium and Northern Ireland verified only too well for political sensibilities (Chapters 12 and 13).

Diversity and Fairness

Mean scores for groups of recruits assigned randomly to one of eleven different forms available for each test are contained in Table 11.4. The group of 367 recruits contains those who were involved in the proving studies already described. This group acts as a baseline comparison for the large group of 1512. The descriptive statistics for the whole group and males and females are also included in Table 11.4 for easy reference. All recruits improve with practice but with no memory for identical items because they do not exist – only an item type is similar. There was great variation between recruits, and between groups of recruits. Test forms did show variation, but only to a degree that could have been accounted for by individual differences and the different group compositions on any one occasion. In all analyses carried out, test form did not emerge as a significant overall effect, all other things accounted for, as the p-values in Table 11.4 show. By far the most important influence on performance was the *Air Force Qualifying Test Score (AFQT)*. When the effect of the entry qualification was controlled for, the sex and group test differences were lessened. If these groups had been compared without controlling for AFQT, then the results would undoubtedly have been misleading. Group differences existed but not on every test, and not on every occasion. Differences between male and female averages are very small in most tests and show effect sizes of minor importance only in *Number Fluency* and in *Orientation.* Females do better in *Error Detection* tasks, consistent with many more research studies, but again, the effect size is of little practical importance. Within the context of traditional male and female dispositional patterns, these tests are considered to be as fair as might be possible.

The second part of Table 11.4 details the effects of an unstable score on the reliability of the test forms. Two groups are examined, those with no unstable scores and those with one or more negative scores when each of the six test results is adjusted for guessing. Three sets of findings are shown for four different groups of recruits. The first is for all 1512 recruits for whom a complete data set was obtained. Two more groups are identified within this total sample. One of these is a set of 1311 who had no negative score after adjustment for guessing. The group of 201 recruits that remains had one or more negative scores.   A negative score in computer-delivered tests is a dependent variable with a multitude of possible independent causes within individuals.

Figure 11.10: Practice, Test Form and Reliability Effects on Performance

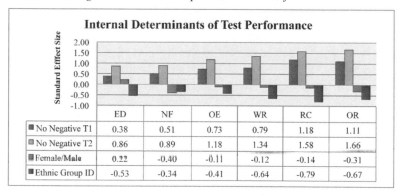

External Influences on Test Scores

	ED	NF	OE	WR	RC	OR
■ Reps	0.31	0.16	0.19	0.19	0.19	0.39
▢ Forms	0.24	0.33	0.22	0.33	0.18	0.23
■ Reliability	0.48	0.39	0.51	0.51	0.49	0.61

EXTRA AND INTRA-INDIVIDUAL EFFECTS ON RELIABILITY AND PERFORMANCE

Two illustrative charts conclude this section on performance factors. The first shows the relative force of different test construction elements. These are not part of the psychological profile of individuals. They are *external* influences. What will affect the score of any individual most strongly, a repetition with a different test form, being given a different form from one's neighbour, or the reliability of the test as a whole? Figure 11.10 gives a clear answer. Unreliability will have a far greater effect than either a second try at the test, or the form of the test administered. In all tests, the effect of repetition or test form are easily encompassed by ensuring that the border zone of any individual score, the standard estimate, is known and employed when decisions about acceptance or rejection are taken.

Figure 11.11: Internal Dispositions and Test Performance

Internal Determinants of Test Performance

	ED	NF	OE	WR	RC	OR
■ No Negative T1	0.38	0.51	0.73	0.79	1.18	1.11
▢ No Negative T2	0.86	0.89	1.18	1.34	1.58	1.66
■ Female/Male	0.22	-0.40	-0.11	-0.12	-0.14	-0.31
■ Ethnic Group ID	-0.53	-0.34	-0.41	-0.64	-0.79	-0.67

Figure 11.11 is concerned with the relative strength of factors that are not external or construction in origin, but could more properly be described as *internal*, or part of the parcel of influences brought to the test by the applicant. What are the effects of scores that seem to be the outcomes of guessing or other motivational factors? Are female and ethnic group identities more or less important than the presence of unstable scores? The results are clear. If the series is produced without any negative score on the first trial, mean scores are about .75 of a standard deviation higher, and more than one standard deviation higher on a second trial. These are large differences. Sex and group identity effects are much less by comparison. One should

remember, though, that these group effect sizes do not control for AFQT differences. When this is done, the sex and Group ID effects are much less.

THE FAIL-SAFE MECHANISM

As a consequence of these results, a unique fail-safe mechanism was built into the computer administration to warn when any test score may be unstable. *An unstable score is one that after adjustment for guessing, using the confidence scoring approach described in Chapter 3, approaches zero within the limits of the standard error of estimate of any zero score.* The system allows a retest of that test and a complete retest can be automatically ordered. When this happens, the original test scores are overwritten using second trial norms to ensure equity. To the best of our present knowledge, no other testing system has the capacity to employ retest norms based on multiple forms except the *British Army Recruit Battery*.

TEST SCORES AND QUALITY OF LIFE IN THE USAF AT LACKLAND.

The data in Table 11.4 can be scrutinised further. With 201 recruits having one or more negative or random scores out of a total of 1512, the probability of having one or more random scores in the test series is about one in eight, or 13%. Suppose one knew how a recruit feels about life at Lackland while undergoing basic training. A reliable indication was possible because a number of quality of life questions were asked of the recruits, and the details of these are found in Chapter 16. One question above all seemed to be a vital indicator of motivation during the training period. *Wanted to quit because life was not what you expected?* Questions on the quality of life and personality scales, were responded to on a six interval scale of frequency, *Always, Usually, Often, Sometimes, Rarely, and Never*. When the responses to this question were cross-tabulated with the categories of having produced one or more random scores, the Chi-Square statistic was highly significant. The result of a large likelihood ratio was salutary. The probability of producing a random score is only 13% without knowledge of the quality of life perception of the recruits: but it increases to 70% after the motivation screen is applied. '*Keypressers*' were not well-motivated to persist: and they surfaced in Chapter 16 among those for whom service life was not a totally happy event.

VALIDITY BY DATA REDUCTION: CONSTRUCT VALIDITY

With a very large sample of recruits, knowledge of what the tests measure is increased because the chances of interpreting chance differences in patterns of correlations are very much reduced. For the rest of this section, only 1311 recruits are used, because operationally, no subject who had a n unstable score would be included in real-life use of the tests. This has the effect of increasing the consistency of the recruits, but of decreasing the range of the tests very slightly. A simple correlation matrix of the first and second test results revealed close similarity if not perfect agreement. The availability of the Armed Services Vocational Aptitude Battery results for each subject permits a more extensive analysis of the Lackland *Tests*. First test scores adjusted for guessing are correlated with the ASVAB individual test results and the matrix is reduced to its basic dimensions. The factor analysis of the first test trial with the ASVAB results is shown in Table 11. 5.

WANTED TO QUIT BECAUSE LIFE WAS NOT WHAT YOU EXPECTED?

Table 11.5: Factor Analysis of Lackland Tests and ASVAB Battery results (N=1311)

TESTS	Factor1	Factor2
Odds and Evens	.736	.277
Number Skills	.730	.336
Word Rules	.698	.380
Reasoning Categories	.603	.349
Orientation	.598	.408
Error Detection	.594	.140
ASVAB: Math Knowledge(MK)	.537	.369
ASVAB: Coding Speed(CS)	.465	-.031
ASVAB: Numerical Operations(NO)	.456	-.032
ASVAB: Arithmetic Reasoning (AR)	.577	.588
ASVAB: Elec. Info.(EI)	.186	.785
ASVAB: Mechanical Comprehension(MC)	.344	.768
ASVAB: General Science(GS)	.280	.732
ASVAB: Auto & Shop(AS)	.045	.667
ASVAB: Word Knowledge(WK)	.262	.596
ASVAB: Paragraph Comprehension(PC)	.340	.512

THE ASVAB at LACKLAND

Psychometric g is a principal components chimera? Maybe not, but an artefact no less.

Note: Extraction Method: Maximum Likelihood.
Rotation Method: Promax with Kaiser Normalization.

The familiar two-factor structure associated with this type of analysis emerges once more. One factor is the strong working memory factor (*Capacity to Process Information*) shared by the numerical and coding speed components of the *Armed Services Vocational Aptitude Battery*. The other is the ASVAB verbal-educational knowledge and achievement factor that tests as much of what the subject knows through schooling as it does any particular aptitude. The two factors correlate .395 in this sample. In previous sections using paper-and-pencil versions, the same structure emerges. The results produce the fundamental division between acquiring information and the power to process it. The two dimensions are not wholly independent of each other. They contribute to the definition of all-round capabilities that are the products of processing capacity, education and a number of other contributing factors, including social opportunity, motivation and interests.

THE LAST STEP: VALIDITY BY PREDICTING ASVAB CLASSIFICATIONS
The *Armed Services Vocational Aptitude Battery* results contain not only scores for individual tests, but composites that are used for allocation of individuals to broad occupational categories. These include the *Air Force Qualifying Test Score* and several other indices, including *ASVAB Administration (Clerical) ASVAB General Duties, ASVAB Mechanical Services and ASVAB Electrical Maintenance*. These indices were used as criterion or dependent variables and the *Lackland Tests* were entered into stepwise regression equations to find out how well they predicted various work-related profiles for training. The results are shown in summary form in Table 11.6.

Table 11.6: Predicting Occupational Profiles using Lackland Tests

Occupational Profile	R	R2	ED	NF	OE	WR	RC	OR
					Rank Order Of Entry			
Air Force Qualifying Test Score	.61	.38	4	1	-	5	3	2
ASVAB Administration (Clerical)	.53	.28	2	1	-	3	-	-
ASVAB General Duties	.60	.36	4	1	-	5	3	2
ASVAB Mechanical Services	.35	.12	3	4	5	2	-	1
ASVAB Electrical Maintenance	.55	.33	4	1	6	5	3	2

As before, the number of recruits used for the regression study was 1311, providing good stability. The multiple correlations with the various *Armed Services Vocational Aptitude Battery* composite indicators and the proportion of variance explained are given. The order in which the tests are entered into the equation shows their relative importance under each test heading. The results might be said to exceed expectations, because the technical components of the various *Armed Services Vocational Aptitude Battery* profiles are essentially knowledge-based. Nevertheless, there are useful concurrent validity coefficients with every profile except *ASVAB Mechanical Services* because it is derived from a heavily weighted test of mechanical knowledge. The *Lackland Tests* do not claim to measure acquired knowledge thresholds. Instead, they emphasise processing capabilities. In fact, the results in Table 11.6 support the different emphases in the *Lackland Test* programmes from the ASVAB and define their complementary role.

CONCLUSIONS ON THE LACKLAND TEST FORMS IN USA
The test and retest norm base for computer-delivered versions in the USA exceeded 3,000 recruits aged 18-27 years. The extensive and comprehensive study of the use of computer-delivered forms generated by algorithms with more than one thousand recruits, for whom extensive background information was generously provided by the USAF, replicated in large measure the proving study. In that work, accuracy was a strong indicator of subject persistence. The same type of analysis derived from scores adjusted for guessing dramatically revealed the need to ensure that test results were an adequate sample of subject capabilities. Test scores that are unstable lead to retesting with parallel form tests immediately if necessary, later if a new session is required. That can only be done fairly whenever retest norms are available and retest reliabilities are high, as proven here.

The *Lackland Tests* were designed to ensure that tests are fairly administered, not biased against males or females or any ethnic or social group. The computer-delivered series pursued these goals with more than anticipated success. Finally, validity studies within and across cultures are confirmatory of paper-and-pencil operational and quasi-operational trials. The tests invariably test the same skills and capacities and they predict classifications made by other criteria. They are also sensitive, but not overly so, to different levels of preselection by other methods, such as high-school and graduate diploma achievement. Finally, when put into the same frame as the ASVAB tests, whose content is outlined in Chapter 9, their working memory nexus reveals the *overwhelming educational and informational basis of any*

ASVAB psychometric general or group factors. It is a reasonable conclusion to take all references to 'psychometric g' as far as the ASVAB is concerned as no more or less than a statistical artefact, rather than a construct-referenced interpretation. Psychometric *g* is not Spearman's g, nor for that matter, Carroll's *g* as a hierarchical outcome from a number of related group factors, first determined by Godfrey Thomson (1939), who was visited in Edinburgh by Carroll in 1947.

THE BUNDESWEHR TRANSFORMATIONS

by Johannes Wulf with Thomas Kutschke
Senior Psychologists, German Armed Forces Personnel Psychology Group

It is my great pleasure to introduce this chapter reflecting cooperation with Dr. Irvine over the past decade. Although the Psychological Service of the German Armed Forces had known of his early work (see the ABC-tests or BARB), collaboration was initiated while Thomas Kutschke, who was to become one of our co-workers, participated in a scientific exchange program affiliated with the United States Air Force at San Antonio, Texas, in 1998. Thomas had the privilege of working with Dr. Irvine (at The United States Air Force Laboratory, Brooks Air Force Base) in the field of personality and computerized psychometrics. Their many meetings ensured familiarity with item generation, the sphere of *radicals and incidentals* and the benefits from having almost infinite equivalent test forms available. This chance association turned out to be fruitful for trials of item generative tests by a team in the German Armed Forces Personnel Psychology Group. Joint efforts led first to the construction of some paper and pencil test versions in 1999, applied to trainees in several German Air Force training units; and finally resulted in a computerized version of basic recruit screening test forms, for the first time encoded in a language other than English.

Working together marked an important milestone. *A British test approach valid for predicting military training outcomes was translated and adopted for use by a NATO member not part of the British or Anglo-American technical cooperation agreements.* Another European NATO nation, Belgium, followed by using similar tests in French and Flemish for recruitment some years later. Thus, the early studies with German conscripts provided an 'advanced guard' contribution to validity generalization of the Lackland Tests (*Tests for Selection and Interviews* as distributed by Mindmill).

I was fortunate to be a member of the team organizing and administering the computer-delivered test trials in Germany in the year 2002. Beginning in the year 1998 we had developed a new test platform called CAT4, which allowed us to handle all new kinds of tests. But with the computer delivered test trials we were encouraged to organize in 2002, we were facing challenges, for which we were not prepared:

- It turned out rather difficult to run the test software on the German LAN, because we had planned to create all tests on our own test platform.
- The special interface we used to operate the computers was not compatible with the tests, which required a mouse.
- The test results could not be transferred immediately in our database.

The difficulties were resolved. The team operating from Bonn, and staff in the test administration centres nationwide were curious about this new approach; and more than willing to overcome the limitations of the CAT4 system. Everybody contributed ideas and hard work to make the project successful. And it was worth it. One of the outstanding results of the German trials was that the composite *Intelligence*

Score generated by the existing German Armed Forces Test Battery could be well predicted by the scores of only four tests of a second generation of computer-delivered tests that we called *The Bundeswehr Experimental Test Battery*. With a specific focus on working memory capacity and processing speed, and a testing time of only nineteen minutes, it demonstrated the power of multiple parallel forms to replace lengthy tests with fixed item banks.

Unfortunately, due to budget cuts in those days, and different priorities, adopting this new approach for regular use within the German Armed Forces was not to happen. Nevertheless, military psychologists in Europe, and especially François Lescrève in Belgium, became aware of our experience. We like to think that the decision to implement similar tests operationally in Belgium was in part due to Bundeswehr successes. Things have changed even since 2003. Initial screening for jobs is often internet based. The new challenge of internet testing should be able to foster the need for robust, short and reliable pre-testing with multiple equivalent forms. With that in mind, I personally hope very much that cooperation will continue in a generation of tests that have come of age since their birth in the 1980s and their adolescence in Germany!

CHAPTER 12

PSYCHOMETRIC COUNSEL FROM EUROPE

A second English language item-generation system described in Chapters 10 and 11 was standardised on a large USAF recruit sample during 1998-99, after initial paper-and-pencil analogues had been used to select applicants to a regional police force in the UK, (Irvine, 1998). It had been examined with the ASVAB as an established frame for comparison. After 1999 it was trialled in Germany (Irvine, Kutschke and Wober, 2000; Irvine, Wulf, Schambach, Kutschke and Walker, 2003). Installed in Belgium in 2006 for recruits to its armed forces, it has been in operation since then in recruiting offices regionally and centrally in the Brussels reception headquarters where additional screening occurs.

EUROPEAN TRANSLATIONS

The Bundeswehr Experimental Test Battery Paper-and-Pencil Versions

Computer-Delivered Trials in Germany

Operational Use in Belgium: The GCTB Tests 2006-2012

The European studies were to provide two recruitment contexts comparable to what had gone before in the United Kingdom and the United States. The German work was against the background of conscription, and with an already existing selection system in operation, using a variety of tests comparable to the ASVAB. Concurrent validation was possible, when test scores from every source were collated from a national sample of conscripts. And there was one other similarity: in Germany, as in the United States, trials with paper and pencil tests were followed by computer-delivered versions. In Belgium, the second generation of tests went a step further than trials conducted in Germany, going operational in 2006 as the actual selection system, just as their BARB parents had done in 1992 within The United Kingdom, offering predictive validity on follow-up as well as construct definition concurrently. In these circumstances, the European language studies were a vital challenge to the effectiveness of evidence centred design in action.

Although the principles of back-translation for cross-cultural tests were well-known and used throughout, there was no previously published work on translating item generative tests from one language to another, and at the same time translating from one military context to another. Because of these different demands, the German and Belgium journeys were to make historical demands on the robustness and resilience of item generative tests. In Europe, the system had to undergo proving trials in three languages apart from English, French, German, and Flemish (Belgian Dutch). Could identical multiple parallel forms be generated within each user language? Did they predict outcomes well? Did they measure the same qualities regardless of language and recruitment policies? Were they fair to different language groups? The issues were many and the results, confirmatory or not, were to prove decisive.

TRANSLATING TESTS

The key to translating multiple parallel form generation of tests is the design[1] of the test 'engine'. The engine is a code that obeys the rules for generating items for each different test. This uses a unique test 'grammar' (Bejar, 1986 a, Irvine, 1990; Irvine Dann & Anderson, 1990) to produce items in series consistent with the theoretical cognitive framework necessary for the production of parallel forms (see Chapter 2). The multilingual 'grammatical' content of each different test engine is determined by cross-cultural back-translation of its key elements[2] and final audit methods (Brislin, 1986). These protocols ensure parallel item production necessary for *linguistically equivalent representation of the items in identical order for each language used.*

A useful analogy is to liken each test form to be used in different languages to a banknote in Euros, where the only apparent difference is a numerical random number that identifies it, even if the not itself contains national symbols. By using the same random number seed to generate a test form for more than one language of administration, *identical item order within every test type was assured.* These procedures were in place for the Dutch, French and German versions tried and verified on recruits to the armed services of Belgium and Germany. The European data sets in this chapter were derived from samples collected from nation-wide recruiting offices. Because other test and classification data were currently available, reliability estimates were supplemented by appropriate content, construct and criterion validity studies. The Belgian system, known as the GCTB, has been operational from 2006 through 2014.

THE BUNDESWEHR EXPERIMENT

Paper-and-Pencil Versions: Origins and Scope

Results: Descriptives Parallelism Reliability

Translations as Radicals

Validity: Inferences about Function

THE BUNDESWEHR EXPERIMENT: TRIALS WITH CONSCRIPTS

Chronologically, the work of extending the utility of item generative tests began in Germany. Like others before it, a preliminary study (*Arbeitsberichte Psychologischer Dienst der Bundeswehr Nr. 1/2000*) used paper-and-pencil analogues of tests generated by computer. Details of this work are available in Irvine, Kutschke and Wober, (2000). However, the success of paper-and-pencil parallel forms, when two trials were given to a sample of 250 recruits, led to decision to a further proving trial with item-generative tests delivered, administered, scored and reported by computer, after minor amendments to *Error Detection* and *Number*

---

1   By Richard Walker

2   Thomas Kutschke, Johannes Wulf and Yves Devriendt were invaluable as bilingual advisors.

Skills. These were contained in an executable file capable of running within the then existing German CAT4 test platform. An indication of the extent of the already existing German selection battery is given in the list of measures available for comparison with the *Bundeswehr Experimental Test Battery* (BETB). Progress made during the decade by the Bundeswehr authorities in the development of computer-delivered adaptive tests can be found in publications by Wildgrube 1980; Nauels & Wildgrube, 1981; Wildgrube,1990; Storm, 1995. These are by no means exhaustive, but they are the sources most likely to be available to readers.

THE BUNDESWEHR EXPERIMENTAL TESTS

Label	Title	Time (mins.)
ED	**Error Detection Test**	4
NF	**Number Skills Fluency**	5
RC	**Reasoning Categories Test**	8
OR	**Orientation (Locations) Test**	6
OE	**Odds And Evens Test**	4
WR	**Word Rules Test**	4
AB	**Alphabet Test**	4
TI	**Transitive Inference**	4

Note: The Alphabet and Transitive Inference tests were confined to the computer-delivered battery

Throughout, the system is referred to as the *Bundeswehr Experimental Test Battery* (BETB). This unofficial label is used for convenience only. Detailed specifications about what these new test items were to be, how they were to be sequenced, and how answer keys were to be constructed were provided in English and then translated into German. These were discussed fully with officials in the Bundeswehr, and only after detailed checks on translations, were analogue German language forms produced for paper-and-pencil trials prior to a computer-delivered survey on a nation-wide basis.

SCOPE AND CONTEXTS

A national sample of approximately 300 conscripts completed the paper-and-pencil version, and a further 400 participants completed a computer-delivered version of *The Bundeswehr Experimental Test Battery* and the then current *Bundeswehr Entry Tests,* the complete report of which is published as Irvine (2003)[3]. Comprehensive result tables are available in that and in Irvine et al. (2000). In short, the results of *The Bundeswehr Experimental Test Battery* can be summarised under headings of parallelism, reliability and validity.

THE EXPERIMENTAL TEST BATTERY

The test types of *The Bundeswehr Experimental Test Battery*, like all others in this volume, derived from theoretically consistent item-generative principles. The computer delivered variants nevertheless place more emphasis on working memory than the paper and pencil analogues. Whatever the mode and language of delivery,

---

3 Thanks are extended to Thomas Kutschke, Sybil Schambach and Johannes Wulf for cooperation in producing this version, whose results are the basis of this account.

however, each test has additional specific variance that is non-random, such as verbal, numerical and spatial attributes. The skills and knowledge demanded were, as in all other contexts, the minimum levels to be expected of people completing a normal school curriculum. In fact, elementary school children aged 11 can complete these tests quite comfortably once they understand fully what each test is about. The tasks in *The Bundeswehr Experimental Test Battery* were chosen to be fair to minorities and, as far as nature allows, fair to both men and women.

The insert provides the time limits in minutes for the administration of the tests used in both paper-and-pencil and computer delivered formats. In general, the results are presented in summary form in order to make the trends and conclusions clear and precise. Much preliminary analysis was carried out in order to explore every possibility.

OFFICIAL GERMAN TESTS
A number of measures were provided by the German Ministry of Defence, including the test centre identification number, results of *The Bundeswehr Entry Tests* aptitude tests, and age. No participant was identified by name or country of origin. *The Bundeswehr Entry Tests* were administered by computer using a console interface. Some aptitude tests are adaptive. Other tests are timed, having fixed numbers of trials at a specific task. Each score is now briefly described as a reference point for their use in trials with the new tests.

1. *Intelligence Test Theta and Standard Score/Value.* This composite consists of adaptively (2-PL Birnbaum) administered items out of three different item pools (figural reasoning, number and verbal reasoning/comprehension).
2. *Verbal Reasoning and Figural Reasoning Scores.* See above, but integers used for standardised values 1 to 7.
3. *Mathematical Facility Scores.* The item pool consists of geometrical, arithmetic problems, numerical comprehension tasks (not a number fluency test, not speeded).
4. *Mechanical Comprehension Scores.* These are derived from a number of items demanding understanding of mechanical principles.
5. *Electronic Comprehension Test.* Principles and applications of electrical engineering, e.g. Ohm's law.
6. *Orthographic (Spelling) Test.* This is a multiple-choice test of correct word identification from four different spellings of the same word.
7. *Reaction Time Test.* The participant has to press 0, 1 or 2 out of 6 keys on the console depending on which (or none) of 6 stimuli have been presented. The response is correct if all stimuli have been recognised. Those stimuli are a triangle, a square, a circle, a cross, a high pitch and a low pitch sound.
8. *Radio Operator Test.* The participant has to discriminate the letters R, W, K presented acoustically as Morse signals. After being trained, the participant has to run three trials of 50 signals each, the signals being presented faster from trial to trial. This is a highly speeded test; a maximum of 150 items administered by headphones.
9. *Auditory Discrimination Test.* Two sounds are presented sequentially. Participants decides which one was higher; or if both have the same pitch. They are mono sounds presented on both ears. The differences between those two sounds range from 32 Hz to 5 Hz, the pitches range from 820 Hz to 940 Hz.

10. *Signal Detection Test.* Four optical stimuli (flashing circles, short flash, long flash) are presented. Participants reproduce the order of those short or long stimuli: (short - long – short - long for example) by pressing keys on the panel. There are 20 short-long patterns of light signals to detect and encode by pressing buttons on the console. The short signals last 200 msec; the long signals 700 msec; the time between the signals is 300 msec. resulting in a highly speeded test.

Tests are scored either by estimating ability thresholds through adaptive formulas, or by raw scores that are then transformed by a uniform metric. A *Theta* score is the ability parameter estimated for each of three adaptive tests of *Verbal Reasoning, Mathematical Facility and Figural Reasoning.* A general aptitude parameter *Intelligence Theta* (or intelligence), is the sum of those three thetas. All four thetas have been standardised. The ten tests were as important in Europe as the ten ASVAB tests were in the United States. They were the core results essential for validity studies.

CATEGORIES USED IN THE ANALYSIS
Every care had to be exercised in the partition of variance between the experimental parallel test forms. The following categories were used in the analyses of the test scores.

1. *Test Forms:* Three parallel forms of each of *The Bundeswehr Experimental Test Battery* tests were administered at random to each participant. A *Test Form* variable was created to identify each form of every test administered. *Test Form* was used as a random factor in all ANOVAs.
2. *Age and Education Levels:* Although conscripts comprise a population with a very restricted age range, age was found to correlate negatively with test performance. Younger participants were better performers than older ones. Consequently, age was a necessary covariate in assessing test form effects. Type of school attended before induction was also available. This category was expected to relate to scores on the computer-delivered tests.
3. *Training Regiment Allocation:* Recruits were allocated to different training regiments depending on their results in the comprehensive Bundeswehr entry tests described above. This category, like the type of school attended, provided a concurrent validity platform.
4. *Filter Variable of Test Competence:* The filter variable is called *Test Competence.* Exclusion of a random score in any test ensured a database of respondents for whom one might assume that the tests were understood and completed satisfactorily. This filter identified *keypressers* among United States Air Force recruits. In Germany, *Test Competence* was also used as a category in assessing variations in test parallelism.

PAPER-AND-PENCIL VERSIONS: ORIGINS AND SCOPE

This study followed discussions in the United States Air Force Laboratory, San Antonio, Texas[4], on the feasibility of translating item-generative cognitive tests that were then undergoing intensive standardisation, reliability and validity trials, into

---

4   With Thomas Kutschke.

a context where they could undergo similar trials with comparable populations in Germany. These informal meetings were followed by a review in Bonn late in 1998 at the German Ministry of Defence, and a formal agreement for the trial under licence of the test series was concluded. In summary, the initial aim was to administer paper-and-pencil analogues of computer-delivered tests to a national sample of about 300 male German conscripts in a number of different training regiments. The test results used to allocate these recruits to different training regiments were to be retrieved from records and collated with individual test results. Finally, group membership categories were established, including regiment allocation, education standard and, where relevant, occupation in civilian life.

Methods
Two paper-and-pencil parallel forms of each test were administered in a simple crossover design applied randomly to cohorts within a number of different training regiments. Half of the subjects had Form 101 first; and half had Form 102. In the second trial, the alternate form was given. The analytical methods used included the scoring of response data to adjust scores for guessing; screening of data for confounding effects; the use of multivariate analysis of variance to assess form and trial effects; estimation of reliability; regression and correlational analyses.

RESULTS: PARALLELISM RELIABILITY PRACTICE
Reliability over forms was, for tests with a short time limit, in the range (.79 - .94) good to excellent, averaging .89. A composite score derived from all of these tests with unit weight would yield a reliability coefficient in excess of .97. When averages for different forms of the tests were compared, only *Error Detection* showed a form difference of any real importance. This type of difference was obtained in some early versions of the *Error Detection* series, of which this is an example. In March 1999, adjustments were made to the generation control processes for this and *Number Fluency*. Results revealed that form differences had disappeared in first and in second trials during which test forms were randomly assigned. Comparing the mean trial values revealed the size of trial effects over forms. There were, as one might expect, practice effects that are not functions of remembering the right answer from repetition of an identical test because the design ensured that a different second form was administered. Instead they are true fluency or strategic effects. Such effects were well known by the time that the German trials were complete, as the studies with prior exposure to item types had shown in the UK with army and navy entrants and in the USA. The paper-and-pencil German trials were indicators of how consistently the item types were behaving. The effects of practice on selection can be very much reduced, or removed if necessary, by the use of pre-test booklets containing practice examples (Tapsfield, 1993a, 1993b) and adjusting norms accordingly.

Test Robustness: Comparative Cross-National Results
To compare results from different recruit populations is to invite criticism especially if these are cross-national and/or cross-cultural. The writer has *always* advocated extreme caution in the interpretation of such outcomes (Irvine & Berry, 1988, Ch. 1). Perhaps no harm can ensue if the sole purpose is to gain an inkling of *how robust the tests might happen to be in spite of uncontrollable background differences in applicant populations.* Accordingly, Table 12.2 shows first trial means for *comparable paper-*

and-pencil tests administered to German male recruits, UK male police applicants and USA Air Force recruits (predominantly male in the initial purposive sample).

Table 12.1: Cross-National Paper and Pencil Parallel Forms

GROUP	N	ED 1	OR 1	RC 1	NF 1	OE W1 (S)
			AVERAGES			
GER	250	27	21	17	39	39 (47)
UK	4500	30	23	20	41	43
USA	300	28	22	19	40	40
			RELIABILITIES			
GER Rtt		.78	.84	.90	.94	.91(.91)
UK Rtt		.78	.86	.82	.92	.87
USA Rtt		.68	.84	.80	.80	.85

On the basis of these results, test form effects due to regional disparities in development and educational opportunity appear minor, if not altogether minimal. The effect sizes (largest overall mean difference less than .25 SD units) are so small that more detailed investigation may reasonably be expected to show the same homogeneous pattern of results. The relevant finding is the stability of performance of different parallel forms with language groups in different services in different countries: and the overall internal consistency of the tests, shown in the lower half of the table.

TRANSLATIONS AS RADICALS
Translations into German have proved effective, but the mean for the symbol version of *Odds and Evens* has been included to compare with the language version in German. When the symbol version of Odds *and Evens* was created (see Chapter 7) note was taken of the similarity, when vocalised and read, of the German expressions *'gerade'* (even) and *'ungerade'* (not even or odd). Figure 12.1 gives an example of the item forms. Moreover, as the example shows, the German expressions were no longer monosyllables[5], as the equivalent English words are. Difficulty was expected to increase in German because of language specificity and the increase on short-term memory incurred by polysyllables (Baddeley, Thomson, & Buchanan (1975). The confirmatory study by Ellis and Hennelly (1980) involved bilingual Welsh children, where numerals in Welsh were polysyllabic and tended to decrease performance in number memory-span tasks compared with performance in English. Welsh-English bilinguals confirmed this effect as it showed that children had larger digit spans for English numbers than for Welsh numbers, which take longer to pronounce. This series, and discussion of the Welsh language finding by Baddeley (1981) were the cognitive theory background for what was to be essentially an experiment where the effects of the symbol and language versions of *Odds and Evens* in German could be contrasted.

---

5   'Even' in English might pass as monosyllabic when pronounced, as it tends to be,' evn', or perhaps a syllable and a half!

Figure 12.1: Identical German Odd-Even Items in Language and Symbol Format

Regel	Zahlen	Antwort
		F1
Gerade Ungerade Ungerade	**Drei Fünf Eins**	[0] [1] **[2]** [3]
		F2
		F2
○ ◆ ◆	**Drei Fünf Eins**	[0] [1] **[2]** [3]

When the scores were examined, the symbol version always showed a major improvement effect size over the verbal version of nearly one standard deviation unit, while the reliabilities are identical. Further clarity is provided by the comparison of English and German schoolchildren's attempt at simple arithmetic problems in working memory (Adams & Hitch, 1997). Two experiments investigated the extent to which children's mental arithmetic performance is constrained by working memory rather than their arithmetical competence. A span procedure measured the limit on English- and German-speaking children's ability to add together pairs of numbers graded in difficulty. Results were remarkably similar in both contexts, consistent with the notion of working memory as a general-purpose resource with dynamics that are unaffected by to the detailed nature of operations. As was apparent in the Bundeswehr study, working memory was the key to item difficulty, not its specifics. In passing, this particular example reveals once again how the comparison and publication of cross-national attainments with strict control of cultural and linguistic contexts is ethically correct, and, unlike a large number of cross-national educational attainment league tables has no political significance, but considerable scientific value (cf. Irvine,1969, 1983).

LANGUAGE MAKES A MARK

Translations as Radicals

Odds and Evens harder as 'Even' and 'Not Even'?

VALIDITY: INFERENCES ABOUT FUNCTION
There are three main issues: what constructs are measured by paper-and-pencil tests; what they predict; and how sensitive they are to group memberships, such as education levels and training regiment allocations.

Construct Validity by Factor Analysis
By including the basic test battery already given by the German Ministry of Defence and by data reduction methods, common factors in the array of tests used can be estimated. The results were all very similar to what had been found in previous studies where the tests had been placed in the same network as existing selection tests, such as AET 86 in Britain and the ASVAB in the United States. Two factors were extracted. One factor identifies the German Ministry of Defence tests, and the other the new tests. The factors correlated at about .65 to .67, indicating the presence of a higher-order

general factor. This result is very close to the finding realised in the United States. The new tests correlate with the United States Armed Services Vocational Aptitude Battery to almost exactly the same degree. Regardless of where they have been used in the past, the new tests always identify a strong working memory factor, closely allied to reasoning and fluid intelligence and a strong predictor of rate of learning new procedures. There is no reason to change that interpretation when they are used with a group whose first language is German. The United States Armed Services Vocational Aptitude Battery has been shown in previous extensive studies to produce a verbal-educational construct that is very much a function of acquired knowledge.

Concurrent Validity by Regression
Operational definitions of what may be measured by the new tests can be gathered from attempts to predict scores on tests used by the German Ministry of Defence. The new tests are used as independent variables, and the indices provided by the tests actually in use by the German Ministry of Defence as dependent variables. Coefficients predicted the German Ministry of Defence IQ Standard 7 Point Classification by using all the information available in sequential trials of the tests. A stepwise regression function was fitted, showing that the correlation can reach .704 by using the information from the *Locations (OR), Number Fluency, and Error Detection* scores from Trials 1 and 2. A quasi-operational analysis was conducted using *only the scores from the first trial.* This analysis produced a multiple R of .672, with a common variance of 45.1 percent in which the significant predictors were *OR First Score, NF First Score, ED First Score.*

VALIDATION

Constructs,

Concurrent Validities

and Training Regiment Classifications

Other regression analyses on individual Ministry of Defence Tests showed equally promising results. Almost invariably, the first test to enter into the regression equation, regardless of target, was *Orientation 1 (Locations)* a spatial reconstruction task based on verbal directions. However, *Odds and Evens (Symbol), Number Fluency* and *Error Detection* all made substantial contributions depending on the target. Their frequent contributions are sympathetic with the wide canvas of the tests used by the German Ministry of Defence, involving working memory, figural representation, attention span and speed of encoding. These results also show that some of the tests used have specific knowledge and variance due to biological factors that are not captured by the trial tests. These *Bundeswehr Entry Tests* include *Mechanical and Electrical knowledge and Auditory Thresholds.* Nevertheless, the item-generative test types even in paper-and-pencil form, provided screens for intelligence or information processing capacity, with some confidence in the outcomes for accuracy, fairness and low cost of production and administration if used in computer-delivered fashion.

Concurrent Validity by Group Classification
Validity can be estimated by group membership status when this membership is what we have described elsewhere as a low-inference variable. Allocation to different occupations in civilian life, and to training regiments in the army as the result of aptitude testing is another such low-inference variable. Figure 12.2 shows the

item-generative tests to have marked correspondence with the official allocation of conscripts to qualitatively different training regiments. The least able were trained in duties regarded to be less demanding, while the most able could be assigned to technical roles.

Figure 12.2: First Score Test Means by Training Regiment

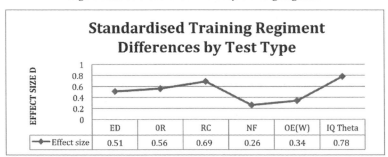

The chart shows a D effect of 0.78 SD units on the official *IQ 7 Point Theta* scale used to assign conscripts to one or other of these two training regiment extremes. *Reasoning Category* and *Orientation* provide the largest dispersions among the item-generative tests. In combination, the trial tests came close to matching the dispersion of the *Bundesministerium IQ Theta* general classification index. In the computer-delivered version, it was possible to examine other categories. For example, length and type of education are differential treatments; and membership of one minority group or another each provide an index from which assumptions about different levels of aptitude have been made, but not always with certainty.

THE COMPUTER-DELIVERED TRIALS IN GERMANY

In the computer delivered trials, *three* parallel forms of each test were administered randomly by Bundeswehr officials to cohorts within a number of different test administration centres, involving more than 500 participants across the country. Computer delivery, scoring and report mechanisms were automatic. The standard computer delivered test interface was by mouse with a restricted cursor. Mouse practice was provided for each participant. All tests had graduated instructions and a final set of five practice items. *If fewer than four were answered correctly, the practice items were repeated again.* Progression from the second practice set to the test itself is automatic. Time limits for the tests of *The Bundeswehr Experimental Test Battery* were the same as those shown in Table 12.1. *The Transitive Inference* and *Alphabet Test*, both included in the computer-delivered trials, were timed at 4 minutes.

THE BUNDESWEHR ENTRY TESTS AND OTHER MEASURES
Concurrent measures were, as before, provided by the German Ministry of Defence, including results of aptitude tests. Categories for comparison of effects included test centre identification number, education level, and age. No participant was identified by name or country of origin. Additionally, a variable was created to identify each form of every test administered. Although conscripts comprise a population with a very restricted age range, in previous analyses, age was found to correlate negatively

with test performance. Younger participants were better performers than older ones. Consequently, age was a necessary covariate in general linear analysis of variance models for assessing test form effects. All details can be found in Irvine (2003), but summary descriptions are included for interpretation of the results.

Operational Methods
Three parallel forms of each test were administered randomly by Bundeswehr officials to cohorts within a number of different test administration centres. Protocols were provided and software was expertly installed at these centres by Johannes Wulf whose comment shows what changes were needed. The participant interface was by mouse. *The cursor was always restricted in movement, so that it could never disappear off screen; and practice in mouse use was provided.* Time limits for the tests of *The Bundeswehr Experimental Test Battery* were shown in a previous insert. The analytical methods used included the scoring of response data to adjust scores for guessing; screening of data for confounding effects; the use of multivariate analysis of variance to assess form effects; estimation of reliability; regression and correlational analyses. The results are in summary form as far as possible; in order to make the trends and conclusions clear and precise. Much preliminary analysis was carried out in order to explore every possibility.

COMPUTER DELIVERY

Three Parallel Forms

Difficulty Levels

Constructs Across Cultures

Group Memberships and Concurrent Validities

Test Competence

COMPUTER DELIVERED RESULTS: FORMS AND RELIABILITY
The means and variances of the three forms of the tests were consistently close. Particularly impressive were the high individual test reliabilities and the very small effect sizes when the three parallel forms of the tests were compared with each other. Table 12.5 shows the significance values for analyses of variance conducted on all three parallel forms of the tests used in the computer delivered study. Examination of all potential test score functions showed the test forms to have little or no bearing in individual scores.

The effect sizes of the minimum form differences are only a fraction of a standard deviation in extent. The smallest difference is 0.01. In short, the two most congruent parallel forms of each test need no further equating. The maximum effect size (D_{max}) for the largest observed mean difference between any pair of three forms occurs in *Word Rules* where it is 0.38 of a standard deviation unit. This is never repeated elsewhere. The laws of chance dictate that at least one such result could emerge from more than twenty different comparisons from the same sample. Be that as it may, because the standard error of estimate of a single score is always used to fix border zones, the between-form effect is less than the within-form effect of normal measurement error.

Table 12.2: German Computer-Delivered Forms Parallelism and Reliability

	Average Scores, Variance					Effect Size, Significance			Reliability
	Form1	Form2	Form3	ALL	SD	D max.	D min.	P value	Rtt
ED	32	33	33	34	6	.18	.06	**.40**	**.81**
RC	9	9	11	13	8	.17	.02	**.25**	**.94**
OR	17	15	16	18	7	.28	.10	**.12**	**.84**
NF	36	38	36	40	13	.08	.01	**.48**	**.92**
OE	27	29	28	32	9	.16	.03	**.43**	**.92**
WR	30	26	29	32	10	.35	.10	**.05**	**.92**
TI	12	12	11	14	6	.13	.01	**.59**	**.88**
AB	115	98	128	100	26	.12	.05	**.65**	**.96**

Difficulty: Percentage Correct and Mean Log Latency Scores

For each participant, the percentage correct and mean log latency per item measured in centiseconds were also recorded. ANOVAs were carried out on all of these results in the progress report (Irvine et al., 2003) and they show little if any effects. In short, the test forms are consonant with each other in terms of average item difficulty measured by percentage correct or average time taken to complete each item. On the other hand, *Age* and *Test Competence* were always significant, even with relatively small numbers. These effects are evaluated in the relevant sections.

A Lesson Learned

One should not overlook or ignore the relatively low scores on the *Reasoning Categories* test reported in Table 12.5. These seem out of place. With hindsight, it was in need of investigation to discover why it proved so difficult for conscripts in the computer-delivered version. Thomas Kutschke suggested that the expression 'living' in German did not cover organic material except animals, causing confusion when trees and other non-animal growing plants are referred to as 'living'. Once more, translation was seen to be a possible radical that would change item difficulty. Similarly, the USAF performance on the *Number Skills* test was much lower than might be expected by European standards. This result is perhaps more easily explained by number skills educational effects than the *Reasoning Categories* differences. The experience with the *Reasoning Categories* test in German meant that strict back-translation procedures were employed for operational versions in Belgium.

LANGUAGE MAKES ANOTHER MARK

Reliabilities

Estimates of reliability (internal consistency over forms) are lower bound because of deliberate range restriction. Only those subjects who had none-chance scores in every test were used for these calculations. Reliabilities for tests with a short time limit range from very good to excellent in the range .81 to .96. The lower-bound estimate for the reliability of a composite of all tests in *The Bundeswehr Experimental Test Battery* remains at the paper and pencil version estimate of .97.

CONCURRENT VALIDITY: GROUP MEMBERSHIP EFFECTS
No test is ever devoid of group membership effects. The important issue is to put those that are observable into perspective. The chart accompanying Figure 12.3 does this by showing the relative strengths of group membership by using Cohen's d, as in other similar contexts. All mean differences observed by comparing the highest and lowest membership groups are on the same relative scale in standard deviation units.

Figure 12.3: Moderators of Test Performance

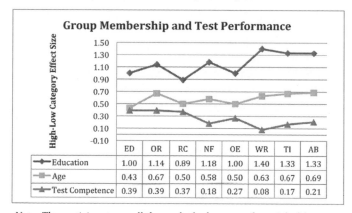

Note: The participants are all those who had an error-free trial of the tests.

Previously, training regiment classification was used as means of estimating concurrent validity; and this was possible because the paper and pencil trials were conducted at the training regiments themselves after classification The computer delivered version was not able to include regiment allocation, because it had not been made when the data was gathered at recruitment offices throughout the country. Nevertheless, other forms of group membership, by which the concurrent validity of tests might be revealed, were available. These were *educational level reached prior to conscription, age, and a control variable of test competence*, where the occurrence of any random score in the series of eight tests was enough for classification into a group for whom computer delivered test delivery might have formed a barrier. Each group effect is addressed in turn.

Education Level
Level of education was recorded for participants. Three finite groups were identified, depending on the type of secondary school course completed: *Hauptschulabschluss* (Group1); *Realschulabschluss* (Group 2); and *Allgemeine Hochschulreife* (Group3 including University/College Entry Qualifications). The effect of level of education on all of *The Bundeswehr Experimental Test Battery* and on the *Bundeswehr Entry Tests* was assessed by analysis of variance tests. Predictably, every F ratio, with one exception, was highly significant; and the effect sizes separating top and bottom groups were large, being one standard deviation or more.

Age as a Package Variable at Conscription

Ages at conscription occupy a very narrow range, from seventeen to early twenties. The younger participants are more effective performers than older ones, more than a standard deviation separating youngest from the oldest cohorts. Because this is so, and there is no such thing as an elderly conscript, the consistent negative correlations with age (Table 12.6) were unusual, suggesting that age was a label for some underlying social factor. According to officials in the German Ministry of Defence, older conscripts had among their number immigrants and residents from the former East Germany whose first language was not German. The age-related performance differences could be an artefact of a two year delay in conscripting Russian-speaking migrants from areas of the former USSR (Kazakhstan and Siberia). *In such circumstances, age categories are package variables offering evidence of test validity by minority language group membership.*

Test Competence as an Unknown

An unusual group classification on this occasion was the filter variable first used in the *Lackland Test* experiments in the United States. As was done in the United States, two groups were created: those who had no chance score or equivalent in any of *The Bundeswehr Experimental Test Battery* tests and those who had one or more scores failing to meet the criterion of acceptability. If a participant had one random test score among all those attempted, this was a loss of test competence for reasons not readily apparent. This variable showed that underlying

TEST COMPETENCE

What Does a Random Score Measure?

domains, such as persistence or quality of life effects (see Chapter 11) can be measured by response patterns to cognitive tests. It is a trait measured by more than one method, a form of convergent validity. Notable effect sizes separate the groups for *Error Detection, Orientation and Reasoning Categories*. Random test scores on the day do not show potential ability like education level or age at conscription. Nor is score definition aided by its category width. Test competence review in the German trial was to prove important for a decision by the Belgian authorities to offer an immediate retest, using second trial norms, to any recruit with an unstable score in any one of the tests used.

CONSTRUCT VALIDITY

Construct validity largely depends on the structure of the correlations among tests, where there are theoretical markers for the underlying meaning of test scores. The extensive marker set provided by *Bundeswehr Entry Tests* was analogous to the use of the ASVAB in the United States but unique among the European languages. The intercorrelations of the tests proved to be very similar to those encountered internationally, and to the paper-and-pencil versions of *The Bundeswehr Experimental Test Battery*. As in the United States when the *Lackland Tests* were combined with the with the ASVAB tests, two basic factors, one of working memory and the other of aptitudes based on acquired knowledge, were reproduced. The two constructs correlated close to .70 in the German language analysis, a result that is consistent with other studies. The extent of this correlation indicates the presence of a higher-order general factor of intelligence commonly found in populations of extended range. Conscripts provide such a population. To conclude, there is convergent validity because different tests and approaches measure the same dimensions. These were also signs of discriminant validity or uniqueness in *the Bundeswehr Entry Tests* of *Signal Detection and Choice Reaction Times* identified by the presence of the working memory markers.

CONCURRENT VALIDITY BY REGRESSION

Operational definitions of what may be measured by the new tests can be gathered from attempts to predict scores on tests used by the German Ministry of Defence. The new tests were used as independent variables to predict the overall grade of the recruit, *Intelligence Theta*. The *Intelligence Theta* score was predicted from the results of four tests, *Transitive Inference. Number Facility, Word Rules and Orientation*, with a multiple R of .70. *Cost-benefits of using only a few tests of short duration as a mass screening strategy are considerable. To reach a correlation of .70 with IQ Theta took only 19 minutes of testing time, involving a test session of 30 minutes after instructions and practice.*

NINETEEN MINUTES TO THETA

High Multiple Correlation with Official Recruit Classification

---

THE GERMAN LANGUAGE STUDIES: CONCLUSIONS

Macdonald went across cultures and languages when he tested Askaris. Test instructions were translated, new forms were added, content and construct validity were confirmed and criteria identified if not predicted through no fault of his own. BARB tests underwent the same scrutinies and lessons were learned. A limited but valid analogy holds for the German language trials. The BETB tests were forerunners of operational use for recruit selection in Belgium, although that was not the purpose at the time. The German language translations largely confirmed the content, reliability and behaviour of the original English language versions and they showed promise in screening conscripts accurately in a very short testing time. Two additional, if in hindsight obvious, lessons were learned. Languages make a difference to what kinds of information are processed and the speed with which information can be accessed, reconstructed and applied to solving problems. Second, cohorts identified by categories may not be what they seem. Age among conscripts was not a potential causal influence. Age may not wither performance as a high-inference variable masking a low-inference (Irvine, 1983, pp.48-49) category, in this case plausibly identified as German language proficiency. Test competence is an outcome that has no certain meaning, but whose effects on reliability are not minimal. These lessons were to be applied in the operational use of Flemish and French versions in Belgium, an account of which now follows.

BELGIUM: THE OPERATIONAL CAMPAIGN

by François J. Lescrève
Lieutenant-Colonel (Ret.), Belgium Defence Force,
Advisor and Organizer, International Military Testing Association

Selection for the Military is an old story. The Bible[6] already gave a first practical solution to the problem. The problem at stake is actually quite simple: provided that the recruiting circumstances are fair in terms of compensation for the anticipated level of required performance and involved risks, and the recruiting services do their job in advertising the vacancies to the right audience, chances are that a large number of applicants apply for a set of differentiated vacancies. The question at hand then turns into: *"Who among the applicants is to be enlisted and for what trade?"* Rational and economically sound approaches to solve the question most often include the assessment of pertinent traits or competencies that, when combined, allow the prediction of future performance. Things however have changed in the last couple of decades. One could say that up to the end of eighties, performance prediction was the ultimate goal for selection and classification systems. Nowadays, things are a bit more complicated. Allow me to develop two facets: the youngsters' attitude and the political climate.

In earlier days, one could assume that performance scores reflected ability levels as the vast majority of recruits would perform to the best of their ability given the socio-cultural context of these days. This is no longer true. Nowadays, youngsters continuously assess their situation; and will not hesitate to leave the Military when they feel that the cost of

staying in outgrows actual or anticipated benefits. This is a serious challenge to the current predictive validity paradigm that assumes that both predictor and criterion measurements are based on the best possible performance level of the individuals. Attrition research data therefore need to be incorporated in the assessment of selection tools quality.

After the fall of the Berlin wall and the perceived collapsing of the threat of a massive Soviet invasion of Western Europe, the efficiency of the Military in Western Europe was no longer seen as the ultimate goal to reach. Instead, politicians emphasized things such as gender fairness, minority and national linguistic representation. Selection tools were no longer only assessed in terms of predictive validity but also, if not mainly, in terms of gender and minority fairness or in short, defensibility. At the turn of the century, I personally was assigned as project officer to review the recruiting systems for the Belgian Armed Forces by the francophone socialist Minister of Defence, André Flahaut. The very concept of item-generative tests and their implementation as realized by Professor Irvine fitted wonderfully well in the search for assessment tools that combine sound psychometrics while addressing concerns of gender and cultural or linguistic fairness. The virtually unlimited series of parallel forms allow applicants to practice: which ensures that instructions are well understood and applicants have the opportunity to familiarize themselves with the different

---

6   The Bible: Judges 7, 4-8.

types of items. Retesting, sometimes at multiple occasions, is also handled elegantly. And finally, by the nature of items that are generated in Professor Irvine's system, gender and cultural fairness is ensured. I therefore was very pleased that the GCTB was implemented as the basic selection tool for the Belgian Defence Forces.

OPERATIONAL VERSION WITH BELGIAN RECRUITS

Geautomatiseerde Cognitieve TestBatterij **(GCTB)**

Operational Requirements

Flemish and French Language Applicants

Parallelism and Difficulty

Validation Infantry, Officers, Pilots

Diversity - to be continued

OPERATIONAL USE IN BELGIUM: THE GCTB TESTS 2006-2012[7]

Belgium in the nineteenth century was referred to as *The Cockpit of Europe* because it had been the site of more decisive European battles than any other country. In the twentieth century it was the theatre of conflict in two world wars. In the twenty-first century perhaps a far-reaching psychometric military campaign about the construction and operational use of modern psychometric tests for recruitment should be expected in that complex and vibrant country with traditional north-south cultural boundaries. In fact, the work of Lescrève, referenced and elaborated in Chapters 2 and Chapter 14, was perhaps the most sophisticated computer-delivered assault on the trench warfare of paper-and-pencil military testing in the era. The culmination is seen in his application of the payoff model he pioneered using data from a number of NATO sources in comprehensive reports (Lescrève, 2002, NATO 2007). His early work from 1980 onwards involved the early transcription and development of traditional paper-and-pencil tests for use in a complex allocation system, first with conscripts and latterly with volunteers. The model was computer-resident, based on ability profiles and stated vocational preferences collated with vacancy needs at the time of recruitment. Accepted by commanders, officials and politicians, it was a much admired model seldom, if ever, emulated within Europe or elsewhere.

Largely because of the already existing climate within the Belgian Defence Force, a contract was signed to deliver an automated test battery, known officially as the *Geautomatiseerde Cognitieve Test Batterij* (GCTB). It was specified as a stand-alone parallel form test series controlled by the secure Belgian Defence Force (BDF) intranet system operating in recruiting centres throughout Belgium. All potential recruits were to be tested under supervised conditions in the language of choice, Flemish[8], French and German[9]. Moreover, each automatically generated parallel form had to have its unique set of items in identical order for each language group. Ten parallel forms of each of the six tests listed in Table 12.3 immediately below were created and assembled. No other recruiting system operating today has this multilingual parallel

---

7   This review was submitted, approved and discussed at a progress meeting held in Brussels in May, 2011.

8   'To come back to your book, if you want to indicate the language spoken in Flanders and include the notion that it is slightly different from the language spoken in The Netherlands, I would suggest you use the term 'Vlaams' (Flemish), the language spoken in 'Vlaanderen' (Flanders). So for instance, you could change "Nederlands" (Belgian Dutch) into "Vlaams" (Belgian Dutch)'. This clarification by François Lescrève is gratefully acknowledged. Flemish has been used and the abbreviation VLA applied as necessary.

9   Although a German language version is available, there were so few German -speaking applicants that no results for this group have been reported. Instead, full data for the two major linguistic divisions in Belgium are always reported.

forms capability. Examples of these tests in analogue and computer-screen format have already been provided in Chapters 10 and 11. Comparisons with previous work were not the main purpose. The GCTB was not, as in Germany, an experiment but an operational battery. Recruitment in Belgium presented new multilingual challenges to automatic item-generation. Given official regulations for the use of tests to ensure equality of opportunity, devising an operationally acceptable system was not a simple task. This section of the chapter deals with issues that required special study during its inception and progress. Results address test consistency, fairness to different regional and language groups, appropriateness for recent immigrants and strategies for persistent repeat applicants. The independent follow-up of the battery has also been unique, with careful attention to detail in different training contexts by Belgian military psychologists. Their concerns reflect the central importance of the validation of the tests in two official languages with all the attendant political overtones.

THE DATA SOURCES

The new GCTB tests operated in a 'black box' that made no inroads upon an existing recording and delivery system named HERMES, which operated nation-wide in a closed secure network, producing reliable and verifiable results. Policy decisions dictated two operational requirements. First, separate norms had to be provided for the two main language groups, French and Flemish; and for any other volunteers who spoke German. Second, because a potential recruit may attempt the test series on more than one occasion, first and second attempt norms were established. Six of the tests introduced for the German study were chosen as the screening battery. From these, separate quotients

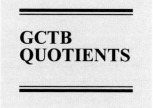

GCTB QUOTIENTS

were created to correspond with existing classification concepts. These test groups are shown in Table 12.3. GCTB data were analysed at key points beginning with the installation of the GCTB in 2006, and continuing annually until 2011. Basic data, organised in SPSS files from which all calculations derived, were provided by BDF officials. Calculations are rounded where possible to conserve space.

Table 12.3: The GCTB Quotients and a General Index of Capability

Test	Verbal Quotient	Memory Quotient	Numerical Quotient	Spatial Quotient	General Reasoning Quotient	General Index Quotient
Alphabet Order	X					X
Word Rules	X	X				X
Odds and Evens		X	X			X
Number Fluency			X			X
Spatial Orientation				X	X	X
Deductive Reasoning					X	X

To give an indication of the extent of the work completed, summary results from all the applicants tested during the period, are organised in Table 12.11, giving enrolments for the major language groups, for female and male entrants and by volunteer applications by application for rank. This shows the scale of the enterprise, with results on a grand scale from a population of applicants, as distinct from a random sample. GCTB data for 2006, 2008 and 2011 are used throughout. Basic SPSS files, from which all calculations derive, were provided by BDF officials. All calculations are rounded to whole numbers where possible to conserve space. None of the views expressed are those of the BDF authorities. The comprehensive 2011 review results in Table 12.9 are a reference marker provided from an independent account by Annemie Defranc, Associate Psychologist, BDF given on September 8, 2011 in Brussels (Defranc, 2011), of the operational use, from November 2006, to December 2010 of *Geautomatiseerde Cognitieve TestBatterij* (GCTB). In this period, 11,423 French Language (FR) applicants and 10,474 Flemish Language (VLA) applicants were tested. *In all tables the subscript FR indicates French and VLA indicate applicants who speak Flemish.* Throughout, the applicants are referred to by their language categories, as Flemish and French. These do not imply nationality.

GCTB 2006-10

POPULATION RESULTS:

Language Used, Males and Females, and Ranks

GENERAL CLASSIFICATION RESULTS

The group ability quotients from the very large numbers of applicants in Table 12.4 are derived from summing z scores of groups of the six tests. They are shown in a traditional BDF format adopted by BDF in previous record systems and retained by the authorities, with a mean of 10 and standard deviation of 4. This conventional system had been in use for many years with the previous entrance tests. For administrative convenience, it was adopted in calculating the general survey quotient, known as the CTI. These quotients show similarities and differences by salient groups, *always* distinguished by language preferred for testing.

Table 12.4: General Ability Quotient (CTI) Results by Categories

GROUPS	N	Mean	SD	GROUPS	N	Mean	SD
All FR	11423	10.4	*4.0*	**FR Officers**	1235	13.7	*3.3*
				FR NCOS.	1959	11.8	*3.5*
All VLA	10474	10.9	*3.8*	**FR Other Ranks**	7319	8.8	*3.9*
Men FR	10346	10.3	*4.0*	**VLA Officers**	1570	14.0	*3.0*
Women FR	1077	11.0	*3.9*	**VLA NCOS.**	2129	11.7	*3.2*
				VLA Other Ranks	5816	9.3	*3.7*
Men VLA	9292	10.8	*3.8*				
Women VLA	1182	11.6	*3.6*				

To summarise, applicants speaking Flemish have slightly higher average general training quotient scores than French-speaking applicants. Other ranks score a lot lower than NCOs and Officers, the effect size differences between officers and other ranks exceeding one standard deviation. This is an important result because the applicants *volunteer* for rank status *prior to testing*, providing a self-referent criterion of current validity never repeated elsewhere. Women seem to score higher than men, if the male-female distinction is not adjusted for rank status proportion differences, as Chapter 14 analyses of differential item functioning reveal. *Results for individual tests with large samples are shown for populations in the all-inclusive Table 12.5.*

INDIVIDUAL TEST RESULTS

The composites provide the big picture of the consequences of introducing the GCTB as a replacement for a previously existing and well-established group of tests for selecting volunteers to the Belgian armed forces. From all points of view, no harm was done and some intuitive certainty emerged from the differentiation of scores by the ranks applied for, with its occupational opportunities. This still left the need to show that individual tests performed adequately as far as different language groups, reliabilities, parallelism and repeated applications were concerned. The relevant results are shown in the remaining tables.

Table 12.5: Summary GCTB Statistics (2006-2010) on Populations of 11,423 French and 10,474 Nederlands Language Applicants

CATEGORIES	INDIVIDUAL TEST RESULTS						
	AB	WR	OR	NF	OE	TI	CTI
Language							
FR French	101	28	14	35	33	22	10.4
VLA Flemish	96	33	16	38	34	26	10.9
Overall SD	*29*	*10*	*7*	*13.5*	*11*	*9.5*	*4*
Mean Diff.	5	5	2	3	1	4	0.5
Effect Size	*0.17*	*0.50*	*0.29*	*0.22*	*0.09*	*0.42*	*0.13*
Reliability							
Test Retest FR	.86	.81	.74	.89	.81	.82	.90
Test Retest VLA	.87	.74	.69	.87	.79	.77	.91
Int. Consist. FR	.96	.89	.88	.92	.90	.90	.97
Int. Consist. VLA	.96	.88	.87	.94	.91	.89	.96
Parallelism							
Effect Size FR	*.09*	*.10*	*.06*	*.13*	*n.s.*	*.06*	*-*
Effect Size VLA	*.09*	*.08*	*.06*	*.13*	*n.s.*	*.06*	*-*

Language Differences
Table 12.5 details the infrastructure of the GCTB battery. There is a general tendency for Flemish language applicants to perform better than French applicants, except, and for reasons that have as yet to emerge, in the *Alphabet Test*. Effect sizes are not

always large enough to engage the separate language norms policy adopted by the government. They range from .09 to .50 of a standard deviation, but only two tests, involving verbal reasoning (TI) and verbal categories (WR) discriminate sufficiently to make separate norms an outcome. These results would make score norms for some composite indexes directly applicable regardless of the language used to apply for entry.

Reliability
Two forms of reliability are reported, parallel form test-retest reliability and internal consistency over all forms. The test-retest reliability was derived from 1088 Nederlands and 1725 French language applicants who attempted the GCTB on more than one occasion. The intervals varied between test sessions, so that the figures are affected by random time lapses and, of course, random allocation of parallel forms on subsequent test occasions. Internal consistency estimates based on samples of over 2000 applicants in each language group are consistent with the high reliabilities for USAF personnel.

Parallelism
In Flemish and French the official languages, the GCTB battery contains 10 parallel forms of each of the six tests used. Forms are assigned to individual applicants at random. The form of the test is recorded for each applicant. With this information, one may determine how closely the mean scores of the forms agree with each other. In Table 12.6 the largest mean differences among the ten parallel forms of each test are compared and then they are divided by the population standard deviation. With over 10,000 applicants since 2006, each form has had more than 1,000 exposures. With such large numbers a severe test of parallelism is the result.

Table 12.6: Parallel Form Comparisons 2011

Subtest	Lang.	Sig.	Form*	Subtest	Lang.	Sig.	Parallel Form*
AB	ONE	p<.001	AB102	NF	VLA	p<.001	NF102
					FR	p<.001	NF102
WR	VLA	p<.07		OE	VLA	P>.54	--------
	FR	p<.01	WR102		FR	p>.09	--------
OR	VLA	P>.13	--------	TI	VLA	p>.12	--------
	FR	p>.08	--------		FR	p>.99	--------

Even a minor mean difference will be significant if subjected to analysis of variance with test form as the category. All largest mean differences among each test type were shown to be significant at the .001 level of probability, except for *Odds and Evens*, but of course what is important is the effect size of that difference for each test. The effect sizes are negligible, so that no bias against any applicant is encountered by allocation to any one form. The sample sizes for each of the 10 forms of the tests were in the 200-300 range. The results are therefore unlikely to change with the addition of more cases. Of 120 parallel forms in use, there is evidence to suggest that only 2 should be actively considered for replacement. Nevertheless, two forms of the

Alphabet Test and three of the *Number Skills* test were reviewed for study and possible replacement.

IMPROVEMENTS OVER TIME

The independent review of 2011 also indicated an increase in performance during 2007 and 2008 after the successful introduction of a Pretest Booklet. This was issued to all applicants prior to testing after being translated from an English version provided by the contractor. The pretest booklet was possible because it provided analogues of the actual test items and offered no compromise to the random allocation of one of 10 parallel forms of each test type used on the day of testing at one of the regional offices, known nationally as *Maisons de Defence*.

TIME WILL TELL

Pretest Booklets and Practice

Pretest Booklet Introduction Post 2006.

GCTB test scores for the population from 2006 when the tests were first introduced, and in 2011 when a study of Differential Item Functioning (DIF) was commissioned, are shown in Table 12.7. The results give insights into language group differences and improvements over time associated with the introduction of the *Pretest Booklets*. Unlike previous results with controlled and accidental effects, the inference is made from test averages in years prior to the introduction of the original English versions into Flemish and French.

Table 12.7: Changes over Time: 2006-2011

GCTB 2006-10

Detailed Examination of Parallel Forms

	AB	WR	OR	NF	OE	TI
	Individual Test Averages					
FRENCH						
2006 Results	104	27	13	36	30	21
2011 Results	105	30	15	35	38	23
Effect size d'	*.03*	*.33*	*.29*	*-.07*	*.73*	*.21*
FLEMISH						
2006 Results	94	31	15	36	31	24
2011 Results	98	34	17	38	38	27
Effect sizes d'	*.14*	*.33*	*.29*	*.15*	*.64*	*.32*
POP. SD	**29**	**10**	**7**	**13.5**	**11**	**9.5**

The different language group improvements are consistently small. Improvement over time is greatest in the *Odds and Evens* test, suggesting that applicants in 2006 were unsure about how to do this test. The issue of a pretest booklet ensured familiarity with the unusual item type and results improved. If the improvements over time are compared by language groups, the relative improvements are the same for both groups. Experimental trials and operational use both confirm the effects of previous exposure to test item types. Small as they were, the practice effects observed made different norms *for repeat applicants* an essential part of operations in Belgium to ensure fairness.

Comparative Effects Of Trying Again to Enlist
The 2011 data for repeat applicants is reproduced in Table 12.8. Clear trends are evident. *Those who repeat have average initial test scores in the lowest 34 percent of applicants, for the most part one SD below the mean.* Raw score improvements in individual tests were variable, largest in *Orientation* and *Word Rules* and lowest in *Number Fluency.* Effect size varied

> **TRY, TRY, TRY AGAIN.**
>
> *Special Results with Persistent Applicants*

from .80 to .30 standard deviation units. The average performance of Flemish and French second-time applicants is equivalent, as are their relative improvements

Table 12.8: Test Repetition for French and Flemish Language Groups 2011

LANGUAGE GROUP	RESULTS	AB	WR	OR	NF	OE	TI
Flemish 1st	Mean	65	20	9	21	22	16
Flemish 2nd	Mean	73	25	13	23	26	19
	N	171	171	171	171	171	171
	Std. Dev.	*23*	*9*	*5*	*11*	*11*	*8*
EFFECT	**SIZE**	.34	.50	.80	.18	.33	.38
RETEST	**RELIABILITY**	.83	.79	.66	.84	.75	.74
French 1st	Mean	75	18	8	21	23	14
French 2nd	Mean	86	24	12	24	30	17
	N	275	275	275	275	275	275
	Std. Deviation	*24*	*9*	*5*	*10*	*10*	*7*
EFFECT	**SIZE**	.44	.60	.80	.30	.58	.42
RETEST	**RELIABILITY**	.82	.67	.61	.84	.73	.71

No increase is so small, however, that it can really be ignored and if repetition increases the probability of recruitment for those of less than average ability. Test-retest reliabilities for the much reduced ability range is as good as might be expected, and in some tests, much better than one might have hoped. Given the overall pattern of score increase and the special nature of the re-test sample, second time norms could not be compiled from this data set, but from data obtained from a national sample having more than one trial with different parallel forms.

Policy and Practice

In any event, official government policy demands that different norms be used for each language group; and that second-time test norms be used to guard against any unfair advantage that familiarity with the test requirements may engender. Such a policy makes test application and use relatively simple, although it does not, by itself, always guarantee fairness to both French and Flemish language users. Nevertheless, the test results demonstrated here show that such differences as do exist with automatic item-generation tests are minor compared with what might be, if literacy and numeracy thresholds for understanding and performance were at the post-secondary level. Hence, given the nature of the tests and their raw score results, different norms for Flemish and French language groups, when more than one attempt to be accepted into the BDF is made, might well be a politically defensible policy decision, whatever the psychometric debate might be.

**LANGUAGE
GROUP NORMS:
A FACT OF LIFE**

ALL-IMPORTANT VALIDITY STUDIES

It is possible to summarise briefly the work carried out on validating the GCTB by looking at concurrent, construct and criterion validity outcomes. Concurrent validity is simply demonstrated by the very large differences in mean scores when applicants are compared by the type of opening in BDF that they wanted to fill. Even if there were no other evidence, the detailed results in Table 12.9 are the only example of a self-referent criterion known in the recruitment literature.

The applicants apply to have a career in these ranks. If successful, they are given the rank appropriate to the job demands. Accordingly, Belgian applicants are already self-chosen for ambition and perceived ability levels. They provide a concurrent criterion for the success of the GCTB tests. Table 12.9 shows that in both language groups, there are large performance differences separating officers, non-commissioned officers and other ranks. Applicant group averages are clearly separated by voluntary rank preference, substantial differences shown as standard effect sizes that increase linearly from enlisted to non-commissioned officer and officer applicants. The importance of the results should not be underestimated. The GCTB individual tests undoubtedly identify recruits with different aspirations. It is a valid screen for volunteers self-chosen for ability.

The descriptive statistics also affirmed that the individual tests of the GCTB battery have good homogeneity across language groups; and that observed mean differences between language groups are relatively small. Evidence for adequate representation of language group similarity is provided by the large numbers of first time test scores available. The group means are very similar and the variances comparable.

**TESTS NOT
FAIR FOR
REJECTS?**

*Item Difficulties for
Persistent Applicants*

Table 12.9: Means and Variance by Ranks for French and Flemish Language Groups 2011

LANG	RANK	N	AB	WR	OR	NF	OE	TI
	OFFICER	*408*	121	34	19	44	44	29
			25	*8*	*7*	*13*	*9*	*9*
FRENCH	NCO	*735*	112	32	16	39	41	25
			25	*8*	*6*	*12*	*10*	*9*
	ENLISTED	*2234*	100	28	14	33	27	22
			26	*9*	*7*	*12*	*12*	*9*
	ENL v.	*NCO*	.46	.44	.29	.46	.33	.33
d Effect	*ENL v.*	*OFF*	.81	.67	.71	.85	.58	.78
	NCO v.	*OFF*	.35	.22	.43	.38	.25	.44
LANG	RANK	N	AB	WR	OR	NF	OE	TI
	OFFICER	*471*	114	38	21	47	44	32
			26	*8*	*6*	*13*	*9*	*9*
FLEMISH	NCO	*612*	101	36	18	39	40	28
			27	*9*	*7*	*13*	*10*	*9*
	ENLISTED	*1909*	92	33	15	35	36	25
			26	*9*	*8*	*13*	*11*	*9*
	ENL v.	*NCO*	.35	.33	.38	.31	.36	.33
d Effect	*ENL v.*	*OFF*	.85	.67	.75	.92	.73	.78
	NCO v.	*OFF*	.50	.33	.38	.62	.36	.44

Note: Sds for tests in italics

Figure 12.4: Comparison of Item Difficulties for Parallel Forms and by Selection Status

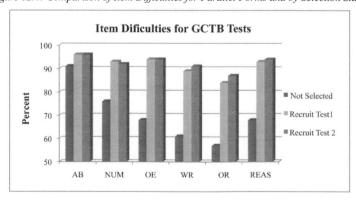

TESTS WITH REJECTED APPLICANTS?

Comparison of the differences in performance of those recruited and those not accepted was made in Figure 12.4. There are two salient observations. First, the tests are reliable even among those who are not accepted. This means that their failure cannot be attributed to any fault in the technical construction of the test forms. Second, the effect size differences in test performance in standard units are very large. Test variance usually embraces a range of 6 standard deviations. The gaps suggest that those selected are very much above the performance level of those not admitted to the BDF.

The Difficulty of the Tests for Rejects
Large differences in test scores between successful and rejected applicants cannot, as was demonstrated on the last section, be due to a difference in reliability. The tests must differ in difficulty for those who succeed and those who fail. But how difficult are the tests for those who are not admitted? Are they so difficult that they are outside the boundaries of test acceptability?

Figure 12.4 provides a most compelling result. The overall average difficulty of two multiple parallel form test items are shown for all applicants. These are compared with the difficulties of items for those who were not accepted. Apart from the *Alphabet Test*, where the difficulties are very close, the items are more difficult for those who are rejected; and for optimum use items should not fall below an average difficulty of 50%. Nowhere does the item difficulty of a single test fall below this mark for rejected applicants. While in general the items are more difficult for those who fail to be admitted, that is in itself a consistent finding showing that test items successfully discriminate between acceptable and unsuitable candidates. In fact, the aim of providing test items that are relatively easy to solve, ensuring that the main difference is diligence due to attention and working memory effectiveness, seems to have been realized in these results.

CONSTRUCT VALIDITY
When the GCTB tests were correlated with each other, in 2006 and 2011, in both official languages, using large data sets, the matrices for both language groups were virtually identical, and a large general factor accounted for most of the variance. Table 12.10 indicates a very close fit regardless of language or cohort differences in the five year interval.

Table 12.10: Factor loadings 2006-11 by Language Group

Fluid Intelligence a Raven Attribute?

GCTB Test General Factors 2006-11						
Year	French Factor Loadings					
	(AB)	(NF)	(OE)	(OR)	(TI)	(WR)
2006	.750	.773	.839	.761	.774	.830
2011	.727	.753	.841	.736	.758	.807
	Flemish Factor Loadings					
	(AB)	(NF)	(OE)	(OR)	(TI)	(WR)
2006	.754	.777	.858	.738	.831	.801
2011	.688	.759	.836	.736	.784	.788

Working memory tasks that lend themselves to item-generation modelling have emerged strongly in the last two decades and it is important to emphasise the strong general working memory component of the GCTB, first found in the 2006 data, and replicated in 2011 almost without change in both official languages A number of studies have shown that the English language versions produced a single general factor with highest loadings on tests depending on the attentive allocation of working memory resources. The Belgian Flemish and French language factors, following the German results, define general ability consonant with working memory, the multilingual consistency being a major contribution to cognitive science.

FACTORS AND THEIR MEANING

Working Memory

Linguistic Congruence

QUOTE THE RAVEN[10] - (N)EVERMORE?
A separate attempt was made by BDF officials to relate the results of the individual GCTB tests to a total score on the *Raven's Progressive Matrices* test with 704 Flemish language volunteers. The CTI produced a correlation of .48 with the total test score, and individual tests ranged between .30 for the *Alphabet Test* and .43 for *Orientation*, with an average of .40, accounting for 16 percent of the individual variance. Some concern was expressed at the low correlation. But this is not an isolated example as a report in the technical cooperation series (TTCP, 1997, pp, 29-30) where similar correlation sizes were observed between ARCOM and *Raven's Advanced Progressive Matrices* in an officer cadet entry. Again, concern was raised. What might these limited agreements imply? In the annals of test literature, much has been claimed but little proved for the qualities of *Raven's Progressive Matrices* (Cf. Hunt, 1974; Irvine, 1967, 1969). It is a figural, but certainly not non-verbal test of reasoning as video evidence of participants' lips moving while completing the items almost invariably reveals[11]. It has a large specificity and according to the late Sir Cyril Burt (see Chapter4), who supervised the creation of the test by Raven in his Master's degree, it is certainly not 'a test of pure g' nor an absolute measure of general 'fluid' intelligence as some have asserted[12].

The result does not make the GCTB composite any less powerful an indicator of fitness for military service. It confirms that the paper-and-pencil version of *Raven's Progressive Matrices*, even if transferred screen by screen for computer-delivery, has a limited working memory element. This conclusion is justified from all current and previous correlational studies undertaken with the GCTB individual tests.

CRITERION VALIDITY WITH PILOT APTITUDE
Perhaps the most unexpected finding from a number of criterion studies carried out independently by the officials of the BDF psychology unit was a pass-fail result from pilot training, albeit with a small sample. Of 34 applicant selected for training by the lengthy

---

10   With apologies to Earl Hunt.

11   I first saw this in Zimbabwe, in 1960. Anyone administering the *Progressive Matrices* test could witness this. I have never understood thereafter why so many psychologists refer to *Raven's Matrices* as non-verbal, with all the systematically misleading consequences that have attended debate on the meaning of a score derived from it. Figural, yes, non-verbal, certainly not. Pure g? Nonsense!

12   Personal communication, July, 1967

psychomotor pilot aptitude tests, 24 failed and 11 passed. The CTI mean difference calculated from the Test battery results was almost a complete standard deviation, with a correlation of .40 with pass-fail. However, the standard error of this correlation is plus or minus .17, so caution is required before any generalisation can be made. If this trend persists, then the GCTB is an inexpensive pre-screen for pilot aptitude.

Pilot Aptitude Factors.

Previous analysis of the correlations of the English language versions of the tests used in the GCTB with the all of the ASVAB tests, given in Chapter 7, show that the division between this factor and the ASVAB acquired knowledge factor was also clear. However, any opportunity to extend construct validity by inclusion with tests that are not supposed to have a general screening function, is as welcome as it may be unique. In the BDF, an opportunity to examine the GCTB tests alongside a comprehensive aviation screening tests was presented, albeit with a limited sample size. The pilot aptitude battery consisted of 13 computer-delivered tests using a complex interaction system with hand and foot controls. In both French and Nederlands air crew applicants, the six GCTB tests defined a working memory factor in the pilot aptitude battery, linking with aptitude battery elements labelled *patterns, views, sequences, hands,* and *concentration:* and was somewhat distinct from a second group of psychomotor tests. A third doublet of the *Number Skills* and a test for pilots named *Number Operations* was also recognised. The clear definition of the tests in the GCTB offered by the pilot aptitude and ASVAB comparisons is both consistent and confirmatory.

> **PUT IT UP THE FLAGPOLE TO SEE IF IT WILL FLY**
>
> *Pilot Aptitude Predicted*

THE ATTRITION CRITERION PROBLEM PERSISTS.

An extensive review of the capability of CTI to predict training outcomes was carried out by BDF officials, with mixed results. Much doubt about the usability of estimates of suitability for various military roles has existed since Macdonald's day, in Chapter 1. In Chapter 14, there is a complete review of efforts to combat attrition over the past 30 years in the United States and elsewhere. When the figures are compared cross-nationally, not much has changed. Perhaps the most telling commentary of all is implicit in the reported drop-out rates for Belgian other ranks, including special infantry companies. *Of a reported follow-up of 3,477 recruits, a total of 1,269, or 37% failed to complete training.* The similarity with reported British attrition rates for infantry is remarkable (Chapter 14).

The average effect size of the CTI difference between staying in and leaving was 0.21 sd units, the drop-outs having the poorer score. This value is border zone for utility. What was important was the very much restricted range of the CTI scores. Whereas the population SD is 4.0, the infantry range was 2.8 SD units. This ensures that any correlations with criteria are curtailed through range restriction. Attempts, given range restriction, to predict outcomes in other ranks and NCO training battalions yielded results similar to those experienced by Jacobs (1996) Hampson (1997) and others using BARB tests. Correlations were predictably low, where they existed, but a pattern of significant relationships emerged in a group of approximately 300 Flemish enlisted men and women were in the .23 range, not much different from the normal kinds of relationships encountered in unsupervised criteria used in basic training, seen in BARB studies in the UK and similar analogues in Australia as seen in Chapter 5. The pattern seems to be consistent globally. Early drop out is not predicted by cognitive tests. If the recruits survive basic training, then a relationship with 'on the job' phase two results will ensue.

PERFORMANCE OF OFFICERS IN ACADEMIES

As for officers, where results in the academic programme of the military academy were related to CTI scores, there was no success in predicting written examination outcomes. Nor, indeed, was there any prior assertion that there might be. Modest prediction of academic progress was achieved by relating recorded secondary school mathematics scores to examination criteria, but the magnitude of the correlation was no greater than those achieved for NCOs and other ranks, being averaged at .26 for academic and overall performance in year one. Ratings based upon a review and pre-enlistment interview by professional psychologists were also predictive to the same degree.

These results confirm what we already know to be true. The contexts of training success in military cultures around the world are an uncompromising command environment where individual success - or perhaps survival - depends on maintaining self-esteem while carrying out tasks designed to instil and maintain discipline. Cognitive screening tests will always be necessary, but they have seldom provided more than limited predictive power. They are necessary, but not by themselves sufficient to ensure success or lessen drop-out any known validity study. The GCTB tests successfully grade applicants, they predict the acquisition of procedural knowledge, they screen for pilots whose training demands complete mastery of new procedures.

What else can they do that has not been demonstrated hitherto? One fundamental politically correct question yet remains to be answered using known psychometric procedures. *Do the GCTB items discriminate against minorities, even within language groups with different norms for acceptance into the BDF?* Could this possibly be determined with 10 different multiple parallel forms automatically generated? The next chapter addresses these problems in detail. The results could well have been part of a complete chapter devoted to the Belgian operational studies. Perhaps they should have been, but the affinity with the German language experiments was the determining influence. In Chapter 13, the affinities of the Belgian language groups and the Northern Ireland sectarian groups as examples of different diversity studies were too close to ignore. The Belgian work is given full prominence at the start of the chapter, so that it can be read directly after this conclusion.

THE EUROPEAN CAMPAIGNS

At the beginning of the chapter questions about the translatability, robustness and utility of multiple parallel form tests in different languages and military organisations were raised. The results of the detailed validity studies, concurrent, construct and predictive, show that confidence in the evidence centred design features of the system can be maintained. The tests within the different batteries have proven utility. Paper-and-pencil analogues were as effective as computer-delivered tests. Practice and pre-test information resulted in gains, so that second-attempt norms were devised to ensure fairness. Last, but certainly not least, multiple form parallelism was maintained regardless of language.

Perhaps a final word of caution is permissible. Translation was found, in collaboration with German and Belgian colleagues, to be a *radical* exercise. It is not *incidental* to the test form and meaning. Language is the inevitable radical that makes demands on processing resources with consequent effects on difficulty. Cross-cultural psychologists have been aware of this for many years. Perhaps it is time for mainstream schools of empirical investigation analysing the results of questions 'translated' for use in military and other cultures to observe this principle with great care. Performance comparisons dependent on gross averages from 'identical' tests in diverse contexts, sectarian as well as linguistic, are common. As the next chapter shows, first in Belgium, to round out its operational requirements using computer-delivered tests and then in the United Kingdom with earlier paper-and-pencil versions they are dangerously misleading. As a counsel to perfection, some might wish to read the first section of Chapter 13 as a most welcome, if unexpected extension of the Belgian work, as it indeed was.

CHAPTER 13

THE POLITICS OF PSYCHOMETRICS: DIVERSITY OR ADVERSITY?

So far, the emphasis has been on the qualities of item generative tests used in a number of military organisations and in four different languages. Enough has been written to demonstrate their acceptability under the famous dictum[1] that tests should be technically sound and administratively convenient. But Alec Rodger always stressed that the real issue is, and perhaps always will be, for any democratic society, that tests must first and foremost be politically defensible. Indeed, the easiest way to provoke an enquiry into tests used for selection to any training programme, apprenticeship, college, occupation, or military force is to allege or to suggest that any single test might not be fair to all prospective entrants. In fact, the rise of the 'non-verbal' test could be directly attributed to the mistaken notion that the use of figural items could make tests 'more fair' to educationally disadvantaged applicants.

THE POLITICS OF PSYCHOMETRICS

Computer-Delivered Solutions in Belgium

Minitests for Flemish and French Applicants

Belgian, Immigrant or Guarded Responses?

GCTB Fair to All

Paper-and-Pencil in Northern Ireland

Diversity or Adversity?

Tests as Part of a Succession of Barriers

Fallacies of Sectarian Comparisons

Because the computer-delivered multiple parallel form tests have had exposure in Europe and America, a broader and more detached look can be taken at the question of test fairness, because no defence is being offered for their continued use. Parliament is not about to create a judicial enquiry into the use of item generative tests. The issues underlying verdicts on fairness are explored in three different situations.

1. Computer-delivered tests in Belgium among officially defined minorities in both French and Flemish language groups.
2. Paper-and-pencil tests used in Northern Ireland Police force applicants from self-defined sectarian groups for two years in succession.

This overview attempts to make clear the many qualifications that logically attend any and all analytical outcomes, given the nature of the information available. The outcomes are no more than examples of what might be found everywhere. As a consequence,

---

1   Attributed to the late Professor Alec Rodger, Birkbeck College, University of London, my thesis supervisor.

what might, and more importantly, what might not be inferred from various categories used to compare scores and item properties, sex differences, ethnicity, language groups. At the outset, the aim is not to make a summative judgment on the functions of items in the different test batteries. That is for others to do when all the data necessary for such a judgment is to hand. Perhaps the overwhelming issue remains. Is it ever possible to convince those who may feel unfairly treated that the argument is complete? Even more intriguing, perhaps, can fairness be evaluated if multiple parallel forms are used with seemingly different items in each parallel form of the test? Would it be possible if each applicant, as in BARB, had a unique parallel form?

PART 1: BELGIAN DIVERSITY: MALE AND FEMALE, ETHNICITY AND LANGUAGE

Fairness was a question that had to be answered in Belgium, where ten different parallel forms of each test were operational at any one time. An official enquiry was launched by the authorities. Although no such enquiry had been made about the tests that had been replaced by the GCTB, in spite of a widely held view that items in these tests discriminated against minorities[2], the opportunity to conduct a unique enquiry for an entirely new series was apparently grasped.

A key methodology question underlay all of this. How well and accurately could immigrant or minority group status, however defined, be determined from responses to questions asked of potential recruits? Without certainty, the results would be indeterminate, if not a matter of public concern. Given the importance of finding a way forward in a multiple parallel form context, the prospect of finding answers with a study of the items of a test battery actually used to select from a nation-wide group of applicants is a rare event. Microanalysis of individual item types is different in its potential consequences from comparisons of test average scores across groups. If differential item functions are evident, then the tests themselves - not the social characteristics of members of the groups identified as reference groups and focus groups - come under scrutiny. The Belgian Defence Force (BDF) initiated just such a project to examine the behaviour of the GCTB towards its recognised minorities. The official aim of the *GCTB Diversity Project* was to review with reference to appropriate language and minority classifications, the item content and characteristics of the six tests that were included in the GCTB.

COMPUTER-DELIVERED QUESTIONS IN BELGIUM

Who Defines Minorities?

How to Isolate Items in Multiple Forms?

How to use Differential Item Functioning for Minorities Within Language Groups

STUDY PARAMETERS AND CONSTRAINTS
Currently, the modern *GCTB Test Battery* of six individual tests used to select applicants for service in the BDF is computer-delivered. There are ten parallel forms of each

---

2   Personal comment of a former Belgian military psychologist.

of the six tests, involving over 3,000 individual items in total in operation at any one time. The difficulties of isolating and thereafter assessing the impact of any *single* test *item* on minority groups in a national recruiting context render an operational solution virtually impossible without years of work, thousands of participants and at great cost. In a real-world context of national recruitment, there are several constraints affecting the possible methods used to obtain an accurate item data set. In highly sensitive selection contexts where the stakes are high, scientific constraints cannot be seen to alter the approved recruiting procedures. Nevertheless, the end result has to be capable of investigation using modern psychometric methods of item calibration. The administrative aspects of data collection protocols required consideration of the effects of various potential hazards, including test content representation; sample equivalence; and language effects. Finally and critically, the undoubted effects of increasing total test times on recruit performance by adding test items to those that are normally presented to each recruit. A study of the amount of time necessary to add to the existing battery was made, contrasting high and low scoring cohorts. The GCTB Diversity Project committee then considered how best to solve the problems of representing the parallel form content inherent in the structure of the six different tests that form the GCTB Battery introduced in 2006.

One of the proposed short-term solutions was to have all candidates undertake a complete GCTB battery of six tests, using only *one form of each test*. This would have ensured that all answered identical items while they were actually undergoing selection. However, the history of test use in competitive situations suggests that a single computer-delivered test form would quickly be compromised, as Wainer (2002) dramatically revealed. Given a campaign to steal its content, it could be quickly rendered useless in today's technological climate. Once the test items were distributed nation-wide in careers offices, and thereby known, later candidates seeking admission to the BDF could gain unfair advantages over early participants; and officials decided the risk was unacceptable.

THE MINITEST SOLUTION

A solution was proposed and accepted, after consultation, by the BDF authorities. A new parallel form of each of the six GCTB tests was generated. From each test, two different stratified random samples each of eleven items were extracted. The choice of the final samples of items to be used was made by the BDF, who had, after expert review, to be satisfied that the items were grammatically correct and that verbal equivalence in all official languages was maintained. The eleven item series for each of the six tests thus provided are known as the *GCTB Minitests*. In all, 66 items were analysed for potential bias.

The sets of eleven items were to be administered *after* the completion of each of the six tests, so that they did not require new instructions for the item type. This had one very important consequence. *The GCTB battery actual test scores, made immediately prior to completing the sets of eleven items could be used as the method of equating ability levels.* This meant that the items considered

COMPUTER-DELIVERED DIVERSITY IN BELGIUM

The Minitest Solution

for bias effects were not part of the ability score, ensuring experimental independence. These items were to be administered to recruits who volunteered, by completing an appropriate background questionnaire, compiled by BDF, to participate in the diversity project. Examples of the various computer screens used in item presentation for the six tests were shown in Chapter 11. They are an indication of the number of screens required for presentation and the deliberate application of the principle that less is more.

OFFICIAL CRITERIA FOR FOCUS AND REFERENCE GROUPS

"DIF research on our tests made use of the previous definitions of the Flemish government.

'A person with a nationality of a country outside the European Union or person of whom at least one parent or two grandparents have a nationality of a country outside the European Union'. Based on this definition it will be on the basis of the first five questions on this questionnaire that is determined whether someone is native or not."

CRITERIA FOR ETHNICITY AND/OR MINORITY STATUS
The officials of the Belgian Defence Force provided the definition upon which minority status was subsequently assigned, and included in the given data set, to applicants. Those accorded minority status served to form the *focus group* for item analysis, and the majority, categorised as native Belgians were the *reference group*. Minority definition is in the insert. From this official definition in use by the Belgian Defence Force, an *Origin* category was defined and provided for data analysis. Minority status was assigned from the responses of the applicants to five questions in the participant agreement administered by BDF.

The implications of assignment to categories from applicant responses are not insignificant. How did they respond and why? One of the great commentaries on response styles is given in Guilford (1954, pp. 451-456). The factors influencing responses and several methods of taking them into account are all laid out with exemplary brevity and precision. More than half a century later, little has changed to make Guilford's cautions redundant. Questionnaires are there to be answered, true, false, fact or fiction. And in the study of Differential Item Functioning, the basis upon which migrant status is assigned, was the profile of the first five questions in the questionnaire. The effect of the order of these items in the questionnaire on response set cannot be calculated. *Of course, the most obvious response set in any voluntary questionnaire is not to complete it - Avoidance, or as has been used in this analysis, a category of Omit/Guarded.*

In the French Language group, of 2,999 no-duplicate responses, 315 did not complete the question on national origin. Of the others, 356 of the remainder were classified as of external (non-native) origin. In short, the numbers being classified as one of two potential minorities (ethnic or guarded) were almost equal. In the Flemish sample of 2933 non-duplicate test results, 170 were declared to be of foreign extraction, while 222 did not complete the question and could be classified as having a non-compliant or guarded response style. The trends in language groups are similar, although the pro-portions are different (22% French, 13% Flemish).

OBSERVATIONS ON SAMPLE CHARACTERISTICS AND STATISTICAL INFERENCE

Just what may be inferred from the actual Differential Item Functioning results may be a function of group identity, real or imagined. In the end, it largely depends on the size, structure and representativeness of the samples provided. Some simple observations that may help to inform the discussion of any empirical findings are provided below.

Figure 13.1: Test Mean Effect Sizes by Language and Military Rank

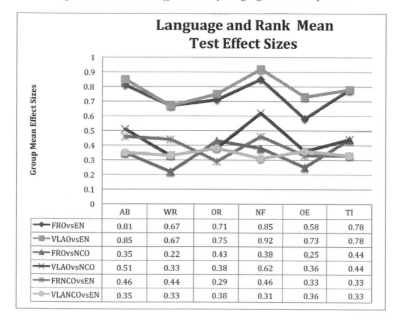

	AB	WR	OR	NF	OE	TI
FROvsEN	0.81	0.67	0.71	0.85	0.58	0.78
VLAOvsEN	0.85	0.67	0.75	0.92	0.73	0.78
FROvsNCO	0.35	0.22	0.43	0.38	0,25	0.44
VLAOvsNCO	0.51	0.33	0.38	0.62	0.36	0.44
FRNCOvsEN	0.46	0.44	0.29	0.46	0.33	0.33
VLANCOvsEN	0.35	0.33	0.38	0.31	0.36	0.33

Figure 13.1 shows[3] average effect size differences by language group and rank categories. The effect sizes in standard form have been used as a consistent framework for mean comparisons among tests with different variances. *The results are almost identical to those seen in the recruit populations in the previous chapter, so that representativeness may be assumed.* The implications of the resulting patterns for ability group balance, and their potentially large effects on the equivalence of within-category structures, are self-evident. Regardless of language, there are large differences in performance on the tests used on the day, prior to administering the items earmarked for Differential Item Functioning scrutiny. Largest effect sizes separate Officers from Enlisted candidates, averaging .76 s.d. units, but these are diminished to an average .38 s.d. units approximately when Officers are compared

---

3   In the chart the following abbreviations are used: FR-French Language; NL-Flemish Language; O-Officers; NCO-Non-Commissioned Officers; EN-Enlisted Other Ranks vs-versus.

with NCOs and NCOs are compared with enlisted participants. Even so, there are other important concerns.

1. *Non-Randomness.* Because the participants were *volunteers* among all applicants over a constrained period, random population samples are not available. This means that the volunteer samples will be purposive. This constraint makes correct inferences from statistical analyses difficult at worst and subject to debate at best. To ensure that any observed item differences are not due solely to volunteer sample bias, careful stratifying, and controls within contrast groups are required.

2. *Potential Confounds.* At the outset, cautionary comments on the nature and structure of the Belgian Defence Force purposive samples are offered, because of the need to be precise in the degree of confidence that can be placed in the outcomes of the analyses that were performed.

> ## CROSS-CULTURAL CAUTIONS
>
> *'Stimulus identity in the vernacular does not guarantee either equivalent performance or identical strategies or similar control processes when subjects solve logical problems posed by the stimuli.'*
>
> *(Irvine 1983, p.55)*

3. *Language Divisions.* There are separate groups of French and Flemish speaking applicants, for whom policy decisions mean that different norms must be applied to different language group entrants. Figure 13.2 is an example of the technical test construction *linguistic radicals* that could lead to this decision: but it is not itself the complete political argument. Careful examination of tests shows that some items types require different numbers of words or syllables to express the same meaning in French and Flemish. In translation, having to alter the form of an item can make a different demand on working memory than if it had fewer elements. An example of this was shown in the previous chapter with the Odds and Evens items in German when verbalisation was replaced by symbols.

Figure 13.2: Odds and Evens Syllable Effects in Flemish, French and German

Regels	Aantallen			Antwoord	
gelijk gelijk oneven	2	4	5	[0] [1] [2] [3]	Q1

Règles	Nombres			Assortiments	
pair pair impair	2	4	5	[0] [1] [2] [3]	Q1

Regel	Zahlen			Antwort	
gerade gerade ungerade	2	4	5	[0] [1] [2] [3]	Q1

The same influence exists in French and Flemish, where the nine syllables are needed in Flemish and only three in French to encode in working memory the verbal categories 'odd' and 'even' for number matching. Even at this stage, it is possible to use our knowledge of the theory of item performance to predict that some types of items with identical meanings will prove more difficult, and more time-consuming, in one language than another. Cross-cultural psychologists gave cogent examples of these effects decades ago, (Cole, Gay & Glick, 1968, Gay & Cole, 1967 pp. 79-83). Irvine (1983, p. 55). When the languages themselves prevent the assurance of total equivalence, to attribute any observed different item behaviours across language groups to bias or faults would be tendentious. There is an official policy of different norms for different language groups in Belgium.

4. *Repeated Applications.* Next, Belgian Defence Force policy ensures that an applicant can come forward on more than one occasion in an attempt to reach a given standard for entry as an enlisted, non-commissioned or commissioned officer. This leads to duplicate raw scores that use parallel form norms taking account of previous exposures to test types These raw scores were preserved, and included in the original data files, but were removed prior to our analyses.

5. *Duplicate Scores.* Without the removal of duplicate scores following initial application, the samples would be compromised with repeated measures that would confound all results dependent upon independent samples. A considerable number of repeat scores had to be removed from the given data. In the French language group, a total of 625 duplicate scores were removed, leaving 2999 applicants whose data included first time efforts only. In the Netherlands group, a total of 191 duplicate scores were removed, leaving a purposive sample of 2933 first-time applicants.

6. *Female and Male.* Men and women applicants were not equally represented in the two major groups. In the Flemish sample, 280 were women and 2652 were men. In the French language cohort, 236 were women and 2763 were men. Most important, men and women are present in unequal proportions in the three basic application categories, Enlisted, NCO and Officers. These inequities make any simplistic comparisons of averages impracticable. Moreover, there are very few female applicants compared with males. It is therefore undesirable to discuss outcomes on the basis of female and male differences without attempting to control for *extraneous factors*, but are inherent in the different structure of male and female applicant populations. Without foresight, errors of inference are very likely, particularly in Differential Item Functioning protocols.

7. *Differential Ability Levels.* The important regulator of group membership, apart from ethnic, female-male and language groupings has to be the effect of different capacity to understand the items and process information levels upon each of the different tests. Accordingly, individual test scores made at the same time as the minitest items were administered were recorded to enable ability groups to be the main hierarchical classification, and other group memberships to be nested within these. It is quite possible, for example, that a single recruit could be in different ability classification groups for each test.

8. *Increased Test Times.* If the time spent on the tests increases markedly with the addition of extra items, performances will worsen as the recruits become tired as they make progress through the six tests. Recruits of relatively poorer capability will suffer most, because, as the preliminary analyses showed, they take longer as they struggle with the test items.

OVERVIEW
The outline of multiple data constraints has been important for ensuring that the correct inferences are made from empirical analyses. There is, however, no certainty of unequivocal conclusions from even the most enlightened statistical attempts at clarity when complexity defies control. There is one certain guarantee however. Attempts to equate ability groups before embarking on are a recognised principle of any analytical framework and these attempts were made and judged. All the results given in the pages that follow are constrained by the realisation that the data to hand will have first to demonstrate that it is fit for its declared purpose. And this may not always be possible.

Data Categories
Data was received from   involving approximately 3,000 volunteers in each of the major language groups, Flemish and French. The following seven modifications were taken in the interests of clarity and removing any ambiguities. Reasons are clearly summarized in the next page inserts collated to provide a convenient reference frame for the results that follow.
1. All duplicate (second and subsequent GCTB results) applicant scores were removed.
2. Because there is no nation-wide method of defining minority status, the definitions of ethnic origin as provided by Belgian Defence Force were employed to provide minority focus groups for comparison with majority reference groups.
3. Male and female identity was used in association with other relevant groupings.
4. Questionnaire response style was used to identify a *Guarded* category.
5. Other recruit categories, including rank, were used where appropriate.
6. As a consequence of these preliminary investigations into group membership, the examples that follow, are mainly confined to the French speaking applicants.
7. However, an independent academic enquiry at the University of Ghent verified these results by another method and extended them to the Flemish Group (Brouwer, Fontaine and Mylle (2012). A short summary of this concludes the Belgian Differential Item Functioning section.

DIFFERENTIAL ITEM FUNCTIONING STATISTICS.
The Mantel-Haenszel (M-H)   statistic was used throughout and, wherever a significant value of non-conditional independence was observed at the ,05 level of probability, the M_H *ln* function of this was converted to the ETS Delta statistic (Holland and Thayer, 1986). The Delta statistic ensured the classification of items, where Differential Item Functioning might be indicated, into three types, A, B, and C, of which only the latter would require possible intervention. Logistic regression, although a potential alternative examination of Differential Item Functioning was not used because of data considerations.

The following inserts are summary reference points for the study prior to detailed results.

DIF PROCEDURES QUALIFIED

There are significant differences in performance between Language groups, regardless of group membership within the language groups. There are additional structural differences that imply that the two applicant populations, French and Flemish, are different.

Majority reference group performance is always better than that of any of the other minority focus groups classified by their questionnaire response patterns.

The absolute numbers and relative proportions of respondents in the various minority sub-categories are undeniably small, raising the distinct possibility of Type 1 and Type 2 errors of inference when cells did not reach minimum numbers required for uncorrected estimates based upon ability levels.

Male and Females are unevenly represented in various recruit application military training groups, rendering direct male-female comparisons tendentious.

Non Native and Omit (Guarded) respondents show no significant mean differences in any test within the French language group, but there are significant differences for the same classification in the Flemish group.

MATCHING CRITERIA

The need to match reference and focus groups in ability or attainment bands as narrow as possible is well understood. Actual test scores made on the first application, independent of the Minitest items were used to develop matching bands. Given sufficient numbers, percentile or perhaps deciles categories could be employed. However, the following constraints were forced upon the analyses.

There were only 356 French language minority applicants as defined by Belgian Defence Force; and only 170 Flemish minority recruits. These limited numbers presented problems, even using non-parametric cross tabulations of item and group characteristics within the language groups.

The usable ability categories were therefore very wide, being no smaller than quartiles for French and thirds for Flemish language groups. Performance categories were calculated from the first attempt scores provided for each test, adjusted for guessing.

Other possible minority groups were examined and used where assumptions appeared to be justified by data patterns.

Female and male performance differences were explored using what matching data was available from very small numbers of female applicants.

ILLUSTRATIVE RESULTS

The examples that follow are neither definitive nor summative. Emphasis is given throughout to results from the French-speaking cohort for two reasons: first, the great majority of non-native applicants claim French as their official language; second, those who failed to complete the questionnaire provided an additional incentive to explore the pattern of item responses in a focus group defined solely by the actions of the respondents on the day of recruit test performance. A beginning is made by examining an obvious military minority, women. The procedures outlined in this example were repeated at length with other identifiable minority enclaves.

Table 13.1: Male and Female Mean Differences (French Language)

	AB	WR	OR	NF	OE	TI	N
Female Other Ranks	110	29	12	31	37	21	158
Male Other Ranks	101	29	17	38	38	27	2442
Female Officers	130	35	19	42	44	28	78
Male Officers	120	34	19	45	46	29	321
All Females	117	31	14	34	40	24	236
All Males	104	30	15	36	38	23	2763
French Language All	**105**	**30**	**15**	**35**	**38**	**23**	**2999**

Notes: Mean scores are adjusted for guessing and rounded.

Unwrapping Male and Female Packages[4]
Alleged male and female group differences have had a long and perhaps systematically leading influence on tests and testing. All kinds of speculation has accompanied male and female average differences in test performance, few if any having scientific credibility. Even so, the possibility of Differential Item Functioning with adverse impact on recruits of either sex is an obvious first step, because the pursuit of fairness is a necessary goal of selection in the Belgian Defence Force. Table 13.1 is a simple summary of the pattern of average score differences involving men and women. There are various differences, some of which are significant, but whose effect size is always minor. Even a cursory examination, however, shows that to infer performance differences from a simple male-female category split would be an error, because the proportions of men (12%) and women

MEN AND WOMEN COMPARED

It's all a Matter of Getting Things in Proportion

---

4   Male and female are attributes associated with genetic differences, and they are not semantic categories. Hence the semantic term gender has been avoided as a term to describe the groups.

(33%) applying to be officers proved, on examination, to be quite different. One third of all female entrants are officer candidates, compared with one in eight males Officer applicants require to demonstrate educational attainments appropriate for military academy entry. *The influence of female officer recruits on the overall female test means is disproportionately great compared with that of males, rendering a direct female-male comparison inappropriate.*

Consequently, to compare the responses to individual items of females and males who want to join the Belgian army, without making inadvertent errors of inference from empirical findings is an exercise in itself. *In the following Differential Item Functioning analyses, male and female are compared only after they are equated for performance level on the test, so that disproportionate representations do not exist.*

Table 13.2: Possible DIF Items by Different Male and Female Classifications

Groups			Test Items		
Male vs. Female Alone	NF10,11				AB5,9
Male vs. Female by Ranks	NF10,11	OR7,8,9		TI 1,7,10	AB5,8
Male vs. Female by Quartiles	NF10,11		OE4		

Table 13.2 has results using various male and female comparison groups, where the Mantel-Haenszel hypothesis of conditional independence was rejected at the .05 level or less. The comparisons show attempts to discover whether Differential Item Functioning exists, acknowledging that any straight male and female comparison is biased because of the different proportions of officer and other rank candidates in the groups. Next, given these realities, an attempt was made to compare men and women *only within their officer and other ranks cohorts.* Finally, a control by ability levels for each test was introduced by slicing the data into quartiles, the smallest division feasible with the small numbers involved. The numbers and types of items vary, of which only two appear to be consistently identified, not, as legend might have predicted, in visual orientation, but in simple number calculation. The *final analysis, by ability quartile stratification,* the best available recommended approach, produced only three items among all those compared, requiring attention. All were of Delta values not requiring intervention.

The small numbers involved in the comparisons gives rise to very real possibility that the total number of items identified, twelve, are no more than might be expected when one in twenty of a total of 198 calculations on the same sample could occur by chance. Finally, the correct answer percentage *for the numerical items exceeded 90%,* so that even if these results did not arise by chance, the *impact*[5] of the item would be negligible on the final scores of all but a tiny minority of applicants. The purpose of the exercise with male and female applicants was to *illustrate the potential*

IS IT NOW ALL TOGETHER IN FRENCH?

---

5   M-H results do not provide, by themselves, a commentary on impact (cf. Holland and Thayer, 1986, p. 2.)

hazards of using broad categories involving small numbers without exhausting the possibilities of classification within what is commonly described as a 'package' variable containing a number of hidden elements. The application of the same forensic approach is witnessed in the following results from French language minorities identified through questionnaire responses.

'Non-Natives' Identified by Questionnaire
Definitions of non-native (sometimes referred to as *nouveaux Belges*) status were applied by the BDF authorities to voluntary replies to a number of officially sanctioned questions. Subsequently, a total of 356 applicants whose origins were adjudged to be non-native, were identified[6]. Re-examination of the data showed that *another 315 applicants had not agreed to answer the questions.*

WHO WANTS TO BE AN IMMIGRANT?

Yes!

No!

I'm Not Telling?

They were a cohort of approximately the same size as those judged to be non-native. Comparisons involving these two groups revealed some unexpected findings. Table 13.3 gives a summary of mean differences among various French Language and Flemish groups identified by questionnaire.

Table 13.3: Simple Summary of Group Mean Differences

	AB	WR	OR	NF	OE	TI
FR Native	105	31	15	36	39	24
FR Not Native	103	26	13	33	36	22
FR Omit(Guarded)	101	27	13	33	36	21
VLA Native	97	35	17	38	38	27
VLA Not Native	94	27	14	32	34	22
VLA Omit(Guarded)	91	32	16	35	36	25

Most of the mean differences involving comparisons of the native and other two defined groups, non-native and omit (guarded) are statistically significant The comparisons between the two French-speaking minority groups, not native and guarded, identified by questionnaire replies, are non-significant. Wherever significant differences existed in the Flemish minority cohorts, the effect sizes were nonetheless small. The analysis outcomes show that the performance profile for non-native and omit/guarded French Language respondents is identical: and both of these groups have the same level of performance deficit compared with the majority. From this result, an extended exercise in the use of the Mantel-Haenszel procedure was devised, but only within the

---

6   By Annemie Defranc, who kindly provided the SPSS categories for this group.

French language cohort. It was feasible to define a combined questionnaire derived minority group, and increase the numbers who could be regarded as a questionnaire response typology, *omit/guarded and non-native*. Because, as the contrasting mean profiles show, the *Flemish non-native and omit/guarded groups were not comparable*, this exercise was not repeated with the Flemish cohort.

ITEM DIVERSITY: FRENCH LANGUAGE GROUPS COMPARED
The increase in numbers classified as a plausible focus group (non-native and omit/ guarded combined), was the aim of the strategy. The combination permitted more confidence to be placed in using the size of the groups within quartile scores used for performance matching and decreased the possibility of errors of inference.

Table 13.4: Summary of M_H Results for French Data Structures

Groups Compared	Quartiles	M_H Items	ETS Deltas		
			A	B	C
Native vs. Non-Native	Yes	8	3	5	-
Native vs. Omit/Guarded	Yes	13	8	3	2
Non-Native vs. Omit/Guarded	No	4	2	2	-
Native vs. Combined Groups	Yes	10	6	4	-

Table 13.4 provides, for the French language, the results of reference and focus group comparisons with the corresponding Mantel-Haenszel outcomes. In the table the ETS categories for action on all 66 items under review is used. Only C items would be judged worthy of renewal, B items would need review, while A items could be ignored because their effects were so small. If attention were to be focussed only on items emerging as C in their need for omission, the numbers so identified are few enough to have occurred by chance from repeated analysis of the total numbers at risk. This would not preclude their scrutiny, but it would inspire caution before ascribing causes.

THE FLEMISH LANGUAGE APPLICANTS

When the same protocol was applied to define reference and focus groups in the Flemish Language group, attempting to increase the focus group size, there were obvious, and statistically significant mean differences between those who were identified as non-natives and those who failed to complete the questionnaire. This meant that the non-native focus group could not be enhanced by inclusion of omit/guarded respondents. The focus group was confined to fewer than 200 participants, making the use of quartiles as ability matching determinants impractical.

As a last resort, upper middle and lower thirds of the verbal concept *Word Rules* test were used to conduct a pilot analyses of NL Word Rule MINI items, those being the most likely to be of interest because of their vocabulary requirements.

FLEMISH SPIRIT OF INDEPENDENCE?

Even so, the ability groupings derived were marginal to say the least. Table 13.5 demonstrates the imbalanced numerical structure of the division into thirds for the Flemish language cohorts of native and non-native origins. In spite of the outcome, showing that *two thirds of the non-native group* were assigned to the *lower* third quartile, an exploratory analysis was duly performed. The result showed that whereas five *Word Rule* miniitems were flagged by the Mantel-Haenszel procedure, only three items were flagged among 44 minitest items in all of the remaining tests (OR, NF, OE, and TI) when the same *Word Rule* thirds criterion was used to group applicants in the remaining tests by an indicator of Flemish language efficiency.

Table 13.5: Performance Indicators for the Flemish Word Rules Test

Group		Word Rule Lower, Middle, Upper, Thirds			
		Lower	Middle	Upper	Total
NL Majority	Count	796	826	915	2537
	% within Origin	**31.4%**	**32.6%**	**36.1%**	**100.0%**
	% of Total	29.4%	30.5%	33.8%	93.8%
NL Minority	Count	105	46	17	168
	% within Origin	**62.5%**	**27.4%**	**10.1%**	**100.0%**
	% of Total	3.9%	1.7%	.6%	6.2%
Totals	Count	901	872	932	2705
	% of Total	**33.3%**	**32.2%**	**34.5%**	**100.0%**

This result suggests that command of the Flemish language appeared to be an important intervening variable of unknown variation among individuals. Clearly, much needs to be done to clarify the nature of the proposed non-native groups among Flemish applicants. And this was not a matter capable of immediate resolution at a distance.

A WELCOME INDEPENDENT ACADEMIC REPLICATION

This study was subsequently replicated under contract to the Belgian Defence Force by an independent group at Ghent University (Brouwer, Fontaine & Mylle, 2012) *using a larger sample, but containing the participants who had formed the initial study in this chapter*. Table 13.6 shows the increased sample size. The authors' abstract shows the methods and results in summary. The number of items correct and response lag time were recorded for each item. The factorial structure in the four groups was determined, resulting in the same factorial structure in the Flemish vs. French subgroups as well as in the Belgian vs. foreign (Nouveaux Belges) subsamples, evidence that the

MULTIMETHOD COMPARISONS:

Confirmation by Belgian Academics

tests measure the same construct in all groups. Language and ethnicity groupings were examined for item bias and checked for average differences. Out of the six subtests, only some items of the *Word Rules Test* showed a need for review, but they were not overly biased. Finally, there was no significant differential item functioning found across the four groups. Moreover, there were no differences found when men and women were compared.

Table 13.6: External Diversity Study Breakdown

	Flemish	**French**	**Totals**
Belgian Native	3619 (45.8%)	3303 (41.8%)	6922 (87.6%)
'Nouveaux Belges'	290 (3.6%)	679 (8.6%)	969 (12.2%)
	3909 (49.4%)	3982 (50.4%)	7891 (100%)

Most significant for psychometrics perhaps, the authors used a different method to test for item equivalence, namely *multiple regression analysis*, investigating all potential litem-bias possibilities. Their exhaustive analyses of each item reached the same conclusions as the previous study, that bias effects were negligible where minorities were concerned. In particular, when the traditional language division that has marked Belgian history was the focus, there emerged inconsistent *radical* language effects that might well be regarded as random variation in three items. In the *Word Rules* series of eleven items, one item showed the French language group to be faster, but in another the Flemish group were faster! In the *Orientation* task, the very first item showed the Flemish group to be faster. The effect sizes were negligible, no statistic suggesting more than a review. In calculating effects for each language group all 66 items were analysed, involving a total of 132 items for a multitude of different calculations on each one; and only three items were brought to the attention of the analysts, who were unable to offer a cause.

STORY OF DIFFERENTIAL ITEM FUNCTION FINDINGS IN BELGIUM

Exhaustive preliminary analysis of the data provided by Belgian Defence Force was undertaken. The examination of six tests, each involving a set of 11 Minitest items, using broad category ability focus and reference groupings determined by the data structure, revealed very few items requiring examination and/ or action.

French. A total of 10 items from were isolated by the Mantel-Haenszel procedure in the French language group, of which 6 were A items and 4 were B items. The largest number (4 items, 2 A type and 2 B type) were in the *Word Rules Tests*, indicating that language development was an intervening variable likely to influence item behaviour in French language minority groups.

Flemish. A limited Flemish language analysis was carried out in spite of the doubtful sample size. The results follow similar trends to the French data, with very few items being identified as worthy of attention. Because a very wide ability matching frame, of upper, middle and lower thirds was employed, forced by extremely small non-native numbers that increased the risk of Type 1 and Type 2 errors, specific instances have been omitted. Once more, the number of items appears very small and the apparent intervening effect of language proficiency was observed.

Female and Male. Appropriate caveats were exercised in the analysis of male and female differences. After the exercise of what controls could be employed, there appeared to be no item bias affecting the status of women recruits.

Replications. Independent replications with different methods and larger samples confirm the overall result pattern and lead to the same conclusions of no discernible bias in the GCTB individual test items.

DISCUSSION

The original study was devised to overcome the difficulty of Differential Item Functioning analysis when multiple parallel forms make comparisons of individual items very difficult. Because items are deliberately designed to be different, one could wait for many thousands of participants to complete identical items that very infrequently occur at random in the many forms of the tests in use. To provide only one form for as long as it took to produce large enough samples of Flemish and French language users was thought to be operationally impracticable. The answer was to provide an innovative and convenient design by randomly sampling items from a randomly generated test form. This selection of items by a committee comprised a minitest to be applied at the end of the particular test under scrutiny, obviating the need for new instructions. This solution, approved by the Belgian authorities, permitted Differential Item Function analyses using focus and reference groups in both languages. From the French language data provided by Belgian Defence Force, the numbers classified as focus groups, women, non-native residents and others, were not large enough, if treated independently, to permit comparisons using deciles and/or percentiles as ability strata. Quartiles were used as the means of exerting partial control on the differential ability proportions within groups. Even this solution was found to be impractical in the Flemish cohort.

CHAPTERS 12 AND 13

IS THE GCTB A MULTILINGUAL MULTIPLE PARALLEL FORM INNOVATION FIT FOR PURPOSE?

Moreover, the small number of items identified as worthy of attention, if not of action, did not behave uniformly across quartiles or at a risk ratio demanding removal of the item type. The work of the academic Ghent group provided a classic replication where the same results were revealed by different methods and approaches to verification. Other methods of DIF in items were employed on the given data, yet the results were not able to be interpreted outside the constraints of group sizes and their as yet unknown internal structures. *At the forefront of every type of analysis carried out, has been the uncertainty of the non-native minority groups boundaries and their limited size,* even when hypothetically combined to produce one larger French language minority with no other than an empirical basis for their combination. The initial major investigation could not have taken place without the efforts made by the Belgian Defence Force[7] to provide large amounts of data in impeccable detail and their cooperation in providing a copy of the IMTA presentation by Brouwer, Fontaine and Mylle (2012).

PART 2 ULSTER: A SECTARIAN CULTURAL CONTEXT

For some years, prior to 1996, the *Police Service of Northern Ireland* (PSNI) recruited from a large number of applicants by announcing and advertising a competition for entry; and thereafter, usually three times a year, applying a single psychometric test of verbal reasoning to select those most likely to succeed in training after background checks and references were considered. In response to changing circumstances, not least of which was a commonly held belief that the single test used as a selection device, unchanged over several years, had been compromised by coaching agencies, the Personnel Division of the Police Service of Northern Ireland (PSNI) commissioned a study of a new test series. The changes to recruitment tests in the UK introduced by BARB five years previously were known to government recruiting agencies, but at that time in Northern Ireland, the introduction of any tests even remotely resembling the BARB system could have produced a public outcry from those sectarian groups who perceived the British Army as an occupying force. Guidelines to ensure reliability, validity, fairness and resistance to compromise were provided. Any new tests for the Police Service of Northern Ireland had to be unique; and with the guarantees in the insert, predate the *Lackland Tests* and The Belgian GCTB By March 1998, all work required to consider the future operational use of the tests was complete. A climate of extreme social sensitivity demanded fairness to men and women, different age groups and traditional sectarian groups, catholic and protestant. In the account, the chapter follows a protocol for multiple parallel form recruitment test trials and

PRECURSORS OF THE GCTB IN ULSTER

§ *Be of more than one single type to provide a representative balance of skills likely to predict training success*

§ *Meet psychometric standards of reliability and validity currently accepted by professional bodies*

§ *Be easy to administer in group paper and pencil form after appropriate training*

§ *Be capable of being understood and completed by literate secondary school students*

§ *Not demand specialised knowledge likely to place groups with such knowledge at an advantage*

§ *Have multiple parallel forms to prevent compromise*

---

7   Thanks are particularly extended to Annemie Defranc for providing much assistance with data description; and to Dr. Patrick Kyllonen for a helpful commentary on an earlier draft of a report co-authored with Arlene McGurk of *Mindmill* for a seminar with general staff that was the source of this chapter.

use. The ultimate if unspoken criterion for their acceptance was political defensibility. Administrative convenience and technical soundness were taken for granted. The pursuit of excellence, nevertheless, was the goal of the new generation of tests that emerged in Northern Ireland. The results shed further light on issues of fairness to minorities because of an outline of their operational use in two successive cohorts of applicants where they were only one stage in an elaborate multi-stage procedure. First, those stages are examined to find out what influence the tests seemed to exert.

AN APPARENT SELECTION PROCESS – HOW FAIR WAS IT?

Reliable and valid tests are basic tools in the process. How they actually contribute to and affect a lengthy selection system in a complex society is quite another question. Details of actual progress through the police service selection system, which had *four successive stages,* ability tests, personal assessments, physical tests and a medical examination, became available long after the work on tests was concluded and the tests were being used in the annual competition. A faxed summary document, apparently originating from an official source (Dalton, 2000) was the point of origin[8]. From this, on the assumption that the figures outline a reflection, if not an actual account, of applicant success at the various stages, it was possible hypothetically to follow the progress of women (F) and men (M) and the three different sectarian affiliation groups (G1, stated sectarian affiliation majority: G2 stated sectarian affiliation minority; G3, no stated religion) from application, test results using a completely new parallel form for each test, assessment interviews, and medical examinations to survival as potential recruits. How many survivors were there? What were the major trends in survival? Table 13.7 was constructed from the faxed account of the progress of two successive cohorts of applicants to the NIPS. It provides reported numbers through four barriers to acceptance. Figure 13.3 provides a convenient overall summary pattern from two annual cohorts listed. What do the different barriers reveal about equal opportunity across the now familiar divides of gender and sectarian identity? Clearly, different percentages from each of the five different groups, female, male and the three sectarian categories progress at each selection stage. To summarise, men, women and the largest sectarian group have a one in twenty chance of acceptance. Only one in forty of the two remaining sectarian groups appear to have been accepted. Some elaboration is offered to account for their progress.

BECOMING A MEMBER OF THE ULSTER CONSTABULARY

Men and Women
The relative success of men and women begins with the number of application forms returned. In all, 2125 men and 1229 women were undertook the tests. After the tests were given, 11% of men and 13% of women entered the second stage, termed

---

8   A faxed summary was sent to the writer from a most reliable source: but no official confirmation was sought. Hence the comments that follow are hypothetical only, without prejudice, and are not meant to be more than an example of what might be found in any similar context.

'Assessment' and most likely a security clearance. Survivors from this stage then underwent first physical and then medical tests: and in those stages the numbers were reduced further. Only 4.8% of the original male applicants made it through the physical tests, but 5.6% of females did. Finally, after the medical examinations, 4.2% of man and 4.1% of women applicants were eligible to be recruited. The medical examination appeared to be the final levelling factor that had reduced an apparently persistent female advantage of one to two percent that existed from the ability test stage until the medical examination had been completed. When all was said and done, equal proportions of women and men were survivors of a rigorous process where the chances of survival, from application to acceptance were 25 to 1 against for men and women alike.

Figure 13.3: PSNI Recruit Progress by Stages and Special Group Categories

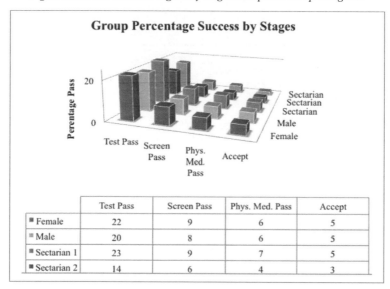

	Test Pass	Screen Pass	Phys. Med. Pass	Accept
■ Female	22	9	6	5
■ Male	20	8	6	5
■ Sectarian 1	23	9	7	5
■ Sectarian 2	14	6	4	3

Sectarian Origin
Could the same equalities exist when cross-tabulated with the recorded affiliations of the applicants? Cohort I is now examined closely. Of those entering the competition after application forms had been returned, there were 2310 applicants in Group1; there were 747 in Group 2; and in Group 3, *whose members had no recorded religious affiliation*, there were 297. After all the stages had been completed, 5.4% of Group 1 entrants had apparently survived, 2.5% of Group 2 entrants, and 2% of Group 3 entrants, a ratio of two Group 1 members to one of all the rest. Among men and women the proportions entering the last three stages after the test screen had been completed were close, but the test results by affiliation status showed no parity when compared at the first barrier. Whereas 17.8% from Group 1 had gone forward, after completing the tests, to the last three stages, security assessment, physical and medical, only 10.5% and 8% from Groups 2 and 3 respectively had made it past the test stage. This gap, where twice as many from Group 1, compared with the rest, had been chosen, is maintained to the end, when, as in the men and women study, approximately 4% overall were finally eligible to be recruits in the police force. *Survivors from Group 1 entrants were one in 25, whereas survivors from entrants in the other two groups were one in 40.*

Table 13.7: Successive Cohort Progress in Police Service of Northern Ireland Recruitment Stages by Sex and Sectarian Categories

Stage	Cohort H						Cohort I						Combined Cohorts					
	F	M	G1	G2	G3	Total	F	M	G1	G2	G3	Total	F	M	G1	G2	G3	Total
Applied	995	1830	2134	431	260	2825	1229	2125	2310	747	297	3354	2224	3955	4444	1178	557	6179
Tested	723	1312	1586	307	142	2035	929	1644	1826	558	189	2573	1652	2956	3412	865	331	4608
Screened	166	279	376	40	29	445	203	313	413	79	24	516	369	592	789	119	53	961
Physical	83	121	179	16	9	204	70	103	139	26	8	173	153	224	318	52	17	377
Medical	65	120	162	15	8	185	60	98	128	22	8	158	125	218	290	37	16	343
Passed	48	96	125	12	7	144	51	91	117	19	6	142	99	187	242	31	13	286
	F	M	G1	G2	G3	Total	F	M	G1	G2	G3	Total	F	M	G1	G2	G3	Total
Percentage	4.8	5.2	5.8	2.8	2.6	5.1	4.1	4.3	5.1	2.5	2.0	4.2	4.5	4.7	5.4	2.6	2.3	4.6

Notes: F: Female; M: Male; G1: Sectarian Majority; G2: Sectarian Minority; G3: No Stated Sectarian Identity

THE SOCIAL AND OPERATIONAL CONTEXTS OF TRIALS

WERE THE TESTS FAIR?

The faxed hypothetical record of progress apparently shows that the test outcomes were not equable as far as sectarian membership was concerned, but they were reasonably close as a screen for ability in men and women. However, the Belgian study showed that group identity was a misleading category if it were left as a gross package with contents hidden away. Could a detailed review of test results in the Police Service of Northern Ireland show the same outcome? The insert begins with the goal of understanding the cultural context, Macdonald's Askaris had not disappeared over the psychometric horizon. Policing in Northern Ireland was perhaps just as unique a situation for test adaptation. When new tests were proposed, sensitivity about the fairness of the selection system was evident from the start of discussions about how to change the system that had existed in the past. Annual advertisement and an open competition were the requirements, but the tests had to be seen to represent in an even-handed fashion, the underlying structure and proportions of applicants of various affiliations, persuasions and dispositions. Fairness to men and women and to groups with different religions was not only socially just, it was politically essential. How could this be demonstrated as part of a continuous process with different stages?

THE PSNI CULTURE

Policewomen, and indeed front-line soldiers, sailors and air force personnel, are still a distinct minority in most democratic societies.

For minority groups, police work is universally of much lower occupational prestige than in majorities: and in Northern Ireland, the police service was not held in high esteem by the Catholic minority community, which perceived the officers to be mainly Protestant and biased.

If the law were administered by a police force whose composition was perceived as neither fair nor equitable, resolution of age-old grievances, real or imagined, would be difficult to reach.

NATURE OF THE TASKS AND THEIR USE

The parallel form specifications for the proposed study required that the tests be referenced to known cognitive dimensions; that mental models for the tasks be predicated; and that there be no item bank for any test, only a series of algorithms for its construction in real time in the computer. Essentially, the theoretical frames described in Irvine, Dann & Anderson (1990) and Irvine (2002) were relevant to the construction of a brand new set of tests bearing no outward resemblance to any in operation at the time within the armed services in the UK. Five tests were derived directly from these principles. The tasks within each test tended to be invariant within each test, and working-memory based. Each, however, had specific variance in a domain that is non-random. Paper-and-pencil examples were previously shown in Chapter 10. The tests used were *Error Detection, Number Skills, Locations, Reasoning Categories and Odds and Evens:*

Nevertheless, a special study was undertaken to assess, within the unknowns of applicant qualifications and motivations, the degree and extent of sensitivity of the tests to sectarian membership. First, the protocols for test use were fixed to set the stage for the results that ensued. These included test formats, time limits, and trial preparations.

- *Test Formats* In keeping with practices current at the time, a paper-and-pencil format for test delivery was provided, in the knowledge that future versions might well be computer-delivered. Hand scoring was accompanied by a computer-based system providing norms from the numbers of right and wrong answers for each test.
- *Time Limits* Candidates were not convinced that a short test was adequate as a gateway to a major employment opportunity. With instructions and demonstrations to be added, the total time required for the session was projected at one hour. This outside limit was not exceeded, the norm being about 50 minutes.
- *Trials* A number of preliminary trials with trainees were conducted in the run-up to quasi-operational simulation. These had various outcomes: test instructions using focus groups of potential administrators; time limits that maximised test reliability, and training of test administrators. A 'train aswe mean to operate' principle assumed groups of 30 people involved two administrators, one a demonstrator and the other a timekeeper and proctor. Roles were rotated to ensure competence in either one.

A QUASI-OPERATIONAL TRIAL

To create a context for standardisation and validation, a trial of all five tests with potential recruits was organised for October 1996. All applicants for entry were tested with the existing test and with the experimental tests. Only the existing test was used to make decisions about entry. The experimental tests were for standardisation of testing procedures and scoring methods. Preliminaries with 350 candidates showed that the tests appeared to be administered successfully by the teams of presenters who used the standard instructions and procedures developed with them. Calculations were based on a random stratified sample of 350 participants, of whom 195 were males and 155 were a specially augmented female group. This was an approximate ten percent sample of all those who entered the competition in 1997 and was of sufficient size to provide stable estimates of all test functions. Illustrative norms were produced for all five tests and expressed as percentiles.

Pilot Study Results

The distributions and reliabilities of the tests were in the range very good to excellent. Comparison of the intended use of the tests, providing an index of *Recruiting Training Potential*, with the existing selection test showed that their use could provide much increased separation at the top end of the applicant ability range. The data collected to this point allowed tentative validity analysis using the test used to select recruits as a marker, and comparison of previously selected recruit trainees with unselected applicants. The best fit was obtained by a combination of *Reasoning Category (verbal) Number Skills (working memory) and Locations (spatial orientation)*, after adjustment for guessing. Every time a test was added, the correlation increased significantly, until final value of .57 was reached. These are quasi-predictive studies based on current data. The second set of analyses focused on what the tests mean when they are analysed as a group in a search for their internal structure. The result was the customary strong general factor underlying all tests currently in use. This concurred with the use of a composite index of the Police Service of Northern Ireland paper-and-pencil test scores called *Recruit Training Potential*. The sample of 350 showed negligible average score differences between males and females, no bias in the results from various testing centres, and good fits for parallel forms. A comprehensive study with a much larger group was necessary before the questions of fairness to all could be resolved.

REPLICATIONS WITH POPULATIONS OF APPLICANTS

A replication with two successive year groups of applicants was possible. In the first year of study, 2013 applicants undertook the tests. In the second year, there were results from a further 2754. Both cohorts took the same types of tests. The test forms were parallel to those given to the sample in the operational try-out with one exception. The *Number Skills* test was made marginally more difficult than that administered to the proving sample of 350, so that comparison of test results was not possible for that test. The data was supplied only after the competition for the yearly intakes had been completed. The nature of the study enabled more details on applicants to be recorded, in particular the age on application. This made a scrutiny of test results possible, and showed that there was one more lesson to be learned. The overwhelming official concern, apart from confirmation of the pilot study results, was how the test characteristics answered the politically sensitive question of their fairness to minorities, including women and two main religious groups for many years seen to be opposed in aims and direction. The results affecting these major concerns are in Table 13.8.

Table 13.8: Test and CPI Index Results for Two Successive Annual Competitions

Applicant Group		Capacity to Process Info.	Error Detection	Reasoning Categories	Number Skills	Odds and Evens	Orientation
Year 1	N	2013.0	2013.0	2013.0	2013.0	2013.0	2013.0
	Mean	**100.1**	**30.8**	**19.5**	**41.8**	**41.8**	**22.7**
	Std. Dev.	15.0	6.4	7.9	15.6	12.0	8.2
Year 2	N	2574.0	2574.0	2574.0	2574.0	2574.0	2574.0
	Mean	**99.9**	**29.5**	**20.0**	**40.3**	**43.1**	**23.3**
	Std. Dev.	15.0	7.1	8.1	15.3	11.6	8.1

Methods and Results for Review of Group Differences

Among cross-cultural psychologists there have always been severe reservations about the conventional approach of comparing broad categories of applicants with tests of any persuasion (see Irvine and Berry, 1988, Chapter 1), but particularly in a study like this one. The tests themselves were designed to contain no material or skills where properly motivated groups chosen at random could be disadvantaged. Nevertheless, the question of fairness is not theoretical, but empirical. The results now presented are derived

DEFINITIIVE OUTCOMES

Two Cohorts Tested

Parallel Form Averages Indistinguishable

from these two annual intake groups totalling 4587 potential recruits. But first, one can look at the results for each year, as an indication, *ceteris paribus*, of how parallel the tests were. The means and standard deviations of all measures are remarkably close. Although significance tests show that the tiny observed mean differences are significant because of the very large sample sizes, the effect sizes are negligible, and so small that no two parallel forms would have any adverse effect on an applicant's chances of success whatever the year of application.. *In fact, the individual test results, averages and spread of scores, are so close as to be all that might ever be expected from two parallel forms of each test given in two successive years to applicants for the same type of job.* Further analyses showed that the underlying structure of the tests remained unchanged from year to year. A large general factor emerged in both tests, just like the one found in the pilot study. This result means that the *Capacity to Process Information* index is stable.

SECTARIAN CATEGORY STRUCTURES, THEIR WEIGHT AND INFLUENCE

Other known influences in test scores were identified. Apart from test form differences, and fairness to sectarian groups, there were two other factors likely to affect the outcome of results. One was the *age* of the applicant because the age limits were between 18 and 50 years, a very large range. The other was the *gender or, more correctly the sex* of the applicant. .Whatever else may be said about membership of minority groups, age and sex differences are more or less permanent and seldom a matter for dispute. They are not to be dismissed simply because they are obvious and subject to traditional social prescriptions about roles and the ability to fulfil them. Given a data set as extensive as the one available, the opportunity to look beyond the simple female-male categorisation arose. *When the potential influence of age and sex differences*

UNPACKING THE CATEGORIES ONE MORE TIME

How valid are comparisons of test performance based on traditional minority categories in Northern Ireland?

on test results was evaluated, the question of **performance** by groups whose sectarian *affiliations were different could then be addressed, not in isolation, but with due regard to the weight of other influences within them. What was the outcome?* If the Belgian experience is any indication, the results were not unexpected even with paper-and-pencil versions of the tests.

To carry out the necessary analyses, four age groups were created from the age distribution, using quartile (25%) divisions. Sex differences were available, and personnel officers assigned sectarian affiliations, from completed application forms. The assignment of status was translated for this purpose into three anonymous sectarian and non-sectarian groups, Group 1 the majority sect, Group 2 a designated religious minority and Group 3 a third, unknown minority group of undeclared or unknown, or indeed no religious affiliation. Other information judged relevant was the test centre attended. This was recorded to check on possible bias associated with the effects of different test administrators. No bias was detected and all centres had the same average and spread of scores. *With this information, sectarian affiliation could be broken down to assess the influence of its components. The religion of the applicant was not a final indivisible category that could stand alone. Like the atom, it could be split. However, split or not, the category has had a permanent effect in Northern Ireland for centuries: and fosters demonstrations, parades and disturbances even today.*

UNPACKING THE CATEGORIES

In the two-year period under review, the proportions of male and female and of different age groups within each affiliation group were found, so that the underlying influences on the applicant categories could be, if not determined wholly, then at least partly understood as a distinct possibility. Figures 13.4 and 13.5 are pivotal, because they isolate the relative influence of test forms which would be *construction incidentals* against what might be termed *social incidentals* like sex and age ratios in isolation from and within each group.

Figure 13.4: Test and Social Incidental Effects on Test Scores

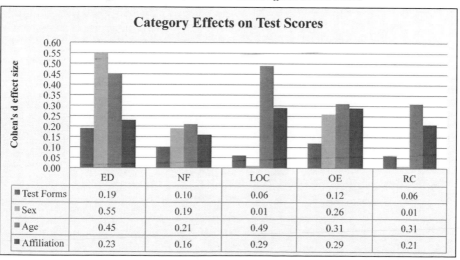

	ED	NF	LOC	OE	RC
■ Test Forms	0.19	0.10	0.06	0.12	0.06
■ Sex	0.55	0.19	0.01	0.26	0.01
■ Age	0.45	0.21	0.49	0.31	0.31
■ Affiliation	0.23	0.16	0.29	0.29	0.21

Effects of Dispositional, Social and Test Form Factors
Each of these factors had an influence on the test averages. If they had been left as raw scores, they would not have been comparable. To illustrate the influence of test forms, sex differences, and age groups, the largest mean differences in any comparison were transformed as effect sizes in standardised values that can be compared directly.

Figure 13.4 provides a summary of the strength of various influences on the tests in this standard form. It shows that different categories exert different effects on test scores, and not to the same degree for every test

Close examination of the patterns in Figure 13.4 how just how much the categories vary in their effects on the individual tests that are by no means equally affected by group identities. Notably, age is the most consistent determinant of group variation, regardless of the test in use. This is the salient feature to bear in mind when progressing to Figure 13.5, one of the most revealing as far as unpacking traditional minority group classifications are concerned. Eight out of a possible twenty mean maximum differences were large enough to exert a noticeable effect, four of these associated with age groups, two with male and female identity, and two with affiliation. Differences between parallel forms from year to year were very small and exert no influence on individual rank orders. The advantages in effect size are for females for Group 1 over others and for younger groups over older groups.

Scrutiny of sectarian affiliation shows that the proportions of males and females within each group are more or less constant for Groups 1 and 2, but alter dramatically within Group 3. Sex differences in test achievements could then affect group affiliation averages inconsistently, because of these different proportions. The same conclusion can be drawn about the effects of age on test scores. Because age affects the results, then the averages of affiliation groups could appear to differ *because the proportions of the four age groups in each affiliation category are inconsistent.* Hence, any single affiliation category contains within itself a potential package of influences making direct comparison of test results for the three sectarian groups inappropriate. They are simply not able to be compared as if all the potential effects on test scores were distributed in random samples within sampling error.

SECTARIAN GROUPS

Age Withers Them but Custom does Not Stale their Infinite Variety

Don't Forget the Service Rank Influence on Belgian Women's 'Superiority'

No Religion A Guarded Response?

Figure 13.5: Religious Affiliation Proportions Unpacked

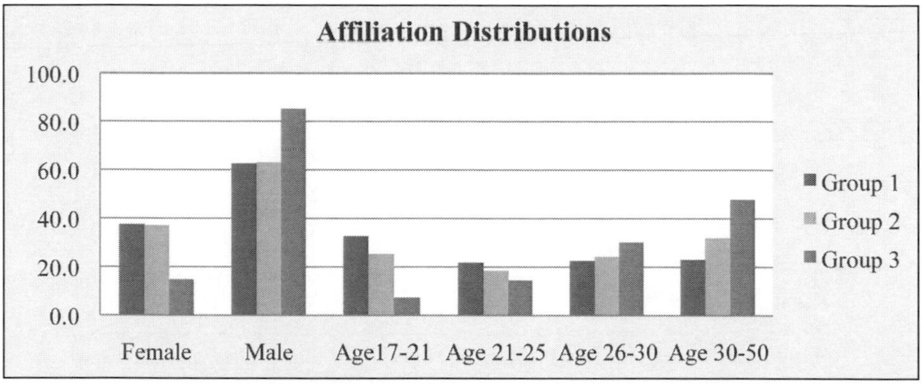

Affiliation Distributions

Affiliation Groups		Sex Group		Age Group				Total
		Female	Male	18-21	22-25	26-30	30-50	18-50
Group	1	1274	2125	1113	739	765	782	3399
Group	2	319	543	218	159	209	276	862
Group	3	48	276	24	47	98	155	324
	Total	1641	2944	1355	945	1072	1213	4585
	Total %	35.8%	64.2%	29.6%	20.6%	23.4%	26.5%	100.0%

From these results, with the prior knowledge that affiliation groups differ markedly in their proportions of sex and age distributions, any observed differences between affiliation groups could not be attributed solely to that categorisation without committing a gross error of inference. This conclusion is not markedly different from results of tendentious comparisons of *Raven's Progressive Matrices* scores across ethnic groups and generations, criticised by Irvine (1983c) and described as a *reductio ad absurdum*.

However, there is one more valid point. How *difficult* were the test items for men, women and different age groups? What proportions of the questions were answered correctly? If the individual questions were drastically different in difficulty level, for men or women or young or old, then the tests themselves could be said to be unfair. The items on the whole were as difficult for males as for females; and variations across the age groups were minor, with older groups marginally less accurate, most differences being within one percentage point. In short, as in Belgium, there was no differential impact on performance due to item difficulty variation among groups.

A CONSISTENT MEASURE: CONSTRUCT VALIDITY

Next, what the tests measured in the centres had to be fit for purpose. A general index of recruit potential (CPI) was the goal. The correlation pattern is very similar to that found in the preliminary work with small samples, and so are the factor loadings. Reliabilities are good to excellent and the reliability of a composite CPI is estimated at .96, giving a very small border zone for a cut-off point.

Table 13.9: Correlation Matrix and Factor Loadings (N=4385)

	ED	**NUM.**	**OE**	**LOC.**	**RC**	**TEST**	**FACTOR**
ED	1.000	.523	.595	.499	.453	ED	.718
NF	.523	1.000	.568	.467	.411	NF	.676
OE	.595	.568	1.000	.540	.529	OE	.787
OR	.499	.467	.540	1.000	.630	OR	.735
RC	.453	.411	.529	.630	1.000	RC	.698
Reliability	.78	.88	.92	.90	.85		

Note: Factor Matrix Extraction Method: Maximum Likelihood.; 1 factor extracted and 5 iterations required.

From this *very large sample of close to five thousand applicants*, one may draw some conclusions having in mind the data reduction method applied was objective, and relied on the strict criteria applied by the method of Maximum Likelihood, which extracted only one general factor or influence in the tests. This replication demonstrated the robust parallel form function of the system, permitting the generation of as many forms as are necessary to guard against compromise by loss of tests or theft of items. In addition, the construct validity of the tests was reaffirmed. A single *general factor of information processing capacity in working memory* (CPI) accounts for a substantial part of the variation among individual subjects.

TEST FAIRNESS – WHAT ARE THE FACTS?

The results of the actual test scores made and the Capacity to Process Information (CPI) index score were conclusive. Differences between sects in the younger age groups were such as one might expect through random fluctuations in the groups. There was a trend to lower performance in the two minority groups, Group 2 and Group 3, but the differences are so small that they are unable to be interpreted as affecting the overall outcome. Older applicants, those aged between 30 and 50 from minority groups have a depressed performance compared with younger people from their own sectarian group and with those of the same age in the majority Group 1. If the candidates were to be chosen by the CPI index than the border zone derived from statistical confidence limits would be large enough to include all who had a chance of success, with sectarian membership an irrelevance. Age would be much more important than religious denomination or lack of it. The tables in the first part of the Police Service of Northern Ireland review shows that sectarian categories were associated with a reduced chance of acceptance from an early stage. The test study shows that the categories themselves are misleading if different internal structures are ignored, just as in Belgium. Both aspects of this chapter permit some generalisations.

SECTARIAN AGE AND SEX CATEGORIES AS UNOPENED PACKAGE LABELS
The results of any studies undertaken for reasons of political defensibility are not meant to lessen the importance of producing personnel policies that are open,

accountable to public scrutiny and defensible. The tests used in the study had to be shown to be equable within the parameters of psychometric methods of inclusion rather than exclusion. Where group equity is a criterion of political correctness in tests, these differences have still to be uncovered and explained. In this detailed analysis, such differences as are verifiable are never attributable to any single category of membership. The differences that are there for any one category have to be qualified by detailed knowledge of membership of other groups nested within that group. Seeing sectarian differences disappear when the differences due to age and gender within these social groups are brought out and are controlled for. Sectarian membership by itself in applicants for the Northern Ireland Police Service is a prime example of what we have defined as the *unopened package label variable*. When its contents are identified, the label on the package is seen to have no bearing on test results in the package itself. Moreover, the verifiable package contents, age and sex, are also dispositional: that is they are a permanent part of the applicant's biological make up. They seldom if ever undergo any significant change at the time of application. Sectarian and other forms of membership on the other hand are learned social phenomena: and like all social categories that are not verifiable by documentation, may be subject to strategic change when high stakes are involved.

SECTARIAN AND SEX DIFFERENCES

The Very Last Word

Unopened Packages are Dangerous Psychometric Deliveries Bringing Untold Misery to Recipients

The final link in the argument concerns a factor that has not been an explicit part of the discussion thus far. It will not have escaped the careful reader that there is another ghost in the machine present in the results on sectarian affiliation. Those whose sectarian membership is categorised as 'unknown' must include persons whose religious affiliation is non-existent or concealed by being guarded (cf. the Belgian patterns) in responding to the question about affiliation; and this group appears on the surface to perform least well of all the socially identified groups. Does this mean that the tests discriminate against people for whom no religious category exists? The only worthwhile conclusion is that he *Unknown* category is just as much a package of social influences on test performance as Group 1 or Group 2 and that none of these alone is a viable factor against which to judge test fairness.

To conclude, the available evidence from Belgium and Northern Ireland does not show that the tests were biased against males, or older age groups, or any socially identified group, just that there are small performance differences associated with each of these categories. The test items do not discriminate unfairly against applicants of any dispositional or social type. On the contrary, the result patterns confirm that applicant group categories are complex packages of physical, social, educational and motivational influences; and that it is impossible to generalise from any single category about the fairness of the results of tests used in the selection procedure.

This multiple parallel form venture was in many ways a landmark. New tests were devised that proved to be robust in parallel formats. Political defensibility was pursued but in the knowledge that the complexities of sectarian affiliations would not provide answers acceptable to citizens in pursuit of change. *But success was measured in revealing how technical soundness could prevent unjustifiable conclusions about the attribution of cause and effect to group identities.* Selection, though, is not simply about tests results. It is often a multi-stage process with no published accountability indices. This is what was discovered about the outcomes when the tests created were seen as only one stage of the process. At the beginning of the Northern Ireland review, a plausible process of selection was outlined, with questions about its fairness implied. If it is looked at again, the conclusion is simple. Summaries such as that in Table 13.7, without the accompanying analysis of group infrastructure, will be misleading. When results of recruitment tests used in Belgium were reviewed, with more sophisticated methods of investigating test fairness available, the same issues of group identity and equity for minorities, characterised by linguistic divisions in the country, were raised and resolved. The tests were fair to all. To have judged them by broad social categories unpacked, was not fair to the tests or to their members.

GROUP VARIATION IN THE USAF STUDIES: A FOOTNOTE

Variation due to dispositional characteristics such as sex and social class is always visible in ASVAB tests with an educational origin, particularly in verbal, mechanical and electrical knowledge. However, not much evidence for category variation is available on working memory tests in general or in computer-delivered versions in particular. A retrospective was conducted on the applicant sample of 1512 USAF recruits tested at Lackland AFB. Apart from those recruits identifying themselves as Black and White, which formed the main categories, there

Mustn't Forget the United States

were extremely small groups stating that they were of Hispanic, Asian or American Indian origin. Differences existed, but for what reason it was impossible to determine. After much examination of test results, there appeared to be too many variables within these small packages to enable full examination of observed mean differences. These included male and female, education levels, preselection by ASVAB results, as well as the pattern of different occupational interests and motivational profiles, which are all discussed in Chapter 11. However, male and female and ethnic group differences in the tests used in Project A are reported in Campbell and Fiske (2001, pp. 273 et seq.). During the last fifty years the writer has long advocated caution in the interpretation of all such results (Irvine, 1968 a, 1986b), and the principles laid down for ethnic group comparisons have not altered either with new technology or by the passage of time, Applicant populations are seldom if ever directly comparable, a conclusion in the USA as well as Belgium and Northern Ireland.

POLITICAL DEFENSIBILITY IN QUESTION

When the results from Cohorts H and I in Table 13.1 first came to hand, it was difficult to reconcile the origins of the observed differences between the affiliation groups with the actual test results from the two successive trials conducted, whereas the female outcomes largely confirmed what was expected from the test results. No obvious explanation emerged from the statistics gathered in the test trials to explain different progress through the system associated with religious affiliation or the lack of it. The summary document did not permit a breakdown of the affiliation groups by age and male-female ratios. Without knowledge of the components of the 'package' variables, sex-derived or political in origin, results such as these, if an actual outcome verified and made public, are more than likely to be interpreted from an entrenched social or political viewpoint. Technically sound as the tests had proved to be, apparent inequities in success ratios are never going to be politically defensible even if they are based on misconceptions. And that, above all, is the lesson to be learned from this unique exercise in the recruitment of policemen and policewomen in Northern Ireland.

Apparent sectarian imbalance is not foreign to Belgian social climates, where political attempts to equate probabilities of success are based on different norms for different language groups. As official Belgian government policy, it has nevertheless to stand up to the incontestable conclusion that different norms may make it easier for members of one language group to be accepted, because the norms are not identical. Once more, political decisions may demote psychometric rigour to a lower rank. This is a very important issue for the use of tests in any context where there arises the abiding issue of different test performance associated with linguistic, ethnic or sectarian identity. And the writer has no perfect answers to the practicalities of it. Nor for that matter has any psychologist living or dead. Whatever technical solutions may have been provided by the authorities to put any testing policy in place to deal with minority groups, they can invariably be questioned and challenged. No test survives an accusation of bias for long.

WISDOM AFTER THE EVENT

There are, therefore, precepts that arise from these two quite different studies. In Belgium, a government policy about fairness exists, and different norms are acceptable as a policy in that country, even if that policy could be challenged technically as being potentially unfair to one of the two language groups, Flemish or French. In Ulster, no policy existed at the time of test administration so that the unspoken question of sectarian or sex bias would always arise. Given unknowns in any national testing enterprise one may perhaps be forgiven for giving some advice as a coda to these two examples.

The really important need is to capture the authority's policy about what in their view constitutes fairness. Any policy-based protocol should clearly establish specifications for the study; and then guarantee if the tests met them, that there would be no barrier to their use and acceptance. One should not be tempted to begin what might be considered by experts to be an entirely appropriate study and then find it vetoed because of unspoken policy reasons which were always the issues at stake in the first place. Language groups in Belgium and sectarian groups in Northern Ireland would be among the first to protest any test results that highlighted long-standing political divisions that psychometrics is powerless to close.

Part 4:

The Shape of Things to Come

THE SHAPE OF THINGS

by **Michael D. Matthews, PhD**
Deputy Head and Professor of Engineering Psychology Department of Behavioral Sciences and Leadership U.S. Military Academy West Point

In this section, Dr. Irvine provides a comprehensive review of the past and contemporary efforts of psychologists to understand, predict, and improve soldier retention. What characteristics can be measured prior to induction into the military that predict retention and job performance? What is the relative importance of physical, cognitive, and attitudinal characteristics in selecting soldiers who find their work satisfying, are competent, and want to remain in the military? After induction, how might assignment and training be improved to increase job performance and retention? We know that aptitude and general intelligence are important, but what about the impact of non-cognitive factors such as vocational interests and personality? The answers to these questions are of vital concern. The days of the disposable, interchangeable soldier are ended. We know from hard experience that raw kinetic power is insufficient, by itself, to ensure victory. We must match the right soldier to the right job, train them properly, reward and motivate them, and keep them far longer in the active duty force than in the past. Modern command, control, intelligence, and weapons systems cannot function in the absence of skilled soldier/ operators.

I have argued that psychology is the most important science for ensuring success in modern military operations (M. D. Matthews, *Head Strong: How Psychology is Revolutionizing War*, Oxford University Press, 2013). Perhaps nowhere is this more apparent than in selecting and retaining a military force. The days are long gone when

the necessary prerequisites for serving effectively in the military were a strong physique, the ability to learn rudimentary battle drills, and the aptitude to operate relatively simple weapons systems. In those days, selection and placement was comparatively easy, since most soldiers could perform most jobs equally. In contrast, today's military consists of hundreds of different occupational specialties, most requiring highly specific technical skills. It may take months or even years, and costs vast sums of money, to train a soldier to be highly competent in the skills required in his or her job. Both the economic and operational significance of building state-of-the-art selection and assignment protocols is clear. Failure to retain highly skilled soldiers perpetuates costly recruiting and training of replacements, and erodes the combat readiness of the force.

Notably, success in 21st century war hinges on skill sets that have not traditionally been associated with the military. In an era where an action taken by a low ranking soldier can be instantly shared via the social media to the entire world, all soldiers must be culturally, socially, and politically savvy. These certainly represent learnable skills, and to some extent they may represent attributes and innate [or acquired] aptitudes. Retention is dependent upon selection, assignment, and training (as well as dynamic, organizational factors such as moral and cohesion). Psychology is the "go-to" science in developing ways of measuring, developing, and shaping these critical skills.

Finally, and perhaps crucially, only about 25 percent of human performance – in virtually all domains – is attributable to aptitude. Turned around, that leaves 75 percent of performance that is largely left unexplained. Aptitude testing traces its roots to the groundbreaking efforts of psychologists in World War I, who forged the early development of aptitude and intelligence testing. For the reasons already stated, modern military psychologists are beginning to unpack the other 75 percent of factors that shape performance and retention. These chapters provide a view not only of where we have been with respect to improving retention, but also to where we are going.

CHAPTER 14

THE ATTRIBUTES OF ATTRITION: A THANKLESS QUEST?

The abiding problem of recruitment is not initial selection from those who apply, but retaining those who are accepted. Generally, the selection tests seldom predict with any great degree of accuracy successful performance in the first phase of training. Once this barrier is passed, correlations with further training increase markedly. One more conclusion. Up to one third of recruits leave during initial training: and their selection tests fail to identify them. The last three chapters of the book are an attempt to identify those at risk. There are three familiar stages: the attrition culture; evidence for test use; and validation of measurements.

The current chapter examines previous efforts to deal with attrition in the United Kingdom, the United States Belgium and Germany. It features a large number of initiatives in the construction and use of self-report questionnaires, the use of compensatory screening models, commentary and decisions by policy makers. As an essential key to understanding the constant pattern of attempts to reduce attrition followed by policies of inactivity, the chapter concludes that attrition is not due to a set of attributes within recruits that can be pursued and predicted at the outset, but is the result of a process with its causes in the treatment prescribed for individual recruits by instructors and squad members alike.

Chapter 15 asks if psychological theory can build a scientific framework for the pursuit of attrition. Several strands are followed that characterise the process of attrition as a logical result of military culture. Different internal forms of screening of applicants and trainees are compared. Psychometric evidence for traits that have been associated with drop-outs is reviewed. It all leads to the construction of a set of tests, personality, vocational, quality of life and body clock adaptation to life styles. The chapter ends with a summary description of these inventories, developed at Lackland and used to identify recruits with different perspectives on the six weeks of life there. The last, Chapter 16, focuses on measures of physical, mental and social health of the United States Air Force inductees, female and male. Fitness for purpose was demonstrated in various ways. The sexes can be identified accurately from question patterns. Safeguards against faking are shown to work in various inventories, personality and vocational interests included. Wanting to quit the force was a key question whose responses sharply identified those with unstable personality tendencies and poor quality of life. Much later, use of the health related quality of life inventory with Royal Marines was to show that attrition could be predicted from a small number of questions after the instructors had decided who would stay or go among those recruits previously selected for personal qualities.

The three stages follow Macdonald's five lessons: what is the culture of attrition, what tests could be used, how could they be presented, how scored; and with what validity? Perhaps the five lessons appear as hindsight, as well they may. Chapter 16 used the work with 1500 recruits undergoing training at Lackland Air Force Base to construct and employ a number of measures that offer convincing evidence of individual attrition risk. The Lackland work was completed well before it was linked with a report on military motivation (Irvine, 1995) a preamble for non-cognitive tests in military training and selection. Only when attrition became apparent as the storehouse of knowledge where the Lackland studies belonged, did links emerge and some coherence develop.

INTERNATIONAL PURSUIT OF ATTRIBUTES

The move to create BARB, its deployment, validation and extension all showed that the task of generating tests from theory and computer algorithms could succeed. In the twenty year period of its nation-wide use in Britain it had produced a new set of tests for every recruit, with predictions of success in training that were comparable to most and better than some. When an entirely different set of tests based upon the same principles and benefitting from experience, was introduced first in the United Kingdom, then in the United States, Germany and Belgium, they were no less successful and proved capable of dealing with female and male, sectarian, linguistic and ethnic diversity among recruits, with no ill-effects and minimal need for item alterations. Unlike their predecessors they were, above all, capable of daily exposure in computers nationwide without fear of compromise or undue influence. Pre-test booklets removed the effects of coaching for a test in use. Unlike the adaptive item-response theory forms, common-core items that could be stolen and passed on were never required. Almost two decades later, however, with such an achievement, one might be expected to leave the selection of recruits right there. But attrition during initial training, an issue that has differed only in degree for centuries, but never in kind, continues to be a major concern internationally.

A THANKLESS QUEST ?

Recruit Attrition and Military Motivation: The British Effort

The USA Studies: Wars of Attrition?

Europe: Belgian and German

Inside the CULTURE of Attrition

One recent comprehensive account of numerous national attempts to deal with recruitment NATO (2007) provides details of recruits first selected by ability and aptitude tests, followed by security and criminal record screen and medical examinations, who either failed to complete basic training, or exercised their options to leave the service after an initial short term involvement, usually not exceeding six months. Such widespread interest in military motives and personal dispositions is not without good reason, because the crossing of each one of three service career thresholds – recruitment, deployment and repatriation, requires a lifestyle modification. During the time spent in any one of the three career phases, different demands are made on physical and mental health: and with these demands, there come changes in health-related quality of life. Moreover, there are casualties at every stage; attrition during recruitment training; deaths and wounds on deployment;

post-traumatic disorders, alcoholism and domestic violence on repatriation. What might be done to ensure that the correct decisions are made for individuals at each stage under is not a matter of routine. But decisions are more likely to have positive outcomes when fully informed. The issues are fully revealed in attempts to identify those who would be at risk in Britain, the United States, Belgium and Germany, countries where item generative tests were trialled and used.

RECRUIT ATTRITION AND MILITARY MOTIVATION: THE BRITISH EFFORT:

The failure of many countries with volunteer services to reduce wastage from attestation to the end of recruit training is not due to any one cause. In particular, recruiting agencies have not been able to meet the demands of British Army field commanders. The problems of supply and demand have been further exacerbated by the fact that of the 98,000 soldiers in the British Army, 7,000 have been said to be unfit for duty[1]. Overall, the army is reported to be short of 4,000 soldiers; but it is the infantry, which should be composed of 25,000 soldiers, where the crisis is hitting hardest. Almost every one of the infantry 36 battalions is reportedly under strength. To maintain the infantry - who have been most involved since the invasion of Iraq in 2003, and who are deployed in southern Afghanistan[2], at least 5,000 new men are needed annually. Written evidence, considered by a UK parliamentary committee in 2003-2004, showed how widespread and consistent basic training attrition rates were (Phase 1 Wastage 23%), and from BARB scores at the recruit offices (43%). Phase 2 wastage, during specialised training after the completion of basic induction, was much less, averaging 3.4% annually. That fundamental difference between wastage at basic training level and during specialised training is reflected in the difference in predicting success at each level, limited in phase one, better in phase two, (Jacobs, 1997).

ATTRITION IN BRITAIN AFTER BARB

Heavy Losses in the Front Line

Social Attributes: The Hampson Review

The Stress Construct: Kiernan's Attribute Study of 1,000 Infantrymen

Johansen's Quest: Situational Attributes Personal Appraisal Frame

HEAVY LOSSES IN THE FRONT LINE

Recent official details on attrition among British infantry recruits, being the soldiers most likely to be deployed on active service, are also available: and the outcome is consistent with European rates for enlisted volunteers, and equally disturbing. Although similar to the Belgian outcomes, the losses are particularly difficult to sustain, and perhaps to rationalise. *The recruit in an infantry training battalion may have already completed basic training satisfactorily.* Procedural knowledge and

---

1   Figures quoted in this paragraph from an article in The Daily Telegraph 24 February 2008

2   And called upon for any security emergency at home, for example, at a week's notice to man posts during the Olympic games as a result of commercial contract failures.

basic survival skills have been learned. Table14.1[3] sets out the numbers of infantry recruits who commenced their basic training at the United Kingdom Infantry Training Centre at Catterick (ITC(C)) and who failed to complete their training from 2004 to 2010. One third of all those assessed as suitable by BARB *(The British Army Recruit Battery)* and completing other medical and security checks failed to complete the infantry training course. A success in basic training can be a failure as an infantry soldier. The UK Army website currently estimates the overall average cost of recruiting and training is £19,000 per person. From this, the total cost to the taxpayer of infantry training attrition alone from 2004 to 2009 can be estimated at £113.9 million. The costs in other specialist branches can be no less for every dropout, and is probably greater. The financial losses are substantial, but the implications for commanders are, or ought to be, serious enough to raise questions if not of training competence, then of selection policy. Current statistics issued by the MOD website for 2008-12 show the total outflow rate at an average 9.5%, half of which was voluntary, and one quarter leaving after completion of term of service.

Table 14.1: British Infantry Attrition During Recruitment

	Entry	**Failed to Complete**	
Year	**Total**	**Number**	**Percentage**
2009-10	2,969	910	30.7
2008-09	3,828	1,141	29.8
2007-08	3,458	1,180	34.1
2006-07	3,398	1,037	30.5
2005-06	2,517	892	35.4
2004-05	2,420	837	34.6
Totals	**18,590**	**5997**	**32.3**

Note: Figures for 2009-10 are as at 20 November 2009.

If such a large failure rate were experienced in any private organisation, it could not be tolerated for long without the company experiencing considerable financial difficulty. As far as personal costs are concerned, the cost of loss of self-esteem for the failures cannot be estimated, only guessed at, but the knock-on effects to the taxpayer can be calculated, and with some certainty. What is it about specialised infantry training that causes three out of ten previously successful recruits into failures?

SOCIAL ATTRIBUTES: THE HAMPSON REVIEW
Perhaps any major shift of emphasis towards the end of the century comes as no surprise when viewed against the history of military attempts to find the causes of attrition and to introduce remedies. After all, the last complete, and eminently practical account of successful working practices involving personal quality appraisal in all three UK services was fifty years old (Vernon & Parry, 1949, Chapter 9): and finding a copy in print even then was not easy. The high proportion of recruit withdrawals,

---

3   Official figures supplied by a UK government minister in response to a question in the United Kingdom parliament.

sanctioned or voluntary, was the main and proverbial issue, as the figures showed year after year. For decades, no objective measures of military motivation involving personal qualities and dispositions had been in use and a programme of research and development was introduced to seek a solution. Five years after BARB went into use, Hampson (1996, 1997a,b) extended the range of variables from tests to social attributes. She published a longitudinal study of attrition in the army using a cohort of more than 5,000 recruits with three goals. The study consisted of five main parts.(a) review of relevant literature: (b) familiarisation visits to army training regiments (c) collection of interview data: (d) analysis of selection and training data (e) survey of recruits during phase one training.

Table 14.2 reveals how Hampson was able to identify a number of underlying factors that separated survivors from drop-outs in a large scale study of more than 5,000 army recruits while BARB was in full flow. The left hand column shows what verifiable factors, apart from the BARB general training index score, identified those who remained in training, having produced a better performance than those who left the service. In the right hand column are factors having no apparent effect. Because there were more than 5,000 recruits surveyed, there were significant statistical effects but the effect sizes were very small, so that the gain for any one factor seemed no better than the gain from the BARB score. Surprisingly perhaps, no discriminant function analysis involving all of the measures to predict stayers and drop-outs is reported. There is, however, an account of the attributes of the *Personal Qualities Applicant Profile* (PQAP) that was constructed to identify qualities needed for survival.

THE HAMPSON REVIEW

- *To find valid social screening measures for use in selection that would identify recruits likely to leave during Phase I training.*

- *To recommend how the measures could be applied*

- *Thereafter to suggest such changes to the selection process and Phase I training as were likely to reduce the numbers who choose to leave*

Table 14.2: Prediction of Training Risks: Factors Affecting Withdrawals

Significant Differences	No Effective Differences
Personal Qualities Applicant Profile (PQAP)	Member of Uniformed Group (Cadets)
The British Army Recruit Battery (BARB)	Family Links to the Service
NCO Potential	Length of Training
Educational Background	Female or Male Status
Previous Army Experience	Family Reasons for Leaving
Expectations & Socialisation	
The Effects of Relegation	
Timing of Discharge as of Right (DAOR)	

Interviewers who delivered the *Personal Qualities Applicant Profile* gave ratings of personal turnout, sociability, emotional maturity and stability, drive and determination, physical strength, self-reliant experience, reaction to discipline and regimentation, army life experience and, in conclusion, an overall rating. Hampson (loc. cit. p. 198) concludes by advising on the construction of a general purpose structured system to predict individuals likely to leave during Phase 1 training. Although Johansen (2011, 2012) stated that she had no prior knowledge of this work[4] she nevertheless set out during the following decade, to devise just such a framework before introducing an extension to BARB. Her own attempts to reduce attrition are detailed later in the chapter.

THE STRESS CONSTRUCT: KIERNAN'S ATTRIBUTE STUDY

Hampson's findings were to precede those of Kiernan, who enlarged the attribution horizon by examining the role of stress during training. *This moves the focus from pre-enlistment attributes to a study of the process of recruit acceptance in Phase 1.* He confirmed the effects of stress factors in young British Naval and Marine recruits when a number of related studies began to emerge. Stress was the area of concentration where extensive research was carried out by the Royal Navy and details are found in various sources, including Bridger (2008); Bridger, Brasher, Dew& Kilminster (2008); Jackson, Agius, Bridger & Richards (2011); Munnoch & Bridger (2008a); and Munnoch & Bridger (2008b). A search for the means to predict those individuals likely to fall by the wayside because the influences of various stress factors were not in their favour was begun, as it had been in the USA and Belgium, among other NATO organisations. Nevertheless, although originating in the Naval Medical Research Centre, Kiernan's (2011) as yet unpublished doctoral thesis is undoubtedly one of the high points of research into United Kingdom infantry recruit attrition. Two battalions of infantry joining between September 2002 and March 2003 were followed, using a total sample of 1,000 men who were invited to take part. A biographical questionnaire was completed prior to infantry training. Weekly

---

WE ARE BUT WARRIORS FOR THE WORKING DAY

Henry V Act 4 Scene 3

'Within the entire population, 11.3% (n=112) did not know their father; however 84.3% (n=834) came from homes where their father was in employment, with only 4.4% (n=43) of fathers having not worked. The majority of the sample (53.1%, n=517) achieved GCSE (General Certificate of Secondary Education) results of grade C or below, with only 14.8% achieving grade B or above in all subjects. Most notable was that over half of all respondents (53.3%, n=533) reported being in trouble with the police prior to enlistment.'

(Kiernan, loc. cit. p. 103)

---

4   Personal communication January 21, 2013

monitoring occurred and the training outcome (pass/fail) was recorded. Variables in five biodata categories *(Demographic & Physical Measurement, Education, Outdoor Education, Non-Physical Activity and Conduct and Behaviour)* were used to examine their association with training outcome.

Kiernan's Results: Recruit Enclaves

The results were compelling. Of the study cohort, more than a third of the recruits (n=362) failed to complete infantry training. Within this failure group six out of ten left at their own request and one in seven were dismissed. In all, seventy-five percent of training attrition was attributable to difficulties in adapting to service life, with recruits either choosing to leave or being compulsorily discharged. These proportions are remarkably consistent with those reported by Tranent & Laurence (1993), twenty years ago in the United States. However, a small minority, less than five percent, were transferred to other training depots even if they were unsuitable for infantry training. Most revealing, perhaps were Kiernan's insights into the formative years of those volunteers who aspired to life in infantry regiments, specially noted in the insert. These boundaries define a recruit enclave of minority, if not sub-cultural, social status. Even so, Kiernan shows that there were other critical self-report biodata factors associated with higher odds of failure: absence of female siblings; aggressive coping strategies; use of the drug ecstasy; evenings per week spent at the family home prior to enrolment; truancy, frequently changing schools, and unsatisfactory classroom behaviour (Kiernan, loc cit. pp.103-105). Kiernan integrated all of his findings: first to find out whether prediction of failure was practicable; and thereby to develop an increased understanding of the impact that antecedent factors and training experiences contributed to training failure. In addition, the analysis of comments from interviews with recruits leaving and commandants' reasons for failure suggested that there was *a marked difference between the wellbeing needs and emotions of recruits who failed training and the behavioural prescriptions for British Army Infantry success.*

> ## 'HE WHICH HATH NO STOMACH TO THIS FIGHT, LET HIM DEPART'
>
> **Henry V Act 4 Sc.3**
>
> *'Cognitive dissonance and varying extremes of stress were reported by those recruits that failed during the transition to military life.'*
>
> **(Kiernan, loc. cit. p. 4).**

Custom and Conflict

Although Kiernan was able to use the results to predict the odds of success and failure for each recruit following in-depth interviews, and to construct a biodata screening questionnaire, the improvement in predicting attrition was still, in his view, not large enough to justify operational use. Nevertheless, the elements in a broad-based framework for attrition among infantry - culture conflict, minority recruits versus the ruling army establishment - emerge from the work as a whole and these are definitive. Not since Schneider's work in 1947 on the social dynamics of disability in training has there been such a sensitive and accurate analysis of the organisation of a military command environment with its echoes of and analogies with life in total institutions (Goffman, 1961) which Kiernan clarifies and discusses at length.

JOHANSEN'S QUEST: SITUATIONAL ATTRIBUTES

More was to following Britain after the turn of the century. According to Johansen (2011), the commonly held beliefs, officially sanctioned, about drop outs during initial training were that they lacked commitment due to poor motivation. In particular the values of recruits and military culture were in conflict, partly because entrants had no realistic idea of what they were signing up to. Moreover, many could not cope with elementary training demands, such as physical readiness, inability to follow verbal orders and comprehend simple texts. Finally, personal histories, lack of support and family concerns also took their toll.

> **JOHANSEN'S REVISIONS:**
>
> **Situational Grading**
>
> **Personal Appraisal Frame**
>
> **Private Enterprise**
>
> **No More BARB after 2014?**

Given such a perspective, Johansen (2011, 2012) provides two short accounts at conferences of current recruiting practices in the UK where BARB still runs its course: and what the future may hold following a complete revision. During the past decade, she directed studies to improve selection in the British Army by supplementing BARB's composite score of suitability for initial training (GTI) with appropriate ratings of personal fitness for purpose. The need for re-appraisal was prompted by a number of factors affecting attrition, among them high drop-out in initial training, a recruitment surge acerbated by a shortage of training places, and first-come entry practices where quantity was valued over quality. Administrative changes were required; but only if valid measures of personal qualities could be added and were shown to reduce wastage.

Johansen's Personal Appraisal Frame.
Two conference presentations by Johansen (loc. cit.) contain outlines with some results of what constituted a major change of focus during the past decade. Applications would be followed by at least two phases, attendance at the recruitment office with new selection tests and a regional residential appraisal centre. The decisions to accept or reject were made in the second stage after medical physical and behaviour during a number of team tasks were incorporated into an overall grade of recruit potential.

Only the briefest indications of what was involved in the various measurements are visible in the published visual presentations. However, the final acceptance criterion was a grading measure, apparently a weighted composite of best-fitting assessments. Four domains are indicated by the supposed structure. Three of those, labelled commitment, effort and suitability apparently owe their origins to the *Individual Development & Assessment Tool (IDST)* originally developed at the selection centre and involving ratings on a number of qualities deemed essential to success. BARB, basic skills and run time[5] continued to define attainment. All the other qualities appear to emanate from the *Individual Development & Assessment Tool* whose qualities included ratings from various sources on *selfless commitment, discipline, courage, integrity, respect, military awareness and expectations, loyalty, motivation for joining, personal circumstances, resilience, maturity.*

Table 14.3: Current Two-Stage British Army Recruitment Procedures

Primary Stage Recruiting Office	Secondary Stage Selection Centres
BARB General Trainability Index	Medical
Literacy	Physical Tasks
Numeracy	Ice Breaker
English Speaking and Listening	Military Lesson
Interviews (3)	Selection Officer's Interview
Individual Development &	Team Tasks
Assessment Tool (IDST)	Overall Grading Measure

    The grades were awarded on a five category descending scale from A through D, and information about their effectiveness in reducing attrition is given in Johansen (2012). Figure 14.1 shows the percentage of two categories of withdrawal, voluntary and 'unsuitable' for each type of grade awarded from 2009 to 2011, involving 14,126 recruits. The graph is linear with percentage increases of almost the same size for each successive grade. Summed over the two categories of withdrawal types, A grade soldiers (16% of recruits) had a one in five chance of withdrawal, B grades (51% of recruits) one in four, and C (27% of recruits) and D (6%of recruits) grades, one in three.

Figure 14.1: Percentages Voluntary and Unsuitable 2009-11 (N =14,126)

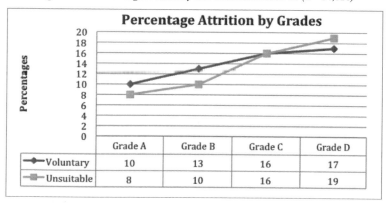

	Grade A	Grade B	Grade C	Grade D
Voluntary	10	13	16	17
Unsuitable	8	10	16	19

---

5   The run time is the time it takes a candidate to run a mile and a half at the selection centre. For the IDST Johansen took data from a year's recruits, divided them into 6 groups and then allocated a score of 1-6 depending on how fast they ran.

Because only one in six applicants received an A grade, the costs of attrition are very dependent on withdrawals from lower echelons when the numbers are counted overall. Just how feasible it would be during a time of low recruitment to reject all except the highest grades is a moot and possibly political point. The linear patterns of results of grading were consistent in the four regional centres throughout the United Kingdom. Johansen also admitted that in the five year period, 24,570 applicants were graded *after attending the residential centres*, but only 18,109 entered training subsequently, a loss of 26 percent overall, to be added to the cost of failures at initial and subsequent training. Attendance at the residential centres was a powerful intervening, perhaps causal event. Attrition becomes, as her work shows, a category of considerable width, unlike falling off a bicycle, which has no discernible width whatsoever. Finally, Johansen's 2012 presentation exposes a major departure from the traditional organisation of military selection in Britain. The government has contracted it out to private enterprise. The effects can only be guessed at.

THE USA STUDIES: WARS OF ATTRITION?

If proof of the almost universally high attrition rates regardless of service arm during recruitment were required, there are official reports in the United States Congress. Gebicke (1997a, 1997b) in published testimony to a United States Congressional Sub-Committee gives a detailed accounting of the high costs of attrition. The drop-out rates of US military recruits during basic training for 2002 showed the Army and Navy lost 14% of recruits, the Marine Corps 12% and the Air Force 7%. In every situation, recruits drop out for physical reasons, including injuries: but many have previously undisclosed physical or mental ailments, as well as performance-related difficulties. In the USA, where figures are available, the costs are similar to those quoted for the UK. To recruit new service members exceeds $10,000 per person, while the cost of initial entry training is $35,000 on average.

Table 14.4: The US Military Recruitment Stages

Recruiter Contact	Selection	Classification	Swear-In/
• Ability screens	• AFQT	• Job & Career Info.	• Swear-In
• Moral, financial,	• Background	• School guarantee	• Delayed Entry
and educational	affidavits	• Ship date	Program
screens	• Medical exam	• ASVAB scores	• Ship to RTC

Table 14.4 is an outline of the four stage allocation programme (NATO, 2007, Section 2H) used in the United States, very similar to systems used elsewhere, and indicative of the attempt to assess relevant attributes, based upon the history of success and failure in recruitment, seen in both historical and immaculate detail in Trent's 1992 work.

Table 14.5: Trent's 1992 Breakdown of Attrition in The US Military, 1992

Criterion Measure Status	No.	Percent	Criterion Measure Status	No.	Percent
Total Followed Up	*50,513*	*100*	*Attrition Reason*		
Completed Term	**36,053**	**71.4**	**Erroneous Enlistment**	**603**	**1.2**
Total Attrition	**14,460**	**28.6**	**Fraudulent Entry**	**596**	**1.2**
			Pregnancy/Parenthood	**837**	**1.7**
			Total Incidental	*2,036*	*(4.1)*
Attrition Reason					
Training Performance	**2,588**	**5.1**	*Attrition Reason*		
Medical Discharge	**2,341**	**4.6**	**Desertion**	**157**	**0.3**
Behavioral Unsuitability	**2,374**	**4.7**	**Sexual Deviance**	**220**	**0.4**
Alcoholism/Illegal Drugs	**1,727**	**3.4**	**Civil/Criminal/Military Court**	**350**	**0.7**
Serious Offense	**1,412**	**2.7**	**Other**	**1,255**	**2.4**
Total Behavioural	*10,442*	*(20.5)*	*Total Miscellaneous*	*1, 982*	*(3.8)*

Table 14.5 is adapted from a breakdown originally provided by Trent and Quenette (1992).

USA ATTRITION: QUESTIONNAIRE CONFLICTS

Trent's Lost Case
ASAP

Project A
The ABLE Questions

Alley and Matthews
VOICE

Department Of Defense
Calls it Quits

Kubisiak's Tri-Stage
Analyses: A Last-Ditch
Attempt at Clarity?

TRENT'S LOST CASE

Unquestionably, in the United States, the most comprehensive of a series of studies of attrition, its origins and attempts to deal with it in all its manifestations occurred during the period 1986 -1993; and published as a comprehensive report by the Department of Defense (DOD), edited by Trent and Laurence (1993). The results of this work are discussed in more detail later, but among its references is a prior paper by Trent and Quenette (1992) in which details (loc. cit. pp. 6-8) of a three-year follow up of a sample of more than 50,000 recruits derived from an initial survey of more than 120,000 are given. For a three-month period, service applicants for active duty in the United States military (N = 120,175) were administered one of two forms of a questionnaire known as the *Armed Service Applicability Profile* (ASAP). Each ASAP form contained 130 items about personal, school, and work experiences in a multiple choice format. The military performance of subsequent accessions, a huge total (N = 55,675), was tracked during their first three years of service, a remarkable effort at what cost of energy and satisfaction can hardly be imagined.

Nowhere are there comparable details of *reasons for attrition* with such large numbers of personnel. Moreover, the general pattern of reasons and relative importance has been unchanged over the past two decades (NATO, 2007 Section 2H2). Behavioural failures accounted for 20 percent, and incidental and miscellaneous reasons together were less than half this amount, showing that 72 percent of all losses within a three-year follow-up period were dismissals for behavioural reasons, not deemed to be voluntary. That time in the services was to be was to be but a short part of occupational history is the grim revelation (Trent & Quenette, loc. cit. p.7) that 25 percent of losses (3615 of 14,460) occurred within 57 days and 50 percent (7230) of losses had separated within 344 days of entry.

A Succession of Rearguard Actions: TRENT ASAP, ASP, ABLE, CSM, VOICE:
The road to a small, reliable and valid number of honestly answered questions needed to provide a reduction in wastage was to prove, and still is, long, rocky and tortuous with no guarantee of success or approval. In the Trent and Laurence volume, no fewer than four different attempts were made to introduce questions that would reduce wastage in a ten year period. They included attempts by all three service arms, each apparently with its own team of scientists; and they produced ASAP (Trent, 1993), an *Adaptability Screening Profile* (ASP) adapted from ABLE (White, Nord, Mael & Young, 1993), and a *Compensatory Screening Model* (CSM) outlined by McBride, (1993) and VOICE (Alley et al, 1976, 1977).

Table 14.6: ASAP Questions With Maximum Discriminability

Total Item Discrimination Cluster

Social	*Vocational*
1 Smoke	12 Have had more full time jobs
2 Start smoking early	15 Not plan on making service a career
4 Have a tattoo	13 Have applied for more jobs
10 Stay out more on weekends	
Educatioal	*Criminal*
3 Suspended from school at younger age	11 Have been in trouble with police
7 Have thought about quitting school	
8 Parents unhappy about school grades	
9 Lower grades in school	
14 School grades lower than they expected	

ASAP in The Front Line
In retrospect, no lengthy campaign to reduce wastage by using follow-up methods of precision and thoroughness has ever matched that of Trent and his associates in the decade prior to 1993, when the final report was published showing how adequately the issues had been covered in the numerous reports, published and unpublished: Trent, (1987); Trent, Atwater, & Abrahams (1986); Trent, Folchi, & Sunderman (1991); Trent, & Quenette (1992); Walker, (1988); Waters, (1989); Wise, Hough, Szena, Trent, & Keyes (1989).

After producing parallel forms of ASAP (*Armed Services Adaptability Profile*), carrying out checks for reliability, investigating fake response potential, ethnic and male-female fairness, and follow-ups in all three service arms to establish predictive validity, Trent concluded (1993, pp. 88 et seq.) that after a five-year period, there was a .64 *d* effect size score difference separating successful completion of service term and those who failed to complete, and that a useful correlation of .32 over the long term existed between ASAP scores and staying-in and leaving for any reason. Despite all the positive signs, the DOD abandoned research into ASAP. According to Trent, this decision was the result of concerns that use of the form would produce an undesirable climate of faking, coaching, test compromise and producing unreliable norms for military entry (loc cit. p. 93). It is worthwhile listing the most powerful questions in Trent's ASAP form, because they constituted a small number of the proposed total of 50 in each of two parallel forms. These have been grouped for convenience but their original numbers have been retained because they are the rank order of their power to discriminate between survivors and drop-outs over the review period. The questions are undoubtedly personal and depend on veracity for their effectiveness. Opacity is not a part of their function. Clearly, they could be isolated and coached, especially if they were published on any website, official or otherwise, leading to mendacity. Intuitively, they may seem to make sense, but their very nature as empirical rather than theoretical outcomes was the subject of much discussion, leading to the attempt to produce ASP from the constructs in ABLE, and in all probability, the compromise CSM model that relied on verifiable and historical facts.

ABLE and CSM: Logistics
The other rival models, described fully in the volume by Trent and Laurence, were produced by different, and reportedly rival organisations. The Army research group provided a form (ASP) based on the constructs of ABLE, the US Army's attempt to produce a personality screen with predictive validity for training success. The CSM model was devised to explore the possibility of admitting to the services those who did not have the basic educational requirement of a high school diploma. McBride (1993, p. 166) outlines the model as one where each applicant's attrition risk would be estimated individually, and the screening decision would depend on the probability of that risk and not solely on the level of education reached. The risk equation could contain age, aptitude scores, marital status, and other relevant variables in addition to education level.

ALLEY'S VOICE: Job Dissatisfaction Unheard
The Air Force too had a VOICE in all of this (Alley, Berberich, & Wilbourn. 1977; Alley, Wilbourn, & Berberich 1976; Alley & Matthews, 1982). VOICE, perhaps the most comprehensive military vocational interest inventory ever devised, described in immaculate technical detail by Alley and his associates, has within it a Predicted Job Satisfaction Score (PJS) devised by relating VOICE scores to subsequent ratings of job satisfaction by the recruits. A vast, virtually unreported study by Matthews (1982) followed 36,759 male and 12,909 female entrants for 36 months in their initial tour of duty. At each 12 month interval there was a linear increase in the numbers who left the service corresponding to the degree of predicted dissatisfaction with the job. Lowest job satisfaction scorers rates for leaving were 16, 32, and 40 percent at 12, 24 and 36 months. Corresponding leaving rates for the highest PJS scorers who were

happy at their work were 5, 15 and 26 percent, yielding substantial odds-ratios. Search of the literature shows no sign of operational implementation of the PJS score subsequently, although studies with forms of VOICE adapted for army use showed that vocational interest scores had value in predicting job efficiency (Campbell & Knapp,, Chs. 10, 16).

Gebicke's Intuition: It's The Treatment, Stupid!

.......about one-third of the separating recruits we interviewed told us that they were subjected to "humiliating" treatment and that this treatment contributed to their desire to leave the military. We were told that drill instructors frequently used obscene language, although such language is prohibited by service regulations. Although we cannot generalize from our interviews, what we heard from recruits reinforced Army, Air Force, and Rand studies, which concluded that negative motivation has a detrimental effect on some recruits' desire to stay in the military. (loc. cit 1997a, Ch.0. para.6)

DEPARTMENT OF DEFENSE DECLARES CEASE FIRE

These are by far the most comprehensive data sets on a perennial attrition problem. This and other data was widely available when the DOD[6] investigated the enduring attrition problem and Gebicke's (1997a, 1997b) reports were tabled. Gebicke begins the first of these with a summary statement outlining the reasons for failure to survive basic training losses with a total loss of 25,000 in a single year. The median loss rate over all service arms was 11.9% in the first six months. Gebicke ends his executive overview with a closing remark that some may find surprising after the work by Trent and his associates on introducing biodata.

'The main reasons for the high attrition rate during the first 6 months are that (1) the services' screening of applicants for disqualifying medical conditions or pre-service drug use is inadequate and (2) recruits fail to perform adequately because they are in poor physical condition for basic training or lack motivation. Although the services are greatly concerned about attrition, their goals for reducing attrition are based on inconsistent, incomplete data and are unrealistic.' (loc.cit. 1997a, Ch.0. para. 1)

He concludes his statement with this verdict.

'Currently, DOD defines a "quality" recruit as one who has a high school degree and has scored in the upper mental categories on the Armed Forces Qualification Test. Despite historically meeting DOD's benchmarks for quality, all of the services continue to experience early attrition, thus suggesting that certain elements that make a quality recruit are not captured in the current standards.'   (loc. cit. 1997a, Ch.9 para. 0)

Lack of 'capture' is the alleged and official reason. What was there to capture that is not already in the net provided by ASVAB, interviews, search for criminal records and a medical examination? Perhaps Gebicke himself was aware of the

6   Department of Defense

hazards of recruit culture being in the hands of instructors, rather than in the heads of the recruits in basic training.

KUBISIAK's
TRIPARTITE
FRAME

Pre-Enlistment

Remedial

Organisational

THE 30 YEARS SEARCH FOR ATTRITION

One might have hoped for victory over the enemy of attrition a decade later. In fact, the published record shows that these four lengthy attempts were the forerunners of a series of many to capture essentials by interventions from each branch of the US armed services. Studies to reduce attrition, reviewed dispassionately and constructively by Kubisiak and co-authors (2009). A summary is in Table 14.7.

Table 14.7: USA Attrition Intervention Frameworks

Dimensions	Strategies
1: Pre-Enlistment	**Realistic Job Previews**
	Smart Allocation Systems
2: Remedial	**Quality of Life Early Warnings**
	Counselling
	Academic Interventions
	Physical Fitness Interventions
	Incentive Programs
3: Organisational	**Leadership Strategies and Policies**
	Radical Training Regimen Relativity

Three phases in a search for a cure were revealed, pre-enlistment, remedial, and organisational . When subdivided, with nine categories in total. Kubisiak *discovered more than forty approaches in the period following Gebicke's reports.* These are grouped in an intervention framework (see Sections 1 and 2) of seven categories: *Counseling, Realistic Job Previews, Social Support Programs, Leadership Strategies and Policies, Physical Fitness Interventions, Remedial Programs and Incentive Programs.*

Analysis revealed qualified support for most approaches, except psychiatric interviews, with most favourable odds-ratio outcomes associated with remedial companies during recruitment focussing on morale improvement. *It seems hardly possible that no fewer than 59 different approaches had taken place since the pioneering Trent and Laurence account in 1993, many with clear evidence of wastage reduction, and not always for the same reason.* Screening, counselling, interventions, behavioural therapy, leadership modification, training courses have all severally seemed to increase the chances that recruits will complete their terms of service. But these activities were not part of a coherent and planned effort. Like Topsy, they just growed. Kubisiak's third division, organisational, recognised that although there had been positive gains by altering the treatment of recruits, nothing would happen unless policies changed to make them extensive. Action to apply the results as part of a coherent recruitment policy has not been forthcoming in spite of consistent international attention by all NATO countries (Lescrève, 2007).

EUROPE: BELGIAN AND GERMAN VOLUNTEERS

BELGIUM SINCE 2006

The 2006 introduction of the GCTB series in Belgium has been the reason for official interest in the validity of the tests; and data showing their effects was provided in Chapter 10. As part of the process, volunteer dropout rates among those making the grade on the GCTB tests, followed by medical examination and interviews by psychologists were recorded between 2007 and 2010 (de Franc, 2010). Of a total of 3,477 enlisted other ranks personnel for whom records existed, 1269, or *36.4 Percent had left the service*, and 2208 remained. Among Fusiliers, elite combat troops, four out of ten among 316 entrants failed to complete basic training. Of officers, the wastage rate was 17.3 percent of a 428 total. By any standard, these unexplained losses are hard to accommodate in a country with a relatively small defence force. One should also remember that Belgium's state-of-the art batch processing model with all its sophistication (see Chapter X), introduced by Lescrève, and had been in operation for more than a decade, but the losses seemed comparable with those of far less sophisticated methods of allocation. As a reminder of the completeness of the Belgian Defence Force recruit framework, the outline first shown in Chapter 2 is repeated here.

Table 14.8: Outline of Three-day Selection Sequence in BDF

Day1	**Day2**
Information (Part 1)	Medical Examinations[7]
Intellectual Potential Test[8]	*Lunch*
Lunch	Physical Fitness Tests
Motivation Test	**Day3**
Information (Part 2)	Interviews
Biodata Form[9]	
Additional Tests (as required)	

Typically, procedures such as these, as witnessed in the UK and USA have formed the basis of relatively inconclusive attempts to predict outcomes from self-report biodata questionnaires, social background checks, criminal records, interest inventories, situational exercises. Examples of how they might succeed, however, were provided in the visionary compensatory screening models, introduced 20 years ago by Lescrève, (1993, 1995a, 1995b, 1996,1997a, 1997b, 1998) but evident only in their unique use in Belgium. From 2006 as commander of a special unit investigating attrition in Belgium, Lescrève was instrumental in the production of the NATO (2007) major review of recruitment internationally.

---

7   Candidates who pass the medical selection are admitted to the physical fitness tests. The others are sent home after the lunch break.

8   Candidates who pass the Intellectual potential test may continue. The others are sent home after the lunch break.

9   Experimental tests or tests for specific entries.

GERMANY FOLLOWING THE END OF CONSCRIPTION IN 2011.

When the multiple parallel form test series was trialled in Germany in 2000-2003, the Bundeswehr was a conscripted force. This policy meant that the national samples trialled could be regarded as representative, establishing firm anchor norms for future development. The conscripts had to serve at least six, but could volunteer to remain for as many as twenty-three months. This situation was to change irrevocably. The last 12,000 conscripts entered the services on January 3, 2011, and by July of that year, only volunteers were to be recruited for the Bundeswehr. The policy was not without debate, but once in place, it evoked much interest from the press, once the first cohort of volunteers reported on July 3, 2011.

The first available news report (*The Local,* 2011) was about early attrition. It stated that the daily newspaper *Hannoversche Allgemeine Zeitung (HAZ)* reported on Friday 22 July that 14 percent of recruits in one battalion in Lower Saxony had quit in the preceding three weeks of the new system. At a Berlin battalion, the drop-out rate was said to be 10 percent. Officially, a third of withdrawals were for medical reasons, but reports of disenchantment with life in a recruit barracks were mentioned, including one reported incident of recruits standing to attention for two hours before entering a building to answer a single question. Whatever the truth of these allegations, there was more tangible evidence of drop-outs to come in the newspaper providing news in English about Germany (*Strategy Page,* 2011). Its report on December 26 revealed that of the first batch of 3,459 volunteers admitted on July 3, 2011, close to 1,000 of them (28%) had left the service. Apparently, one in five was asked to leave because of unsuitability, but others left because they had received a better job offer in the interim, or had received word that they had been accepted for college and university entry. Lack of official figures to date has meant reliance on such reported sources, but no denials of the initially reported drop-out rates and circumstances have been reported in the press. All that might reasonably be concluded is the similarity of the rate of attrition to other, official statistics from neighbouring and allied NATO countries.

THE LESCRÈVE QUESTION

What is it about first phase recruit training that makes attribute assessment redundant?

INCREASING INTERNATIONAL CONCERNS

To date, presentations at the International Military Test Association (IMTA) annual conferences since 2004, namely, Aubecq (2010); Bownds & Mehay (2004); Fang & Bender (2010); Fisher (2011); Harris, White, Eshwar & Mottern, J. A. (2005); Irvine (2004); Koundakjian (2012); Lane (2006); Latchman (2008); Latchman & Michaud (2010); Latchman & Arseneau (2012); Lee (2010); and Lescrève (2007) show that, across national boundaries, services and personnel ranks, they are in every respect searching for the means to predict comparable rates of attrition and to deal with it in ways that are fit for purpose. In all of these reports, just as in the UK, the USA, and in the overall view of NATO (2007), there is no evidence of an effective policy of implementation following the extraordinary amount of research carried out in the past thirty years. Typically, studies such as these are inconclusive attempts to predict outcomes from self-report biodata questionnaires, social background checks, criminal records, interest inventories, situational exercises. All of these approaches raise a basic question, which in deference to his leading role in the area of attrition for NATO, one might define as: *The Lescrève Question.*

Seeking an answer is all the more important because of the strong evidence of the relative, even if variable, success of cognitive tests in predicting second-phase training outcomes, once survival is assured. Briefly, recruit basic training must today be recognised as a near-random intervening variable that nullifies all attempts to use it as a criterion of selection success or failure.

INSIDE THE CULTURE OF ATTRITION

Possibly, all attempts to identify those at risk of leaving are doomed because the nature of the variable is, like weather, an empirical one without any theory for its definition or accurate forecasting. To sum up, almost invariably, recruits are required to complete a number of cognitive tests of training capability, but the process does not end there. Medical examinations are undertaken during security checks. The degree and extensiveness of the system is a matter for each nation to decide. Clearly, even if BARB, ASVAB, and other national aptitude tests help to predict training success of those who remain in the service, they do not predict early attrition in a military culture. The social web page has had its effects on how applications are processed. For example, a current MOD website encourages application on line, using a 17 item role discovery questionnaire, asking personal questions, giving advice and details of local recruitment offices. Seldom, however, has screening routinely extended to determining emotional stability and temperamental suitability (Deu, Srinivasan and Srinivasan, 2004) for military entry, although the Belgian authorities are a notable exception. What is it about the motivation required for success in basic training, the first encounter with the requirements of military cultures, that might make screening prior to or during military service a matter of success?

There is, of course, a second parallel culture with its behavioural prescriptions. This is the culture of main-line psychology itself, with its rites of initiation, rites of passage and sanctioned procedures. Psychologists, though, have no status conferred on them by the *University of Life* that exists in the culture of basic training, because they seldom, if ever, undertake it or live in a total residential environment within a command culture. Few academic or occupational psychologists have completed any form of military basic training, although perhaps some psychologists have worked in prisons, and some less fortunate than others may have attended command-style private boarding schools.

The methodological lessons from many years of work in cross-cultural psychology (Irvine, 1986; Irvine & Berry, 1989); and more recently, work in the field of health-related quality of life (see under Irvine et al., 1990-1994, Irvine 2002, 2004). are immediately applicable to assessing motivational aspects of basic training and service on deployment, although main-line psychology has been slow to apply them, often regarding its techniques as interesting oddities. The lessons of cross-cultural psychology are simple. If psychologists are to provide credible measures of motivation for use by military commanders, they must first acquire probationary status by acquiring an insider's view of the target culture. A little imagination transposes this advice to basic training battalions. Training manuals uncover what is demanded at what stage; the physical activities on and off the parade ground, and off-duty recreations reveal energy levels. In the squad billet what all people wear as off-duty personal gear and equipment, what they download to their MP players, and forms of discourse can be observed. The degrees to which recruits are able to conform to demands and conventions define them as accepted squad members, or isolate them as 'outcasts'.

Four Corners of the Recruit Universe
Websites by experts offering advice to recruits prior to induction provide a key to understanding why so much importance is attached to behaving in new and perhaps unaccustomed styles, like operating in a foreign land with a different currency, with local customs to be observed and rules of interaction to be scrupulously followed. The prescriptions of contributors about appropriate behaviour during training are undoubtedly accurate: and they are overwhelmingly procedural. Four elements of recruit training define the content of what has to be captured is basic training; and they set boundaries to the kind of data that could be collected to account for attrition.

Self Esteem and Military Structure
Without well-being derived from accomplishments during training, life becomes progressively harder for recruits everywhere. For more than 50 years, it has been well known that in social contexts of 24/7 barracks-based training with no counter-control on the behaviour of instructors, many recruits enjoy a poor quality of life: and are destabilized when unable to cope with adverse physical and degrading social experiences (Schneider, 1947). Official accounts in a UK House of Commons Defence Committee Report (HMSO, 2005) are illustrated in the next page insert.

If one were to devise a questionnaire about life as a recruit, opinion within military culture is sure about one domain that needs definition and subsequent appraisal. Self-esteem arising from group status in training and/or combat is the most widely recognised intervening variable in retention. Occupational stress is the construct universally associated with initial training demands. Historical and current resources underpin this conclusion (Bridger, Dew, & and Kilminster, 2008; Bridger, Dew, Munnoch and Kilminster, 2009; Bridger, Dew, Sparshott, and Kilminster, 2010; Merton, 1940; Schneider, 1947; Vernon and Parry, 1949; Irvine, 1995, Irvine, Kyllonen & Roberts, 2000). Self-esteem can be assessed using direct and opaque psychometric methods, as the detailed case studies among recruits, and complementary evidence, have shown (Irvine, 2004a, 2004b, 2005, 2006). How self-esteem is regulated within

---

THE FOUR CORNERS

Basic training constitutes a unique and universal military acculturation experience, closed to outsiders

Basic training is a rite of initiation conferring status in a 24/7 command environment

Achieved and ascribed group status both determine levels of self-esteem in recruits

Personal self-esteem is a critical determinant of individual training survival

OFFICIAL COMMENTARY FROM THE HOUSE OF COMMONS, 2005

SNCOs and JNCO s provide the majority of training and supervision. The training is designed to induct trainees into the military ethos and develop their self-discipline, teamwork and fitness. Training days are highly structured, no leave is given and the immaturity of recruits is recognised through high supervision levels both during working hours and out-of-hours. (HMSO, 2005, p 119, para. 110).

'We heard evidence of recruits who wanted to leave the Army outside of this time restriction who, having been refused permission to leave, went AWOL. On their eventual return to their training unit they were put on a charge.   Mr James told us of the experience of one particular recruit:

'*…there was an article in a newspaper about a boy who was going AWOL from Deepcut . Every time he went back, he was being beaten up….I was put in touch with the boy directly and spoke to him on a number of occasions. The story he told me was quite horrific. So I phoned Ron Laden [Commanding Officer at RLC Deepcut], and I said: "Ron, remember what you told me—the WRVS, the WI, the Army, reputation—your fellows are just knocking hell out of this lad. What are you doing? Why are you doing it?" "Yeah", he said, "but he's useless; he just keeps running away". I said: "But you keep beating him up." "No, no, no," he said, "he just runs away all the time". I said: "Ron, honestly, I have spoken to the boy and if he is no good send him away from the Army. Why are you doing this?'(HMSO loc. cit. p. 17, para.103)*

'*We believe that it is better for Service men and women to be committed and motivated while training for their chosen career and note the potential risks to the wellbeing of recruits being in the physically and mentally demanding training environment against their will.' (HMSO loc. cit.p.18, para.105)*

the culture itself is the clue to successful identification of those who will fail to achieve it by being outcasts.

The Structural Backbone: Squaddy Attributes
Self-esteem derives almost completely from being an accepted member of the squad. The colloquial slang term 'squaddy' which is a *positive affiliative/familial diminutive* derived from the squad, or the basic operational combat unit. *Positive affiliative/familial* (cf. Jacquie, Charlie, Freddy, Maggie) diminutives generally have 'y' or 'ie' endings, and they are particularly prevalent in British soccer and cricket teams. A nickname with such an ending usually is a sign of acceptance if not actual endearment. A headline in the UK Newspaper of the Year for 2012[10] on July 16 reads "Calls for furious *squaddies* to get Games bonuses" when a security firm's failure to provide staff for the London Olympic

---

10   The i Newspaper, published by Independent Print Ltd. London, UK.

Games had to be solved by calling in regiments newly returned from deployment in Afghanistan, resulting in leave cancellations. There is no doubt from the headline that the soldiers deserved endearment. They were not to be described as 'troops' in a monosyllable.

How does everyday language describe negative reactions to prospective or actual failures? The security firm failing to produce the required number of agents for safeguarding Olympic events was accused of 'staggering stupidity'. Its executives were likely to be labelled in negative terms using *negative affect mono-syllabic derogatories* (none of which, note, have affiliative diminutive endings)[11]. It would certainly be customary in platoons to talk of the people responsible for costly calamities, as 'prats' (ineffectual, clumsy persons cf. pratfall falling on one's prat or back-side); 'nerds' (irritating and/or strange persons who do not conform to group mores); 'wimps' (ineffectual persons of weak and somewhat effeminate nature) or 'geeks' (peculiar or otherwise dislikeable persons, who, in comparison with the group, are overly intellectual). These labels are common in military language, when it is not putting emotion under a stiff-upper-lip quarantine. There are other characteristics that will produce stigmatisation from within the squad, including undue deference to authority, and the use of barrack-room law for self-advancement. Superior officers are most likely to describe such platoon members as 'unlikely to be career soldiers', and, therefore, in 'Thatcherite' language, as 'not one of us'. Once again, the common language of the target culture contains three themes and criteria for identifying outsiders: lack of fitness; lack of affiliation; and lack of masculine identity.

My Mates Image
A second, confirmatory metaphor about what good 'squaddies' are like was provided by a television commercial about *Marmite*, a yeast extract that is 'flavourful and nutritious and good-for-you'. The commercial showed pictures and images of 'squaddies' road-running and shouting in time to their paces and in unison 'Marmite - My Mate!' almost in the same cadence as Left-Right, both parts of the phrase being indistinguishable from each other (*Ma-Mite*) in the south-eastern England dialect used in the commercial. The medium and the message are built around three important aspects and recurring images of basic training in the commercial - physical fitness, affiliation (team-membership, my-mateship), and masculinity. Masculine predispositions are not to be confused with homosexuality, because traditional military role-behaviour is overtly, and often by regulation, heterosexual in its orientation.
Squaddy members are the first to notice signs of possible failure, because in small, closed, total environments, performance is invariably public. Hence, potential or actual incompetents are both easy to identify. They are perceived as difficult to carry in a squad competition; or when extra drill is required by the whole squad because of failure or perceived shortcomings by any one individual; or when lives may be at risk during deployment on active service. Individuals whose dispositions are unsuited to the requirements of the culture as revealed by its popular image - the trinity of fitness, affiliation and masculinity - will be isolated and subject to various formal (superior officer) sanctions or peer ('squaddies') social restriction. These will serve to improve their status or to cause their removal.

---

11   Nick Buckles, head of the security firm described by Simon Hoggart, The Guardian, 17 July, 2012 as a 'stunned fish', fish being a monosyllable.

Measurement and Intervention

The selection question from the perspective of an insider's view of the problem of adaptation to military culture to achieve status, then becomes one of determining two outcomes: one of defining propensities to fitness for purpose, affiliation and masculinity (at the very least) as part of a personal quality structure (dependent variables), and the other of measuring personal quality success level (criterion specification) within a command or empowering structure. The psychological screening problem reformulates the operational form of the outcomes in this way. If the dimensions indicated by the insider's view are valid, there are at least two issues.

- What combinations of these qualities are required as prerequisites for entry?

- Do these qualities in training and subsequent deployment roles prevent departure by decree (involuntary discharge) or by inclination (voluntary discharge)?

Consistent with the process undergone in creating multiple parallel form cognitive tests, both theoretical and administrative reviews were needed to find plausible answers to the difficulties of identifying those at risk of dropping out in basic training, where attrition is most severe. The next chapter outlines these approaches.

CHAPTER 15

ATTRITION SCREENS: CONVENTION, PRACTICE, THEORY

THEORY COMPONENTS IN THE PROCESS OF ATTRITION

From analytical psychology diagnoses on the insights gained by extended interviews that reveal more than the subject knows

From learning theory, the need to observe behaviour in context; how to apply universal methods of shaping and fixing desirable patterns of behaviour; and how to avoid inducing neurotic and anxiety-laden states is relevant in the appraisal of training procedures. Or, if training procedures are not modifiable, to select those who are dispositionally capable of surviving in less than optimal training situations

From biological models, the extent to which outcome behaviour may be predicted by measuring only a few robust, and fundamental personality dimensions

From social interaction theory the need to account for observed differences in success rates from platoon to platoon and battalion to battalion in terms of social pressures and forces amounting to occupational stress within the organisation itself

In early chapters, underlying cognitive models of attention, working memory, visualisation and reasoning were seen to be essential in choosing the items used in BARB and subsequent ability tests. They were not used until item generative tests were designed as multiple parallel forms from relevant theory. The research into attrition shows that these tests made no appreciable difference to drop out in initial training. The problem was to find out what attributes would: and when they should be used. The same issues as surrounded the cognitive tests reappeared. What evidence to use in their construction, how to present them, score and validate them. *Questions had to be asked of recruits, but what kinds of questions and in what contexts?*

All self-report inventories carry with them implicit or explicit motivation theories. Models of motivation, just like ability theories, are as frequent and as diverse as schools of psychology. They can be summarised for the purposes of illustration and logical progression as dynamic/ developmental, learning, biological, and social interaction models, with various combinations and rapprochements. The functions of these models include adequate description of the domain: theoretical elements that can be tested by a number of methods of verification and falsification once items are constructed consistent with the theory. In short, any new venture in screening for military suitability needs to know where its theoretical origins lie, so that the product is subject to all necessary psychometric techniques of verification. How relevant are psychological theories for solving the numerous problems associated with military attrition? The insert summarises the potential of mainstream contributions. Their impact depends on the realisation that attrition is a process and not by itself a predictable state of mind prior to recruitment. First, though, a look at screening models within military contexts, owing all or nothing to the theories in the insert that might be relevant to interpreting the results.

MILITARY SCREENS

Bureaucratic

Medical

Social

Personality

Ratings and Halos

MILITARY SCREENS: BUREAUCRATIC, SOCIAL AND PSYCHOMETRIC

Theories of motivation to succeed emerge from different schools of psychology, each of which might adduce a causal explanation for success or failure. Regardless of explanation, there exist essentially three different military conventions for assessing individual differences in fitness to serve, bureaucratic, social and psychometric. Personal quality procedures can be grouped under three simple headings, bureaucratic, where a review of individual qualities is carried out by a committees under regulations; social, where the group informally or formally decides if its members succeed in fulfilling its prescriptions for acceptable behaviour; and psychometric, where reports from applying specially constructed tests and inventories are used to make decisions, often using computer algorithms, depending on how well the measures are known to predict good and bad outcomes. Any procedure can make use of tests from any source and with their scores implicitly or explicitly reflect origins in one of the main psychological models under review. The bureaucratic and social screens are part of the ongoing process of attrition itself. The psychometric approach has traditionally been external. If it were to be introduced as an aspect of life for personnel in the services, its form has yet to be decided before embarking on any new prediction of attrition risk.

THE BUREAUCRATIC MODEL: INTERVIEWS AND REVIEWS BY COMMITTEES
The bureaucratic assumption implies that basic question-and-answer interviews will be conducted: and that the interview will be interactive. That is, that the sequence of questions asked will depend on the answers provided. The questions to be asked will be those that groups deem relevant to success or failure, informed by appropriate reference frames. The rationale is derived from analytical psychology. People will reveal in conversation more about themselves than they are consciously aware of, if you know what you are looking for. Additionally, the interview stage is invariably thought of as a reward, (cf. the dynamic pleasure principle). Nothing is more demotivating than being left off the short list, or more encouraging than being invited to attend. Second, the interview has interactive flexibility denied to standardised tests,

which still tend to provide information regarded by employers as only supplementary to the interview itself. The 'psychology' of the interview as an indispensable ritual of a superstitious[1] nature in the display and exercise of power by management exists in that judgement of more than fifty years ago. Its reliability has always been open to question.

Alec Rodger and the Royal Navy
None of this is very new. An attempt to provide a foundation for bureaucratic procedures based on interviews and reviews can be seen in the early work of the National Institute for Industrial Psychology in the thirties and forties to introduce structure to the interview. The publications of Oldfield (1941), and perhaps above all, Alec Rodger (1954) resulted in a synthesis called *The Seven Point Plan*. This called for systematic and orderly accretion of information about the following seven relevant characteristics of candidates: *physical make up; attainments; general intelligence; special aptitudes and skills; interests; disposition; environmental circumstances and support.* Although Rodger gave scientific advice to the Navy for many years, the longevity of this structure has more to do with the sheer contextual, or cultural, consonance than influence. It is, or ought to be, accepted for what Rodger said it ought to be - a starting point or *'rough sketch of a scientifically defensible system for the assessment of occupational potentialities' (p.16)*. Jones's (1984, pp. 69-70) bureaucratic frame is a direct-line, if original, descendant of its ancestor. It was put into practice in this way. A synthesis of the qualities necessary for a commissioned officer's performance in the Royal Navy was operationalised both by constructing appropriate instruments and by specifying what the interview procedure should involve. Jones's list of *the structured stages of the pre-assessment interview* in chronological

> **JONES: AN INTERVIEW FOR COMMITTEES**
>
> *completion of a candidate personal history form*
>
> *an interview conducted using standard procedures and core questions*
>
> *a report form compiled after review of the first two stages by the interviewer*
>
> *a reference from the candidate's last educational institution*
>
> *a headquarters reappraisal of all evidence*

order is in the insert. At this juncture one has to ask how reliable and how valid these systematic procedures were, because the most common criticism of interviews is, as traditional wisdom reveals, their lack of effectiveness *because they are unreliable.* Not every procedure can be accused of unreliability, though. The correlation between a headquarters reappraisal of all candidates' fitness for training conducted by Jones

---

1   Superstition is the continuance of behaviours based on irrational explanations. If interviews are as unreliable as the evidence shows, there is no justification, in terms of the probability that they will improve outcomes, for their use.

and all the evidence submitted by the field interviewers provided an upper-bound[2] index of reliability. This was .85. In numerical terms, 80 percent of field assessments were verified by the bureaucratic review at headquarters. This offers a big advance on unstructured interviewing outcomes When the various components of the stages were correlated (see footnote) with actual performance at a two-day assessment centre programme of tests and performance measures, a validity study was possible. A multiple correlation of .71 was achieved using all relevant pre-screening information The importance of military case studies like those produced by Jones is considerable, since they are seldom reported in such detail. This particular bureaucratic interview model provides evidence of being both functional and coherent but it has seldom been replicated. There was no follow-up to show if the interview was related to attrition.

Women's Royal Naval Service

'careful, steady, conscientious, reliable, experienced and teachable'

WRNS Structured Interviews:

80,000 men in 1943

2.69 Percent rated Unstable

Referral Rates from 2.8 to 9.7 Percent

WORLD WAR 2 CONSCRIPT UNSUITABILITY: EFFECTIVE FEMALE DIAGNOSES

Efforts to uncover temperamental unsuitability during the Second World War are much criticised by supporters of the view that judgements about military unsuitability are seriously flawed. Psychiatrists in the USA were ridiculed for wrongly screening volunteers who later served with distinction (Wessely 2004, Jones et al. 2000, and Rona et al. 2006). However, no mention was made in any one of these reviews of the success of female *Personnel Selection Officers* in the British armed services who interviewed conscripts and then referred those believed to be at risk for further psychiatric assessment (Vernon and Parry, 1949, pp. 155-160). Women's Royal Naval Service (WRNS) personnel assistants conducted short structured interviews of conscripts. In a single year, 1943, at the height of the war they interviewed 80,000 men. Of these 2.69 percent were rated as unstable. These 'suspects' were referred to psychiatrists; who decided what course of action to take with those who were referred. They were not all excused service. Almost half were thought to be useful in some capacity for a year, another fifth for six months' trial, and the remained, one in twenty, were rejected. Psychiatrists declared WRNS personnel to be accurate 75% of the time. Referral rates by the interviewers varied from 2.8 to 9.7 percent averaging 6.3 percent. Those remarkable interviewers found to be most accurate were judged by their supervisors to be *careful, steady, conscientious, reliable, experienced and teachable.*

---

2   Upper-bound, because the Headquarters review had all the previous information at its disposal, and HQ decisions were not made independently of that information. The file on the candidate was part of the HQ input, resulting in some degree of autocorrelation. Dr. Collis reports the same finding from 1995 analyses of Admiralty Interview Board ratings.

BACK TO BASICS: CONFUSION AND CONFLICT IN MEDICAL REVIEWS

Interviews take many forms, as the 1943 US Navy cycle in the next section exemplifies, not least of which are conducted by Medical Officers. More recently, there have been British historical reviews in which World War 2 assessments in the United States for active service exclusion are largely discounted. (Jones, Hyams & Wessely, 2003; French, Rona, Jones & Wessely, 2004; Rona, Hooper, Jones, French & Wessely 2004; Wessely, 2004). In contrast, psychiatrists' judgements are revered above all others and have a permanent place in the valuation and devaluation of other psychological currency. Rona (2004) and colleagues have referred to a "Gold Standard" (GS), in assessment of temperamental unsuitability. This is no more or less than the judgement of a psychiatrist. In one study, the poor results of validating inventory classifications with Medical Officers' diagnoses following receipt of self-report inventories is underlined (French et al., 2004). The blame is laid at the door of the inventories.

However, low correspondence is a predictable consequence of first not training and then supervising the Medical Officers on the use of the inventories, of which there is no mention (French et al., 2004). The contrast with the successful WRNS interviewers is clear. Interviews are not all the same. These articles in medical journals assert that it is not possible to identify personnel at risk reliably, either prior to recruitment or pre or post deployment, amounting to a denial that a complete psychological profile has any relevance and predictive power in identifying the temperamentally unsuitable soldier (Rona, Hooper et al. 2006).

Before and After Deployment: The Wessely Doctrine

While the material on recruitment screening is cogent and relatively straightforward, the epidemiological literature on the effects of deployment on mental health is vast and complex. Green et al. (2008) and Fear et al. (2010) each list more than 50 sources in recent reviews of the effects on health of deployment. Whereas there can be little doubt about the *effects* of deployment on individuals, family and medical services, considerable confusion exists about the *identification of pre-deployment risk factors*. Perhaps the essentials of *a climate of doing nothing* to assess temperamental suitability of personnel for warfare in countries where the indigenous population offers little or no support to those deployed, is contained in the Liddell-Hart Lecture of 2004 (Wessely, 2004), termed the Wessely

THE WESSELY DOCTRINE.......

- *Once a psychiatric disorder is found, by all means treat it*

- *But neither screening beforehand nor debriefing on return can be justified, because there is no evidence that there are predispositions to breakdown*

- *There are only a number of known risk factors whose prevalence might emerge only after a non-estimable period of time has elapsed*

- *Additionally, all interventions before actual proof of disorder are likely to produce a climate of uncertainty and fear of risk itself, which is unpatriotic*

doctrine. Psychological risk factors are not proven, nor are they readily diagnosable from self-report data. Hence, the use of psychological profiles to exclude those who are likely to be at risk by the emotional, and for many, traumatic, demands of initial deployment and subsequent service, denies the birthright of every citizen to serve one's country for no credible scientific reason. This cannot go unchallenged when the work by Hoge et al. (2002) shows that among a one-year cohort of US personnel, almost half of those hospitalised for the first time for a mental disorder left the service, compared with only one in eight admitted for any other reason. Waiting until breakdown happens is associated with a high level of attrition, if not its cause. Conflicting transatlantic opinions are the norm. The difficulties are compounded when the available *medical epidemiology survey* methods are examined, by summarising the methodology of a number of empirical studies. An appropriate review of *psychological* findings is found later in the chapter. This seems only proper, because depth analysis of the references in the Jones et al. (2003) publication nevertheless reveals that 84 percent were published *before* 1990; *and not one reference is made to a psychology journal.* What then, could psychology offer given doubt and confusion and disagreement among the medical sources themselves?

QUESTIONABLE PRACTICES

Surveys involving large numbers of respondents are the stuff of medical opinion about causes and treatments of mental illness in the armed forces. In examining the fine print, the basic transcultural lesson from Macdonald's Askaris seems not to have been learned by many medical researchers. There is little or no evidence from a number of UK medical studies that popular civilian inventories used in surveys of British military personnel have been

THE VOICES IN THE WILDERNESS

'*There is a lack of information on the relevance of currently available standardised personality assessment measures to the military and moreover, British military population. The use of commonly used measures in the Armed forces in the absence of appropriate military norms would be questionable, since they are not a representative cross section of society and therefore cannot be readily compared to normative student, psychiatric or general populations typically used as standardisation samples. Indeed, where measures are available, these tend to have been validated on non-British populations rendering direct comparisons difficult. The military rationale for a comprehensive research and develop-ment strategy in the area of temperament and suitability would appear necessary. The cross-cultural differences in military selection, training and roles would indicate a clear need for a British contribution to the development of appropriate assessment tools, norms and evidence-based practice.' Deu, Srinivasan, & Srinivasan (2004)*

subjected to cultural restandardisation. The need for such pre-cautions is cited in an important and virtually ignored discussion on what constitutes temperamental unsuitability provided by MOD psychiatrists, Deu, Srinivasan, & Srinivasan (2004). Against the popular tide, they stress the need for instruments to help with diagnoses; and a clear understanding of differentiating factors in temperamental unsuitability for military service. This opinion is well supported by a study of the various surveys purporting to investigate the use of self-report questionnaires administered to service personnel. For example, in the watershed article by Rona, Hooper et al.(2006), and its successors, Fear et al. (2010), Rona et al (2012), show that various health functions in military personnel were assessed by the unstandardized contents of their inventories:

- The questions about health consisted of a checklist of previous or current health problems,
- Self-rated health from the 36-item Short Form Health Survey. Symptoms of common mental disorder were measured with the *12-item General Health Questionnaire (GHQ-12)*
- Probable post-traumatic stress disorder with the *17-item National Centre for PTSD Checklist (PCL-C)*
- Alcohol use with the *10-item WHO Alcohol Use Disorders Identification Test (AUDIT)*

Binary outcomes in posttraumatic stress, mental disorders and abuse of alcohol from replies to the collection of questions were cursorily defined without showing distributions, with the following individual score cut offs:

PCL ORIGINS:

"The psychometric properties of the PTSD Checklist (PCL), a new, brief, self-report instrument, were determined on a population of 40 motor vehicle accident victims and sexual assault victims using diagnoses and scores from the CAPS (Clinician Administered PTSD Scale) as the criteria." (Blanchard et al. 1996)

EPIDEMIOLOGICAL MENDACITY?

"The main barriers to health screening were lack of trust, perceived low quality of healthcare, and perceived lack of concern within the institution about work environments and home life.....Screening was considered worthwhile, but many confided that they would not honestly answer some items in the questionnaire (French, Rona, Jones and Wessely, 2004, p.153).

- 50 or more for the PCL (which we have termed probable post-traumatic stress disorder),
- 4 or more for the GHQ-12 (which we have termed symptoms of common mental disorder),
- 16 or more for the AUDIT (usually defined as hazardous use, termed alcohol misuse).

These would normally be introduced by psychologists after careful psychometric checks and balances on reliability and validity. There is no such evidence (Rona et.al. 2006; Fear et al. 2010; Rona et al. 2012). One can take as an example of the problems with using civilian medical checklists the short PCL checklist so often quoted in these surveys. What are its psychometric hallmarks? The commonly quoted PTSD checklist (Blanchard, Jones-Alexander, Buckley and Formeris, 1996) has surfaced as a core contribution to a number of medically recommended scales. This inclusion seems impressive until the quotation from the original publication is read in the insert. Much of what is represented here can be applied to medically-based inventory research carried out in military contexts. To use civilian inventories without offering proof of standardisation in a specific military context seems hardly credible. These strictures could, nevertheless, be regarded as lay concerns of no apparent face validity. However, identical reservations are voiced by the accredited medical researchers themselves. The second insert of relevance contains cautions against questionnaire use because of climates of distrust among military personnel who are asked to complete them. In psychometric terms, this means assessment of social desirability response profiles (cf. Bochner & Van Zyl, 1986) guardedness and faking in military personnel, of which there are no examples in any of the British work quoted here. *Briefly, in epidemiological studies of military personnel, originating in medical journals, there has been no indication of the reliability, validity, and perhaps critically, liability to*

**US NAVY 1941-2
SOCIAL ACCEPTABILITY LIST**

1. *Does he like the Navy?*

2. *Is he quickly obedient?*

3. *Does he complain a good deal*?*

4. *Is this man fit for sea duty?*

5. *Is he cheerful and industrious?*

6. *Does he keep himself neat and clean?*

7. *Does he have many friends in Coy.?*

8. *Would you like to have him in your division?*

9. *Does he learn Navy routine as well as most?*

10. *Does he take part in games and activities off duty*

*Negatively scored

known response style distortion and distrust by military personnel of conventional civilian inventories. It would, in all fairness be entirely inappropriate to leave the impression that all surveys follow the British example. The work in the United States on the need to validate civilian inventories, including the PCL checklist is extensive, the following examples being typical (Adler, A. B., Wright, K. M., Bliese, P. D., Eckford, R. D., & Hoge, C. W., 2008; Bliese, P. D., Wright, K. M., Adler, A. B., Cabrera, O., Castro, C.A.,& Hoge, C. W., 2008; Bliese, P., Wright, K., Adler, A. B., & Thomas, J., 2004; Dickstein, D., Suvak, M., Litz, B. T., & Adler, A. B., 2010; Hoge, C.W., Castro, C. A., Messer, S. C., McGurk,D., Cotting, D. I., & Koffman, R. L., 2004; Wright, K. M., Huffman, A.H., Adler, A. B., & Castro, C. A., 2002; Wright, K. M., Thomas, J. L., Adler, A. B., Ness, J. W.,Hoge, C. W., & Castro, C. A., 2005; and Wright, K. M., Bliese, P. D., Thomas, J. L., Adler, A. B., Eckford, R. D., & Hoge, C.W. 2007). Added to the confusion over the veracity of responses in the social context of military surveys are conflicts about the need to validate them in the same culture. Given extensive technical differences about the administration and construction of medical questionnaires for screening and diagnosis, what alternatives may be of most worth to decision-makers? The first step is to see attrition and the identification of possible personnel at risk not as a prior medical, but a current social process, consistent with Schneider's (1947) classic framework that is dealt with in the ensuring sections.

SOCIAL SELECTION IN A WARTIME ENVIRONMENT
The account (Garstle, Wagner & Lodge 1943) of a seven-day screening process in the US Navy includes a social questionnaire about the acceptability of conscripts. It became part of an official system of appraisal that took a week to conclude and had all the traditional elements, physical, psychiatric, psychological tests, and bureaucratic review. Questionnaires were completed by recruits themselves, and by section leaders. Personnel identified as being of doubtful status by this method occurred at the second induction stage, where 'suspects' were identified. These unfortunates were subjected to further screening, but importantly, at a social level within the unit itself. Here was a way of identifying if not 'suspects' then potential 'outcasts'. The inclusion of screening questions to determine whether or not recruits, *once admitted to the service*, can cope with the culture of learning designed to produce combat readiness through immediate obedience, has seldom been a direct requirement of military biodata inventories. Social network screening by peers or section leaders within military groups is seldom made public knowledge. Yet commanders undoubtedly pay great attention to informal reports of role unsuitability. If these reports are field-based in deployment there is every reason to pay attention because lives are at risk. The ten item questionnaire is reproduced here only as a wartime example, noting that today it might well be used within a health-related context to assess quality of life. In fact, only if the responses to these questions were positive, could the recruit be set to enjoy life as it then existed in recruit camp. The questions are typical of prescriptions for acceptability in World War Two: and to some extent still hold today.

VIRTUAL SOCIAL/CULTURAL SCREENS IN UK MILITARY TODAY
Social screens involve primary interventions for 'the sick soldier'. These are implemented during induction, by using two types of 'health' screening, one by commanders, and the other by peers, or 'mates'. Both are believed to be widespread

in recruit battalions: and the most obvious is the *command* screen. Interventions by commanders involve routine and snap inspections, finding faults, identifying offenders, shouting at them, giving extra tasks to the individual and collectively to the platoon, singling out on parade those identified as failing to come up to standard, and as a last straw, reporting them to a higher authority. Many sources do not find the command screen either too punitive or more than what should be expected in a normal training environment.   Gebicke (1997) devotes a complete section to leadership, with evidence that abusive language, lack of supportive counselling and concern for faltering recruits increase early dropout rates.

Certainly, few charges on the basis of such behaviour are laid against NCOs who are the main implementers of a command screen. Officers are not present at every training session: but they expect to be kept informed so that the screen has the legitimacy of approval by the officer with duty of care. The operation of the command screen has its origins in the goal of military culture and the rejection of weakness. The second *social* screening procedure applied by one's own erstwhile comrades is widely reported to be just as powerful. Misfits are jeered at, made fun of, ignored and have no friends or companions. Posing a threat to survival, they must be dealt with summarily and within the framework of living together in billets. It follows, from the characterisation of the sick soldier by Schneider seen in the relevant inserts, that the threat has to be isolated and dealt with by isolating those designated as misfits by the 'disrespect' of instructors. There is no possibility of counselling, often a sign of stigma. They become outcasts.

CONCLUSION: THE MANY PATHS THROUGH ATTRITION

Social screens are perhaps only too successful at removing those whose face does not fit. This is only one outcome of life in a new culture. Not all are negative. To be specific, some learn eagerly in a platoon-regulated environment.   Others, with reluctance, develop coping strategies. Still more find ways out, consciously or unconsciously according to *analytical* theories by avoiding pain through being ill, a strange anomaly. More understandable is the material on matching interests with job allocation. Of those that leave of their own accord, there is no perceived match between current job characteristics and self-awareness of personal qualities: and hence, no prospect of career satisfaction.

ATTRITION ATTRIBUTES: MILITARY PSYCHOMETRIC ALTERNATES

For users of tests in occupational selection, validity remains the central issue.   If questions identifying recruits at risk of leaving the service are to be asked, the approach adopted has to be right one. The popularity of self-referent scales is evident in the large share of the occupational market they command, although little is reported about the results of vast amounts of data they generate annually (Irvine, 1989a).   The standard discussion of the relative strengths and weaknesses of forced-choice and norm-referent measures exists in Cronbach, (1990, Chapters 12 & 13). In that review, the theoretical questions about validity of self-report questionnaires are no different now than they were when Vernon (1953) wrote what is regarded by many as still the classic introductory text on the use of personal assessments.   What is measured by these instruments; and, of just as much concern, what theory of the processes governing their use by assessors qualifies their validity? In this section, personality scales used in military contexts are compared with each other; and ratings of characteristics are examined.

Multi-Scale Approaches: Some Military Options

Critics and reviewers of multidimensional personal scales assert, for example, that two of the most influential personality inventories, *Cattell's 16 PF* (1949) and *Jackson's PRF* (1984) have hundreds of questions; and, respectively, 16 and 20 different dimensions. Critics of large inventories, on the other hand, express concern at interpreting, and counting upon a single correlation from a large set of scores when five percent of any set of correlations from large data sets could occur by chance (Blinkhorn & Johnson, 1990). Multi-dimension methods of assessment may fail to emphasise that the separate parts of large inventories are more often than not intercorrelated with each other. They seldom, if ever, retain their claims to independence. Factor analysis methods, (Tupes & Christal, 1992, Carroll, 2002) have reduced inventories with many scales to a much smaller number of latent dimensions. What are they, and what influence do they have in practice?

MILITARY PERSONALITY

BIG FIVE

ABLE

PRF

Christal's Big Five in the USAF

The debate on just how few personality functions it takes to provide adequate descriptions of people at work continues, although the Big Five framework first proposed by Tupes and Christal in a USAF report in the 1960s and reproduced many years later) and given a great deal of scrutiny since, (Digman & Inouye, 1986; McRea & Costa, 1987; Hough, Barge and Kamp, 1987; Tellegen, 1985; Beard, 1990; Salgado, 1998) from their responses to many questions. The first two of these reported studies show the reduction of large inventories to five dimensions. Since its inception, the framework suggested by Christal has been subjected to extensive analysis, with hundreds of studies. Carroll (2002) exemplifies many who regard the five factor model as incomplete and liable to further reduction and challenge, largely because many of the personality statements do not access the motives, attitudes and beliefs that coexist with the behavioural statements. The five factor domains as listed are possibly bi-polar.

> **Extraversion/ Surgency vs. Introversion/Timidity;**
> **Agreeableness/ Affiliation vs. Coldness and Independence;**
> **Conscientiousness/ Responsibility vs. Disorganisation/Impulsivity;**
> **Emotional Stability vs. Negative and Defensive Feelings;**
> **Cultural Adaptation/ Active Exploration of the Environment vs.**
> **Closed, Narrow-mindedness and Slowness to Change.**

Carroll's own analysis suggests that Tellegen's (1985) proposed hierarchical structures may have credibility. Tellegen's three higher-order dimensions, (a) *Positive Emotionality* and (b) *Negative Emotionality* and (c) *Constraint* are described with data to support the structures in a refinement of the *Minnesota Multiple Phasic Inventory*

(Watson & Clark, 1994). These domains exist as 'higher order group factors' deriving from the original components of the Big Five. *Positive Emotionality* involves *Big Five Extraversion* and the proactive aspect of *Conscientiousness*; *Negative Emotionality* includes *Big Five Neuroticism and Agreeableness*; and *Constraint* covers the restrained aspect of *Conscientiousness* and much of *Openness to Experience*. In short, the *Bigger Three*[3] accounts for relationships among the *Big Five* – and so on *ad minimum*, but not without ongoing debate.

US ARMY ABLE INVENTORY

In an attempt to create a new instrument for manpower decisions, Hough et al (1987) devised 10 new, but carefully referenced scales for trial in the personality/ biodata domain among US Army recruits. However, these beginnings were to expand to a 15 scale inventory labelled ABLE (*Assessment of Background and Life Experiences*) and whose construction and eventual use in composites are detailed in Campbell & Knapp, (loc. cit. pp 287-293). From the results of this and vocational interest applications derived from Alley's VOICE (Alley, Berberich, & Wilbourn. 1977); Alley, Wilbourn, & Berberich 1976; Alley & Matthews, 1986), the following composites were derived by data reduction methods, adding to those derived by Hough.

> **Leadership Potential (*Dominance*)**
> **Internal Control** *(Socialisation)*
> **Achievement Motivation (*Work Orientation Energy Level, Self Esteem*)**
> **Dependability (*Conscientious, Traditional Values, Nondeliinquency*)**
> **Adjustment (*Emotional Stability*)**
> **Cooperativeness** *(Likeability)*

JACKSON'S PRF: THE ROYAL NAVY TRIALS

In Britain, Beard's (1990) study of Naval Officer Cadets showed that Jackson's 20 *Personality Research Form* (PRF) scales reduced to 5 second-order factors in their British Royal Naval College training context where naval officer recruits were given a comprehensive set of measures including cognitive tests. Note, parenthetically, the correspondence between these individual difference dimensions and the hypothesised group behaviours under command learning conditions in the previous section. How far are these factors influenced by interactions with learning in command environments?

> **Dominant Achievement Motivation** *(Control)*
> **Gregarious and Exhibitionist Social Influence** *(Extraversion)*
> **Self-Referent, Cautious, Rule-Governed Behaviour** *(Dependability)*
> **Defensive, Touchy and Aggressive Behaviour** *(Hostility)*
> **Caring, Empathetic, Supportive Behaviour** *(Affiliation/Nurturance)*

Beard correlated the factor scores from the five clusters with interest factor scores derived from the *Jackson Vocational Interest Survey*. The five personality factors combined with the vocational choice factors in recognisable trait-like groupings, producing third-order constructs of considerable explanatory power. In fact, they were later used in another study to distinguish accurately Naval Technicians, Clerical Aides and Marine Commandos with 90 percent accuracy, as Table 8.6 shows.

---

3   My nomenclature and italics only.

Naval Job Classification: Incremental Validity

In Chapter 8, describing the work in the Royal Navy, vocational interest and personality measures in the job classification of United Kingdom Royal Navy personnel were added to standard cognitive measures. The addition of interest and personality tests to typical aptitude tests applied at entry produced dramatic increments in predicting actual training regimens. The aim was to use these measures to predict the actual job classifications of recruits in training. Three job categories were available: Royal Navy Artificers *(Technical)*; Royal Marines *(Combat)*; and Women's Royal Naval Service (WRNS) *(Mainly Logistic Support)*. Using discriminant function analyses, it was possible to classify these entrants first by initial ability test scores; and then to note improvements leading to 90 percent accuracy by adding in cumulative fashion vocational interest followed by personality test scores. A summary of these results (Beard and Collis, 1991) is in Table 8.6. This was not an isolated result involving the use of interest and personality test scores. An important review of empirical studies of structural, environmental and personal factors influencing military turnover can be seen in Sümer, (2004). Nevertheless, the potential of this work was never realised in the official use of vocational interest and/or personality tests. The main reasons, parallel to those in the USA, were administrative, reinforced *by a widespread belief that such measures were open to faking when jobs were at stake.* Computer delivery of tests now provides many safeguards against guarded and socially desirable responses. The next chapter shows how the incremental validity paradigm for the Royal Navy was used to classify USAF recruits as females or males using similar test results with safeguards against faking.

MILITARY INVENTORIES

The Official Demurral;

No guarantees against faking

CONCLUSIONS AND PRESCRIPTIONS

Qualities associated with job demands are defined. Different approaches testify to the appraisal of motivation in as few dimensions as can be conveniently dealt with. Nevertheless, there has been continued reluctance to use self-report questionnaires because of the lack of any internal beacon to shed light on the veracity or mendacity of response patterns.

EXTERNAL RATINGS OF PERSONAL QUALITIES AND THE MAGIC NUMBERS

Perhaps the most dramatic study in the literature of occupational classification, military or otherwise, based on the ratings of personal and situational qualities is described in three articles by Christal (1968 a, b) and Christal & Bottenberg (1968). Credibility arises out of their origin in one of the very few reported large-scale studies of what happened when ratings of job attributes were rated by professionals who were both trained and experienced.

Christal (1968a), by what enviable powers of influence and persuasion one may only guess at, had 22 colonels rate 3,575 jobs in the US Air Force in terms of their demand levels. Here, the sample size was the number of jobs. Of a possible 200 factors that might have influenced the policy of each of these senior officers, only nine were consistently captured in the regression functions set up to determine what was in the beholder's eye, or perhaps ego, or even more realistically the beholder's working memory aided by references. These nine then became the actual regression weights for implementation of the policy determining final job level. Although nine elements realised a full regression model of .92 to define job grade, a very good fit was achieved by only 5 dimensions (a) the complexity, variety and level of job activities; (b) the scope and significance of the planning involved for job execution; (c) special training requirements; (d) degree of importance and independence of judgements involved; and (e) the levels and ranks of agencies or individuals involved in communications (loc. cit. p.38).

The reduction of many job level factors by senior officers to parsimonious percepts constituting less than 5 percent of the original 200 thus provides an empirical parallel to self-induced reductionism in personality inventories. The study proved to be extremely influential and its regression model has been employed widely. Nevertheless, reasons for the empirical parsimony of the five dimensions in the equation determining job level have never emerged. The observed reductionism in ratings is nevertheless a fact of life. Human nature dictates that very few dimensions of behaviour among recruits will be perceived and then used to make a rating of success or failure.

Civilian Rating Dimensions: Psychiatrists and Psychologists
Another historical landmark study, where behaviour ratings of large samples by experienced psychiatrists and trainees were analysed by data reduction methods is to be found in one of the most extensive and strangely enough, least noticed works (Lorr & Suziedelis, 1969) in the published literature. A sample of 525 patients was rated by a nation-wide sample of trained psychiatrists in the USA; and 290 normal adults were rated by 254 students of psychology who had known them for at least one year. *Personality checklists totalling 160 items used in both patients and, normal adults, were reducible by factor analysis to 5 latent dimensions of rater perception.* The first four were perceived in both normal and patient groups. As before, actual scale names are clustered with the authors' construct label in italics.

> **Affiliation, Agreeableness, Nurturance *(Nurturance)***
> **Dominance, Competitiveness, Aggressiveness, Exhibition *(Control)***
> **Sociability vs. Detachment *(Gregariousness)***
> **Inhibition, Submissiveness, Abasement *(Dependency)***
> **Unstable Aggressive Behaviour in Patients *(Hostility)***

The last of the five factors emerged from the patient studies only and was described as *Hostility*. The reduction of the ratings in the checklist to domains parallel with those described by Christal as from the large number of items used in personality self-report inventories is close and a plausible basis for consensus. Even this concordance does not signify closure for many critics, but ratings have one inescapable quality in common that has always seemed to dominate.

RATINGS: THE HALO EFFECT
The most intriguing, and theoretically consistent, extension of the observed persistent reductionism involving adjectival descriptions of personality traits, is witnessed in

task group activities and discussions rated by trained observers (Herriot, Chalmers & Wingrove, 1985; Wingrove, Jones & Herriot, 1985); although there was no accounting for the group mechanisms that could be involved. The paper by Jones, Herriot, Long, & Drakely 1991) on assessment centre processes, shows that supposedly different personal qualities assessed by panels rating relatively large numbers (N=576) of potential officers on synthetic dimensions made up of several component parts at a central assessment centre reduce to *a single personal characteristics factor* with the following loadings, (*Leadership Potential .81, Character and Personality .86, Career Commitment .80).* The consistency of the intercorrelations among the dimensions used by the raters shows the power of their opinions in determining an order of acceptance in the assessment centre. This rank order is in turn correlated with a factor revealing ratings on *Effective Intellect* .91 and minor loadings on three personal clusters.

THE HALO EFFECT

Good at Everything

or

Good For Nothing?

The correlation between the factors reveals the higher order general 'halo' or evaluative dimension, a construct showing longevity without adequate explanation in the occupational lexicon (Vernon, 1953, pp. 115-119 and 137-138; Cooper, 1981) and paralleled perhaps in the positive and negative emotionality poles of Tellegen (1985). Whatever the source, the assessments could all be reduced to one overarching dimension with two poles, positive and negative. Those who are acceptable in the eye of the beholder are seen to be good at everything; and those not acceptable might well be judged good for nothing. In fact, multiple regressions of ratings on an Overall Average Rating taken as the measure to determine order of suitability approach .90. As such they capture perfectly group consensus on recruitment policy. They do not, of course, necessarily predict with accuracy personal qualities assessed by any other than the raters' own judgements. Nor are they related to role performance. Halo effects transferring to recruits thought to be unsuitable are a necessary conclusion from much of the insider accounts of what happens once they are seen to hinder the progress of a platoon.

THE ATTRITION PROCESS: ARE PSYCHOLOGICAL THEORIES RELEVANT?

Models of individual differences in motivation patterns and level must account for variance in individual efforts by 'squaddies', who are made to learn both by their instructors and by their peers. Each one of these models, inserted at the beginning of the chapter as a hallmark, has some contribution to make to the measurement of motivation by psychologists. Their relevance and importance in the study of attrition, nevertheless, is an empirical issue if they are used in the construction of inventories and questionnaires designed to identify those at risk. However, the conclusion of the review in the previous chapter was plain. The search for personal attributes necessary to survive the process of attrition has not met with success. Perhaps the way forward is to examine the process itself from a perspective that will help to ameliorate it. Psychological models of process are potential contributors, but to what degree?

Developmental and Dynamic Models

One might begin by acknowledging that the introduction to military life can be a painful experience. The work of early analysts, such as Freud, Adler and Jung, focussed on the treatment of abnormalities by individual psychoanalysis and counselling, and are often referred to as *analytical* models. For the most part, they assert that motives are of an unconscious nature, the central core of which is the pleasure principle. People will, without necessarily being conscious of it, be driven to seek what is pleasurable and avoid what is painful. One unusual example of the use of analytical concepts in the military literature is the work of Schachter (1959).

TWO INFLUENCES

Dynamic or Analytic Learning,

Social and Biological

Concentrating on affiliation, he examines birth order and its association with success as a fighter pilot, at first glance a long stride. From the point of view of the fundamental influence of childhood emotions, first-borns are supposed to be more prone to fear and anxiety than those born after them. Schachter examined the fighter pilot statistics available at the time. Whatever the original family size, there were fewer fighter 'aces' in the Korean war who were first born than would have been statistically expected.

Thwarting the satisfaction of unconscious pleasure-principle needs by parents, teachers, carers and partners can lead to neurotic behaviour that is self-perpetuating. Later proponents of this perspective on the motives for actions include analysts Karen Horney and Erich Fromm, who added a social dimension to motivation development, to include the generally accepted notion of actively coping with the environment through learned stratagems and defensive devices. Although dynamic or analytic theories are both seductive and pervasive, and have enriched the ways in which people are described and understood not just by psychologists, but by writers and the public at large, they are generally untestable because different motives may be attributed by individual analysts to interpret any form of action. It is this seemingly endless interpretive framework that makes dynamic theories, based on hidden motives, limited in the extent to which they can be validated. In fact, the most persuasive evidence for the enduring nature of the difficulties associated with analytical theory use can be found in the classic source volume, with its multiple examples, by Lindzey and Hall (1965).

Learning Theories of Personality Development

In contrast to dynamic models, learning theories of personality development are concerned only with behaviour that can be observed. In their strictest form according to Watson, motives, emotions, consciousness and mind cannot exist because they cannot be observed. To insist that they exist or cause events is, by definition, illogical. Skinner's contribution to this area was to show how learned behaviour could be induced by rewards and punishments, and also unlearned or radically altered by the same mechanism. In later practical work, he introduced the notion of 'the token economy', whereby people in total, command environments, such as correctional institutions, or asylums (Goffman, 1961), could be induced to modify their behaviour when desirable behaviour was rewarded directly by a tangible reward, or indirectly by tokens that could be used in exchange for the reward. These principles are seen in action today in commerce. They are used to modify the behaviour of normal people in open environments. They are witnessed, for example, in the award of air miles points for using a particular airline, or other incentives to showing purchasing 'loyalty' or consistency towards a single brand, most notably perhaps, supermarkets and hotel chains.

Neurotic behaviour can be induced by inconsistent and capricious use of rewards and punishments (see especially Mehrabian, 1970). How learning is organised during basic training will make a big difference to the way that squad members will respond. However, there are individual differences in how recruits and combat personnel respond to fixed treatments and routine sequences. Eysenck (1953), with a form of biological learning typology attempted to bridge the gap between general laws of learning and individual differences in motivation. He distinguished four personality quadrants, based on two dimensions, *stability-instability*, and *introversion-extraversion* and asserted that people learn in ways consistent with their personality profiles. For theorist like Eysenck, all 'squaddies' learn but some learn more, and more comfortably, than others depending on aspects of personality that can, unlike dynamic motives, be measured objectively. Individual differences in recruit learning under fixed and non-adaptive conditions would, according to this theory, depend on the reaction of the nervous system, already predisposed biologically, to patterns of rewards and punishments.

ATTRITION AS A SOCIAL PROCESS DURING TRAINING

Social interaction theories of motivation, with no analytic ancestors, are less frequent in psychology, but they more than abound in sociology, which is perhaps why they are absent from textbooks on personality theories. There are sociological macro theories of motivation such as those associated with Durkheim and Weber. Learning and working in small, self-contained environments (*gemeinschaft*) is different from learning and working in industrialised factory-like large organisations *(gesellschaft),* for the simple reason that different forms of motivation are associated with achievement in each one. This does not mean that motives are not universal, just that their expression will be modified by the organisational variables that permit their expression in action through role acquisition. Much effort has been devoted in the past to identifying personal traits and social attributes that would in a selection process predict attrition. A shift in emphasis from selection to studying behaviour during training as a means of understanding and dealing with it is a required psychological alternative.

EXCHANGE THEORY IN MILITARY CULTURES
The application of social learning theory in one specific form, exchange theory, is particularly helpful whenever commanders motivate squaddies by ordering them to carry out drills, exercises or combat manoeuvres without question and without debate. Exchange theory (French & Raven, 1959; Secord & Backman, 1964 Ch. 8) applied to group learning predicts that the long-term use of any *one* of a number of sources of social power (reward, coercion, referent, expert and legitimate) by a commander has predictable consequences for its members, in a platoon or elsewhere.

COMMAND STRUCTURE: 24/7 GROUP EFFECTS

Dependency on the rewards offered by the commands of the leaders;

Irritability and aggressiveness by group members to each other;

Low frequency of suggestions from group members to leaders;

Dissatisfaction with quality of life;

High quantity and low quality of productivity.

COMMAND STRUCTURE: THE 24/7 COPING STRATEGIES

Withdrawal physical (I leave voluntarily or get a medical discharge for 'sore back'.) and emotional (Water off a duck's back. I am out of here in eight weeks so I feel very little whatever happens.)

Form alternative relations to balance the cost (The DI is only one instructor. The PE man said I did the assault course well.)

Reduce the status of the leader by making the leader's satisfaction less (Exaggerated deference amounting to 'taking the mickey' within limits.)

Form coalitions with other members (If we stick together we can beat this.)

It means, in the different military rites of passage, that *individuals will modify aspects of their normal behaviour pattern in exchange for status, unless the price is too high.* What is the price in the attrition process? The price is fixed, and has been for centuries - the motivational costs of learning under a command structure where *coercion and rewards and punishments* are used constantly. The command is never personal: by saluting an officer one honours the rank, and not the person with the rank. Prolonged and invariant 24/7 command leadership produce the effects on group members shown in the left panel. This means that those selected must have personal coping strategies to function adequately in this type of social learning climate. If the individual costs are too high, then motivational strategies of cost-reduction have to operate to maintain equilibrium by reducing anxiety.

These, in the inserts on the social context of training, can be seen alongside command structures. Just how well one could assess the prevalence and effects of continuous existence under severe command conditions is an unknown. Given the overwhelming need to preserve status and not be regarded as in any sense as socially undesirable, *the probability of adverse comment or personal distress in identifiable questionnaire replies about how commanders are perceived is remote,* as had already been admitted by psychiatrists conducting surveys with a variety of self-report inventories imported from civilian sources This knowledge, however, did little to persuade the same authors that their epidemiological studies could be fraught with, if not error, then bias. Clearly, any attempt to identify recruits at risk by asking questions has to have built-in safeguards against mendacity or guarded responses such as those seen in the Belgian and Northern Ireland responses to questions about ethnicity and sectarian identity.

STRUCTURAL DETERMINISM: LIFE IN SQUADS
Behaviour in social contexts largely depends on the nature of the society in which it occurs: but military units are unique in their demands. This is no new flash of insight. The unsurpassed analysis of the fundamental goal of military society, involving the rigours of recruit training, and by implication, life on deployment has existed for more than half a century. No one has been more precise about military

---

SCHNEIDER'S DETERMINISM

Army ...training is...the efficient execution of the masculine role of toughness, ruggedness, ability to 'take it' – which is the aim of successful combat. The sick evade this specific role by acting in precisely the contrary fashion: they are neither tough nor rugged, but unable to 'take it'. From the cultural perspective alone, the sick role is the direct negation of the major goal of army....culture'. (Schneider, 1947, pp 323-333.

SCHNEIDER'S CULTURAL DETERMINANTS: IDENTIFYING THE THREAT

From the cultural perspective alone, the sick role is the direct negation of the major goal of army....culture' David M. Schneider, 'The Social Dynamics of Disability in Army Basic Training' Psychiatry, 10, 1947, pp. 323-333.

'He was singled out by the NCO Instructors as the weak link. That disrespect was passed down from the officers to the NCOs to the recruits, and everyone bullied him.' Scott Knowles, The Sun Newspaper, 04/12/04

goals and their absolute requirements, demanding unique social interaction and sanctions, than Schneider, whose contributions to sociology are universally acknowledged. Qualities of fitness, affiliation and masculinity may have limited value in today's politically correct commercial environments. The platoon is a social context just as powerful in its own right as the command structure. Its own learning environment is dynamic, in the sense that it undergoes change. Without conformity to the masculine role, obligatory because of demands in basic training and deployment, life is by definition difficult if not impossible for those who are perceived by 'squaddies' and superior officers alike, as misfits due to physical frailty or mental illness, regardless of their other capabilities.

Nowhere is rejection more apparent than in the social dynamics that surround one of the most common routes out of basic training, sickness and medical discharge for ailments that are not treated in hospital. For the squad member, a medical discharge may be acceptable if proved genuine, while a voluntary discharge for an undisclosed complaint calls in question the basic attributes of fitness, affiliation, and masculinity. Where sympathy and support may be extended in initial stages to the soldier having difficulties, this turns to aggression, scapegoating and exclusion from platoon membership when individuals hinder the platoon in its quest for status, signalled by, 'toughness ruggedness and the ability to take it'. With a sick person in the platoon, goal attainment (for example in the recruitment catchphrase (*Being the Best*) is unlikely, if not denied. According to Schneider, all those belonging to medical and voluntary withdrawal categories do not, and indeed cannot, achieve membership status within platoons by the very nature of the prescribed demands of the role. Given this knowledge, those seeking medical discharge for non-hospitalised ailments, for voluntary discharge, and those withdrawn for 'recruitment procedure irregularity' may have sought an 'honourable' way out.

SCHNEIDER'S CULTURAL DETERMINANTS: NEUTRALISING THE THREAT

'This threat is neutralized by isolating it and insulating the group from it.' David M. Schneider, 'The Social Dynamics of Disability in Army Basic Training' Psychiatry, 10, 1947, pp. 323-333.

'He often used to have to eat on his own in the chow hall because nobody wanted to sit next to him.' Scott Knowles, The Sun Newspaper, 04/12/04

'If you are mentally ill or in any way ill in the Army you are 'outcasted' and that is not good when you are living in close proximity to everyone else.' Ben Close, former Coldstream Guardsman (BBC News 15 June, 2010)

SOCIAL FITNESS FOR PURPOSE

Fitness is not simply a physiological matter, and, for those who suggest that it be appraised prior to enlistment, there is a psychological aspect to the pursuit of fitness. That aspect may be the clue to what may prove to be the core part of the social interaction selection process. People who are fit for purpose will also have interests and attitudes that show it, as the monumental work by Alley (1976, 1977, Alley & Matthews, 1982) on military vocational interest scales proves. Similarly, those who are affiliative and masculine in orientation will reveal leisure interests and attitudes and will value behaviour consonant with platoon success. In short, basic training success will display a modal interest, value and attitude profile that is associated with successful platoon membership, conformity to the role requirements and job satisfaction. Vocational interest follow up (Matthews, 1982, p.1) based on using Alley's VOICE with Air Force personnel showed that 'an orderly and significant relationship between predicted job satisfaction and attrition' existed at two and three years' distance from recruitment.

Many failures will not have these interests, nor will they value the same things, nor will they have concordant attitudes. These will either fight to survive, or they will find avenues of escape. Dynamic theory suggests the flight phenomenon is more likely than the fight option. At least, the flight route is taken by more than two-thirds of those who leave basic training. To use everyday speech, 'Their face did not fit. They were not cool. They did not have what it takes'. In the squad there are social demands and occupational stresses as important as externally imposed rewards and punishments.

OCCUPATIONAL STRESS

The construct of occupational stress is directly relevant to life in recruit camp. The most recent and directly relevant accounts are by Macpherson (2011) and Jackson, Agius, Bridger & Richards (2011). Both provide comprehensive literature reviews of the nature and consequences of occupational stress. A number of stress studies have emerged from the Royal Navy research group (Bridger 2008; Bridger, Brasher, Dew & Kilminster 2008; Munnoch & Bridger 2008a; and Munnoch & Bridger 2008b). But direct studies on the measurement of stress and its effects in military contexts are few. Jackson et al. (2011) recently conducted a study of occupational stress in 476 army recruits where unmodified but specially administered civilian inventories were successful in predicting 85 percent of those who were asked to leave. Other physical and personal factors previously thought relevant did not contribute to the array of predictors. The results of Macpherson's unique work on Royal Marine Commandos in training under stress are discussed in Chapter 16, where *Health Related Quality of Life* (HRQOL) measures were employed with others. Only ten questions were needed to predict successful trainees undergoing perhaps the most stressful training available.

FIT FOR PURPOSE

Why, Hal, 'tis my vocation, Hal. 'Tis no sin for a man to labour in his vocation'.

Henry IV Part 1, Act1, Sc. 2

STRESS

'That beads of sweat have stood upon thy brow, like bubbles in a late-disturbed stream'.

Henry IV Part 1, Act2, Sc. 3

KNOWING THAT AND KNOWING HOW IN NEW TEST CONSTRUCTION

This chapter has asserted that theory in the mind of the test constructor prescribes what to measure. An important addition to the conventional approach is knowing that metaphors, models and measurements combine to produce a coherent argument for the kinds of knowledge needed to predict basic military role successes and failures that are motivational in origin. The goal in the context of a stressful and novel experience is to determine what inferences can be made from the samples of statements made by those in a volunteer culture of basic training, in order to determine the possibility that they are at risk from rejection and failure. One must also know how to go about measuring what is necessary for integration within a computer-delivered system that leaves a very important, but strictly defined role for recruiting and training officers.

Initial interpretation is, nowadays, easily within the compass of an expert system in the computer. The recruiting officer role can be as wide as is necessary. What, though, has psychometrics to offer recruitment officers in their roles, or to counsellors during training?

ALL IS NOT LOST: UNDERUTILISED PSYCHOMETRIC EVIDENCE

In spite of any concerted attempts to use psychometric evidence that is associated with dropping out of training, or being asked to leave, there is sufficient to make a case for non-cognitive assessments. There are several published psychological sources providing detailed empirical findings that identify positive and negative qualities of who wish to work in military organisations. In particular, many of them relate to attrition in recruiting camps. For specific conclusions, the following sources are important. Talcott, Haddock, Klesges, Lando, & Fiedler (1999) found that of the four most common reasons for failure to complete training a critical risk factor was *instability*. Other well-identified personal dispositions predicting early attrition included *a lack of maturity and motivation* (Jensen, 1961), *emotional instability* (Plag, 1962), *overdependence* (Quick, Joplin, Nelson, Mangelsdorff, & Fiedler, 1996), and, most frequent of all, *depression* (Carbone Cigrang, Todd, & Fiedler, 1999; Cigrang, Carbone, Todd, & Fiedler, 1998; Lubin, Fiedler, & Whitlock, 1996, 1999). Positive training outcomes were marked by *optimism* (Carbone, Cigrang, Todd, & Fiedler, 1999), and *self-confidence* (Turner, Dixon, Caulfield, & Wolfe, 1999). Additionally, (Fiedler, Oltmanns, & Turkheimer, 2004) there have been studies of self-reports compared with peer evaluations.

Among the most authoritative and technically complete publications, however, is Holden's study of the effectiveness of a short personality inventory in predicting attrition in the Canadian forces (Holden & Scholtz, 2002; Magruder et al., 2002). Using a sample of 423 non-commissioned recruits in a 10-week Canadian Forces basic military training course, Holden reports that *recruits differed significantly from civilians in terms of psychological adjustment.* Recruits who failed to complete training were more similar to civilians than those who were successful; *and the inventory Depression scale significantly predicted recruit training course release.* Complementary mental health studies are evident in Hoge, Lesiger et al., (2002, 2005); Creamer, Carboon, et al. (2003); Barrett, Boehmer et al. (2005). These severally address the aetiology of psychiatric disorder in military contexts and include attention to measures of health-related quality of life (Voelker et al. 2002; Booth-Kewley et al.2003) with recommendations that Health Related Quality of Life surveys should be periodic for military personnel.

Finally, for those who may entertain doubts about the need to assess the veracity of military self-report data, attention could be directed to Irvine, (2006), Kyllonen (2006) and Roberts, Schulze and Kyllonen, (2006). Equally notable is the recent work of Cigrang, Carbone, Todd, & Fiedler (1999) on mental health attrition from Air Force basic military training. Recruits recommended for discharge often had a history of depression, expressed a lack of motivation to continue in the military, were reporting suicidal ideation, and typically had withheld information on their mental health history during their Military Entrance Processing Station interviews[4].

---

4   This enquiry is reported in Sackett and Mavor (2006) as being a single question about having a history of mental illness; and they recommend a comprehensive questionnaire (p.190)

Table 15.1: *Descriptions of Tests Created for Use in USA Study of 1500 Recruits*

Cognitive Tests	Vocational Interests	Quality of Life	Psychometric Big-Five -Plus -One Inventory	Body Clock
Lackland Tests* Multiple choice items	*Jobs and Occupations Inventory* (JOIN)* Likert scale responses to all items	*Health Related Quality of Life* (Military Version)	The Self Inventory* Likert scale response to single-sentence items	*Biological Adaptation to Day and Night Situations (BANDS)** Likert scale response to items
Six individual test of information processing capability	15 Broad job profiles each of seven items in four families	Three scales based on extensive work in the medical field.	Big Five Factors **Reactive Interactive Nurturant Intellective Disposition**	Three source rationale for three scales.
Error Detection Number Skills Odds and Evens Orientation Reasoning Categories Word Rules	**Environment Business Physical Creative Arts and Media Nurturing and Caring**	**Physical QoL Social QoL Emotional QoL**	Plus **Proactive**	**Morning Style Evening Style Sleep Debt Account**
Computer and paper-and-pencil	Computer and paper-and-pencil	Computer and paper-and-pencil	Computer and paper-and-pencil	Computer and paper-and-pencil
Rtt .80 to .91	**Rtt. 72 to .86**	**Rtt. 82 to .90**	**Rtt. .89 to .81**	**Rtt. .79 to .92**

Note: *Tests Asterisked* are all fully standardised components of The Mindmill Tests*

During the late 1990s, the goal was to devise measures for specific use in military training contexts. In the United States, what to devise and measure, with the ASVAB results already assured, was the challenge. Above all, the subculture of USAF basic training was well understood as a relatively benign example of military culture at large, so that few if any false trails might beckon to the unwary. The operational need was for new and shorter tests of motivation, interests, and quality of life, in addition to the multiple parallel form cognitive tests. Moreover, they had to be *military* tests, not, as in so many medical epidemiological studies, civilian forms introduced without adaptation. They were all developed afresh: and Table 15.1 summarises the output and serves as a convenient reference while they are outlined individually.

PSYCHOMETRIC GENERATION FOR RECRUITS IN TRAINING

The material on attrition shows that identifying those at risk is an internal matter. The opportunity to devise and introduce a comprehensive series of psychometric tests for use among military recruits while in training does not arrive often, if at all. In 1997-98, the situation at Lackland Air Force Base was such that it might be attempted. In fact, it proved possible to complete a programme of test construction trials in the relatively short time available. The test administration centre was particularly suitable, because enlisted men and women from all over the USA come to Lackland for basic training. Although purposive, they were a nationally representative sample of volunteers; and they carried with them their ASVAB results on file. Whatever else was measured was to be referenced against the tests used for their enlistment. The key to completion of the work was excellent support from all concerned, including the recruits themselves. Brooks Air Force Base had been an important test development laboratory for many years, but by the end of the decade it no longer was a psychometric research centre of international fame. Its staff were scattered to the winds, and its programmes were closed. If Macdonald's lessons were to be learned, the work had to be done at Brooks in its last days.

THE COGNITIVE BATTERY
The six tests of the battery are described with their validation data in Chapter 10. They identified the working memory foundation necessary for learning procedures. At the completion of the study, ten forms of each test in their computer-based forms were deposited in the archives of the Air Force Laboratory for future experimental use by the USAF. The ten component scores of the ASVAB were on record, completing a cognitive frame of reference.

WITHIN LIMITS: A PERSONAL APPRAISAL SYSTEM
In addition to developing forms of the Armed Services Vocational Aptitude Battery, its scientists had produced VOICE, a lengthy vocational interest inventory with good validity. In the period 1990-94 Christal's TS-D personality test arising out of his *Big Five* work with Tupes in the 1960s was republished in 1992 and revised following extensive discussion about its trait adjectives and personality questions with Goldberg. Admirable as this potential foundation was, the time required to administer these, and others, including the multiple parallel form cognitive tests were too much for the system to handle. Shorter, equally useful alternatives had to be found before the goals of the project could be realised. Moreover, there was no extant *Health Related Quality of Life* inventory standardised on military personnel; and the need for measures of self-esteem among recruits was evident.

THE SELF INVENTORY: DESIRABILITY, FREQUENCIES, CATEGORY WIDTH
Measures of motivation were deemed essential; and there was already an inventory standardised on USAF personnel available. Years of work by Christal produced the Air Force TS_D personality inventory, measuring the Big Five domain, using 110 statements and 64 trait adjectives. In spite of satisfactory results, it could not be completed quickly: and there remained some misgivings, perhaps minor in themselves, but noted in the pursuit of improvement and perfection, if possible. The Self Inventory (S_I) was the outcome of a decision to create a series of measures parallel to Big Five, but with additions and with a question and response format completely different from that preferred by Christal. The new measures of military motivation arose from cooperation with Christal that began in 1984. Information was exchanged and files of data were scrutinised until his sudden death a decade later. There were three issues that were apparent in the review of TS-D and that were taken into account in the development of the *Self Inventory*.

Table 15.2: Examples of the Self Inventory Items

Examples of The Self Inventory Scale Items

S_I Proactive	**S_I Nurturant (Agreeable)**
I am self-confident, assured	I am kind to people
I prefer to take on responsibilities	I feel sorry for people on welfare
I set out to win: I do not back down	I am pleasant and agreeable
I achieve difficult targets	I respect the feelings of others
S_I Interactive (Extraversion)	**S_I Intellective Habit of Mind (Openness)**
If a party is dull, I get it going	I enjoy applying theories
On social occasions I approach people	I think hard
I really enjoy talking	Philosophical discussions bore me
I am a shy person*	I enjoy intellectual discussions
*Reverse scored	with my friends
S_I Reactive (Conscientious)	**S_I Dispositional**
I set a timetable for my work...	I feel nervous
I keep things neat and organised	I sleep soundly
I check every detail	I feel tense
I like to have everything in its place	I worry about how things
	might go wrong

First, a principle component analysis of 205 trait adjectives analysed by Christal (Personal Communication, April, 1993) showed that the rank order of the loadings of the first component correlated .96 with rank order of the *average* of all individual responses to each item. The popularity of the item, estimated from a scale of how 'characteristic' the trait adjective was of the person making the response, corresponded to its loading almost exactly. This suggested a need for a check on social desirability as an underlying dimension among recruits - not an unusual occurrence. No social desirability indices existed in TS-D; but internal checks on social desirability and guardedness were built into S_I as a result and the TS-D itself was subjected to a fake social desirability vs. true experiment.

Next, of the 110 statements in the Christal inventory, rated on a seven category continuum from very strongly agree through neutral to very strongly disagree 35 contained a quantifier in the expression, such as *sometimes, always, a lot*. The possibility of variation when such quantifiers were used was the result of two influential papers by Steve Newstead and colleagues at Plymouth (Newstead & Collis, 1987; Newstead, Pollard, & Riezebos, 1987). Their findings resulted in re-writing all the S_I item statements without quantifiers and the use of the same recommended six point response dimension of frequency - *Always, Usually, Often, Sometimes, Rarely, Never* - not only in S_I but in JOIN, MRQOL and BANDS. This system meant that all the inventories had the same frequency dimension regardless of item type. This was a big change in comparison with many inventories where the response types were many and varied. There was one important lesson to be learned from the revisions by Christal, and this concerned the response mechanism on screen, using a mouse cursor as the standard. By 1998 in the USA, very few recruits had not used a mouse interface. In any case, practice with a constrained cursor was mandatory prior to test administration. Figure 15.1 shows the standard screen format adapted from Christal's suggestion that a linear display would be better replaced by a semi-circular mode, so that the extremes would not be neglected.

Figure 15.1: Standard Format for All Inventory Items on Screen

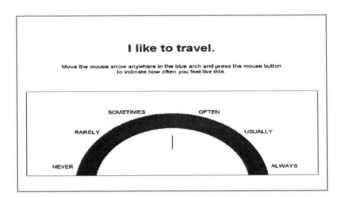

Finally, the *category width* of individual trait words and traits present in statements was uncontrolled in the Christal inventories, in both the trait words and the response mechanism for, which used the low frequency expression 'characteristic' of me. This in itself had an enormous category width, so that any new inventory had to avoid confusion arising out of categories that permitted wide individual variation. The work by Hampson, John, & Goldberg (1986), and Hampson, Goldberg, & John (1987) was critically important in narrowing the width of trait expression so that ambiguities, and as (Horst, 1957, p. 291) asserted many years ago, recognising that ipsative mean points for replying to questions with qualifiers or quantifiers are *individual*, not group referenced.

Table 15.3: The Self Inventory and Christal's Big Five (OCEAN)

Christal Big 5	S_I Nurturant	S_I Reactive	S_I Interactive	S_I Disposition	S_I Intellective	S_I Proactive
Agreeableness	.681(.800)	.393	.287	-.270	.125	.219
Conscientious	.292	.709(.787)	.097	-.263	.254	.424
Extraversion	.285	.154	.817(.784)	-.384	.173	.525
Neuroticism	-.264	-.417	-.152	.761(.839)	-.256	-.403
Openness	.067	.256	.028	-.085	.811(.807)	.316
Reliabilities	.82	.84	.86	.84	.82	.84
Means	68	63	62	37	60	60
SDs	9	11	11	10	11	11

Note: Intercorrelations from Lackland 367 Computer-Delivered Respondents.Figures in brackets from 192 paper-and-pencil responses. Reliabilities and descriptives from 1512 recruits in current study

All of the acquired knowledge from its diverse origins was employed in the writing of the items and their scoring format. It did much to shape the nature of S_I statements, the Likert six point response scale with no neutral point to be used as a possible guarded preference, and to foster built-in checks on that and social desirability. The aim was to provide a short form corresponding to the five factor model and to add one other domain, seen as a subscale of TS-D but never made explicit, namely the *self-assertive or proactive* domain associated with leadership and resiliency. Table 15.2 has examples of the items used in S_I with labels and corresponding *Big Five* domains. It was trialled on several occasions before being standardised on results from the final Lackland study group of 1502 recruits. The comparative results of Table 15.3 are self-explanatory, the goal of a smaller inventory with six domains parallel to the *Big Five* being realised with high correlations and good reliabilities.

Table 15.4: Items Predicting S_I Dispositional Scale Score

Item Stem	
Nurturant	**Habit of Mind**
People think I am not very helpful.	Understanding complex material is hard for me.
I feel sorry for others down on their luck.	Curiosity plays a big part in my mental life.
I am pleasant and agreeable.	I am interested in new ideas and inventions.
I find it easy to put up with difficult people.	I enjoy intellectual discussions with my friends.
	Philosophical discussions bore me
Reactive	
I ease off when I could be working.	
I do much, much more than is expected of me.	**Interactive**
If need be, I have not told the whole truth.	I am a shy person.
When a task bores me, I do something else.	I do not like to be alone for any length of time.
	If I can, I avoid meeting new people.
Proactive	I am uncomfortable if I am the center of attention.
I am self-confident, assured.	If a party is dull, I get it going
I have to be in control of decisions.	I keep myself to myself.
I thrive on competition.	
I scare easily.	
I get even with people who cross me.	
Making money is the bottom line for me.	

NEGATIVE MOTIVATION: VERACITY AND OPACITY IN NERVOUS DISPOSITIONS

The material on health related quality of life in Chapter 15 confirms that the most important predictor of poor quality of life at Lackland AFB is the *S_I Dispositional Scale,* which is essentially designed to identify those with a nervous disposition. Given that such scales have proven useful in Canadian military contexts (Holden and Scholz, 2002) and in other Lackland research of Carbone et al., (1999) and Cigrang, Carbone, Todd, & Fiedler, (1998), there are operational issues to resolve. The veracity of self-reports of anxiety and depression has been doubted by many. Who, after all, is ready to admit a number of qualities not acceptable in a military context? In this study, individual *Self Inventory* items that are *not* part of the *Dispositional Scale* were regressed against the actual scale scores. These hidden, or opaque questions were the clue. Opacity checked the veracity or mendacity of the profile. Those items, not part of the *Dispositional* scale but contained elsewhere in the S_I inventory, that provided opacity are in Table 15.4.

The result was a very large multiple correlation of .794 accounting for 62.5 percent of the variance. *Given this size of correlation, it is possible to isolate all outliers whose actual scale scores are significantly less - or indeed greater - than the predicted scores.* The size of the multiple R identified only 228 recruits out of 1500 whose veracity might have to be pursued. If mendacity were present, there would doubtless be a strong odour in the interview room.[5]

QUALITY OF LIFE (M_RQOL) AMONG RECRUITS

HRQOL

The Three Factor Framework

Although the concept of *Health-Related Quality of Life* (HRQOL) is a relatively recent addition in medical science as an index of accountability, the potency of its constructs are well understood, particularly by pharmacological companies, who are largely responsible for its exponential growth since 1990. A search for the exact phrase 'health-related quality of life' in a search engine will produce over four hundred thousand references. Although empiricism in HRQOL is universal, theory is perhaps less well formulated; and like all theories for relatively new concepts, subject to debate.

Contributions to theory for measuring Health-Related Quality of Life took place over a period of seven years while investigating HRQOL among chronic diseases involving separate groups of asthma, gastric and hypertensive patients (Bamfi, Olivieri, Arpinelli, De Carli, Recchia, Gandolfi, Norberto, Pacini, Surrenti, Irvine, & Apolone, 1999;

Figure 15.2: M_RQOL Structure

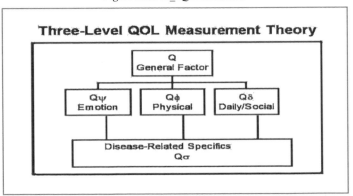

THE FOUR JOIN ENVIRONMENTS

BUSINESS ENVIRONMENT

Business Operations & Management

Office Services & Sales

Computing Science & Support

Hotels, Food & Travel Services

CREATIVE ARTS AND MEDIA ENVIRONMENT

Writing and Editing

Media and Entertainment

Music Performance & Production

Visual Arts

Beauty, Fashion & Style

PHYSICAL ENVIRONMENT

Construction & Engineering

Protection & Military Services

Earth Science & The Natural Environment

Physical Fitness, Leisure & Sports

NURTURING AND CARING ENVIRONMENT

Medical & Health Services

Teaching and Social Services

De Carli, Irvine, Arpinelli, Bamfi, Olivieri, & Recchia G.1. 1995, 1998; Irvine, Hyland, Wright, Recchia, Del Negro, & De Carli, 1992; Irvine, Wright, Recchia, De Carli, & Zanferrari, 1993; Irvine, Wright, De Carli, & Recchia, 1994). Extensive analysis of HRQOL protocols for each chronic disease led to the identification of key domains in the formulation of self-reported patient QOL. General perceptions of wellbeing or malaise were functions of specific statements from three domains – *emotional states, physical activities and social interactions*. These domains were always positively correlated and provided a causal framework for the production of a general factor.

Figure 15.2 shows the structural frame arising out of the chronic diseases studies listed in Chapter 16, and used in the construction of the inventory for recruits. Specific statements about quality of life could be classified into three dimensions, and these three could be used to produce a general scale of coping with health effects on quality of life. *Note that a general index was a consequence of individual questions in three areas, not an overarching determinant, comparable to g, Spearman's or otherwise.*

If the theory were to transfer to the state of HRQOL brought about by recruit training conditions, then Health-Related Quality of Life in basic training could be identified through and measured reliable items describing the three domains. This application of the health-related quality of life theory derived from medical research led to the construction of a simple self-report inventory whose aim was to identify recruits at risk of leaving the service. Items were constructed only after reviews involving serving USAF personnel, and study of the Lackland training environment and its demands. Cross-cultural experience was once again invaluable in item definition. Construction, standardisation and validation were based on the results of 1512 voluntary USAF recruits at Lackland Air Force Base, in 1998-9 during their last week of basic training. There were 999 male and 513 female respondents. For construct validation, a large reference frame of independent measures was available.[6]

JOIN: How JOIN Was Designed, Constructed And Validated

The decision to create a short form for assessing vocational interests did not come easily, because Brooks was the home of VOICE.   Regardless of its impeccable qualifications, VOICE, like most vocational choice forms had two features that were barriers to their use, analysis and interpretation. One was its length when a number of other measures had to be given in the single time slot available. The other was its forced choice format. Although, like the Christal personality questionnaire, Alley's VOICE (Alley, Wilbourn, & Berberich 1976; Alley, Berberich, & Wilbourn, 1977; Alley & Matthews, 1982) was a reality having avoided the pitfalls of older inventories, and had proved that it could predict job dissatisfaction in the USAF with follow-up of departures from the service, it was just too long to fit into the schedule. An alternative had regrettably to be found.

The result was a trial with a printed form with instructions that looked like the short examples. The central purpose of JOIN is to present a wide range of related work activities in the shortest possible framework. Once choices are made, and these are assessed for strength of interest, a more-fine-grained appraisal is pos-sible. Only at this stage does the person completing the inventory finally set those activities of low interest to one side. To achieve these goals, 250 different activities were selected, and then grouped in related clusters of three, to represent not a single occupation, but the kinds of things people do when they work at different types of jobs. The examples are typical.

Groups of words describe certain work tasks and equipment used at work. How often have you thought about working like this? Circle the word that describes how often you have thought about it.

1. JOIN007	Computers /Data Processing/ Websites	Always Usually Often Sometimes Rarely Never
4. JOIN031	Security / Surveillance / Control	Always Usually Often Sometimes Rarely Never
5. JOIN072	Clothing / Design / Fashion	Always Usually Often Sometimes Rarely Never

Interests were sought for job categories involving similar skills and social contacts. Clustering had the great advantage of reducing the number of items needed to show interest in a vocational area, rather than any one specific role. This notion was in line with the adaptive allocation system devised by Lescrève where negotiation could take place if related vacancies had to be filled. *By grouping them, the number of questions asked was reduced from over 200 to fewer than 100 and category width deliberately broadened to represent not one job, but rather a job type.* Then the frequency scale was applicable to find out *how often* people had considered getting involved in them.

---

6   Information Processing Capability (Tests for Selection and Interviews: T_SI), Motivational Profiles (The Self-Inventory: S_I). Job Activity Preferences (Jobs and Occupations Inventory: JOIN), Biological Adaptation to Night and Day Situations: (Circadian Propensities BANDS), Health-Related Quality of Life in the Workplace (Military Version): (HRQoL_W). Other measures included all US Air Force ASVAB results, gender and ethnic status.

Computer-Based JOIN

A special version of JOIN was produced for the computer. In it, the questions were given one at a time. There were only 81 questions in the preliminary version. First analyses showed 13 clusters of items in the 81 questions. These were studied and matched with other trends in the results to produce 15 scales with the reliabilities necessary to provide a profile of work activity preferences. The 15 scales are presented in a smaller number of areas that are related to each other. Reliabilities were satisfactory for scales with seven items. The highest score for any single subscale of seven items is 42, and the lowest possible is 7. JOIN is not lengthy, nor does it ask people to reject outright any type of work activity. More important, it was constructed for today's job opportunities. By combining scores from scales that are part of a family of interests, four general work areas are represented. These and their sub-groups are all shown in the insert. Each has its special focus points, and there are fifteen in all. The report generation system is interactive, following the ranking of the most preferred occupational choices. A complete printout of the qualities of the first and second job choices is provided for discussion with counsellors. The computer-based version of JOIN has been very popular in work with school leavers since 2008 carried out by Mindmill in Northern Ireland and elsewhere.

BE THERE WHEN.......?

§ *BANDS Morning Style: A preference for doing things early in the day*

§ *BANDS Evening Style: A preference for doing things later in the day or in the evening*

§ *BANDS Sleep Debt Account: Tendency to accumulate a sleep debt on a regular basis*

§ *BANDS Body Clock Regularity Scale*

BANDS

In all forms of life, there is a response to degrees of light and darkness, which can be called Biological Adaptation to Night and Day Situations. These initials (B.A.N.D.S.) form the name of this inventory for use with normal people[7]. Human beings have a cycle of response that covers a 24-hour period, unlike many species of plants and birds, whose growth or migration cycles are seasonal. There are four sources of influence on the adaptation patterns of individuals, apart from the body chemistry, taken for granted.

THE FOUR BANDS SCALES

To measure these attributes and dispositions, an inventory of four scales was constructed, each scale being based on one of the four major factors affecting ability to focus on the tasks in hand. The rationale for developing BANDS among recruits was the knowledge that fast deployment over time zones was subject to jet lag. Knowledge of the degree of cognitive adaptation necessary from individuals with different biorhythms was considered appropriate, although it was not an immediate focus for identification of dropouts.

---

7   Richard Roberts was the driving force behind the production of BANDS.

DISCUSSION

The various inventories were subjected to rigorous review before they were used. They were not conceived as part of any new theory construction. They were meant to be applied in the military structures for which they were intended. The result was a broad spectrum of information from which to construct personal appraisals of life as a recruit in training. From their deployment at Lackland, identifying recruits and serving personnel for whom counseling rather than attrition and mental distress in its various forms became a viable option. The last chapter shows how this conclusion was reached.

CHAPTER 16

THE PSYCHOMETRICS OF RECRUITMENT AND ATTRITION

Results from all of these scales were available in an attempt to assess the relative usefulness of non-cognitive supplements to the regular ability screens applied to recruits. It seemed axiomatic that the health related quality of life among recruits in training would exert a major effect on a desire or capability to finish the course. Accordingly, the first look at potential links to attrition was what factors had affected the health of the recruits while at Lackland AFB. Two approaches were taken. One asked simple questions about health status. The second was to assess the validity of health related quality of life questions in assessing the risk of attrition. Some years later, an opportunity to test the potential of the results arose when an independent evaluation took place in a company of Royal Marine Commandos. There was one vital difference. The Lackland data was collected in the last week of training, where there were no drop-outs: but the Marine results were collected before decisions were made to pass or fail. Operational use was a consummation greatly to be desired.

PHYSICAL AND MENTAL HEALTH AMONG USAF RECRUITS

The Physical Sick Role: Health Status, Aches, and Pains

As part of the validation programme for *The Self-Inventory,* participants were asked a number of simple health questions fronting the *Health Related Quality of Life* inventory, enquiring after their general health status, whether they were on prescription drugs, how often they reported sick, and whether they were injured during training. The Insert gives a basic summary of the replies.

The outcome was surprising to some extent, in that thirty percent said they were not usually in good health; one in seven was injured, although no specifics were asked for; and one third reported sick at least once, all during a six-week period. A number of recruits were on prescription drugs, females at forty-three per cent being almost half of their number, twice the male percentage, suggesting possible use of contraceptives as

THE SICK ROLE CALL?

70 % report usually in good health

1 in 7 injured during training

34% reported sick at least once during a six week period

22% of males on prescription drugs

43% of females on prescription drugs

the reason. However, all had survived to the last week, when the tests took place. They were survivors and had not left or been asked to leave. Was there more to be discovered from quality of life enquiries to graduates from Lackland apart from a collection of physical symptoms, a number of minor injuries and prescriptions for on-going complaints or conditions?

ACHES, PAINS, NERVOUS DISPOSITIONS

Figure 16.1 shows clearly that the *Dispositional* (Equable) scale of *The Self-Inventory* was sensitive to individual differences in general health, and the frequency of aches and pains, headaches and the degree of tolerance of noise in the living quarters. The charts contrast the effect size of average differences on the *Dispositional* scale when those with low frequencies *(rarely, never)* of symptoms are compared with those who have high frequencies *(usually, always)* on the questions about injury, aches and pains, headaches, use of prescription medicines, and good general health. The effect sizes are dramatic. To elaborate, the average score of the *Dispositional* scale was 37. A low score indicated a normal disposition and a high one a nervous disposition. Only 22.6 percent of those who reported seldom if ever having aches and pains had scores greater than 40. This contrasts with 57.9 percent of those who reported having aches and pains often and usually scoring over 40. Those with frequent aches and pains were twice as likely to score over 40 as those with few or none. In addition, they reported on some aspects of communal living in the USAF. We asked them in the *Health Related Quality of Life* inventory if the *noise in the dormitories annoyed them; how frequently they might have experienced headaches and other aches and pains; if they needed more time to think; how they liked the food on offer.* Why were these questions part of the survey?

Figure 16.1: Symptoms of Neurosis

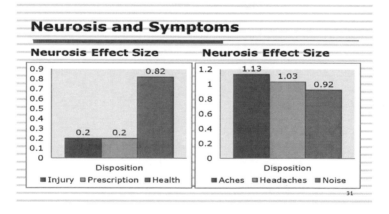

These questions were deliberately fashioned to assess *Health-Related Quality of Life;* but they had also proved during World War Two symptomatic of those unlikely to succeed in military operations (Bennett and Slater, 1945). This virtually unknown paper by Bennett and Slater is remarkable for three reasons. First, it shows an original approach to finding recruits whose dispositions made them proven risks on active service. Second, Slater's precise mathematical proof of the effectiveness of key items is even now not likely to be understood by many: and was far too labour intensive to employ in time of war. Last, it had no further reference in military psychometrics in spite of its originality, or even, perhaps, because of it. In that, it shares with the panoply of meticulous research into causes of attrition, the distinction of official neglect. The *Dispositional* scale of the *Self Inventory* was used to compare those who were at the opposite ends of the response frequencies for six physical questions. Large differences in the *Dispositional* scale were associated with replies to four of them, general health, aches, headaches and tolerance for noise, contrasted with only minor and negligible association with the use of prescription drugs or an injury during training. Mental health was not an independent domain.

FOOD, COMMUNAL LIVING, THINK TIME

The questions about *food quality, life in barracks and time to think* were also related to differences in the *Dispositional* scale. The average effect sizes when the two extremes of the response scale *(always vs. never)* were compared were once again beyond the 0.25 level necessary for concern and possible intervention. Figure 16.2 shows the different effects of living in a 24/7 command environment with strangers, with food prescribed rather than a matter of individual preference, and where the pace of life is regulated by the need to learn new procedures. Results show clear trends. Responses to three different questions all showed that those with a negative view of these three circumstances also had quite different emotional climates from those who adapted easily to the cultural changes.

Figure 16.2: Communal Living and Dispositional Tendencies

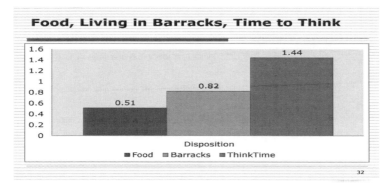

Food quality and shared dormitory facilities were more trouble for those scoring highly on the *Dispositional* scale than for those within the normal range. The largest effect size of more than one standard deviation was associated with those recruits who *needed more time to think*. They lacked composure. *The Lackland Tests* were given on the same day. If they need more time to think, what effect did the health questions show when put against test performance?

HEALTH AND COGNITION

However, there was one other caveat. If health symptoms affected the responses to motivation questions, they could just be a general malaise that affected efforts put into carrying out the cognitive tests three days prior to departure.

Figure 16.3: Health Factors and Information Processing

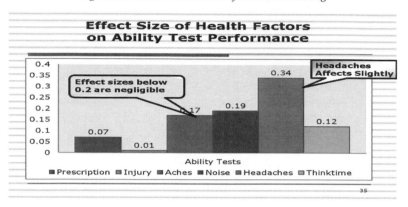

Figure 16.3 puts all the physical symptoms into an array against the general information processing index of training suitability derived from the battery of computer-delivered multiple parallel form tests administered at Lackland. Invariably, the effect sizes of comparing high and low ability test performance associated with the various symptoms reach a noticeable level of importance only as far as headache frequency is concerned. Headaches can be expected to interfere with cognitive performance to some extent. In other words, although the motivational scales demonstrated extensive criterion validity, in that emotional disturbance can predict the frequency of occurrence of physical and mental attributes, performance on widely-used cognitive tests could not be predicted with any similar degree of success.

PERSISTENCE AND QUALITY OF LIFE
Overall performance was not apparently affects by health factors. But there is more to test scores than the outcome. Randomness is an outcome, but what motivates it? Previously, in Chapter 10, the result of grouping those who had made a random score in the test sessions was detailed. A short reminder is useful in the *Military Quality of Life Scale* (M-RQOL) context. With 201 recruits having one or more negative or random scores out of a total of 1512, the probability of having one or more random scores in the test series is about one in eight, or 13%. Suppose one knew how a recruit feels about the quality of life at Lackland. One question *Wanted to quit because life was not what you expected?* was a valid indicator of motivation during the training period. The probability of producing a random score is 13% without knowledge of the quality of life perception of the recruits; but it increases to 70% after the motivation question response pattern was applied. '*Keypressers*' were not well-motivated to persist: and they were among those for whom service life was not a happy event.

HEALTH RELATED MOTIVATION
Without doubt, *The Self-Inventory* and M_RQOL measure qualities distinct from cognitive ability tests: and these are appropriately defined as motivational attributes associated with mental state disorders that will produce physical symptoms. But that was only the beginning. Because six weeks of life in a USAF induction camp was hardly akin to lengthy combat training regimens, physical strength and resilience were not fundamental antecedents to military quality of life. The question to be answered was how were dispositions in recruits related to measureable quality of life outcomes,

provided that equally reliable measures of personality dimensions and health related quality of life, specifically constructed for military purposes, could be used?

VOCATIONAL PROFILES FOR MILITARY RECRUITS

The next campaign was designed to determine the limits of the use of self-declared interest in a military role. It takes a complementary approach. In particular, the study is secure in the knowledge that interest measures are associated with studying harder to achieve prerequisite skills for occupational success; and with Matthews (1982) work with VOICE showing clearly how long Air Force personnel were likely to remain in any employment that is consonant with individual interests. Two questions about their use for enhanced selection procedures are addressed here. They were the political concerns that doubted the reliability and veracity of replies to the questions in the inventories. How trustworthy are self-report interest scales? How much more can they offer recruitment agencies than ability tests?

THE VOCATIONAL INTERESTS OF RANDOM NUMBERS
A perennial issue in the use of vocational inventories is their propensity to produce profiles that are the result of near-random responses. Where there are many jobs derived from many items, it is possible that 1 in 20 of the profiles could be produced by chance. No one has bettered the implicit criticism of Burnham and Crawford's (1935) methods in an aptly titled paper *The Vocational Interests of a Pair of Dice*. They rolled the dice on both the *Bernreuter Inventory and The Strong Vocational Interest Blank* to produce profiles equally likely for a scoutmaster or journalist.

Table 16.1: Military Interest: Rolling the Dice at Military.com.

Chance Item Label	Chance Item Label	Chance Item Label
28 Work with electronics	25 Learn foreign languages	48 Learn to skydive
8 Sing in a musical variety show	47 Fight fires	10 Conduct research studie
50 Build a radio	42 Fight crime & drugs	19 Train others to reach their goals
13 Work with aircraft, cars, tanks, ships	24 Work with TV, Radio or broadcasting	30 Lead a project team or committee
4 Construct wooden furniture	19 Train others to reach their goals	29 Work in a science or medical lab
23 Write news, speeches	13 Work on aircraft, cars, tanks, ships	43 Learn pharmaceuticals
Actual On-Line Job Suggestions	Actual On-Line Job Suggestions	Actual On-Line Job Suggestions
Communications and Information Computer Systems Aircraft Maintenance Vehicle Maintenance	Vehicle Maintenance Nuclear Munitions Civil Engineer, Electrical Engineer	Contracting Superintendent Education And Training Helper Acquisition Manager

Accordingly, with the benefit of hindsight from Burnham and Crawford, the dice were rolled again as a precaution for this study, in two different vocational contexts. The first was an attempt to replicate a real-life context where an on-line source was accessed and six items in a 50 item inventory were checked at random on three different occasions. In particular, guidance was sought on the availability of US Air Force vacancies. Table 16.1 reveals the items checked and the responses from the computer about what vacancies were available from the randomly expressed interests. Admittedly, the information provided by the dice was scant, but on inspection, the site responses may appear to be ill-matched to what was made available.

In all fairness, the exercise was repeated with *JOIN*, the inventory being filled in from a set of random numbers generated for responses 1 through 6 representing an interest scale from Never to Always for each item. *Briefly, when this was done, the broad categories results persistently showed a random fluctuation around a mean of 53 and a standard deviation of 3. No category score was ever more than 1 SD distant from the mean generated at random.* Any set of responses from an applicant that came within these limits would be judged unreliable. By invoking these checks and balances, it was possible to guard against randomness in JOIN and to remove the age-old criticism against the use of such questionnaires.

PREDICTING COMMITMENT TO MILITARY SERVICE
The central operational question we addressed was the extent to which commitment to a military career was evident among USAF male and female recruits. Was JOIN equally sensitive to the needs of female and male entrants? Once more, the issue of responding in a socially desirable way to be consonant with a preferred job, was a focus of attention. Moreover, response patterns were shown to predict the strength of this commitment obliquely,

Reliability? Veracity ?

Safeguarding Vocational Interests

from indirect measures. In operational contexts, the actual stated commitment is compared with the predicted measure derived from other sources. The scale used as the outcome variable was the *JOINSERV (Military and Law Enforcement)* subscale of the Jobs and Occupations Inventory. The predictor variables were the items of the remaining vocational interest scales, not obviously connected with service in military organisations, and the six personality scale measures from *The Self-Inventory*.

Table 16.2 shows those items within the *JOIN Inventory* that can be used to predict the *MILITARY & LAW ENFORCEMENT* scale scores of individuals. They are arranged by positive and negative weights for males and females to provide easy comparisons. The patterns of both groups are very similar, suggesting validity generalization across genders. When the *JOIN Inventory* variables were used alone, the male correlation was .768 and the female .812. This check on faking in high stakes testing serves to dispel standard objections to the use of vocational choice instruments.

Table 16.2: Military Interests Using JOIN's Non-Military Scale Positive Items.

Positive Female	Positive Male
Hunting / Shooting / Fishing	Sailing / Camping / Hiking
Sailing / Camping / Hiking	Hunting / Shooting / Fishing
Air Traffic / Control / Decisions	Air Traffic / Control / Decisions
Autos / Motorcycles / Repair Shops	Physical Activity / Outdoors / Adventure
Drafting / Blueprints / Scale Models	Languages / Translations
Sports / Coaching / Playing	Welding / Riveting / Metalwork
Physical Activity / Outdoors / Adventure	Environment / Pollution / Prevention
Animals / Dispensary / Cure	Surveys / Buildings / Sites
Physics / Chemistry / Mathematics	Gymnastics / Body-Building / Fitness
History / Politics / Economics	Customs / Immigration / Regulations
Customs / Immigration / Regulations	Acting / Rehearsing / Performing
	Discos / Clubs / Casinos
	Autos / Motorcycles / Repair Shops

Negative Female	Negative Male
Farms / Animals / Crops	Farms / Animals / Crops
Diets / Exercise / Health Farms	Filing / Xeroxing / Faxes
Libraries / Museums / Galleries	Diets / Exercise / Health Farms
Bills / Expense Sheets / Returns	Clothing / Design / Fashion
	Music / Arranging / Composing
	Opinion Polls / Forecasting / Statistics
	Carpentry / Plumbing / Masonry

Note: Dependent Variable: MILITARY & LAW ENFORCEMENT Scale

RELIABILITY, VERACITY AND OPACITY

The importance of this accurate prediction of military commitment of men and women from oblique sources is that it holds in spite of quite different gender landscapes. The regression equation to predict military interest from items that are not visibly related to life in any of the services can be written and the outcome revealed. The discrepancies between actual and predicted interest in military careers for any individual applicant become the point of interest for follow up. Individual outliers can be identified within any specified standard deviation bandwidth and interviewed thereafter. These results lend growing confidence in the assessment of interests that predict a long career in the services if the job corresponds with the expressed wishes of the recruit. With checks for reliability and veracity from within the inventory itself, there is a strong case for its use.

TELL ME THE TRUTH. ARE YOU A MAN OR A WOMAN?

IS THE RECRUIT FEMALE OR MALE? CLASSIFICATION BY ATTRIBUTES

A definitive study (see Chapter 8 Table 7) had already been completed (Beard & Collis, 1991) in the University of Plymouth to investigate the role of vocational interest and personality measures as adjuncts to conventional ability screening tests. The aim was to use these measures to predict the actual job classifications of recruits in training. Three job categories were available*: Royal Navy Artificers (Technical); Royal Marines (Combat); and Women's Royal Naval Service (WRNS: Mainly Logistic And Keyboard-Related Functions).* Using discriminant function analyses, it was possible first to attempt to classify these entrants into their service categories by initial ability test scores; and then to note improvements in accuracy by adding in cumulative fashion vocational interest test and then personality test scores. Dramatic increments in predicting actual training regimens were apparent, with a success rate of ninety percent.

With this precedent in mind, proving a parallel in the new cultural framework provided at Lackland AFB was a challenge. There was no indication of the branch of the service allotted to the recruits. But we did know if the recruits were male or female. *If the sex of the recruit could be identified from the test results alone, then the first step to their use in a more comprehensive arena could be considered.* Hence, in the initial analyses of data from the representative cohort of 1500 US Air Force recruits who completed the battery at Lackland Air Force Base, San Antonio Texas, USA during 1998-99, we posed two questions. *What degree of accuracy identified interest in a military career among males and females from their test scores? Could the extent of interest in USAF service be checked for veracity?* These questions have been answered unequivocally. There was one more. *As a primary concern, did a gender landscape of predictors emerge from the results?*

FEMALE AND MALE LANDSCAPES
These were neither idle nor academic questions, because of policy changes governing female participation in operational roles in active service. Because gender was a dispositional and habituated attribute that seldom underwent any significant change, the success or failure of psychometric tests to differentiate accurately males and females was an acid test. Only if some success were to be registered here, then more work could be undertaken to estimate precisely the chances of pursuing a career in a military context. Identifying males and females from test results using the techniques already proven in 1991 at the University of Plymouth was the next priority.

Table 16.3: USAF Male and Female Classification Using Psychometric Test Results

Predictors	Females	Males
	Classified%	Classified%
ASVAB Component Tests	73.0	85.8
ASVAB + Big Five from S_I	75.8	86.0
ASVAB + S_I Big Five + JOIN	84.6	91.4
ASVAB + Individual Test Items	89.0	97.2

Table 16.3 shows an outcome of not unreasonable practical use. Like its Royal Navy predecessor, it reveals an increasing accuracy of classification of male and female recruits, but using 1500 Lackland Inductees, of whom 513 were females and 999 were males. This was a promising start to the full exploration of the power of non-cognitive tests in identifying attributes among recruits. A further check was made using a logistic regression based on the same variables. This provided probabilities of successful allocation to gender-role consonant with job categories, with an overall accuracy of 91.3%. Inspection of the overall patterns showed 4 Ability, 19 Personality and 26 Interest items were needed in the single discriminant function required to classify them. Although the aptitude scores were necessary, they were not sufficient in themselves. Additionally, the qualitatively distinct male and female landscapes were intuitively certain, beginning with the customary *v:ed* or verbal-educational advantage of females, offset by *k:m* or mechanical-spatial propensities of males. These ability differences are just the skeleton.

The body of evidence was augmented by clearly differentiated male and female interest items, and finally anchored by the long-term suspicion that women are in the majority when the job needs conscientious and detail-focused mind sets, which were surfaced by personality items. Not without concern for those who advocate front line roles for women was the result showing that only 11 percent of female recruits could fit the profile landscape of males, sharing ability, interest and motivational attributes. *If maleness were the criterion for entry to the services, and a sex-fair 'blind' approach adopted by using the test results from anonymous internet sources, only eleven percent of women would have been wrongly admitted, and three percent of men wrongly excluded.* No other comparable success rate exists in the history of military psychometrics!

There are not only differences in aptitude capabilities, there are distinct vocational interest and motivation patterns, clearly recognizable and substantiated in the long history of research on differences associated with females and males. Military motivation by sex of entrant could be modelled. Once in training, however, could motivation to enlist be maintained? Occupational stress was guaranteed for men and women, and with it challenges to mental health and quality of life. How accurately might the risk of drop-out be assessed, using all the tools at one's disposal?

Table 16.4: Three Factor referenced Scales of Health-Related Quality of Life in Basic Training (N=1512)

Emotional QOL	Physical QOL	Social QOL
Felt discouraged or downhearted?	Felt threatened (picked on) by people in the flight?	Wanted privacy, but couldn't have any?
Worried about your ability to succeed?	Found some PT exercises too hard to do?	Been sleeping badly?
Worried about things that might happen?	Been blamed for letting the flight down?	Found that living in dorms makes you feel uncomfortable?
Been afraid that you wouldn't pass the course?	Been breathless during PT activities?	Had your sleep disturbed?
Worried more than most people?	Had problems walking 300 yards quickly?	Deliberately avoided someone in the flight?
Felt tense?	Had difficult day-to-day relationships in the flight?	Taken a personal dislike to person(s) in the flight?
Had panicky feelings?	Had trouble marching in step with the flight?	Lost your temper?
Become mentally exhausted (tired like never before)?	Forgotten where you put things?	Been restricted in your social life?
Wanted to quit because life was not what you expected?	Been made fun of by people in the flight?	Been aware that sharing facilities can make life difficult?
Been unable to think straight?	Forgotten a drill movement?	Had headaches?
Felt like not doing anything anymore?	Not been able to remember things?	
Been hassled by the pace of life around you?	Had problems climbing flights of stairs?	
Complained to your family about what was happening to you?		
Wanted to go home to be with your own friends?		
Needed more time to think?		
Mean 44.0 Std. Dev. 14.3 Cronbach's Alpha .911	Mean 23.5 Std. Dev. 7.2 Cronbach's Alpha .793	Mean 32.8 Std. Dev. 8.1 Cronbach's Alpha .761

Table 16.5: Scale Intercorrelations and General Factor Loadings (N=1512)

	Emotional QOL	Physical QOL	Social QOL	Coping QOL	G Factor Loading
EmotionalQ0L	1	.659	.651	.558	.862
PhysicalQ0L	.659	1	.558	.582	.788
SocialQ0L	.651	.558	1	.385	.717
Coping Skills	.558	.582	.385	1	.653

Note: Extraction Method: Maximum Likelihood. 1 factor extracted. 4 iterations required.

MILITARY QUALITY OF LIFE (M_RQOL) AMONG RECRUITS

The concept of *Health-Related Quality of Life* (HRQOL) is a relatively recent addition to outcome accountability whose potency is well understood in medical science, particularly by pharmacological companies. A search for the exact phrase 'health-related quality of life' in a popular search engine will produce over four hundred thousand references. Although empiricism is universal, theory is perhaps less well formulated; and like all theories for relatively new concepts, subject to debate. The development of theory for measuring *Health-Related Quality of Life* by the present author took place over a period of seven years while investigating HRQOL among chronic diseases involving separate groups of asthma, gastric and hypertensive patients (Bamfi , Olivieri , Arpinelli, De Carli, Recchia, Gandolfi, Norberto, Pacini, Surrenti, Irvine, & Apolone,1999; De Carli, Irvine, Arpinelli, Bamfi, Olivieri, & Recchia G.1. 1995, 1998; Irvine, Hyland, Wright, Recchia, Del Negro, & De. Carli, 1992; Irvine, Wright, Recchia, De Carli, & Zanferrari, 1993; Irvine, Wright, De Carli, & Recchia, 1994). Extensive analysis of patient protocols led to the identification of key domains in the formulation of self-reported HRQOL, regardless of the chronic disease studied. General feelings of wellbeing or malaise were functions of three domains – *emotional states, physical activities, and social interactions.* These domains were always positively correlated and provided a causal network for the production of a general factor with category width restricted to the domains and limited by the construction of specific questions.

THE M_RQOL INVENTORY SCALES
Consistent with a culture-relevant development process, the first draft for the inventory of items was produced only after discussion with USAF personnel about aspects of recruit training and from direct observation of recruit and drill instructor behaviour. After review and editing, the scales themselves were constructed after factoring all the items in the draft form, using maximum likelihood factoring and extracting three factors. Following Varimax and Promax rotations, the items with the highest leadings on the three factors were subjected to scale reliability analysis. Table 16.4 lists the items for the three scales, descriptive statistics and correlations, with internal consistency estimated using Cronbach's alpha coefficient. Inspection of the items in permits verification of the three domains, emotional, physical and social. Each scale reaches a satisfactory level of internal consistency. Distributions approached normality and proved to be capable of further definition by using the extensive array of context variables in regression analyses. The three factor-determined scales are

used as measures of HRQOL for the sample of 1512 USAF recruits.

By isolating items that loaded on all three factors, a short general scale of *Military Recruit Quality of Life (M_RQOL)* was produced, with good internal consistency. The scale, referred to in tables as *M_RQOL Coping* was able to use items from all three aspects of quality of life: and is intended as a counselling tool .capable of being given in an interview. The scale is included with an *M_RQOL 'Outcasts'* subscale in Table 16.10. The *M_RQOL Coping Scale* was also subjected to microanalysis by regression using non-cognitive measures. It was possible to predict the *Coping Scale* scores (R= .679) using the scores from the three independent HRQOL factors, the score on *Interest in Military Service*, morning tendency from the BANDS inventory, sex/gender and age. *Coping skills were accompanied by better Health-Related Quality of Life, greater interest in Military Service, preferring to be active in the morning, being male and being older on entry.* Much later, similar work with US Marine Corps members and their families was discovered (Kerce, 1996; Schwerin, Michael, Glaser & Uriell, 2002). These extensive studies showed how HRQOL scores, derived from questionnaires specially created for Marine contexts could predict outcomes such as job satisfaction, welfare support, re-enlistment prospects and likelihood of long-term enlistment.

Validation Outcomes from M_RQOL

Validation of the quality of life scales from the sample and data characteristics consisted of group comparisons and construct validation by microanalysis of the scale scores using the extensive array of psychometric data available for regression analyses. The large sample size permits inclusive and detailed stepwise regression.

Personality Profiles and QOL

Table 16.6 shows the intercorrelation of the *Health-Related Quality of Life* and the *Self-Inventory* scales based on a sample of 1445 participants for whom error-free responses for cognitive measures were observed, including confidence scores. The importance of the comparison lies in the relative size of the relationship between the *Dispositional* scale and the *Health Related Quality of Life* measures, compared with the much smaller correlations with the rest of the *Self-Inventory.*

Table 16.6: Intercorrelations of Quality of Life and The Self-Inventory Scales

	Proactive	Disposition	Interact	Intellect	React	Nurture
EmotionalQ0L	-.299	**.684**	-.178	-.215	**-.363**	-.179
PhysicalQ0L	-.273	**.485**	-.192	-.161	**-.347**	-.229
SocialQ0L	-.094	**.432**	-.087	-.082	**-.323**	-.241

Those with a poor emotional quality of life declared a more a nervous disposition. And there were modest correlations with a lack of attention to detail and dislike of restrictions and rules. Of course one does not know if the personality trends existed prior to enlistment or were a function of very recent recruit experience. There is simply a strong association on the day.

Table 16.7: Female and Male HRQOL Differences And Effect Sizes

Sex	Emotional	Physical	Social	Coping
Female	45.2	24.5	34.5	46.7
Male	43.4	22.9	31.9	47.4
Total	44.0	23.5	32.8	47.2
Std. Dev,	14.3	7.2	8.1	7.0
M v. F Effect Size	0.12	0.22	0.32	0.10
Probability(N=1512)	.017	.000	.000	.063

Sex and Ethnicity Differences and HRQOL

Validation by category assumes, from previous research findings, that there are significant differences in HRQOL during recruit training when men and women are compared. In general, women have found service life more difficult to cope with than men and they have proportionately less success in their careers. Baumgarten's (2004) work on use of support services confirms this generally accepted outcome; and one would predict a poorer HRQOL in basic training for women than men. Table 16.7 shows the results of group comparisons translated into the three domains and coping skills. Higher scores in the scales are associated with poorer HRQOL in men and women. Female recruits show a consistent trend to a less satisfactory QOL in all three domains and in the coping skills scale, although not all group means are significantly different from each other. Significance with such a large sample size is not important in operational terms. There are only two effect sizes worthy of attention, *Physical and Social*, the latter being the more pronounced, showing a one-third standard deviation difference. In short, the physical demands and social climate of basic training are more salient in female perceptions of aspects of life at this particular time in their careers.

Ethnic Groups

Participants declared their affiliation with one of the ethnic groups used by the authorities for records purposes. When these were used to reveal the extent of variations, the results of were not such that would indicate the need for special care and attention to groups. The largest effect size of 0.46 standard deviation units separating the best and worst *Social* quality of life perceptions contrasted Asian and Hispanic (best), and Black and Other (worst). However, these are isolated differences compared with those who wanted to quit the service and those who did not, as the results that follow amply demonstrate.

RECRUITS AT RISK: WANTING TO QUIT

Consistent with accounts of emotional instability of recruits as the prime reason for quitting basic training given physical fitness, the *Emotional Scale* was the main criterion of risk. Poor emotional well-being was predicted by nervousness and anxiety *(The Self-Inventory Dispositional Scale)* with a value of .684. Clearly, those with a poor quality of life score were also revealing an unstable dispositional profile. An even stronger prediction occurred when other measures were added in a multiple correlation. These included high sleep debt score indicating sleep disturbance *(BANDS Sleep Debt Scale),* and lack of self-confidence *(The Self-Inventory Proactive Scale).* In all, seven predictor variables *(S_I Dispositional, BANDS SLEEP, S_I Proactive, JOINSERV Military & Law Enforcement, S_I Interactive, S_I Reactive, S_I Nurturant)* produced a final multiple R of .72. The multiple R overall was verified when calculated separately for men and women, (Males .718, and Females .677).

The overall size of the relationship with scores external to the quality of life *Emotional* scale once more provided a check on the consistency of the response pattern for any individual and offers a check on potential faking, if suspected. Consistent with the intercorrelation patterns in Table 16.6, the first element to enter into the regression equation is the *Dispositional Scale* of *The Self-Inventory.* Of course, in addition to not knowing how nervous they were before entry, their quality of life standings before recruit training are not known. The fact remains that health-related quality of life was severely depressed for some recruits during the final week of training when the tests were given.

THE DIRECT QUESTION: WANTING TO QUIT
A check on veracity or mendacity was welcome. But there was more to come. A second strand of evidence comes from *a single pertinent question* in the quality of life inventory.

'THE' QUESTION

***Qual. 060*: Wanted to quit because life was not what you expected?**

The frequency response distributions for this question showed that 11% had wanted to quit in the frequency range *Often-Always.* These must be seen to be among those most likely to have found military life hard to accept. Surprisingly perhaps, only a little over half (52% of the sample) had *never* thought of quitting at any stage: 23% had *rarely* thought of quitting, while the remainder, a quarter of them, had thought of quitting at some time or other. This, it might be noted, in a military training environment regarded as benign compared with many. Replies to this single question could be referenced to the whole array of responses, in particular indicators of motivation, personality, vocational interests and quality of life. The results of comparisons of the salient response category groups were definitive.

When those who had thought of quitting *Always, Usually or Often* are compared with the remainder who *Never, Rarely or Sometimes* considered leaving basic training, the means and effect sizes of pertinent regression variables in Table 16.8 reveal several substantial differences, the highest belonging to the *Emotional QOL and S_I Disposition* scores, as might be expected. All of the observed differences were statistically significant, but in addition, the effect sizes are of operational importance. Because of small numbers in the distribution of the statement indicating a desire to leave, males and females were not separated in this table.

Table 16.8: Mean Differences and Effect Sizes for Quitting Frequency

| | Often –Always | | Never-Sometimes | | |
	Mean	SD	Mean	SD	Cohen's d
JOINSERV Military	21.8	9.3	24.0	10.1	-0.32
HRQOL					
Emotional Q0L	64.9	11.6	42.2	12.8	**1.81**
Physical Q0L	29.5	9.0	22.9	06.7	**0.98**
Social Q0L	39.1	7.6	32.3	07.8	**0.87**
PERSONALITY					
Dispositional Scale	45.4	10.5	36.6	09.3	**0.95**
Proactive Scale	56.5	11.6	60.7	10.3	**-0.41**
Interactive Scale	60.7	12.4	63.0	11.3	**-0.19**
Cognitive Scale	57.6	10.5	60.0	10.8	**-0.22**
Reactive Scale	58.0	10.1	63.7	10.5	**-0.54**
Nurturant Scale	66.6	9.3	68.4	08.6	**-0.21**
	N	169	N	1414	

NERVOUS DISPOSITIONS AND QUALITY OF LIFE

As far as *The Self-Inventory* is concerned, the large effect size of the *Dispositional Scale* is further evidence if its validity. *Personnel who are of a very nervous disposition were far more likely to wish to leave the service than those who were not so challenged. The Proactive and Reactive scales were also useful indicators. The results show that those most likely to want to leave were less conscientious and less self-reliant than those who had no doubts about remaining in the Service.* The ranks of these effect sizes were considered before compiling the summary profile of those Air Force recruits who frequently considered leaving the Service. Other effect sizes of the motivation scales are minor, simply confirming statistical evidence of a substantial degree of destabilization at the end of recruit training.

Short Scales for Identifying Coping and Outcasts

These general trends led to a further refinement, the provision of short scales for use in interviews. Applied psychometrics isolated items that were represented on all three factors; and an attempt was made to first to construct a short scale of *General Coping Skills* in recruit training. At the same time, an *Outcasts* scale was derived from only five items. These are contrasted in Table 16.9.

Table 16.9: General Basic Training Coping and Outcasts Scales

SHORT GENERAL COPING SCALE	OUTCASTS SCALE
Felt confident, sure of yourself?	**Been blamed for letting the flight down?**
Been accepted by others in the flight?	**Felt threatened (picked on) by people in the flight?**
Increased your self-respect?	**Had difficult day-to-day relationships in the flight?**
Remained in good spirits (active, upbeat)?	**Been made fun of by people in the flight?**
Physically felt strong?	**Taken a personal dislike to person(s) in the flight?**
Coped with new people easily?	
Felt happy?	
Done parade ground drills correctly?	
Coped with service demands?	
Been able to keep pace with the workload?	
Mean 47.2	**Mean 10.1**
N 1512.0	**N 1512.0**
Std. Dev. 7.0	**Std. Dev. 4.2**
Cronbach's Alpha .80	**Cronbach's Alpha .73**

The *General Coping Scale* is an overall short quality of life composite derived from factor analysis of all of the items. It was also subjected to microanalysis by regression using non-cognitive measures. It was possible to predict the general coping skills scale scores (R= .679) using the scores from the three independent[1] HRQOL factors, the score on Interest in Military Service, BANDS Morning Tendency, sex/gender and age. *Basic training coping skills were, to sum up, accompanied by greater interest in Military Service, preferring to be active in the morning, being male and being older on entry.*

IDENTIFYING SCHNEIDER'S SOCIAL SCREEN OUTCASTS

For Schneider (1947), outcasts are *necessary conditions* of military life, because they represent threats to the fundamental aim of military life, toughness, resilience and the ability to take it. The creation of a five item sub-scale to identify outcasts was possible from the HRQOL questionnaire. For a five item screen, its reliability was acceptable at .73. The addition of one more item, *Been accepted by others in the flight* raised reliability to .75. Scale intercorrelations with the *Health Related Quality of Life* scales were calculated; and a factor analysis replicated the work done with the *General Coping Skills* subscale. The results are similar, with a general factor showing that outcasts are identifiable in the context of military *Health Related Quality of Life.*

---

1   The items in the short scales were removed from the three basic QOL factors before calculating the corelations.

Figure 16.4: Outcast Propensity Compared with Emotional and Ability Levels

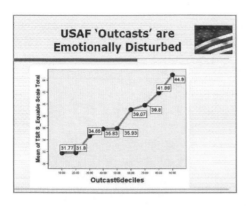

Figure 16.4 is an important contribution to the construct validity of the *Outcasts Scale*. Using the six-item variant, the participants were grouped in deciles, or ten percent intervals. When the average scores of each of the groups was calculated for the *Dispositional Scale* on the *Self Inventory*, and the *Air Force Qualifying Test* composite of the ASVAB. Whereas there is no pattern for outcasts on the ability, or ASVAB scale, there is a linear increase on the scale of emotional security. Those reporting that they were outcasts, to a certain degree, showed a corresponding increase in disturbed feelings. Pre-enrolment cognitive measures gave no inkling of potential loss of self-esteem, but reports of within-group treatment by peers is closely associated with emotional insecurity at the end of basic training. *The attributes for attrition emerge during training and are not identified by tests used prior to induction.*

Checks on Faking an Outcast
The key politically defensible question following all studies of attrition risk has always been how well could other responses predict the likelihood of being outcast, contrasted with pretending to be one? Regressing on the remaining items of the HRQOL scales and *The Self-Inventory* subscales produced a multiple correlation of .74 using 24 variables. So questions *not obviously related to outcast status* in the personality inventory could verify or provide an alternative to the outcast scales if necessary. A built in report function would identify outliers from the correlation function, so that they could be interviewed. Moreover, using only 5 other measures, a correlation of .70 was reached. There were four quality of life items present in the equation, in addition to the S_I *Dispositional Score,* that is in another inventory. In summary, short and well-defined operational scales were produced, capable of indicating adaptive and maladaptive tendencies

OUTCAST?
LET'S CHECK

Deliberately avoided someone in the flight?

Been accepted by others in the flight?

Lost your temper?

Been hassled by the pace of life around you?

during initial training: and if applied at a suitable time with the confidence of the recruits, indicating the need for a counselling interview. The issue of health-related quality of life in training as the prime reason for attrition, but not its cause seemed to be resolved. But there was no sign that its measurement would predict drop-out. That sign had to come many years later.

UNITED KINGDOM DEVELOPMENTS:
PREDICTING ATTRITION AMONG ROYAL MARINES

Previously, in Chapter 8, the detailed and rigorous criterion measures of progress in Royal Marine Commando training in the Royal Navy were held up as examples of how recruit progress in procedural knowledge could be rescored to enable predictions from tests scores to be made. By chance, a study emerged from the same service, showing the value of key questions among a number asked during recruit training in predicting attrition. Thanks to the generosity of W. Macpherson[2] and his colleague, Ms. Dally Virk, it was possible to analyse the entire self-report questionnaire data collected from a company of Royal Marines in training in the UK. Questions that

KEY QUESTIONS FOR COMMANDO TRAINING SUCCESS

1 Personally praises me when I do outstanding work

2 Do you find that living in the grot makes you feel uncomfortable?

3 I have a say in my own work speed

4 Have you or do you take a personal dislike to others in the troop?

5 Have you found the physical side of training too hard to do?

6 Relationships in training are strained

7 Have you felt threatened (picked on by people in the troop)?

8 Encourages recruits to be team players

were contextual adaptations of the Lackland version, labelled as the M_RQOL (*Military Role Quality of Life*) were made available. With minor modifications for use in Royal Marine, as distinct from United States Air Force contexts, the complete

---

2   W. Macpherson first asked for and received permission to use and locally adapt the situations in M_RQOL forms, for example, *troop* for *flight*, *grot* for *dorm* and so on. He kindly allowed me to see the data set and to examine it further. Results were copied to him and his colleague.

inventory was applied with other measures of perceived instructor empathy, the main focus in Macpherson's (2011) research. His study of the effects of occupational stress and empathy between training staff and a cohort of recruits in this particular training period showed that 83 passed and 34 failed to be accepted as front-line commandos. When, with his permission, a discriminant function was calculated on those identified as pass or fail, using all the empathy and quality of life questionnaire items available in the study, the correct identification percentage of passes and failures was 83.2%.

More importantly, perhaps, only eight questions were needed to identify those who passed first time and those who did not. The eight questions listed reflect different aspects of physical, social and emotional quality of life moderated by the perceived empathy of NCO instructors in each training group of seven commando trainees. The unique aspect is the authenticity of the data collected in such unique circumstances. Macpherson's officially sanctioned work is an insider's approach, trusted by the men and training staff, and unlikely to be repeated often, if ever. More than a decade after the Lackland validation, a valid confirmation of trends may be attributed to this one-off attempt at applying M_RQOL to recruits. The direct parallel with Macdonald's Askari enterprise is Macpherson's exemplary attempt to adapt military tests to the particularly arduous Royal Marine training setting and the lesson learned. Data is only as good as its origins. This example of the predictive potential of health related quality of life questions, important though it might yet prove to be, is only a small part of his thesis, exemplary in scope and execution.

Motivation Profiles and Quality of Life

Given people in reasonably good health, the centrality of motivation to succeed in recruit training is widely acknowledged. The Lackland and Macpherson studies showed that scales could be constructed to predict the frequency with which recruits expressed a wish to leave the service, to identify those of nervous disposition for whom surroundings were disturbing, and to provide counsellors with useful diagnostic tools. Moreover, and perhaps crucially, in view of widespread official opposition to the introduction of valid and reliable non-cognitive measures, the computer-delivered focus permitted checks on the consistency, if not veracity, of response patterns in critical scales. Although the efforts of the US services to deal with screening for attrition, so ably represented in Kubisiak et al. (2009) are without parallel in scope and energy, the Lackland and Royal Marine Commando materials together serve as an example of what might be achieved to *forecast the risk of withdrawal from initial training with short and sensitive inventories administered during training, not beforehand.* The cause of attrition is not pre-enlistment personal and social differences, but differences in treatments encountered during training for which no reasons exist. If early warnings of drop-out risk are available, then different treatments can be applied to ensure training success[3]. For example, immediate transfer to phase two training where the demands are different: and, given success there, a review of further training requirements.

---

3   For example, immediate transfer to phase two training where the demands are different: and a review of training requirements thereafter. I have always thought that phase two training should precede basic weapons training after a short orientation period, but this may be regarded as heresy, even from someone like me who had survived basic training in 1956 and completed compulsory national service.

CROSS-CULTURAL RECRUITMENT: A GENERATION OF TESTS

This book began by detailing how, across cultures social and military, to create and use evidence centred multiple parallel forms of cognitive tests, consonant with computer construction, and independent of security-prone IRT functions. Because they could assess the core abilities necessary to learn new procedures in military contexts in a very short time, they made adaptive test forms redundant. The benefits are many, from total security, low cost and opportunities for renewal in small time slots. Additionally, they proved robust, fair to both males and females; and met all the criteria for test items fair to minorities in a unique multilingual and multi-ethnic study in Belgium, where, as in Germany, they behaved exactly as they had done in studies in the UK and United States with the original test language. The tests were reliable and valid among combat troops, USAF ground trades, could be used as a pre-screen for Belgian aircrew, identified satisfactory British Army gunners, predicted first and second phase training in the UK and demonstrated their power in predicting learning electric logic gates. All of this was accompanied by very good reliabilities, both internal and parallel form, with consistent construct validity either as a single battery or when accompanied by other, larger test formations, such as the ASVAB and the German Bundeswehr conscript battery. Within the customary and often arbitrary limits associated with all forms of military criteria, the tests were valid predictors of training success.

Even with these successes, there has been continuous concern since the Second World War at the number of recruits who, competent performers in cognitive tests, fail to prove themselves in recruit training and even beyond it, but particularly among front-line infantry. The last part of the book directly addressed various issues of attrition, attempting to show that additional tests of motivation and quality of life reflecting treatment during basic training in The United States Air Force and Royal Marines could successfully identify personnel at risk.

The study at Lackland Air Force Base was notable for one more important result. In using personality, vocational interest and quality of life instruments, not only were direct measures of motivation successful, they could produce indirect, opaque measures of the same qualities that enabled checks on the veracity and consistency of individual scores. Such computer-based interventions are a modern technological response to long-expressed doubts about the veracity of self-reports when jobs and careers are at stake.

The whole is meant to present a positive and optimistic future for recruitment psychometrics, given the political will to implement procedures if not identical, then in parallel form to those first demonstrated in 1986 by a generation of tests whose potential perhaps is not yet fully realised. Concerted attempts to answer *The Anderson Question* have not been easy: but the question itself underlines the need for a psychometric technology that matches the advances in training made by simulators and computers. Test constructors have a long way to go before another generation of tests provides the ultimate reply.

LIST OF FIGURES AND TABLES

TABLES

REFERENCES AND BIBLIOGRAPHY

AACD (1984). *Counsellor's manual for the Armed Services Vocational Aptitude Battery, Form 14.* American Association for Counselling and Development, Alexandria Virginia.

Ackerman, T. A., Gierl, M. J., & Walker C. (2003). Using multidimensional item response theory to evaluate educational and psychological tests. *Educational Measurement: Issues and Practice, 22*, 37-53.

Adams, M. J (1979). Models of word recognition. *Cognitive Psychology, 11,* 133-176.

Adams, J. W. & Hitch, G. J. (1997). Working memory and children's mental addition *Journal of Experimental Child Psychology 67*, 21-38.

Adler, A. B., Wright, K. M., Bliese, P. D., Eckford, R. D., & Hoge, C. W. (2008) A2 Diagnostic Criterion for Combat-Related Posttraumatic Stress Disorder *Journal of Traumatic Stress, Vol. 21, No. 3, June,* 301-308.

Alderton, D. L. (1989). *US Navy new test research.* Paper presented at TTCP Meeting on Computer-Based Testing (Bath, England) ; USNPRDC, San Diego. Calif.

Allen, J. F. (1984). Towards a general theory of action and time. *Artificial Intelligence, 23*, 123-154.

Allen, J. F., H. A. (1985). A model of naive temporal reason. In J. R. Hobs & R. C. Moore, (Ed.) *Formal theories of the commonness world.* Norwood, NJ: Ablex Publishing Corporation, pp. 251-268.

Alley, W. E., Berberich, G. L., & Wilbourn, J. M. (1977). *Development of factor-referenced subscales for the Vocational Interest-Career Examination.* AFHRL-TR-76-88, AD-A046 064. Brooks AFB, TX, Personnel Research Division, Air Force Human Resources Laboratory, June.

Alley, W. E., & Matthews, M. D. (1982). The vocational interest career examination: a description of the instrument and possible applications. *Journal of Psychology, 112*, 169-193.

Alley, W. E., Wilbourn, J. M., & Berberich, G. L. (1976). *Relationships between performance on the Vocational Interest-Career Examination and reported job satisfaction.* AFHRL-TR-76-89, AD-A040 754. Lackland AFB, TX, Personnel Research Division, Air Force Human Resources Laboratory, December.

Allison, R. B. (1960). *Learning parameters and human abilities.* Technical report (ONR 694(00)-NR151-113). Princeton NJ, Educational Testing Service.

Allport, G. W. (1928). A test for Ascendance-Submission. *Journal of Abnormal and Social Psychology, 23*, 118-136.

Allport, G. W. (1961). *Pattern and growth in personality.* New York: Holt, Rinehart.

Allport, G. W. & Odbert, H. S. (1936). Trait names: a psycho-lexical study. *Psychological Monographs, 47,* No. 211, 1-171.

Almond, R. G., Steinberg, L. S., & Mislevy, R. J. (2002). Enhancing the design and delivery of assessment systems: A four-process architecture. *Journal of Technology, Learning, and Assessment, 1*(5). http://www.bc.edu/research/intasc/jtla/journal/v1n5.shtml.

Anderson, J. R. (1980). *Cognitive psychology and its implications*. San Francisco, Freeman.

Arendasy, M., Hornke, L. F., Sommer, M., Häusler, J.,Wagner-Barrick, M. R., & Mount, M. K. (1993). Autonomy as a moderator of the relationships between the Big Five personality dimensions and job performance. *Journal of Applied Psychology, 78,* 111-118.

Arendasy, M., & Sommer, M. (2005). The effect of different types of perceptual manipulations on the dimensionality of automatically generated figural matrices. *Intelligence, 33,* 307–324.

Arendasy, M., & Sommer, M. (2007). Psychometrische Technologie: Automatische Itemgenerierung eines neuen Aufgabentyps zur Messung der Numerischen Flexibilität [Psychometric Technology: Automated item generation of a new item type for the measurement of Arithmetic Fluency]. *Diagnostica, 53(3)*, 119-130.

Arendasy, M., Sommer, M., Gittler, G., & Hergovich, A. (2006). Automatic generation of quantitative reasoning items: A pilot study. *Individual Differences, 27*, 2–14.

Armstrong, R. D., Jones, D. H., & Wang, Z. (1994). Automated parallel test construction using classical test theory. *Journal of Educational Statistics, 19,* 73-90.

Arvey, R. D. & Campion, J. E. (1982). The employment interview: a summary and review of recent research. *Personnel Psychology, 35,* 281-322.

Aubecq, R. (2010). *Monitoring the Performance of the Struggle against Early Attrition.* In Proceedings of the 52nd Annual International Military Testing Association Conference.

Ayers, E., & Junker B. W. (2006). Do skills combine additively to predict task difficulty in eighth grade mathematics? *In Beck, J., Aimeur, E., & Barnes, T. (Eds). Educational Data Mining: Papers from the AAAI Workshop.* Menlo Park, CA: AAAI Press. pp. 14-20. Technical Report WS-06-05.

Baddeley, A. D. (1968). A three-minute reasoning test based on grammatical transformation. *Psychonomic Science, 10,* 341-342.

Baddeley, A. D. (1981). Cognitive psychology and psychometric theory. In Friedman, M. P., Das, J.P., & O'Connor, N. (Eds.). *Intelligence and learning.* New York, Plenum, pp. 479-486.

Baddeley, A. D. (1992). Working memory. *Science, 255 (5044),* 556-9.

Baddeley, A. D., & Hitch, G. (1974). Working memory. In G.H. Bower, (Ed.), *The Psychology of learning and motivation,* (Vol.8, pp. 47-90).

Baddeley, A. D.; Thomson, N; Buchanan, M (1975). Word length and the structure of short-term memory. *Journal of Verbal Learning and Verbal Behavior*, *14*, 575-58.

Bahill, A. T. & McDonald, J. D. (1982). Zero-latency tracking of baseballs and other targets. *Investigative Opthalmology and Visual Science. 22,* 265.

Ballard, D. H. (1981). Generalizing the Hough Transform to detect arbitrary shapes *Pattern Recognition, 13 (2),*111-122.

Ballard, D. H. & Brown, C. M. (1982). *Computer Vision.* Prentice-Hall, New York.

Baker, F. B. (2001). *The Basics of Item Response Theory (2nd Ed.)* ERIC Clearinghouse on Assessment and Evaluation.

Bamfi, F., Olivieri, A., Arpinelli, F., De Carli, G., Recchia, G., Gandolfi, L., Norberto, L., Pacini, F., Surrenti, C., Irvine, S. H., & Apolone, G. (1999). Measuring quality of life in dyspeptic patients, development and validation of a new specific health status questionnaire: final report from the Italian QPD project involving 4000 patients. *American Journal of Gastroenterology, 94,* 730-8.

Barnard, G. A. (1959). Control charts and stochastic processes. *Journal of the Royal Statistical Society.* B (Methodological), *21,* 239-7.

Barrett, D. H., Boehmer, T. K., Boothe, V. L., Flanders, W. D., Barrett, D. H. (2005). Health-related quality of life of U.S. military personnel, a population-based study, *Military Medicine, Jan, 170(1),*87-93.

Bartram, D. (1986). *Development and evaluation of MICROPAT 4.* SP(N) Report TR 184. Ministry of Defence, London.

Bartram, D. (1987). The development of an automated testing system for pilot selection, the MICROPAT project. *Applied Psychology, International Review, 36,* 279-298.

Bartram, D. (1988). *Validation of MICROPAT Version 4. The prediction of RN Observer and Pilot grading outcomes.* SP(N) Report TR 210. Ministry of Defence, London.

Bartram, D. (2006). Testing on the internet: Issues, challenges, and opportunities in the field of occupational assessment. In D. Bartram & R. Hambleton (Eds.), *Computer-based testing and the internet* (pp. 13-37). Hoboken, NJ: Wiley.

Bartram, D., Beaumont, J. G., Cornford, T., Dann, P. L. & Wilson, S. L. (1986). *Recommendations for the design of software for computer-based assessment.* Leicester, UK. British Psychological Society Report.

Bartram, D. & Choi, M. (1988). *Evaluation of three tests of navigation ability.* SP(N) Report TR 209. Ministry of Defence, London.

Battig, W. F., & Montague, W. E., (1968). Category norms for verbal items in 56 categories: a replication and extension of the Connecticut norms. *Journal of Experimental Psychology Monograph, 80, No. 3, Part 2, 1-46.*

Baumgarten, V. A. (2004). *Job Characteristics in the United States Air Force and Mental Health Service Utilization.* Unpublished PhD Dissertation, Arizona State University, Tempe AZ.

Beard, C. (1990). *Vocational interest and personality factors in naval officers under training.* BSc Honours Project Report, Human Assessment Laboratory, Polytechnic South West, Plymouth, UK.

Beard, C. A. & Collis, J. M. (1991). *Personality and Vocational Interests of Naval Officers under training, the prospective utility of objective motivational assessment.* SP(N) Report TR 260. Office of the Senior Psychologist Naval, Ministry of Defence, London, UK.

Bejar, I. I. (1986a). *The psychometrics of mental rotation, (RR-86-19).* Educational Testing Service, Princeton, N.J.

Bejar, I. I. (1986b). *Analysis and generation of Hidden Figure items, A cognitive approach to Psychometric Modelling. (RR-86-20).* Educational Testing Service, Princeton, N.J.

Bejar, I. I. (1986c). *Final Report, Adaptive testing of spatial abilities (ONR 150 531).* Educational Testing Service, Princeton, N.J.

Bejar, I. I. (1990). A generative analysis of a three-dimensional spatial task. *Applied Psychological Measurement, 14,* 237-245.

Bejar, I. I. (1993). A generative approach to psychological and educational measurement. In N. Frederiksen, R. J. Mislevy, & I. I. Bejar (Eds.), *Test theory for a new generation of tests* (pp. 323-359). Hillsdale, NJ: Lawrence Erlbaum.

Bejar, I. I. (1996). *Generative response modelling: Leveraging the computer as a test delivery medium* (ETS Research Report 96-13). Princeton, NJ: Educational Testing Service.

Bejar, I. I. (2002). Generative testing: From conception to implementation. In S. H. Irvine & P. C. Kyllonen (Eds.), *Item generation and test development* (pp. 199-217). Mahwah, NJ: Lawrence Erlbaum.

Bejar, I. I., & Braun, H. I. (1999). *Architectural simulations: From research to implementation*: Final report to the National Council of Architectural Registration Boards (Research Memorandum 99-2). Princeton, NJ: Educational Testing Service.

Bejar, I. I., Fairon, C., & Williamson, D. M. (2002). *Multilingual item modeling as a mechanism for test adaptation: Applications to open ended and discrete items.* International Conference on Computer-Based Testing and the Internet: Building Guidelines for Best Practice (ITC Conference 2002), Winchester, England.

Bejar, I. I., & Yocom, P. (1991). ,A generative approach to the modelling of isomorphic hidden-figure items. *Applied Psychological Measurement, 15(2),* 129-137.

Bennett, E. & Slater, P. (1945. Some tests for the discrimination of neurotic from normal subjects. *British Journal of Medical Psychology, 20,* 271-282.

Bennett, R. (2001). How the internet will help large-scale assessment reinvent itself. *Educational Policy Analysis Archives, 9,* 1-23.

Berger, M. (1982). The scientific approach to intelligence: an overview of its history with special reference to mental speed. In H. J. Eysenck, (Ed.) *A model for intelligence.* Springer-Verlag, New York, pp. 14-43.

Berry, J. W. & Irvine, S. H. (1986). Bricolage, savages do it daily. In R.J. Sternberg & R. K. Wagner (Eds.) *Practical Intelligence.* New York, Cambridge, pp. 271-306.

Berry, J. W., Irvine, S. H., & Hunt. E. B. (Eds.) (1988). *Indigenous cognition: functioning in cultural context.* Proceedings of the NATO Advanced Research Workshop on "Indigenous Cognition and Models of Information Processing", Kingston, Canada, June 15-20, 1986 (NATO ASI Series D, Behavioural and Social Sciences ; no. 41) ISBN 90-247-3671-4. Dordrecht, Martinus Nijhoff.

Bevans, H. G. (1963). *Probability (Confidence) scoring for multiple-choice tests, applied to the Advanced Matrices.* Unpublished paper. Crichton Royal Infirmary, Dumfries.

Bevans, H. G. (1966). *Probability (confidence) scoring for the Standard Progressive Matrices and the Advanced Matrices.* Unpublished Manuscript of Paper presented to the 65th British Psychological Society Annual Conference, Swansea, Wales.

Bhatia, C. M. (1956). *Performance tests of Intelligence under Indian conditions.* London, Oxford.

Birch, R. S. (1981). *The digit-symbol substitution task: An experimental study.* Unpublished BSc project, Plymouth, UK: Department of Psychology, University of Plymouth.

Birke, W., & Wildgrube, W. *Die anwendbarkeit computerunterstutzter adaptiver testmethoden im bereich der. Bundeswehr* (Wehrpsychologische Mitteilungen 1/78). Bonn, Bundesministerium der Verteidigung Psychlogischer Dienst der Bundeswehr, 1978.

Birnbaum, A. (1957). *Efficient design and use of tests of a mental ability for various decision-making problems.* (Series Report 58-16, No. 71-55-23). USAF School of Aviation Medicine. Randolph Air Force Base, Texas.

Birnbaum, A. (1967). *Statistical theory for logistic test models with a prior distribution of ability.* ETS Research Bulletin RB-67-12. Educational Testing Service, Princeton, NJ.

Birnbaum, A. (1968). Some latent trait models and their use in inferring an examinee's ability. In F. M. Lord & M. R. Novick (Eds.), *Statistical theories of mental test scores* Reading, MA: Addison Wesley (pp. 395-479).

Birnbaum, A. (1969). Statistical theory for logistic test models with a prior distribution of ability. *Journal of Mathematical Psychology, 6,* 258-276.

Blanchard, E. B., Jones-Alexander, J., Buckley, J. T., and Forneris, C. A. (1996). Psychometric properties of the PTSD checklist (PCL). *Behavioral Research Therapy, 34,* 669-73.

Bliese, P. D., Wright, K. M., Adler, A. B., Cabrera, O., Castro, C. A., & Hoge, C. W. (2008). Validating the PC-PTSD and the PTSD Checklist with soldiers returning from combat. *Journal of Consulting and Clinical Psychology, 76,* 272-281.

Bliese, P., Wright, K., Adler, A., & Thomas, J. (2004). *Validation of the 90 to 120 day post-deployment psychological short screen.* (U.S. Army Medical Research Unit-Europe Research Report 2004-002). Heidelberg, Germany: U.S. Army Medical Research UnitEurope.

Blinkhorn, S., & Johnson, C. (1990). The insignificance of personality testing. *Nature, 348,* 671-672.

Bliss, L. B. (1980). A test of Lord's assumption regarding examinee guessing behaviour on multiple choice tests using elementary school children. *Journal of Educational Measurement, 17,* 147-153.

Block, J., Weiss, D. S. & Thorne, A. (1979). How relevant is a semantic similarity interpretation of personality ratings? *Journal of Personality & Social Psychology, 37,* 1053-1074.

Bochner, S., & Van Zyl, T. (1986). Desirability ratings of 110 personality trait words. *The Journal of Social Psychology, 125(4),* 459-465.

Bock, R. D. (1983). The mental growth curve re-examined. In D. J. Weiss, (Ed.), *New Horizons in Testing.* New York, Academic Press.

Bongers, S. H., & Greig, J. E. (1997*). An Australian trial of the British Army Recruit Battery - Part 2.* Report of The Air Force Office, Mawson ACT 2607, Australia.

Booth-Kewley, S. & Larson, G. E. (2003). Predictors of psychiatric hospitalization in the Navy. *Military Medicine. Nov,168(11),904*-10.

Bottenberg, R. A., & Christal, R. E. (1961). *An iterative technique for clustering criteria which retains optimum predictive efficiency.* WADD-TN-61-30, AD-261 615. Lackland AFB, TX, Personnel Laboratory, Wright Air Development Division, March, 1961.

Bownds, C. D. & Mehay, S. L. (2004). *An Analysis of Educational Credentials and First-Term Attrition.* In Proceedings of the 46th Annual International Military Testing Association Conference.

Brand, C. R. & Deary, I .J. (1982). Intelligence and "inspection time". In H. J. Eysenck (Ed.), *A model for intelligence.* New York, Springer-Verlag.

Bray R, Fairbank J, Marsden E. (1999). Stress and substance abuse among military women and men. *American Journal of Drug and Alcohol Abuse, 25,* 239-256.

Bridger, R. S. Dew, A. & Kilminster, S. (2008). Occupational stress and strain in the Naval Service. *Occupational Medicine; 58,* 534-539.

Bridger, R. S. Dew, A. Munnoch, K. & Kilminster, S. (2009). Chronic and acute psychological strain in naval personnel. *Occupational Medicine*; *59,* 454-458.

Bridger, R. S. Dew, A., Sparshott, K. & Kilminster, S. (2010). Job strain related to cognitive failure in naval personnel. *Ergonomics, 53,* 739-747.

Brooks, P. G., Dann, P. L. & Irvine, S. H. (1984). Computerised testing, exacting the levy. In *Bulletin of the British Psychological Society, 37,* 372-374.

Brouwers, S., Fontaine, J., & Mylle, J. (2012). *Are the Belgian versions of the automated cognitive test battery culture fair?* Presentation at the 54th IMTA conference, Dubrovnik, Croatia, November, 2012.

Buchtala, W. (1977). Entwicklung eines testinstrumentes fur individualisierte testung durch adaptive parameterschatzung. In W.H. Tack, *Bericht uber den 30. Kongress der Deutschen Gesellschaft fur Psychologie in Regensburg* (Band 2). Gottingen, Hogrefe.

Bunderson, C. V. (1967). *Transfer of mental abilities at different stages of practice in the solution of concept problems.* Princeton, NJ, Educational Testing Service (Research Bulletin RB-67-20).

Bunderson, C. V., Inouye, D. K., & Olsen, J. B. (1988). *The four generations of computerised educational measurement.* Research Report (RR88-35) Educational Testing Service, Princeton, NJ.

Burnham, P. S. & Crawford, A. B. (1935). The occupational preferences of a pair of dice. *Journal of Educational Psychology, 26,* 508-512.

Burt, C. (1917). *The distribution and relations of educational abilities.* Report No.1868. London County Council, London.

Burt, C. (1928). *Handbook of Tests.* London, Staples Press.

Bycio, P., Alvares, K. & Hahn, J. (1987). Situational specificity in assessment centre ratings: A confirmatory factor analysis. *Journal of Applied Psychology, 72,* 463-474.

Campbell, D. T. & Fiske, D. W. (1959). Convergent and discriminant validation by the multitrait-multimethod matrix. *Psychological Bulletin, 56,* 81-105.

Campbell, J. P. & Knapp, D. J. (Eds.) (2001). *Exploring the limits in personnel selection and classification.* Lawrence Erlbaum Associates, Mahwah, NJ.

Campbell, J. P., McCloy, R. A., Oppler, S. H., & Sager, C. E. (1992). A theory of performance. In N. Schmitt & W. C. Borman (Eds.), *Personnel selection in organizations.* San Francisco, CA, Jossey-Bass.

Carbone, E. G., Cigrang, J. A., Todd, S. L., & Fiedler, E. R. (1999). Predicting outcome of military basic training for individuals referred for psychological evaluation. *Journal of Personality Assessment, 72,* 256-265.

Carretta, T. R. & Ree, M .J. (1996a). Factor structure of the Air Force Officer Qualifying Test: Analysis and comparison. *Military Psychology, 8,* 29-42.

Carroll, J. B. (1972). Stalking the wayward factors. Review of Guilford & Hoepfner's *The Analysis of Intelligence* In *Contemporary Psychology, 17,* 321-324.

Carroll, J. B. (1976). Psychometric tests as cognitive tasks, a new "Structure of Intellect." In L. B. Resnick (Ed.), *The nature of intelligence.* Hillsdale, NJ, Lawrence Erlbaum Associates (pp. 17-56).

Carroll, J. B. (1980a). Discussion. In D. J. Weiss (Ed.), *Proceedings of the 1979 Computerized Adaptive Testing Conference.* Minneapolis: University of Minnesota, Department of Psychology, Psychometric Methods Program, 1980, (pp. 449-452).

Carroll, J. B. (1980b). *Individual difference relations in psychometric and experimental cognitive tasks.* Report No. 163, Thurstone Psychometric Laboratory, University of North Carolina, Chapel Hill, N.C.27514

Carroll, J. B. (1983a). Studying individual differences in cognitive abilities, implications for cross-cultural studies. In S. H. Irvine & J. W. Berry, (Eds.), *Human assessment and cultural factors.* New York, Plenum.

Carroll, J. B. (1983b). The difficulty of a test and its factor composition revisited. In Wainer, H. & Messick, S. (Eds.) *Principals of modern psychological measurement,* Hillsdale, NJ. Erlbaum (pp. 257-82).

Carroll, J. B. (1986a). *A critical synthesis of knowledge about cognitive abilities.* Final Technical Report, NSF Grant BNS 8212486. University of North Carolina, Chapel Hill, NC.

Carroll, J. B. (1986b). Defining abilities through the person characteristic function. In S.E. Newstead, S. H. Irvine & P. L. Dann, (Eds.). *Human Assessment, Cognition and motivation.* Dordrecht, Netherlands, Nijhoff, (pp. 213-236).

Carroll, J. B. (1987). New perspectives in the analysis of abilities. In R. R. Ronning, J. A. Glover, J. C. Conoley, & J. C. Witt (Eds.), *The influence of cognitive psychology on testing.* Hillsdale, NJ, Lawrence Erlbaum Associates (pp. 87-142).

Carroll, J. B. (1989). *Some statistics of homogeneous tests, Estimating ability and item difficulty parameters with the person characteristic function.* Manuscript revised for publication. University of North Carolina, Chapel Hill, NC.

Carroll, J. B. (1993). *Human cognitive abilities, A survey of factor-analytic studies.* New York, Cambridge University Press.

Carroll, J.B. (2002). The five-factor personality model, how complete and satisfactory is it? In H. I. Braun, D. N. Jackson & D. E. Wiley, Eds., *The Role of Constructs in Psychological and Educational Measurement.* Mahwah, NJ, Lawrence Erlbaum Associates, pp. 97-126.

Carroll, J. B., Meade, A., & Johnson, E. S. (1991). Test analysis with the person characteristic function, implications for defining abilities. In R. E. Snow & D. E. Wiley (Eds.), *Improving inquiry in education, psychology and social science, a book in honor of Lee J. Cronbach* (pp.109-143). Hillsdale, NJ, Erlbaum.

Cattell, R. B. (1963). Theory of fluid and crystallised intelligence, A critical experiment. *Journal of Educational Psychology, 54,* 1-22.

Cawkill, P. (1992). *A validation study of the T2 test battery against RM other rank training performance.* SP(N) Report TR299. Ministry of Defence, UK.

Cawkill, P. & Collis, J. M. (1991). *The Plymouth Combined ABC Test Battery for Royal Marine other rank entrants, validity and reliability studies.* Senior Psychologist Naval SP(N) Report TR269, Ministry of Defence, London.

Chaiken, S. R., Kyllonen, P. C. & Tirre, W. C. (2000). Organisation and components of psychomotor ability. *Cognitive Psychology, 40,* 198-226.

Chittenden, T. G. (1986). *Experiment to investigate the relationship between intellect and the speed of information processing in working memory*. BSc Honours Project, Department of Psychology, Polytechnic South West, Plymouth, Devon, UK.

Christal, R. E. (1968a). Selecting a harem - and other applications of the policy-capturing model. *Journal of Experimental Education, 36,* 35-41.

Christal, R. E. (1968b). JAN: A technique for analysing group judgement. *Journal of Experimental Education, 36,* 24-27.

Christal, R. E. & Battenberg, R. A. (1968). Grouping criteria - a method which retains maximum predictive efficiency. *Journal of Experimental Education, 36,* 28.

Christal, R. E. (1981). *The need for laboratory research to improve the state of the art in ability testing. Paper presented at the National security* Industrial Association-DoD Conference on Personnel & Training factors in Systems Effectiveness, San Diego, California.

Christal, R. E. (1984).*New cognitive tests being evaluated by TTCP services.* Report to the Technical Cooperation Program Meeting of 1984, USAF Armstrong Laboratory, Brooks AFB, San Antonio, Texas.

Christal, R. E. (1985a). *Learning abilities measurement programme (Project LAMP)* Unpublished Report, USAF Human Resources Laboratory San Antonio, Texas.

Christal, R. E. (1985b). *New cognitive tasks being evaluated by TTCP services.* Unpublished Report, USAF Human Resources Laboratory San Antonio, Texas.

Christal, R. E. (1987). *A factor-analytic study of tests of working memory.* Unpublished Report, USAF Human Resources Laboratory San Antonio, Texas.

Christal, R. E. (1988). *Theory-based ability measurement, The Learning Abilities Measurement Laboratory.* Aviation, Space, and Environmental Medicine, *59(11),* sec. 2.

Christal, R. E. (1991). *Comparative validities of ASVAB and LAMP tests for logic gates learning.* Final Technical Paper for Period November 1989 - March 1991 (AP1991-031). Air Force Systems Command Brooks Air Force Base, Texas.

Christal, R. E. (1992). Author's note on "Recurrent personality factors based on trait ratings". Special issue on the five-factor model, issues and applications. *Journal of Personality, 60(2),* 221-224.

Christal, R. E. (1993). *Principal components of 205 trait adjectives correlated with average 'characteristic of me' rating,* Personal communication received April 1993 at Brooks AFB, San Antonio, Texas.

Christal, R. E. & Kyllonen, P. C. (1986). Individual differences in learning abilities. In T. Sticht, F. Chang, & S. Wood (Eds.). *Advances in Reading/Language Research*, Vol. IV. Greenwich, CN, JAI Press.

Christal, R. E. & Weissmuller, J. J. (1988). Job-task inventory analysis. In G. Gael (Ed.) *The Job Analysis Handbook for Business, Industry, and Government, Volume II.* New York, John Wiley & Sons, (pp. 1036-1050).

Cigrang, J. A., Carbone, E.G., Todd, S., & Fiedler, E. (1998). Mental health attrition from Air Force basic military training. *Military Medicine, 163,* 834-838.

Clark, H. H. (1969). Linguistic processes in deductive reasoning. *Psychological Review, 76,* 387-404.

Clark, H. H. (1970). Comprehending comparatives. In, G. B. Flores, D'Arcais & W. J. M. Levelt (Eds.), *Advances in psycholinguistics.* Amsterdam, North Holland (pp. 294-306).

Clark, H. H. (1973). Space, time & semantics in the child. In T.E. Moore, (Ed.), *Cognitive development and the acquisition of language.* New York: Academic, pp. 27-63.

Clark, H. H. & Chase, W. G. (1972). On the process of comparing sentences against pictures. *Cognitive Psychology, 3,* 472-517.

Clause, C. C., Mullins, M. E., Nee, M. T., Pulakos, E. D., & Schmitt, N. (1998). Parallel test form development: A procedure for alternative predictors and an example. *Personnel Psychology, 51,* 193-208.

Cofer, C. (Ed.), (1976). *The structure of human memory.* San Francisco, Freeman.

Cohen, J. (1992). A power primer. *Psychological Bulletin, 112,* 155-159.

Collins, A. M., & Loftus, E. F. (1975). A spreading-activation theory of semantic processing. *Psychological Review, 82,* 407-428.

Collins, A. M., & Quillian, M. R. (1969). Retrieval time from semantic memory. *Journal of Verbal Learning and Verbal Behavior, 8,* 240-248.

Collis, J. M. (1993). *BARB analogues afloat: criterion validity studies with the Royal Navy.* Paper presented at the 35th Annual Conference of The International Military Testing Association, Williamsburg, VA. Conference Abstracts Book, pp. 386-390. (also as Technical Report, 2-1994 Army Personnel Research Establishment) Human Assessment Laboratory, University of Plymouth, Plymouth, UK).

Collis, J. M., & Beard, C. A. (1993). *The use of personality and vocational measures for allocation of Royal Naval ratings: some preliminary indicators of validity.* SP(N) Report TR (315), Ministry of Defence, under contract to University of Plymouth.

Collis J. M., & Irvine, S. H. (1993d). *The effects of pre-knowledge, retest and types of test administration on computer generated cognitive tasks in a group of royal navy and royal marine entrants.* SP(N) Report TR 314, Office of the Senior Psychologist (Naval), Ministry of Defence, London under contract to University of Plymouth.

Collis, J. M. & Irvine, S. H. (1994). *The Navy Personnel Series, A New Generation of Cognitive Tests.* Human Assessment Laboratory Technical Report 1-94. University of Plymouth, Plymouth, UK.

Collis, J. M., & Irvine, S. H. (1991a). *Predictive Validity and Utility of the ABC Battery with Royal Navy Officers under Training.* SP(N) Report TR 261, Office of the Senior Psychologist (Naval), Ministry of Defence, London under contract to University of Plymouth.

Collis, J. M., & Irvine, S. H. (1991b). *The Plymouth ABC Battery for Artificer Apprentice Entrants. Validity and reliability studies.* SP(N) Report TR 265, Office of the Senior Psychologist (Naval), Ministry of Defence, London under contract to University of Plymouth.

Collis, J. M., & Irvine, S. H. (1991c). *The Plymouth ABC Battery for RN Non-Technician Ratings under Training. Validity and reliability studies.* SP(N) Report TR 266, Office of the Senior Psychologist (Naval), Ministry of Defence, London under contract to University of Plymouth.

Collis, J. M., & Irvine, S. H. (1991d). *The Plymouth ABC Battery for WRNS Rating Entrants. Validity and reliability studies.* SP(N) Report TR 267, Office of the Senior Psychologist (Naval), Ministry of Defence, London under contract to University of Plymouth.

Collis, J. M., & Irvine, S. H. (1991e). *The Plymouth ABC Battery for RN/WRNS Ratings and RM other Ranks under Training. Validity and reliability studies, summary report.* SP(N) Report TR 271, Office of the Senior Psychologist (Naval), Ministry of Defence, London under contract to University of Plymouth.

Collis, J. M., & Irvine, S. H. (1993a). *The ABC Combined Battery for Artificer Apprentices. Further validity studies.* SP(N) Report TR 311, Office of the Senior Psychologist (Naval), Ministry of Defence, London, under contract to University of Plymouth.

Collis, J. M., & Irvine, S. H. (1993b). *The ABC Combined Battery for Royal Marine Apprentices. Further validity studies.* SP(N) Report TR 312, Office of the Senior Psychologist (Naval), Ministry of Defence, London under contract to University of Plymouth.

Collis, J. M., & Irvine, S. H. (1993c). *The ABC Combined Battery for RN/WRNS Non-Technicians. Further validity studies.* SP(N) Report TR 313, Office of the Senior Psychologist (Naval), Ministry of Defence, London, under contract to University of Plymouth.

Collis, J. M., & Irvine, S. H. (1994). *A new generation of ability tests for selection and training. The Navy Personnel Series.* Technical Report 1,1994, Human Assessment Laboratory, University of Plymouth, Plymouth UK.

Collis, J. M., Tapsfield, P. G. C., Irvine, S. H., Dann, P. L., & Wright, D. (1995). The British Army Recruit Battery goes operational, From theory to practice in computer-based testing using item-generation techniques. *International Journal of Selection and Assessment, 3,* 96-103.

Cor, K., Alves, C., & Gierl, M. J. (2009). Three applications of automated test assembly within a user-friendly modeling environment. *Practical Assessment Research and Evaluation, 14,* 1-23.

Costa, P. T. & McCrae, R. R, (1988). Personality in adulthood: A six-year longitudinal study of self-reports and spouse ratings on the NEO Personality Inventory. *Journal of Personality and Social Psychology, 54,* 853-863.

Creamer M., Carbone I., Forbes, A. B., McKenzie, D. P., McFarlane, A. C., Kelsall, H. L., & Sim, M. R. (2003). Psychiatric disorder and separation from military service, a 10-year retrospective study. *Military Medicine, Nov,168(11),* 941-7.

Cronbach, L. J. (1957). The two disciplines of scientific psychology. *American Psychologist, 12,* 671-684.

Cronbach L. J., & Gleser, G. C. (1957). *Psychological tests and personnel decisions.* Urbana: University of Illinois Press.

Cronbach. L. J. & Snow, R. E. (1977). *Aptitudes and instructional metho*ds. New York, Irvington.

CSIR (1962). *The Spiral Nines Test.* Johannesburg. South African Council for Scientific Research, National Institute for Personnel Research.

Daily Express (2000). Recruits who can't take harsh Army life. *Daily Express Newspapers,* September 19, P.6. London, UK. (Attributed to Michael Burke).

Dann, P. L. (1993). *The BARB computer-based testing system.* Report for APRE, Ministry of Defence, UK, Human Assessment Laboratory, University of Plymouth.

Dann, P. L., & Irvine, S. H. (1987). *Handbook of computer-based cognitive tasks.* Centre for Computer-Based Assessment, University of Plymouth, Plymouth, UK.

Dann, P. L., Irvine, S. H. & Collis, J. M. (Eds.) (1991*). Advances in Computer-Based Human Assessment.*, Dordrecht, Netherlands, Kluwer Academic.

De Carli G., Irvine S. H., Arpinelli F., Bamfi F., Olivieri A., & Recchia G. 1. (1995). Development and validation of QPD 32, a specific questionnaire for measuring the quality of life of patients with peptic ulcer. *Minerva Gastroenterological Dietology, 41(4)*,275-82.

De Carli G., Irvine S. H., Arpinelli F., Bamfi F., Olivieri A., & Recchia G.1. (1998). In, Salek S (Ed.) *Compendium of Quality of Life Instruments. (5 vols.).* Chichester, West Sussex, Wiley. V.2, 2H,3, Pg.1-2 (datasheet)., V.2, 2H,3a, Pg.1-6 (instrument).

Defranc, A. (2011). *Unpublished report on the follow-up of the GCTB system.* Personnel Division, Ministry of Defence, Brussels.

De Lucia, P. R. & Cochrane, E. L. (1985). Perceptual information that can be extracted through a ball's trajectory. *Perceptual & Motor Skill, 61*, 143-150.

Dennis, I. (1993). *The development of an item generative test of spatial orientation closely related to Test SP80a.* SP(N) Report TR 307, Office of the Senior Psychologist (Naval), Ministry of Defence, London.

Dennis, I. (1995*). The structure and development of numeracy and literacy tests in the Navy Personnel Series.* Technical Report for the Office of the Senior Psychologist (Naval). Human Assessment Laboratory, University of Plymouth, Plymouth UK.

Dennis, I., Collis, J. M., & Dann, P. L. (1995 October). Extending the scope of item generation to tests of educational attainment. *Proceedings of the 37th International Military Testing Association Conference*, Toronto, Canada.

Dennis, I. & Evans J. St. B. T. (1989). *System architecture for computerised assessment.* Human Assessment Laboratory, University of Plymouth Report for The Army Personnel Research Establishment (Contract 2021/12). Plymouth, UK.

Dennis, I. & Evans, J. St.B. T. (1996). The speed-error trade off problem in psychometric testing. *British Journal of Psychology, 87,* 105-129.

Dennis, I., Handley, S. J., Bradon, P., Evans, J., & Newstead, S. E. (2002). Towards a predictive model of the difficulty of analytical reasoning items. In S. H. Irvine & P. C. Kyllonen (Eds.), *Item generation for test development* (pp. 53-71). Mahwah, NJ: Erlbaum.

Dennis I., & Tapsfield, P. G. C. (Eds.) (1996). *Human abilities, their nature & measurement.* Erlbaum, Hillsdale, NJ.

Detterman, D. K. (1982). Does g exist? *Intelligence, 6,* 99-108.

Detterman, D. K. (1984). Understand cognitive components before postulating metacomponents, etc. Part 2. *Behavioral & Brain Sciences, 7,* 289-90.

Deu, N. Srinivasan, M. Srinivasan, P. (2004). Issues in temperamental unsuitability: re-examining concepts and current practice in the British army. *Journal of The Royal Army Medical Corps, 150, 179-181.*

Devriendt, Y. (1999a). *Test of English for Non-commissioned Officers, TE-NCO, Taaltest Engels voor kandidaat-onderofficieren van het actief kader.* Technisch Rapport 1999 nr.1. S.l., Centrum voor Recrutering en Selectie, Ministry of Defence Brussels, Belgium.

Devriendt, Y. (2000). *Differences between candidate-NCO's on a test of English.* Paper presented at the 42nd Annual Conference of The International Military Testing Association, Edinburgh. U.K., 7th-9th November 2000. Conference Abstracts Book, p. 37.

Devriendt, Y. (2001). De constructie van een Duitstalige testbatterij voor kandidaat-vrijwilligers. Technisch Rapport 2001-2. Centrum voor Recrutering en Selectie, Ministry of Defence Brussels.

Diamond, J. & Evans, W. (1973). The correction for guessing. *Review of Educational Research, 43,* 181-191.

Dickstein, D., Suvak, M., Litz, B. T., Adler, A. B., (2010). Heterogeneity in the course of posttraumatic stress disorder: trajectories of symptomatology. *Journal of Traumatic Stress, 23, No. 3,* 331-339.

Digman, J.M. & Inouye, J. (1986). Further specification of the five robust factors of personality. *Journal of Personality & Social Psychology. 50,* 116-123.

Drasgow, F., & Mattern, K. (2006). New tests and new items: Opportunities and issues. In D. Bartram & R. Hambleton (Eds.), *Computer-based testing and the internet* (pp. 59-76). Hoboken, NJ: Wiley.

Drasgow, F., Luecht, R. M., & Bennett, R. (2006). Technology and testing. In R. L. Brennan (Ed.), *Educational measurement* (4th ed., pp. 471-516). Washington, DC: American Council on Education.

Dubois, P. H. (1965). *An introduction to psychological statistics.* New York, Harper & Row.

Eagling, D. (1989). *A validation study of computer-based cognitive tasks among Polytechnic students.* BSc Honours Thesis, Department of Psychology, Polytechnic South West, Plymouth, UK.

Earles, J. A., & Ree, M. J. (1992). Training validity. *Educational and Psychological Measurement, 54, 7,* 21-725.

Educational Testing Service (1985). *Educational technology research.* Princeton, NJ, ETS.

Ekstrom, R. B., French, J. W., & Harmon, H. H. (1976). *Manual for kit of reference tests for cognitive factors.* Princeton, NJ: Educational Testing Service.

Embretson, S. E. (1995). Working memory capacity versus general control processes in abstract reasoning. *Intelligence, 20,* 169-189.

Embretson, S. E. (1996). Multidimensional latent trait models in measuring fundamental aspects of intelligence. In I. Dennis & P. G. C. Tapsfield, (Eds.) *Human abilities, their nature and measurement.* Hillsdale, NJ, Lawrence Erlbaum Associates.

Embretson, S. E. (1998). A cognitive design system approach to generating valid tests: Application to abstract reasoning. *Psychological Methods, 3,* 380-396.

Embretson, S. E. (1999). Generating items during testing: Psychometric issues and models. *Psychometrika, 64,* 407-433.

Embretson, S. E. (2002). Generating abstract reasoning items with cognitive theory. In S. H. Irvine & P. C. Kyllonen (Eds.), *Item generation for test development* (pp. 219-250). Mahwah, NJ: Erlbaum.

Embretson, S. E., & Daniel, R. C. (2008). Understanding and quantifying cognitive complexity level in mathematical problem solving items. *Psychological Science Quarterly, 50,* 328-344.

Embretson, S. E., & Yang, X. (2007). Automatic item generation and cognitive psychology. In C. R. Rao & S. Sinharay (Eds.) *Handbook of Statistics: Psychometrics, Volume 26* (pp. 747-768). North Holland, UK: Elsevier.

Ercikan, K. Gierl, M. J., McCreith, T., Puhan, G., & Koh, K. (2004). Comparability of bilingual versions of assessments: Sources of incomparability of English and French versions of Canada's national achievement tests. *Applied Measurement in Education, 17*, 301-321.

Estes, W. K. (1974). Learning theory and intelligence. *American Psychologist, 29,* 740-749.

Estes, W. K. (1978). On the organisation and core concepts of learning theory and cognitive psychology. In W. K. Estes (Ed.) *Handbook of learning and cognitive processes*, Vol. 6. Hillsdale NJ, Erlbaum Associates.

Estes, W. K (1981). Intelligence and learning. In M. Friedman, J.P. Das & N. O'Connor, (Eds.), *Intelligence and learning*. New York, Plenum.

Evans, J. St.B. T. (1982). *The psychology of deductive reasoning.* London, Routledge.

Evans, J. St.B. T., & Wright, D. E. (1992). *The transitive inference task* (Technical Report 2-1992 Army Personnel Research Establishment). Human Assessment Laboratory, University of Plymouth, Plymouth, UK.

Evans, J. St.B. T., & Wright, D .E. (1993). *The properties of fixed-time tests, A simulation study*, (Technical Report 3-1993 Army Personnel Research Establishment). Human Assessment Laboratory, University of Plymouth, Plymouth, UK.

Eysenck, H. J. (1953). *The Structure of Human Personality*. London: Methuen.

Eysenck, H. J. (1988). The biological basis of intelligence. In S. H. Irvine, & J. W., Berry. (Eds.). *Human abilities in cultural context.* New York, Cambridge.

Eysenck, H. J. (Ed.) (1982). *A model for intelligence.* New York, Springer-Verlag.

Fairbank, B. A., Tirre, W. & Anderson, N. (1986). Measures of thirty cognitive tasks, intercorrelations and correlations with aptitude battery scores. In S. E. Newstead, S. H. Irvine & P. L. Dann, (Eds.). *Human Assessment, cognition and motivation.* Dordrecht, Netherlands, Nijhoff.

Fang, M. & Bender, P. (2010). *Identifying Contributors to Changes in Attrition Rates*. In Proceedings of the 52nd Annual International Military Testing Association Conference.

Fatimilehin, I. & Hunt, K. (2013). Psychometric assessment across cultures. *Assessment and Development Matters, 5*, 21-23.

Fear, N. T., Jones, M., Murphy, D., Hull, L., Iversen, A. C., Coker, B., Machell, L., Sundin, J., Woodhead, C., Jones, N., Greenberg, N., Landau, S., Dandeker, C., Rona, R. J., Hotopf, M., Wessely, S. (2010). What are the consequences of deployment to Iraq and Afghanistan on the mental health of the UK armed forces? A cohort study. *The Lancet, 375,* 1783-1797.

Ferguson, G. A. (1954). On learning and human ability. *Canadian Journal of Psychology, 8,* 95-112.

Ferguson, G. A. (1956). On transfer and the abilities of man. *Canadian Journal of Psychology, 10,* 121-131.

Fiedler, E. R., Oltmanns, T. F., & Turkheimer, E. (2004). Traits associated with personality disorders and adjustment to military life, Predictive validity of self and peer reports. *Military Medicine, 169, 207-211.*

Fischer, G. H. (1973). The linear logistic test model as an instrument in educational research. *Acta Psychologica, 37,* 359-374.

Fischer, G. H. (1980). Discussion. In D. J. Weiss (Ed.), *Proceedings of the 1979 Computerized Adaptive Testing Conference.* Minneapolis: University of Minnesota, Department of Psychology, Psychometric Methods Program, pp. 436-438.

Fisher, N. (2011). *Exploring Reasons for Attrition in the British Army: A Longitudinal Study.* In Proceedings of the 53rd Annual International Military Testing Association Conference.

French, C., Rona, R. J., Jones, M., & Wessely S. (2004).Screening for physical and psychological illness in the British Armed Forces, II, Barriers to screening - learning from the opinions of Service personnel *Journal of Medical Screening,11,*153-157.

French, J. R. P. & Raven, B. H. (1959). The bases of social power. In D. Cartwright (Ed.) *Studies in social power* Ann Arbor Mich.: Univ. of Michigan Press.

French, J. W., Ekstrom, R. B., & Price, L. A. (1963). *Manual for kit of reference tests for cognitive factors.* Princeton, NJ: Educational Testing Service.

Friedman, M. P., Das, J.P., & O'Connor, N. (Eds.) (1981). *Intelligence and learning.* New York, Plenum.

Fritscher, W., & Koch, E.W. (1975). *Elektronische datenverarbeitung und personal klassifikation im Psychologie dienst der Bundeswehr* (Wehrpsychologische Untersuchungen 3/75). Bonn:Bundesministerium der Verteidigung Psycho-logischer Dienst der Bundeswehr.

Furneaux, W. D. (1952). Some speed, error and difficulty relationships within a problem-solving situation. *Nature, 170,* 3.

Furneaux, W. D. (1960). Intellectual abilities and problem-solving behaviour. In Eysenck, H. J. (Ed.), Handbook of abnormal psychology, Pitman, London, pp. 167-192.

Garstle, M., Wagner, R. L., & Lodge, T. (1943). The inapt naval recruit. *United States Naval Bulletin*, 51, 480-490.

Gebicke, M. E. (1997a). Military attrition: better screening of enlisted personnel could save millions of dollars. General Accounting Office, GAO Series: GAO testimony, GAO/T-NSIAD-97-120. Publisher: Washington, DC 1997.

Gebicke, M. E. (1997b). Military readiness: improvements still needed in assessing military readiness. General Accounting Office, GAO. Series: GAO testimony, GAO/T-NSIAD-97-107. Publisher: Washington, DC 1997.

Gibson J. J. (1979). *The ecological approach to visual perception.* Boston: Houghton Mifflin.

Gierl M. J. & Haladyna T. M., Eds., (2012). *Automatic item generation: theory and practice.* New York, NY: Routledge.

Gierl M. J., & Lai H. (2012a). Using weak strong theory to create item models for automatic item generation: some practical guidelines with examples. In: Gierl MJ, Haladyna TM, eds. *Automatic Item Generation: Theory and Practice.* New York, NY: Routledge. (pp. 47-63).

Gierl, M. J., & Lai, H. (2012b). Using item models for automatic item generation. *International Journal of Testing, 12,* 273-298.

Gierl, M. J., Lai, H., & Turner, S. (2012). Using automatic item generation to create multiple-choice items for assessments in medical education. *Medical Education, 46,* 757-765.

Gierl, M. J. & Leighton, J.P. (2004). Book Review: Item generation for test development by Irvine & Kyllonen, (Eds.) 2002. *Journal of Educational Measurement, 41*, 69-72.

Glas, C. A. W., & van der Linden, W. J. (2003). Computerized adaptive testing with item clones. *Applied Psychological Measurement, 27*, 247-261.

Glass, A. L., & Holyoak, K. J. (1975). Alternative conceptions of semantic memory. *Cognition, 3,* 313-339.

Glass, A. L., Holyoak, K. J., & Kossan, N. E. (1977). Children's ability to detect semantic contradictions. *Child Development, 48,* 279-283.

Goeters, K-M., (1979). *Die anderung der psychometrischen kennewerte und der faktorenstruktur als folge der ubung von tests.* Unpublished Doctoral Dissertation, University of Hamburg, Hamburg.

Goeters, K-M., & Lorenz, B. (2002). On the implementation of item generation principles for the design of aptitude testing in aviation. In. Irvine, S. H. & Kyllonen, P.C. (Eds.), (2002). *Item generation for test development.* Erlbaum Associates, Mahwah, NJ, pp. 339-360.

Goeters, K-M., & Rathje, H. (1992). *Computer-generiete parallel-tests fur die fahigeitsmessung in der eignungsauswahl von operationellem luftfahrtpersonal.* DLR Institut fur Flugmedizin Abteilung Luft-und Raumfahrtpsychologie, Hamburg.

Goffman, E. (1961). *Asylums: Essays on the Social Situation of Mental Patients and Other Inmates.* London, Penguin.

Golby, J. (1989). The relative importance of perceptual information throughout the sections of a cricket ball's trajectory. *Current Psychology, 8*: 188-199.

Gorham, R. (1978). *Verbal ability, previous practice and load on short term memory as determiners of difference in a complex learning task: an experimental study.* Unpublished M.Ed. thesis, Brock University, St. Catherines, Ontario, Canada.

Green, G., O'Neill, D., & Walker, S. (2008). *Welfare and warfare an uneasy mix, personal experiences of and organisational responses to emotional and mental health issues in young ex-service personnel.* Report of University of Essex, Colchester, England, pp. 1-20.

Greene, J. M. (1970). Syntactic form and semantic function. *Quarterly Journal of Experimental Psychology, 22*, 14-27.

Greig, J. E. (1997). *In TTCP (1997), Technical minutes of the 1997 HUM-TP3 meeting at Portsmouth, United Kingdom, August 1997, pp. 41-43:* TTCP-HUM-97-009.

Greig, J. E., & Bongers, S. H. (1996). An Australian trial of the British Army Recruit Battery. *Proceedings of the 58th Annual Conference of the International Military Testing Association.* San Antonio, November 1996.

Greig, J. E., & Bongers, S. H. (1997). *An Australian trial of the British Army Recruit Battery - Part 3, Validity coefficients and factor structure.* Report of The Air Force Office, Mawson, ACT 2607, Australia.

Grenzebach, A. P., & McDonald, J. E., (1992). Alphabetic sequence decisions for letter pairs with separations of one to three letters. *Journal of Experimental Psychology Learning, Memory, and Cognition, 18,* 865-872.

Groen, G. J., & Parkman, J. M. (1972). A chronometric analysis of simple addition. *Psychological Review, 79,* 329-343.

Guilford, J.P. (1954). *Psychometric Methods (2nd Ed.).* McGraw-Hill, New York.

Guilford, J.P. (1956). The structure of intellect. *Psychological Bulletin, 53*, 267-293.

Guilford, J.P. (1964). *Fundamental statistics in psychology and education.* McGraw-Hill, New York.

Gulliksen, H. O. (1950). *Theory of mental tests,* New York: Wiley. (Reprinted in 1987 by Lawrence Erlbaum Associates; Hillsdale, NJ.

Gustafsson, J-E. (1981). *A general model for the organisation of cognitive abilities.* Research Report 1981,06, Department of Education, University of Goteborg, Box 1010, S-431 26, Molndal, Sweden.

Gustafsson, J-E.(1988). *Broad and narrow abilities in research on learning and instruction.* Paper presented at the Minnesota Symposium on Learning and Individual Differences (Minneapolis, 14-16 April). University of Goteborg, Molndal, Sweden.

Hacker Hughes, J. G., Wagner, A., Willkomm, B., & Smykala P. (2004). NATO Research Task Group 20, Stress and Psychological Support in Modern Military Operations: Clinical Sub-Group Initial Report. RTO-TR-HFM-081, Brussels, Belgium.

Hambleton, R. K., & Swaminathan, H. (1985). *Item response theory.* Kluwer Nijhoff, Boston.

Hampson, A. (1997). *Predicting voluntary training wastage.* Proceedings of 39th Annual Conference of The International Military Testing Association Sydney, Australia.

Hampson, S. E., Goldberg, L. R., & John, O. P. (1987). Category breadth and social desirability values for 573 personality terms. *European Journal of Personality, 1,* 241-256.

Hampson, S. E., John, O. P., & Goldberg, L. R. (1986), Category breadth and hierarchical structure in personality studies of asymmetries in judgements of trait implication. *Journal of Personality and Social Psychology, 51,1,* 37-54.

Harris, R. L., & Tapsfield, P. G. C. (1995*). The British Army Recruit Battery Trials of Pre-Test Booklets.* Human Assessment Laboratory Technical Report 10-1995, University of Plymouth, Plymouth, UK.

Hasher, L. & Zacks, R.T. (1979). Automatic and effortful processes in memory. *Journal of Experimental Psychology, 108*, 356-388.

Hector, H. & Hudson, W. (1958). Pattern specificity in a sample of Mozambique tribesmen on the 7-Squares Test. *Journal of the National Institute for Personnel Research, 7,* 156-161.

Hendrickson, A. E (1982). The biological basis of intelligence Part 1, theory. In H .J. Eysenck, (Ed.), *A model for intelligence.* New York, Springer-Verlag.

Hendrickson, D. E (1982). The biological basis of intelligence Part 2, measurement. In H.J. Eysenck (Ed.), *A model for intelligence.* New York, Springer-Verlag.

Herriot, P. Chalmers, C. & Wingrove, J. (1985). Group decision making in an assessment centre. *Journal of Occupational and Organizational Psychology: 58* (4), 265-349.

HMSO (2005). *House of Commons Defence Committee Third Report, Mar 14, 2005*

House of Commons Information Service Session 2004-05 <u>Publications on the internet</u> *<u>Defence Committee Publications</u>*.

Hockey, G. R. J., Maclean, A., and Hamilton, P. (1981). State changes and the temporal patterning of component resources. In J. Long and A. D. Baddeley (Eds.), *Attention and performance, Vol. 9.* Hillsdale, NJ, Lawrence Erlbaum Associates.

Hockey, G .R. J., & Maclean, A. (1986). Direct temporal analysis of individual differences in cognitive skill. In S. E. Newstead, S. H. Irvine, & P. L. Dann (Eds.), *Human assessment, cognition and motivation* (pp. 419-420). Dordrecht, Nijhoff.

Hoge, C.W., Castro, C. A., Messer, S. C., McGurk,D., Cotting, D. I., & Koffman, R. L. (2004). Combat duty in Iraq and Afghanistan, mental health problems, and barriers to care. *New England Journal of Medicine, 351*, 13-22.

Hoge C. W., Lesikar S. E., Guevara R, Lange J., Brundage J. F., Engel C. C. Jr., Messer S. C., Orman D. T. (2002). Mental disorders among U.S. military personnel in the 1990s, association with high levels of health care utilization and early military attrition. *American Journal of Psychiatry, Sep., 159(9),* 1576-83.

Hoge C. W., Toboni H. E., Messer S. C., Bell N., Amoroso P., Orman D. T. (2005). The occupational burden of mental disorders in the U.S. military, psychiatric hospitalizations, involuntary separations, and disability. *American Journal of Psychiatry, Mar., 162(3),* 585-91.

Holden, R. R. & Scholtz, D. (2002). The Holden Psychological Screening Inventory in the prediction of Canadian Forces basic training outcome. *Canadian Journal of Behavioural Science, 34*(2), 104-110.

Holland. P. W. & Thayer, D. T. (1986*). Differential item-functioning and the Mantel-Haenszel procedure.* ETS Program Statistics Research *Technical Report 86-69 (and also ETS RR-86-31).* Educational Testing Service, Princeton, NJ.

Holroyd, S. R., Atherton, R. M., & Wright, D. E. (1995a). The criterion related validity of the British Army Recruit Battery. *Proceedings of the 37th Annual Conference of the International Military Testing Association.* Toronto.

Holroyd, S. R., Atherton, R. M., & Wright, D. E. (1995b). *Validation of the British Army Recruit Battery against measures of performance in basic military training.* Centre for Human Sciences, Report DRACHS/liS3/CR95019/1.0. Defence Evaluation and Research Agency, Farnborough.

Horney, K. (1950). *Neurosis and human growth.* New York: W.W. Norton

Hornke, L. F. (1977). Antwortabhangige testverfahren, Ein neuartiger ansatz psychologischen testens. *Diagnostica, 23,* 1 - 14.

Hornke, L. F. (1978). Vergleich zweier adaptiv-antwortabhangiger teststrategien. *Diagnostica, 24,* 103 - 112.

Hornke, L. F. (2002). Item-generation models for higher-order cognitive functions, In S. H. Irvine & P. C. Kyllonen, (Eds.), *Item generation for test development* Erlbaum Associates, Mahwah, NJ, pp. 159-178.

Hornke, L. F. & Habon, M. W. (1986). Rule-based item bank construction and evaluation within the linear logistic framework. *Applied Psychological Measurement, 10,* 369 380.

Horst, P. (1957). *The factor analysis of data matrices.* Holt, Rinehart & Winston, New York.

Hough, L. M., Barge, B. N. & Kamp, J.D. (1987). Non-cognitive measures: Pilot testing. In N.G. Peterson (Ed.), *Development and field test of the trial battery for Project A.* Technical Report 739, US Army Research Institute for the Behavioral Sciences, Alexandria, Virginia, USA

Hough, P. V. C. (1962). *Method and means for recognising complex patterns.* U.S. Patent 3,069,654.

Hovland, C. I. (1938). Experimental studies in rote-learning theory III. Distribution of practice with varying speeds of syllable presentation. *Journal of Experimental Psychology, 23,* 172-190.

Hunt, E. (1974). Quote The Raven? Nevermore! In Gregg, L. W. (Ed). *Knowledge and cognition*, pp.129-158. Hillsdale, NJ: Erlbaum.

Hunt, E (1980). Intelligence as an information-processing concept. *British Journal of Psychology, 71,* 449-474.

Hunt, E (1981). The design of a robot mind. In M. Friedman, J.P. Das & N. O'Connor, (Eds.), *Intelligence and learning.* New York, Plenum.

Hunt, E. (1987). A cognitive model of individual differences with an application for attention. In S. H. Irvine & S. E. Newstead (Eds.). *Intelligence and cognition.* Dordrecht, Netherlands: Nijhoff.

Hunt, E., Frost, N. & Lunneborg, C. (1973). Individual differences in cognition: A new approach to intelligence. In G. Bower (Ed.). *The psychology of learning and motivation.* (Vol.7). New York: Academic Press.

Hunt, E. & Lansman, M., (1982). Individual differences in attention. In R. J. Sternberg (Ed.). *Psychology of human intelligence.* Hillsdale, NJ: Erlbaum Associates.

Hunt, E., Lunneborg, C. & Lewis, J. (1975). What does it mean to be high verbal? *Cognitive Psychology, 7,* 194-227.

Inpsych Ltd. (1999, 2000). *The Millennium Tests, The Self Inventory and JOIN.* Berwick-Upon-Tweed, Northumberland, UK.

Irvine, C. D., & Irvine, S. H. (1996). Effects of antihypertensive treatment on cognitive function of older patients: effect is not proved. *British Medical Journal, 313,* 166.

Irvine, S. H. (1964). *A psychological study of selection problems at the end of primary schooling in Southern Rhodesia.* Thesis submitted to the University of London in partial fulfilment of the requirements for the degree of Doctor of Philosophy.

Irvine, S. H. (1965). Adapting tests to the cultural setting, a comment. *Occupational Psychology,* 39, 12-33.

Irvine, S. H. (1966). Towards a rationale for testing abilities and attainments in Africa. *British. Journal of Educational Psychology 36,* 24-32.

Irvine, S. H. (1969a). Culture and mental ability. *New Scientist, 42,* 230-231.

Irvine, S. H. (1969b). Figural tests of reasoning in Africa: studies in the use of Raven's Progressive Matrices across cultures. *International Journal of Psychology, 4,* 217-228.

Irvine. S. H. (1969c). The factor analysis of African abilities and attainments, Constructs across cultures. *Psychological Bulletin, 71,* 20-32.

Irvine, S. H. (1979). The place of factor analysis in cross-cultural methodology and its contribution to cognitive theory. In L. H. Eckensberger, W. J. Lonner & Y. H. Poortinga (Eds.), *Cross-cultural contributions to psychology.* Lisse, Swets & Zeitlinger pp. 300-341.

Irvine, S. H. (1981). Culture, cognitive tests and cognitive models. Pursuing cognitive universals by testing across cultures. In M. Friedman, J.P. Das & N. O'Connor (Eds.), Intelligence and learning. New York, Plenum.

Irvine, S. H. (1983b). Testing in Africa and America, the search for routes. In S. H. Irvine & J. W. Berry, (Eds.), *Human assessment and cultural factors.* New York, Plenum.

Irvine, S. H. (1983c). Where intelligence tests fail. *Nature, 302,* 371.

Irvine, S. H. (1983d). Lynn, the Japanese and environmentalism, a response. *Bulletin of the British Psychological Society, 36,* 55-56.

Irvine, S. H. (1983e). Has Eysenck removed the bottleneck in IQ? (Essay review of H. J. Eysenck [Ed.], *A model for intelligence*. New York, Springer-Verlag, 1982). *New Scientist, 99,* 121-122.

Irvine, S. H. (1984). The contexts of triarchic theory. *The Behavioral and Brain Sciences, 7,* 293-294.

Irvine, S. H. (1986a). Approaching the LIQ: new waves and old problems in individual differences. In S.E. Newstead, S. H. Irvine & P. L. Dann, (Eds*.). Human assessment, cognition and motivation*. Dordrecht, Netherlands, Nijhoff (pp. 21-24).

Irvine, S. H. (1986b). Cross-cultural assessment, From practice to theory. In W. Lonner & J. W. Berry (Eds.), *Field Methods in cross-cultural psychology.* New York, Sage pp. 203-230.

Irvine, S. H. (1987a). Functions and constants in mental measurement, a taxonomic approach. In S. H. Irvine & S.E. Newstead, (Eds.), *Intelligence and cognition, contemporary frames of reference.* Dordrecht, Netherlands, Nijhoff.

Irvine, S. H. (1994). *Generative Principles for Foundation Items in Mathematics: Rationale, Examples and Plans.* Report prepared under Ministry of Defence Research Agreement 2021/12 between the Army Personnel Research Establishment (Now DRA) and the University of Plymouth.

Irvine, S. H. (1995). Metaphors, models and measurement in military motivation. Part 1, Radical conceptual analysis. Part 2, Progress Report to September 30, 1995. Part 3, Contextual Frameworks and Operational Definitions, the Self-Report Inventory for Military Motivation (SI_MM) *HAL Technical Report 6-95. Human Assessment Laboratory, University of Plymouth, Plymouth UK.*

Irvine, S. H. (1998a). *The computer-generation of ability tests for adaptive testing in selection and training, A report in the form of a technical handbook.* USAF Air Force Laboratory, Brooks AFB, San Antonio, Texas.

Irvine, S. H. (1998b). *New tests for recruitment, standardisation and validation.* Final Report for The Royal Ulster Constabulary. Inpsych Ltd., Berwick-upon-Tweed, UK.

Irvine, S. H. (2004a). *Innovative self-reports of health-related quality of life in basic training, their measurement and meaning for attrition.* Proceedings of The Annual Conference of The International Military Testing Association Brussels, Belgium, October 2004.

Irvine, S. H. (2004b). *Unwanted behaviours during basic training, a psychometric landscape.* Proceedings of the 7th International Military Mental Health Conference Royal Military Academy Brussels, Belgium, December 2004.

Irvine, S. H. (2005). *Preventive medicine in recruitment: the proven case for extended, automated psychometric testing.* Proceedings of the 8th International Military Mental Health Conference, Prague, Czech Republic, December, 2005.

Irvine, S. H. (2006). *Personal profiles of motivation in basic training, validity, veracity, opacity.* Annual Conference Of The International Military Testing Association Kingston, Ontario, Canada 2nd- 6th October 2006.

Irvine, S. H. (Ed.), (2009). *Mindmill Cognitive Technical Manual.* Mindmill Ltd. Carrickfergus, N. I. (As registered with the British Psychological Society).

Irvine, S. H. (2009) (Ed.) *Mindmill Self-Inventory Technical Manual* Mindmill Ltd. Carrickfergus, N. I. (With further information updated by Arlene McGurk).

Irvine, S. H. (2010). *To screen or Not to Screen, That is the Question.* Invited Address, 13th International Military Mental Health Conference, Amsterdam, September 6-9.

Irvine, S. H. (2013a). *New conflicts, new tests: but an old enemy - attrition.* Paper presented at The International Applied Military Psychology Symposium Bern Switzerland, May 27-31, 2013.

Irvine, S. H. (2013b). BARB after 21 years: the end of a generation? In *Psyche, No.68, Summer 2013, pp. 8-11.* Newsletter of The Psychometrics Forum.

Irvine, S. H. & Berry, J. W. (Eds.) (1983). *Human assessment and cultural factors.* New York, Plenum.

Irvine, S. H. & Berry, J. W. (1988a). The abilities of mankind, a revaluation. In S. H. Irvine & J. W. Berry, (Eds.), *Human abilities in cultural context.* New York, Cambridge.

Irvine, S. H. & Berry. J. W., (Eds.), (1988b). *Human abilities in cultural context.* New York, Cambridge.

Irvine. S. H., & Carroll, W. K. (1980). Testing and assessment across cultures. In H. C. Triandis & J. W. Berry (Eds.), *Handbook of cross-cultural psychology* (Vol. 2, chap. 5). Boston, Allyn & Bacon.

Irvine, S. H. & Christal, R. E. (1994). *The primacy of working memory in learning to identify electronic logic gates.* HAL Technical Report 4 1994-95. University of Plymouth for Ministry of Defence London.

Irvine, S. H. & Dann, P. L. (1991). Challenges of computer-based human assessment. In, P. L. Dann, S. H. Irvine & J. M. Collis (Eds.). *Advances in Computer-Based Human Assessment, Series D* Dordrecht, Kluwer Academic Publishers (pp. 3-25).

Irvine, S. H. & Dann, P. L. (1993). *BARB: Concepts and constructs.* Paper presented at the 35th Annual Conference of The International Military Testing Association, Williamsburg, VA.. Conference Abstracts Book, pp. 396-404. (also as Technical Report, 2-1994 Army Personnel Research Establishment Ministry of Defence) Human Assessment Laboratory, University of Plymouth, Plymouth, UK).

Irvine, S. H., Dann, P. L. & Anderson, J. D. (1990). Towards a Theory of Algorithm-Determined Cognitive Test Construction. *British Journal of Psychology, 81,* 173-195.

Irvine, S. H., Dann, P. L., & Evans, J. St .B. T. (1986). *Item generative approaches for computer-based testing, A prospectus for research.* Report for the Army Personnel Research Establishment, Ministry of Defence, Human Assessment Laboratory, University of Plymouth, Plymouth, Devon UK.

Irvine, S. H., Dann, P. L., Evans, J. St. B. T., Dennis, I., Collis, J., Thacker, C., & Anderson, J. D. (1989). *Another generation of personnel selection tests: Stages in a new theory of computer-based test construction.* Report for the Army Personnel Research Establishment Ministry of Defence, Human Assessment Laboratory, University of Plymouth, Plymouth, UK.

Irvine, S. H., Hyland, M. E., Wright, D. E., Recchia, G., Del Negro, R. & De. Carli, G. (1992). Quality of Life and the Asthma Questionnaire, Measurements and Methods with Italian Patients. *Italian Journal of Chest Diseases, 47,* 273-277.

Irvine, S. H., Kutschke, T., & Walker, R. F. (2000). *Screening conscripts in Germany using item-generative tests* (Report 01/00. Bundesministerium der Verteidigung, Bonn, Deutschland.

Irvine, S. H., Kutschke, T. & Weber, W. W. (2000). *Item-generative tests for the allocation of conscripts in Germany.* Paper presented at the 42nd Annual Conference of the International Military Testing Association, Edinburgh, U.K., 7th-9th November 2000. Conference Abstract Book, p. 13.

Irvine, S. H. & Kyllonen, P.C. (Eds.), (2002). *Item generation for test development* Erlbaum Associates, Mahwah, NJ.

Irvine, S. H. & Kyllonen, P. C. (Eds.) (2010). *Item generation for test development (2nd Ed.).* Routledge, London and New York.

Irvine, S. H., Kyllonen, P. C., & Roberts, R. (2000). *Measuring military motivation, near-perfect prediction of gender role differentiation and vocational commitment among recruits.* Proceedings of The 42nd Annual Conference of The International Military Testing Association Edinburgh, United Kingdom 7th - 9th November 2000.

Irvine, S. H. & Newstead, S. E. (Eds.). (1987). *Intelligence and cognition, contemporary frames of reference.* Dordrecht, Martinus Nijhoff.

Irvine, S. H., & Reuning, H. (1981). Perceptual speed and cognitive controls. *Journal of Cross-Cultural Psychology, 12,* 425-444.

Irvine, S. H., Schoeman. A. & Prinsloo, W. (1988). Putting cognitive theory to the test, group testing reassessed using the cross-cultural method. In G. K. Verma & C. Bagley (Eds.). *Cross-cultural studies of personality, attitudes and cognition.* Macmillan, London.

Irvine, S. H., Wright, D. E., Dennis, I., & Gould, P. (1991). *Time estimation, aiming and tracking - Tp, measurement of individual differences in the performance of military tasks.* HAL Technical Report, University of Plymouth, HAL 3-1991 (APRE) Ministry of Defence.

Irvine, S. H., Wright, D. E., De Carli, G. & Recchia, G. (1994). Limits and paradoxes in cross-national quality of life measurement: stimulus identity or item equivalence? *Quality of Life Research, 3,* 81.

Irvine, S. H., Wright, D. E., Recchia, G., De Carli, G. & Zanferrari, G. (1993). Quality of life measurement. *Monaldi Archives for Chest Disease, 48, no.5,* 549-553.

Jacobs, N. R. (1996). *Validation of the British Army Recruit Battery (BARB) against phase two military training performance measures.* Centre for Human Sciences, Report PLSD/CHS/fiS3/CR96049/1.0 Defence Evaluation and Research Agency, Farnborough, UK.

Jacobs, N. R., Cape, L. T., & Lawton, D. H. (1997). *Validation of the British Army Recruit Battery (BARB) against phase two military training performance measures.* Centre for Human Sciences, Report PLSD/CHS/HS3/CR97018/1.0. Defence Evaluation and Research Agency, Farnborough, UK.

Jacobson, R. L. (1995). Shortfall of questions curbs use of computerised graduate record exam. *The Chronicle of Graduate Education,* January *6,* p.A23.

Jackson, D. N. (1984). *Personality research form manual.* Port Huron, Michigan, USA. Research Psychologists Press.

Jackson, S., Agius, R., Bridger, R. S., & Richards, P. (2011). Occupational stress and the outcome of basic military training, *Occupational Medicine, 61,* 253-258.

Jennings, P. G. (1979). *Searching the page and searching the memory as determiners of differences in a digit-symbol substitution task: An experimental study.* Unpublished M.Ed. thesis, College of Education, Brock University, St. Catherines, Ontario.

Jensen, A. R. (1969). How much can we boost IQ and scholastic achievement? *Harvard Educational Review, 39*, 1-23.

Jensen, A. R. (1982). Reaction time and psychometric g. In H.J. Eysenck, (Ed.), *A model for intelligence.* Springer-Verlag, New York.

Jensen, A. R. (1985). The nature of the black-white difference on various psychometric tests, Spearman's Hypothesis. *The Behavioral and Brain Sciences. 8*, 193-219.

Jensen, A. R. (1988). Speed of information-processing and population differences. In S. H. Irvine, and J. W. Berry (Eds.), *Human abilities in cultural context.* New York, Cambridge University Press.

Jensen, M. B. (1961). Adjustive and non-adjustive reactions to basic training in the Air Force. *The Journal of Social Psychology, 55,* 33-41.

Jervis, B., Allen, E., Johnson, T., Nichols, M. & Hudson, N.(1984). The application of pattern recognition techniques to the contingent negative variation for the differentiation of subject categories. *IEEE Transactions on Biomedical Engineering, BME-31,* 342-349.

Jervis, B., Nichols, M., Johnson, T., Allen, E. & Hudson, N. (1983). A fundamental investigation of the composition of auditory evoked potentials. *IEEE Transactions on Biomedical Engineering, BME-30,* 43-50.

Johansen, D. (2011). *The effectiveness of graded selection in the British Army (Army Recruiting and Training Division (ARTD) UK).* Proceedings of the 53rd International Military Testing Association Conference, Bali.

Johansen, D. & Fisher, N. (2012) *Recruiting partnering project - a step change in recruiting for the British army.* Proceedings of the 54th International Military Testing Association Conference, Dubrovnik, Croatia.

Jones, A. (1984). A study of pre-assessment centre candidate short-listing. *Journal of Occupational Psychology, 57,* 67-76.

Jones, A., Herriot, P., Long, B. & Drakely, R. (1991). Attempting to improve the validity of a well-established assessment centre. *Occupational Psychology, 64,* 1-21.

Jones, E., Hyams K. C., & Wessely, S. (2000). Screening for vulnerability to psychological disorders in the military, an historical survey *Journal of Medical Screening, 10(1),* 40-46.

Jones, M. R. (1985). Structural organisation of events in time. In J. A. Michon & J. L. Jackson, (Eds.) *Time, mind and behaviour.* Heidelberg: Springer, pp. 192-214.

Jou, J. (2003). Multiple number and letter comparison. Directionality and accessibility in numeric and alphabetic memories. *The American Journal of Psychology, 116,* 543-579.

Just, M. A., & Carpenter, P. A. (1980). A theory of reading: From eye fixations to comprehension. *Psychological Review, 87,* 329-354.

Just, M. A. & Carpenter, P. A. (1985). Cognitive coordinate systems: Accounts of mental rotation and individual differences in spatial ability. *Psychological Review, 92,* 137-172.

Just, M. A. & Carpenter P. A. (1992). Capacity theory of comprehension: individual differences in working memory. *Psychological Review, 99, (1),* 122-149.

Kail, R. & Pellegrino, J. W. (1985). *Human intelligence, perspectives and prospects.* Freeman, New York.

Kalisch, S. J. (1980). *Computerised instructional adaptive testing model, formulation and validation.* USAFHRL Report (AFHRL-TR-79-33). US Air Force Human Relations Laboratory, Brooks AFB, San Antonio, Texas.

Kalisch, S. J. (1989). *Use of item response patterns to predict examinee performance.* Paper delivered at Military Testing Association Meeting, November,1989, San Antonio, Texas.

Kass, R. A., Mitchell, K. J., Grafton, F. C, & Wing, H. (1983). Factorial validity of the Armed Services Vocational Aptitude Battery (ASVAB), Forms 8, 9, and 10: 1981 army applicant sample *Educational and Psychological Measurement, 43*, 1077-1087.

Kendall, M. G. (1948). *Rank correlation methods.* London, OUP.

Kendall, M. G. & Gibbons, J. D. (1990). *Rank correlation methods (5th Edition).* London, Edward Arnold.

Kerce, E. W. (1996). *Quality of life in the U.S. Marine Corps,* Navy Personnel Research and Development Centre, San Diego, California 92152-7250 (TN-96-12).

Kiernan, M. D. (2011). *Identifying and understanding factors associated with failure to complete infantry training among British Army recruits.* Thesis submitted for the degree of Doctor of Philosophy Faculty of Medicine & Health Sciences School of Nursing. University of Nottingham, UK.

Killcross, M. C. (1976). *Tailored testing for selection and allocation.* Unpublished PhD Thesis, University of Edinburgh, Scotland.

Kirsch, H. (1971). Der Wegfiguren Test als Auswahlinstrument. *Aviation Psychology.* (Quoted in Goeters, K-M. 1979, p.125).

Kitson, N., & Elshaw, C. C. (1996). *A comparison of the British Army Recruit Battery and the RAF Ground Trades Test Battery* (Report DRA/CHS/HS3/CR96060/1.0). Defence Research and Evaluation Agency, Farnborough, UK.

Kline, P. (1988). The British "cultural influence" on ability testing. In S. H. Irvine & J. W. Berry (Eds.), *Human Abilities in Cultural Context.* Cambridge, New York pp. 187-207.

Kornbrot, D. E. (1988). Random walk models of binary choice, the effect of deadlines in the presence of asymmetric payoffs. *Acta Psychologica, 69*, 109-127.

Kornbrot, D. E. (1989). Organisation of keying skills, the effect of motor complexity and number of units. *Acta Psychologica, 70,* 19-41.

Koundakjian, K. (2012). *Causes of early attrition and the use of retention initiatives: a perspective from Canadian Forces Army.* In Proceedings of the 54th Annual International Military Testing Association Conference.

Kubisiak et al. (2009). *Review of interventions for reducing enlisted attrition in the U.S. military, an update.* (ARI Research Note 2009-13) U.S. Army Research Institute for the Behavioral and Social Sciences, Arlington, VA 22202-3926. (Complete Author List U. Christean Kubisiak, Elizabeth Lentz, Kristen E. Horgen, Rebecca H. Bryant, Patrick W. Connell, Matthew D. Tuttle, and Walter C. Borman (PDRI), Mark C. Young (U.S. Army Research Institute), Ray Morath (ICF International).

Kucera, H., & Francis, W. N. *Computational analysis of present-day American English,* Providence, R.I., Brown University Press, 1967.

Kunda, M., McGreggor, K., & Goels, K. (2009). *Addressing the Raven's Progressive Matrices Test of 'general' intelligence.* E-book report: Design & Intelligence Laboratory, School of Interactive Computing Georgia Institute of Technology, Atlanta, Georgia 30332, USA. *www.aaai.org/ocs/index.php/FSS/FSS09/paper/download/954/1210*

Kyllonen, P. C. (1985). *Dimensions of information-processing speed.* (AFHRL-TP-84-56, AD-A154-778) Brooks AFB, TX, Manpower & Personnel Division, Air Force Human Resources Laboratory.

Kyllonen, P. C. (1986). Theory-based cognitive assessment. In J. Zeidner (Ed.), *Human productivity enhancement, Organisations, personnel & decision-making,* Vol.1 (338-381). New York, Praeger.

Kyllonen, P. C. (1991). Principles for creating a computerized test battery. *Intelligence, 15,* 1-15.

Kyllonen, P. C. (1993). Aptitude testing based on information processing: A test of the four-sources model. *Journal of General Psychology, 120,* 375-405.

Kyllonen, P. C. (1994). CAM: A theoretical framework for cognitive abilities measurement. In D.K. Detterman (Ed.), Current topics in human intelligence (Vol. 4): Theories of intelligence. Norwood, NJ: Ablex.

Kyllonen, P. C. (1996). Is working memory capacity Spearman's g? In Dennis I., & Tapsfield, P .G. C. (Eds.). *Human abilities, their nature & measurement.* Erlbaum, Hillsdale, NJ.

Kyllonen, P. C. (2006). *Solving the faking problem on noncognitive assessments* (Invited symposium, Psychological Assessment and Evaluation). Athens, Greece, 26th International Congress of Applied Psychology.

Kyllonen, P.C. (2010). *The Learning Abilities Measurement Program (LAMP) 1982 - 1999.* Research Report: Operational Technologies, San Antonio, TX.

Kyllonen, P. C. & Christal, R. E. (1986). Modeling learning abilities. In R. E. Dillon (Ed.). *Advances in Testing and Training.* Carbondale, IL, Dept of Educational Psychology, Southern Illinois University Press.

Kyllonen, P. C., & Christal, R. E. (1988). *Cognitive modelling of learning abilities, A status report of LAMP.* (AFHRL-TP-87-66). Brooks AFB, Texas, Manpower & Personnel Division, Air Force Human Resources Laboratory.

Kyllonen, P. C. & Christal, R. E. (1989). Cognitive modeling of learning abilities, A status report of LAMP. In R. Dillon & J. W. Pellegrino, *Testing, theoretical and applied issues.* (pp 146-173) New York, Praeger.

Kyllonen, P. C. & Christal, R. E. (1990). Reasoning ability is (little more than) working memory capacity?! *Intelligence, 14,* 389-433.

Kyllonen, P. C., Roberts, R. D. & Stankov, L. (Eds.), (2008). *Extending intelligence.* Mahwah, NJ. Erlbaum.

Kyllonen, P. C. & Shute, V. J. (1988). *Taxonomy of learning skills* (AFHRL-TP-87-39) Brooks AFB, TX, Manpower & Personnel Division, Air Force Human Resources Laboratory.

Kyllonen, P. C., Tirre, W.C. & Christal, R. E. (1985). *The speed-level problem reconsidered.* Unpublished MS. Brooks AFB, TX, Manpower & Personnel Division, Air Force Human Resources Laboratory.

Kyllonen, P. C., Tirre, W. C., & Christal, R. E. (1991). Knowledge and processing speed as determinants of associative learning. *Journal of Experimental Psychology: General, 120,* 89-108. (Also, [1989] Tech. Paper 87-68, Brooks AFB, TX: Air Force Human Resources Laboratory.)

Kyllonen, P. C., & Woltz, D. J. (1989). Role of cognitive factors in the acquisition of cognitive skill. In R. Kanfer & P. Ackerman (Eds.), *Learning and individual differences: Abilities, motivation, and methodology.* Hillsdale, NJ: Erlbaum. Also [1989] Tech. Paper No. AFHRL-TP-89-5) Brooks AFB, TX: Manpower and Personnel Division, Air Force Human Resources Laboratory.

La Duca A, Staples W. I., Templeton B., Holzman G. B. (1986). Item modelling procedures for constructing content equivalent multiple-choice questions. *Medical Education, 20*, 53-56.

Lansman, M., Poltrock, S.E. & Hunt, E (1983). Individual differences in the ability to focus and divide attention. *Intelligence, 7,* 299-312.

Lane, M. E. (2006). *Predictors of attrition from the U.S. Navy delayed entry program combat centre personnel.* In Proceedings of the 48th Annual International Military Testing Association Conference.

Latchman, S. (2008). *Attrition of new recruits: a cohort analysis.* In Proceedings of the 50th Annual International Military Testing Association Conference.

Latchman, S. & Arseneau, L. (2012). *Demographic and attrition analysis of the MARS officer occupation.* In Proceedings of the 54th Annual International Military Testing Association Conference.

Latchman, S. & Michaud, K. (2010). *Early attrition of army non-commissioned members.* In Proceedings of the 52nd Annual International Military Testing Association Conference.

Laurence J. H. (1993). Education standards and military selection: from the beginning. In Trent, T. & Laurence, J. H. *Adaptability screening for the Armed Forces,* Office of the Assistant Secretary of Defense (Force Management and Personnel, Washington, DC, pp. 1-40.

Laurence J. H. & Waters B. K. (1993). Biodata, what's it all about?.. In Trent, T. & Laurence, J. H. *Adaptability screening for the Armed Forces,* Office of the Assistant Secretary of Defense (Force Management and Personnel, Washington, DC, pp. 41-70.

Leavy, N. & Collis, J.M. (1991). *The use of an audio recording for the transmission of instructions and the administration of the ABC test sessions at the Admiralty Interview Board.* SP(N) Report R 153. London, Ministry of Defence.

Leavy, N. & Collis, J.M. (1991). *The combined ABC test battery: trial at the admiralty interview board 1990/1991.* SP(N) Report TR 282. London, Ministry of Defence.

Leavy, N. & Collis, J.M. (1991). *The Combined ABC Test Battery: Trial at the Commando Training Centre, Royal Marines, Lympstone March 1991.* SP(N) Report TR 290. London, Ministry of Defence.

Lee, D. N. & Reddish, P.E. (1981). Plummeting gannets, a paradigm of ecological optics. *Nature,* 283-294.

Lee, D. N., Young, D.S. Reddish, P.E., Lough, S. & Clayton, T. H. H. (1983). Visual timing hitting an accelerating ball. *Quarterly Journal of Experimental Psychology, 35A,* 333-346.

Lee, J. (2010). *Predicting Basic Training Attrition.* In Proceedings of the 52nd Annual International Military Testing Association Conference.

Lescrève, F., (1993). *A Psychometric Model for Selection and Assignment of Belgian NCO's.* In Proceedings of the 35th annual conference of the Military Testing Association. US CoastGuard, pp. 527-533.

Lescrève, F., (1995a). *The Selection of Belgian NCO's, The Psychometric model goes operational.* In Proceedings of the 37th annual conference of the International Military TestingAssociation. Canadian Forces Personnel Applied Research Unit, pp. 497-502.

Lescrève, F., (1995b). *The use of neural networks as an alternative to multiple regressions and subject matter experts in the prediction of training outcomes.* Paper presented at the International Applied Military Psychology Symposium, Lisboa, Portugal, 1995.

Lescrève, F., (1996). *The psychometric model for the selection of NCO's, a statistical review.* International Study Program in Statistics, Catholic University of Leuven, Belgium.

Lescrève, F., (1997a). *The determination of a cut-off score for the intellectual potential.* Center for Recruitment and Selection, Belgian Defence Force, Brussels, Technical Report -3.

Lescrève, F., (1997b). *Data modeling and processing for batch classification* systems. in Proceedings of the 39th Annual Conference of the International Military Testing Association, Sydney, Australia.

Lescrève, F., (1998). *Immediate assessment of batch classification quality.* In Proceedings of the 37th annual conference of the International Military Testing Association, Internet,www. internationalmta.org.

Lescrève, F. (2000). *Recruiting for the military, a new challenge.* Paper presented at the 42nd Annual Conference of The International Military Testing Association, Edinburgh. Conference Abstracts Book, p. 515.

Lescrève, F. (2007). *Tackling early attrition: research design and metrics in the Belgian Defense.* In Proceedings of the 49th Annual International Military Testing Association Conference.

Lewis-Cooper, C. (1993). *BARB: New horizons in testing.* Paper presented at the 35th Annual Conference of The International Military Testing Association, Williamsburg, VA. Conference Abstracts Book, p. 392-394. (Also as Technical Report, 2-1994 Army Personnel Research Establishment) Human Assessment Laboratory, University of Plymouth, Plymouth, UK).

Lindzey, G. & Hall, C. S. (Eds.) (1965). *Theories of Personality: Primary Sources and Research*, London: John Wiley.

Linhart, H. (1959). Estimation of consistency of psychological tests with dichotomous scoring. *Journal of the National Institute for Personnel Research*, *7,* 162-164.

Lohman, D. F. (1994). Component scores as residual variation (or why the intercept correlates best. *Intelligence, 19,* 1-11.

Lohman, D. F., Pellegrino, J. W., Alderton, D. L. & Regian, J. W. (1987). Dimensions and components of individual differences in spatial abilities. In S. H. Irvine & S. E. Newstead, (Eds.), *Intelligence and cognition, contemporary frames of reference.* Dordrecht, Netherlands, Nijhoff.

Longstreth, L.E (1984). Jensen's reaction time investigations of intelligence, a critique. *Intelligence, 8,* 139-160.

Lord, F. M. (1975). Formula scoring and number-right scoring. *Journal of Educational Measurement, 8,* 147-151.

Lord, F. M. (1980a). *Applications of item response theory to practical testing problems.* Hillsdale, NJ, Erlbaum.

Lord. F. M. (1980b). Discussion. In D. J. Weiss (Ed.), *Proceedings of the 1979 Computerized Adaptive Testing Conference*. Minneapolis: University of Minnesota, Department of Psychology, Psychometric Methods Program, pp. 439-441.

Lord, F. M. (1983). Maximum likelihood estimation of item response parameters when some responses are omitted. *Psychometrika, 48,* 477-482

Lord, F. M. & Novick, M. R. (1968). *Statistical theories of mental test scores*. Reading, Mass., Addison-Wesley.

Lord, F. M. & Wingersky, M. S. (1984). Comparison of IRT true-score and equipercentile observed-score equatings. *Applied Psychological Measurement, 4,* 453-461.

Lorr, M. & Suziedelis, A. (1969). Modes of interpersonal behaviour. *British Journal of Social & Clinical Psychology,* Vol. *8(2),* 124-132.

Lubin, B., Fiedler, E. R., & Whitlock, R. V (1996). Mood as a predictor of discharge from Air Force basic training. *Journal of Clinical Psychology, 52,* 145-151.

Lubin, B., Fiedler, E. R., & Whitlock, R. V (1999). Predicting discharge from Airforce basic training by pattern of affect. *Journal of Clinical Psychology, 55,* 71-78.

Lucas J. W. et al. (2008). *The role of social support in first-term sailors' attrition from recruit training*. Navy Personnel Research, Studies, and Technology Division Bureau of Naval Personnel (NPRST/BUPERS-1) Millington, TN 38055-1000 NPRST-TR-08-1 April 2008. (Full author list Jeffrey W. Lucas, Yuko Whitestone, David R. Segal, Mady W. Segal, Michael A. White, Jacqueline A. Mottern, & Rorie N. Harris.)

Lucas, J. W., Segal, R., Whitestone, Y., & Segal, W. (2010). The role of Recruit Division Commanders in Graduation from US Navy Recruit Training. *Journal of Military Psychology, 22,* 369-384.

Luecht, R. M. (2006). *Engineering the test: From principled item design to automated test assembly*. Paper presented at the annual meeting of the Society for Industrial and Organizational Psychology, Dallas, TX.

Lumsden, J. Discussion. In D. J. Weiss (Ed.), *Proceedings of the 1979 Computerized Adaptive Testing Conference*. Minneapolis: University of Minnesota, Department of Psychology, Psychometric Methods Program, 1980. pp. 442- 443.

Lynn, R (1982). IQ in Japan and the United States shows a growing disparity. *Nature, 297,* 222-223.

MacArthur, R. S., Irvine, S. H., & Brimble, A. R. (1964). *The Northern Rhodesia mental ability survey.* Lusaka, Zambia, Institute for Social Research.

Macdonald, A. (1945). *Selection of African personnel: Final report on the work of Selection of Personnel Technical and Research Unit, Middle East Force*. UK War Office Department DSP, London.

MacLennan, R. (1995). Validity generalisation across military occupational families. *Proceedings of the 37th International Military Testing Association Conference*, Toronto, Canada.

Macpherson, W. G. C. (2011). *Exploratory study: what effect does empathy and cognitive failure in leadership have on occupational stress and well-being in Royal Marines recruit training?* Thesis submitted for the degree of M.Sc. Dept. of Occupational Health and Safety Management, Brunel University, UK.

Magruder, C.D., Holden, R.R., Stein, S.J., Sitarenios, G., & Sheldon, S. (2000). Psychometric properties of the Holden Psychological Screening Inventory (HPSI) in the U.S. military. *Military Psychology, 12,* 267-275.

Maier, M. H., & Sims, W. H. (1986). *The ASVAB score scales: 1980 and World War II (CNR 116).* Alexandria, VA: Center for Naval Analyses.

Mathieu, J., Dubois, P. & Viaene, L. (1997). Asklepios onder de wapens. 500 jaar militaire geneeskunde in België In J., Evrard, R., Mathieu, R., François & R., Moorthamers (Eds S.l., *Wetenschappelijke Vereniging van de Militaire Medische Dienst.* (pp. 355-357).

Matthews, M. D. (1982).*Vocational interests, job satisfaction, and turnover among Air Force enlistees.* Paper presented at the Fourth International Learning Technology Congress, 22-24 February, 1982. (Copy printed by Air Force Systems Command, Brooks AFB, San Antonio, Texas.)

Mayer, R. E., Larkin, J. H., & Kadane, J. B. (1984). A cognitive analysis of mathematical problem solving. In Sternberg, R. J. (Ed.). *Advances in the psychology of human intelligence, Vol.2.* Hillsdale, NJ, Erlbaum, pp. 321-274.

McBride, J. R. (1993). Compensatory screening model development. In Trent, T. & Laurence, J. H. *Adaptability screening for the Armed Forces,* Office of the Assistant Secretary of Defense (Force Management and Personnel, Washington, DC, pp.163-214.

McCloskey, M., & Glucksberg, S. Decision processes in verifying category membership statements. *Journal of Verbal Learning and Verbal Behavior,* 1974, *13,* 237-254.

Mehrabian, A. (1970). *Tactics of Social Influence.* Englewood, NJ. Prentice-Hall.

Mellenbergh, G. J. (1983). Conditional item bias methods. In S .H. Irvine & J. W. Berry, (Eds.), *Human assessment and cultural factors.* New York, Plenum.

Merton, R. K. (1940). Bureaucratic structure and personality. *Social Forces, 18,* 560-568.

Michon, J. A. (1985). The compleat time experiences. In J. A. Michon & J. L. Jackson, (Eds.) *Time, mind and behaviour.* Heidelberg: Springer, pp. 20-52.

Michon J. A. & Jackson, J. L. Eds. (1985). *Time, mind and behaviour.* Heidelberg: Springer.

Miles, R. T. (1957). Contributions to intelligence testing and the theory of intelligence Part 1; on defining intelligence. *British Journal of Educational Psychology, 27,* 153-165

Miller, G. A. (1956). The magical number seven, plus or minus two: Some limits on our capacity for processing information. *Psychological Review 63 (2),* 81-97.

Miller, G. A., & McKean, K. E. (1964). A chronometric study of some relations between sentences. *Quarterly Journal of Experimental Psychology, 16,* 297-308.

Miller, L. T. (1999).Psychometric and information processing approaches to measuring cognitive abilities. *Canadian Psychology, 40 (3),* 241-254.

Mislevy, R.J., (2006). Cognitive psychology and educational assessment. In R. Brennan (ed.) *Educational Measurement (4th edition).* Westport, CT: Praeger, 257-305.

Mislevy, R.J. (2011). *Evidence centered design for simulation-based assessment.* (CRESST Report 800). Los Angeles, CA: University of California, National Center for Research on Evaluation, Standards, and Student Testing (CRESST).

Mislevy, R. J., Behrens, J. T., Bennett, R. E., Demark, S. F., Frezzo, D. C., Levy, R., Robinson, D. H., Rutstein, D. W., Shute, V. J., Stanley, K., & Winters, F.I. (2010). On the roles of external knowledge representations in assessment design. *Journal of Technology, Learning, and Assessment, 8* (2).

Mislevy, R. J., & Levy, R. (2007). Bayesian psychometric modeling from an evidence centered design perspective. In C. R. Rao and S. Sinharay (Eds.), *Handbook of statistics, 26,* (pp. 839-865). North-Holland: Elsevier.

Mislevy, R. J., & Riconscente, M. M. (2006). Evidence-centered assessment design: Layers, concepts, and terminology. In S. Downing & T. Haladyna (Eds.), *Handbook of Test Development* (pp. 61-90). Mahwah, NJ: Erlbaum.

Mislevy, R. J., Riconscente, M. M., & Rutstein, D. W. (2009). *Design patterns for assessing model-based reasoning.* (Large-Scale Assessment Technical Report 6). Menlo Park, CA: SRI International.

Mislevy, R. J. & Sheehan, K. M. (1988). *The role of collateral information about examinees in item parameter estimation.* ETS Research Report (RR-88-55-ONR). Educational Testing Service, Princeton, NJ.

Mislevy, R. J., Steinberg, L. S., & Almond, R.A. (2003). On the structure of educational assessments. *Measurement: Interdisciplinary Research and Perspectives, 1,* 3-67.

Mislevy, R. J., Steinberg, L. S., Breyer, F. J., Johnson. L., & Almond, R.A. (2002). Making sense of data from complex assessments. *Applied Measurement in Education, 15,* 363-378.

Mislevy, R. J., Wingersky, M. S., Irvine, S. H., & Dann, P. L. (1991). Resolving mixtures of strategies in spatial visualisation tasks. *British Journal of Mathematical and Statistical Psychology, 44,* 265-288.

Moyer, R. S., & Landauer, T. K. (1967). Time required for judgements of numerical inequality. *Nature, 215,* 1519-1520.

Mulligan, K., Jones, N., Woodhead, C., Davies, M., Wessely, S., and Greenberg, N. (2010), Mental health of UK military personnel while on deployment in Iraq, *British Journal of Psychiatry, 197,* 405-410.

Munnoch, K. & Bridger, R. S. (2008). An investigation into the relationship between recruit test RT4 scores and mechanical comprehension dependent tasks. *Military Psychology, 20,* 95-101.

Munnoch, K, & Bridger R. S. (2008). Operational performance of a rehabilitation company in royal marines training. *Military Medicine, 173,* 129-133.

Namikas G. (1983). Vertical processes and motor performance. In R.A. Magill, (Ed.), *Memory and control of action.* Amsterdam: North Holland.

NATO (2007). *Recruiting and retention of military personnel (Recrutement et rétention du personnel militaire)* Final Report of Research Task Group HFM-107. North Atlantic Treaty Organisation Research And Technology Organisation Ac/323(Hfm-107)Tp/71 www.rto.nato. int Rto Technical Report Tr-Hfm-107.

Nauels, H.-U., & Wildgrube, W. (1981). Probleme des itempools beim adaptiven testen: pilotstudie zum CAT. *Zeitschrift für Differentielle und Diagnostische Psychologie, 4,* 303-323.

Neimark, E .D., & Estes, W. K. (1967). *Stimulus sampling theory.* Holden, San Francisco. San Francisco CA, Holden Day.

Newstead, S.E. & Collis, J. (1987). Context and the interpretation of quantifiers of frequency. *Ergonomics, 30 (10)*, 1447-1462.

Newstead, S.E., Irvine , S. H. & Dann, P. L. (Eds.). (1986). *Human Assessment, Cognition and Motivation.* Dordrecht, Martinus Nijhoff.

Newstead, S.E., Pollard, P., & Riezebos, D. (1987).The effect of set size on the interpretation of quantifiers used in rating scales. *Applied Ergonomics, 18 (3)*, 178-182.

Orvis B. R., Sastry N., & McDonald L. L. (1996). *Military Recruiting Outlook, Recent Trends in Enlistment Propensity and Conversion of Potential Enlisted Supply.* Rand Corporation Document No, MR-677-A/OSD, Pages, xvii, 68, ISBN, 0833024612.

Page, E. S. (1954). Continuous Inspection Scheme. *Biometrika 41 (1/2)*, 100-115.

Pannone, R. D. (1984). Predicting test performance: a content valid approach to screening applicants. *Personnel Psychology, 37 (3)*, 507-514.

Parkman. J. M. (1972). Temporal aspects of simple multiplication and comparison. *Journal of Experimental Psychology, 95*, 437-444.

Pellegrino, J. W. & Glaser, R (1982). Analyzing aptitudes for learning, inductive reasoning. In R. Glaser, (Ed.), *Advances in instructional technology, Vol.2* Hillsdale, NJ, Erlbaum.

Pellegrino, J. W. & Hunt, E. B (1988). *Assessment and modeling of information coordination abilities.* Paper delivered at Minnesota Symposium on Learning and Individual Differences, Mnneapolis, April 14-16.

Pellegrino, J. W. & Kail, R. (1982). Process analysis of spatial aptitude. In R. Sternberg, (Ed.), *Advances in the psychology of human intelligence, Vol. 1* Hillsdale, NJ, Erlbaum.

Penrose, L. S. & Raven, J. C. (1936). A new series of perceptual tests: preliminary communication. *British Journal of Medical Psychology, 15*, 97-105.

Peterson, C., Park, N., & Castro, C.A. (2011). Assessment for the U.S. Army comprehensive soldier fitness program: global assessment tool. *American Psychologist 66 (1)*, 10-18.

Peterson, N. G. (Ed.), (1987). *Development and field test of the trial battery for Project A.* Technical Report 739, Manpower and Personnel Research Laboratory, US Army Research Institute for the Behavioral and Social Sciences, Alexandria, VA.

Peterson, N. G. & Wing, H. (2001). The search for new measures: sampling from a population of selection/classification predictor variables. In Campbell, J. P. & Knapp, D. J. (Eds.). *Exploring the limits in personnel selection and classification.* Lawrence Erlbaum Associates, Mahwah, NJ, pp. 53-70.

Plag, J. A. (1962). Pre-enlistment variables related to the performance and adjustment of Navy recruits. *Journal of Clinical Psychology, 18*, 168-171.

Poortinga, Y. H. (1985). Empirical evidence of bias in choice-reaction time experiments. *The Behavioral and Brain Sciences. 8*, 236-237.

Poortinga, Y. H. & van der Flier, H. (1988).The meaning of item bias in ability tests. In S. H. Irvine & J. W. Berry (Eds.), *Human Abilities in Cultural Context.* Cambridge.

POPLOG & LISP (2013). *Free Poplog Including Pop-11, Lisp, Prolog, Ml, Popvision Library, Simagent Toolkit.* School of Computer Science The University of Birmingham In collaboration with The University of Sussex: Informatics Department and Centre for Research in Cognitive Science The Free Poplog Portal http://tinyurl.com/PopLog/freepoplog.html.

Posner, M. L., Boies, S. J., Eichelman, W. H., & Taylor, R. J. (1969). Retention of visual name codes of single letters. *Journal of Experimental Psychology Monographs, 79,* 1-16.

Prince, M. J., Bird, A. S., Blizzard, R. A., & Mann, A. H. (1996). Is the cognitive function of older patients affected by hypertensive treatment? *British Medical Journal, 312,* 801-808.

Quick, J. C., Joplin, J. R., Nelson, D. L., Mangelsdorff, A. D., & Fiedler, E. (1996). Self-reliance and military service training outcomes. *Military Psychology, 8,* 279-293.

Rabbitt, P. M. A. (1985). Oh g Dr. Jensen! or, g-ing up cognitive psychology. *The Behavioral and Brain Sciences. 8,* 238-239.

Rasch, G. (1960). *Probabilistic models for some intelligence and attainment tests.* Copenhagen: Danish Institute of Educational Research.

Rasch, G. (1961). On general laws and the meaning of measurement in psychology. *Proceedings of the 4th Berkeley symposium on mathematical statistics, Vol.-1.* Berkeley: University of California Press, (pp. 321-334).

Rasch, G. (1966a). An item analysis which takes individual differences into account. *British Journal of Mathematical and Statistical Psychology, 19,* 49-57.

Rasch, G. (1966b). An individualistic approach to item analysis. In P. Lazarsfeld & N. V. Henry (Eds.). *Readings in mathematical social science* Chicago: Science Research Association, (pp. 89-107).

Ree, M. J., & Earles, J. A. (1991). Predicting training success: Not much more than g. *Personnel Psychology, 44,* 321-332.

Ree, M. J., & Earles, J. A. (1992). Intelligence is the best predictor of job performance. *Current Directions in Psychological Science, 1,* 86-89.

Ree, M. J., & Earles, J. A. (1996). Predicting occupational criteria: not much more than g. In Dennis I., & Tapsfield, P. G. C. (Eds.). *Human abilities, their nature & measurement.* Erlbaum, Hillsdale, NJ.

Ree, M. J., Muffins, C. J., Mathews, J. J., & Massey, R. H. (1982). Armed Services Vocational Aptitude Battery: Item and factor analyses of Forms 8, 9, and 10 (AFHRL-TR-81-55). Brooks AFB, TX: Air Force Human Resources Laboratory, Manpower and Personnel Division.

Resnick, L. B. (Ed.). (1976). *The nature of intelligence.* Hillsdale, NJ, Lawrence Erlbaum Associates.

Restle, F., & Davis, J. H. (1962). Success and speed of problem-solving by individuals and groups. *Psychological Review, 69,* 520-536.

Reuning, H. (1978). *Test Administrator's Manual, Continuous Symbol Checking (Revised Edition)* CSIR Guide K & 62, National Institute for Personnel Research, Johannesburg, SA.

Reuning, H. (1983). Continuous work tests: their scope in cross-cultural contexts. In S. H. Irvine & J. W. Berry, (Eds.), *Human assessment and cultural factors.* New York, Plenum pp. 303-317.

Rips, L. J. (1984). Reasoning as a central intellectual activity. In Sternberg, R. J. (Ed.).(1984a). *Advances in the psychology of human intelligence, Vol.2.* Hillsdale, NJ, Erlbaum, pp. 105-148.

Rips, L. J.; Shoben, E. J,; Smith, E. E. (1973). Semantic distance and the verification of semantic relations. *Journal of Verbal Learning and Verbal Behavior 12 (1),* 1-20.

Roberts. A. O. H. (1959). Artefactor analysis: some theoretical background and practical demonstrations. *Journal of the National Institute for Personnel Research, 7,* 168-188.

Roberts, R. R., Schulze, R., & Kyllonen, P. C. (2006). *ETS Mini-conference on Faking on Noncognitive Assessments.* Princeton, NJ, Educational Testing Service.

Rodger, A. (1954). The seven point plan. *National Institute of Industrial Psychology Paper No.1.* London: NIIP.

Rona, R. J., Hooper, R., Jones, M., French, C,. & Wessely, S. (2004). Screening for physical and psychological illness in the British Armed Forces, III, The value of a questionnaire to assist a Medical Officer to decide who needs help. *Journal of Medical Screening,11,*158-161.

Rona, R. J., Hooper, R., Jones, M., Hull, C., Browne, T., Horn, O., Murphy, D., Hotopf, M., & Wessely S. (2006). Mental health screening in armed forces before the Iraq war and prevention of subsequent psychological morbidity, follow-up study. *British Medical Journal, 333,* 991-994.

Ronning, R. R., Glover, J. A., Conoley, J. C. & Witt, J. C. (1987). *The influence of cognitive psychology on testing.* Hillsdale, NJ, Erlbaum.

Royer, F. L. (1971). Information processing of visual figures in the Digit Symbol Substitution Task. *Journal of Experimental Psychology, 87,* 344-352.

Sackett, P. R. & Mavor, A. S. (Eds.), (2006), *Assessing Fitness for Military Enlistment, Physical, Medical, and Mental Health Standards (2006).* Board on Behavioral, Cognitive, and Sensory Sciences and Education. National Academies Press, Washington, DC.

Salgado J. F. (1998). Big five personality dimensions and job performance in Army and civil occupations: a European perspective. *Human Performance, 11*, 271-88.

Samejima, F. (1983a). *A general model for the homogeneous case of the continuous response.* ONR/RR-83-3, University of Tennessee, Knoxville, TN.

Samejima, F (1983b). Some methods and approaches of estimating the operating characteristics of discrete item responses. In *Principals of Modern Psychological Measurement,* Wainer, H. & Messick, S. (Eds.) Hillsdale, NJ. Erlbaum.

Schachter, S. (1959). Ordinal position and fighter pilot effectiveness. In *The Psychology of Affiliation,* Stanford: Stanford University Press. (See pp. 42-89. Also in G. Lindzey & C. S. Hall (Eds.) *Theories of Personality: Primary Sources and Research*, London: John Wiley, 1965, pp. 114-116.

Schaeffer, E., & Wallace, R. (1970). The comparison of word meanings. *Journal of Experimental Psychology, 86,* 144-152.

Schlechty, P. C. (1976). *Teaching and social behavior.* Boston: Allyn & Bacon.

Schneider, D. M. (1947). The social dynamics of physical disability in Army basic training. *Psychiatry, 10,* 323-333.

Schreurs, B. J. (2001). *Recruitment and selection as social processes, negotiate to reduce the number of back-outs.* Paper presented at the 43rd Annual Conference of the International Military Association, Canberra, Australia, pp. 407-423.

Secord, P. F. & Backman, C. W. (1964). *Social psychology.* New York: McGraw-Hill.

Sheehan, K. M. (1997*). A tree-based approach to proficiency scaling.* ETS Research Report (RR-97-2) Educational Testing Service, Princeton, NJ.

Shepard, R. N. (1984). Ecological constraints on internal representation: resonant kinematics of perceiving, imagining, thinking and dreaming. *Psychological Review, 91*: 417-447.

Shepard, R. N., & Feng, C. A. (1972). A chronometric study of mental paper folding. *Cognitive Psychology, 3*, 228-243.

Shepard, R. N., & Metzler, J. (1971). Mental rotation of three-dimensional objects. *Science, 171,* 701-703.

Sinharay, S., & Johnson, M. S. (2003). *Simulation studies applying posterior predictive model checking for assessing fit of the common item response theory models (ETS RR-03-28).* Princeton, NJ: Educational Testing Service.

Shute, V. J. & Kyllonen, P. C. (1990). *Modeling Programming Skill Acquisition* (Report No. AFHRL-TP-90-76). Air Force Systems Command, Brooks Air Force Base, TX.

Slaven, G., Shariff, A., Pethybridge, R. J. (1999). *The management of stress in the naval service: Stage 1 identification of workplace stressors.* Contract No. 99029. Alverstoke, UK: Institute of Naval Medicine,

Smith, E. E. (1978). Theories of semantic memory. In W. K. Estes (Ed.), *Handbook of learning and cognitive processes* (Vol. 6). Hillsdale, N.J.: Erlbaum.

Smith, E. E.; Shoben, E. J.; Rips, L. J. (1974). Structure and process in semantic memory: A featural model for semantic decisions. *Psychological Review 81 (3),* 214-14.

Smith, E. P. & Graham, S.E. (1987). *Validation of psychomotor and perceptual predictors of armor officer m-1 gunnery performance* . Technical Report 766 U. S. Army Research Institute for the Behavioral and Social Sciences November 1987, Alexandria, Virginia 22333-5600.

Snow, R. E., Kyllonen, P. C. & Marshalek, B. (1984). The topography of ability and learning correlations. In R. J. Sternberg, (Ed.) *Advances in the psychology of human intelligence, Vol.2.* Hillsdale, NJ, Erlbaum.

Spearman, C. (1904). General Intelligence, objectively determined and measured. *American Journal of Psychology, 15,* 201-293

Spearman, C. (1927). *The abilities of man.* London, Macmillan.

Stanko, M. (1979). *Wechsler's Digit-Symbol Test in another culture : Some evidence for the consistent effect of process variables.* Unpublished M.Ed. Project Report, Brock University, St. Catherines, Ontario, Canada.

Stankov, L. (1983). Attention and intelligence. *Journal of Educational Psychology, 75,* 471-490.

Stankov, L. & Horn, J. L. (1980). Human abilities revealed through auditory tests. *Journal of Educational Psychology, 72,* 19-42.

Steege, F.W. & Fritscher, W. (1991). Psychological assessment and personnel management. In R. Gal & D. Mangelsdorff (Eds.). *Handbook of Military Psychology (pp. 7-36).* Chichester, Wiley & Sons.

Steege, F. W. Personnel psychology in the Federal Armed Forces of Germany. In J.W. Miller (Ed.), *The 12th International Symposium on Applied Military Psychology* (C-26-27). London, Office of Naval Research, London Branch Office, 1976.

Sternberg, R. J. (1977). *Intelligence, information processing, and analogical reasoning: the componential analysis of human abilities.* Hillsdale, NJ, Erlbaum.

Sternberg, R. J. (Ed.). (1984a). *Advances in the psychology of human intelligence, Vol.2.* Hillsdale, NJ, Erlbaum.

Sternberg, R. J. (1984b). Toward a triarchic theory of intelligence. *The Behavioral and Brain Sciences, 7,* 269-287.

Sternberg, R. J. (1985a). *Beyond IQ, a triarchic theory of human intelligence.* New York, Cambridge.

Sternberg, R. J. (Ed.). (1985b). *Human abilities, an information-processing approach.* New York, Freeman.

Sternberg, R.J. (1990). *Metaphors of Mind: conceptions of the nature of intelligence.* New York: Cambridge University Press.

Sternberg, R. J. & Gardner, M. K. (1982). *A componential interpretation of the general factor in human intelligence.* In H.J. Eysenck, (Ed.). *A Model for Intelligence.* New York : Springer-Verlag.

Sternberg, R. J. (2008). 'g' g's or jeez: which is the best model for developing abilities, competencies and expertise? In Kyllonen, P. C., Roberts, R. D. & Stankov, L. (Eds.), *Extending intelligence.* Mahwah, NJ. Erlbaum, pp. 267-318.

Sternberg, R. J. & Gardner, M. K. (1982). A componential interpretation of the general factor in human intelligence. In H.J. Eysenck, (Ed.), *A model for intelligence.* New York, Springer-Verlag.

Sternberg, S. (1966). High speed scanning in human memory. *Science, 153,* 652-654.

Storm, E. G. (1995). *Theoriegeleitete Testkonstruktion. Erfassung visueller Analyseleistungen anhand neuartiger, computergenerierter „Eingekleideter. Figur-Aufgaben" (Theory based test construction. Assessing visual perception with new, computer generated embedded figure items).* Arbeitsberichte Psychologischer Dienst der Bundeswehr. Bonn, Bundesminsterium der Verteidigung - P II14.

STRATEGY PAGE. (2011). *German army recruits quit.* Article dated 26 December, 2011, http://www.strategypage.com/htmw/htatrit/articles/20111226.aspx.

Sümer, H. C. (2004). *Individual needs and military turnover.* Paper delivered at the International Military Testing Association Conference, Brussels, October 2004.

Talcott, G. W., Haddock, K., Klesges, R. C., Lando, H., & Fiedler, E. (1999). Prevalence and predictors of discharge in United States Air Force basic military training. *Military Medicine, 164,* 269-274.

Tapsfield, P. G. C. (1993a). *The British Army Recruit Battery: test-retest reliability.* HAL Technical Report, 5-1993 (APRE). Human Assessment Laboratory, University of Plymouth, Plymouth, UK for Ministry of Defence.

Tapsfield, P. G. C. (1993b). *The British Army Recruit Battery, 1993 applicant norms.* (Technical Report, 6-1993 Army Personnel Research Establishment). Human Assessment Laboratory, University of Plymouth, Plymouth, UK for Ministry of Defence.

Tapsfield, P. G. C. (1993c). *BARB Nationwide: inferences from computer-delivered test data.* Paper presented at the 35th Annual Conference of The International Military Testing Association, Williamsburg, VA. Conference Abstracts Book, pp. 380-385. (also as Technical Report, 2-1994 Army Personnel Research Establishment) Human Assessment Laboratory, University of Plymouth, Plymouth, UK for Ministry of Defence).

Tapsfield, P. G. C. (1995). *The British Army Recruit Battery, 1995 applicant norms* (Technical Report, 13-1995. Human Assessment Laboratory, University of Plymouth, Plymouth, UK for Ministry of Defence.

Tapsfield, P. G. C. (1996). *BARB Version BD: A preliminary analysis of experimental tests, a note for discussion*. Human Assessment Laboratory, University of Plymouth Report, December 1996 for Ministry of Defence.

Tapsfield, P. G. C., & Wright, D. E. (1993). *A preliminary analysis of summary data arising from the operational use of the British Army Recruit Battery* (Technical Report, 3-1993 Army Personnel Research Establishment). Human Assessment Laboratory, University of Plymouth, Plymouth, UK for Ministry of Defence.

Tatsuoka, K. M. (1997). *Notes on identification and selection of attributes*. (Comments on Sheehan's paper). Manuscript for circulation, Research Division, Educational Testing Service, Princeton, NJ.

Tatsuoka, K. M. (1997). *Rule-space methodology*. Manuscript of report for publication, Research Division, Educational Testing Service, Princeton, NJ.

Tatsuoka, K. M., & Tatsuoka, M. M. (1978). *Time-score analysis in criterion-referenced tests*. Report of the Computer-Based Education Research Laboratory (CERL Report E-1), University of Illinois, Urbana, Ill.

Taylor, H. C. & Russell, J. T. (1939). The relationship of validity coefficients to the practical effectiveness of tests in selection: discussion and tables. *Journal of Applied Psychology, 28,* 565-578.

Tellegen, A. (1985). Structures of moods and personality and their relevance to assessing anxiety with an emphasis on self-report. In A. Turma & J. Maser (Eds.). *Anxiety and anxiety disorders* (pp. 681-706). Hillsdale, NJ: Lawrence Erlbaum.

THE LOCAL (2011). *Bundeswehr recruits quitting voluntary service.* Article published 22 July. In The Local: Germany's News in English http://www.thelocal.de/national/20110722-36461.html.

Thissen, D. & Wainer, H, (Eds). (2001). *Test scoring.* Mahwah, NJ, LEA Publishers.

Thomson, G. H. (1939). *The factorial analysis of human ability*. London, University of London Press. (1st Ed.)

Thurstone, L.L. (1938). Primary mental abilities. *Psychometric Monographs, 1.* (Whole Number). Also as *Primary mental abilities*. Chicago, University of Chicago Press 1938; and latterly as a Medway Reprint (1975) Chicago, University of Chicago Press.

Trabin, T. E., & Weiss, D. J. (1983). The person response curve: Fit of individuals to item response theory models. In D. J. Weiss (Ed.) *New horizons in testing* (pp. 83-108). New York: Academic Press.

Trent, T. (1987). *Armed Forces adaptability screening: the problem of item response distortion.* Paper presented at the Convention of the American Psychological Association, New York.

Trent, T. (1993). The armed services applicant profile (ASAP). In Trent, T. & Laurence, J. H. *Adaptability screening for the Armed Forces*, Office of the Assistant Secretary of Defense (Force Management and Personnel, Washington, DC, pp. 71-100.

Trent, T., Atwater, D. C, & Abrahams, N. M. *(1986). Biographical screening of military applicants: experimental assessment of item response distortion.* In Proceedings of the Tenth Psychology Department of Defense Symposium, 96-i.

Trent, T., Folchi, J., & Sunderman, S. (1991). Compensatory enlistment screening, A non-traditional approach. *Proceedings of the 33rd Annual Conference of the Military Testing Association,* 565-570.

Trent, T. & Laurence, J. H. (Eds.) (1993). *Adaptability Screening for the Armed Forces. Office of the Assistant Secretary of Defense* (Force Management & Personnel) Washington DC, USA.

Trent, T., & Quenette, M. A. (1992). *Armed Services Applicant Profile (ASAP), Development and validation of operational forms* (NPRDC-TR-92-9). San Diego, CA, Navy Personnel Research and Development Center.

TTCP (1997). *Technical minutes of the 1997 HUM-TP3 meeting at Portsmouth, United Kingdom, August 1997:* TTCP-HUM-97-009.

Tupes, E. C. & Christal, R. E.(1992). Recurrent personality factors based on trait ratings. Reprint of original technical report in Special Issue on the Five-Factor Model, Issues and Applications, *Journal of Personality, 60(2),* 225-251.

Turner, K., Dixon, A., Caulfield, M., & Wolfe, J. (1999, August). *Training preparation, self-efficacy, and emotional adaptation, Impact on Marine Corps attrition.* Paper presented at the APA Annual Convention, Boston, MA.

Ulrich, L. & Trumbo, D. (1965). The selection interview since 1949. *Psychological Bulletin, 63:* 100-116.

USAMEPC (1984). *Test manual for the Armed Services Vocational Aptitude Battery.* United States Military Entrance Processing Command Publication (DOD1304, 12AA) Chicago Illinois.

Van Beirendonck, L. (1998). Beoordelen en ontwikkelen van competenties. Assessment Centers, Development Centers en aanverwante technieken. Leuven, Acco. Verhoeven, C. (S.d.). De automatisering van het CRS. In, R. Vandekerckhove (Ed.). Het Klein Kasteeltje, geschiedenis van een mythe (pp. 120-122). S. l.,

van de Ven, C. & van Gelooven, R. (2006). *Early attrition in the Netherlands' armed forces, a new monitor.* In Proceedings of the 48th Annual International Military Testing Association Conference.

Vernon, P. A. (1983). Speed of information processing and general intelligence. *Intelligence, 7,* 53-70.

Vernon, P. A., & Jensen, A. R. (1985). Individual and group differences in intelligence and speed of information processing. *Personality and Individual Differences, 5,* 411-423.

Vernon, P. E. (1953). *Personality tests and assessments.* London, Methuen, p.165.

Vernon, P. E. (1964). *Personality assessment, a critical survey.* London: Methuen.

Vernon, P. E. & Parry, J. B. (1949). *Personnel selection in the British forces.* University of London Press, London, England.

Verster, J. M. (1983). The structure, organisation and correlates of cognitive speed and accuracy. In S. H. Irvine & J. W. Berry, (Eds.), *Human assessment and cultural factors.* New York, Plenum.

Verster, J. M. (1987). Human cognition and intelligence. In Irvine, S. H. & Newstead, S. E. (Eds.). *Intelligence and cognition, contemporary frames of reference.* Dordrecht, Martinus Nijhoff. pp. 27-140.

Voelker, M. D., Saag, K. G., Schwartz, D. A., Chrischilles, E., Clarke, W. R., Woolson, R. F., & Doebbeling, B. N. (2002). Health-related quality of life in Gulf War era military personnel. *American Journal of Epidemiology, 155(10),* 899-907.

Waag W. L., LT Shannon, R. H., & Ambler R. K. (1973). The use of confidential instructor ratings for the prediction of success in naval undergraduate pilot training. NAMRL1175 National Technical Information Service, US Department of Commerce VA 221.

Wainer H. (2002). On the automatic generation of test items, Some whens, whys and hows. In Irvine, S. H. & Kyllonen, P.C. (Eds.). *Item generation for test development.* Erlbaum Associates, Mahwah, N pp. 287-316.

Wainer, H., Bradlow, E. T., & Wang, X. (2007). *Testlet response theory and its Applications.* New York: Cambridge University Press.

Wainer H., & Messick, S. J. (Eds.), (1983). *Principals of modern psychological measurement.* Hillsdale, NJ, Erlbaum.

Walker, C. B. (1988, October). *The U. S. Army's Military Applicant Profile (MAP).* Paper presented at the meeting of the Defense Advisory Committee on Military Personnel Testing, New Orleans.

Waters, B. K. (1989, April). *ASP 01A and 01B equating.* Paper presented at the meeting of the Joint Services Selection and Classification Working Group, Washington, DC.

Watson, D., & Clark, L. A. (1994). *The PANAS-X: Manual for the positive and negative affect schedule-Expanded Form.* Iowa City: University of Iowa.

Weibull, W. (1951). A statistical distribution of wide application. *Journal of Applied Mechanics, 18,* 293-297.

Weiss, D. J. (1973). *The stratified adaptive computerised ability test.* Research Report 73-3, Psychometric Methods Program, Department of Psychology, University of Minnesota.

Weiss, D. J. (Ed.), (1978). *Proceedings of the 1977 Computerized Adaptive Testing Conference.* Minneapolis, University of Minnesota, Department of Psychology, Psychometric Methods Program.

Weiss, D. J. (Ed.) (1980). *Proceedings of the 1979 Item Response Theory and Computerized Adaptive Testing Conference,* University of Minnesota, Department of Psychology, Computerized Adaptive Testing Laboratory, Minneapolis.

Weiss, D. J. (Ed.) (1983). *New Horizons in Testing.* New York, Academic Press.

Welford, A. T. (1980). *Reaction times.* New York, Academic Press.

Welsh, J. R., Watson, T. W., & Ree, M. J., (1990). *Armed Services Vocational Aptitude Battery (ASVAB): predicting military criteria from general and specific abilities.* (AFHRL-TR-90-63). Brooks AFB, TX: Manpower and Personnel Division, Air Force Human Resources Laboratory.

Wessely, S. (2004). *Risk, Psychiatry and the Military.* The 15th Liddell Hart Lecture. King's College, London, March 2004.

White, L. A., Nord, R. D., Mael, F. A. & Young, M. C. (1993). The assessment of background and life experiences (ABLE). In Trent, T. & Laurence, J. H. *Adaptability screening for the Armed Forces,* Office of the Assistant Secretary of Defense (Force Management and Personnel, Washington, D.C, pp. 101-162.

White, P. O. (1982). Some major components in general intelligence. In H.J. Eysenck, (Ed.) *A model for intelligence.* Springer-Verlag, New York, pp. 44-92.

Whiting, H. T. A. (1968).   Training in continuous ball-throwing and catching tasks. *Ergonomics, 11*: 375-382.

Whiting, H. T. A., Gill, E.B. & Stevenson, J.B. (1970).   Critical time intervals for taking in-flight information in a ball-catching task. *Ergonomics, 12*: 265-272.

Wildgrube, W. (1978a).   *Computergestiitzte hilfen bei der eignungsdiagnostik: problemaufriss.* (Wehrpsychologische Mitteilungen 1/78).   Bonn: Bundesministerium der verteidigung, Psychologischer Dienst der Bundeswehr, 1978.

Wildgrube, W. (1978b).   *Computergestutztes adaptives testen (CAT) – Neueste entwicklungen* (Arbeitsberichte Nr P-3-78).   Bonn, Bundesministerium der Verteididung, Psychologischen Dienst der Bundeswehr, 1978.

Wildgrube, W. (1980).   Computerized testing in the Federal Armed Forces.   In D. J. Weiss (Ed.), *Proceedings of the 1979 Computerized Adaptive Testing Conference.* Minneapolis, University of Minnesota, Department of Psychology, Computerized Adaptive Testing Laboratory, Psychometric Methods, 1980.

Wildgrube, W. (1990).   Computergestutze diagnostik in einer grosorganisation. *Diagnostica, 36, 2,* 127-147.

Wilkins, A. T. (1971).   Conjoint frequency, category size, and categorization time. *Journal of Verbal Learning and Verbal Behavior, 10,* 382-385.

Wilson J. M. G., & Jungner G. (1968). *Principles and practice of screening for disease.* Public Health Paper Number 34. Geneva, WHO,

Wingersky, M. S. & Lord, F. M. (1984).   An investigation of methods for reducing sampling error in certain IRT procedures. *Applied Psychological Measurement, 8,* 347-364.

Wingrove, J. Jones, A. & Herriot, P.(1985).   The predictive validity of pre-and post-discussion assessment centre ratings. *Journal of Occupational Psychology* 58, 189-192.

Wise, L. L., Hough, L. M., Szenas, P. L., Trent, T., & Keyes, M. A. (1989).   *Fairness of the Armed Services Applicant Profile (ASAP), Final report.* Washington, DC, American Institutes for Research.

Woltz, D. J. (1987).   *Activation and decay of semantic memory, An individual differences investigation of working memory,* Report, Manpower and Personnel Division, Air Force Human Resources Laboratory, Brooks AFB, Texas.

Wright, D. E. (1990*).   Item response and theory for item generation, comment and developments* (Technical Report 3-1990 Army Personnel Research Establishment).   Human Assessment Laboratory, University of Plymouth, Plymouth, UK for the Ministry of Defence.

Wright, D. E. (1992).   *IRT modelling using latent variable generalised linear models* (Technical Report, 3-1992 Army Personnel Research Establishment).   Human Assessment Laboratory, University of Plymouth, Plymouth, UK for the Ministry of Defence.

Wright, D. E. (1993).   *BARB and the measurement of individual differences, departing from traditional models.* Paper presented at the 35th International Military Association Conference, Williamsburg, VA. Conference Abstracts Book, pp. 391-395 . (also as Technical Report, 2-1994 Army Personnel Research Establishment) Human Assessment Laboratory, University of Plymouth, Plymouth, UK for the Ministry of Defence.

Wright, D. E. (2002).   Scoring tests when items have been generated.   In Irvine, S. H. & Kyllonen, P.C. (Eds.). *Item generation for test development.*   Erlbaum Associates, Mahwah, NJ pp. 277-286.

Wright, D. E. & Dennis, I. (1992*). Development of a test of mental cube folding for use in officer selection.* Technical Report for Science Air (3), Ministry of defence, London. Human Assessment Laboratory, University of Plymouth, Plymouth, UK for the Ministry of Defence.

Wright, D. E, Irvine, S. H. & Tapsfield, P. G. C. (1992). *Test Lengths and Reliabilities.* HAL Technical Report, HAL1-1992 (APRE) University of Plymouth for the Ministry of Defence.

Wright, D. E. & Dennis, I. (1999). *Exploiting the speed-accuracy trade-off.* Ackerman, Phillip L. (Ed); Kyllonen, Patrick C. (Ed); Roberts, Richard D. (Ed), (1999). Learning and individual differences: Process, trait, and content determinants Washington, DC, US: American Psychological Association.

Wright, D. E, & Tapsfield, P. G. C. (1995). *Reducing BARB Test Times: an initial investigation of the effects on reliability.* HAL Technical Report, HAL8-1995 (APRE) University of Plymouth for the Ministry of Defence.

Wright, K. M., Huffman, A. H., Adler, A. B., & Castro, C. A. (2002). Psychological screening program overview. *Military Medicine, 167*, 853-861.

Wright, K .M., Bliese, P. D., Thomas, J. L., Adler, A. B., Eckford, R. D., & Hoge, C. W. (2007). Contrasting approaches to psychological screening with U.S. combat soldiers, *Journal of Traumatic Stress, 20,* 965-975

Wright, K. M., Thomas, J. L., Adler, A. B., Ness, J. W., Hoge, C. W., & Castro, C. A. (2005). Psychological screening procedures for deploying U.S. Forces. *Military Medicine, 170,* 555-562.

Youden, W. J. (1940). Experimental designs to increase accuracy of greenhouse studies. *Contributions of the Boyce Thompson Institute, 11,* 219-228.

SUBJECT INDEX

ABBREVIATIONS

Alphabet Test	AB
The ABC Trial Tests Paper-and-Pencil	ABC
Assessment of Background and Life Experiences	ABLE
Accuracy Scores Adjusted For Guessing	ADJ
Averaged Evoked Potential(s)	AEP(s)
British Army Entry Tests	AET86
Alphabet Forward-Backward Test	AFB
Air Force Human Resources Laboratory	AFHRL
Air Force /Armed Forces Qualifying Test Score	AFQT
Artificial Intelligence	AI
Army Entry Test 1 Problems	AET1
Army Entry Test 2 Instructions	AET2
Army Entry Test 3 Dominoes	AET3
Army Entry Test 4 Verbal Reasoning	AET4
Army Entry Test 5 Arithmetic Numeracy	AET5
Army Entry Test Battery1986	AET 86
US Air Force Qualifying Test	AFQT
A Natural Deduction System	ANDS
Analysis of Variance Analysis	ANOVA
Army Personnel Research Establishment	APRE
Army Personnel Selection Centre Sutton Coldfield	APSC
Arithmetic Reasoning ASVAB	AR
Army Regular Commissions Board Battery	ARCOM
Army Rumour Service	ARSSE
Royal Navy Artificer Apprentices	ARTAPPS
Auto and Shop Information ASVAB	AS
Armed Services Adaptability Profile	ASAP
NATO Advanced Study Institute	ASI
Adaptability Screening Profile	ASP

Armed Services Vocational Aptitude Battery	ASVAB
Alcohol Use Disorders Identification Test	AUDIT
Biological Adaptation to Night and Day Situations	BANDS
British Army Recruit Battery	BARB
Belgian Defence Force	BDF
Bundeswehr Experimental Test Battery	BETB
British Royal Naval College Dartmouth	BRNC
Computerised Adaptive Testing	CAT
The Complex Learning Assessment	CLASS
Indecx Of Capacity to Process Information	CPI
Coding Speed ASVAB	CS
South African Council for Scientific Research	CSIR
Compensatory Screening Model	CSM
Cumulative Summation Scores	CUSUMS
Discharge as of Right	DAOR
Different Case-Same Pairs Search	DCSPS
Differential Item Function(ing)	DIF
Dann-Irvine Murphy's Laws	DIMS
Directions And Distances	DIRDIS
Deutsche Forschungsanstalt für Luft- und Raumfahrt	DLR
Department of Defense	DOD
Digit-Symbol Substitution Task	DSST
Evidence Centred Design	ECD
Elementary Cognitive Tasks	ECTs
Error Detection Test	ED
Electrical Information ASVAB	EI
Educational Testing Service	ETS
Bundeswehr Aptitude Classification Battery	EVT
French Language Group in Belgium Defence Force	FR
Computer Delivered Test Battery Belgium	GCTB
General Health Questionnaire	GHQ-12
General Science	GS
Royal Air Force Ground Trades Test Battery	GTTB
ETS Graduate Record Examination	GRE
General Training Index	GTI

Human Assessment Laboratory	HAL
Human Relations	HR
Health-Related Quality of Life	HRQOL
Item Characteristic Curve	ICC
Identification Data for Individuals	ID
Infantry Training Centre at Catterick	ITC(C)
Item Response Theory	IRT
Jobs and Occupations Inventory	JOIN
Kuder-Richardson Reliability Estimate	KR20
Learning Abilities Measurement Program	LAMP
Latency Score (Log mean ms. for completed items)	LAT
Letter Checking Test	LCT
Letter Distance Test	LD
Latency Intelligence Quotient	LIQ
The Linear Logistic Test Model	LLTM
Logistic Item Response Modelling	LOGIST
Mean Log Latency Standard Deviation	LSD
Mean Log Latency Standard Error	LSEM
Maisons de Defence Belgium	MdD
Mechanical Comprehension ASVAB	MC
Middle East Selection Project	MESP
Bartram's Pilot Aptitude Battery	MICROPAT
Mantel-Haenszel Statistic	M-H
Mathematics Knowledge ASVAB	MK
Maximum Likelihood Factor Analysis	ML
Ministry of Defence	MOD
Military Quality of Life Scale	M-RQOL
North Atlantic Treaty Organisation	NATO
Non-Commissioned Officer	NCO
Number Distance Test	ND
Number Fluency	NF
National Institute of Personnel Research	NIPR
Naval Personnel Series Tests	NPS
Officer Commanding	OC
Odds And Evens Test	OE

Orientation Test	OR
Percent Accuracy Score	PAC
Hamburg Aerospace Pilot Aptitude Tests	PARAT
Paragraph Comprehension ASVAB	PC
Percentage Correct of Items Attempted	PC
Person Characteristic Curve	PCC
Person Characteristic Function	PCF
Abbreviation for Army Entry Tests 1-5	PIDVA
BARB Projectile Test ('Time Estimation')	PJ
Paper and Pencil Tests	PPTs
Personal Qualities Applicant Profile	PQAP
Quality of Life	QOL
Recruit Training Centre	RTC
Standard Typewriter Keyboard	QWERTY
Qwerty Board Interface	QW
Post-Traumatic Stress Disorder Check List	PCL
Cattell's Sixteen Personality factor Inventory	16PF
Jackson's Personality Research Form	PRF
Police Service of Northern Ireland	PSNI
Post Traumatic Stress Disorder	PTST
Reasoning Categories Test	RC
Symbol Rotation Task	RF
Royal Navy	RN
Royal Navy Recruiting Tests (Total)	RT
Royal Navy Recruiting Tests (Reasoning)	RT1
Royal Navy Recruiting Tests (Literacy)	RT2
Royal Navy Recruiting Tests (Numeracy)	RT3
Royal Navy Recruiting Tests (Mechanical Comprehension)	RT4
Standard Error of Measurement	SEM
The Self Inventory	S_I
Semantic Identity/Distance	SI/SD
Senior Psychologist Naval Department	SP(N)
Symbol Rotation (F) Test)	SR
Trial Linear Wall Tasks	TE1
Trial Parabola/Projectile Tasks	TE2

Trial Moving Objects Task	TE3
Deductive Reasoning Test	TI
Reasoning Tests NPS (Transitive Inference)	TI
Touch Screen	TS
Trait Self-Descriptive Inventory	TSD
Army Entry Test (UK) Classification Index	TSG
Technical Test Cooperation Program	TTCP
Technical Cooperation Program (Australia Canada UK USA)	TTCP
United Kingdom	UK
United States of America	USA
United States Air Force	USAF
Flemish Language Group in Belgium Defence Force	VLA
Vocational Interest Career Examination	VOICE
Wegfiguren Test	WF
Transitive Inference Reasoning Tests (BARB)	WHO
ABC Working Memory Composite	WMEM
Word Rules Test	WR
Women's Royal Naval Service	WRNS